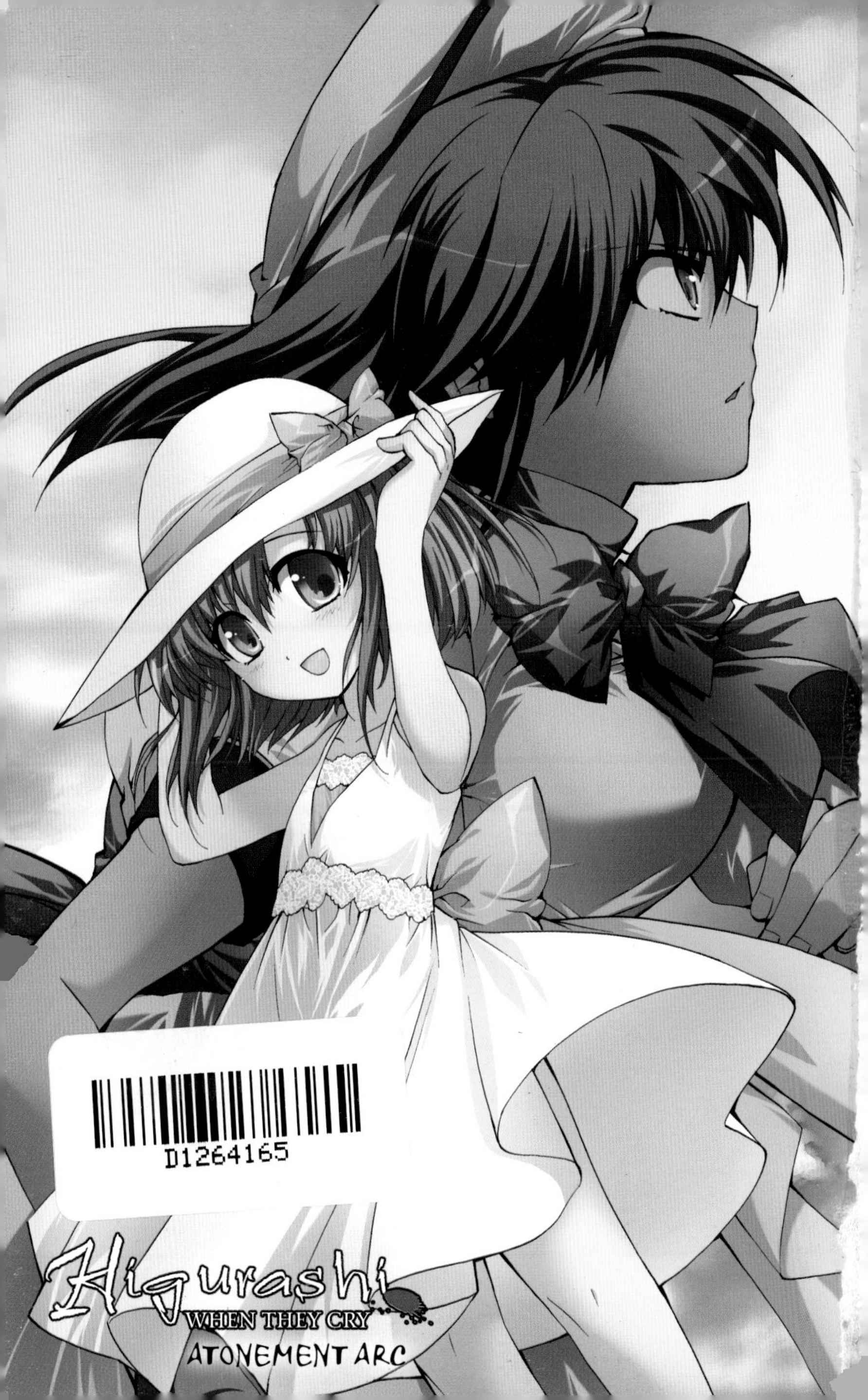
Higurashi
WHEN THEY CRY
ATONEMENT ARC

Higurashi
WHEN THEY CRY
ATONEMENT ARC

4

CONTENTS

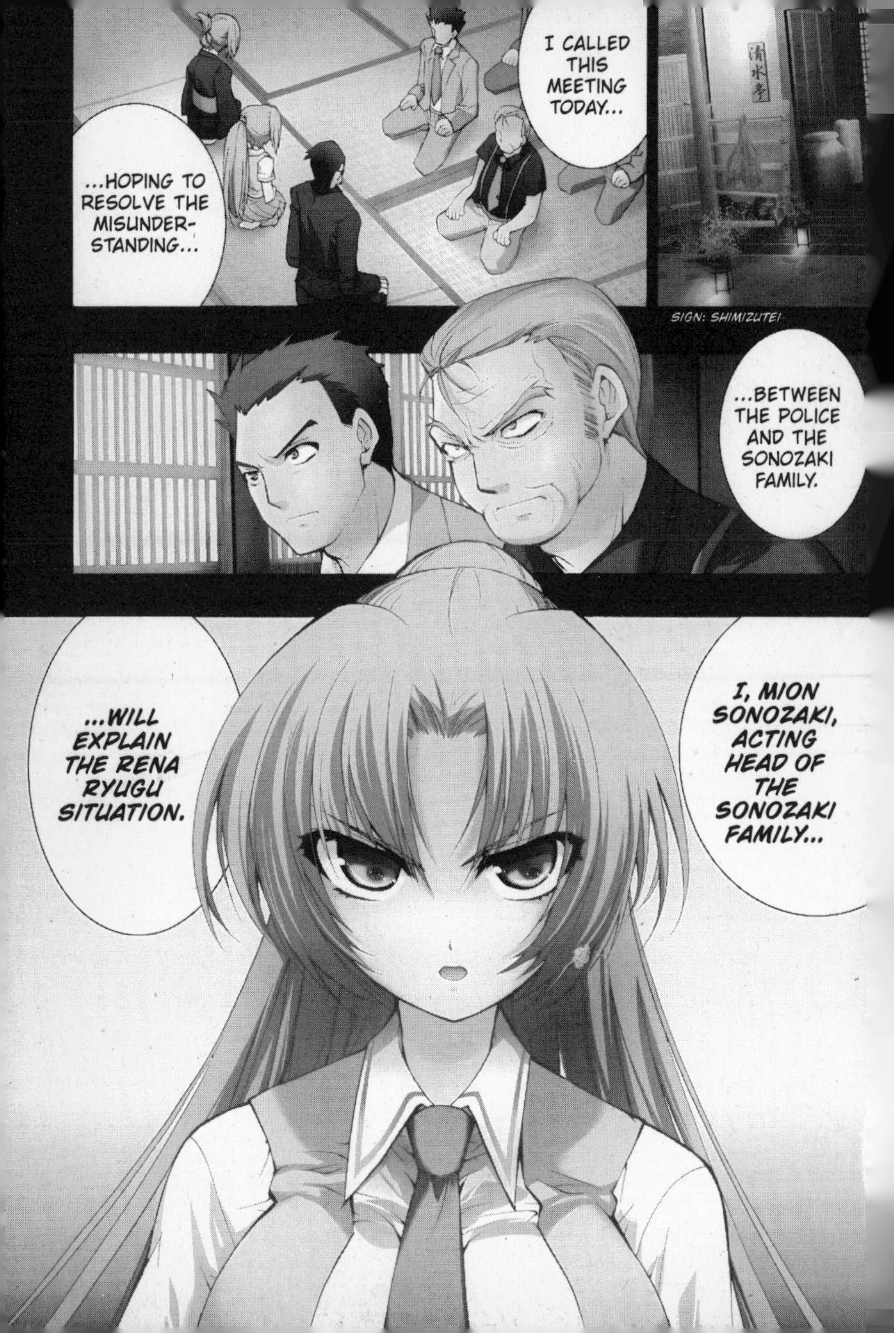
清水亭
SIGN: SHIMIZUTEI
I CALLED THIS MEETING TODAY...
...HOPING TO RESOLVE THE MISUNDER-STANDING...
...BETWEEN THE POLICE AND THE SONOZAKI FAMILY.
I, MION SONOZAKI, ACTING HEAD OF THE SONOZAKI FAMILY...
...WILL EXPLAIN THE RENA RYUGU SITUATION.

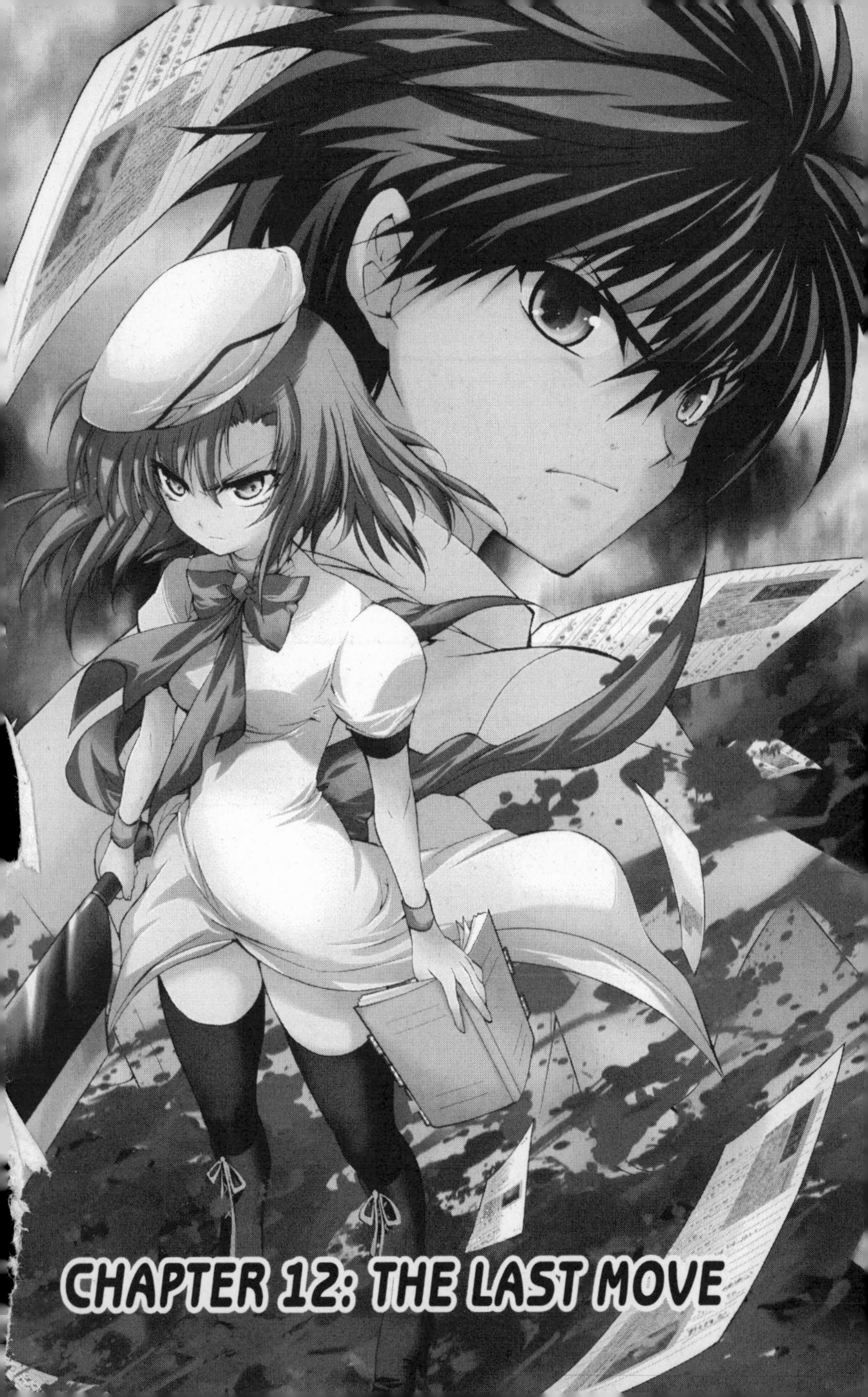

CHAPTER 12: THE LAST MOVE

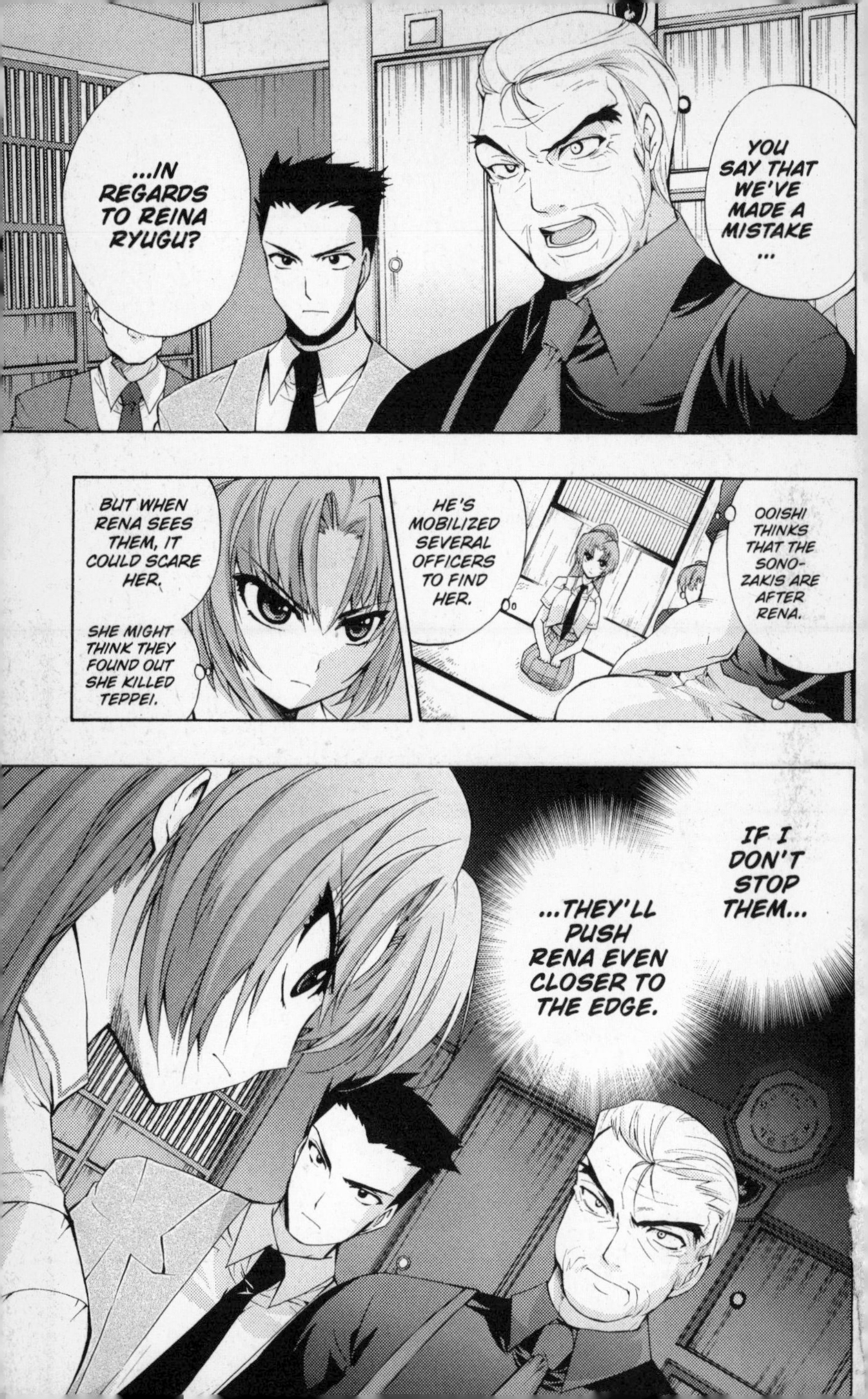
YOU SAY THAT WE'VE MADE A MISTAKE ...
...IN REGARDS TO REINA RYUGU?
OOISHI THINKS THAT THE SONO-ZAKIS ARE AFTER RENA.
HE'S MOBILIZED SEVERAL OFFICERS TO FIND HER.
BUT WHEN RENA SEES THEM, IT COULD SCARE HER.
SHE MIGHT THINK THEY FOUND OUT SHE KILLED TEPPEI.
IF I DON'T STOP THEM...
...THEY'LL PUSH RENA EVEN CLOSER TO THE EDGE.

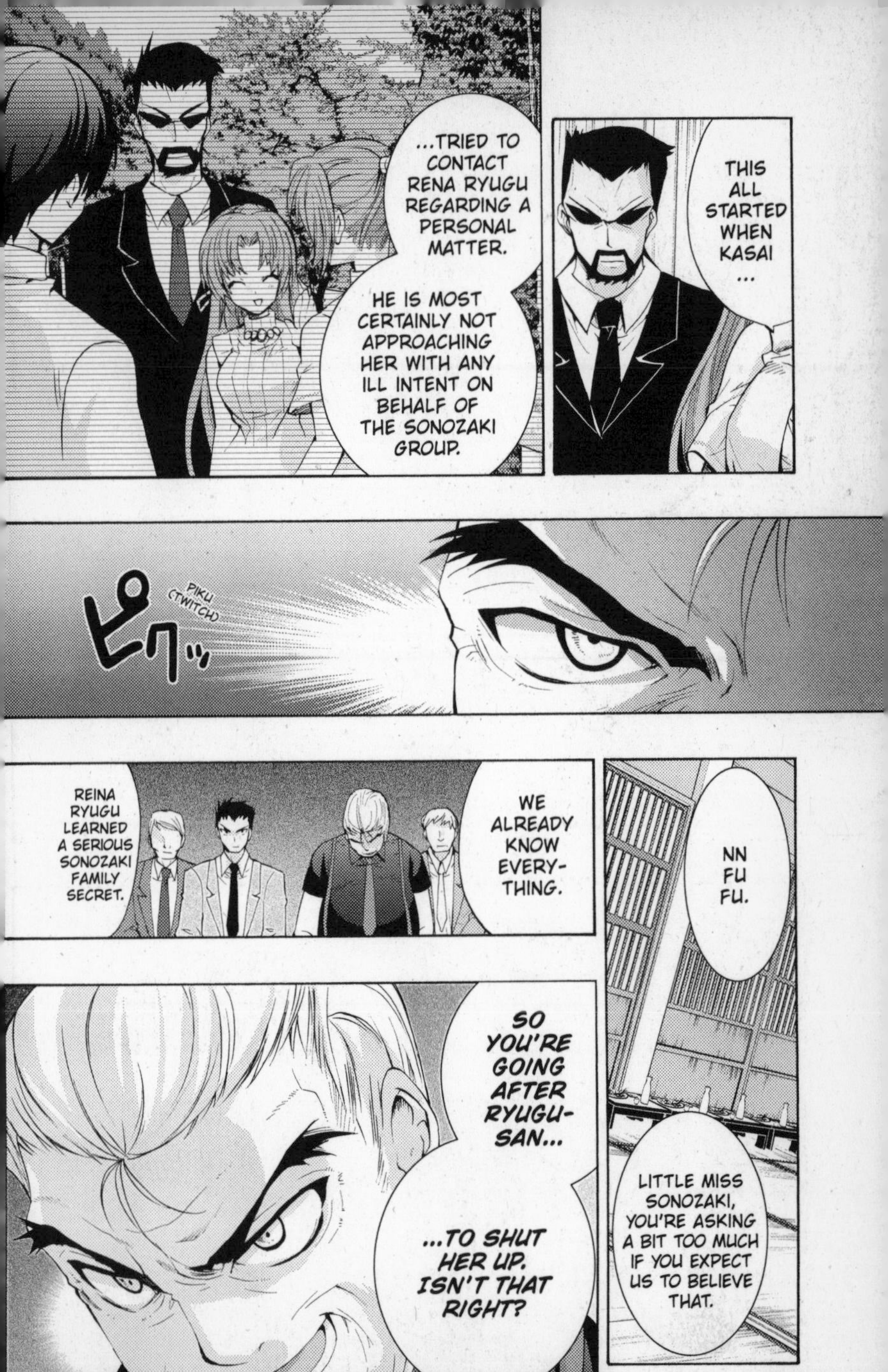
THIS ALL STARTED WHEN KASAI ...
...TRIED TO CONTACT RENA RYUGU REGARDING A PERSONAL MATTER.
HE IS MOST CERTAINLY NOT APPROACHING HER WITH ANY ILL INTENT ON BEHALF OF THE SONOZAKI GROUP.
ピクッ
PIKU (TWITCH)
NN FU FU.
LITTLE MISS SONOZAKI, YOU'RE ASKING A BIT TOO MUCH IF YOU EXPECT US TO BELIEVE THAT.
WE ALREADY KNOW EVERY-THING.
REINA RYUGU LEARNED A SERIOUS SONOZAKI FAMILY SECRET.
SO YOU'RE GOING AFTER RYUGU-SAN...
...TO SHUT HER UP. ISN'T THAT RIGHT?

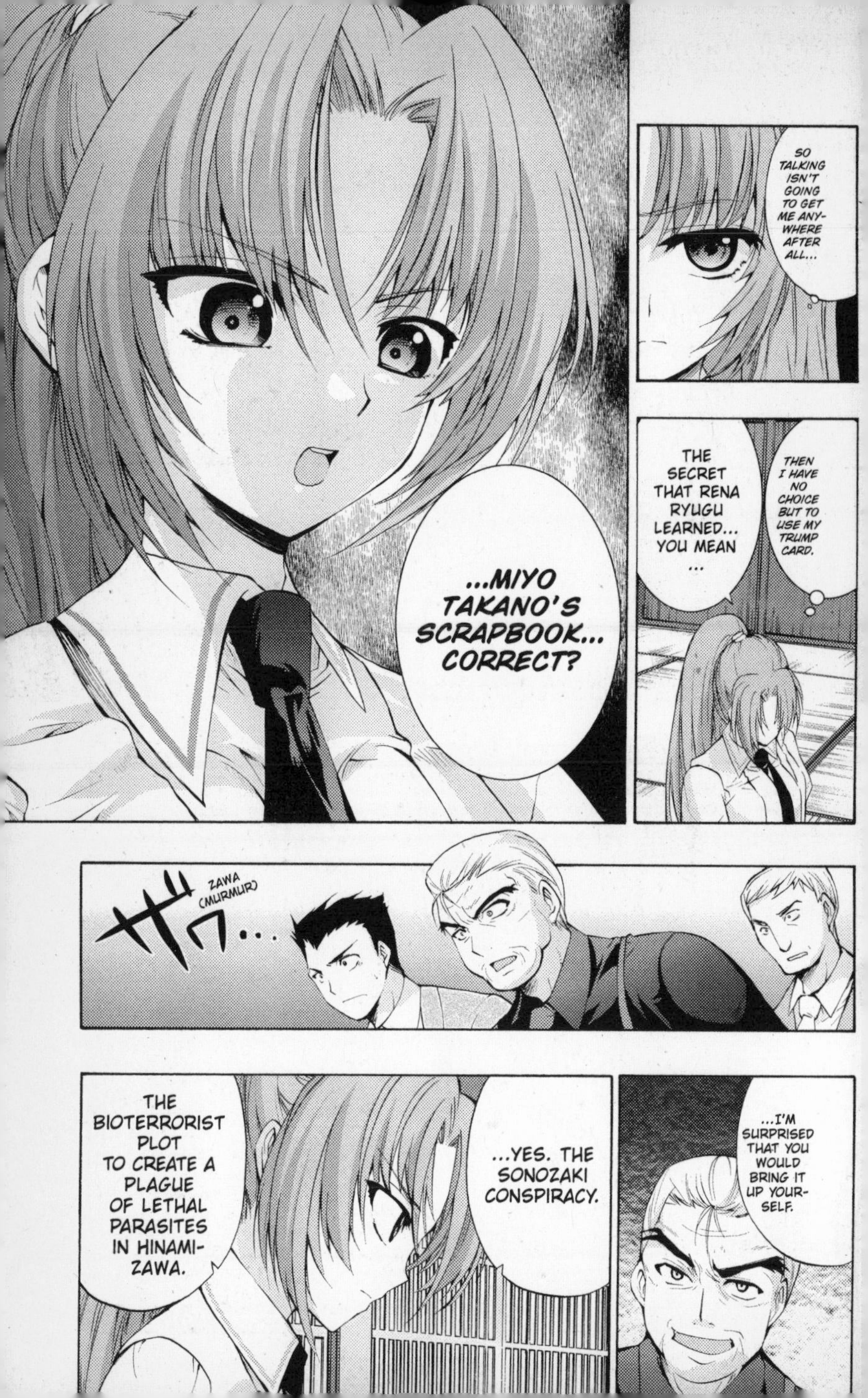
SO TALKING ISN'T GOING TO GET ME ANYWHERE AFTER ALL...
THEN I HAVE NO CHOICE BUT TO USE MY TRUMP CARD.
THE SECRET THAT RENA RYUGU LEARNED... YOU MEAN ...
...MIYO TAKANO'S SCRAPBOOK... CORRECT?
ザワ...
ZAWA (MURMUR)
...I'M SURPRISED THAT YOU WOULD BRING IT UP YOURSELF.
...YES. THE SONOZAKI CONSPIRACY.
THE BIOTERRORIST PLOT TO CREATE A PLAGUE OF LETHAL PARASITES IN HINAMIZAWA.

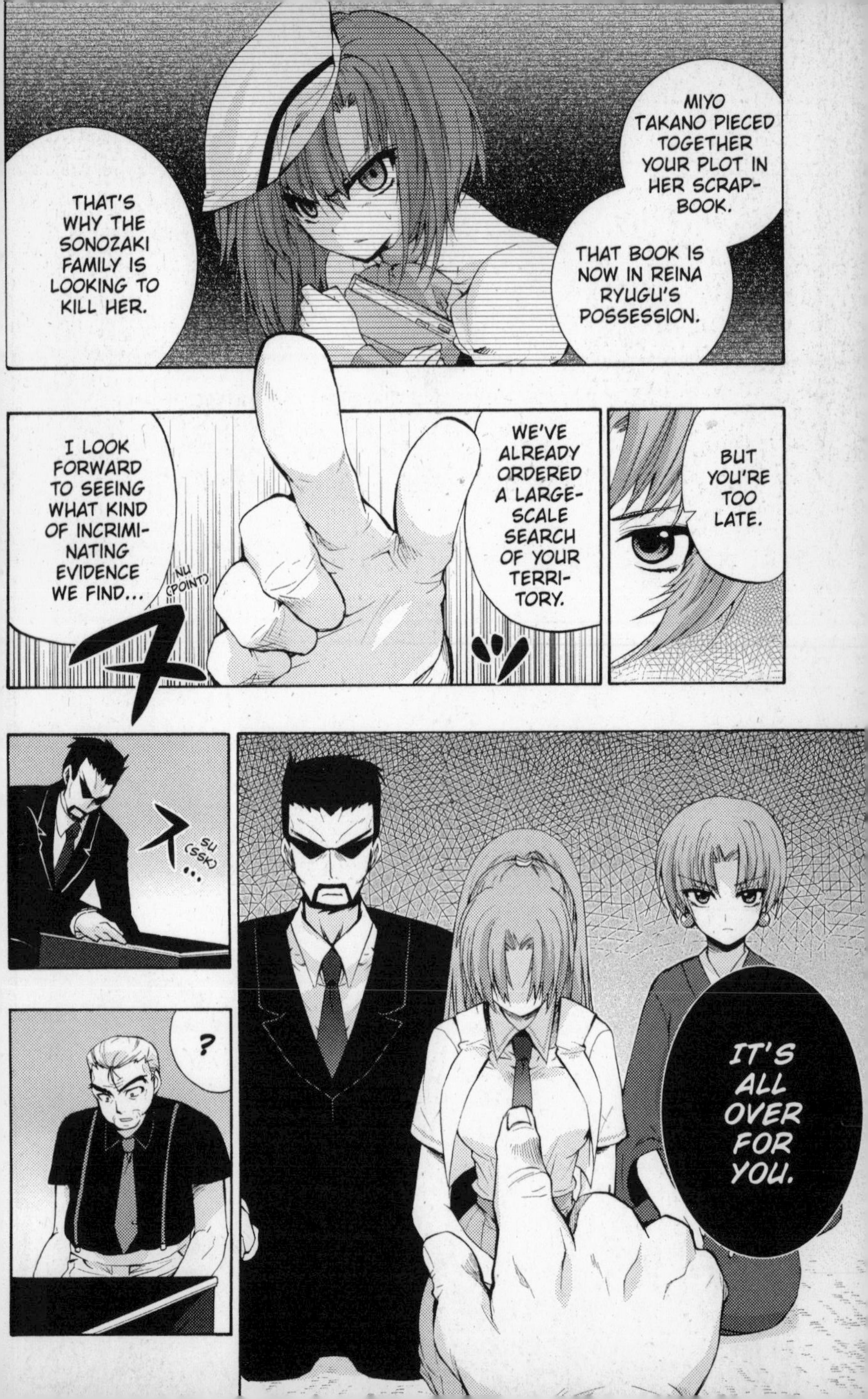

MIYO TAKANO PIECED TOGETHER YOUR PLOT IN HER SCRAP-BOOK.
THAT BOOK IS NOW IN REINA RYUGU'S POSSESSION.
THAT'S WHY THE SONOZAKI FAMILY IS LOOKING TO KILL HER.
BUT YOU'RE TOO LATE.
WE'VE ALREADY ORDERED A LARGE-SCALE SEARCH OF YOUR TERRITORY.
I LOOK FORWARD TO SEEING WHAT KIND OF INCRIMINATING EVIDENCE WE FIND...
NU (POINT)
IT'S ALL OVER FOR YOU.
SU (SSK)
...
?

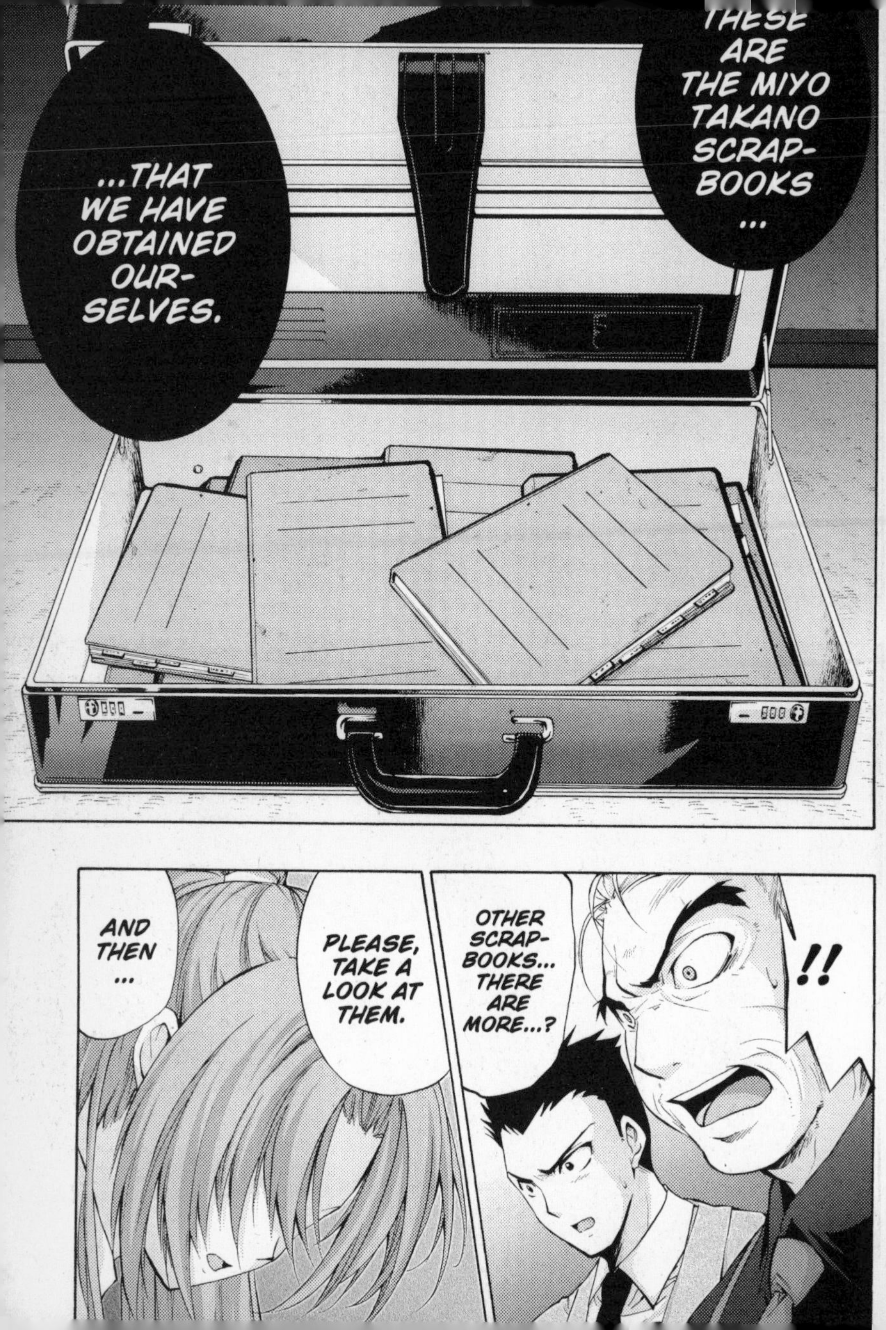
THESE ARE THE MIYO TAKANO SCRAP-BOOKS ...
...THAT WE HAVE OBTAINED OUR-SELVES.
!!
OTHER SCRAP-BOOKS... THERE ARE MORE...?
PLEASE, TAKE A LOOK AT THEM.
AND THEN ...

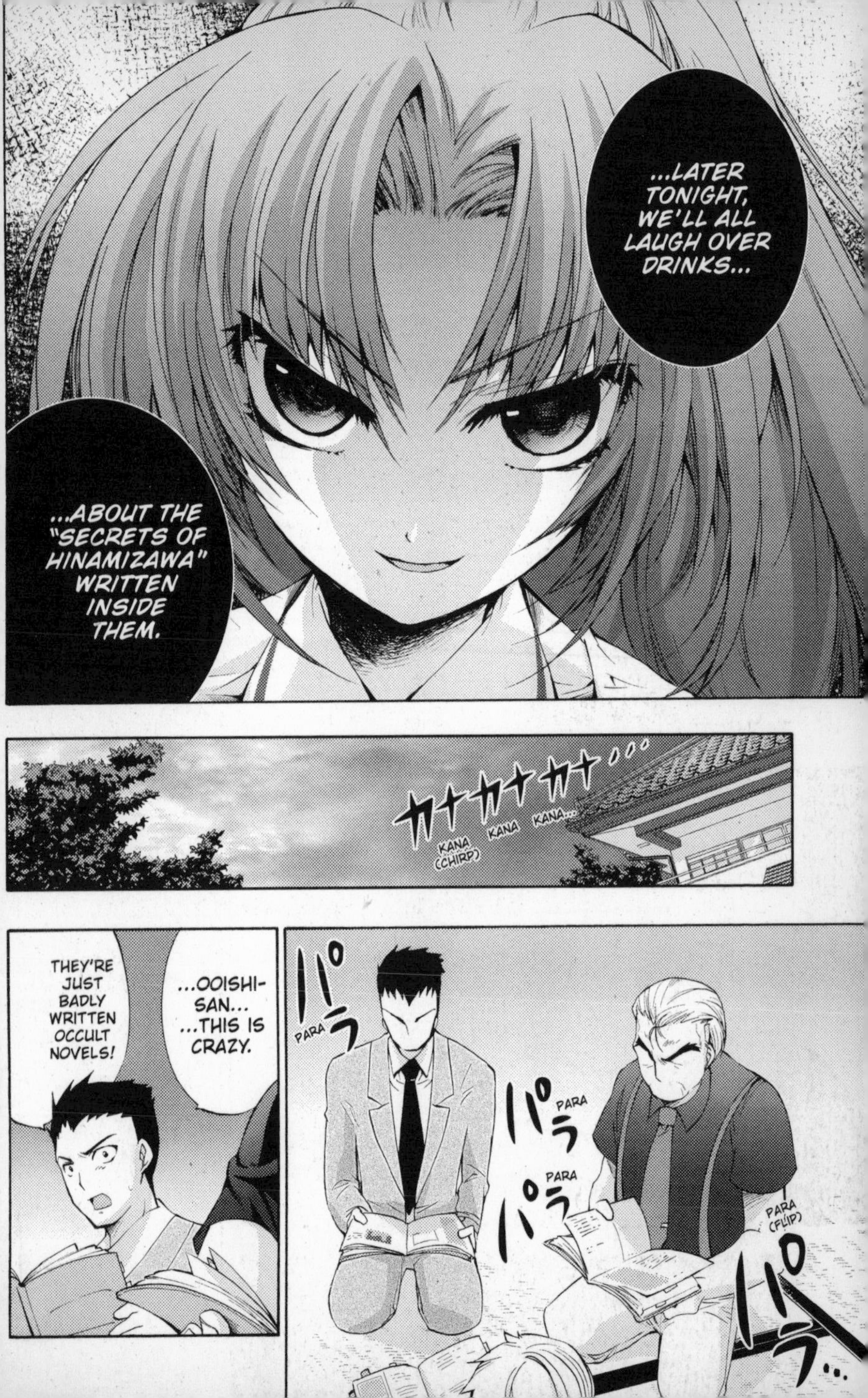
...LATER TONIGHT, WE'LL ALL LAUGH OVER DRINKS...
...ABOUT THE "SECRETS OF HINAMIZAWA" WRITTEN INSIDE THEM.
カナカナカナ
KANA KANA KANA... (CHIRP)
パラ
PARA
パラ
PARA
パラ
PARA
パラ...
PARA (FLIP)
...OOISHI-SAN... ...THIS IS CRAZY.
THEY'RE JUST BADLY WRITTEN OCCULT NOVELS!

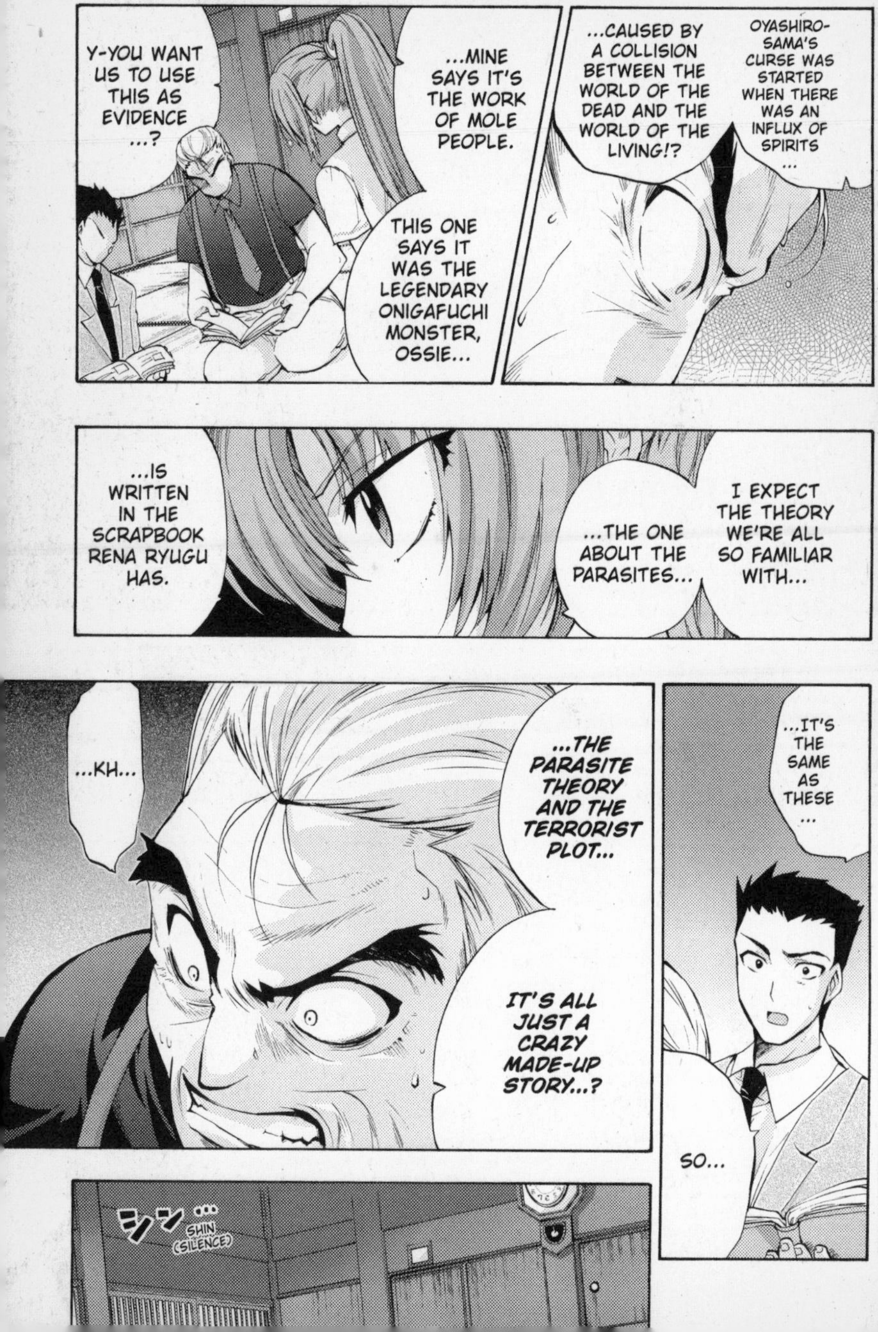
OYASHIRO-SAMA'S CURSE WAS STARTED WHEN THERE WAS AN INFLUX OF SPIRITS ...
...CAUSED BY A COLLISION BETWEEN THE WORLD OF THE DEAD AND THE WORLD OF THE LIVING!?
...MINE SAYS IT'S THE WORK OF MOLE PEOPLE.
THIS ONE SAYS IT WAS THE LEGENDARY ONIGAFUCHI MONSTER, OSSIE...
Y-YOU WANT US TO USE THIS AS EVIDENCE ...?
I EXPECT THE THEORY WE'RE ALL SO FAMILIAR WITH...
...THE ONE ABOUT THE PARASITES...
...IS WRITTEN IN THE SCRAPBOOK RENA RYUGU HAS.
...IT'S THE SAME AS THESE ...
SO...
...THE PARASITE THEORY AND THE TERRORIST PLOT...
IT'S ALL JUST A CRAZY MADE-UP STORY...?
...KH...
シン…
SHIN (SILENCE)

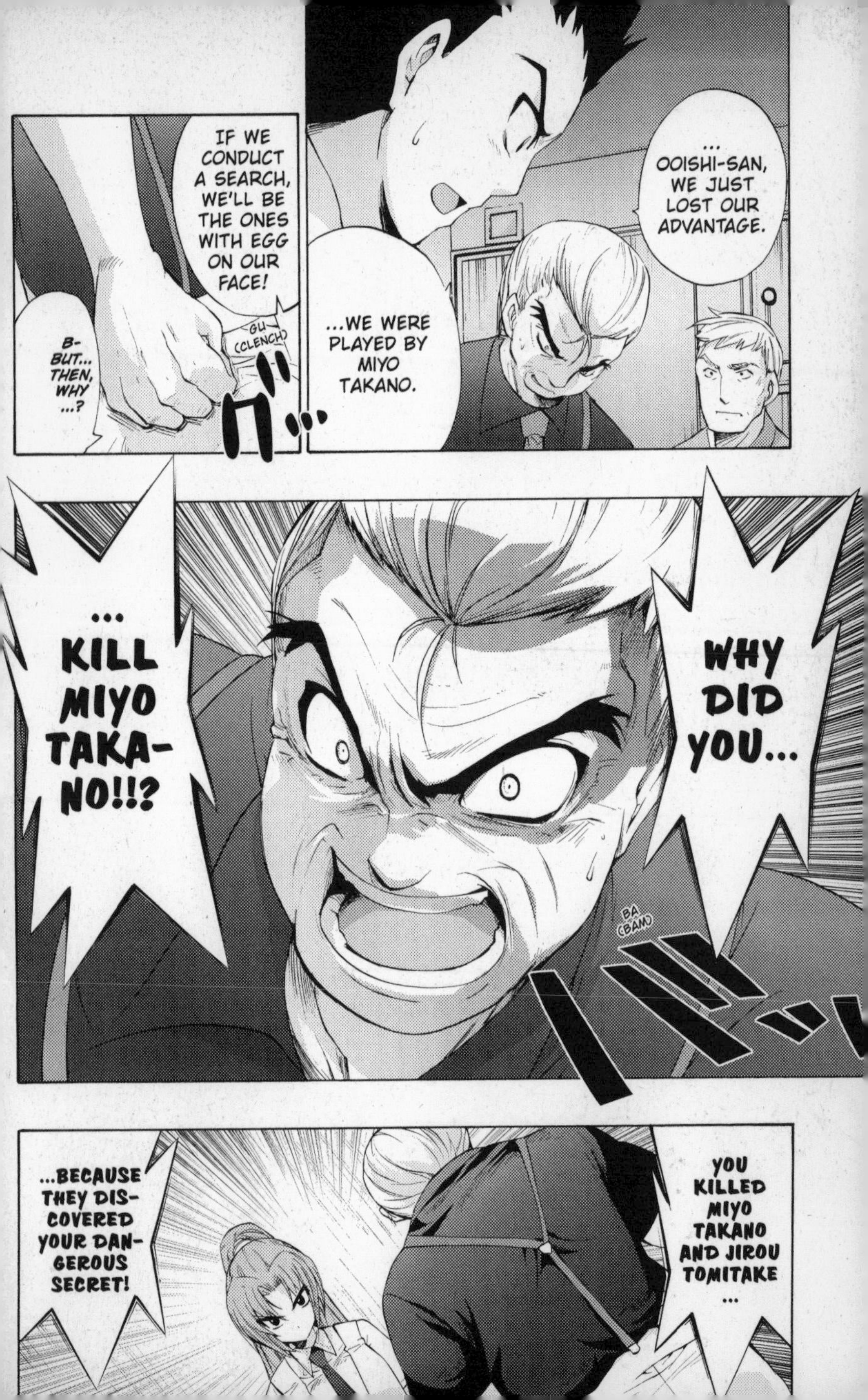
...OOISHI-SAN, WE JUST LOST OUR ADVANTAGE.
...WE WERE PLAYED BY MIYO TAKANO.
IF WE CONDUCT A SEARCH, WE'LL BE THE ONES WITH EGG ON OUR FACE!
GU (CLENCH)
B-BUT... THEN, WHY ...?
WHY DID YOU...
...KILL MIYO TAKA-NO!!?
BA (BAM)
YOU KILLED MIYO TAKANO AND JIROU TOMITAKE ...
...BECAUSE THEY DISCOVERED YOUR DANGEROUS SECRET!

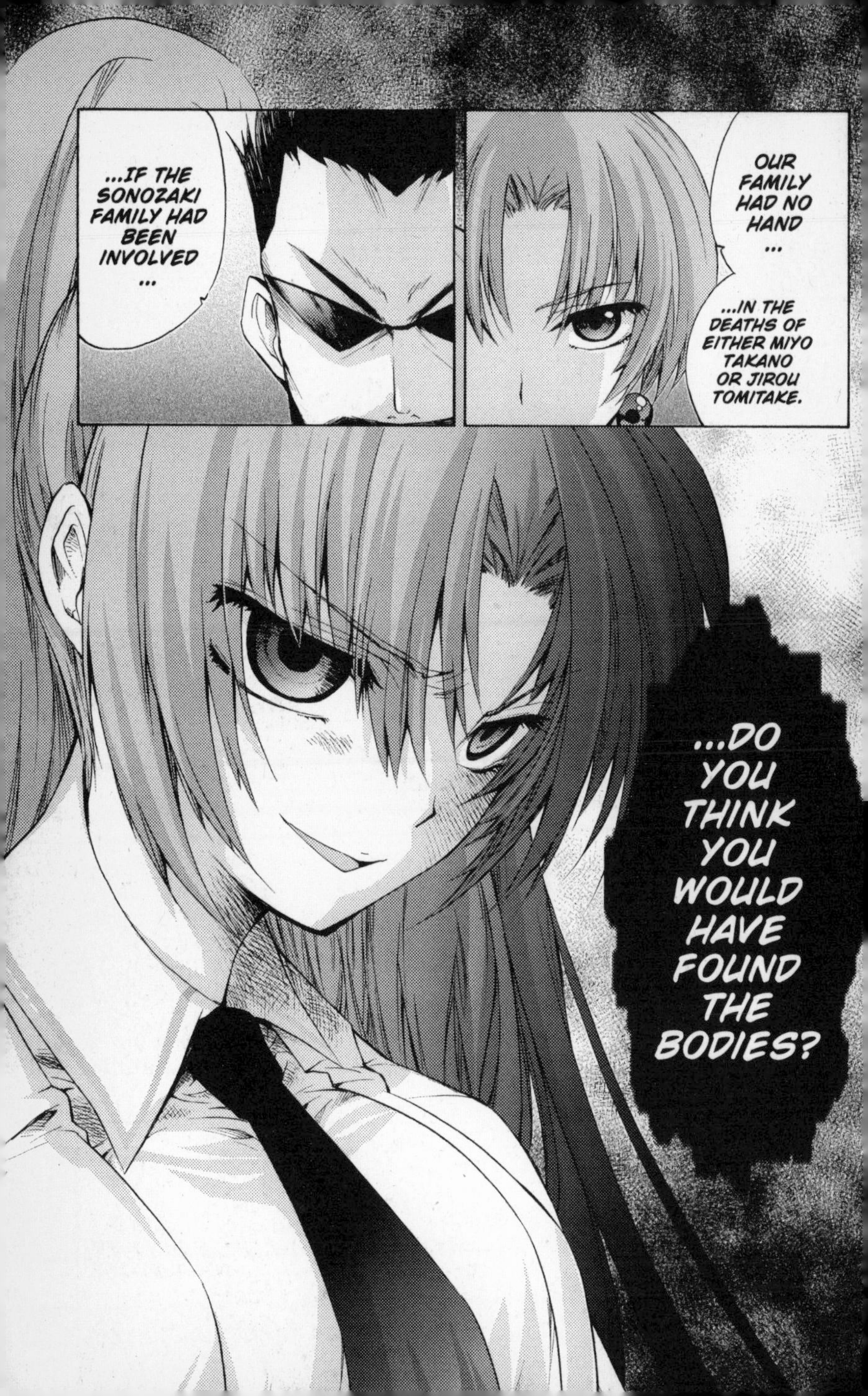
OUR FAMILY HAD NO HAND ...
...IN THE DEATHS OF EITHER MIYO TAKANO OR JIROU TOMITAKE.
...IF THE SONOZAKI FAMILY HAD BEEN INVOLVED ...
...DO YOU THINK YOU WOULD HAVE FOUND THE BODIES?

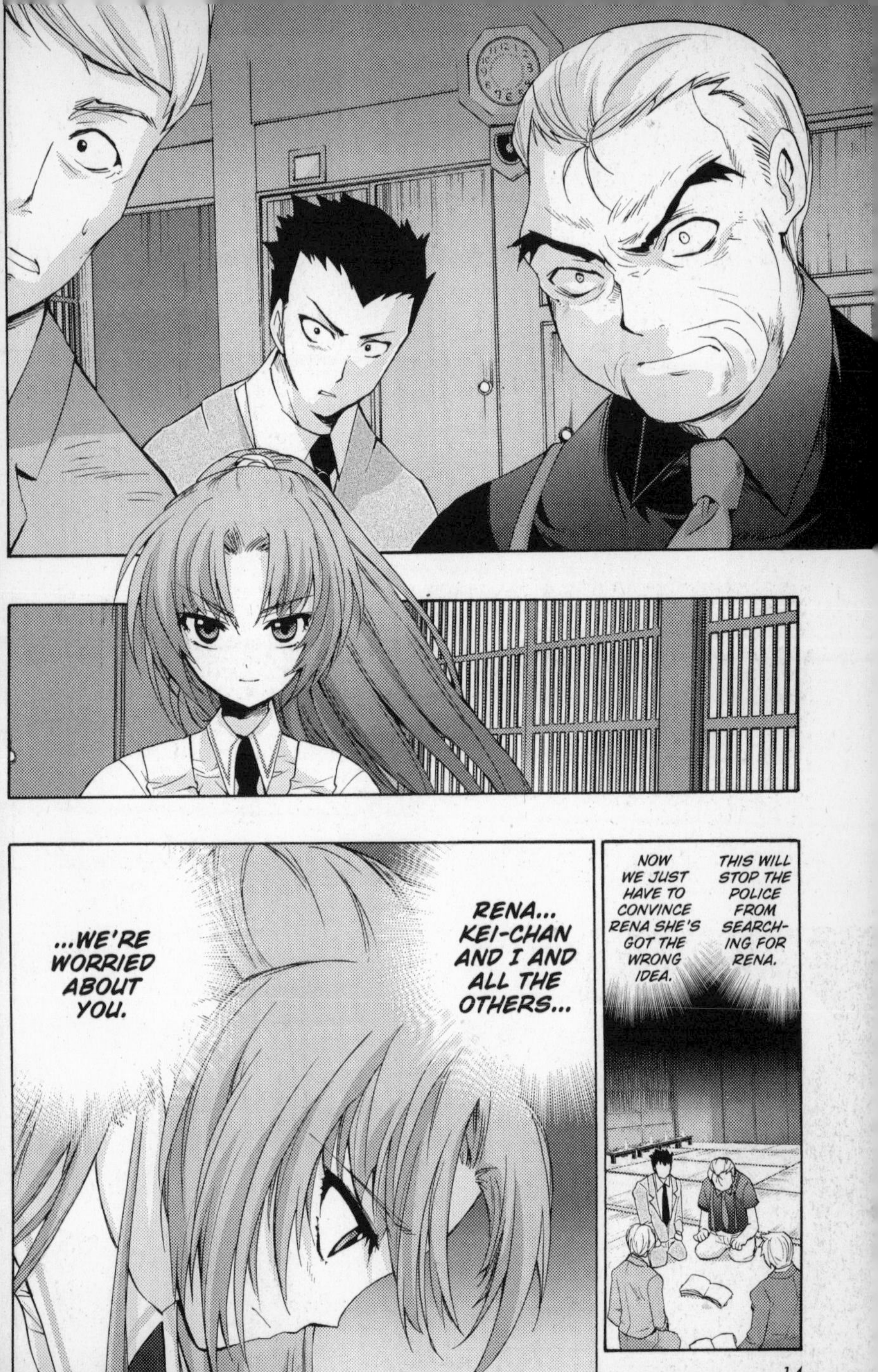
THIS WILL STOP THE POLICE FROM SEARCH-ING FOR RENA.
NOW WE JUST HAVE TO CONVINCE RENA SHE'S GOT THE WRONG IDEA.
RENA... KEI-CHAN AND I AND ALL THE OTHERS...
...WE'RE WORRIED ABOUT YOU.

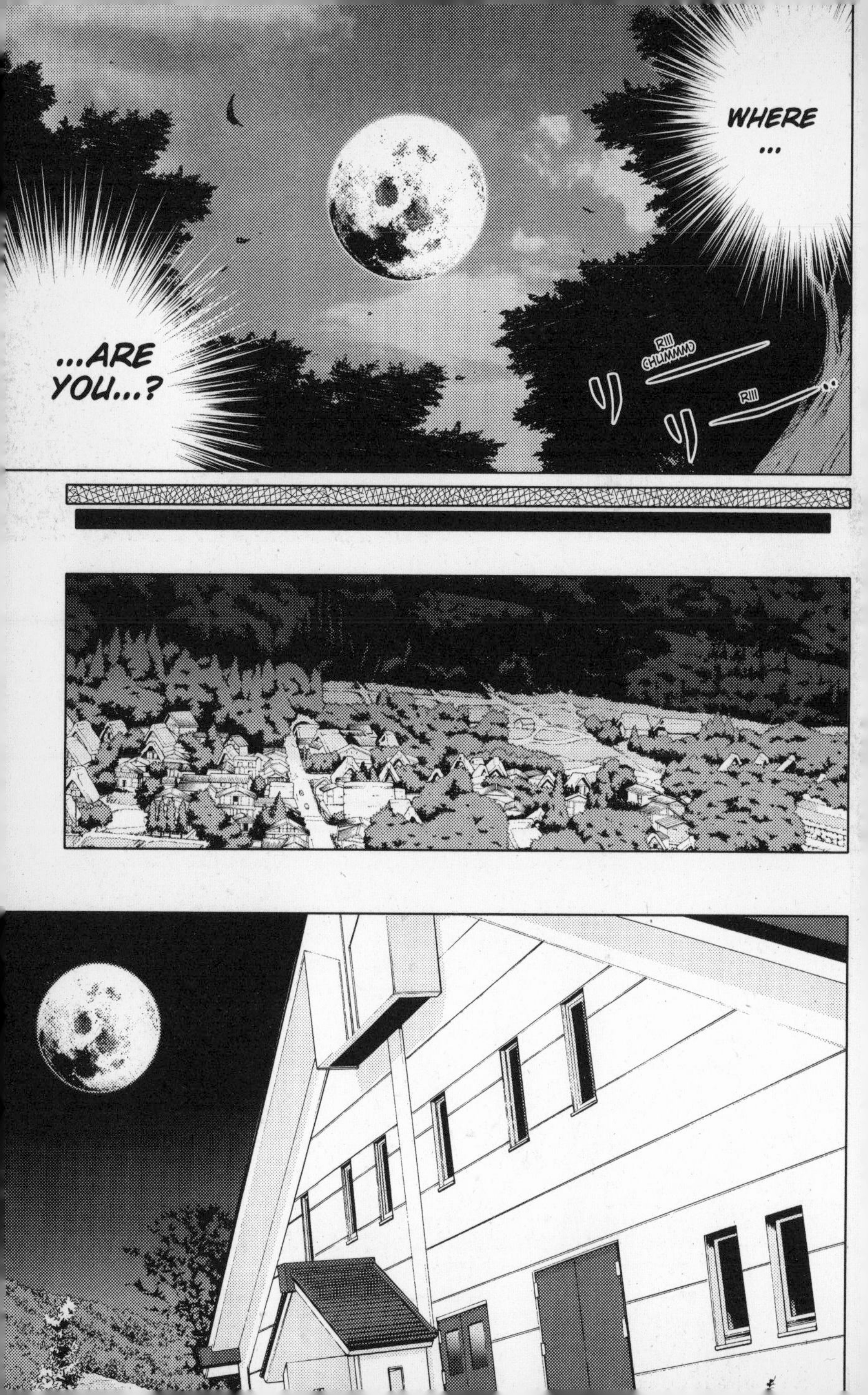
WHERE ...
...ARE YOU...?
RIII (CHLIMMM)
リ
RIII
リ

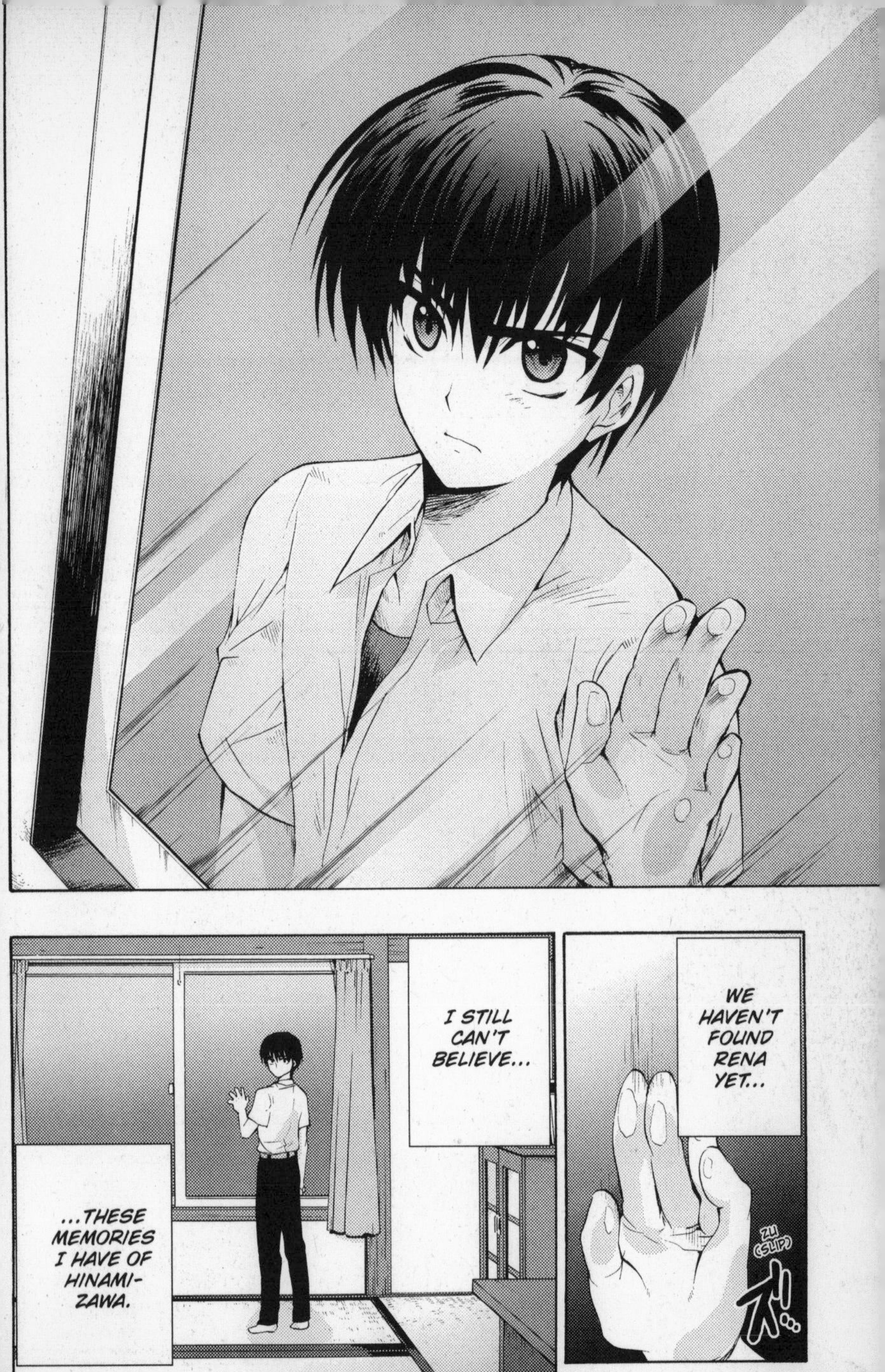
WE HAVEN'T FOUND RENA YET...
ZU (SLIP)
I STILL CAN'T BELIEVE...
...THESE MEMORIES I HAVE OF HINAMI-ZAWA.

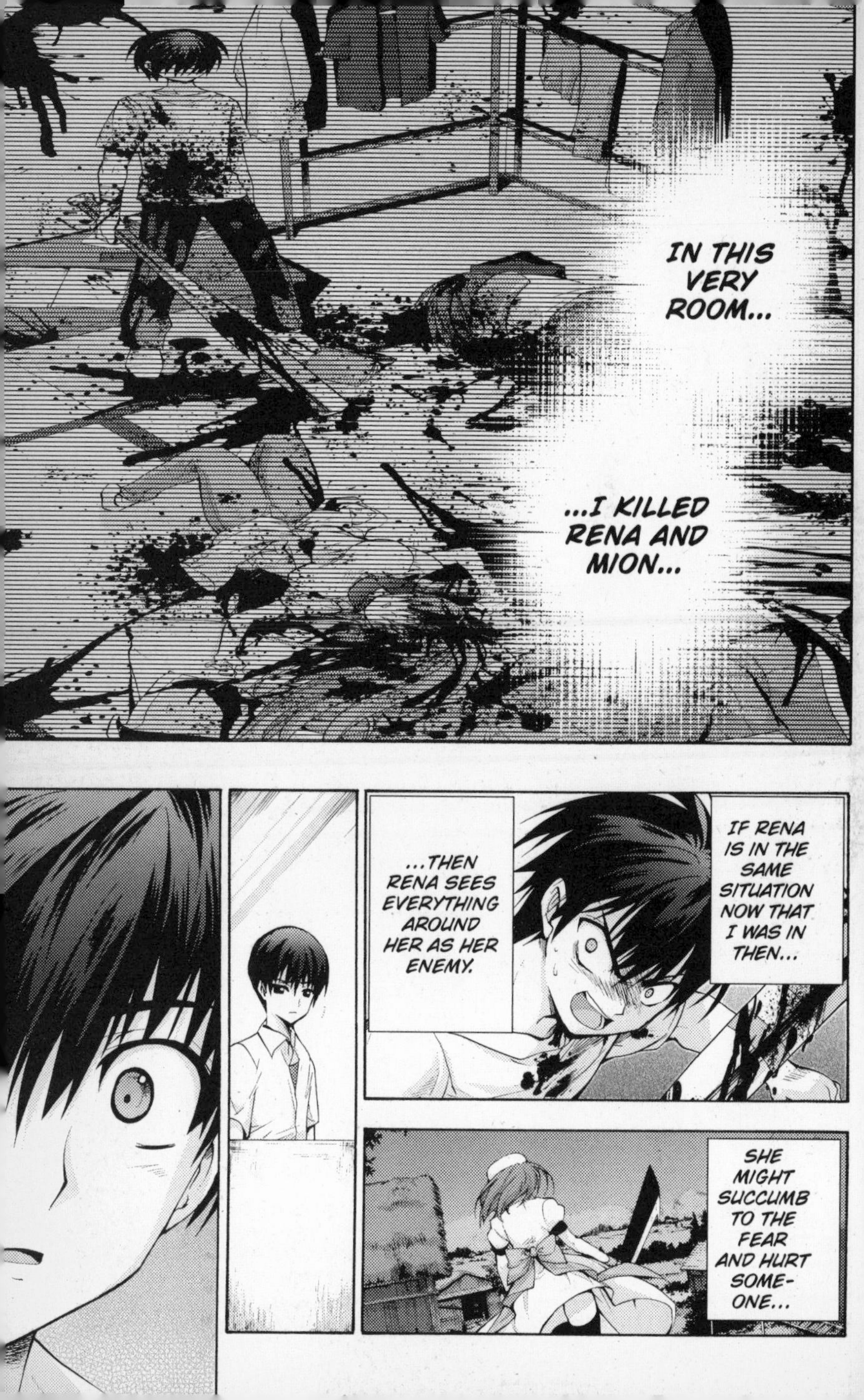
IN THIS VERY ROOM...
...I KILLED RENA AND MION...
IF RENA IS IN THE SAME SITUATION NOW THAT I WAS IN THEN...
...THEN RENA SEES EVERYTHING AROUND HER AS HER ENEMY.
SHE MIGHT SUCCUMB TO THE FEAR AND HURT SOME-ONE...

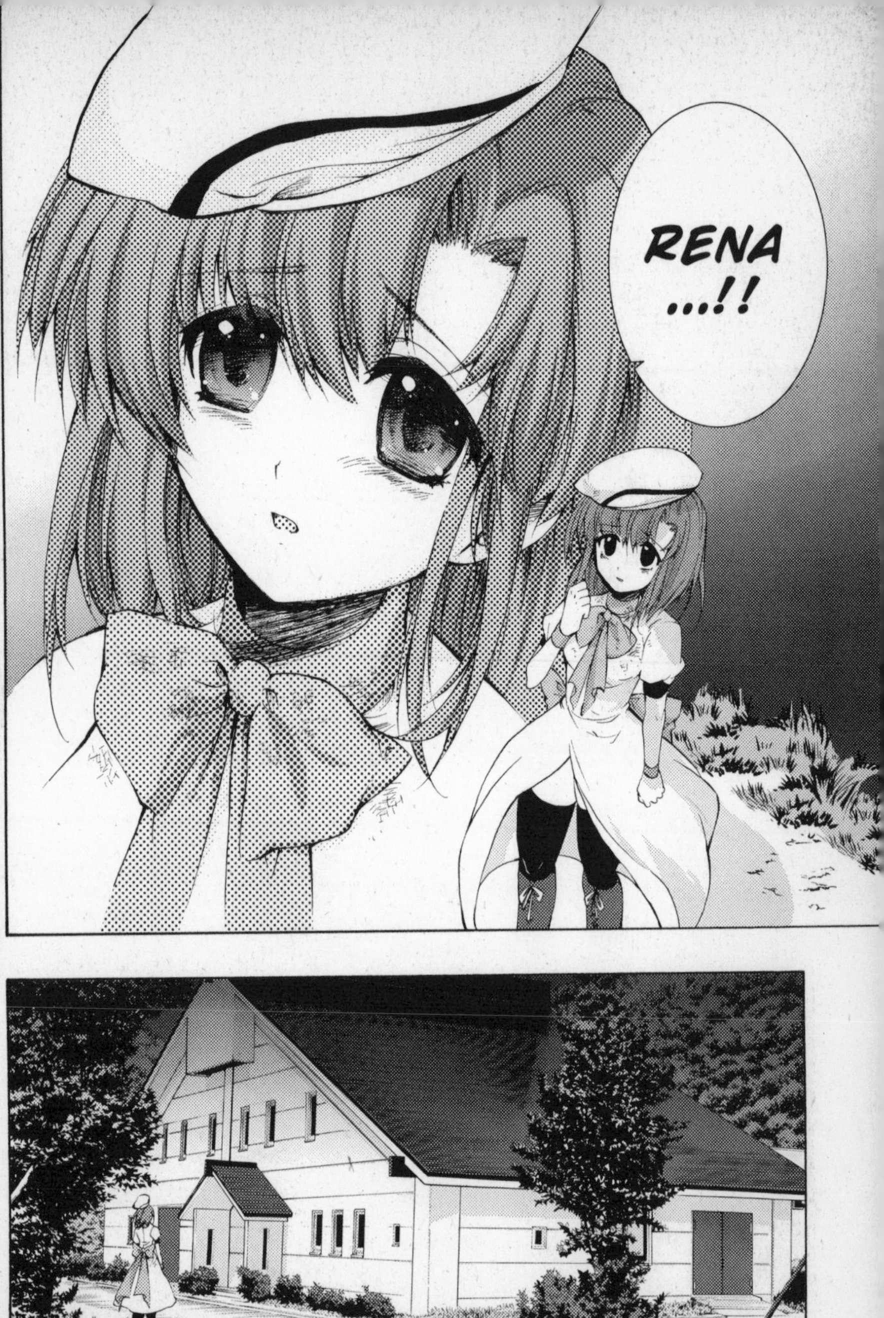
RENA ...!!

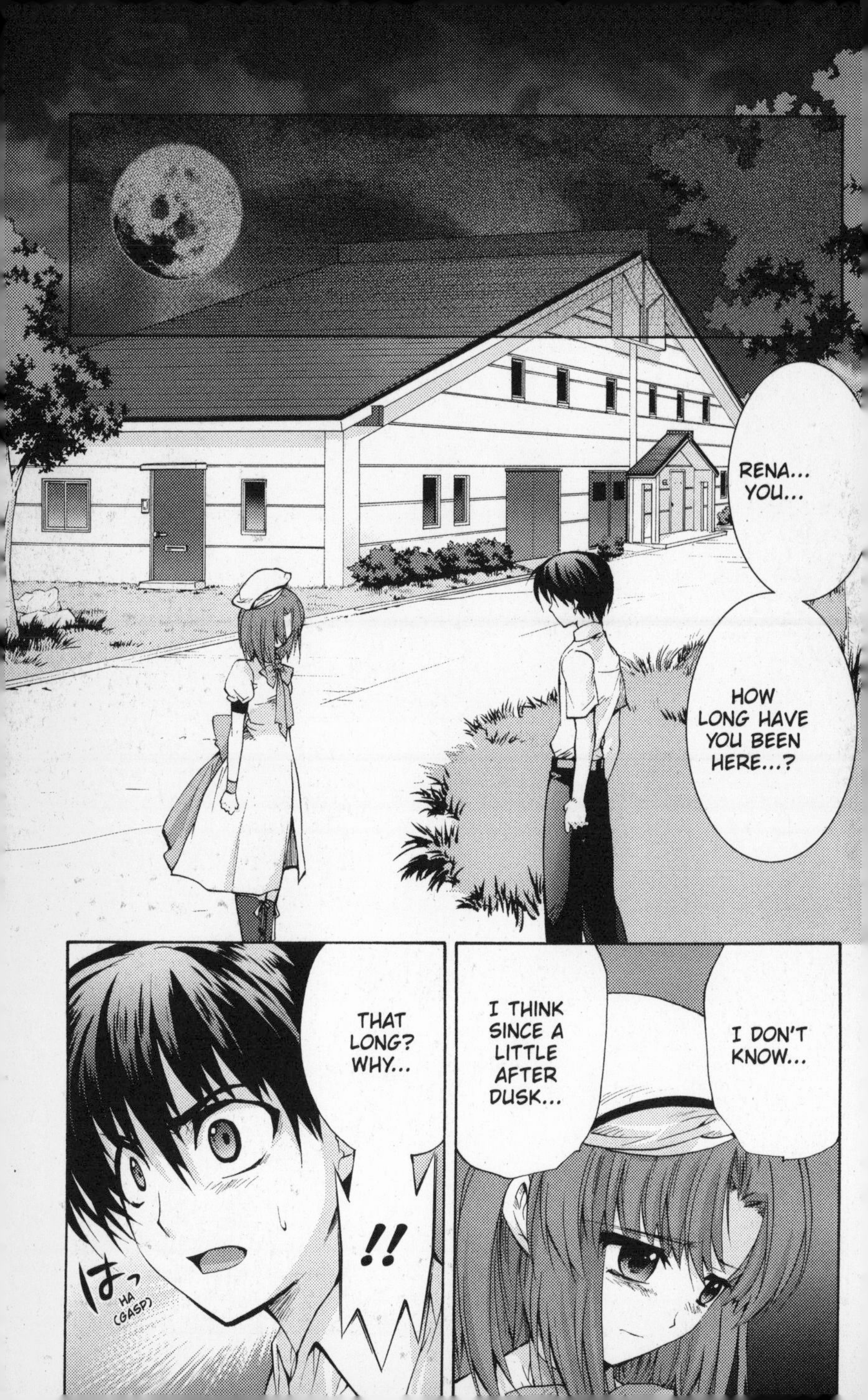
RENA... YOU...
HOW LONG HAVE YOU BEEN HERE...?
I DON'T KNOW...
I THINK SINCE A LITTLE AFTER DUSK...
THAT LONG? WHY...
!!
はっ
HA (GASP)

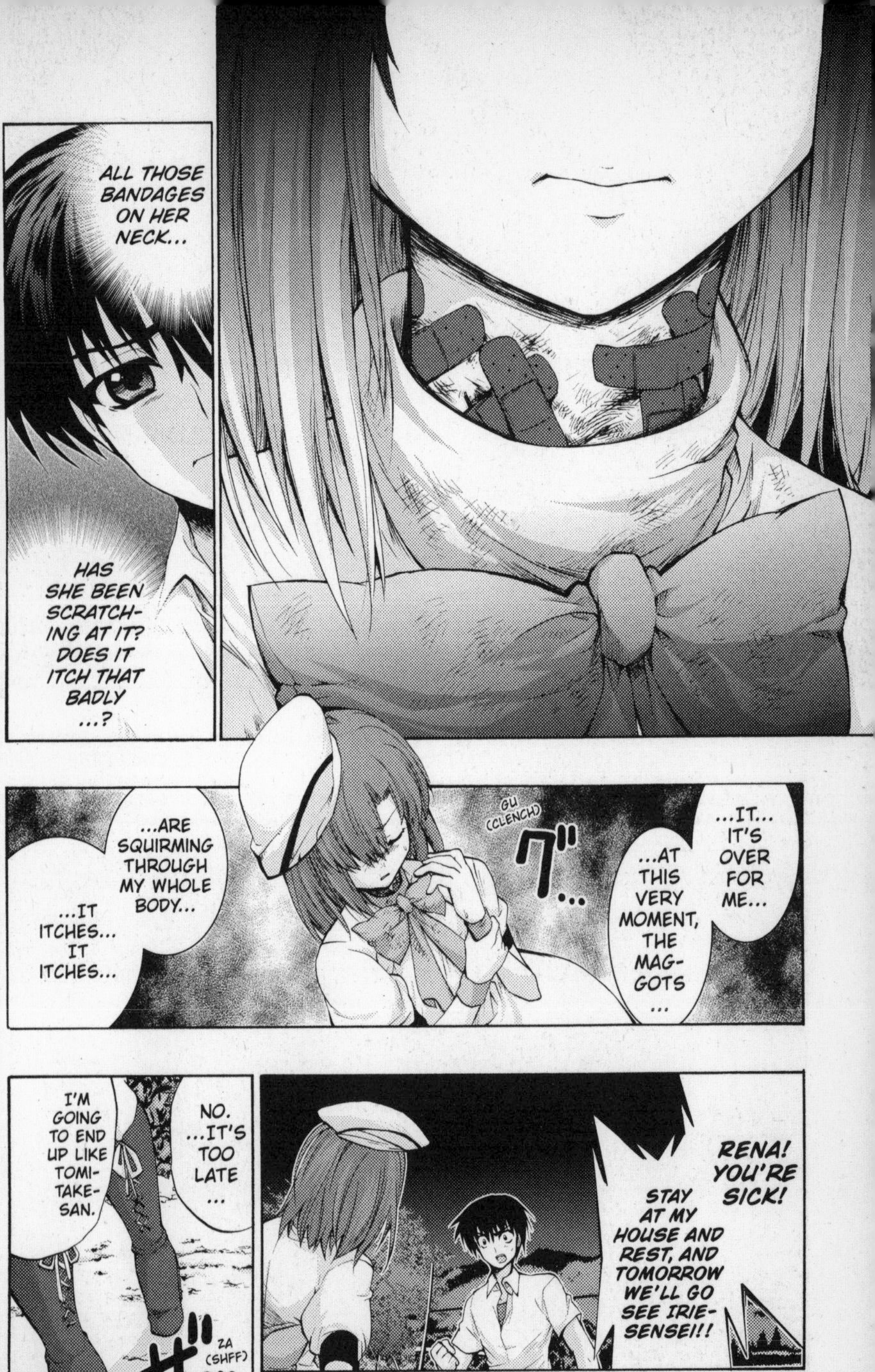
ALL THOSE BANDAGES ON HER NECK...
HAS SHE BEEN SCRATCHING AT IT? DOES IT ITCH THAT BADLY ...?
...IT... IT'S OVER FOR ME...
...AT THIS VERY MOMENT, THE MAGGOTS ...
GU (CLENCH)
グ...
...ARE SQUIRMING THROUGH MY WHOLE BODY...
...IT ITCHES... IT ITCHES...
RENA! YOU'RE SICK!
STAY AT MY HOUSE AND REST, AND TOMORROW WE'LL GO SEE IRIE-SENSEI!!
NO. ...IT'S TOO LATE ...
I'M GOING TO END UP LIKE TOMI-TAKE-SAN.
ZA (SHFF)
ザ...

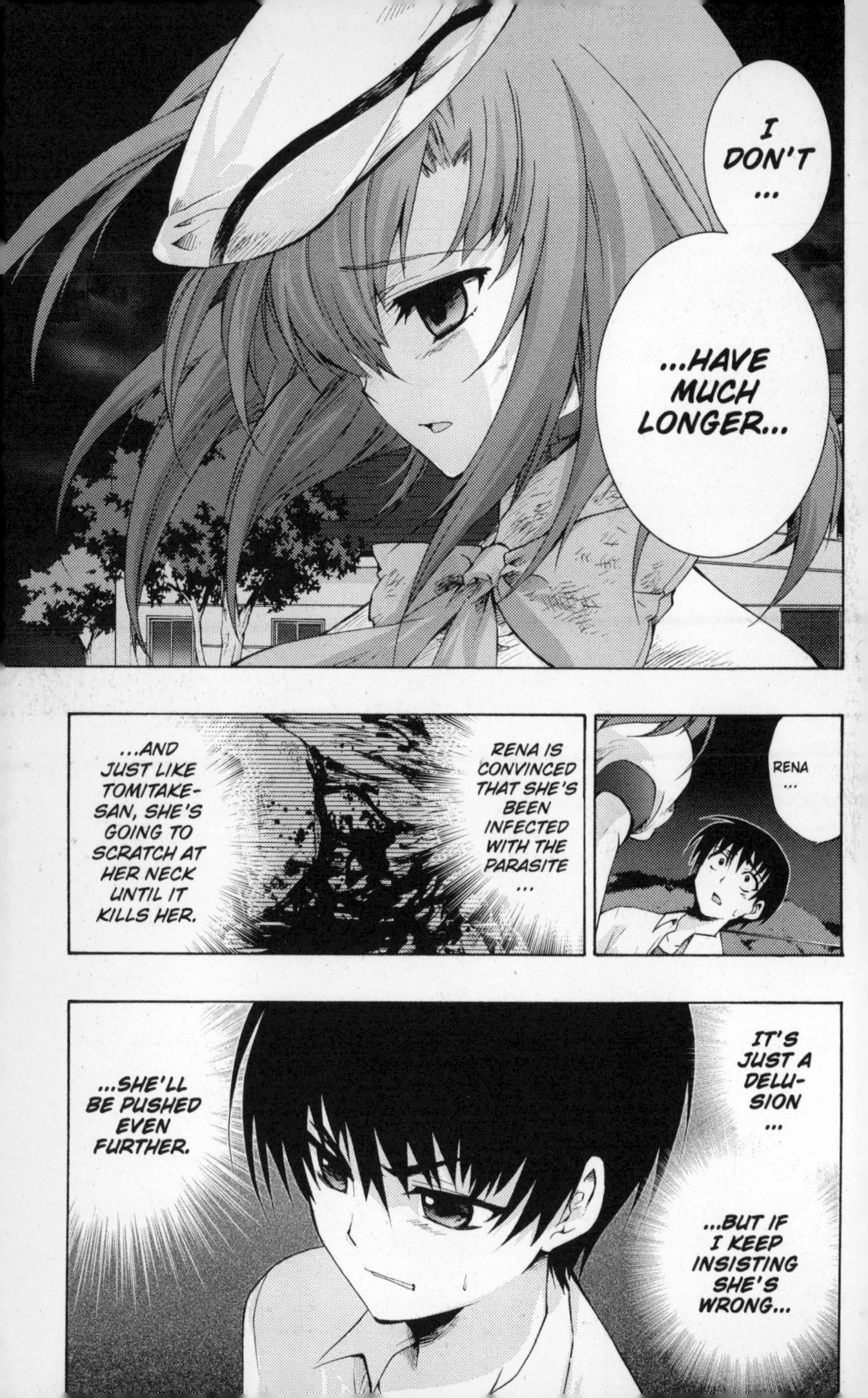
I DON'T ...
...HAVE MUCH LONGER...
RENA ...
RENA IS CONVINCED THAT SHE'S BEEN INFECTED WITH THE PARASITE ...
...AND JUST LIKE TOMITAKE-SAN, SHE'S GOING TO SCRATCH AT HER NECK UNTIL IT KILLS HER.
IT'S JUST A DELUSION ...
...BUT IF I KEEP INSISTING SHE'S WRONG...
...SHE'LL BE PUSHED EVEN FURTHER.

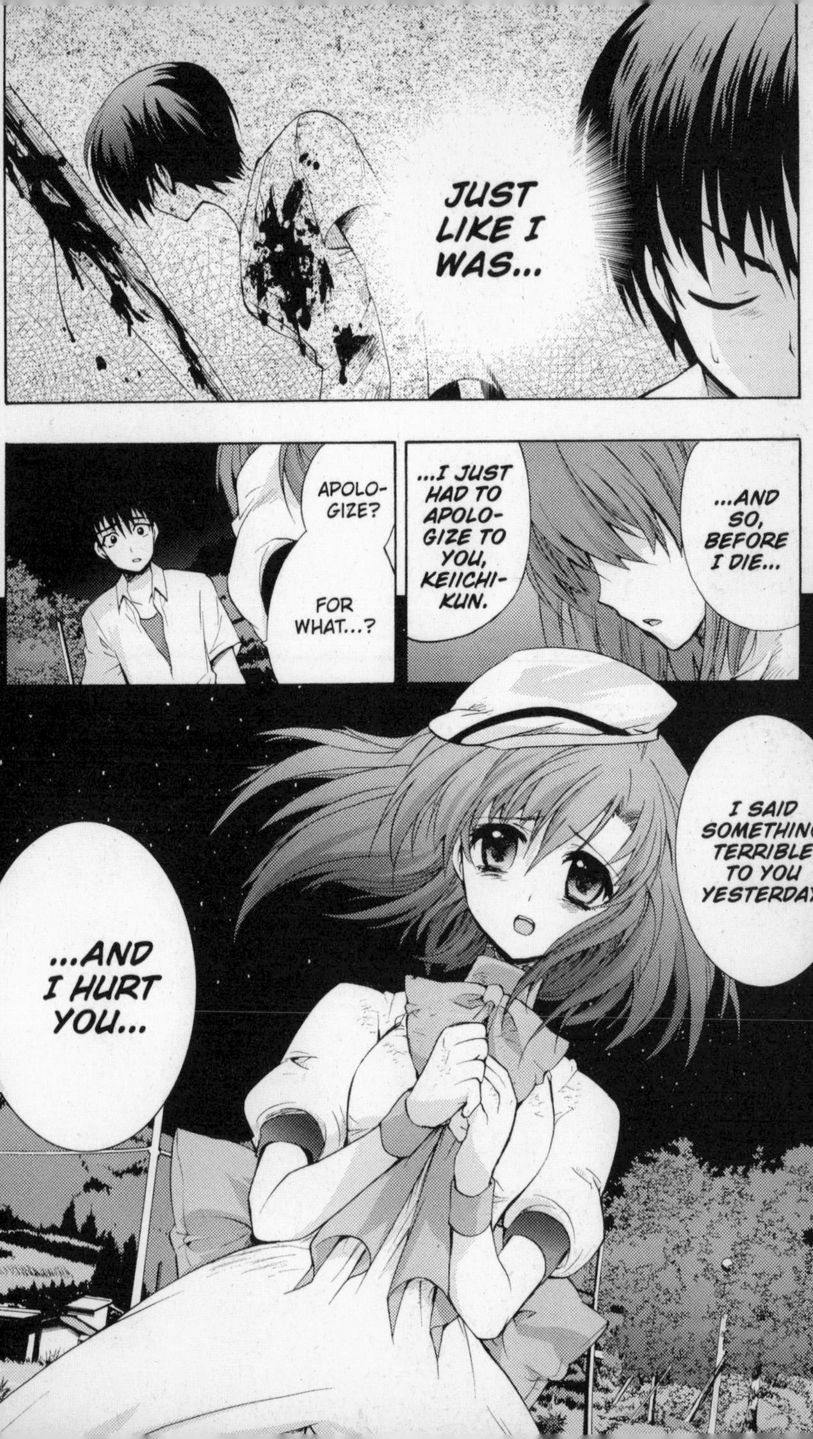
JUST LIKE I WAS...
...AND SO, BEFORE I DIE...
...I JUST HAD TO APOLOGIZE TO YOU, KEIICHI-KUN.
APOLOGIZE?
FOR WHAT...?
I SAID SOMETHING TERRIBLE TO YOU YESTERDAY.
...AND I HURT YOU...

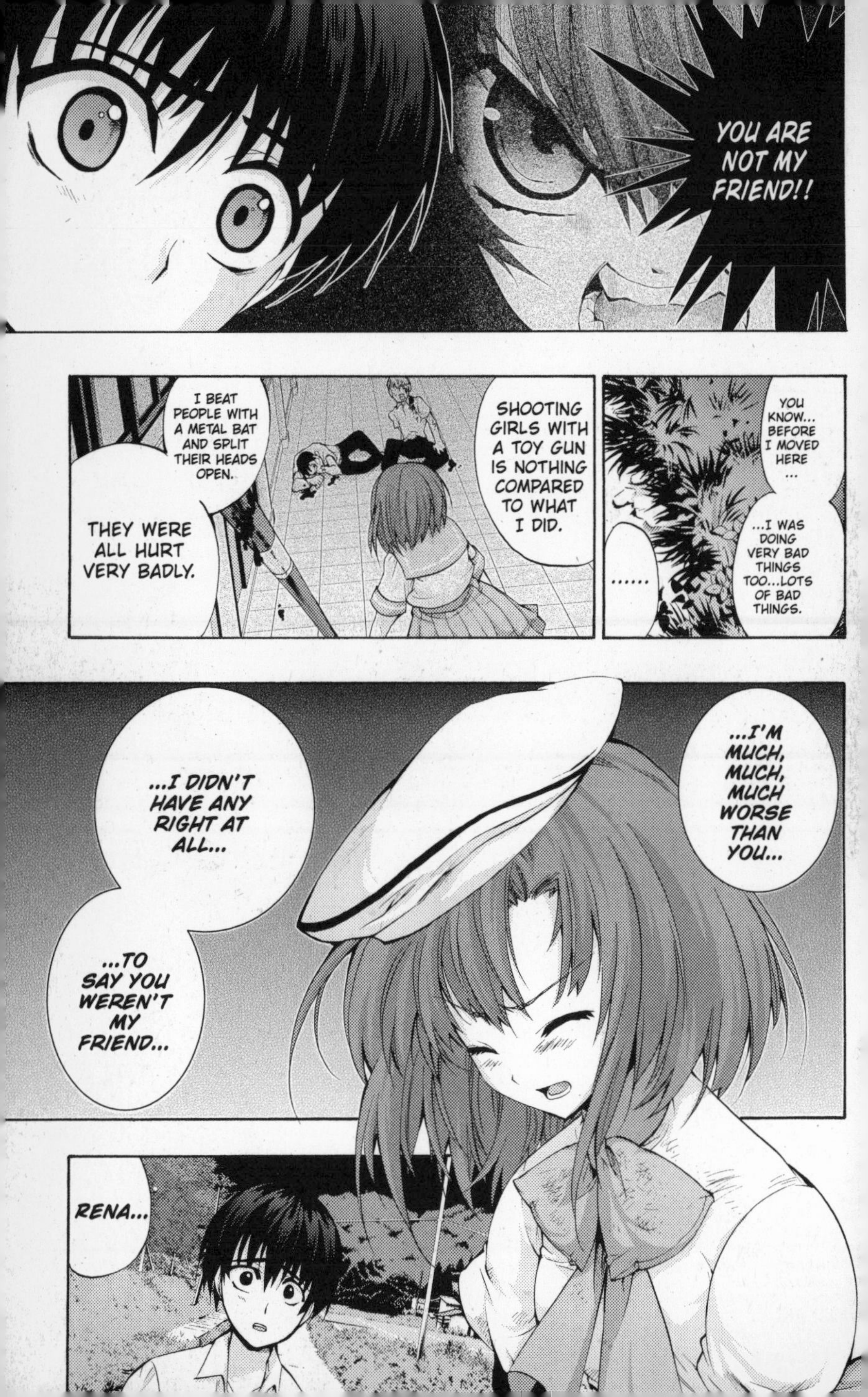
YOU ARE NOT MY FRIEND!!
YOU KNOW... BEFORE I MOVED HERE ...
...I WAS DOING VERY BAD THINGS TOO...LOTS OF BAD THINGS.
......
SHOOTING GIRLS WITH A TOY GUN IS NOTHING COMPARED TO WHAT I DID.
I BEAT PEOPLE WITH A METAL BAT AND SPLIT THEIR HEADS OPEN.
THEY WERE ALL HURT VERY BADLY.
...I'M MUCH, MUCH, MUCH WORSE THAN YOU...
...I DIDN'T HAVE ANY RIGHT AT ALL...
...TO SAY YOU WEREN'T MY FRIEND...
RENA...

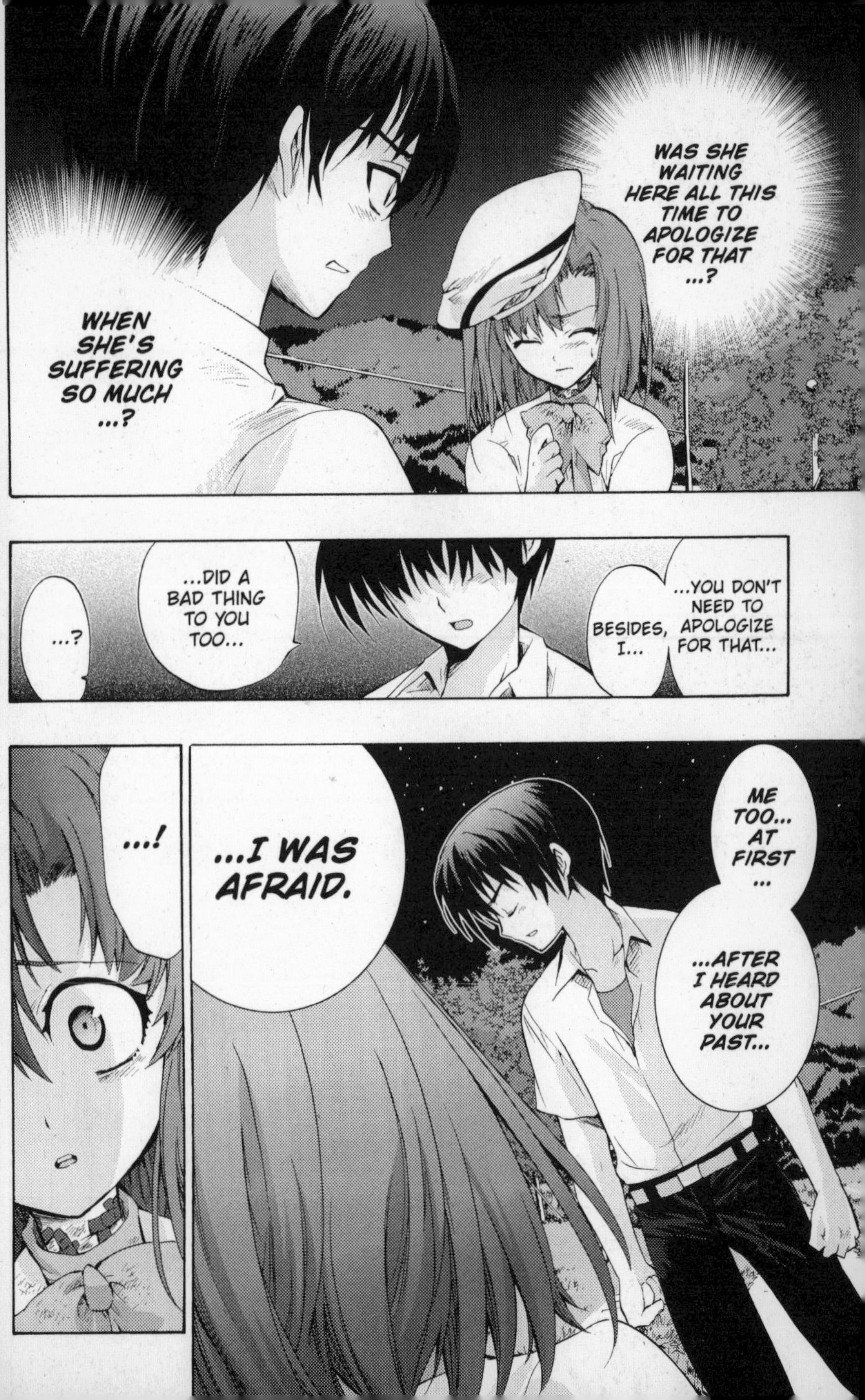
WAS SHE WAITING HERE ALL THIS TIME TO APOLOGIZE FOR THAT ...?
WHEN SHE'S SUFFERING SO MUCH ...?
...YOU DON'T NEED TO APOLOGIZE FOR THAT...
BESIDES, I...
...DID A BAD THING TO YOU TOO...
...?
ME TOO... AT FIRST ...
...AFTER I HEARD ABOUT YOUR PAST...
...I WAS AFRAID.
...!

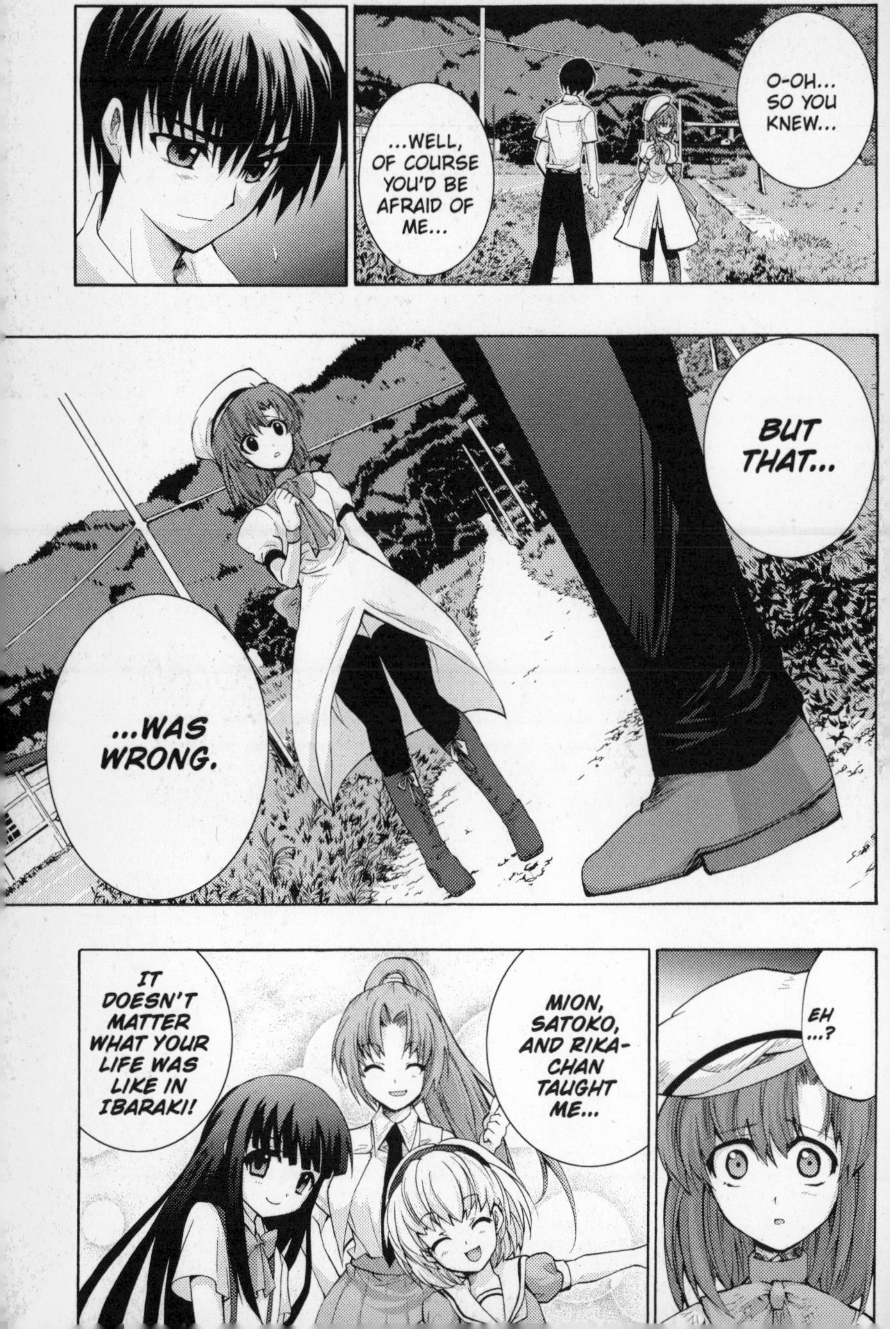
O-OH... SO YOU KNEW...
...WELL, OF COURSE YOU'D BE AFRAID OF ME...
BUT THAT...
...WAS WRONG.
EH ...?
MION, SATOKO, AND RIKA-CHAN TAUGHT ME...
IT DOESN'T MATTER WHAT YOUR LIFE WAS LIKE IN IBARAKI!

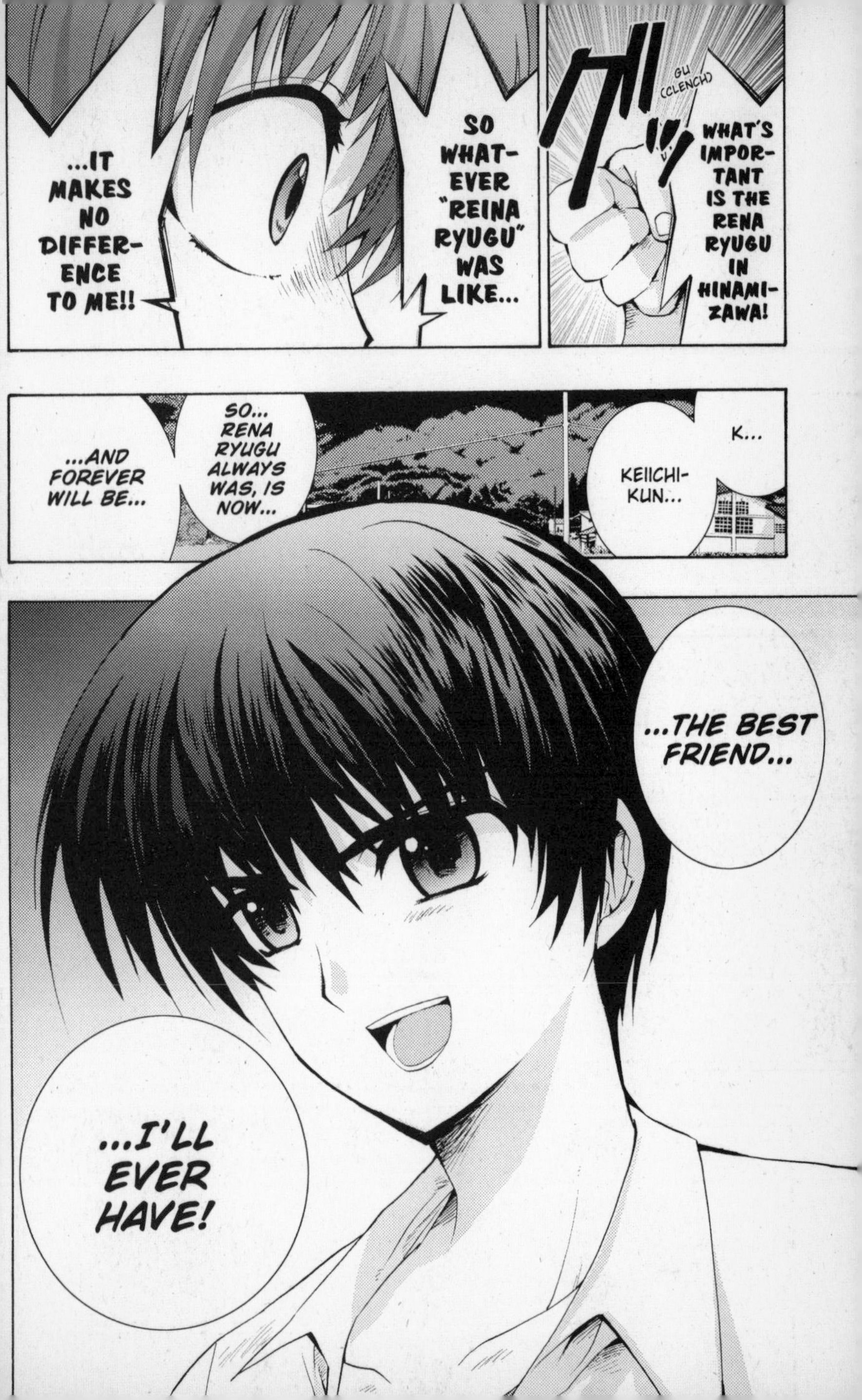
GU (CLENCH)
WHAT'S IMPORTANT IS THE RENA RYUGU IN HINAMIZAWA!
SO WHATEVER "REINA RYUGU" WAS LIKE...
...IT MAKES NO DIFFERENCE TO ME!!
K... KEIICHI-KUN...
SO... RENA RYUGU ALWAYS WAS, IS NOW...
...AND FOREVER WILL BE...
...THE BEST FRIEND...
...I'LL EVER HAVE!

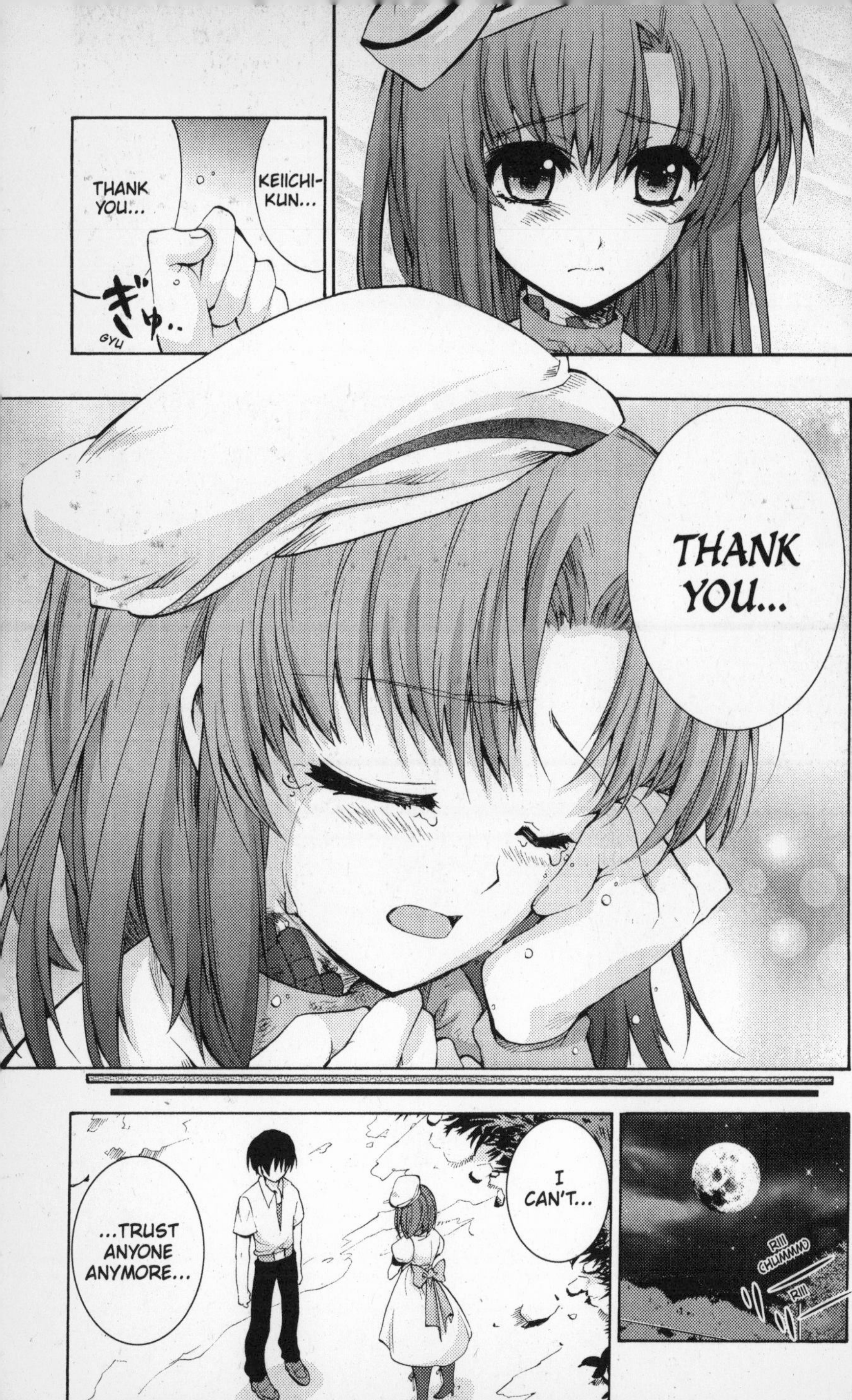
KEIICHI-KUN...
THANK YOU...
ぎゅ..
GYU
THANK YOU...
RIII CHUMMM
RIII
I CAN'T...
...TRUST ANYONE ANYMORE...

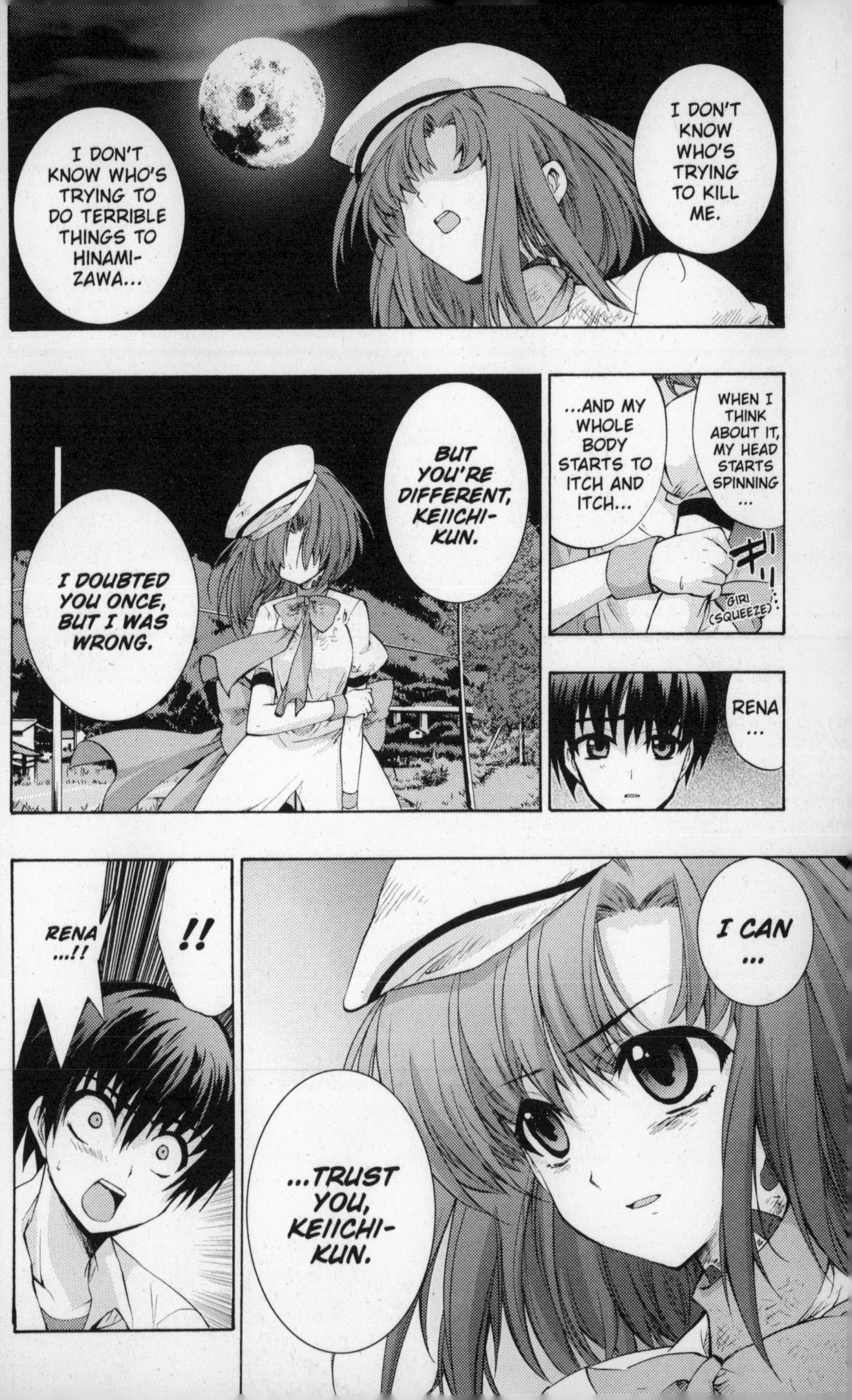
I DON'T KNOW WHO'S TRYING TO KILL ME.
I DON'T KNOW WHO'S TRYING TO DO TERRIBLE THINGS TO HINAMI-ZAWA...
WHEN I THINK ABOUT IT, MY HEAD STARTS SPINNING ...
...AND MY WHOLE BODY STARTS TO ITCH AND ITCH...
ギリ
GIRI (SQUEEZE)
RENA ...
BUT YOU'RE DIFFERENT, KEIICHI-KUN.
I DOUBTED YOU ONCE, BUT I WAS WRONG.
I CAN ...
...TRUST YOU, KEIICHI-KUN.
!!
RENA ...!!

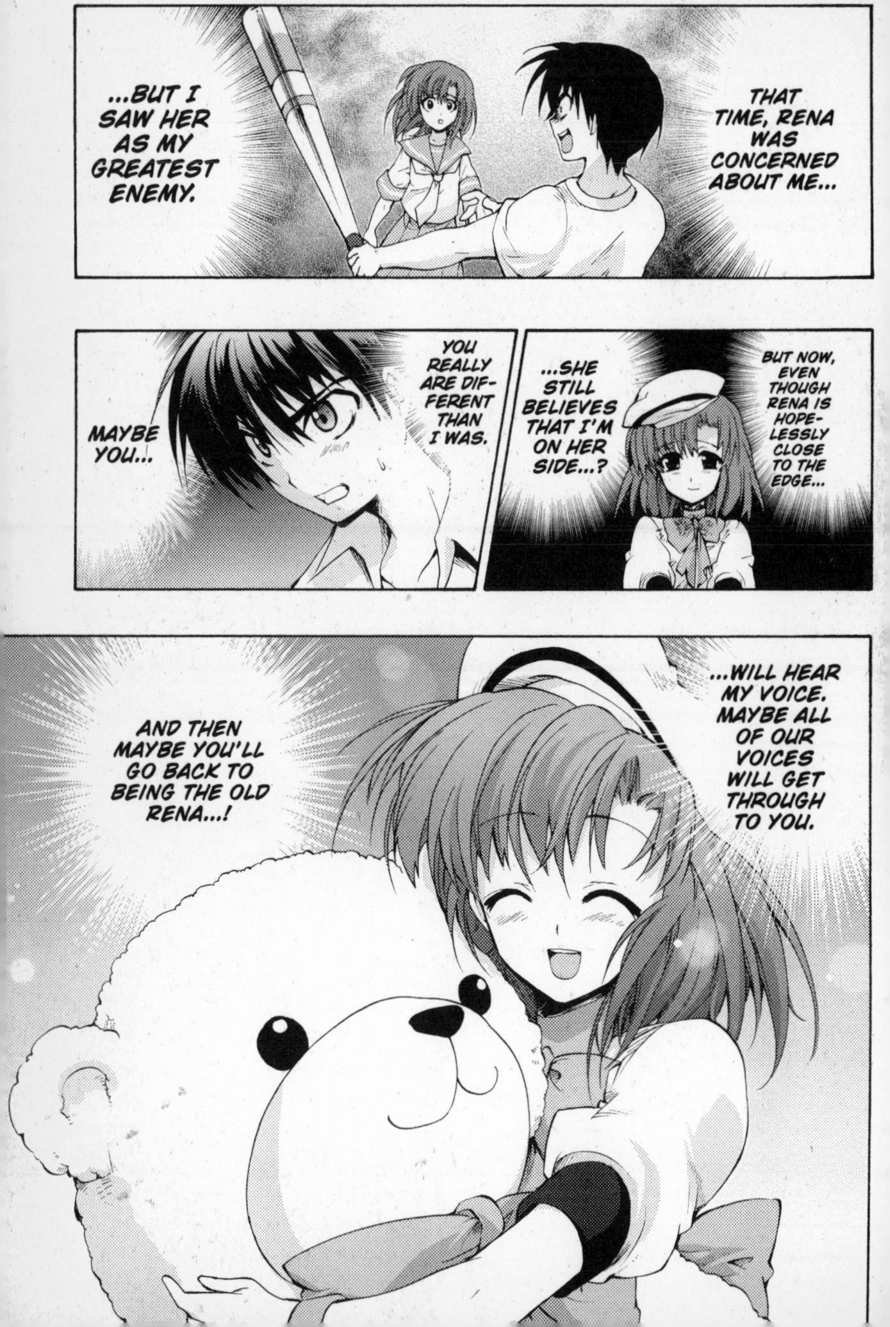
THAT TIME, RENA WAS CONCERNED ABOUT ME...
...BUT I SAW HER AS MY GREATEST ENEMY.
BUT NOW, EVEN THOUGH RENA IS HOPELESSLY CLOSE TO THE EDGE...
...SHE STILL BELIEVES THAT I'M ON HER SIDE...?
YOU REALLY ARE DIFFERENT THAN I WAS.
MAYBE YOU...
...WILL HEAR MY VOICE. MAYBE ALL OF OUR VOICES WILL GET THROUGH TO YOU.
AND THEN MAYBE YOU'LL GO BACK TO BEING THE OLD RENA...!

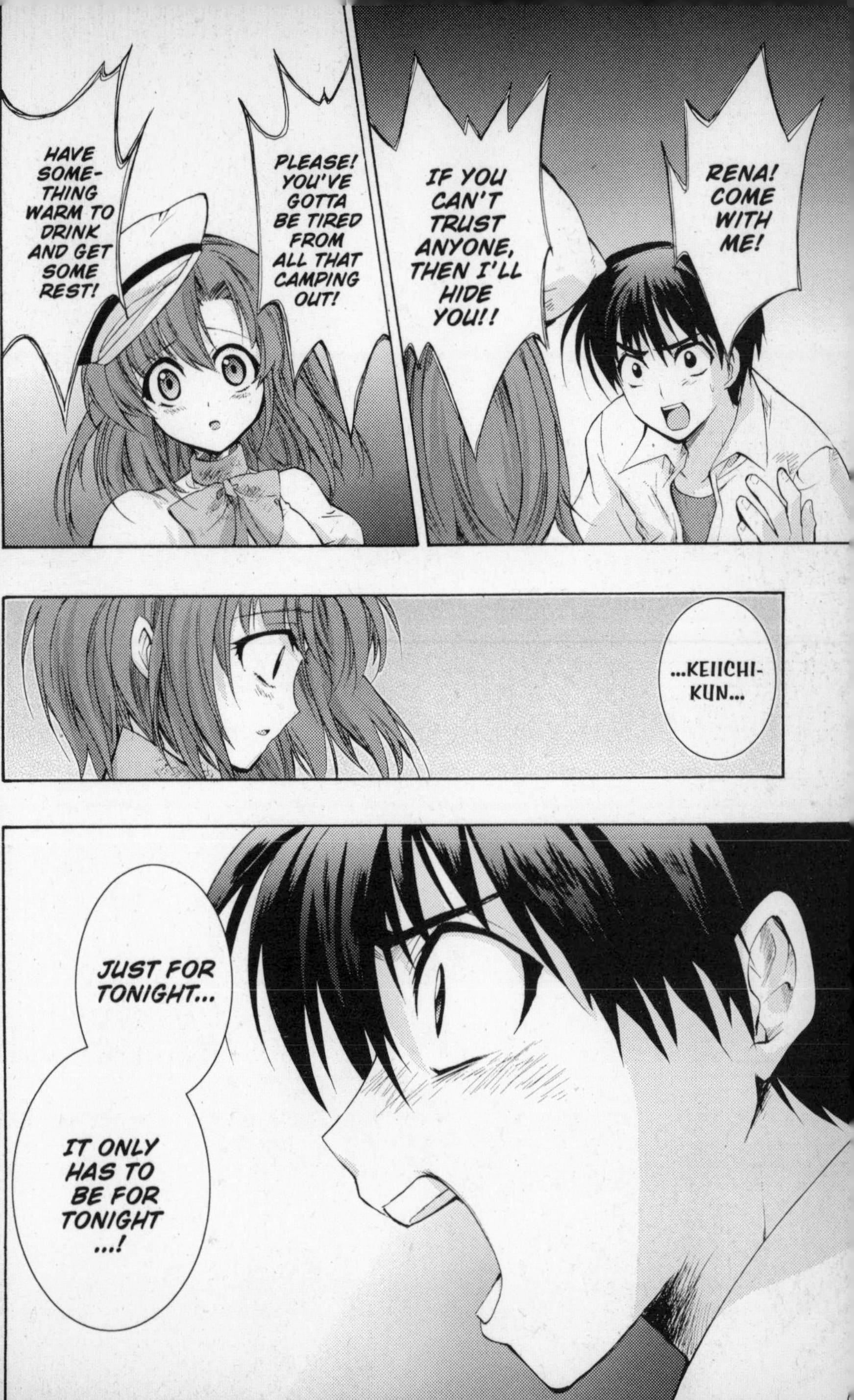
RENA! COME WITH ME!
IF YOU CAN'T TRUST ANYONE, THEN I'LL HIDE YOU!!
PLEASE! YOU'VE GOTTA BE TIRED FROM ALL THAT CAMPING OUT!
HAVE SOME-THING WARM TO DRINK AND GET SOME REST!
...KEIICHI-KUN...
JUST FOR TONIGHT...
IT ONLY HAS TO BE FOR TONIGHT ...!

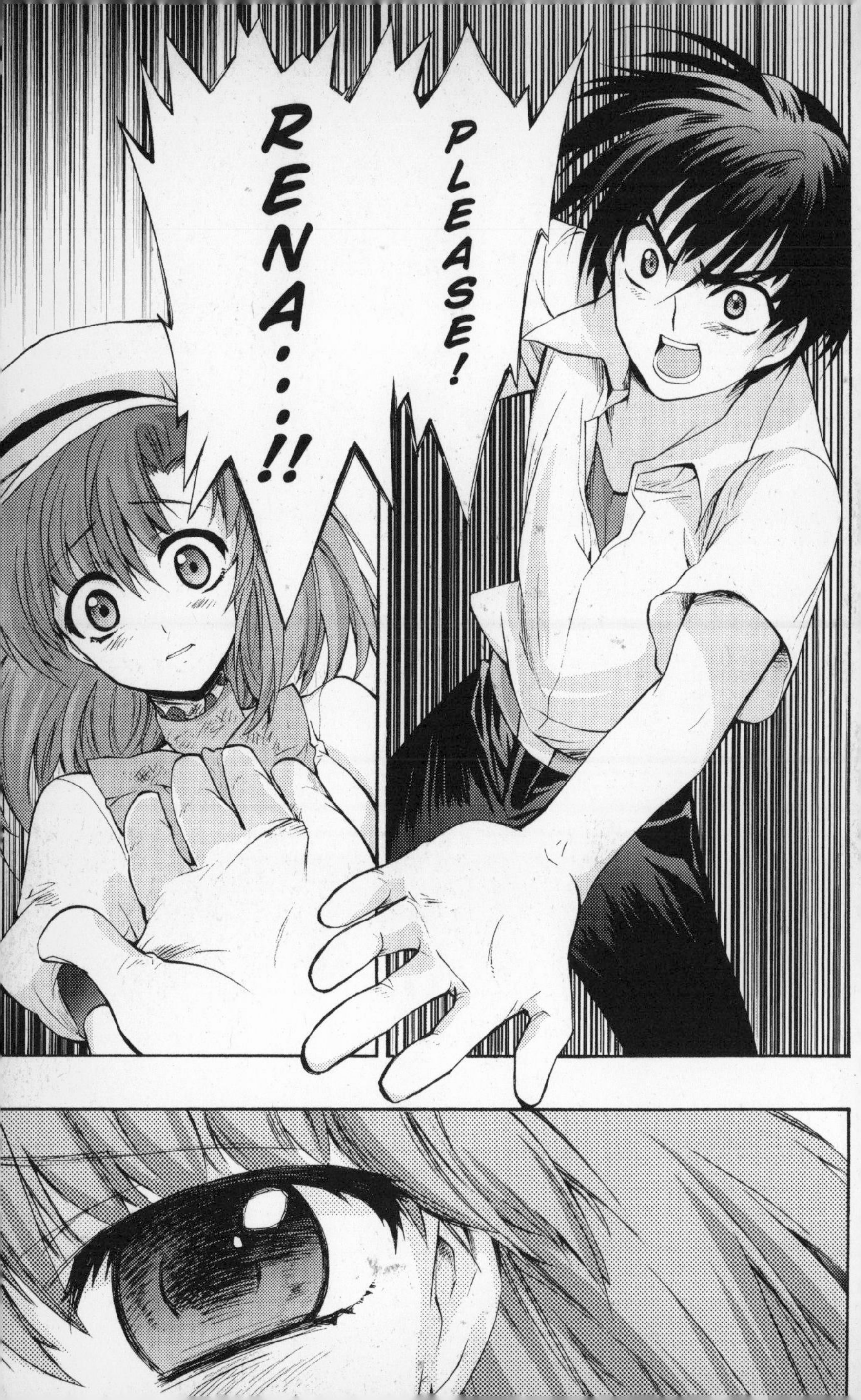
PLEASE! RENA...!!

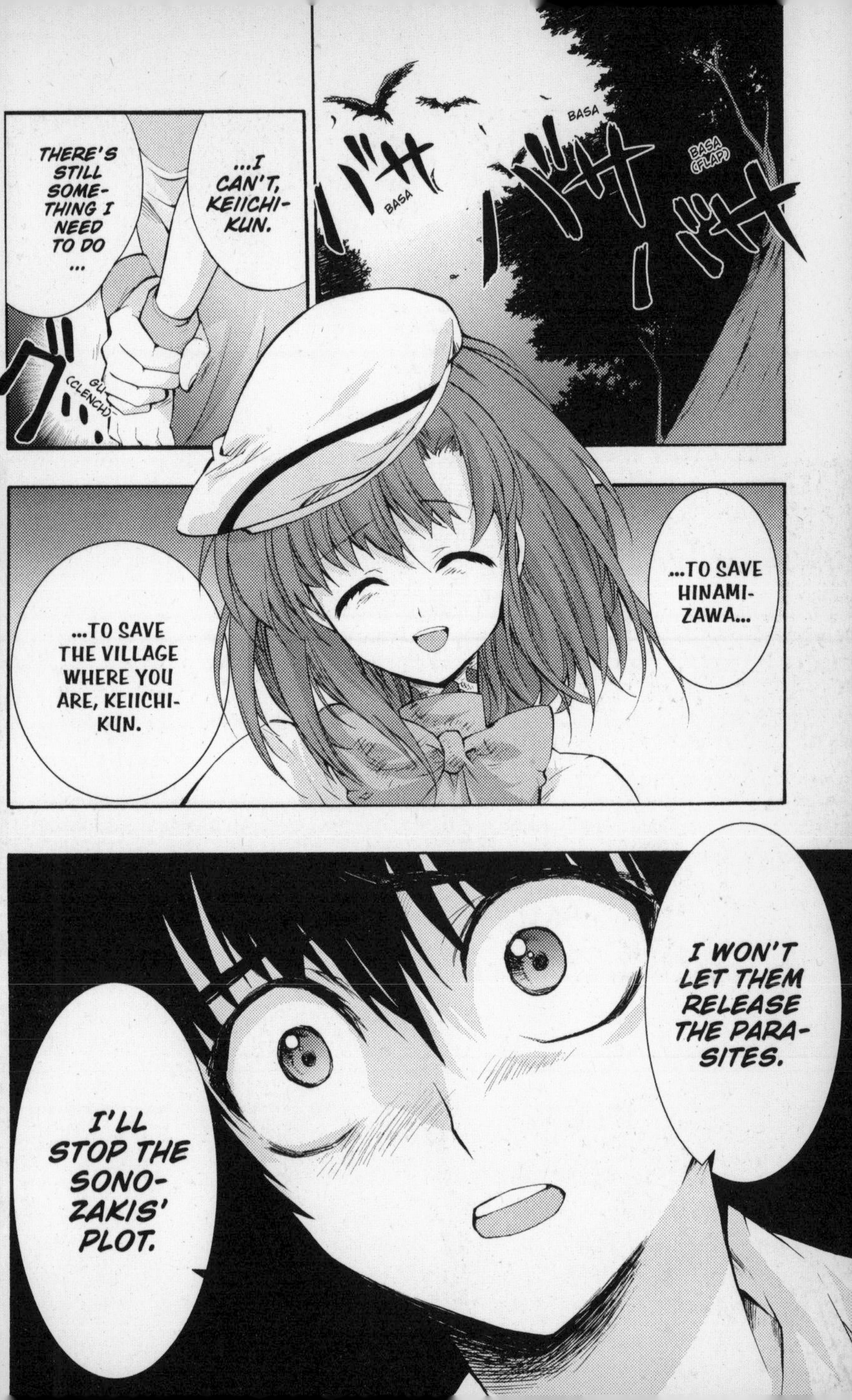

BASA
BASA (FLAP)
BASA
...I CAN'T, KEIICHI-KUN.
THERE'S STILL SOMETHING I NEED TO DO ...
GU (CLENCH)
...TO SAVE HINAMIZAWA...
...TO SAVE THE VILLAGE WHERE YOU ARE, KEIICHI-KUN.
I WON'T LET THEM RELEASE THE PARASITES.
I'LL STOP THE SONOZAKIS' PLOT.

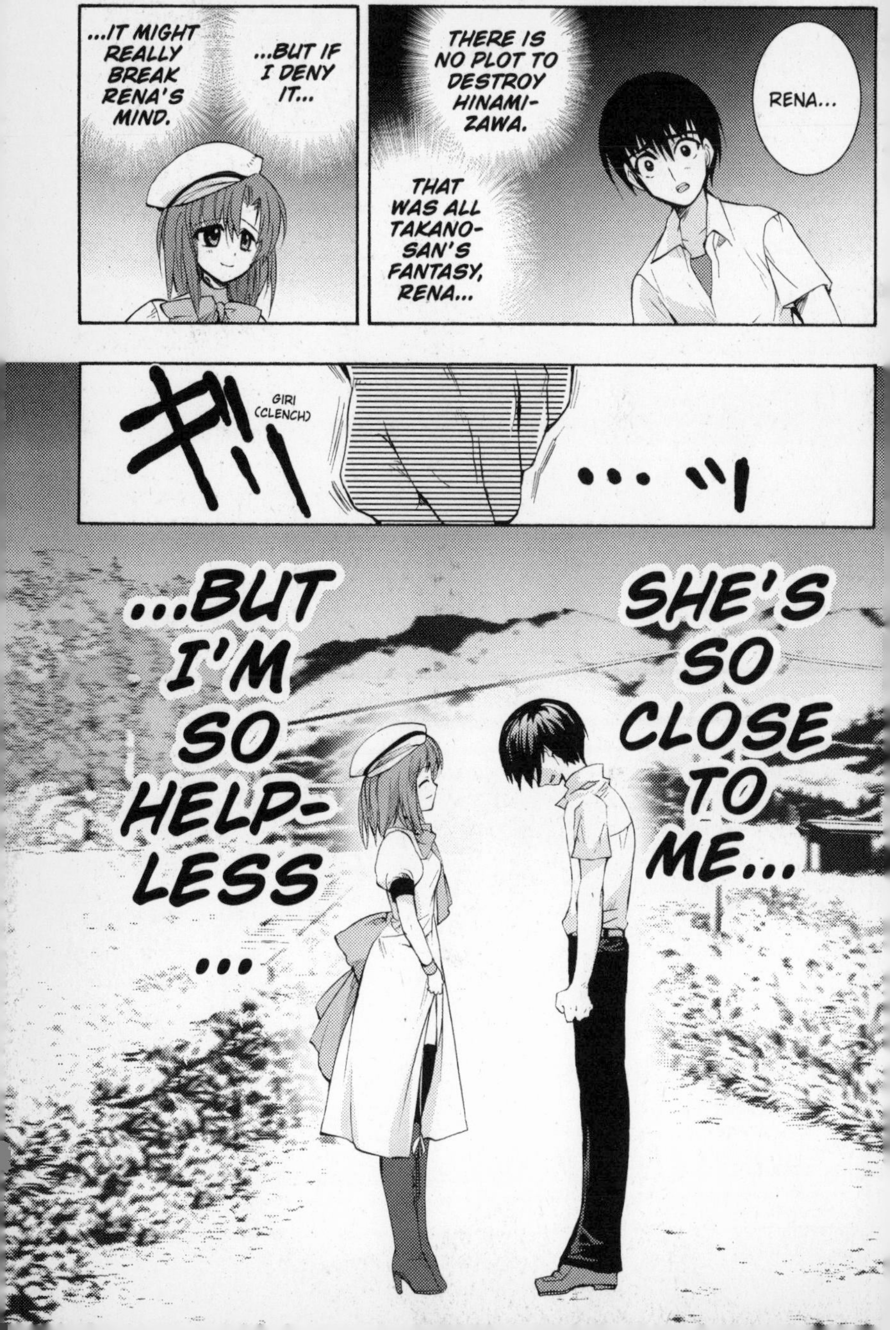
RENA...
THERE IS NO PLOT TO DESTROY HINAMI-ZAWA.
THAT WAS ALL TAKANO-SAN'S FANTASY, RENA...
...BUT IF I DENY IT...
...IT MIGHT REALLY BREAK RENA'S MIND.
...ッ
GIRI (CLENCH)
SHE'S SO CLOSE TO ME...
...BUT I'M SO HELP-LESS...

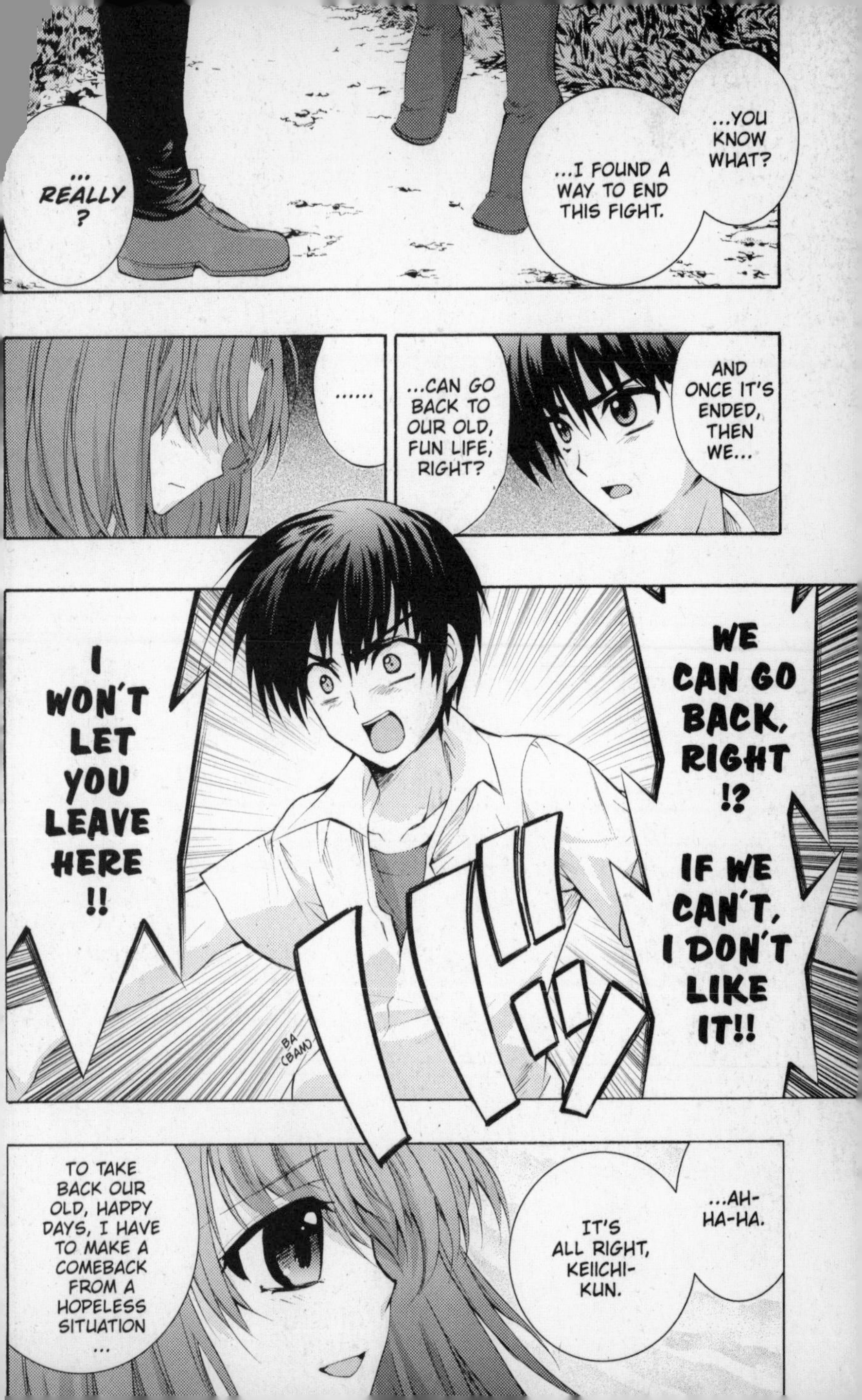
...YOU KNOW WHAT?
...I FOUND A WAY TO END THIS FIGHT.
...REALLY?
AND ONCE IT'S ENDED, THEN WE...
...CAN GO BACK TO OUR OLD, FUN LIFE, RIGHT?
......
WE CAN GO BACK, RIGHT!?
IF WE CAN'T, I DON'T LIKE IT!!
I WON'T LET YOU LEAVE HERE!!
BA (BAM)
...AH-HA-HA.
IT'S ALL RIGHT, KEIICHI-KUN.
TO TAKE BACK OUR OLD, HAPPY DAYS, I HAVE TO MAKE A COMEBACK FROM A HOPELESS SITUATION...

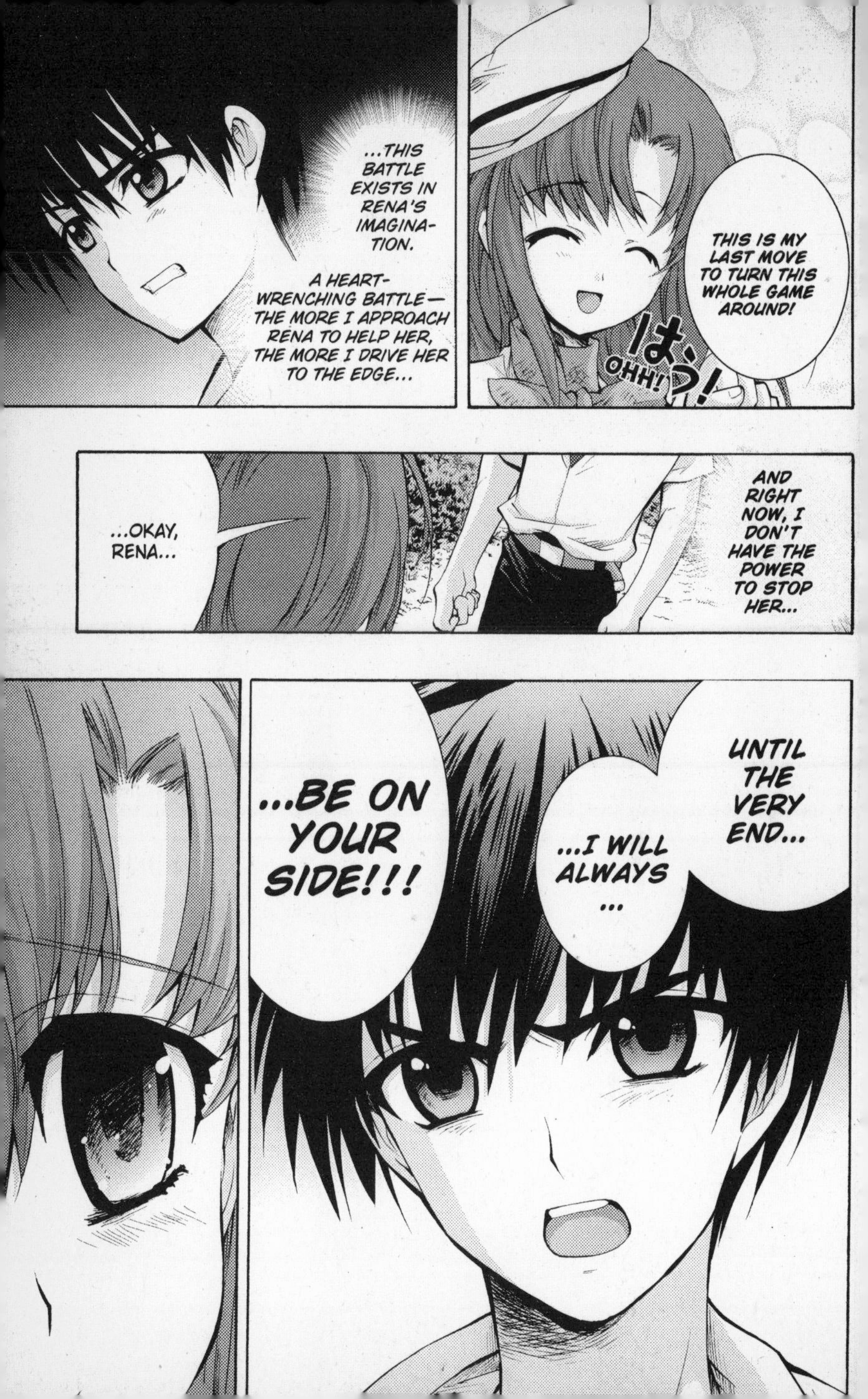
THIS IS MY LAST MOVE TO TURN THIS WHOLE GAME AROUND!
はぅ!
OHH!
...THIS BATTLE EXISTS IN RENA'S IMAGINA-TION.
A HEART-WRENCHING BATTLE—THE MORE I APPROACH RENA TO HELP HER, THE MORE I DRIVE HER TO THE EDGE...
AND RIGHT NOW, I DON'T HAVE THE POWER TO STOP HER...
...OKAY, RENA...
UNTIL THE VERY END...
...I WILL ALWAYS...
...BE ON YOUR SIDE!!!

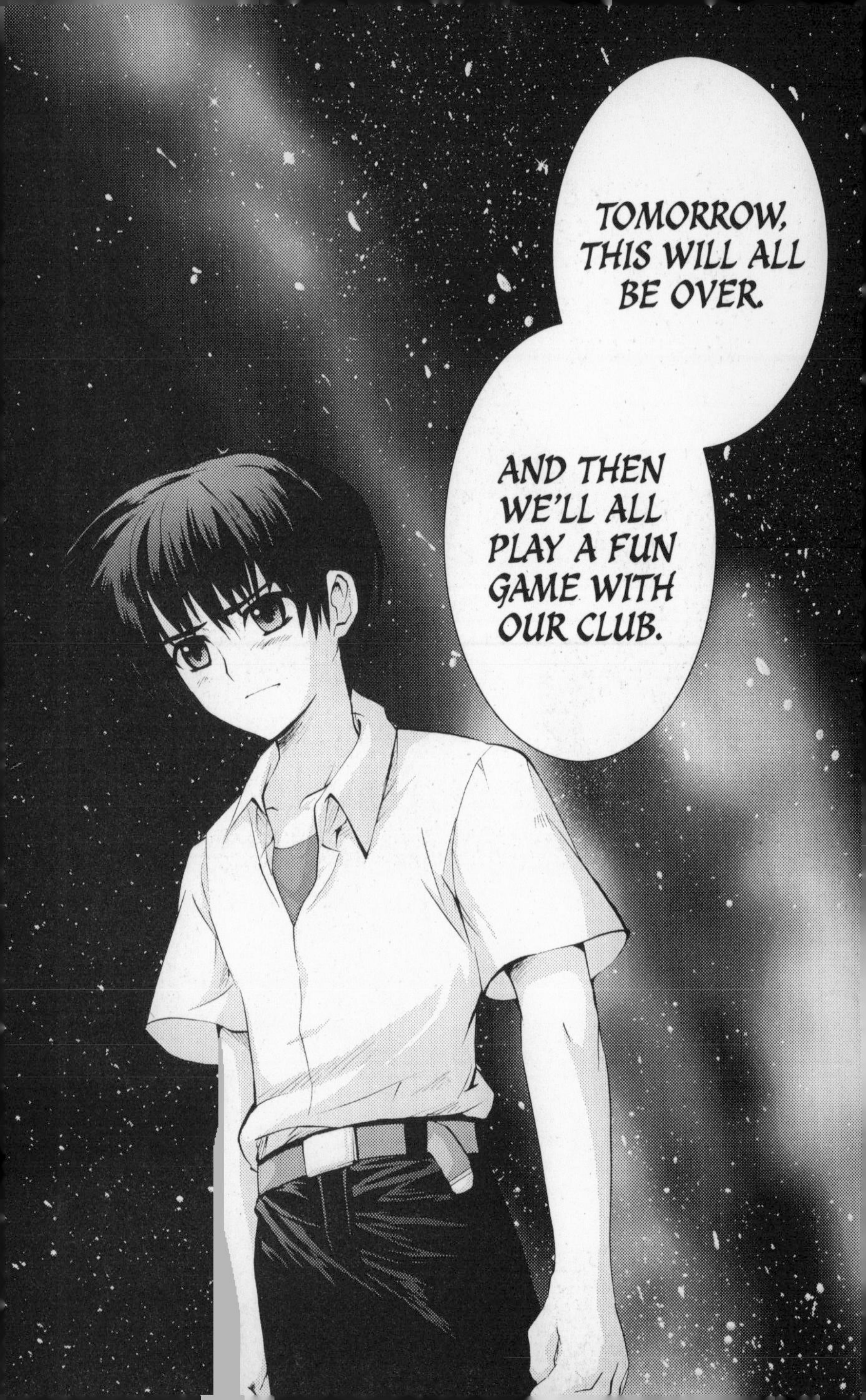
TOMORROW, THIS WILL ALL BE OVER.
AND THEN WE'LL ALL PLAY A FUN GAME WITH OUR CLUB.

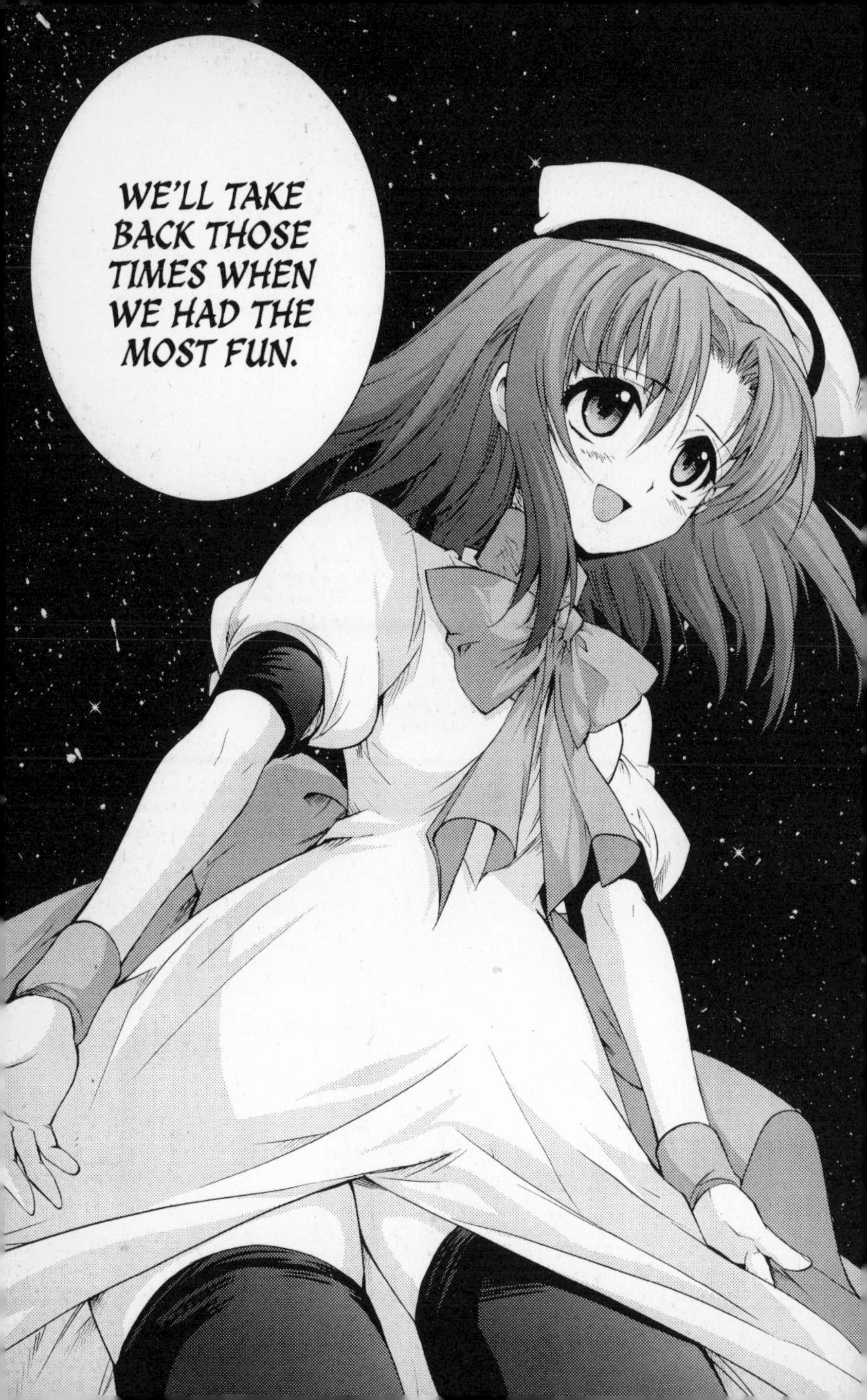
WE'LL TAKE BACK THOSE TIMES WHEN WE HAD THE MOST FUN.

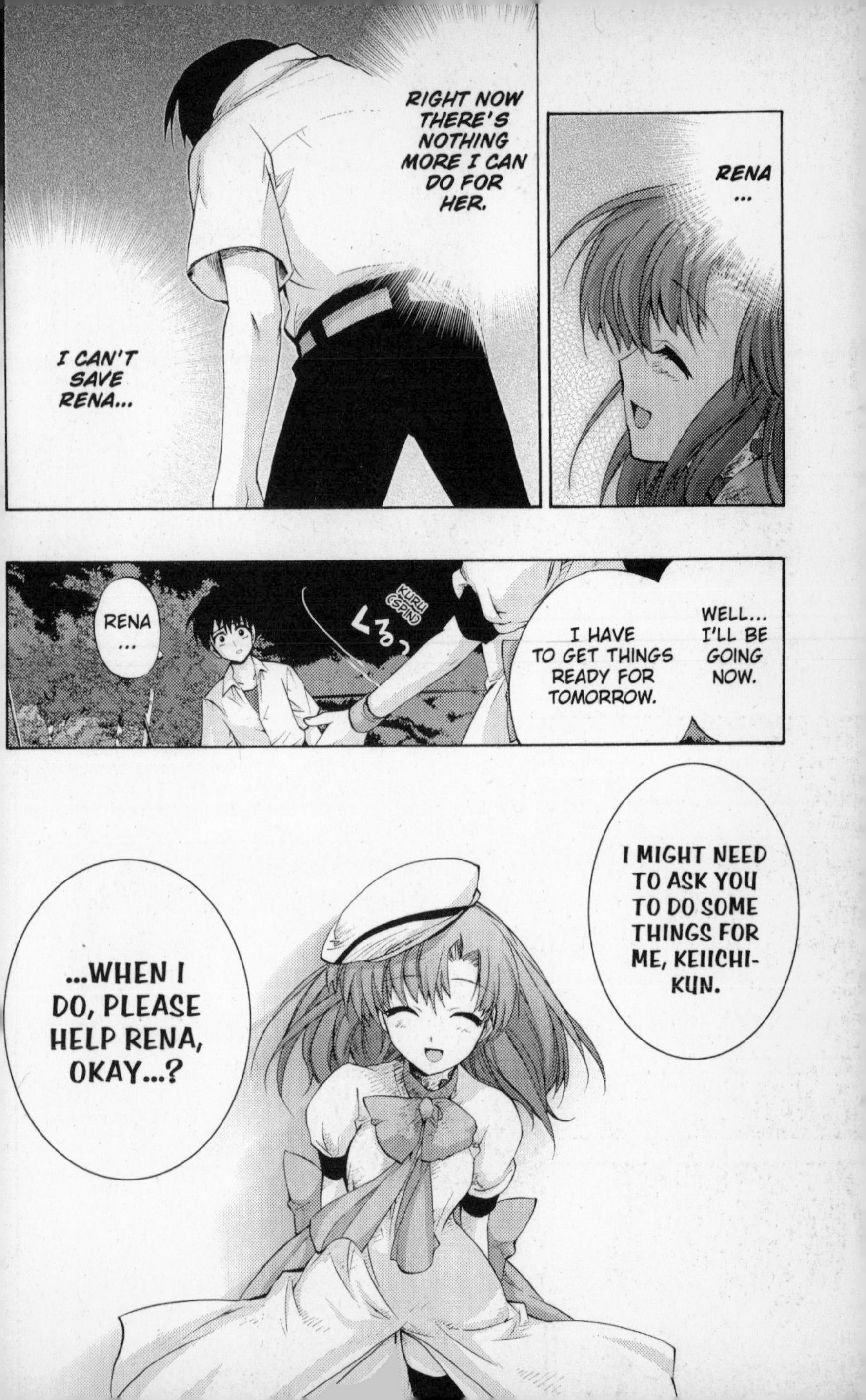
RENA ...
RIGHT NOW THERE'S NOTHING MORE I CAN DO FOR HER.
I CAN'T SAVE RENA...
WELL... I'LL BE GOING NOW.
I HAVE TO GET THINGS READY FOR TOMORROW.
くるっ KURU (SPIN)
RENA ...
I MIGHT NEED TO ASK YOU TO DO SOME THINGS FOR ME, KEIICHI-KUN.
...WHEN I DO, PLEASE HELP RENA, OKAY...?

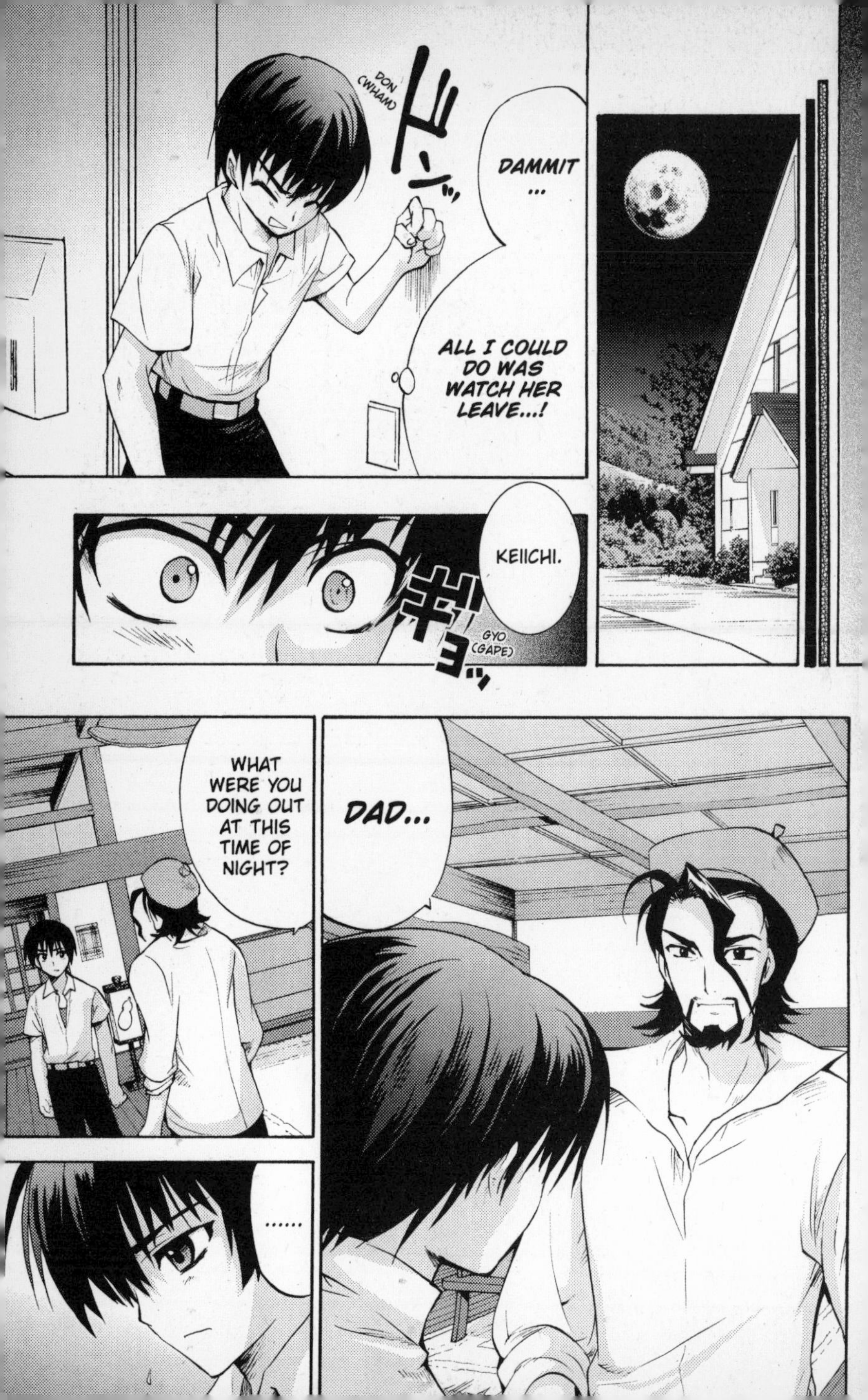
DON (WHAM)
DAMMIT ...
ALL I COULD DO WAS WATCH HER LEAVE...!
KEIICHI.
GYO (GAPE)
DAD...
WHAT WERE YOU DOING OUT AT THIS TIME OF NIGHT?
......

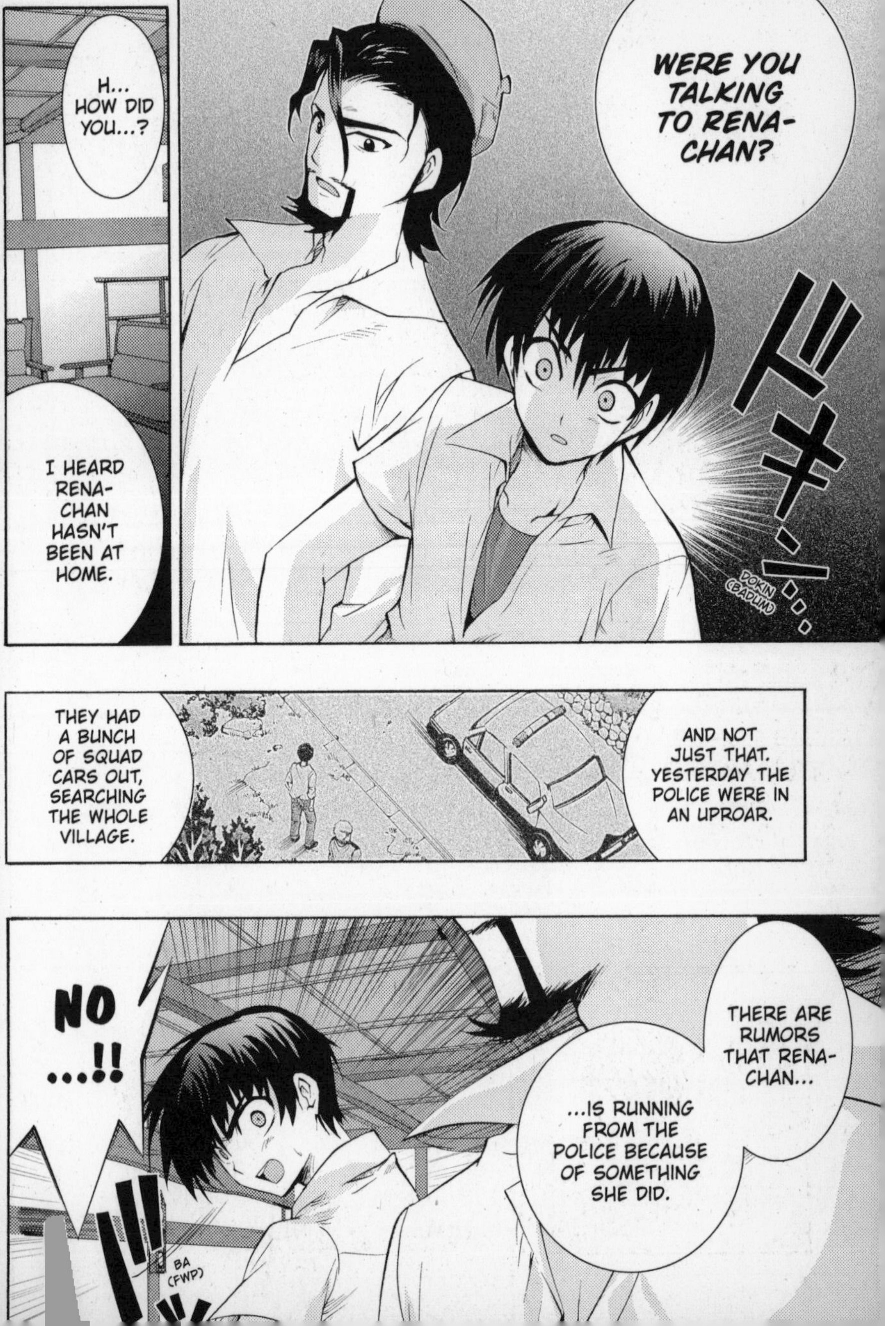
WERE YOU TALKING TO RENA-CHAN?
DOKIN (BADUM)
H... HOW DID YOU...?
I HEARD RENA-CHAN HASN'T BEEN AT HOME.
AND NOT JUST THAT. YESTERDAY THE POLICE WERE IN AN UPROAR.
THEY HAD A BUNCH OF SQUAD CARS OUT, SEARCHING THE WHOLE VILLAGE.
THERE ARE RUMORS THAT RENA-CHAN...
...IS RUNNING FROM THE POLICE BECAUSE OF SOMETHING SHE DID.
NO...!!
BA (FWP)

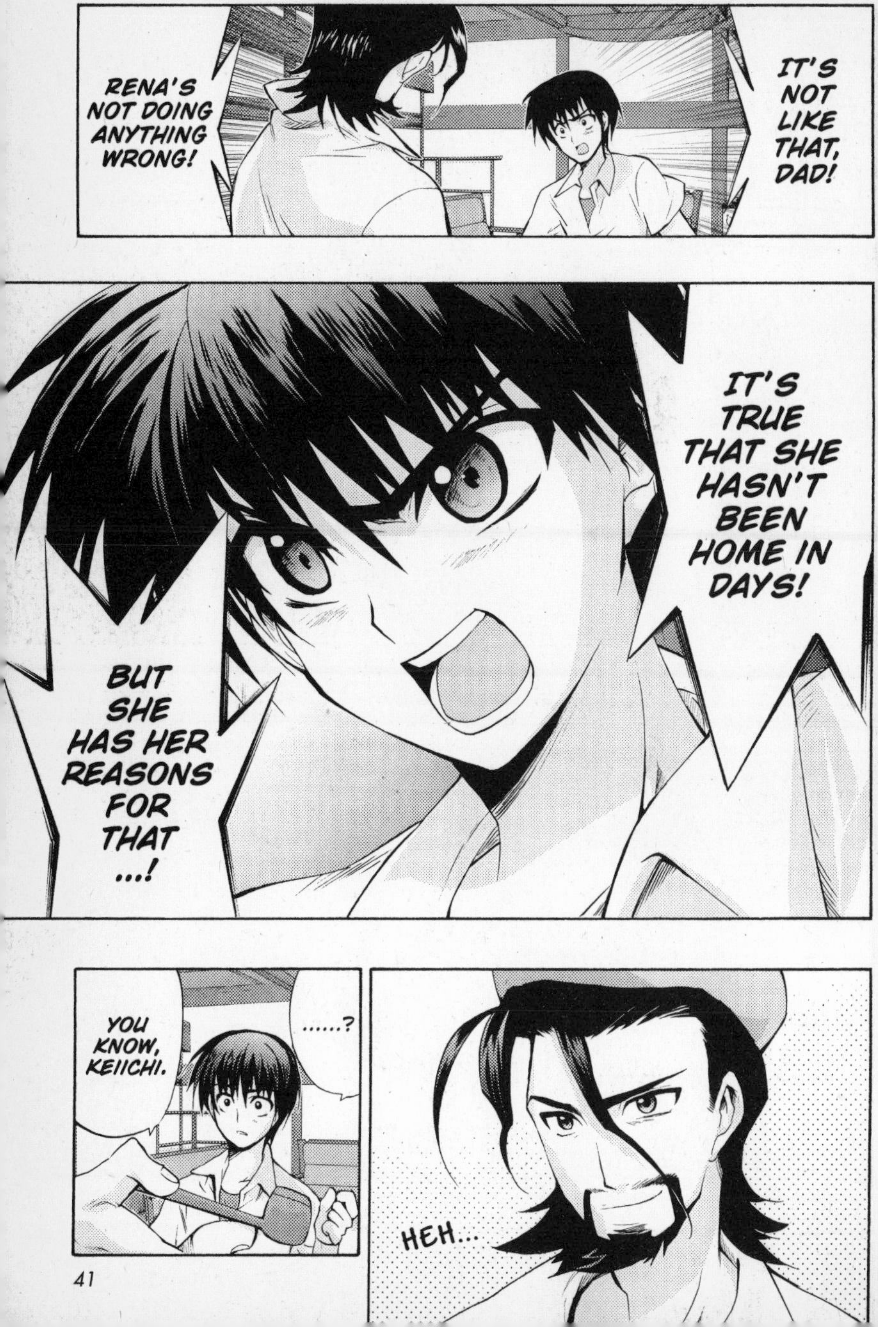
IT'S NOT LIKE THAT, DAD!
RENA'S NOT DOING ANYTHING WRONG!
IT'S TRUE THAT SHE HASN'T BEEN HOME IN DAYS!
BUT SHE HAS HER REASONS FOR THAT ...!
HEH...
......?
YOU KNOW, KEIICHI.

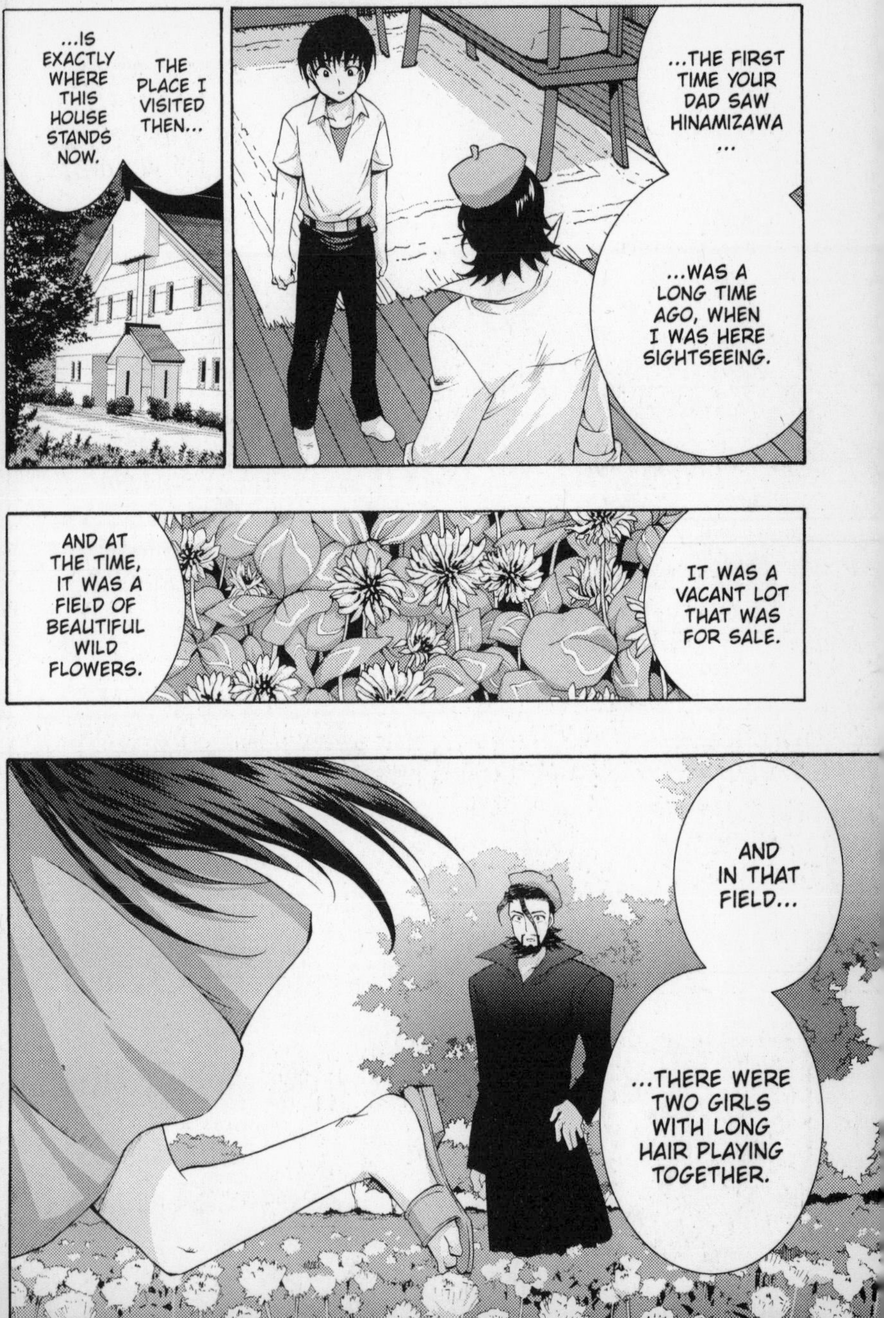
...THE FIRST TIME YOUR DAD SAW HINAMIZAWA ...
...WAS A LONG TIME AGO, WHEN I WAS HERE SIGHTSEEING.
THE PLACE I VISITED THEN...
...IS EXACTLY WHERE THIS HOUSE STANDS NOW.
IT WAS A VACANT LOT THAT WAS FOR SALE.
AND AT THE TIME, IT WAS A FIELD OF BEAUTIFUL WILD FLOWERS.
AND IN THAT FIELD...
...THERE WERE TWO GIRLS WITH LONG HAIR PLAYING TOGETHER.

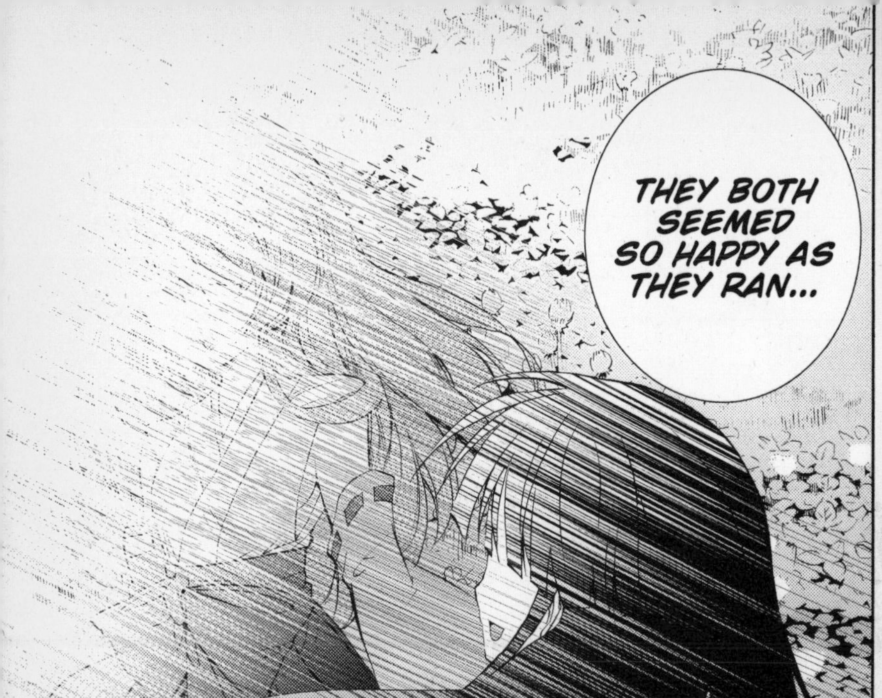
THEY BOTH SEEMED SO HAPPY AS THEY RAN...
...SPINNING AND DANCING THROUGH THE FIELD.
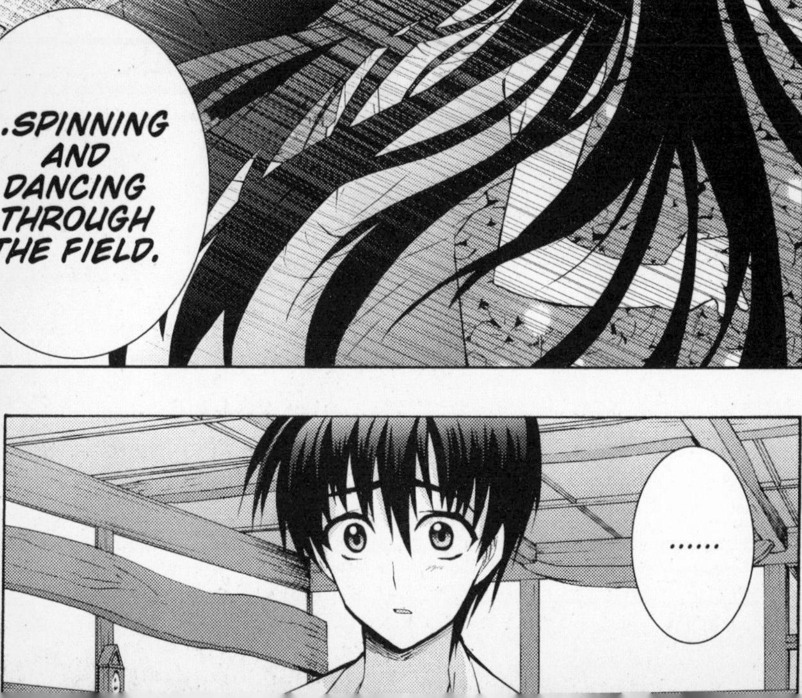
......

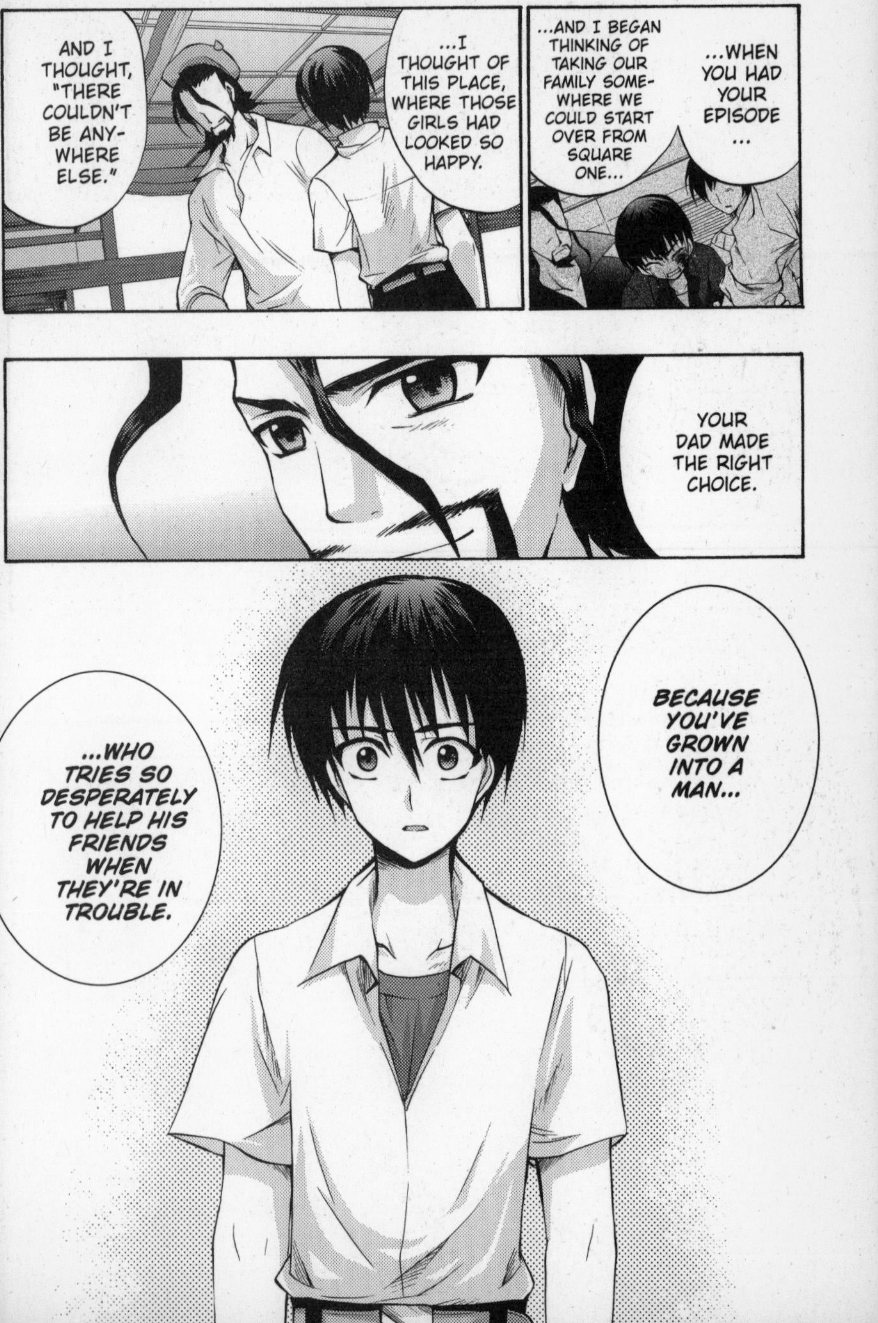
...WHEN YOU HAD YOUR EPISODE ...
...AND I BEGAN THINKING OF TAKING OUR FAMILY SOME-WHERE WE COULD START OVER FROM SQUARE ONE...
...I THOUGHT OF THIS PLACE, WHERE THOSE GIRLS HAD LOOKED SO HAPPY.
AND I THOUGHT, "THERE COULDN'T BE ANY-WHERE ELSE."
YOUR DAD MADE THE RIGHT CHOICE.
BECAUSE YOU'VE GROWN INTO A MAN...
...WHO TRIES SO DESPERATELY TO HELP HIS FRIENDS WHEN THEY'RE IN TROUBLE.

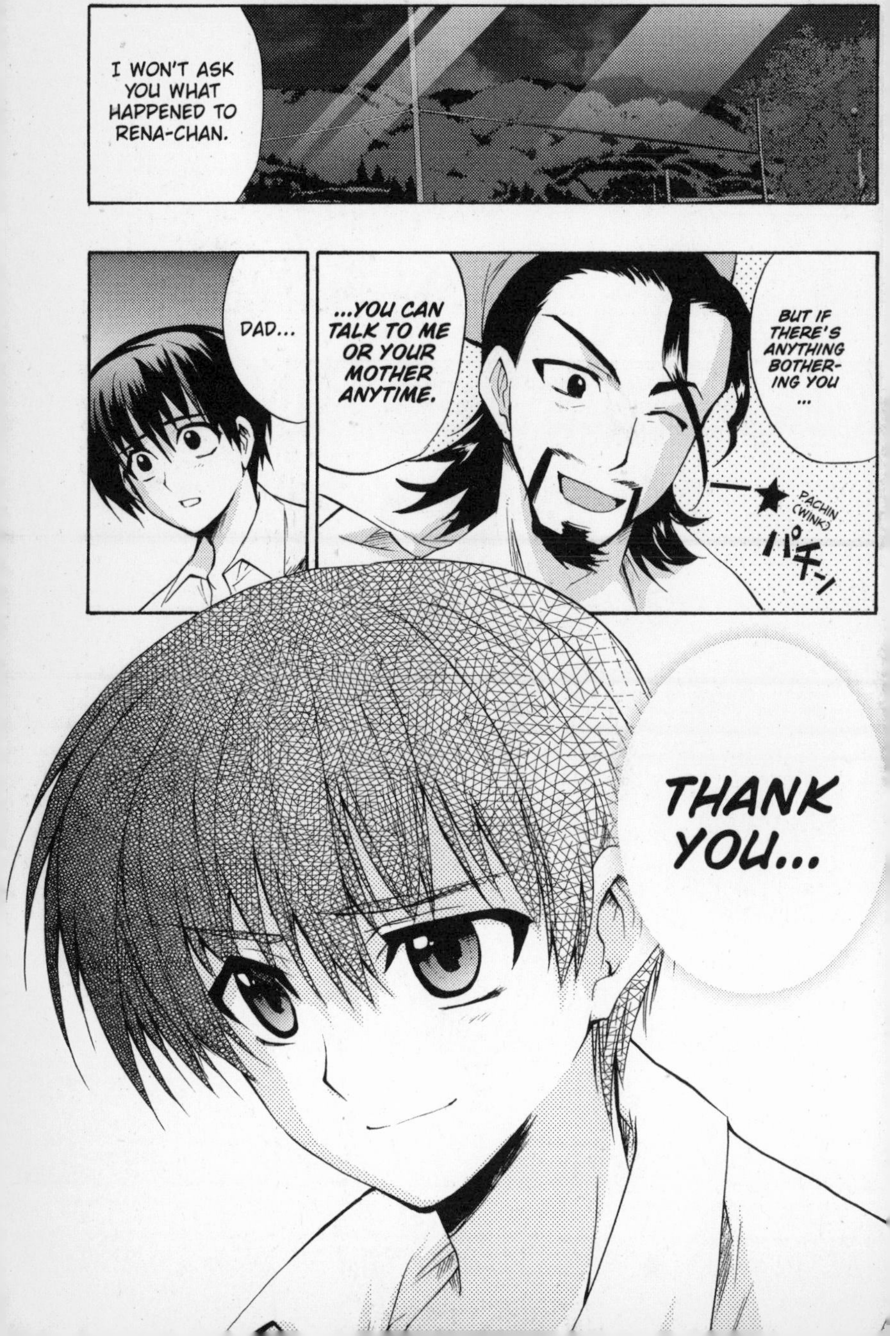
I WON'T ASK YOU WHAT HAPPENED TO RENA-CHAN.
BUT IF THERE'S ANYTHING BOTHERING YOU ...
...YOU CAN TALK TO ME OR YOUR MOTHER ANYTIME.
PACHIN (WINK)
パチーン
DAD...
THANK YOU...

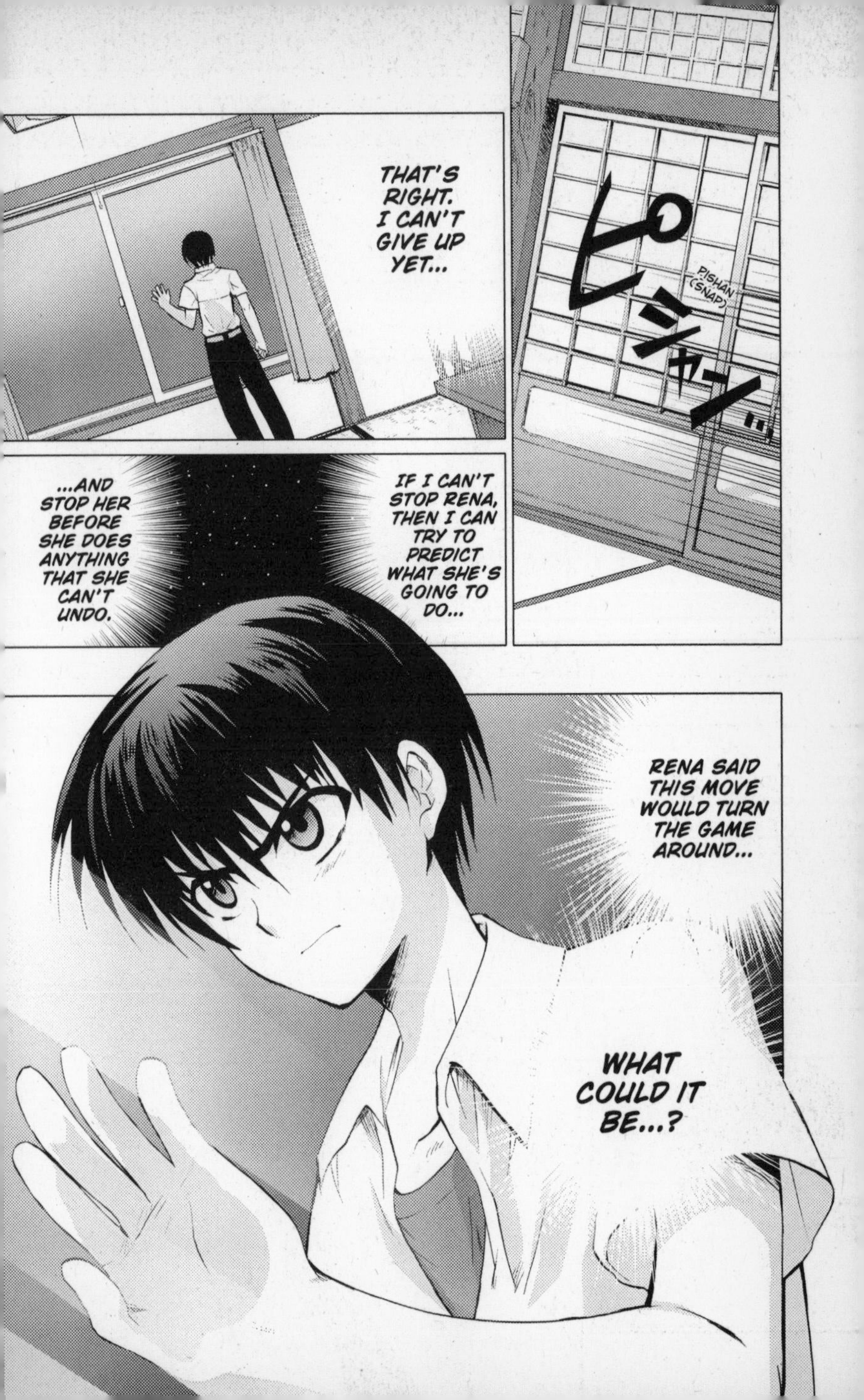
PISHAN (SNAP)
THAT'S RIGHT. I CAN'T GIVE UP YET...
IF I CAN'T STOP RENA, THEN I CAN TRY TO PREDICT WHAT SHE'S GOING TO DO...
...AND STOP HER BEFORE SHE DOES ANYTHING THAT SHE CAN'T UNDO.
RENA SAID THIS MOVE WOULD TURN THE GAME AROUND...
WHAT COULD IT BE...?

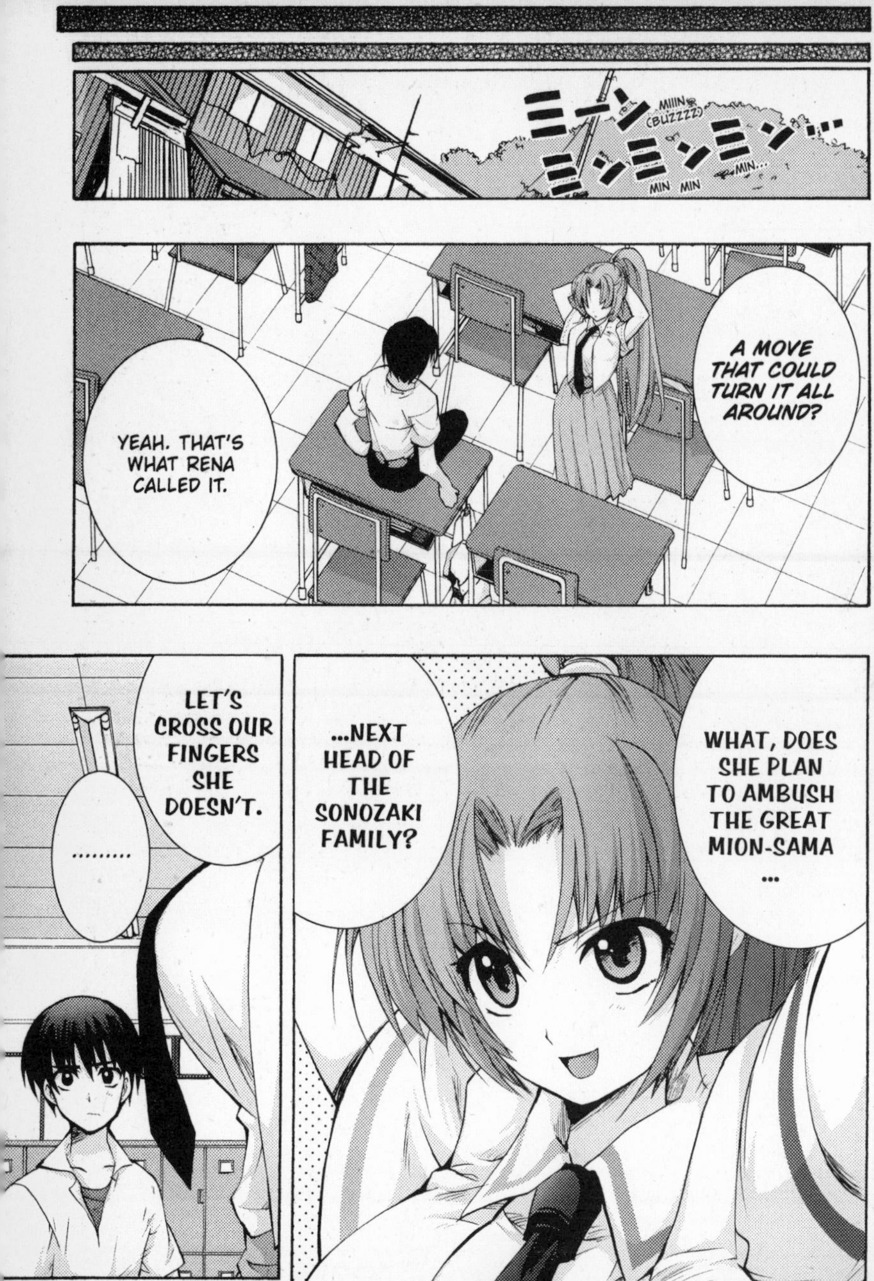
ミーン
MIIIN (BUZZZZ)
ミンミンミン…
MIN MIN MIN...
A MOVE THAT COULD TURN IT ALL AROUND?
YEAH. THAT'S WHAT RENA CALLED IT.
WHAT, DOES SHE PLAN TO AMBUSH THE GREAT MION-SAMA ...
...NEXT HEAD OF THE SONOZAKI FAMILY?
LET'S CROSS OUR FINGERS SHE DOESN'T.
....

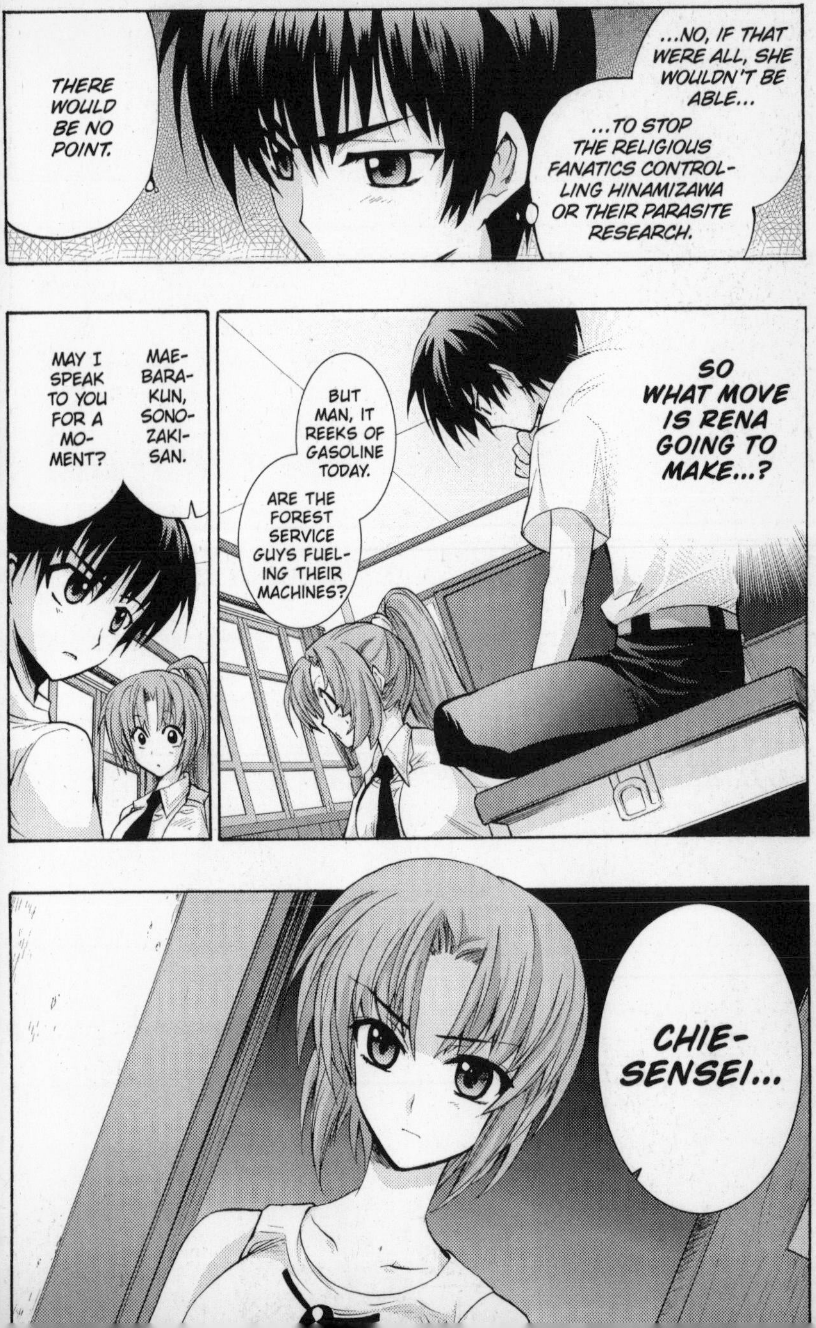
...NO, IF THAT WERE ALL, SHE WOULDN'T BE ABLE...
...TO STOP THE RELIGIOUS FANATICS CONTROLLING HINAMIZAWA OR THEIR PARASITE RESEARCH.
THERE WOULD BE NO POINT.
SO WHAT MOVE IS RENA GOING TO MAKE...?
BUT MAN, IT REEKS OF GASOLINE TODAY.
ARE THE FOREST SERVICE GUYS FUELING THEIR MACHINES?
MAEBARA-KUN, SONOZAKI-SAN.
MAY I SPEAK TO YOU FOR A MOMENT?
CHIE-SENSEI...

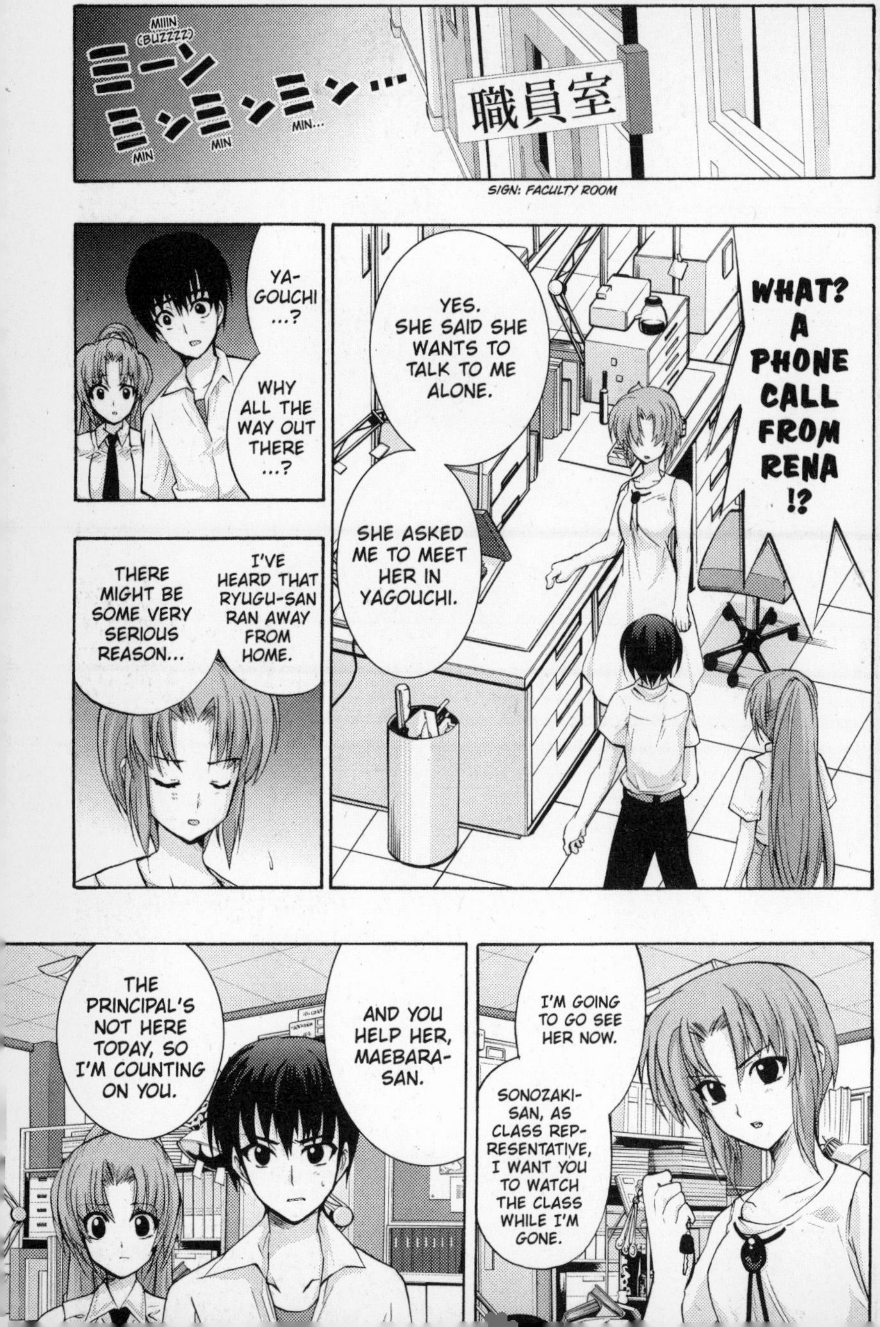
MIIN (BUZZZZ)
ミーンミンミンミン…
MIN MIN MIN...
職員室
SIGN: FACULTY ROOM
WHAT? A PHONE CALL FROM RENA!?
YES. SHE SAID SHE WANTS TO TALK TO ME ALONE.
SHE ASKED ME TO MEET HER IN YAGOUCHI.
YA-GOUCHI...?
WHY ALL THE WAY OUT THERE...?
I'VE HEARD THAT RYUGU-SAN RAN AWAY FROM HOME.
THERE MIGHT BE SOME VERY SERIOUS REASON...
I'M GOING TO GO SEE HER NOW.
SONOZAKI-SAN, AS CLASS REPRESENTATIVE, I WANT YOU TO WATCH THE CLASS WHILE I'M GONE.
AND YOU HELP HER, MAEBARA-SAN.
THE PRINCIPAL'S NOT HERE TODAY, SO I'M COUNTING ON YOU.

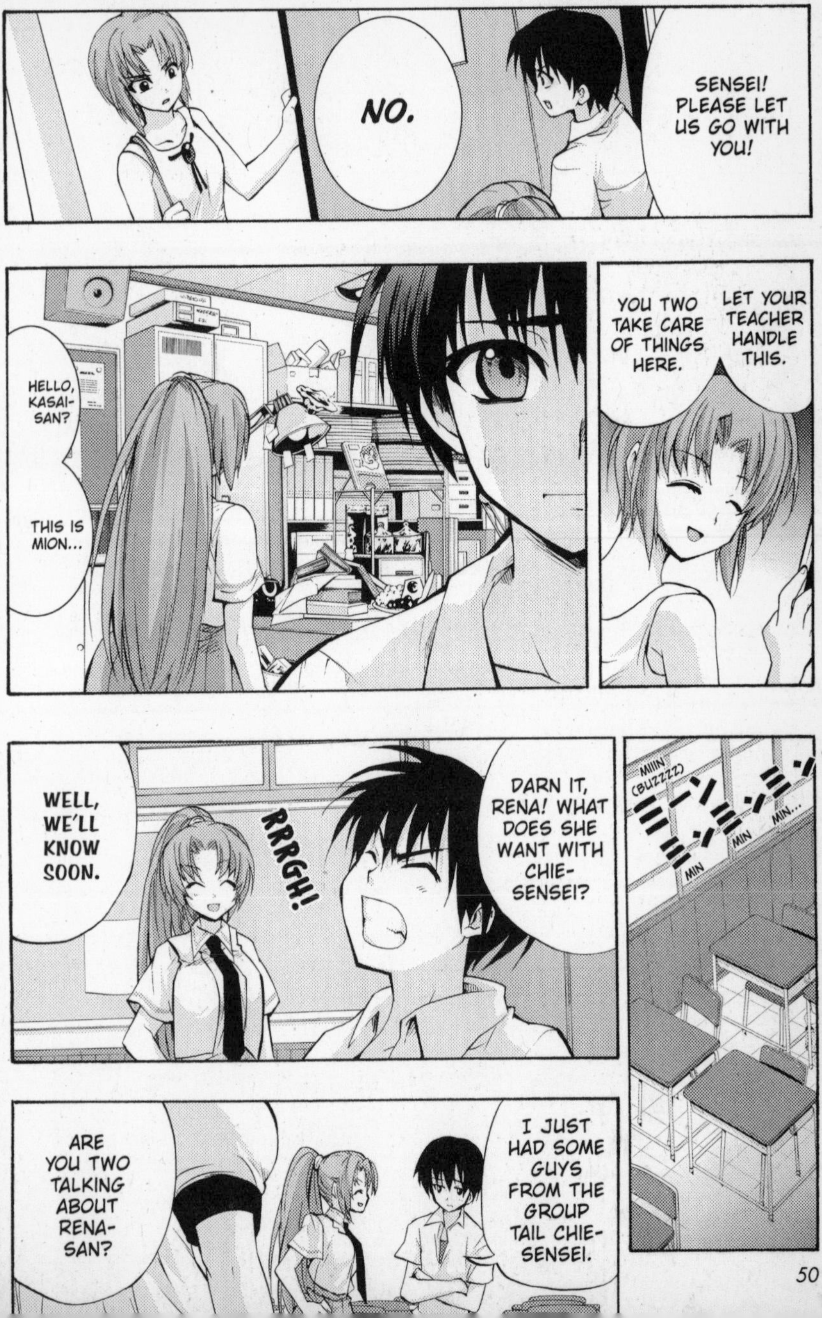
SENSEI! PLEASE LET US GO WITH YOU!
NO.
LET YOUR TEACHER HANDLE THIS.
YOU TWO TAKE CARE OF THINGS HERE.
HELLO, KASAI-SAN?
THIS IS MION...
MIIN (BUZZZZZ)
MIN MIN MIN...
DARN IT, RENA! WHAT DOES SHE WANT WITH CHIE-SENSEI?
RRRGH!
WELL, WE'LL KNOW SOON.
I JUST HAD SOME GUYS FROM THE GROUP TAIL CHIE-SENSEI.
ARE YOU TWO TALKING ABOUT RENA-SAN?

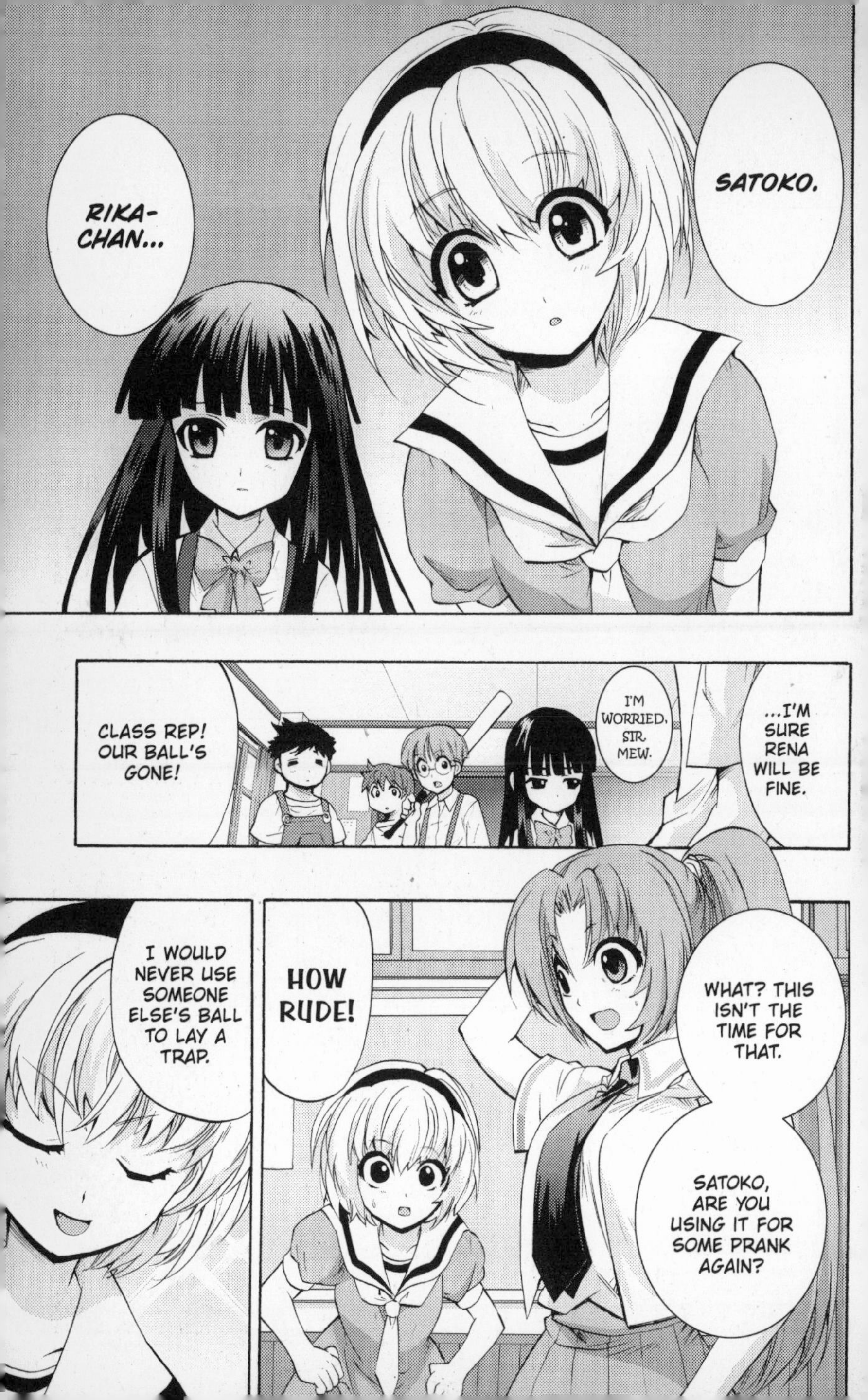
SATOKO.
RIKA-CHAN...
...I'M SURE RENA WILL BE FINE.
I'M WORRIED, SIR MEW.
CLASS REP! OUR BALL'S GONE!
WHAT? THIS ISN'T THE TIME FOR THAT.
SATOKO, ARE YOU USING IT FOR SOME PRANK AGAIN?
HOW RUDE!
I WOULD NEVER USE SOMEONE ELSE'S BALL TO LAY A TRAP.

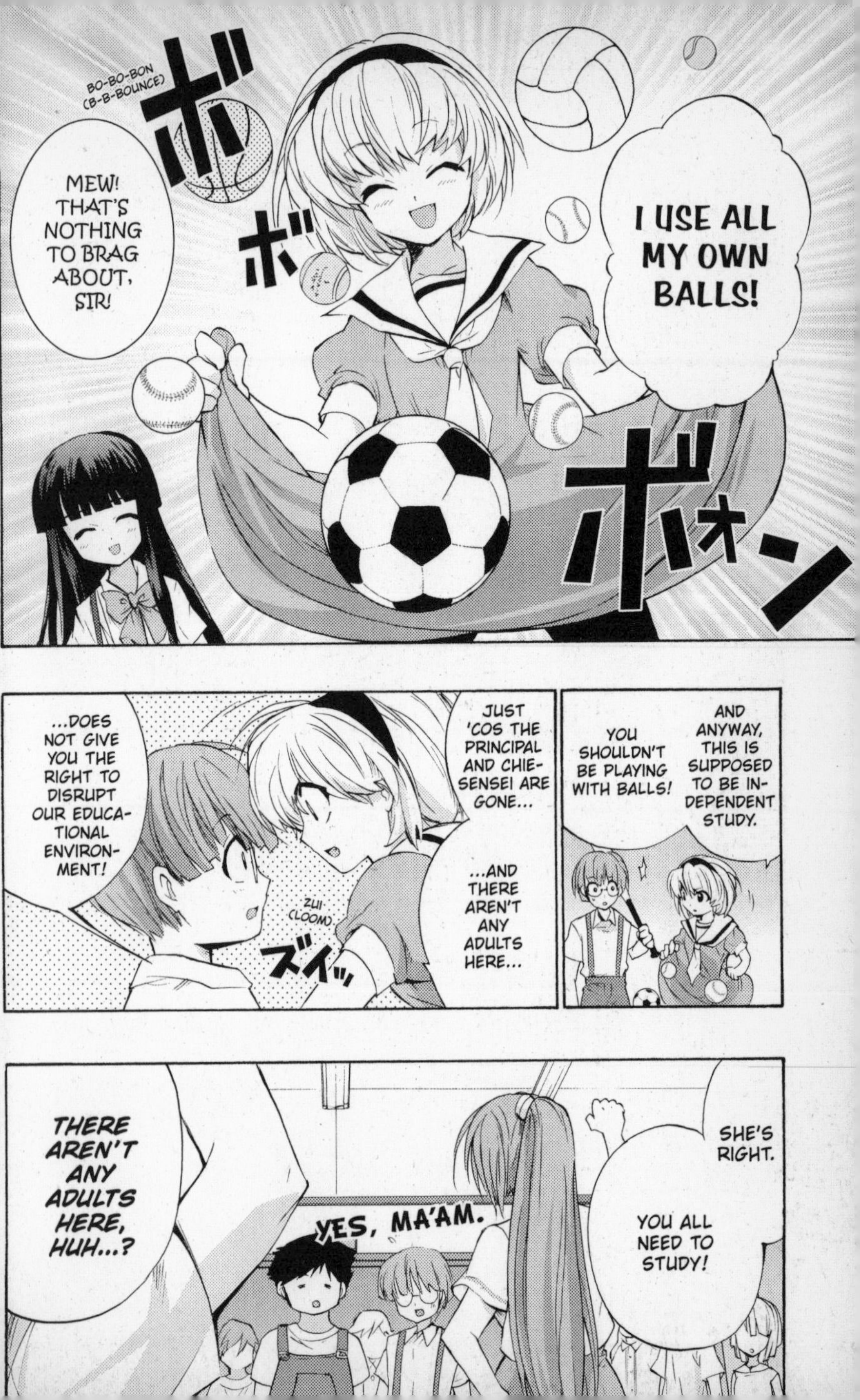
I USE ALL MY OWN BALLS!
BO-BO-BON (B-B-BOUNCE)
MEW! THAT'S NOTHING TO BRAG ABOUT, SIR!
AND ANYWAY, THIS IS SUPPOSED TO BE INDEPENDENT STUDY.
YOU SHOULDN'T BE PLAYING WITH BALLS!
JUST 'COS THE PRINCIPAL AND CHIE-SENSEI ARE GONE...
...AND THERE AREN'T ANY ADULTS HERE...
ZUI (LOOM)
...DOES NOT GIVE YOU THE RIGHT TO DISRUPT OUR EDUCATIONAL ENVIRONMENT!
SHE'S RIGHT.
YOU ALL NEED TO STUDY!
YES, MA'AM.
THERE AREN'T ANY ADULTS HERE, HUH...?

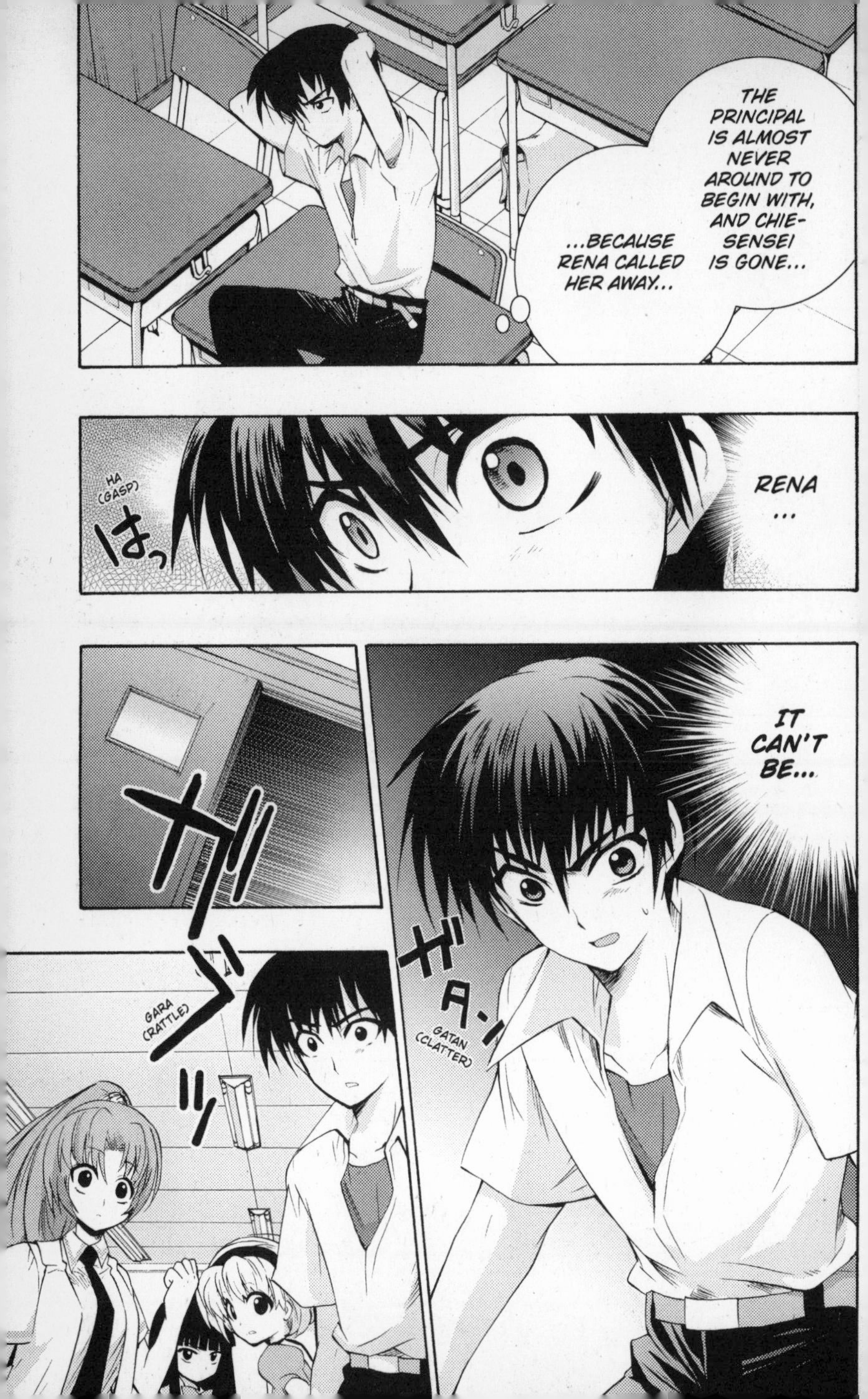
THE PRINCIPAL IS ALMOST NEVER AROUND TO BEGIN WITH, AND CHIE-SENSEI IS GONE...
...BECAUSE RENA CALLED HER AWAY...
RENA ...
HA (GASP)
はっ
IT CAN'T BE...
GATAN (CLATTER)
GARA (RATTLE)

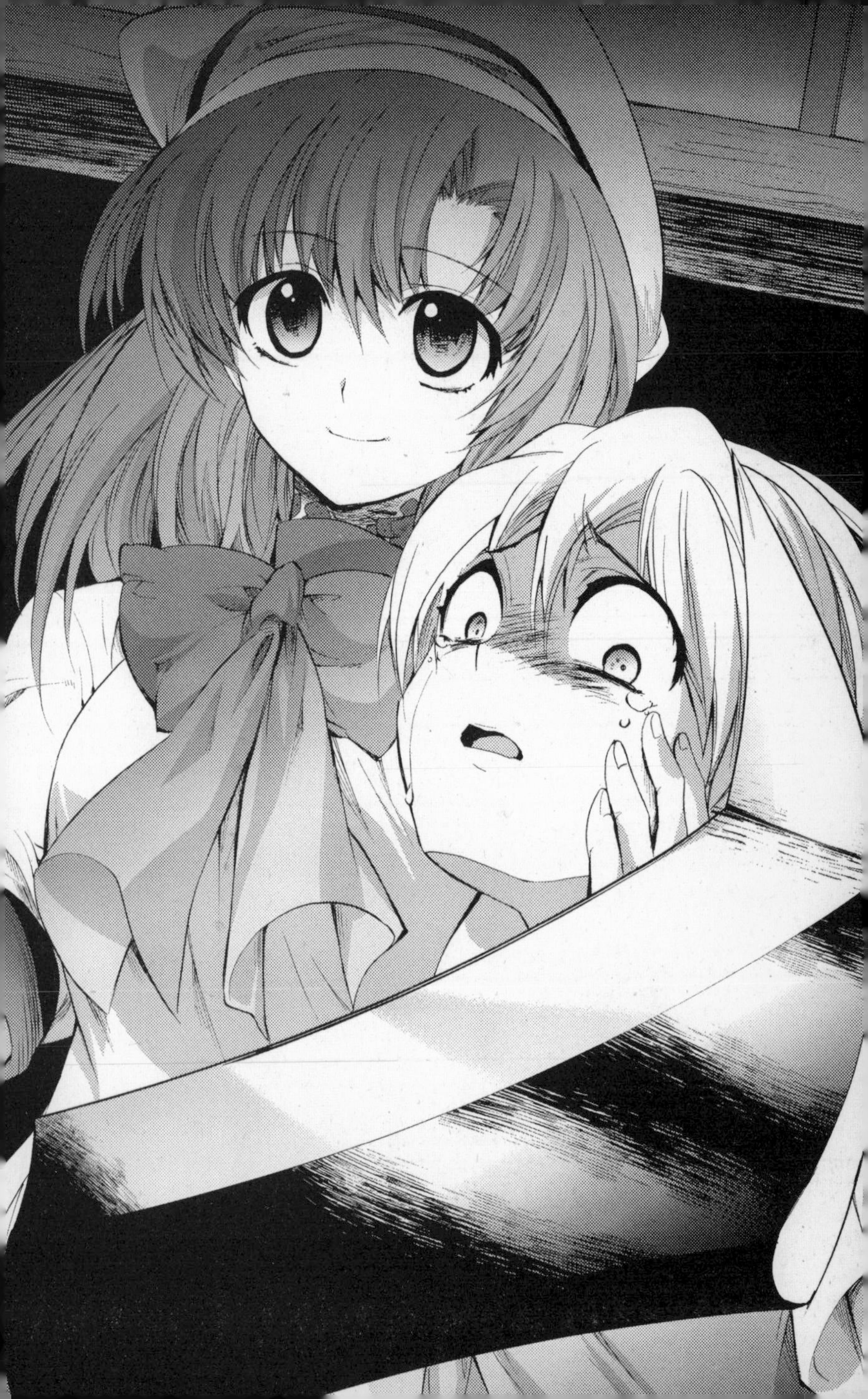

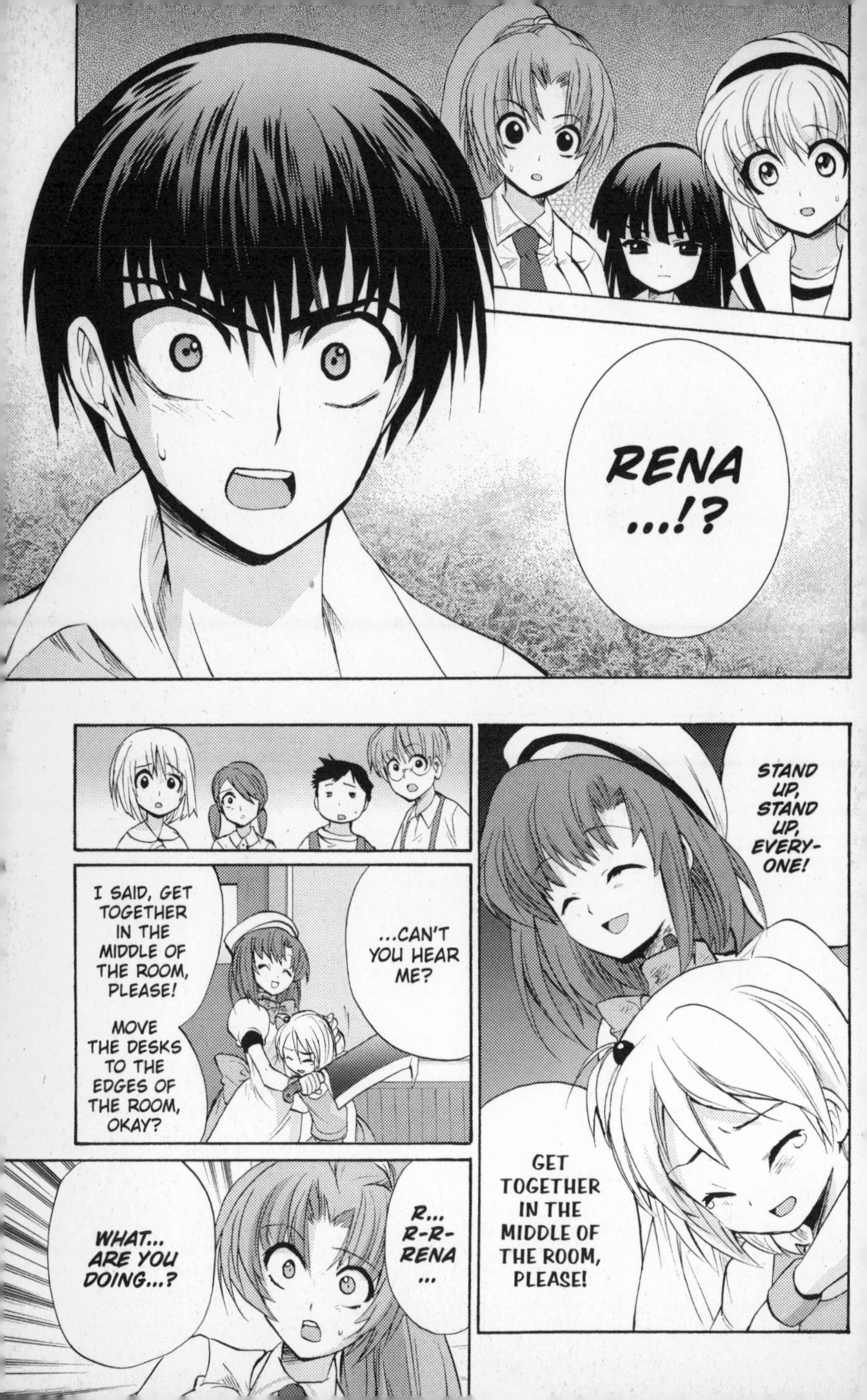
RENA ...!?
STAND UP, STAND UP, EVERY-ONE!
GET TOGETHER IN THE MIDDLE OF THE ROOM, PLEASE!
...CAN'T YOU HEAR ME?
I SAID, GET TOGETHER IN THE MIDDLE OF THE ROOM, PLEASE!
MOVE THE DESKS TO THE EDGES OF THE ROOM, OKAY?
R... R-R-RENA ...
WHAT... ARE YOU DOING...?

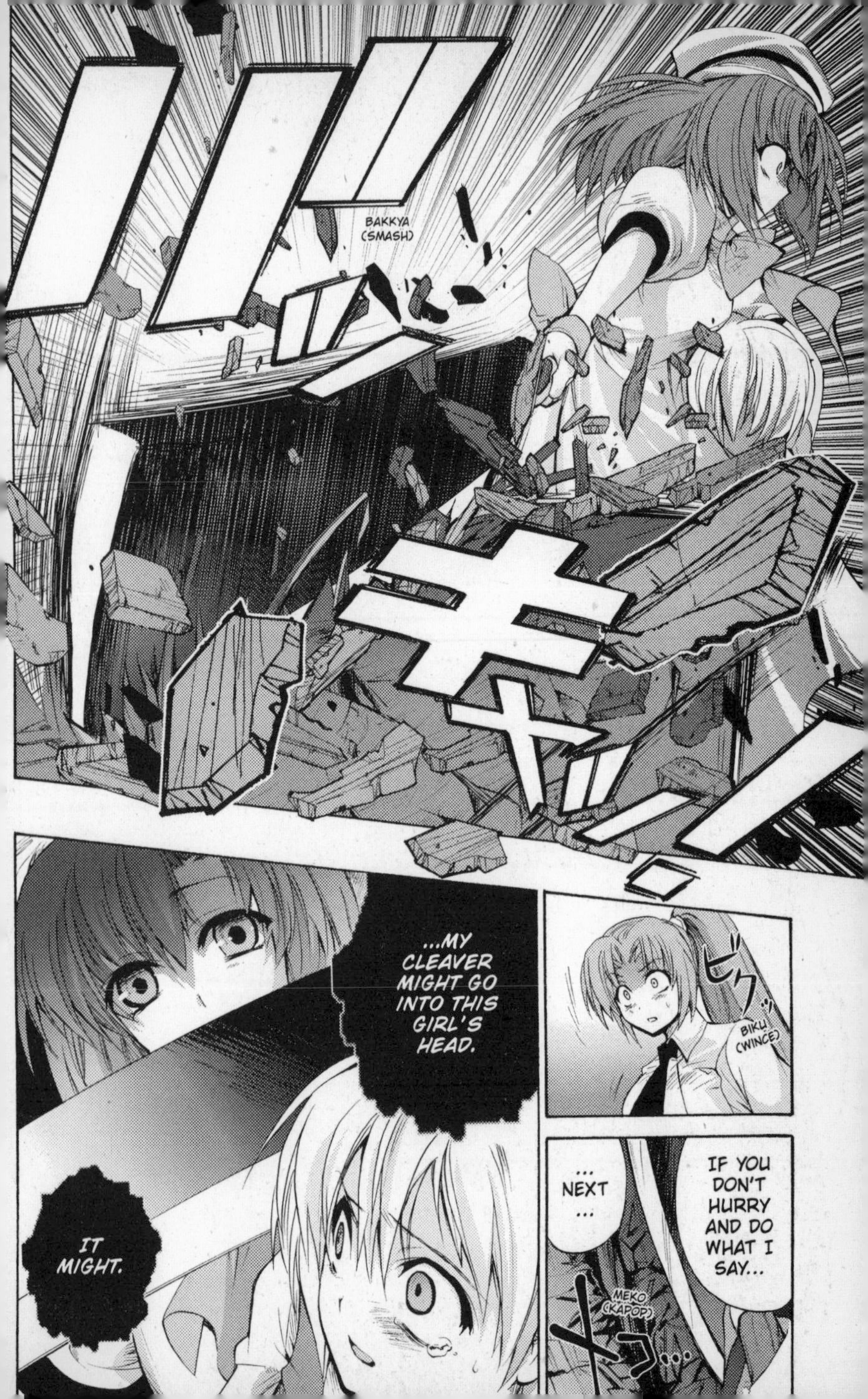
BAKKYA (SMASH)
BIKU (WINCE)
IF YOU DON'T HURRY AND DO WHAT I SAY...
...NEXT...
MEKO (KAPOP)
...MY CLEAVER MIGHT GO INTO THIS GIRL'S HEAD.
IT MIGHT.

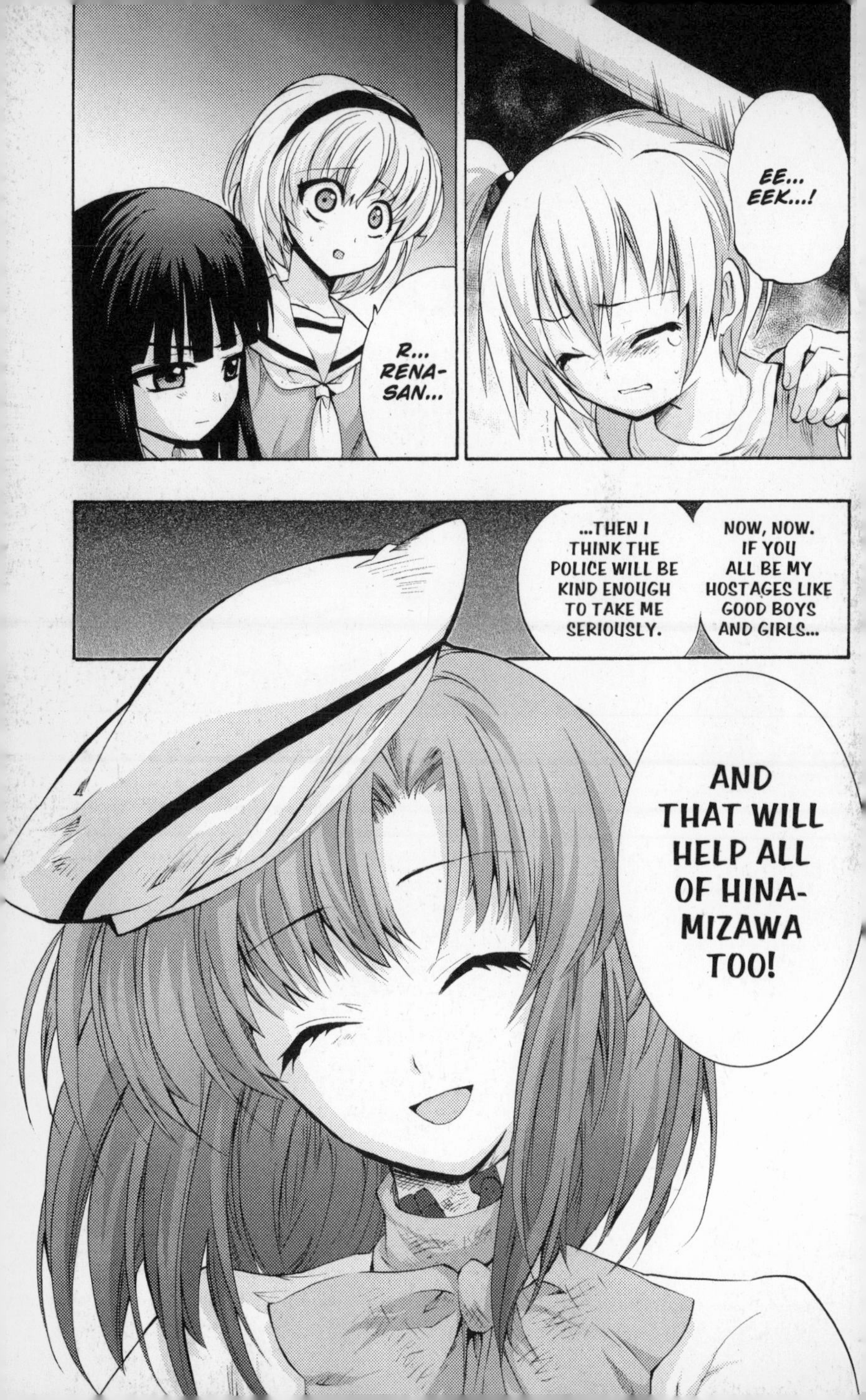
EE... EEK...!
R... RENA-SAN...
NOW, NOW. IF YOU ALL BE MY HOSTAGES LIKE GOOD BOYS AND GIRLS...
...THEN I THINK THE POLICE WILL BE KIND ENOUGH TO TAKE ME SERIOUSLY.
AND THAT WILL HELP ALL OF HINA-MIZAWA TOO!

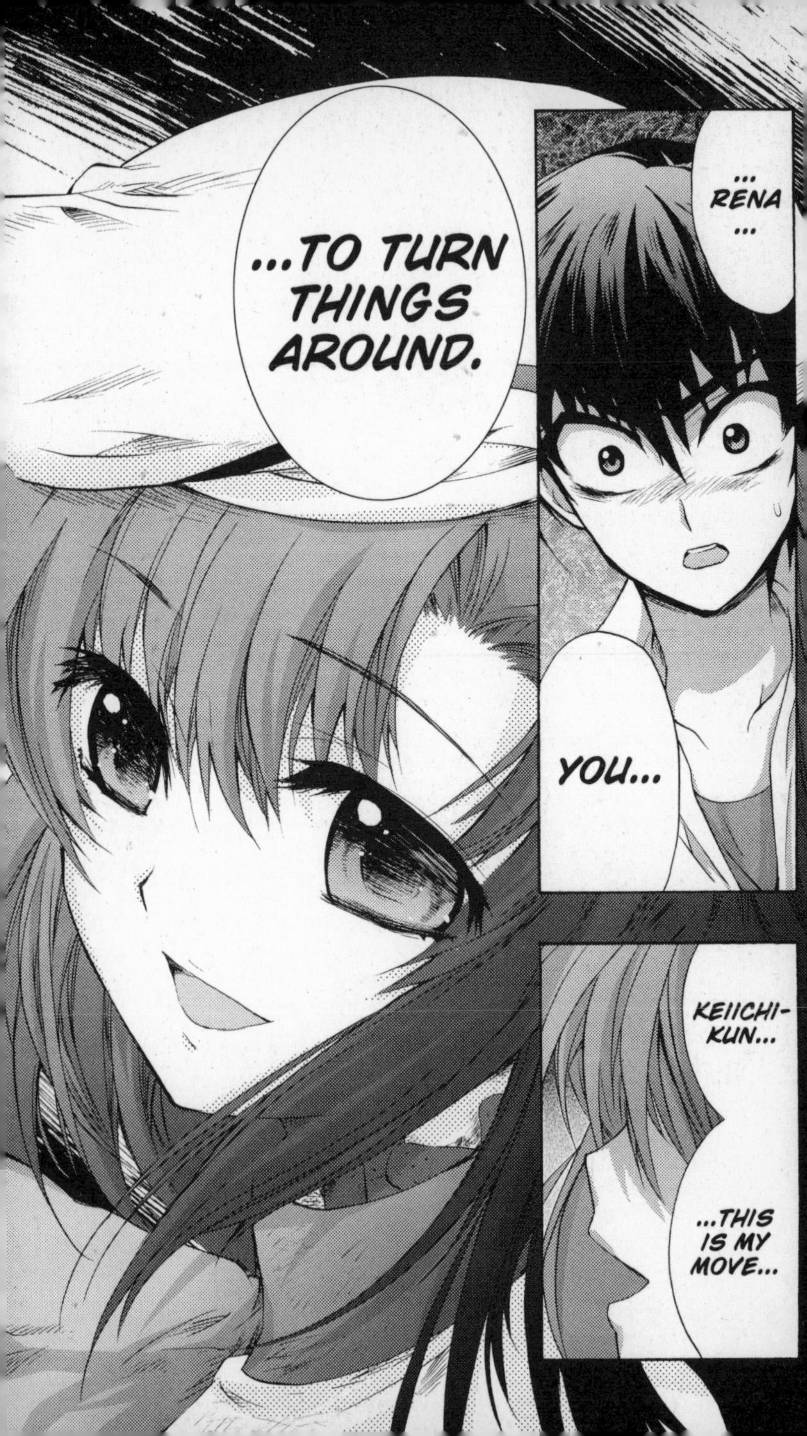
...RENA...
YOU...
KEIICHI-KUN...
...THIS IS MY MOVE...
...TO TURN THINGS AROUND.

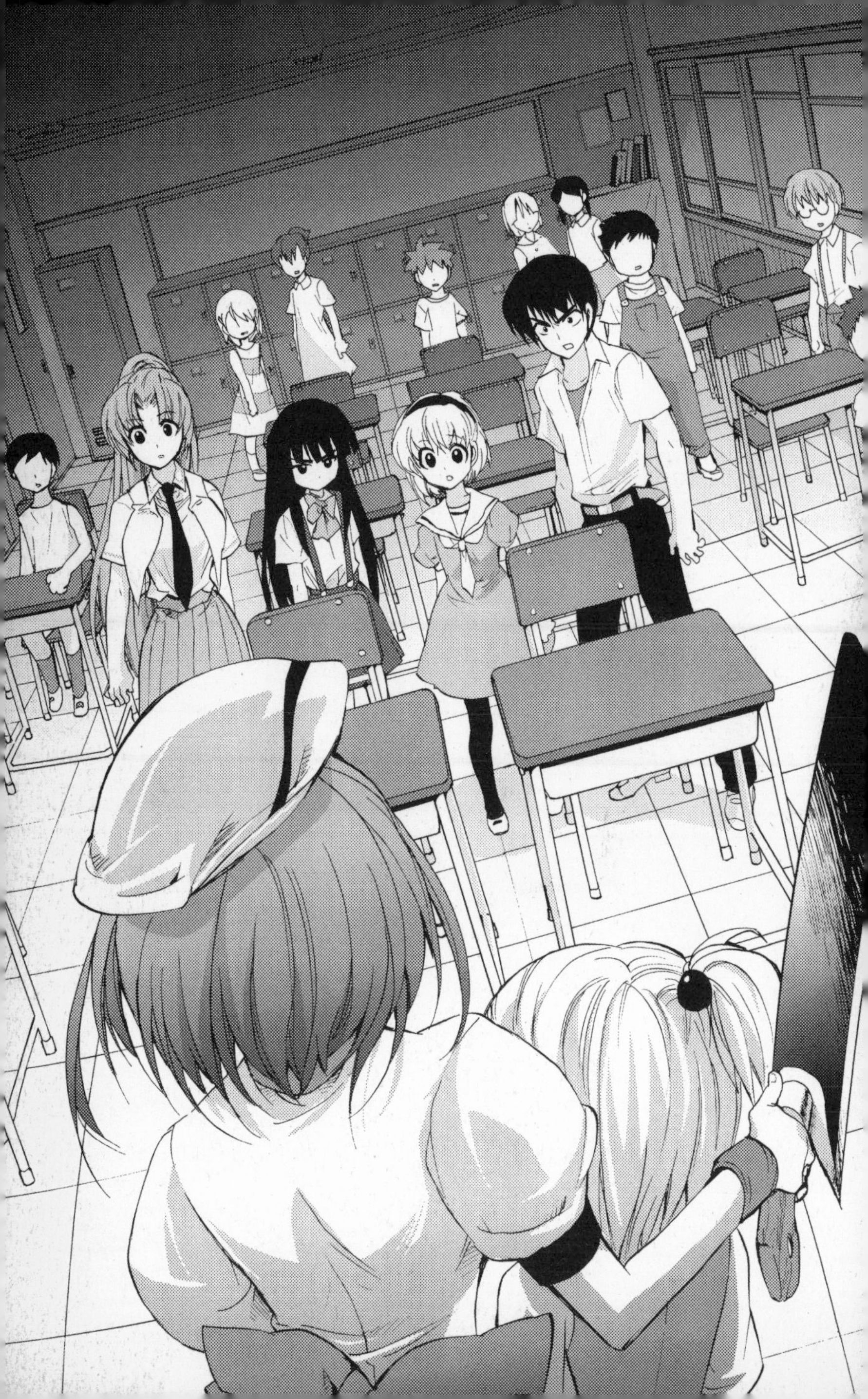

Higurashi
WHEN THEY CRY
ATONEMENT ARC

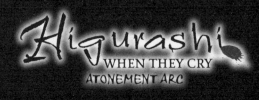

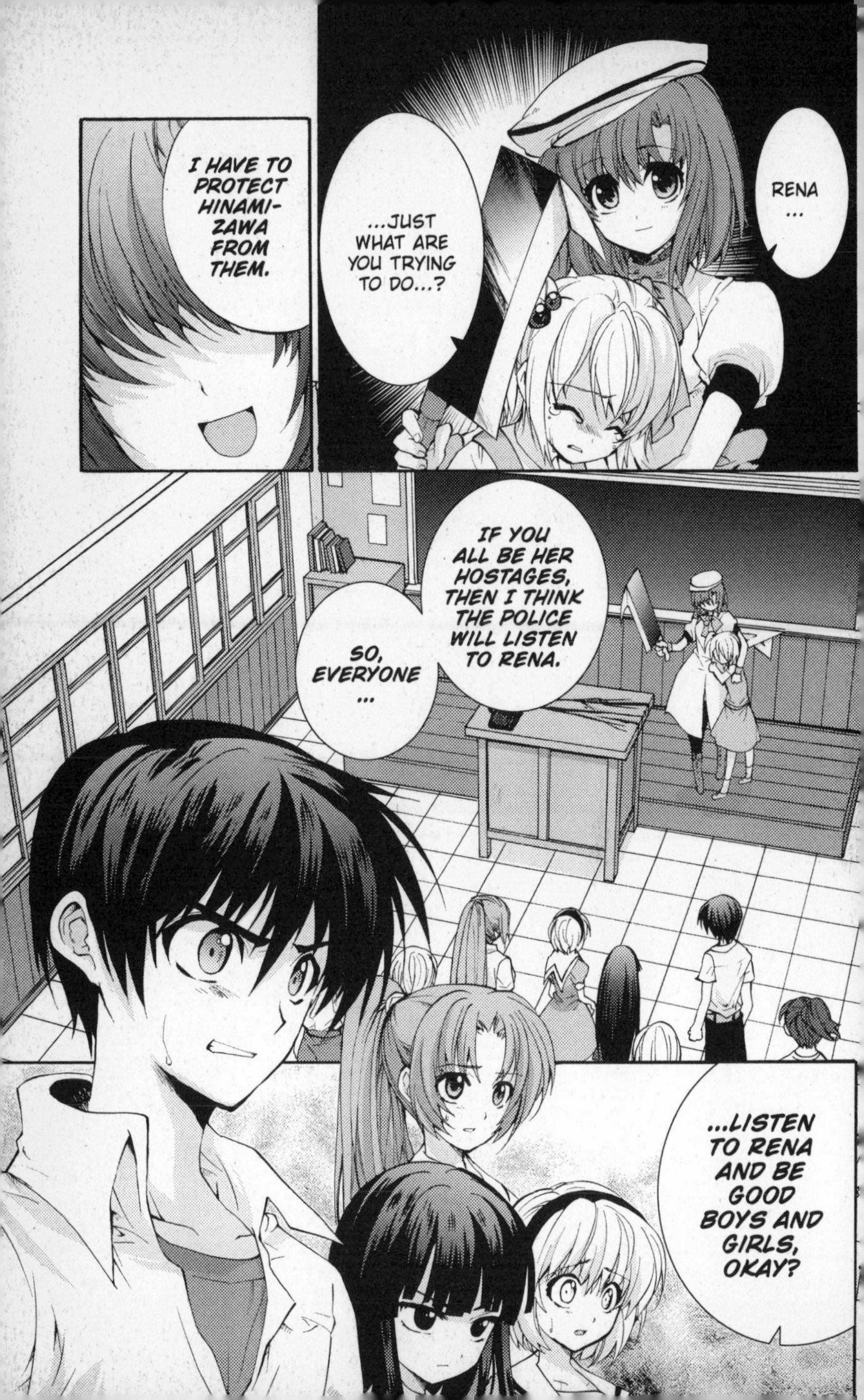
RENA ...
...JUST WHAT ARE YOU TRYING TO DO...?
I HAVE TO PROTECT HINAMI-ZAWA FROM THEM.
IF YOU ALL BE HER HOSTAGES, THEN I THINK THE POLICE WILL LISTEN TO RENA.
SO, EVERYONE ...
...LISTEN TO RENA AND BE GOOD BOYS AND GIRLS, OKAY?

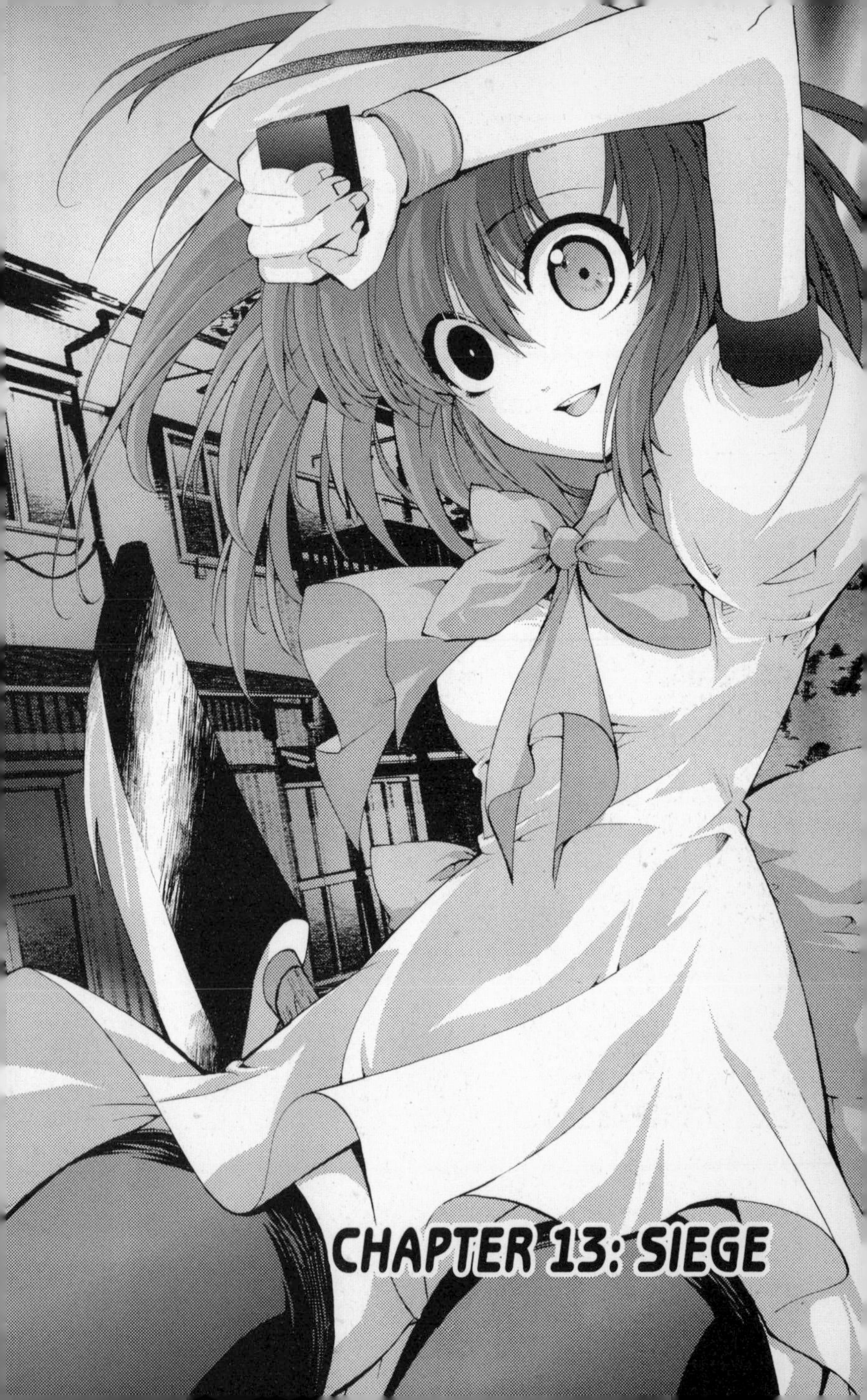
CHAPTER 13: SIEGE

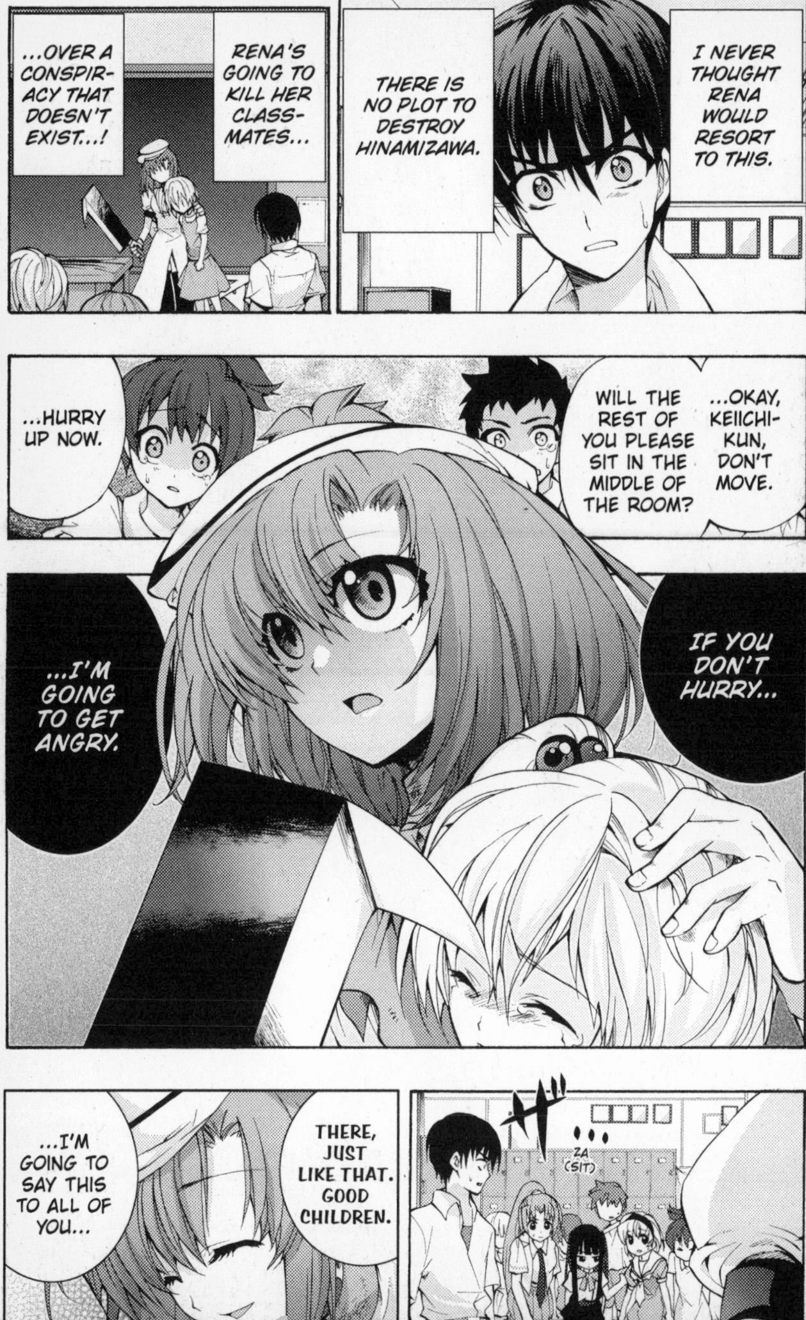

I NEVER THOUGHT RENA WOULD RESORT TO THIS.
THERE IS NO PLOT TO DESTROY HINAMIZAWA.
RENA'S GOING TO KILL HER CLASSMATES...
...OVER A CONSPIRACY THAT DOESN'T EXIST...!
...OKAY, KEIICHI-KUN, DON'T MOVE.
WILL THE REST OF YOU PLEASE SIT IN THE MIDDLE OF THE ROOM?
...HURRY UP NOW.
IF YOU DON'T HURRY...
...I'M GOING TO GET ANGRY.
...
ZA (SIT)
THERE, JUST LIKE THAT. GOOD CHILDREN.
...I'M GOING TO SAY THIS TO ALL OF YOU...

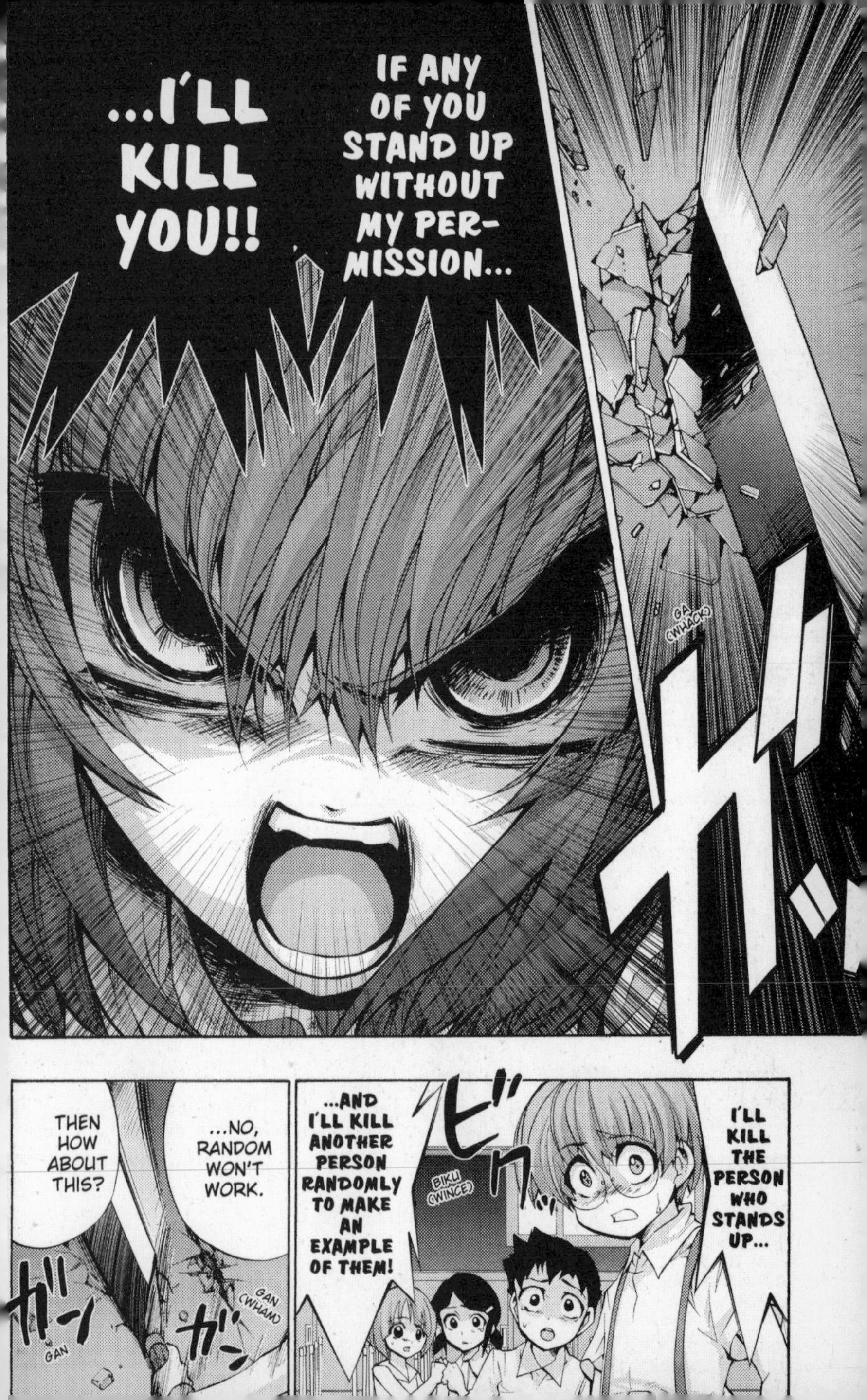
GA (WHACK)
IF ANY OF YOU STAND UP WITHOUT MY PER-MISSION...
...I'LL KILL YOU!!
I'LL KILL THE PERSON WHO STANDS UP...
BIKU (WINCE)
...AND I'LL KILL ANOTHER PERSON RANDOMLY TO MAKE AN EXAMPLE OF THEM!
...NO, RANDOM WON'T WORK.
THEN HOW ABOUT THIS?
GAN (WHAM)
GAN

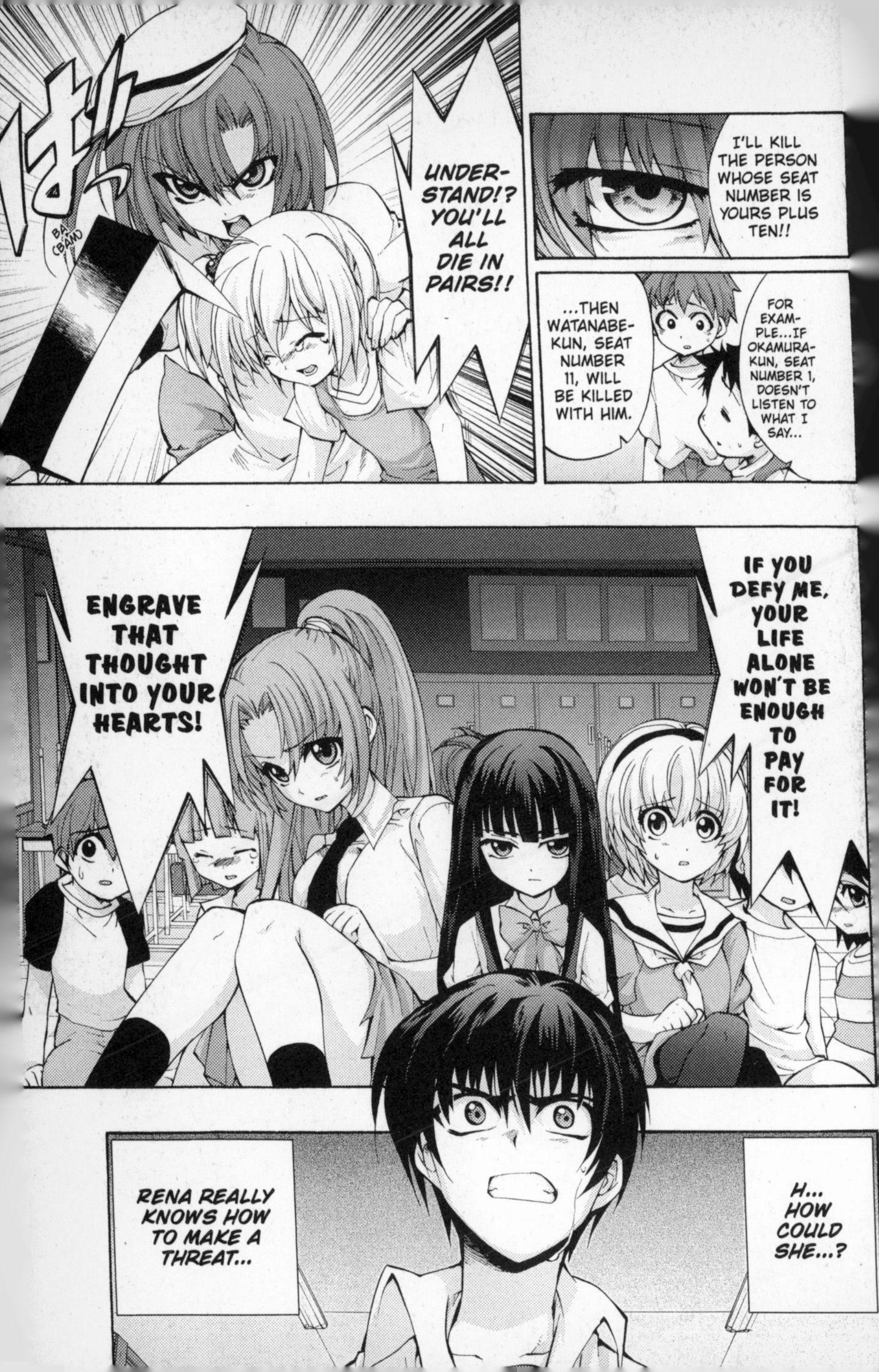
I'LL KILL THE PERSON WHOSE SEAT NUMBER IS YOURS PLUS TEN!!
FOR EXAMPLE...IF OKAMURA-KUN, SEAT NUMBER 1, DOESN'T LISTEN TO WHAT I SAY...
...THEN WATANABE-KUN, SEAT NUMBER 11, WILL BE KILLED WITH HIM.
UNDERSTAND!? YOU'LL ALL DIE IN PAIRS!!
(BAM)
IF YOU DEFY ME, YOUR LIFE ALONE WON'T BE ENOUGH TO PAY FOR IT!
ENGRAVE THAT THOUGHT INTO YOUR HEARTS!
H... HOW COULD SHE...?
RENA REALLY KNOWS HOW TO MAKE A THREAT...

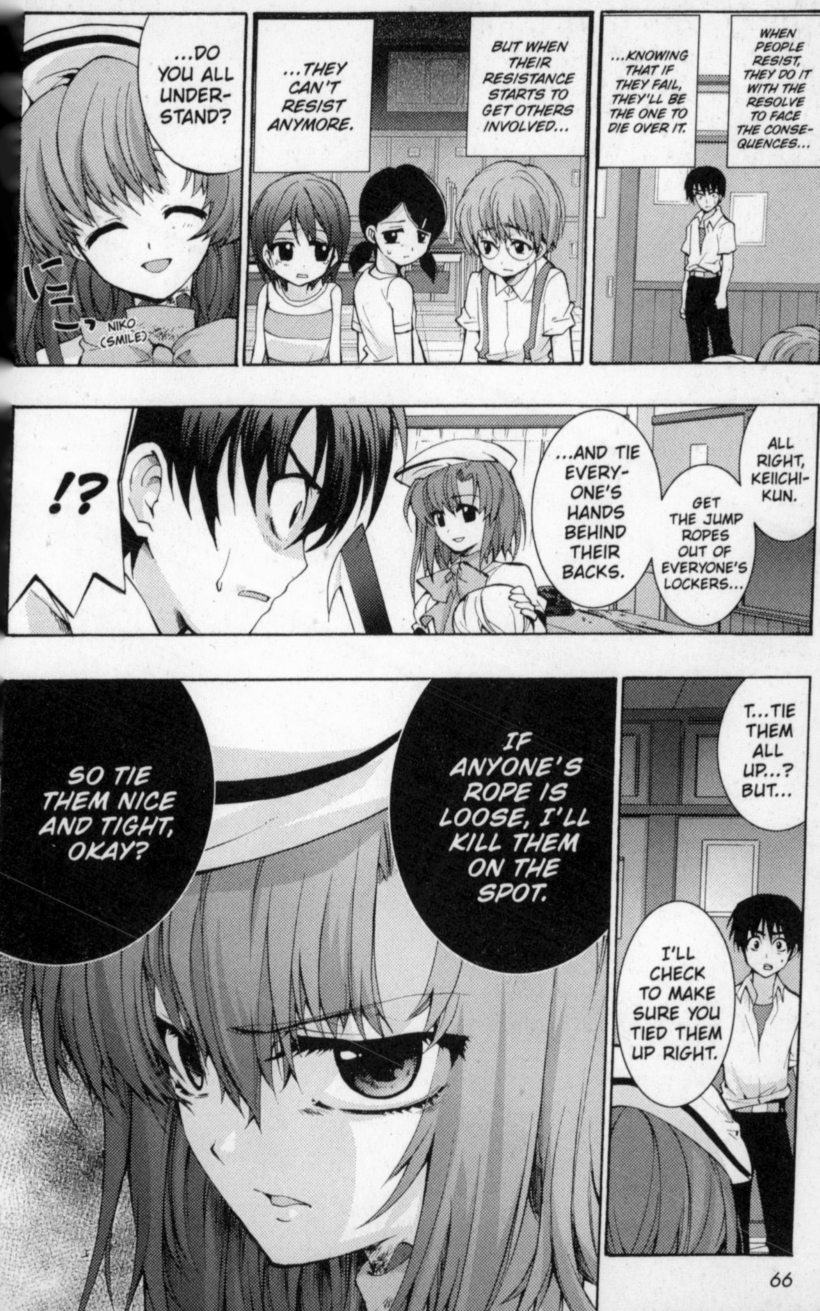
WHEN PEOPLE RESIST, THEY DO IT WITH THE RESOLVE TO FACE THE CONSEQUENCES...
...KNOWING THAT IF THEY FAIL, THEY'LL BE THE ONE TO DIE OVER IT.
BUT WHEN THEIR RESISTANCE STARTS TO GET OTHERS INVOLVED...
...THEY CAN'T RESIST ANYMORE.
...DO YOU ALL UNDER-STAND?
NIKO (SMILE)
ALL RIGHT, KEIICHI-KUN.
GET THE JUMP ROPES OUT OF EVERYONE'S LOCKERS...
...AND TIE EVERY-ONE'S HANDS BEHIND THEIR BACKS.
!?
T...TIE THEM ALL UP...? BUT...
I'LL CHECK TO MAKE SURE YOU TIED THEM UP RIGHT.
IF ANYONE'S ROPE IS LOOSE, I'LL KILL THEM ON THE SPOT.
SO TIE THEM NICE AND TIGHT, OKAY?

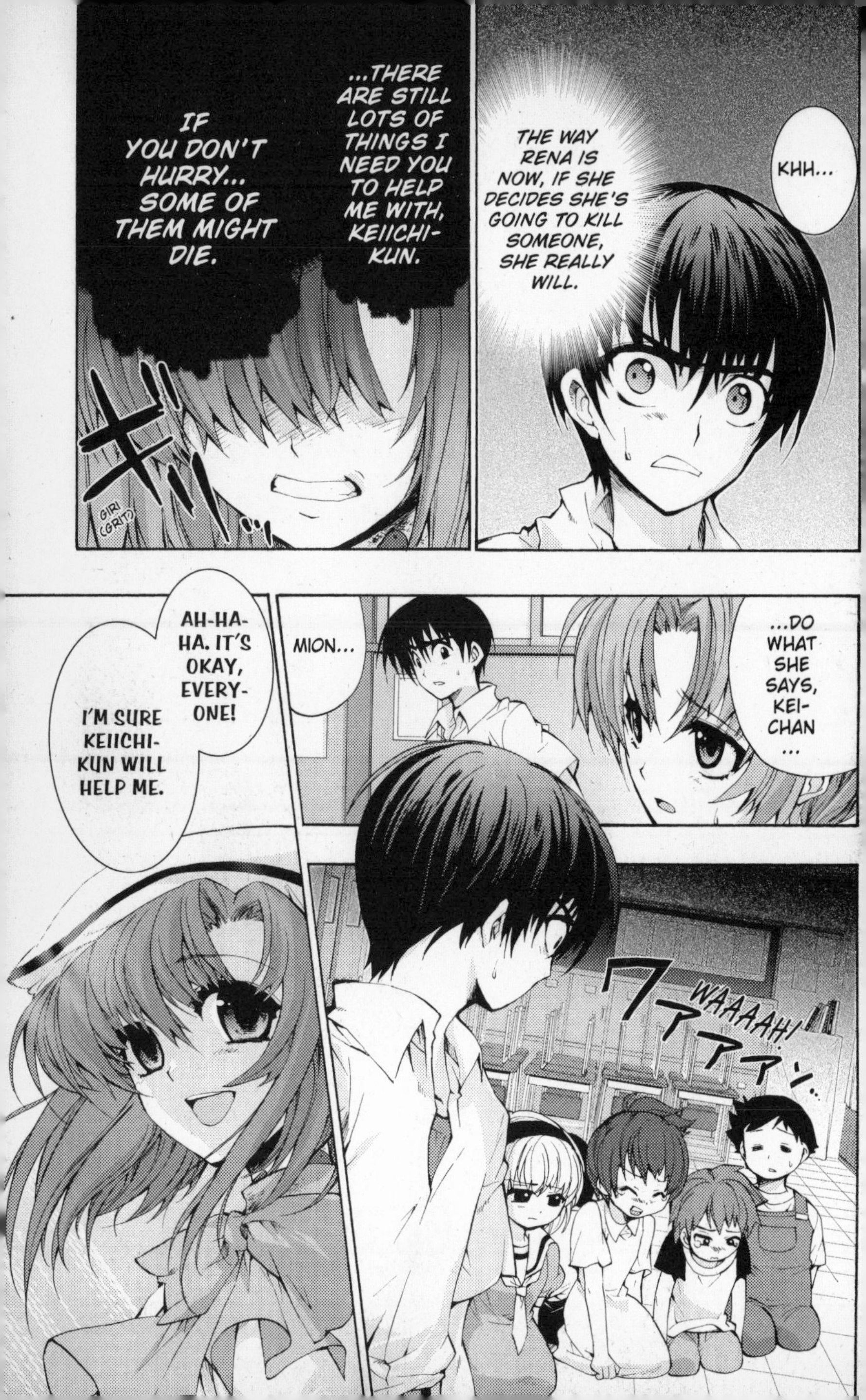
KHH...
THE WAY RENA IS NOW, IF SHE DECIDES SHE'S GOING TO KILL SOMEONE, SHE REALLY WILL.
...THERE ARE STILL LOTS OF THINGS I NEED YOU TO HELP ME WITH, KEIICHI-KUN.
IF YOU DON'T HURRY... SOME OF THEM MIGHT DIE.
GIRI (GRIT)
...DO WHAT SHE SAYS, KEI-CHAN ...
MION...
AH-HA-HA. IT'S OKAY, EVERYONE!
I'M SURE KEIICHI-KUN WILL HELP ME.
WAAAAAH!

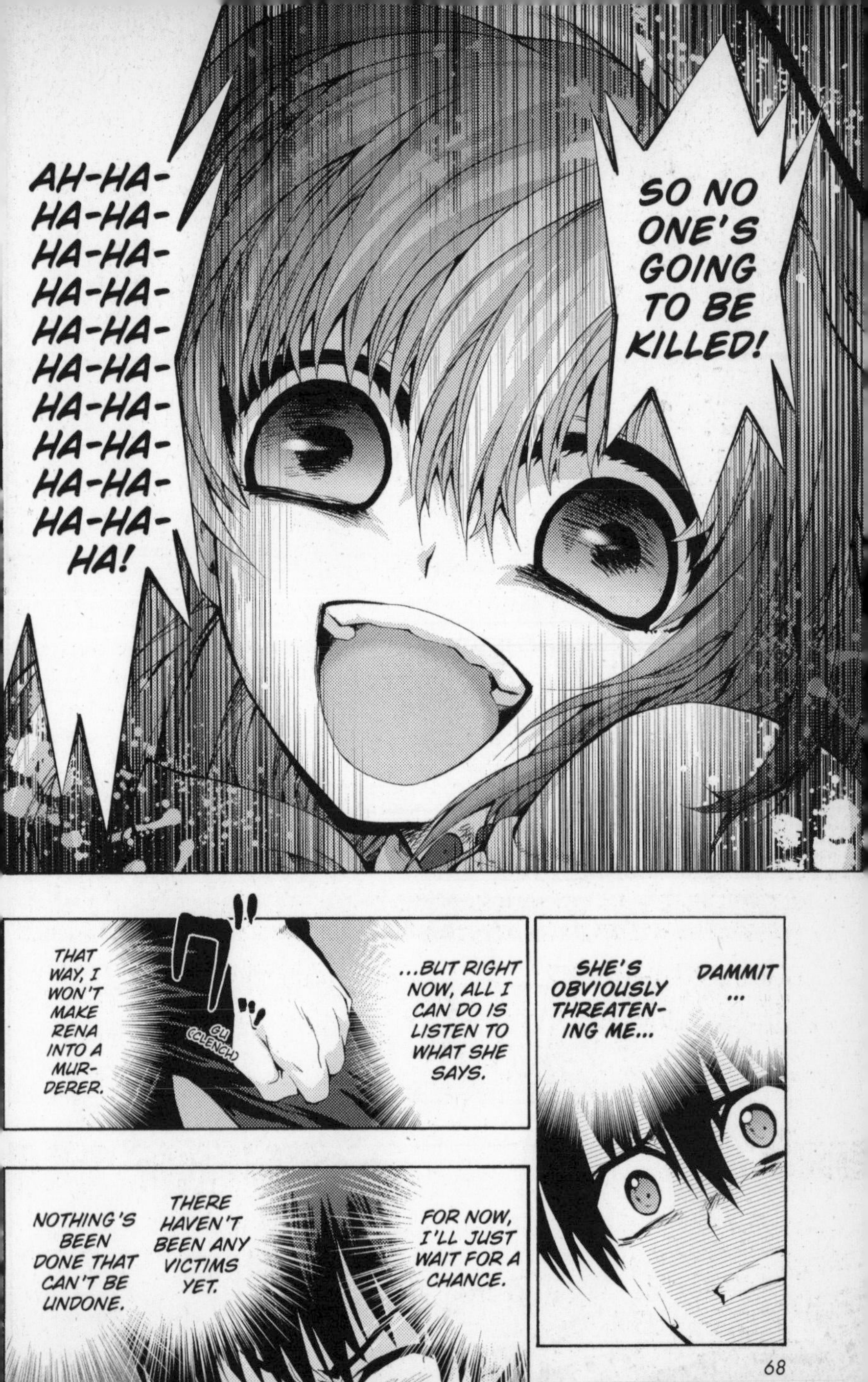

SO NO ONE'S GOING TO BE KILLED!
AH-HA-HA-HA-HA-HA-HA-HA-HA-HA-HA-HA-HA-HA-HA-HA-HA-HA-HA-HA!
DAMMIT...
SHE'S OBVIOUSLY THREATENING ME...
...BUT RIGHT NOW, ALL I CAN DO IS LISTEN TO WHAT SHE SAYS.
GU (CLENCH)
THAT WAY, I WON'T MAKE RENA INTO A MURDERER.
FOR NOW, I'LL JUST WAIT FOR A CHANCE.
THERE HAVEN'T BEEN ANY VICTIMS YET.
NOTHING'S BEEN DONE THAT CAN'T BE UNDONE.

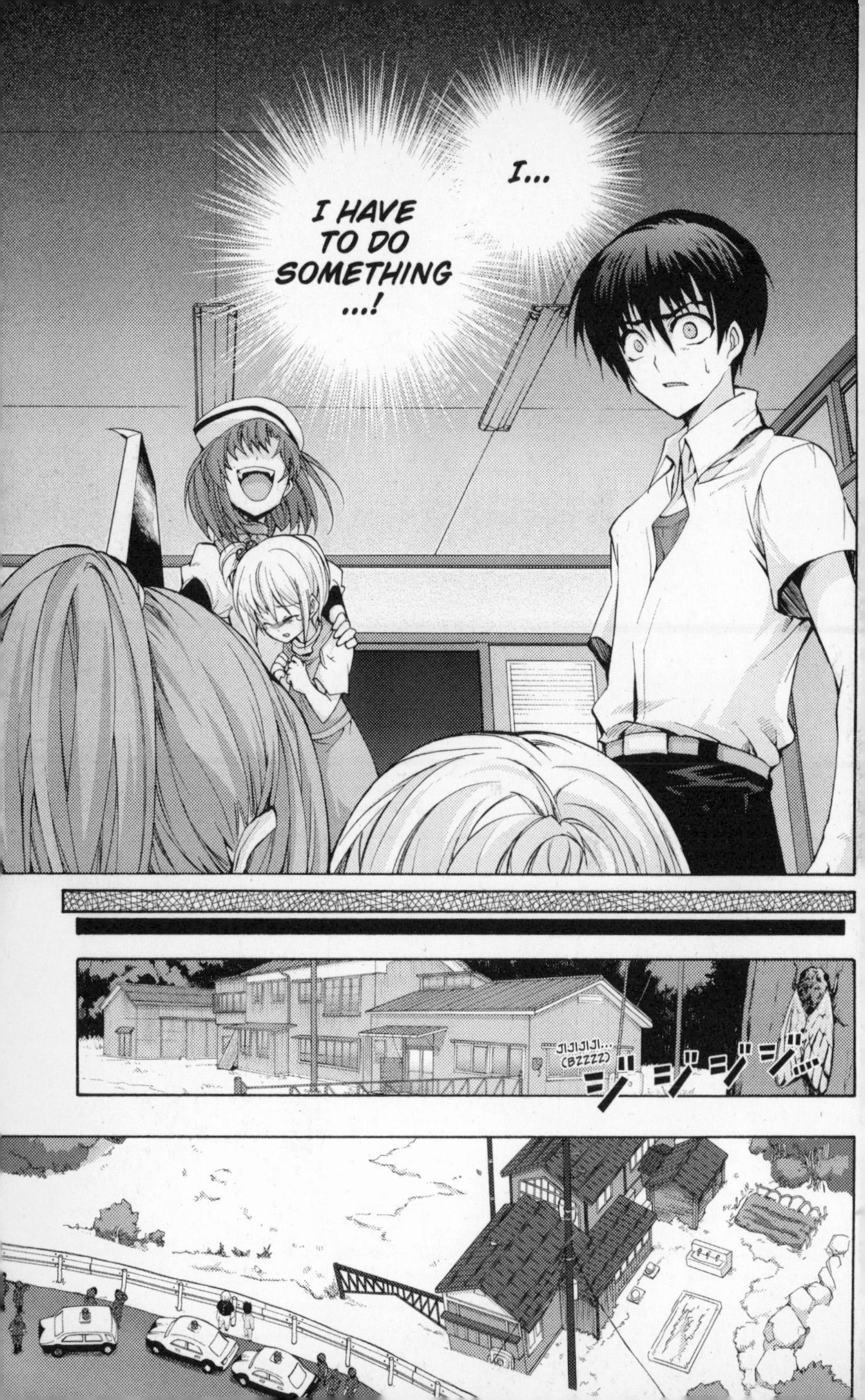
I...
I HAVE TO DO SOMETHING ...!
JIJIJIJI... (BZZZZ)

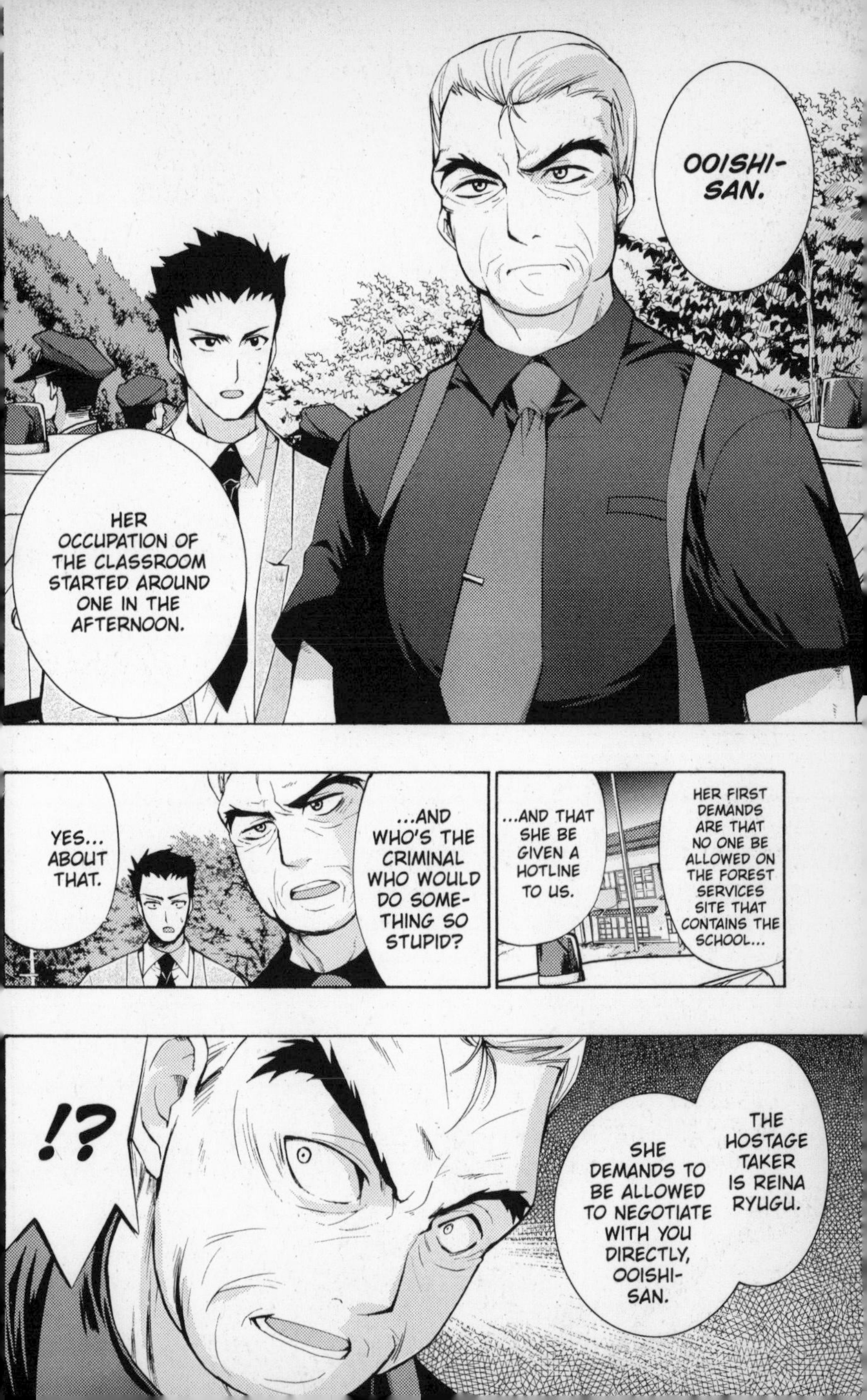
OOISHI-SAN.
HER OCCUPATION OF THE CLASSROOM STARTED AROUND ONE IN THE AFTERNOON.
HER FIRST DEMANDS ARE THAT NO ONE BE ALLOWED ON THE FOREST SERVICES SITE THAT CONTAINS THE SCHOOL...
...AND THAT SHE BE GIVEN A HOTLINE TO US.
...AND WHO'S THE CRIMINAL WHO WOULD DO SOME-THING SO STUPID?
YES... ABOUT THAT.
THE HOSTAGE TAKER IS REINA RYUGU.
SHE DEMANDS TO BE ALLOWED TO NEGOTIATE WITH YOU DIRECTLY, OOISHI-SAN.
!?

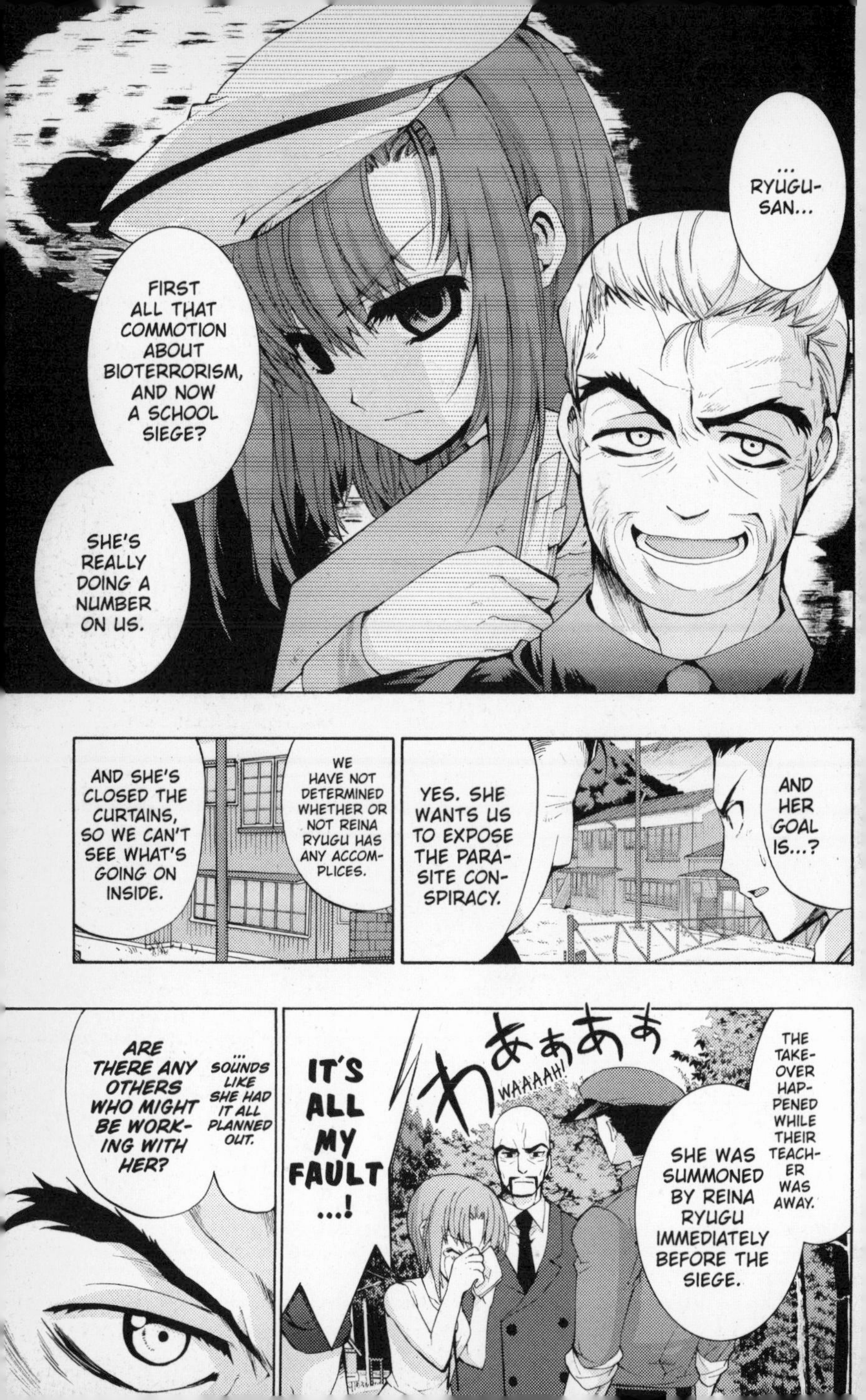
...RYUGU-SAN...
FIRST ALL THAT COMMOTION ABOUT BIOTERRORISM, AND NOW A SCHOOL SIEGE?
SHE'S REALLY DOING A NUMBER ON US.
AND HER GOAL IS...?
YES. SHE WANTS US TO EXPOSE THE PARASITE CONSPIRACY.
WE HAVE NOT DETERMINED WHETHER OR NOT REINA RYUGU HAS ANY ACCOMPLICES.
AND SHE'S CLOSED THE CURTAINS, SO WE CAN'T SEE WHAT'S GOING ON INSIDE.
THE TAKEOVER HAPPENED WHILE THEIR TEACHER WAS AWAY.
SHE WAS SUMMONED BY REINA RYUGU IMMEDIATELY BEFORE THE SIEGE.
わあぁあぁ
WAAAAAH!
IT'S ALL MY FAULT...!
...SOUNDS LIKE SHE HAD IT ALL PLANNED OUT.
ARE THERE ANY OTHERS WHO MIGHT BE WORKING WITH HER?

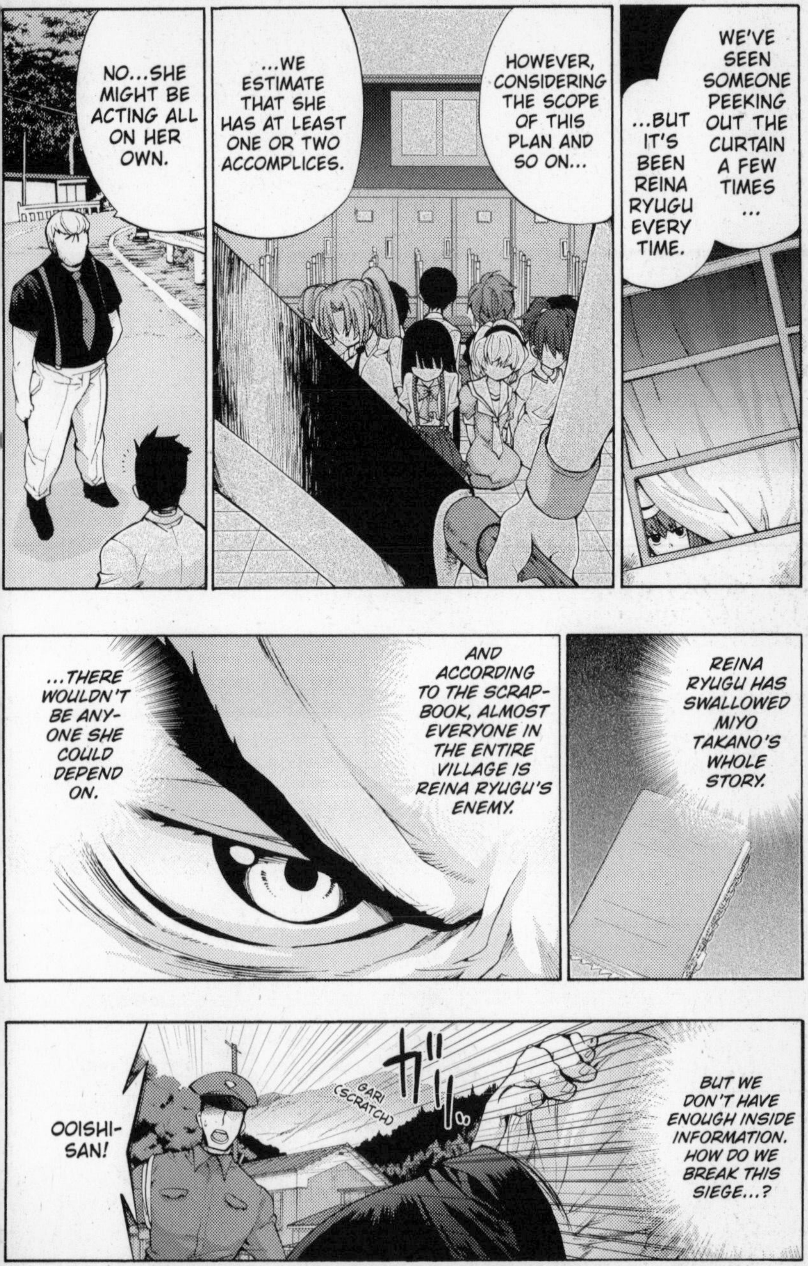
WE'VE SEEN SOMEONE PEEKING OUT THE CURTAIN A FEW TIMES ...
...BUT IT'S BEEN REINA RYUGU EVERY TIME.
HOWEVER, CONSIDERING THE SCOPE OF THIS PLAN AND SO ON...
...WE ESTIMATE THAT SHE HAS AT LEAST ONE OR TWO ACCOMPLICES.
NO...SHE MIGHT BE ACTING ALL ON HER OWN.
REINA RYUGU HAS SWALLOWED MIYO TAKANO'S WHOLE STORY.
AND ACCORDING TO THE SCRAP-BOOK, ALMOST EVERYONE IN THE ENTIRE VILLAGE IS REINA RYUGU'S ENEMY.
...THERE WOULDN'T BE ANY-ONE SHE COULD DEPEND ON.
BUT WE DON'T HAVE ENOUGH INSIDE INFORMATION. HOW DO WE BREAK THIS SIEGE...?
GARI (SCRATCH)
OOISHI-SAN!

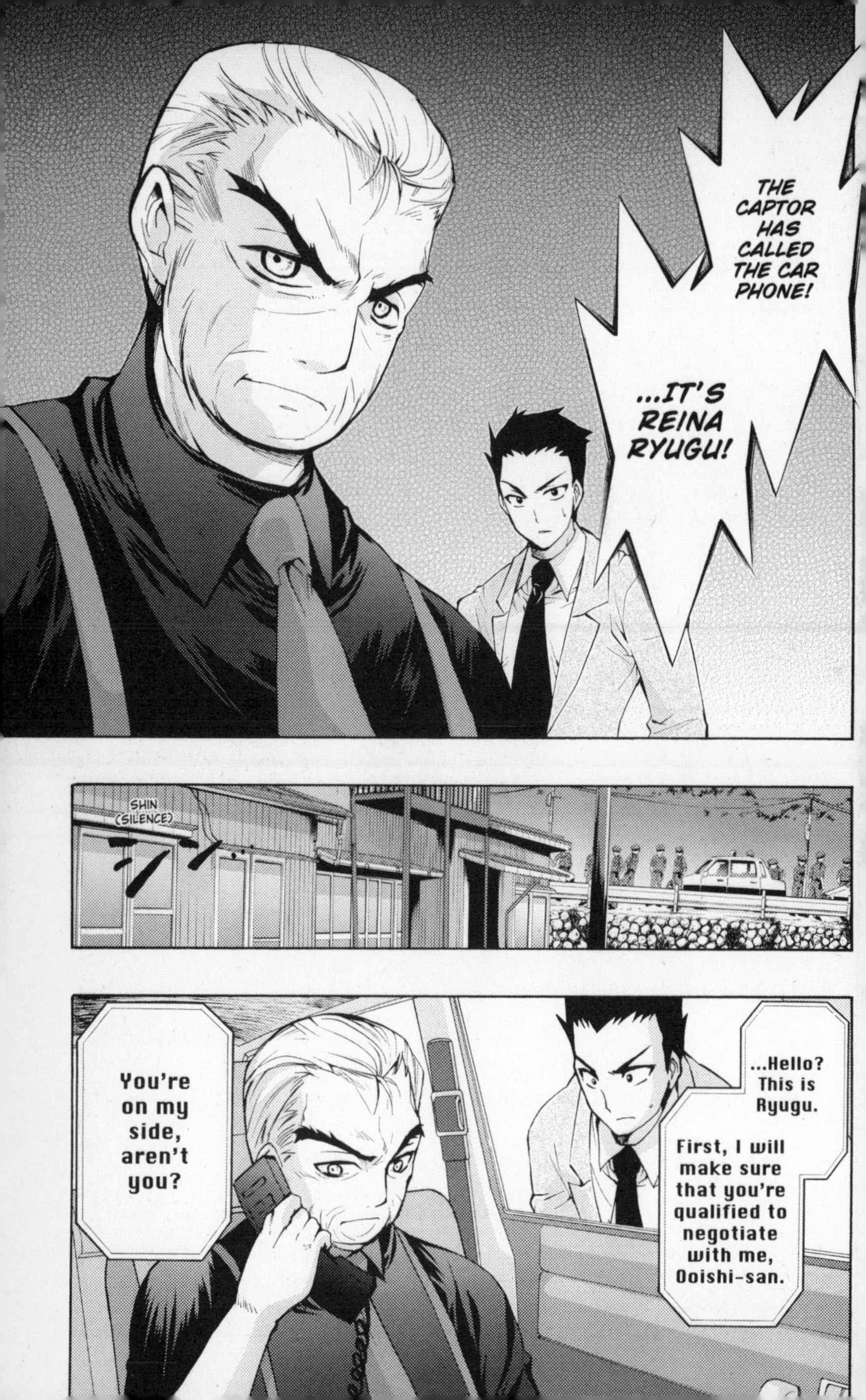
THE CAPTOR HAS CALLED THE CAR PHONE!
...IT'S REINA RYUGU!
SHIN (SILENCE)
...Hello? This is Ryugu.
First, I will make sure that you're qualified to negotiate with me, Ooishi-san.
You're on my side, aren't you?

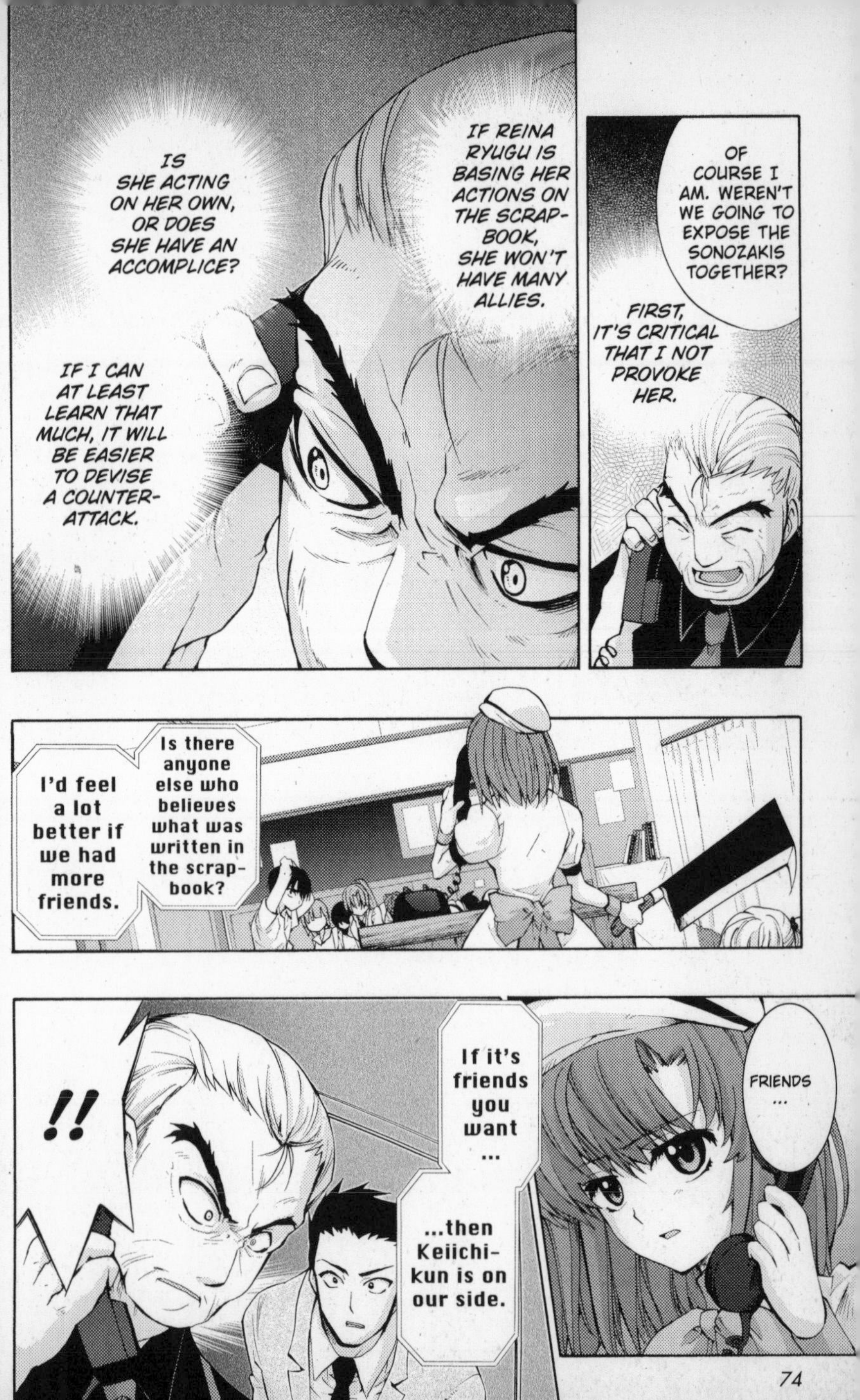

OF COURSE I AM. WEREN'T WE GOING TO EXPOSE THE SONOZAKIS TOGETHER?
FIRST, IT'S CRITICAL THAT I NOT PROVOKE HER.
IF REINA RYUGU IS BASING HER ACTIONS ON THE SCRAP-BOOK, SHE WON'T HAVE MANY ALLIES.
IS SHE ACTING ON HER OWN, OR DOES SHE HAVE AN ACCOMPLICE?
IF I CAN AT LEAST LEARN THAT MUCH, IT WILL BE EASIER TO DEVISE A COUNTER-ATTACK.
Is there anyone else who believes what was written in the scrap-book?
I'd feel a lot better if we had more friends.
FRIENDS ...
If it's friends you want ...
...then Keiichi-kun is on our side.
!!

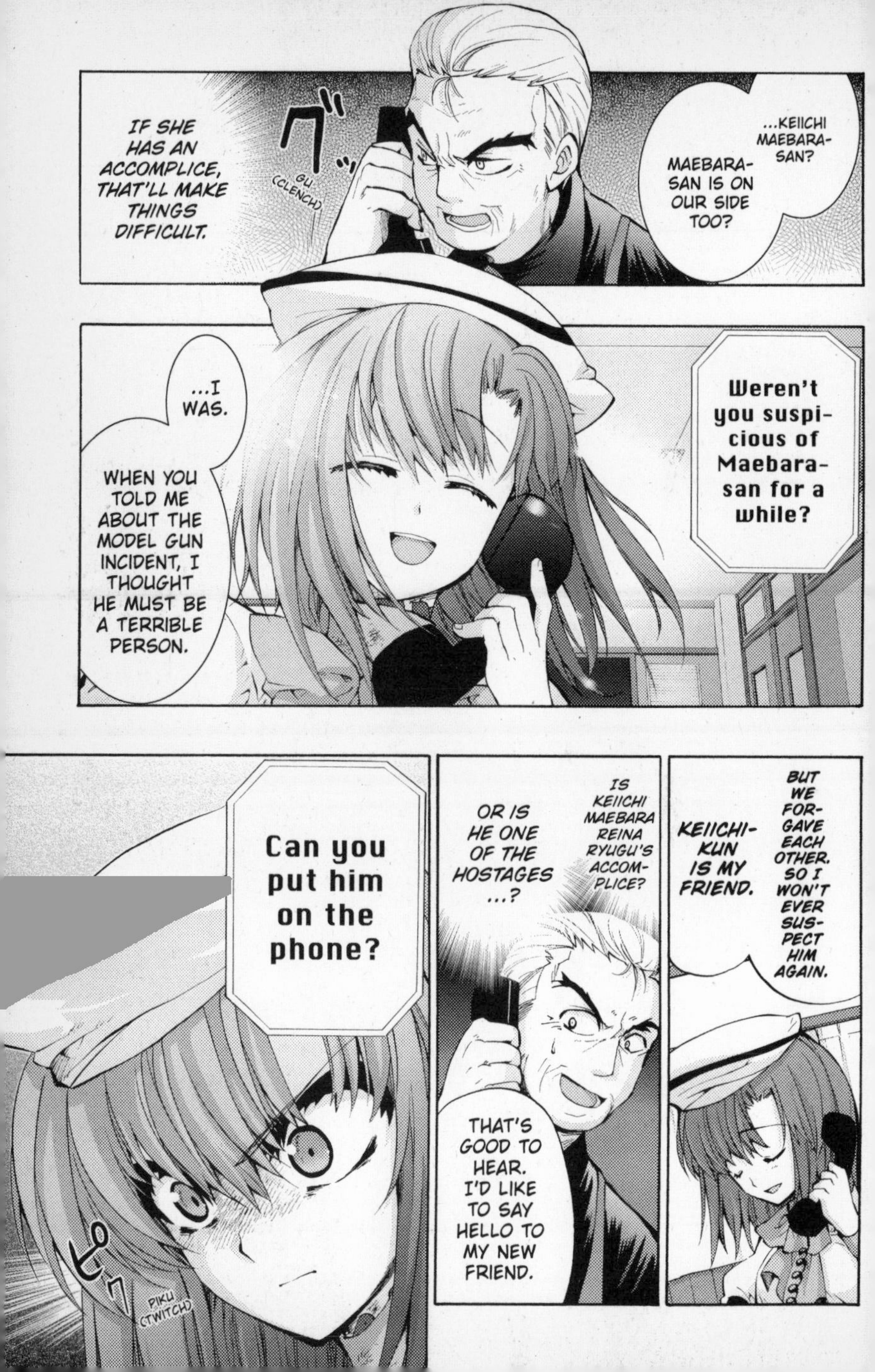
...KEIICHI MAEBARA-SAN?
MAEBARA-SAN IS ON OUR SIDE TOO?
GU (CLENCH)
IF SHE HAS AN ACCOMPLICE, THAT'LL MAKE THINGS DIFFICULT.
Weren't you suspicious of Maebara-san for a while?
...I WAS.
WHEN YOU TOLD ME ABOUT THE MODEL GUN INCIDENT, I THOUGHT HE MUST BE A TERRIBLE PERSON.
BUT WE FORGAVE EACH OTHER. SO I WON'T EVER SUSPECT HIM AGAIN.
KEIICHI-KUN IS MY FRIEND.
IS KEIICHI MAEBARA REINA RYUGU'S ACCOMPLICE?
OR IS HE ONE OF THE HOSTAGES ...?
THAT'S GOOD TO HEAR. I'D LIKE TO SAY HELLO TO MY NEW FRIEND.
Can you put him on the phone?
PIKU (TWITCH)

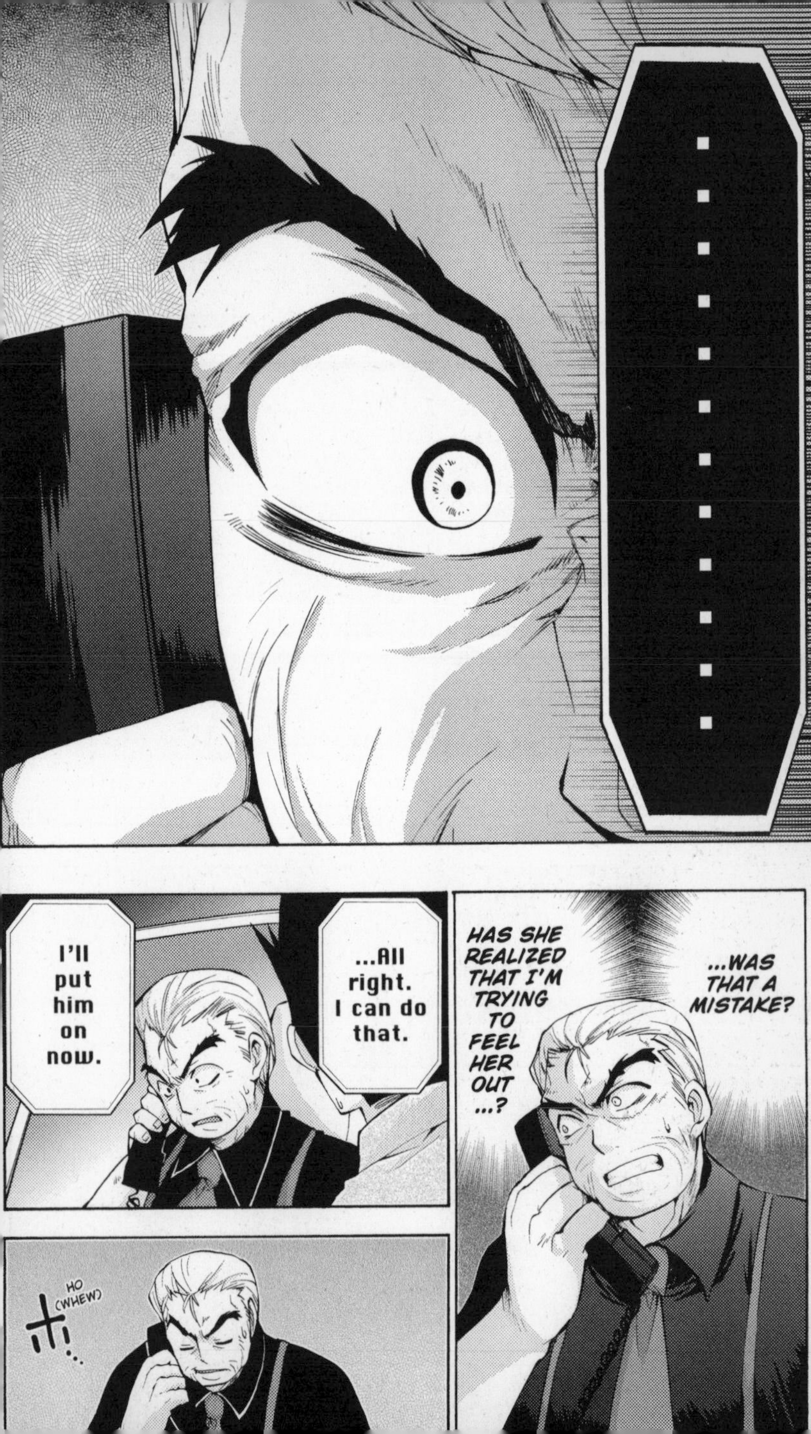
....
...WAS THAT A MISTAKE?
HAS SHE REALIZED THAT I'M TRYING TO FEEL HER OUT ...?
...All right. I can do that.
I'll put him on now.
HO (WHEW)

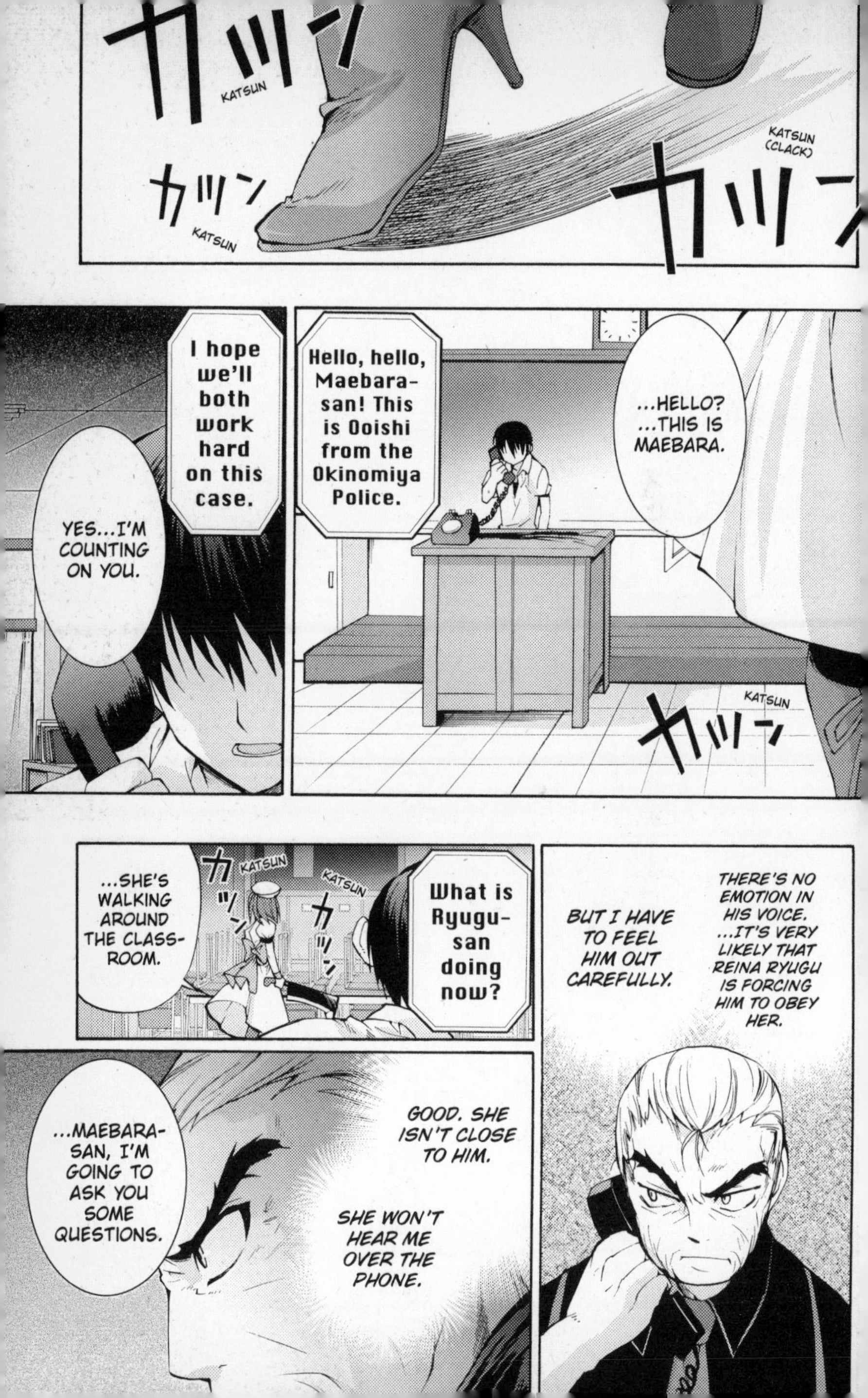
KATSUN (CLACK)
KATSUN
KATSUN
...HELLO? ...THIS IS MAEBARA.
Hello, hello, Maebara-san! This is Ooishi from the Okinomiya Police.
KATSUN
I hope we'll both work hard on this case.
YES...I'M COUNTING ON YOU.
THERE'S NO EMOTION IN HIS VOICE. ...IT'S VERY LIKELY THAT REINA RYUGU IS FORCING HIM TO OBEY HER.
BUT I HAVE TO FEEL HIM OUT CAREFULLY.
What is Ryugu-san doing now?
KATSUN
KATSUN
...SHE'S WALKING AROUND THE CLASSROOM.
GOOD. SHE ISN'T CLOSE TO HIM.
SHE WON'T HEAR ME OVER THE PHONE.
...MAEBARA-SAN, I'M GOING TO ASK YOU SOME QUESTIONS.

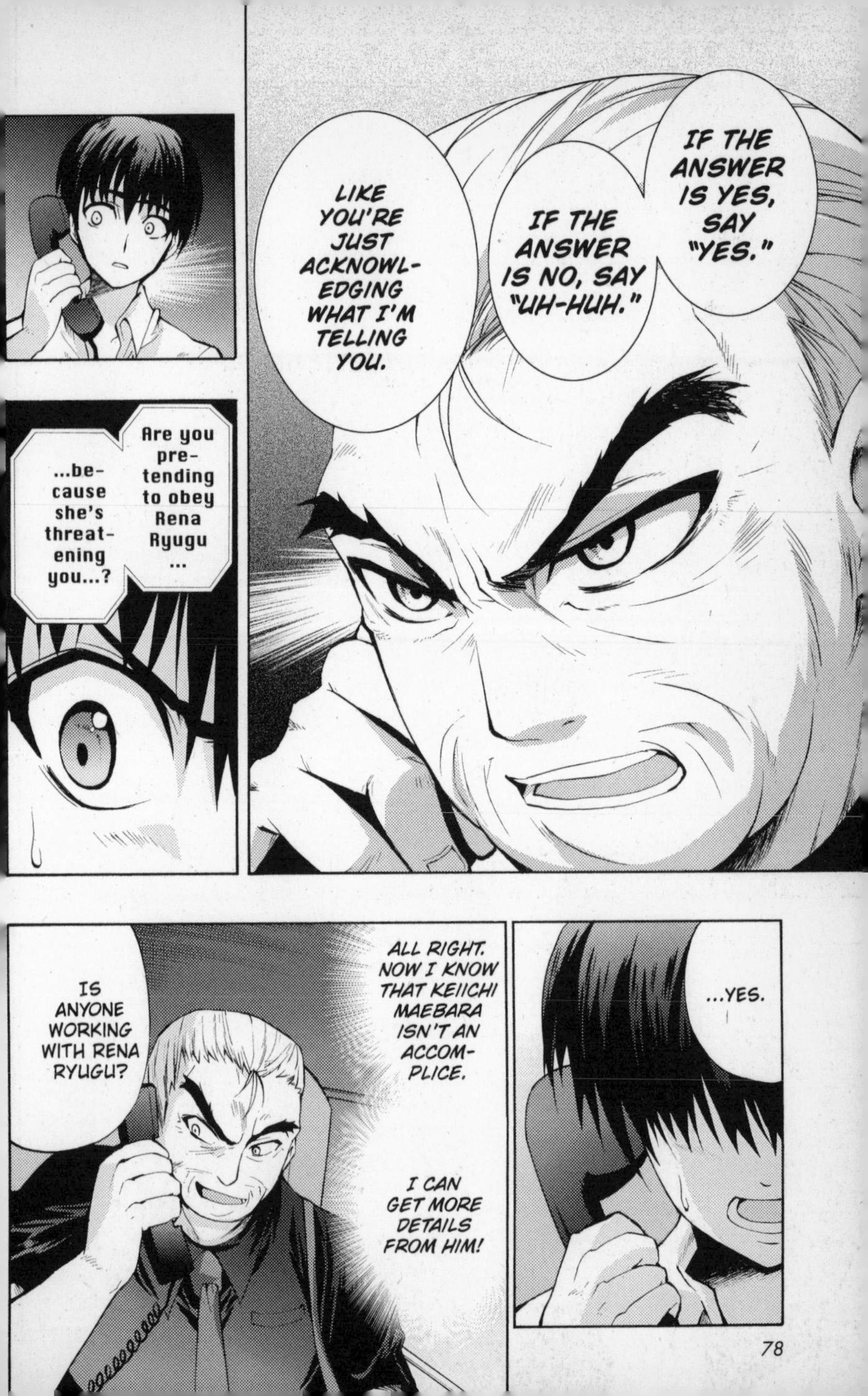
IF THE ANSWER IS YES, SAY "YES."
IF THE ANSWER IS NO, SAY "UH-HUH."
LIKE YOU'RE JUST ACKNOWL-EDGING WHAT I'M TELLING YOU.
Are you pre-tending to obey Rena Ryugu ...
...be-cause she's threat-ening you...?
...YES.
ALL RIGHT. NOW I KNOW THAT KEIICHI MAEBARA ISN'T AN ACCOM-PLICE.
I CAN GET MORE DETAILS FROM HIM!
IS ANYONE WORKING WITH RENA RYUGU?

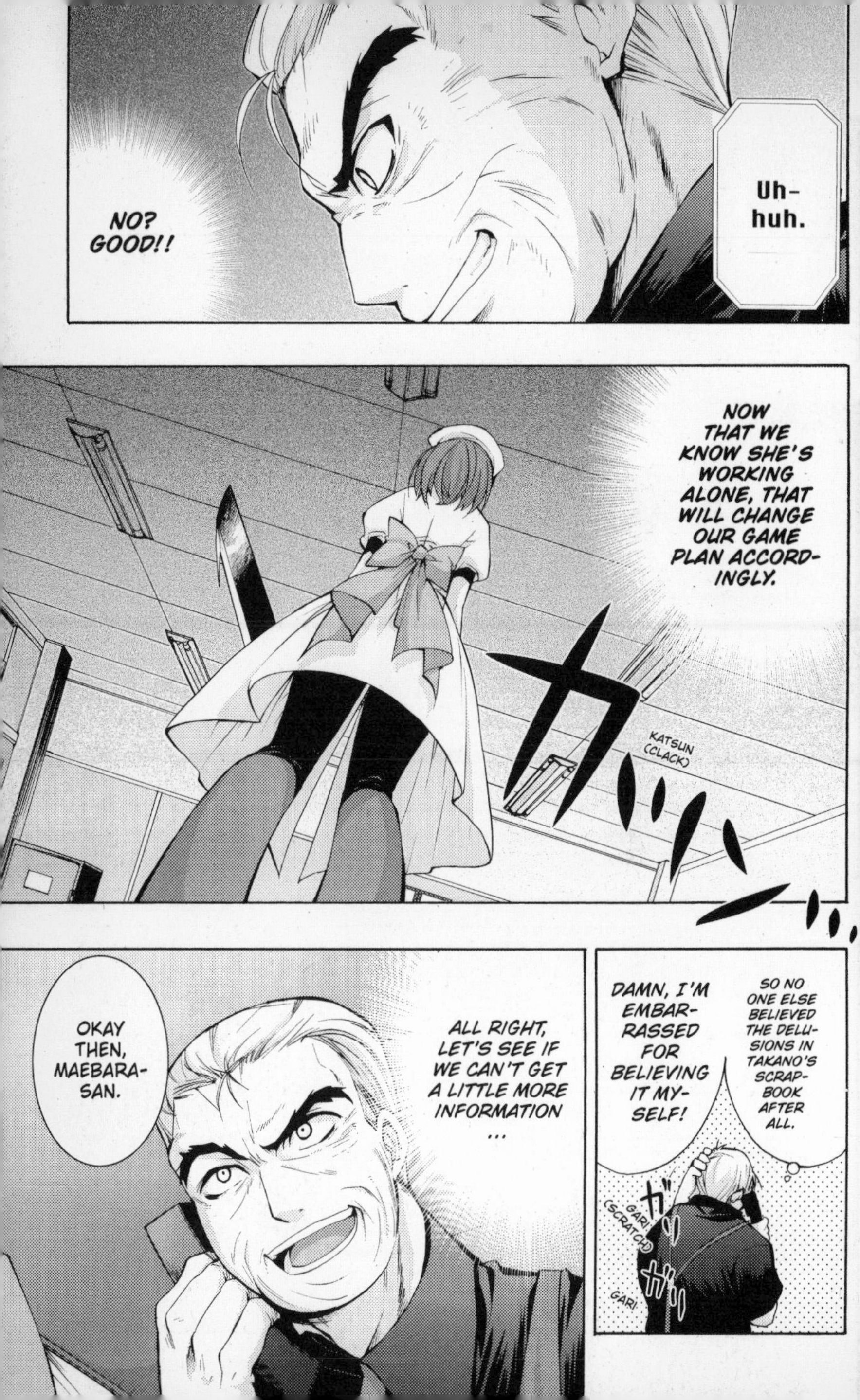
Uh-huh.
NO? GOOD!!
NOW THAT WE KNOW SHE'S WORKING ALONE, THAT WILL CHANGE OUR GAME PLAN ACCORDINGLY.
KATSUN (CLACK)
SO NO ONE ELSE BELIEVED THE DELUSIONS IN TAKANO'S SCRAPBOOK AFTER ALL.
DAMN, I'M EMBARRASSED FOR BELIEVING IT MYSELF!
GARI (SCRATCH)
GARI
ALL RIGHT, LET'S SEE IF WE CAN'T GET A LITTLE MORE INFORMATION ...
OKAY THEN, MAEBARA-SAN.

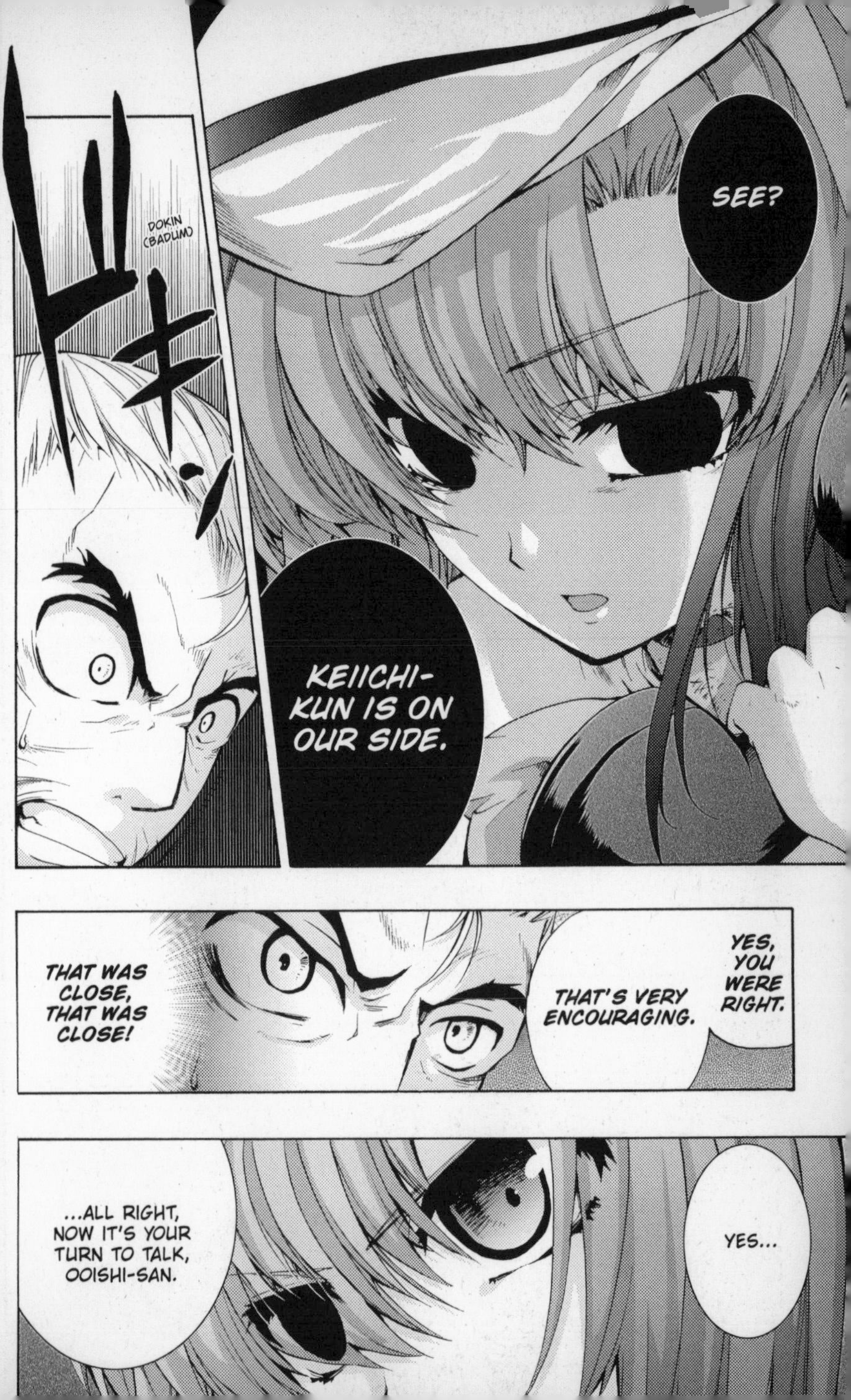
SEE?
KEIICHI-KUN IS ON OUR SIDE.
DOKIN (BADUM)
YES, YOU WERE RIGHT.
THAT'S VERY ENCOURAGING.
THAT WAS CLOSE, THAT WAS CLOSE!
YES...
...ALL RIGHT, NOW IT'S YOUR TURN TO TALK, OOISHI-SAN.

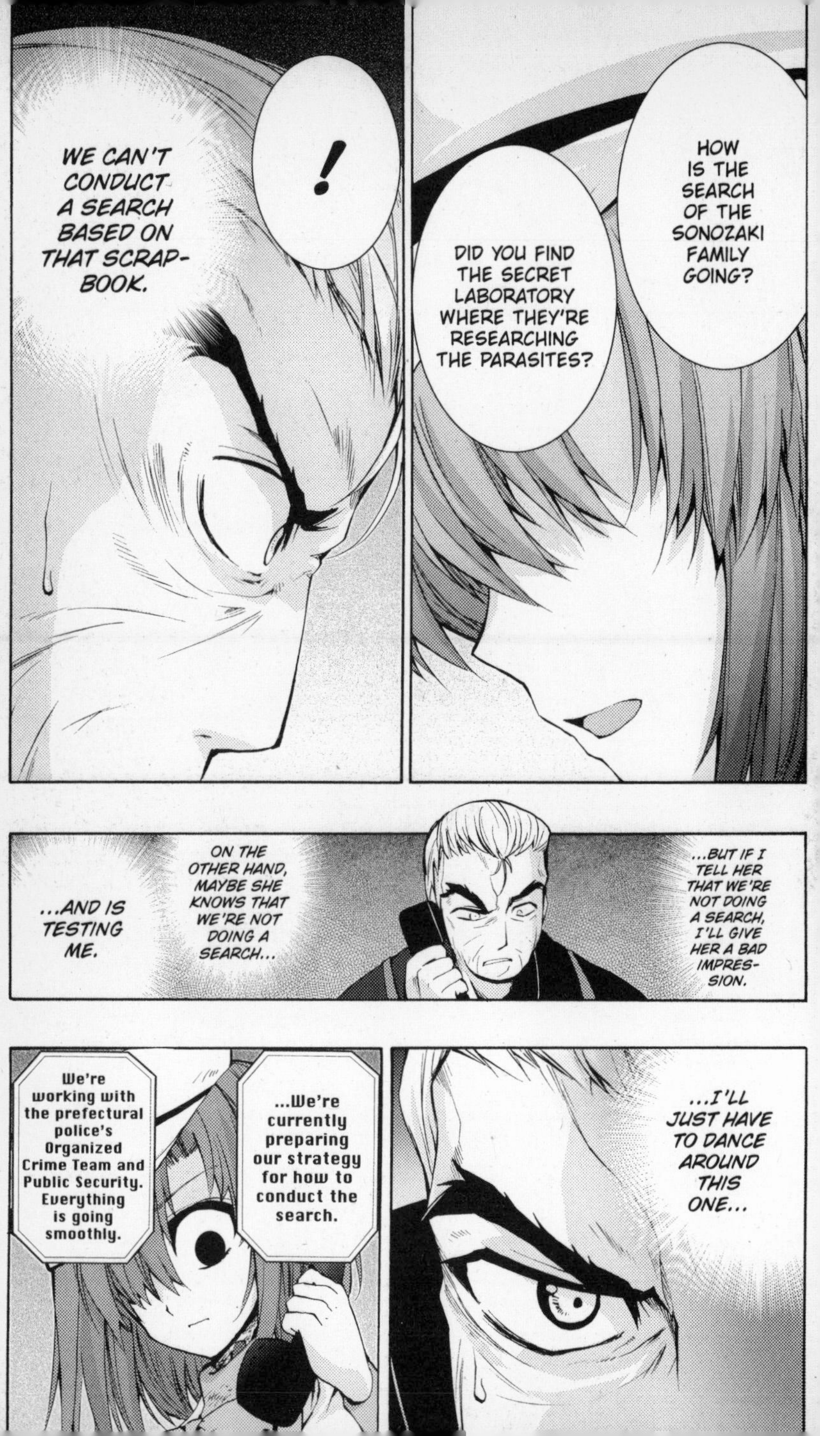
HOW IS THE SEARCH OF THE SONOZAKI FAMILY GOING?
DID YOU FIND THE SECRET LABORATORY WHERE THEY'RE RESEARCHING THE PARASITES?
!
WE CAN'T CONDUCT A SEARCH BASED ON THAT SCRAP-BOOK.
...BUT IF I TELL HER THAT WE'RE NOT DOING A SEARCH, I'LL GIVE HER A BAD IMPRES-SION.
ON THE OTHER HAND, MAYBE SHE KNOWS THAT WE'RE NOT DOING A SEARCH...
...AND IS TESTING ME.
...I'LL JUST HAVE TO DANCE AROUND THIS ONE...
We're working with the prefectural police's Organized Crime Team and Public Security. Everything is going smoothly.
...We're currently preparing our strategy for how to conduct the search.

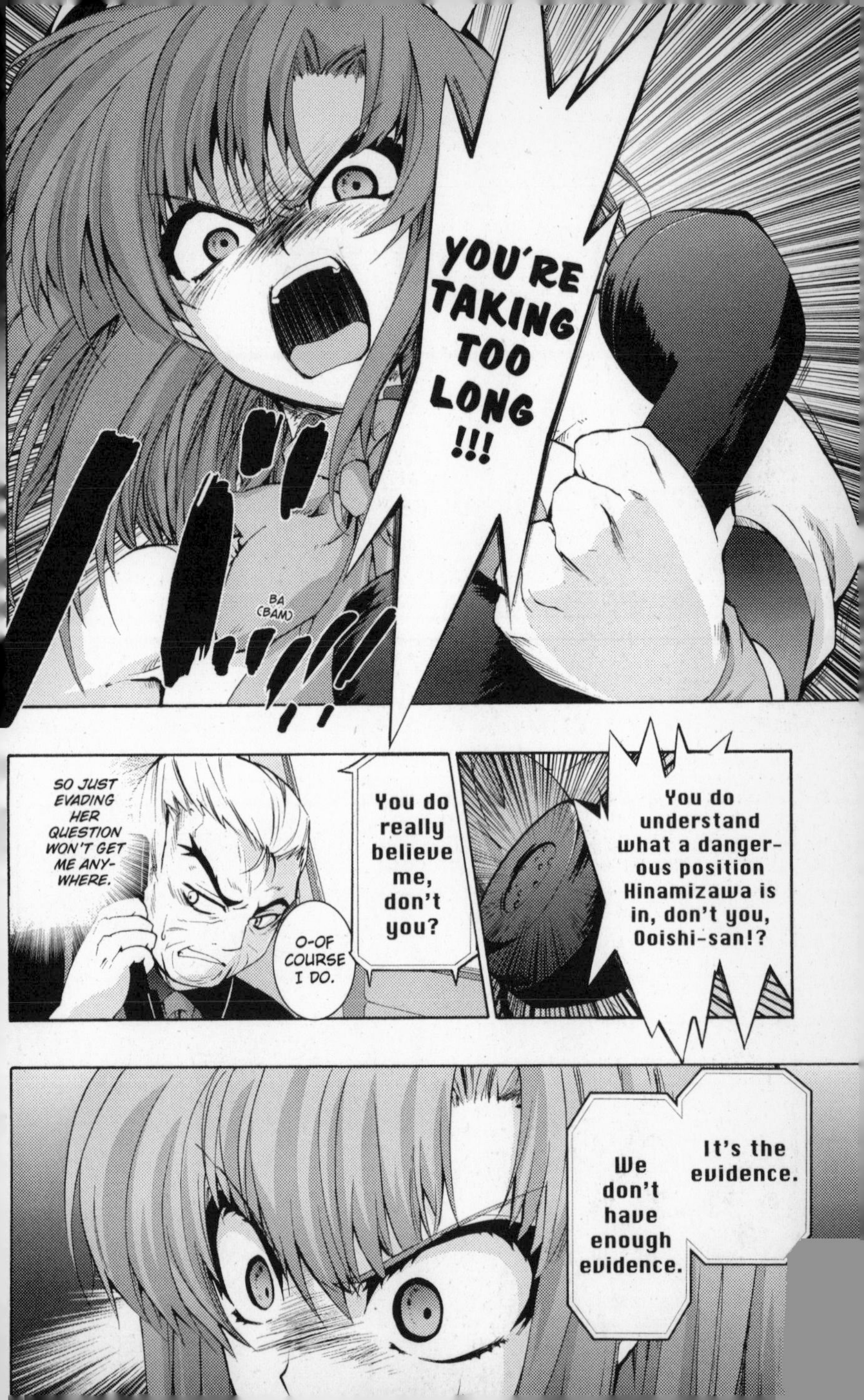
YOU'RE TAKING TOO LONG!!!
BA (BAM)
You do understand what a danger-ous position Hinamizawa is in, don't you, Ooishi-san!?
You do really believe me, don't you?
SO JUST EVADING HER QUESTION WON'T GET ME ANY-WHERE.
O-OF COURSE I DO.
It's the evidence.
We don't have enough evidence.

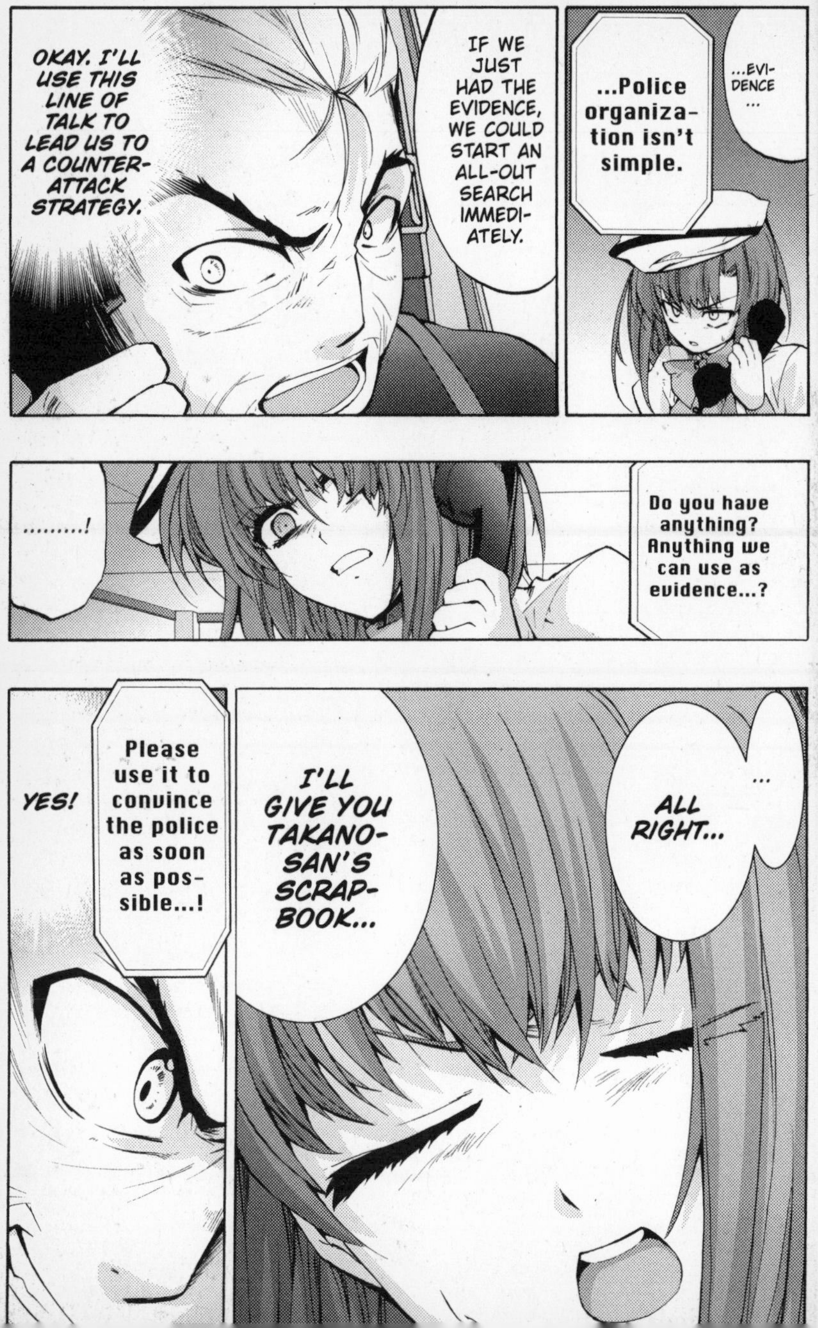
...EVI-DENCE...
...Police organiza-tion isn't simple.
IF WE JUST HAD THE EVIDENCE, WE COULD START AN ALL-OUT SEARCH IMMEDI-ATELY.
OKAY. I'LL USE THIS LINE OF TALK TO LEAD US TO A COUNTER-ATTACK STRATEGY.
Do you have anything? Anything we can use as evidence...?
.........!
... ALL RIGHT...
I'LL GIVE YOU TAKANO-SAN'S SCRAP-BOOK...
Please use it to convince the police as soon as pos-sible...!
YES!

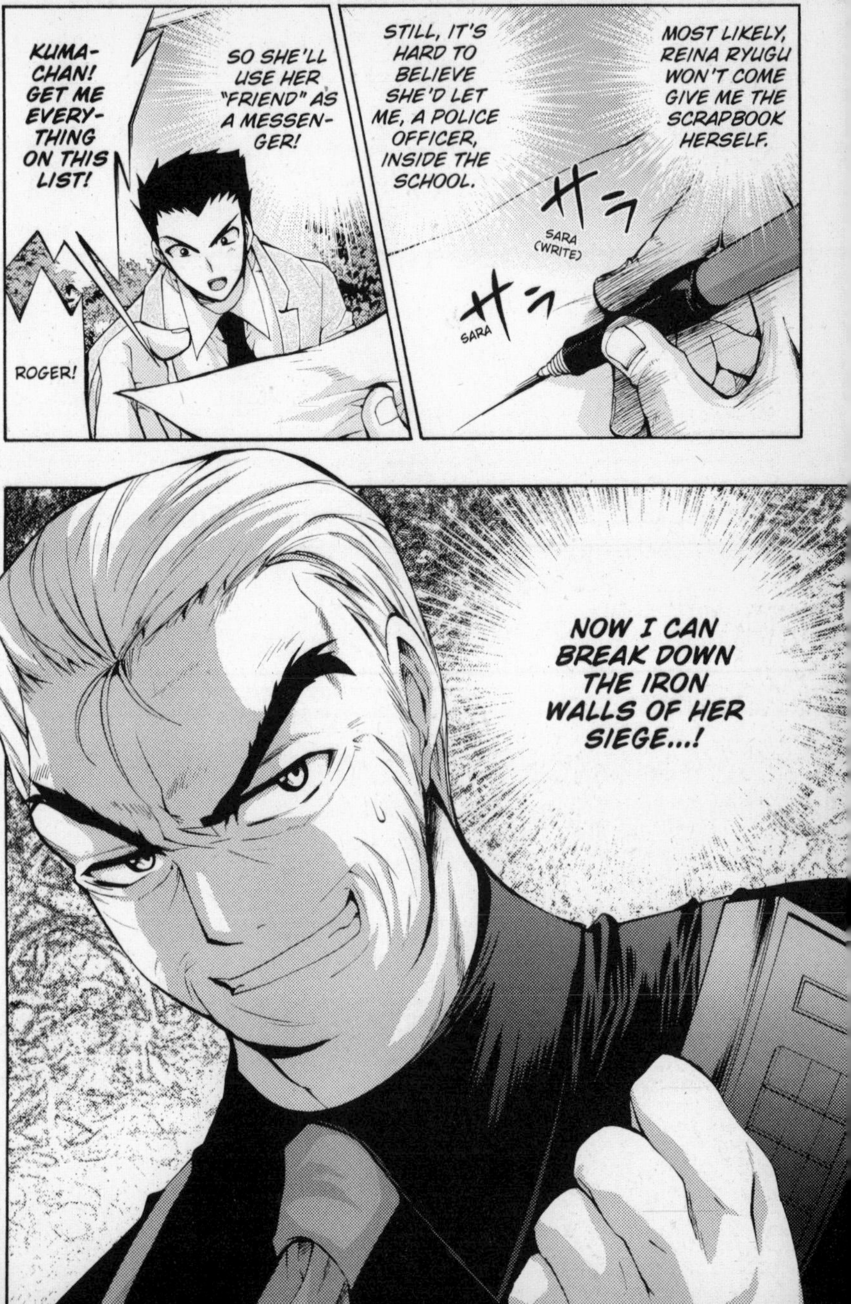
MOST LIKELY, REINA RYUGU WON'T COME GIVE ME THE SCRAPBOOK HERSELF.
STILL, IT'S HARD TO BELIEVE SHE'D LET ME, A POLICE OFFICER, INSIDE THE SCHOOL.
SARA (WRITE)
SARA
SO SHE'LL USE HER "FRIEND" AS A MESSENGER!
KUMA-CHAN! GET ME EVERYTHING ON THIS LIST!
ROGER!
NOW I CAN BREAK DOWN THE IRON WALLS OF HER SIEGE...!

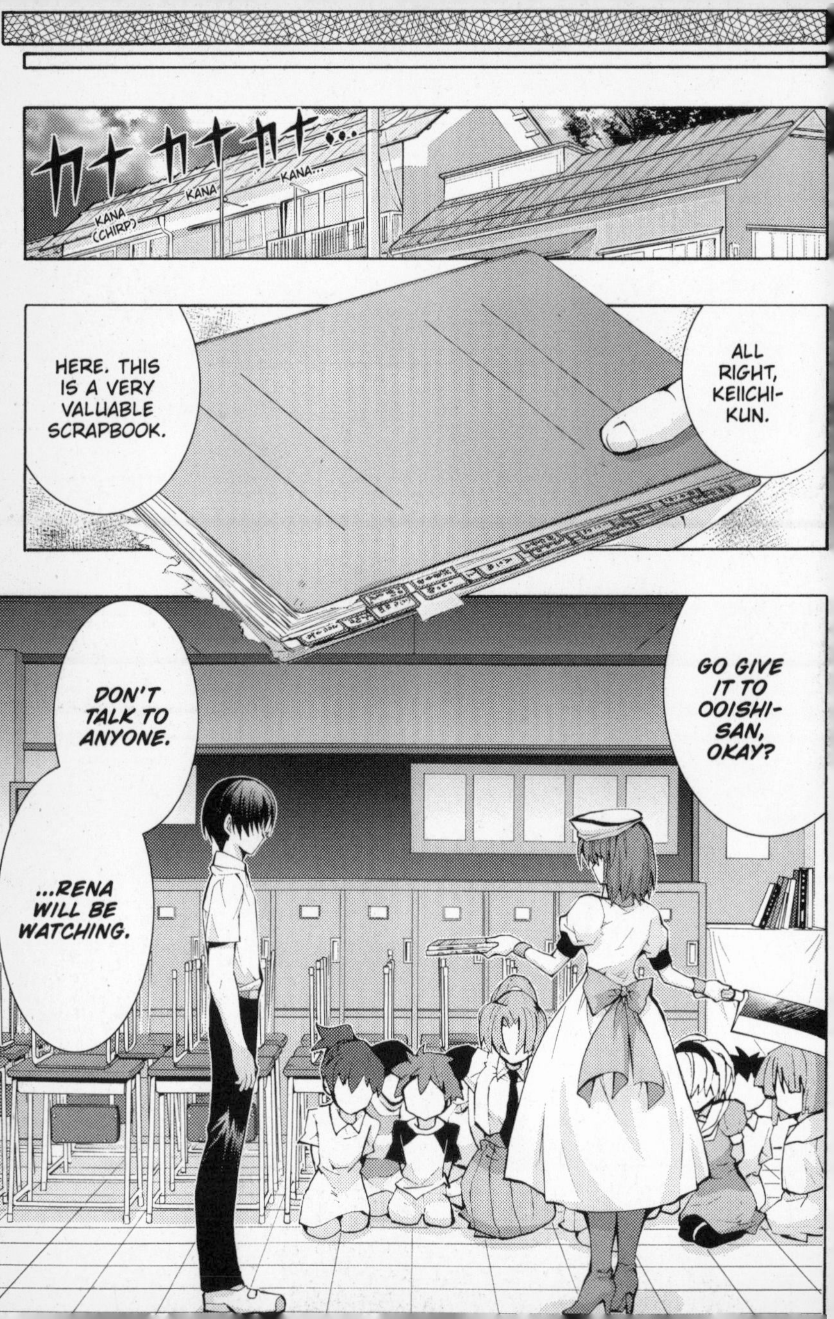
カナカナカナ...
KANA (CHIRP)
KANA
KANA...
ALL RIGHT, KEIICHI-KUN.
HERE. THIS IS A VERY VALUABLE SCRAPBOOK.
GO GIVE IT TO OOISHI-SAN, OKAY?
DON'T TALK TO ANYONE.
...RENA WILL BE WATCHING.

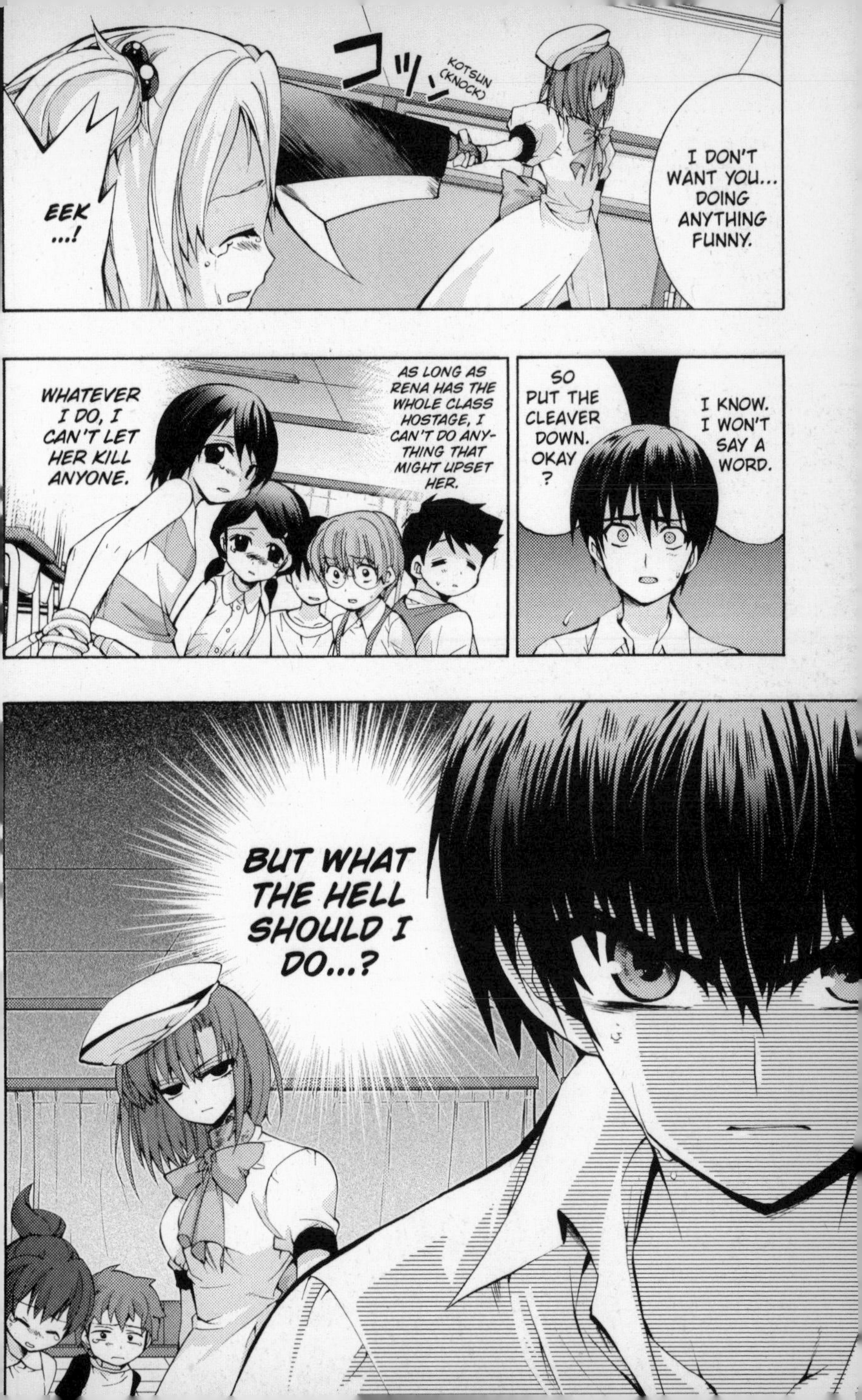

コツン
KOTSUN (KNOCK)
I DON'T WANT YOU... DOING ANYTHING FUNNY.
EEK ...!
I KNOW. I WON'T SAY A WORD.
SO PUT THE CLEAVER DOWN. OKAY ?
AS LONG AS RENA HAS THE WHOLE CLASS HOSTAGE, I CAN'T DO ANY-THING THAT MIGHT UPSET HER.
WHATEVER I DO, I CAN'T LET HER KILL ANYONE.
BUT WHAT THE HELL SHOULD I DO...?

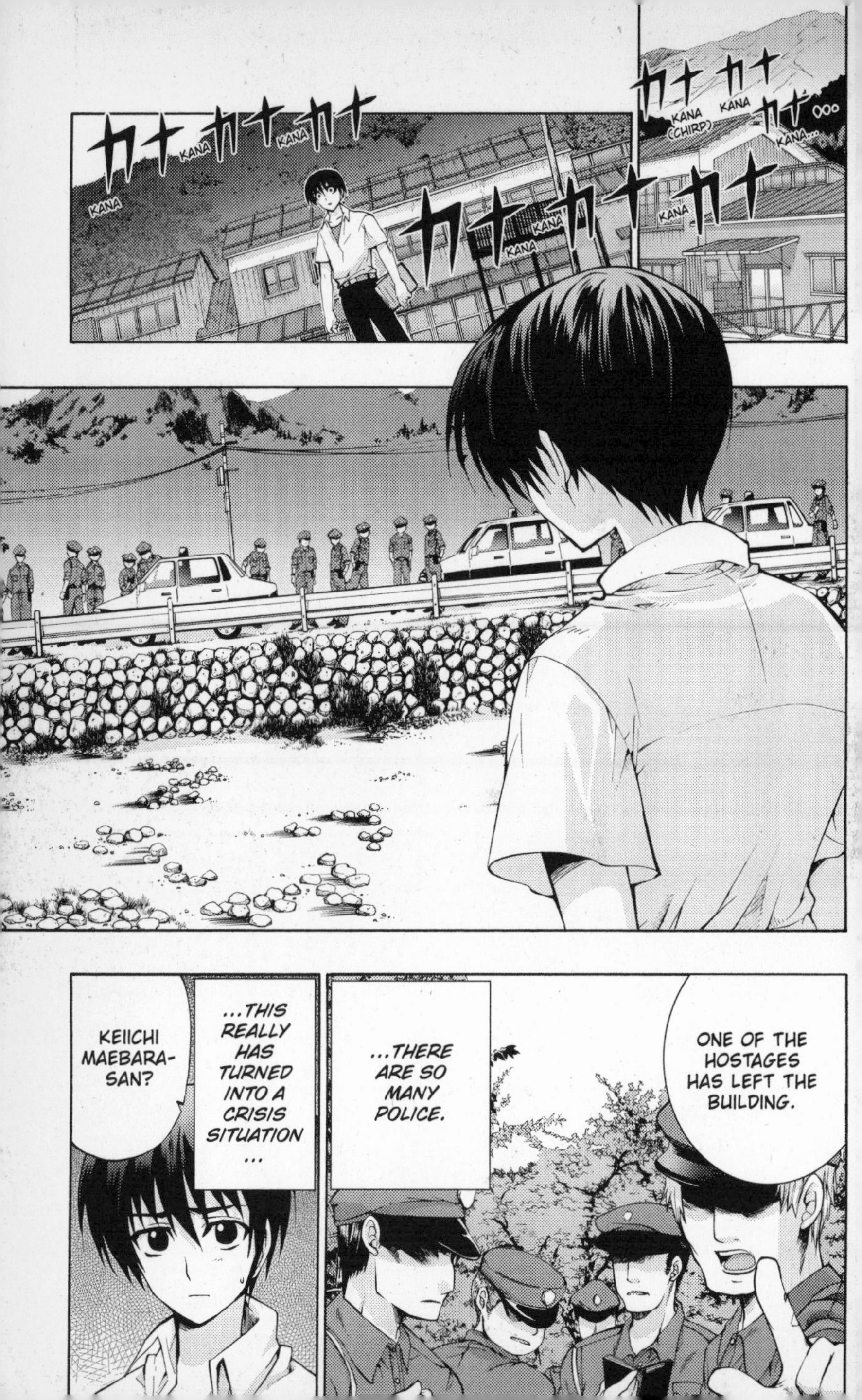

カナ カナ カナ…
KANA (CHIRP)
KANA
KANA…
カナ カナ カナ
KANA
KANA
KANA
カナ カナ カナ
KANA
KANA
KANA
ONE OF THE HOSTAGES HAS LEFT THE BUILDING.
…THERE ARE SO MANY POLICE.
…THIS REALLY HAS TURNED INTO A CRISIS SITUATION…
KEIICHI MAEBARA-SAN?

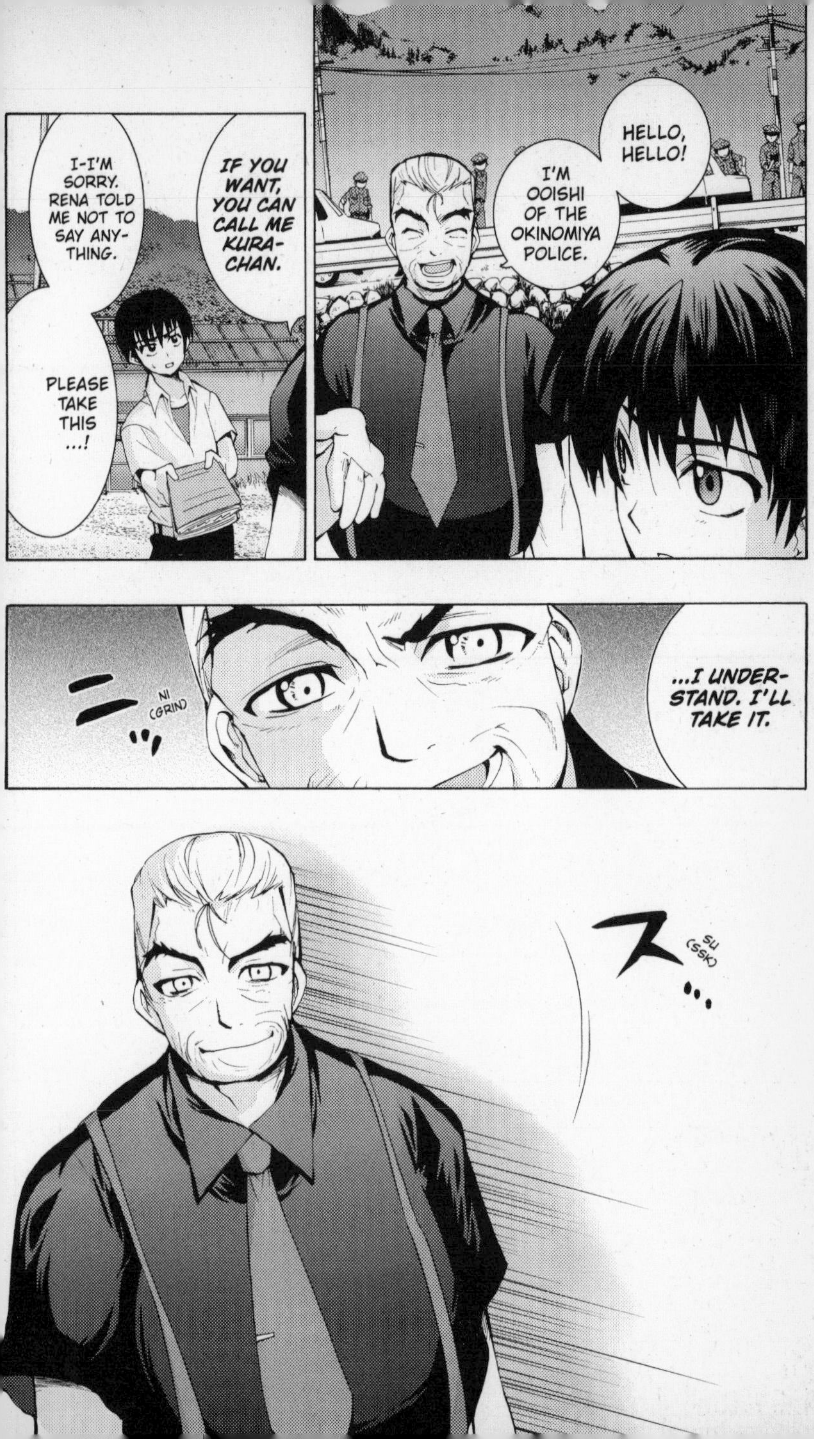
HELLO, HELLO!
I'M OOISHI OF THE OKINOMIYA POLICE.
IF YOU WANT, YOU CAN CALL ME KURA-CHAN.
I-I'M SORRY. RENA TOLD ME NOT TO SAY ANY-THING.
PLEASE TAKE THIS ...!
...I UNDER-STAND. I'LL TAKE IT.
NI (GRIN)
SU (SSK)

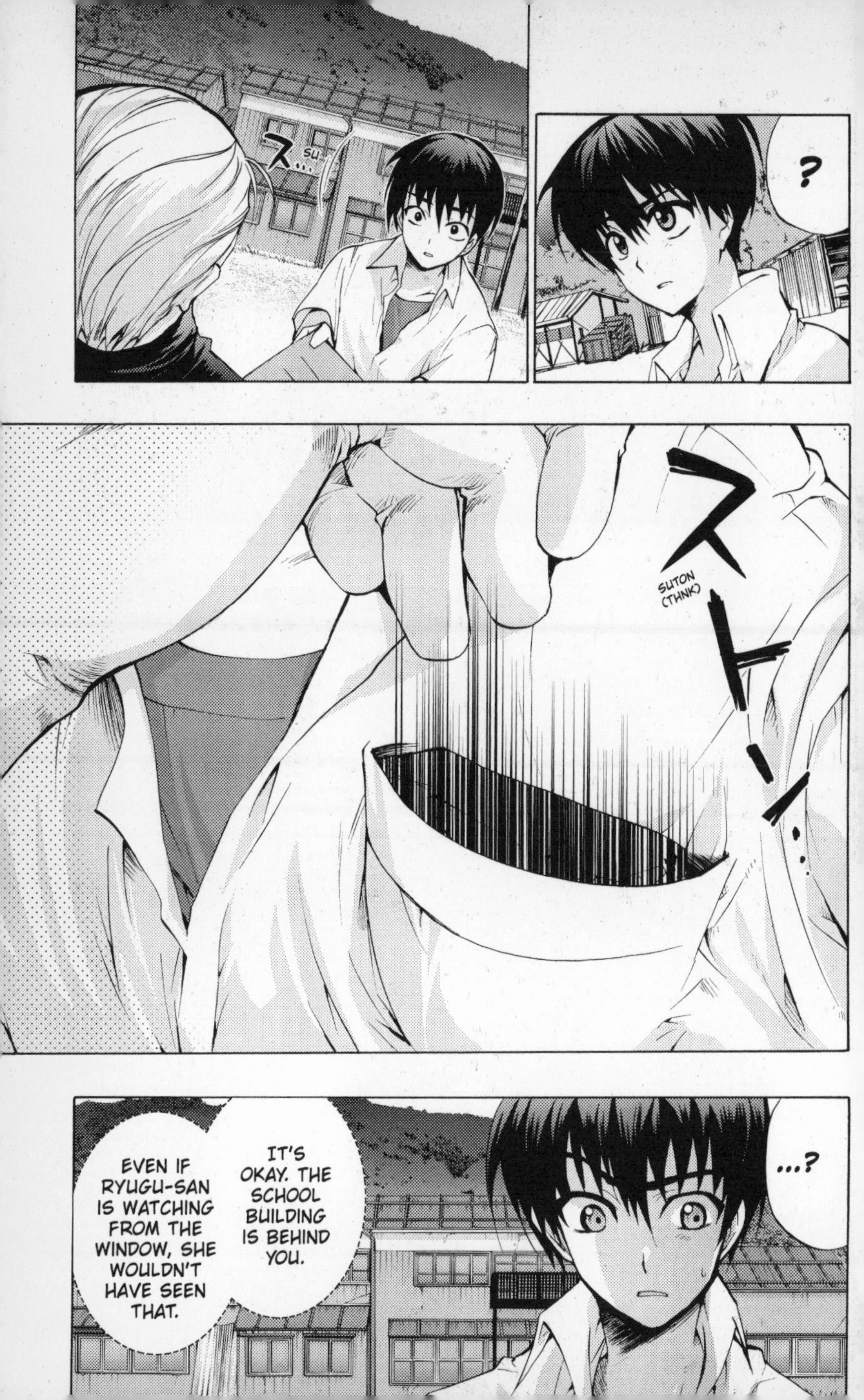
?
ス...
SU
スト
SUTON (THNK)
...?
IT'S OKAY. THE SCHOOL BUILDING IS BEHIND YOU.
EVEN IF RYUGU-SAN IS WATCHING FROM THE WINDOW, SHE WOULDN'T HAVE SEEN THAT.

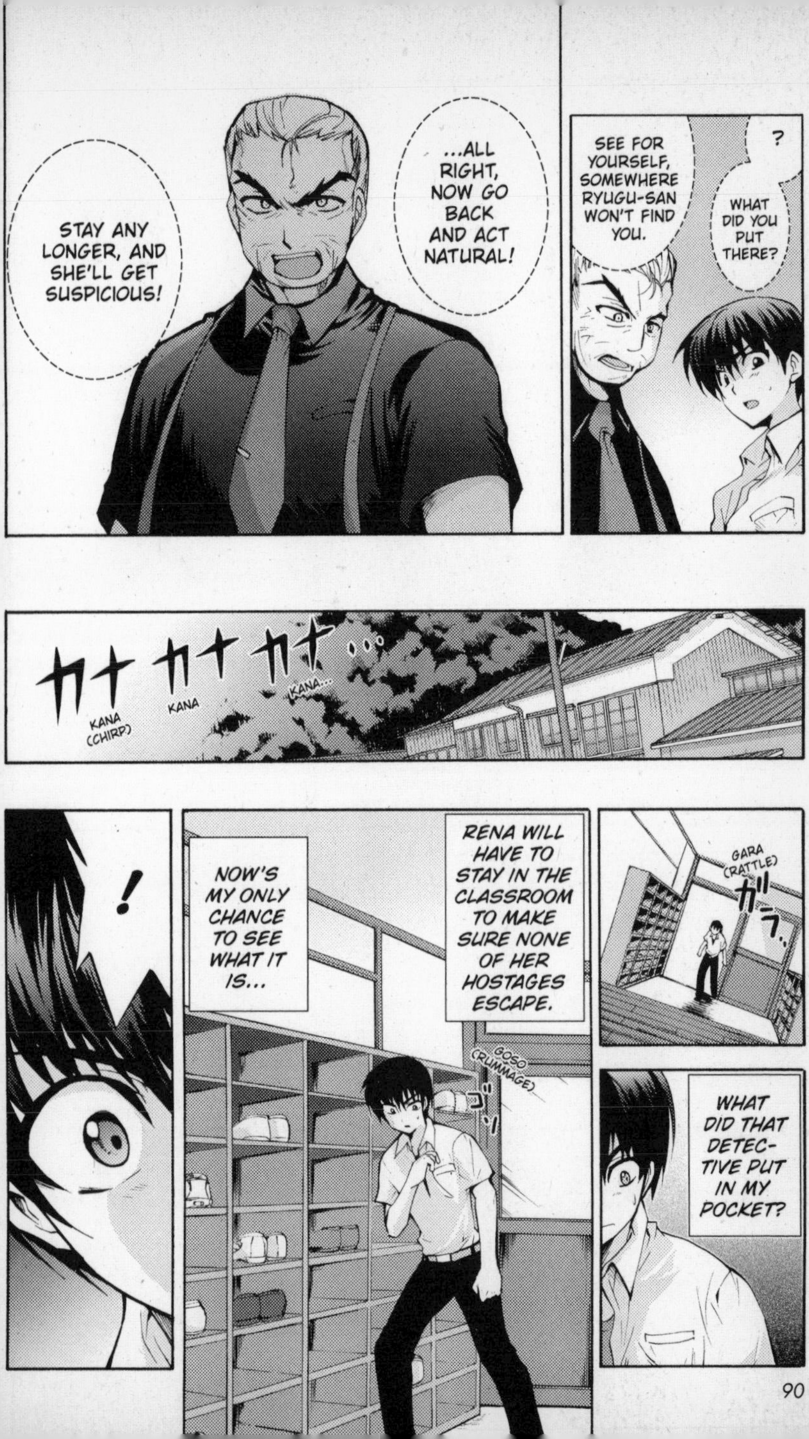
?
WHAT DID YOU PUT THERE?
SEE FOR YOURSELF, SOMEWHERE RYUGU-SAN WON'T FIND YOU.
...ALL RIGHT, NOW GO BACK AND ACT NATURAL!
STAY ANY LONGER, AND SHE'LL GET SUSPICIOUS!
カナ...
KANA...
カナ
KANA
カナ
KANA (CHIRP)
GARA (RATTLE)
ガラ...
WHAT DID THAT DETECTIVE PUT IN MY POCKET?
RENA WILL HAVE TO STAY IN THE CLASSROOM TO MAKE SURE NONE OF HER HOSTAGES ESCAPE.
NOW'S MY ONLY CHANCE TO SEE WHAT IT IS...
GOSO (RUMMAGE)
!

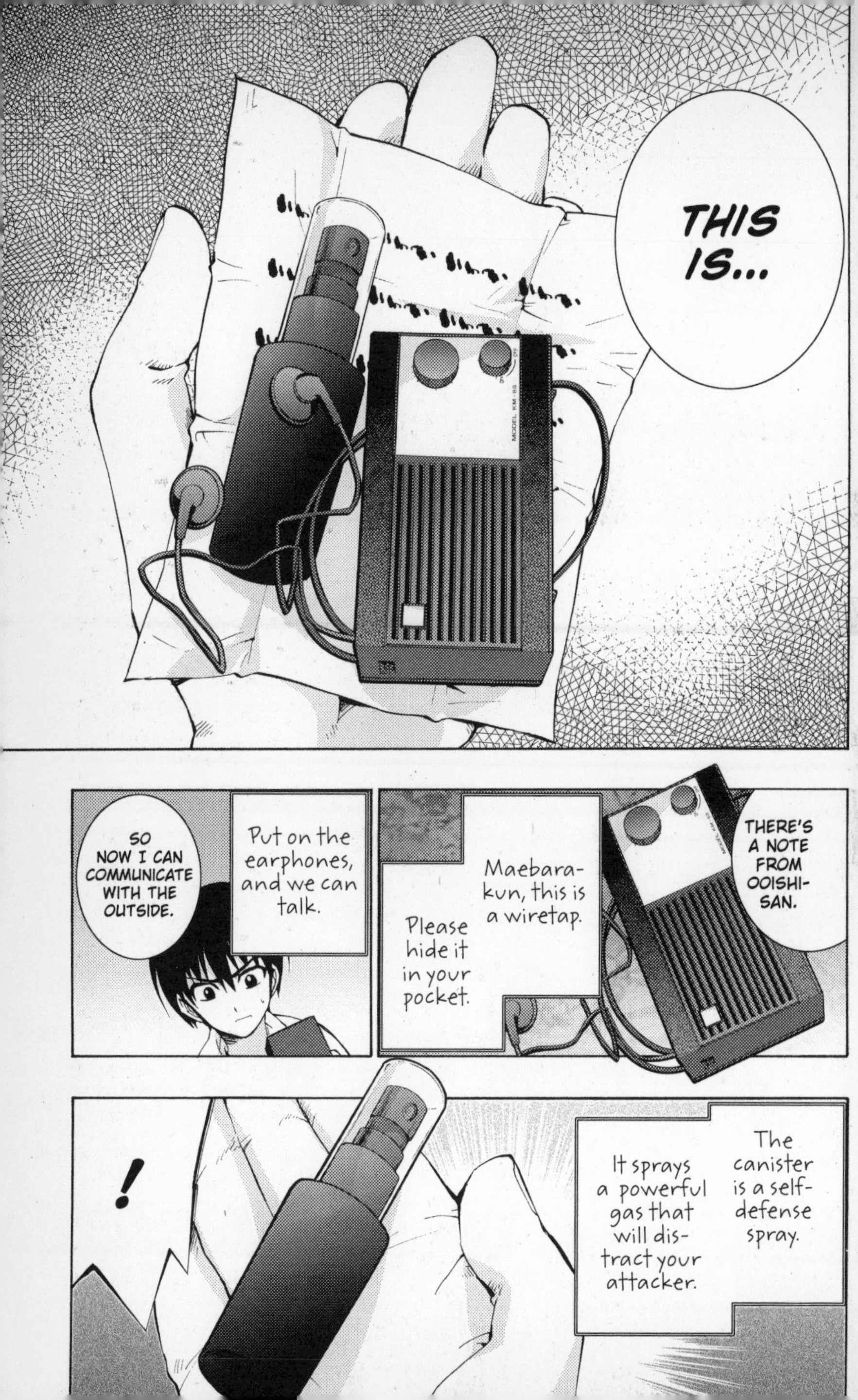
THIS IS...
THERE'S A NOTE FROM OOISHI-SAN.
Maebara-kun, this is a wiretap.
Please hide it in your pocket.
Put on the earphones, and we can talk.
SO NOW I CAN COMMUNICATE WITH THE OUTSIDE.
The canister is a self-defense spray.
It sprays a powerful gas that will distract your attacker.
!

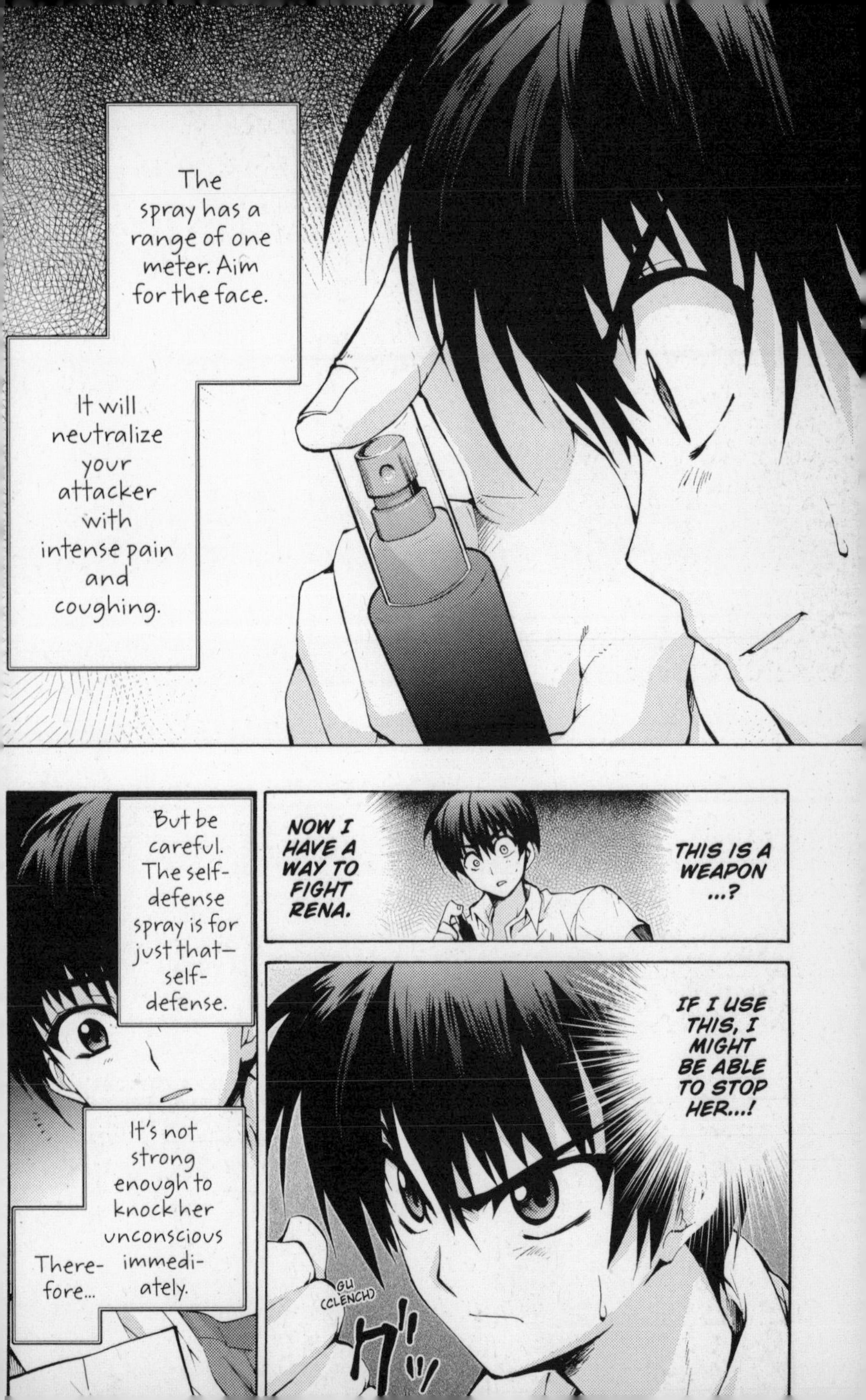
The spray has a range of one meter. Aim for the face.
It will neutralize your attacker with intense pain and coughing.
THIS IS A WEAPON ...?
NOW I HAVE A WAY TO FIGHT RENA.
IF I USE THIS, I MIGHT BE ABLE TO STOP HER...!
GU (CLENCH)
But be careful. The self-defense spray is for just that—self-defense.
It's not strong enough to knock her unconscious immediately.
Therefore...

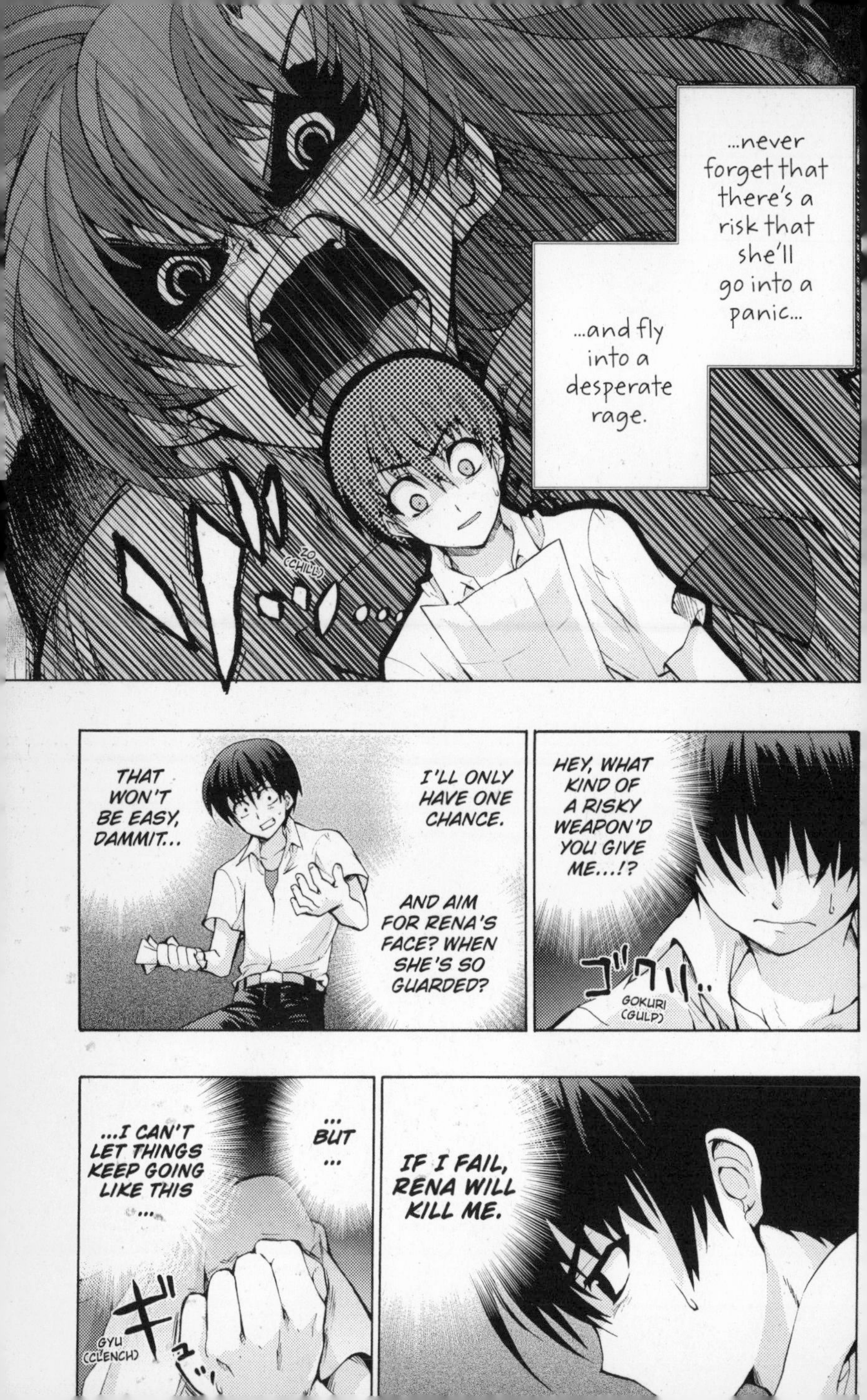
...never forget that there's a risk that she'll go into a panic...
...and fly into a desperate rage.
ZO (CHILL)
HEY, WHAT KIND OF A RISKY WEAPON'D YOU GIVE ME...!?
GOKURI (GULP)
I'LL ONLY HAVE ONE CHANCE.
AND AIM FOR RENA'S FACE? WHEN SHE'S SO GUARDED?
THAT WON'T BE EASY, DAMMIT...
IF I FAIL, RENA WILL KILL ME.
...BUT...
...I CAN'T LET THINGS KEEP GOING LIKE THIS...
GYU (CLENCH)

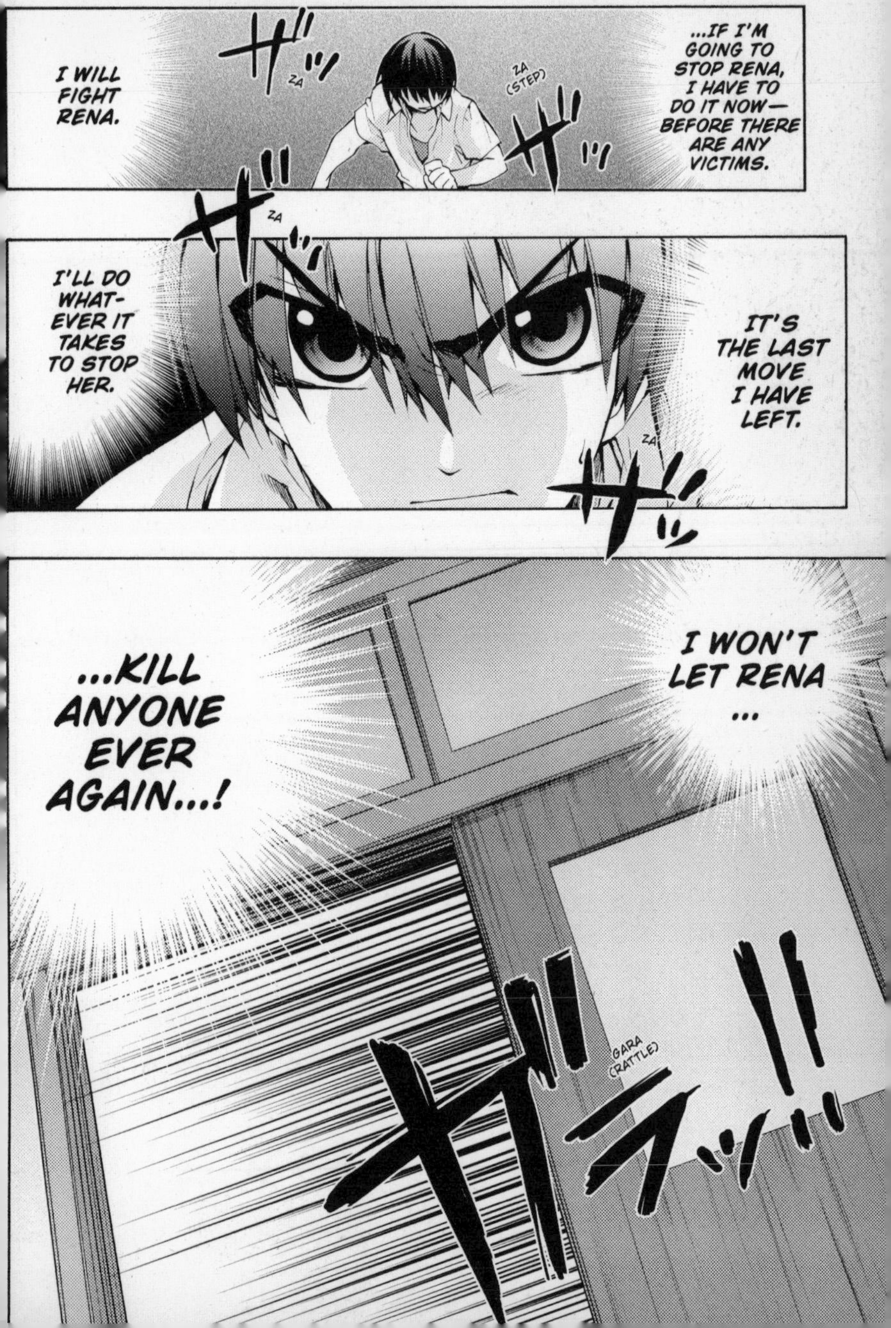
...IF I'M GOING TO STOP RENA, I HAVE TO DO IT NOW—BEFORE THERE ARE ANY VICTIMS.
ZA (STEP)
ZA
I WILL FIGHT RENA.
ZA
IT'S THE LAST MOVE I HAVE LEFT.
I'LL DO WHAT-EVER IT TAKES TO STOP HER.
ZA
I WON'T LET RENA ...
...KILL ANYONE EVER AGAIN...!
GARA (RATTLE)

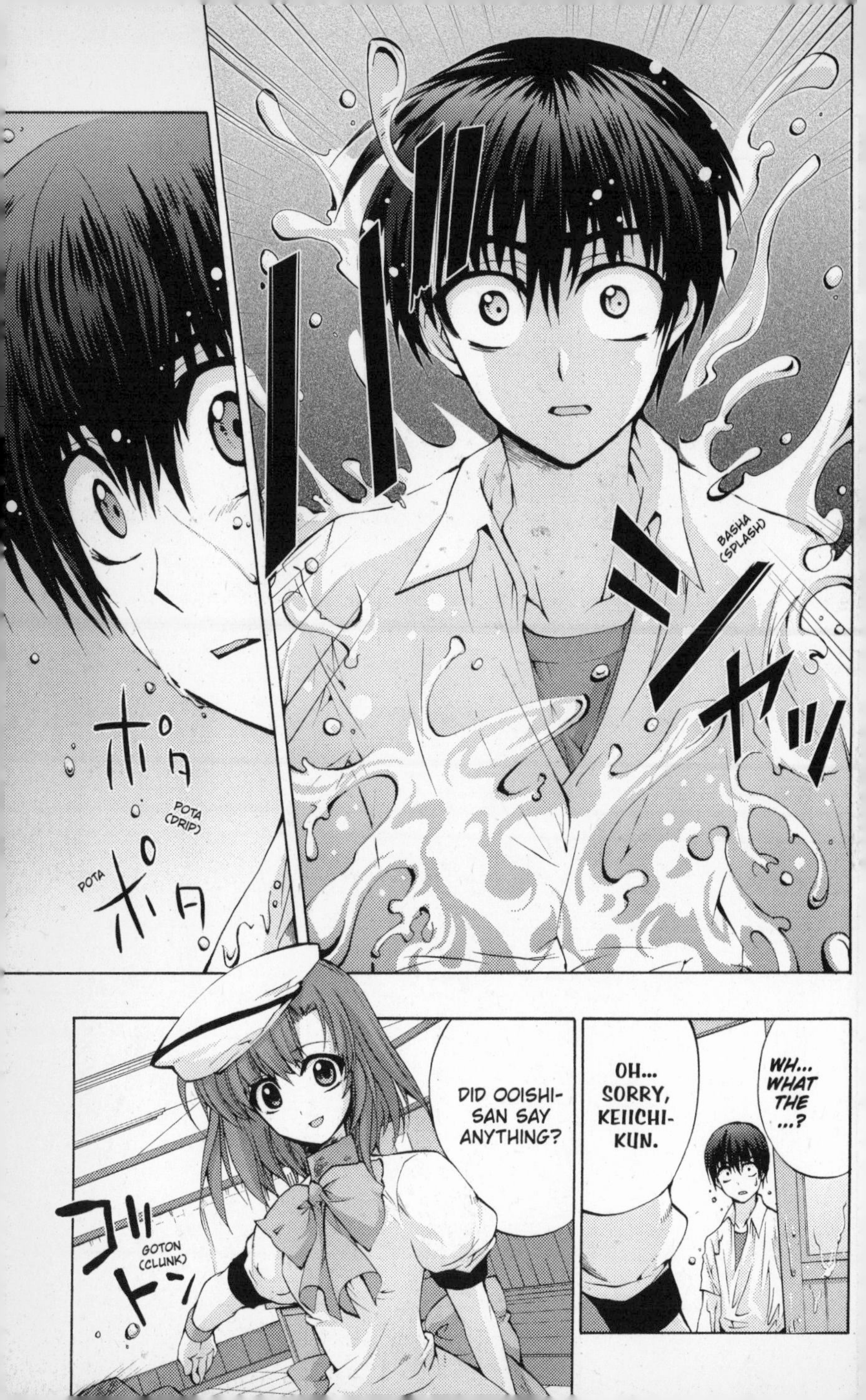
BASHA (SPLASH)
POTA (DRIP)
POTA
WH... WHAT THE ...?
OH... SORRY, KEIICHI-KUN.
DID OOISHI-SAN SAY ANYTHING?
GOTON (CLUNK)

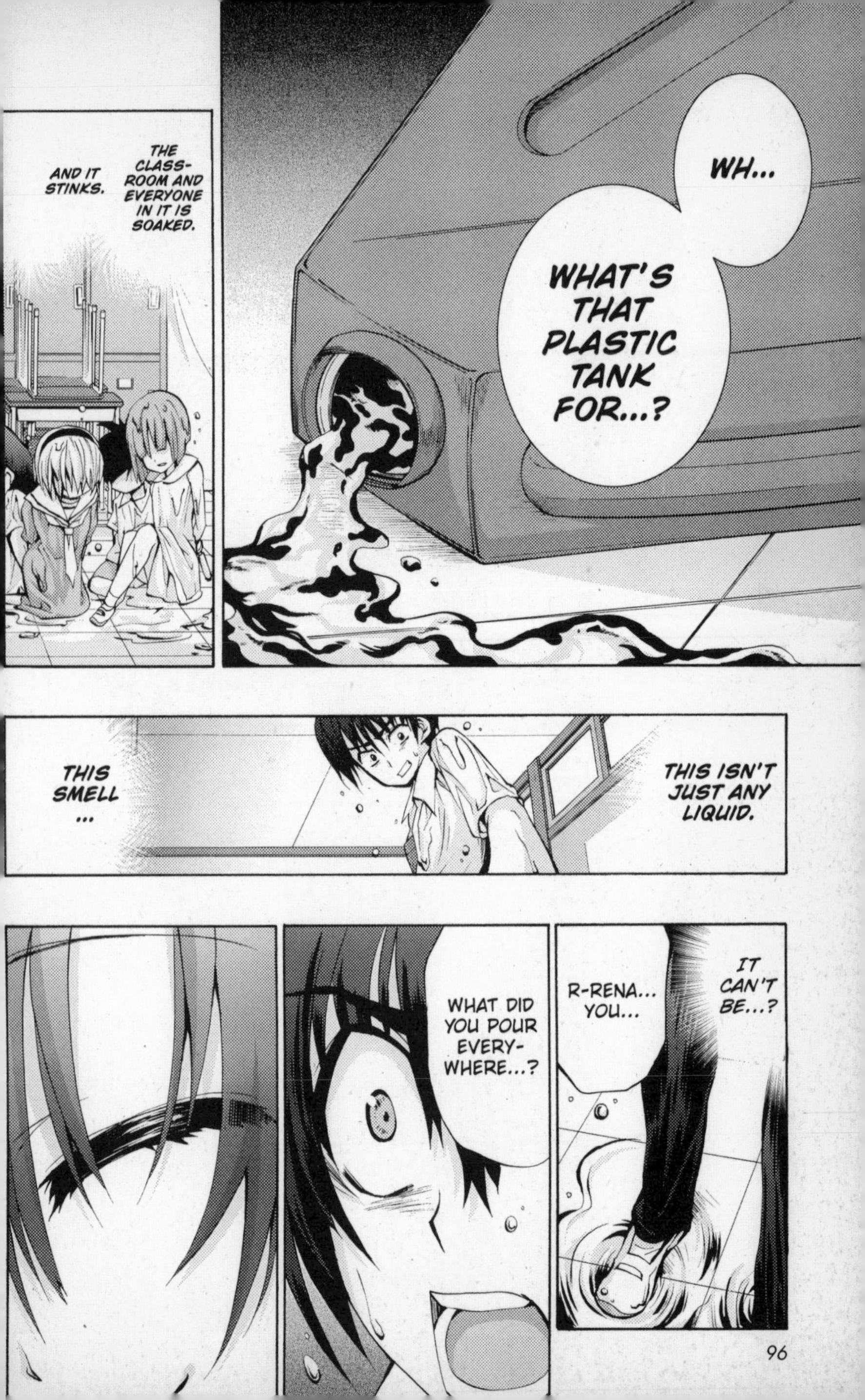
WH...
WHAT'S THAT PLASTIC TANK FOR...?
THE CLASS-ROOM AND EVERYONE IN IT IS SOAKED.
AND IT STINKS.
THIS ISN'T JUST ANY LIQUID.
THIS SMELL ...
IT CAN'T BE...?
R-RENA... YOU...
WHAT DID YOU POUR EVERY-WHERE...?

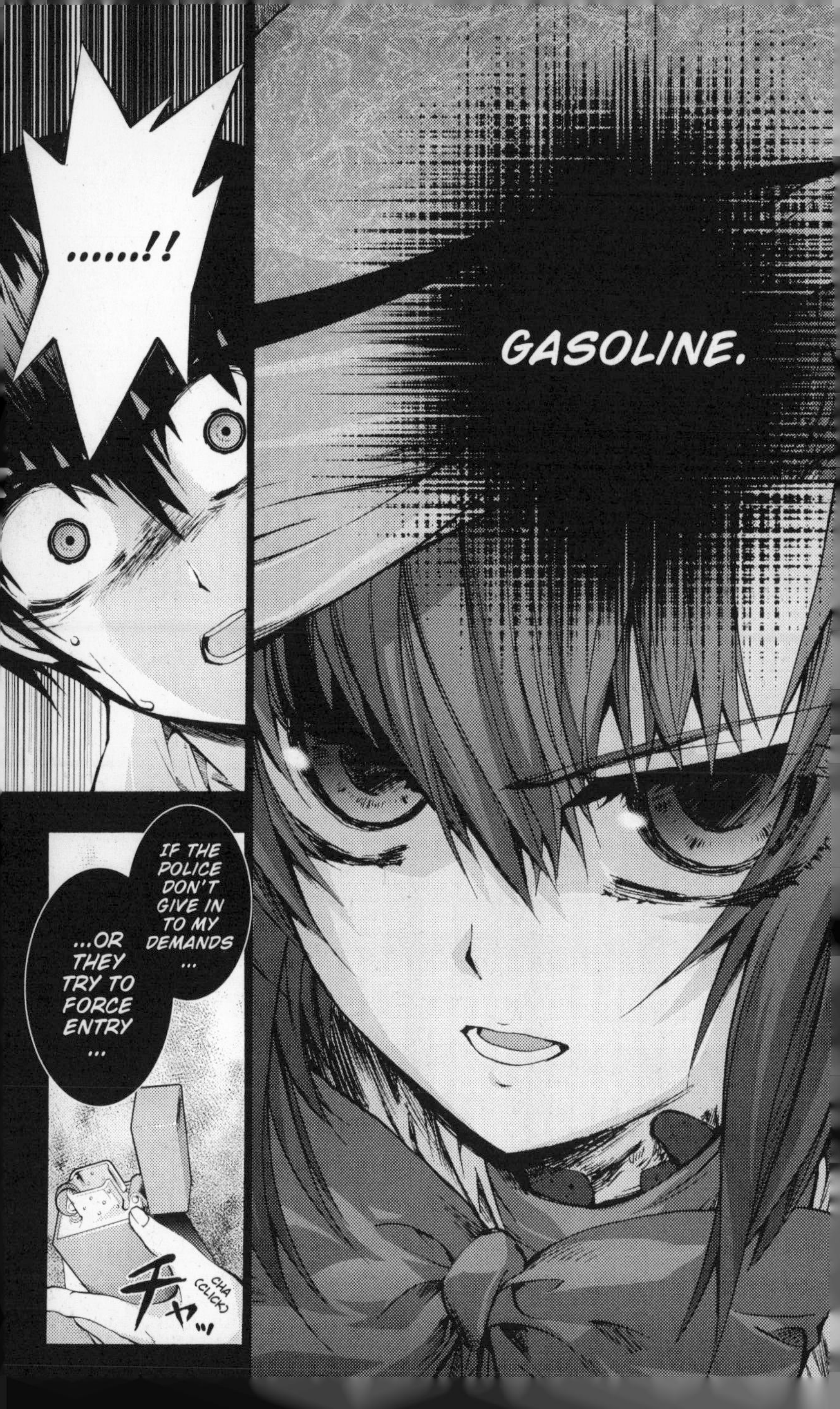
GASOLINE.
......!!
IF THE POLICE DON'T GIVE IN TO MY DEMANDS...
...OR THEY TRY TO FORCE ENTRY...
チャッ
CHA (CLICK)

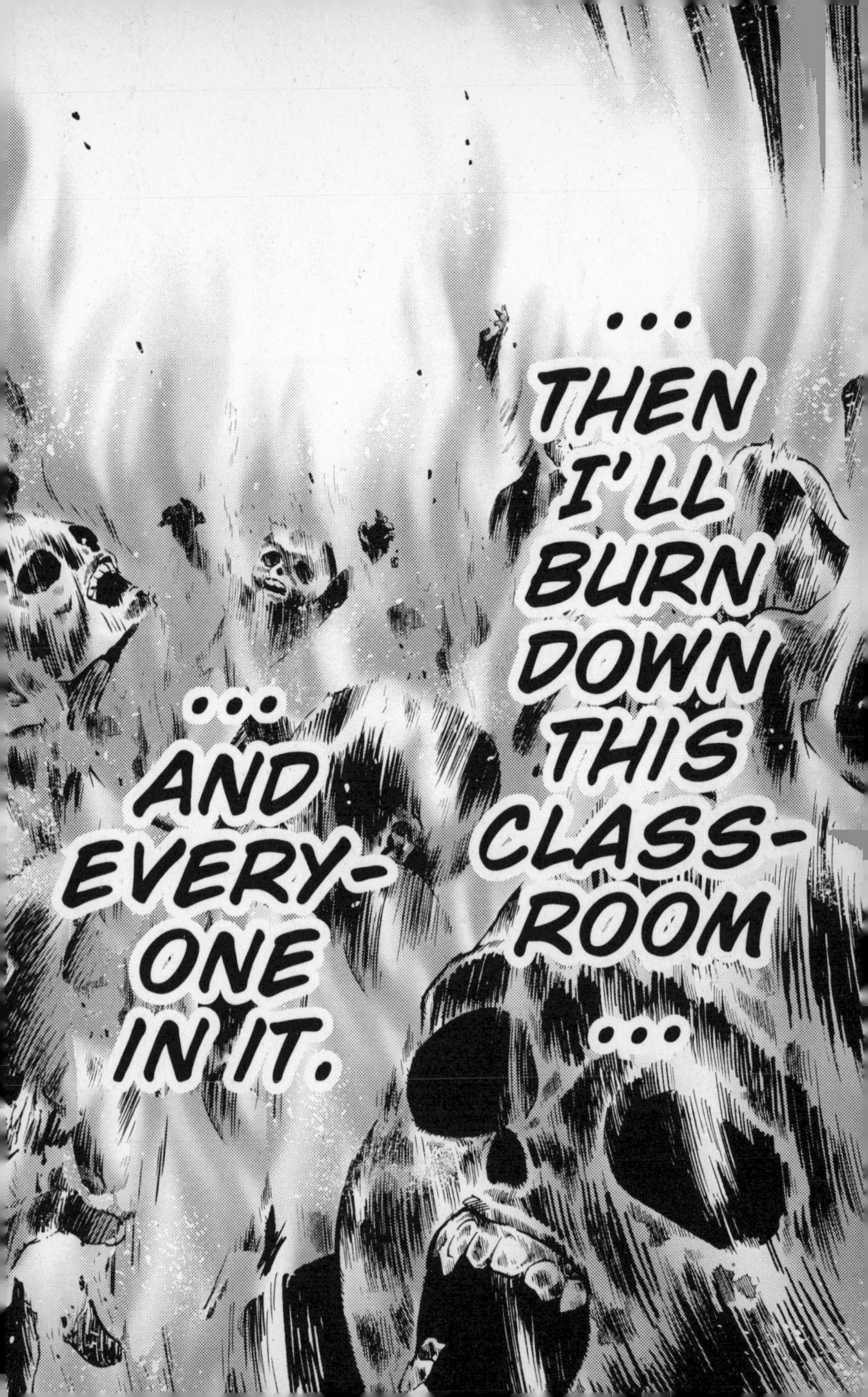
...THEN I'LL BURN DOWN THIS CLASS-ROOM...
...AND EVERY-ONE IN IT.

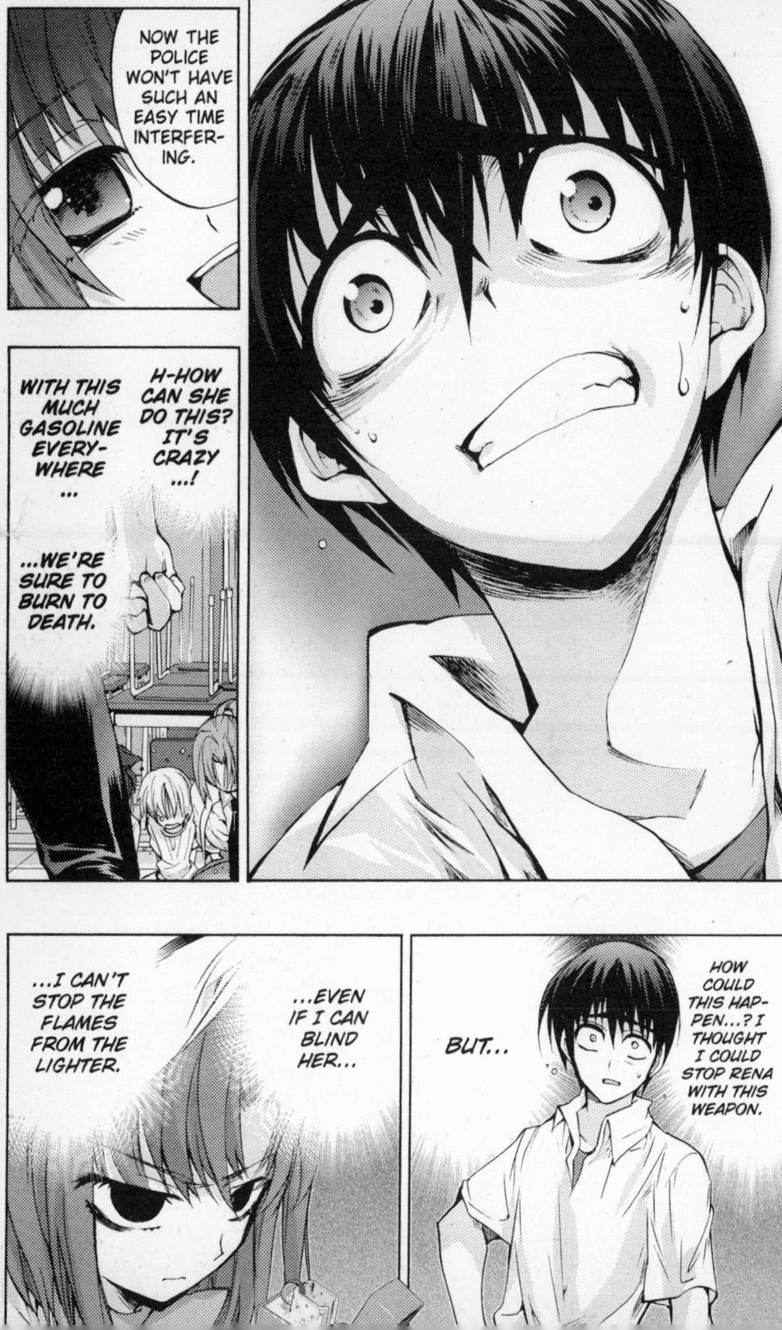
NOW THE POLICE WON'T HAVE SUCH AN EASY TIME INTERFER-ING.
H-HOW CAN SHE DO THIS? IT'S CRAZY...!
WITH THIS MUCH GASOLINE EVERY-WHERE...
...WE'RE SURE TO BURN TO DEATH.
HOW COULD THIS HAP-PEN...? I THOUGHT I COULD STOP RENA WITH THIS WEAPON.
BUT...
...EVEN IF I CAN BLIND HER...
...I CAN'T STOP THE FLAMES FROM THE LIGHTER.

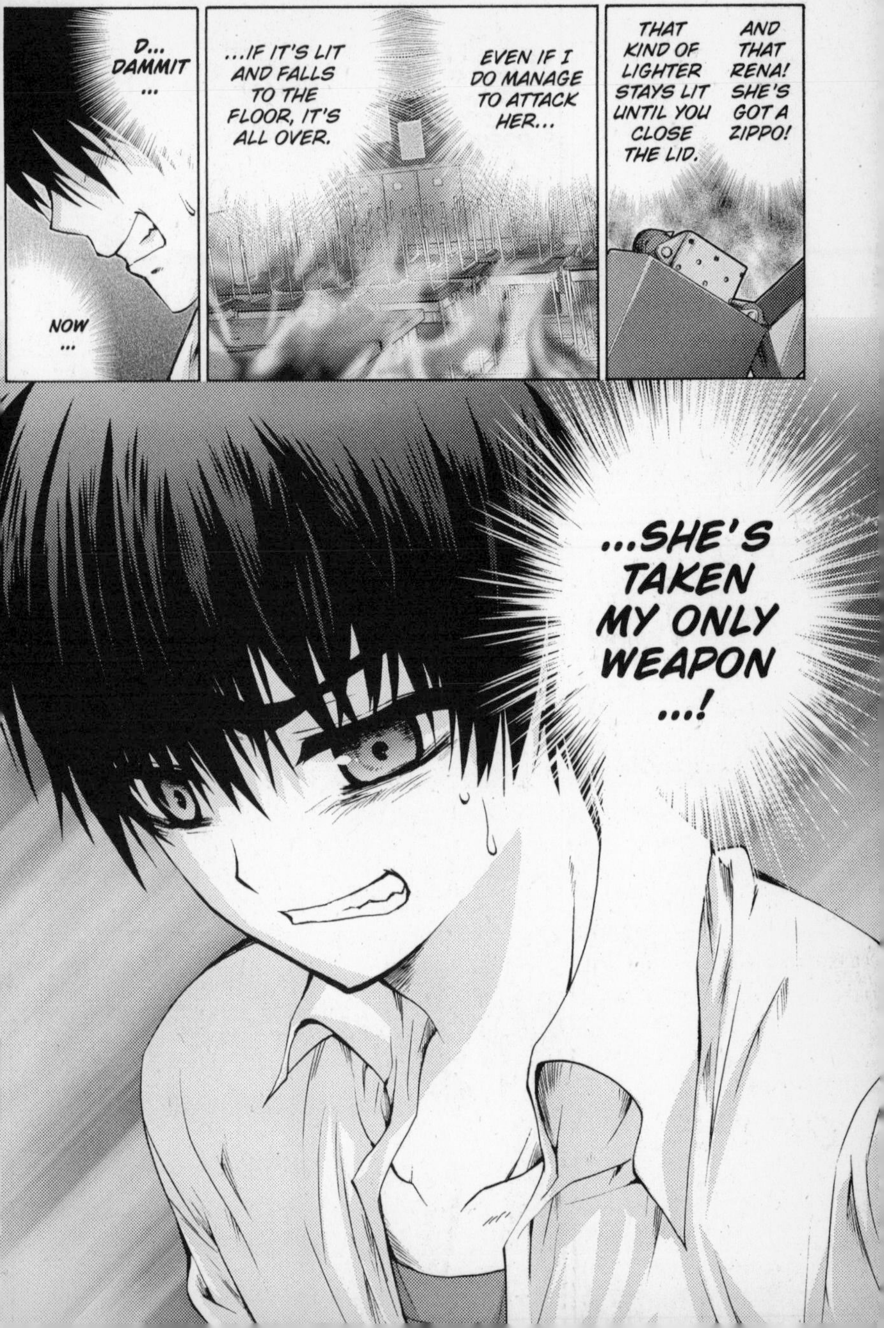
AND THAT RENA! SHE'S GOT A ZIPPO!
THAT KIND OF LIGHTER STAYS LIT UNTIL YOU CLOSE THE LID.
EVEN IF I DO MANAGE TO ATTACK HER...
...IF IT'S LIT AND FALLS TO THE FLOOR, IT'S ALL OVER.
D... DAMMIT ...
NOW ...
...SHE'S TAKEN MY ONLY WEAPON ...!

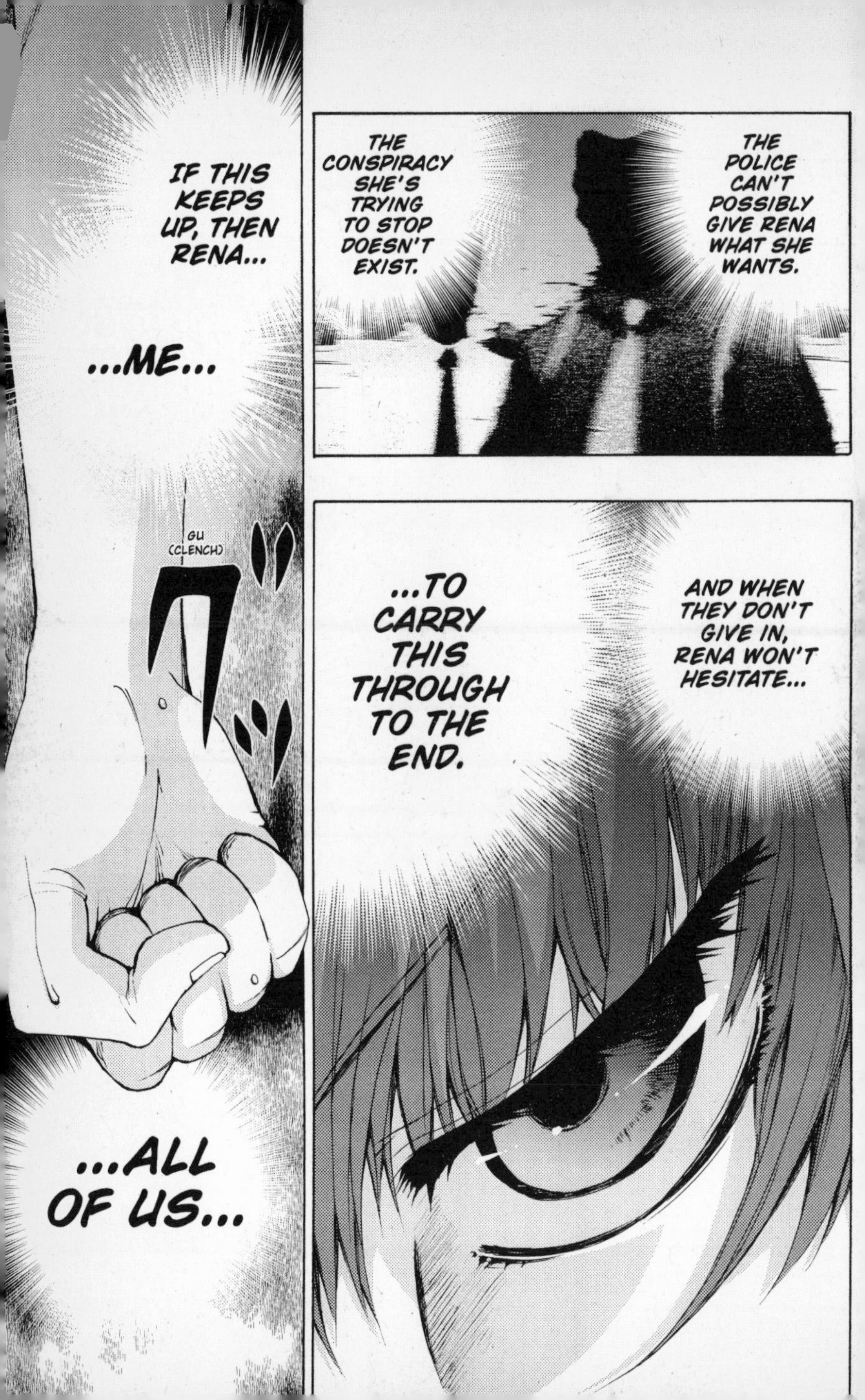
THE POLICE CAN'T POSSIBLY GIVE RENA WHAT SHE WANTS.
THE CONSPIRACY SHE'S TRYING TO STOP DOESN'T EXIST.
AND WHEN THEY DON'T GIVE IN, RENA WON'T HESITATE...
...TO CARRY THIS THROUGH TO THE END.
IF THIS KEEPS UP, THEN RENA...
...ME...
GU (CLENCH)
...ALL OF US...

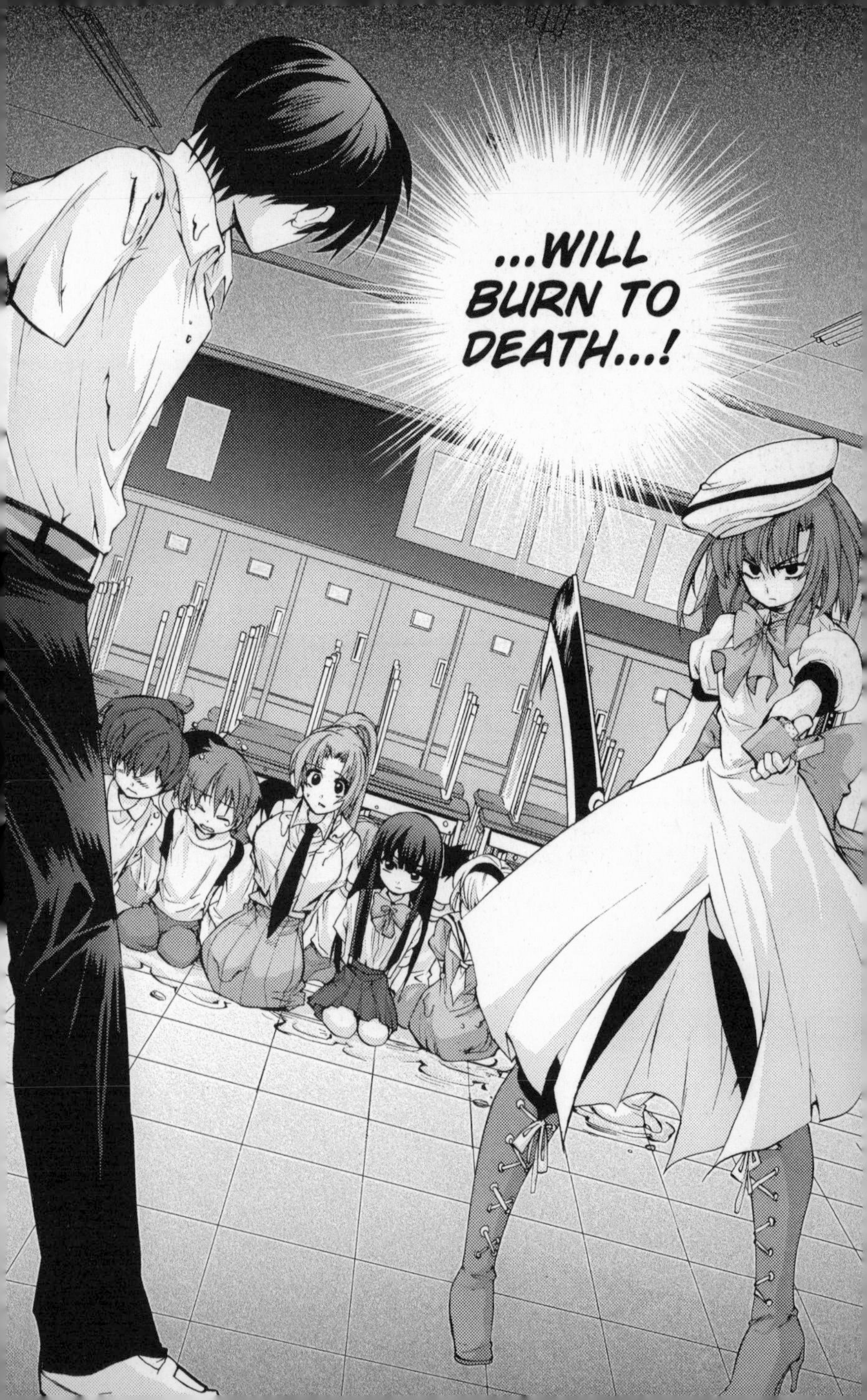
...WILL BURN TO DEATH...!

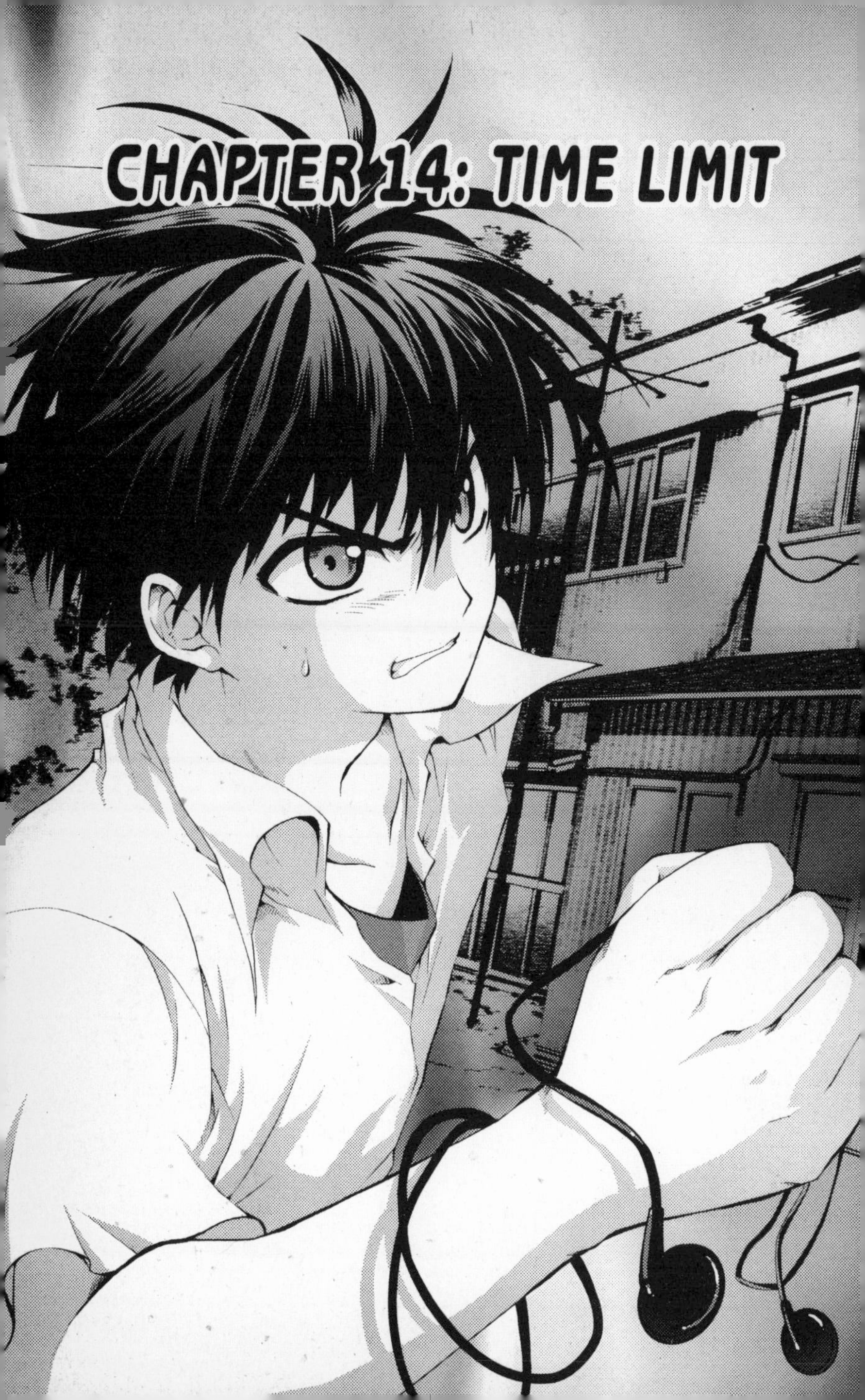
CHAPTER 14: TIME LIMIT

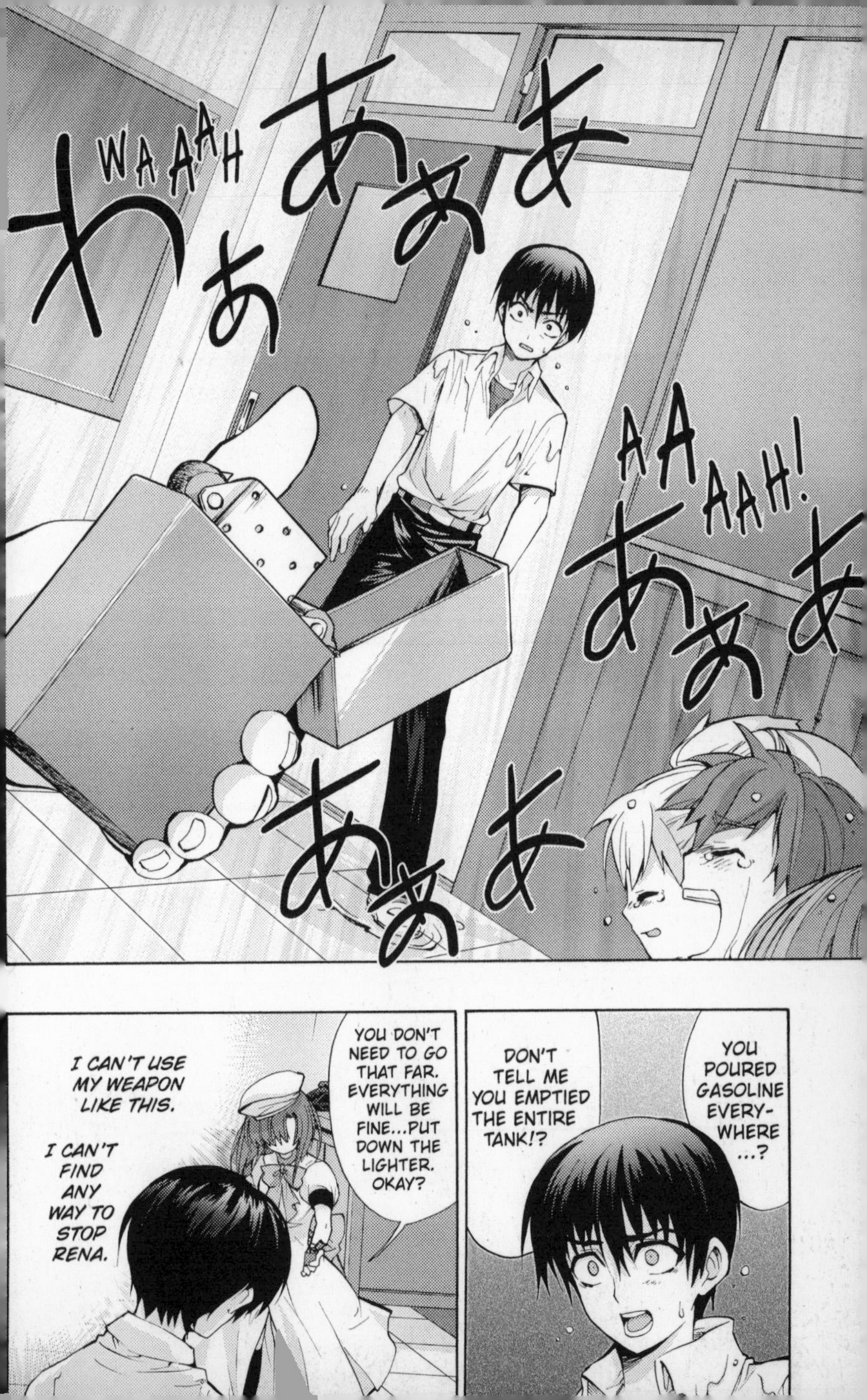
わぁあぁあ
WAAAH
あぁあ
AAAAH!
あぁあ
YOU POURED GASOLINE EVERY-WHERE ...?
DON'T TELL ME YOU EMPTIED THE ENTIRE TANK!?
YOU DON'T NEED TO GO THAT FAR. EVERYTHING WILL BE FINE...PUT DOWN THE LIGHTER. OKAY?
I CAN'T USE MY WEAPON LIKE THIS.
I CAN'T FIND ANY WAY TO STOP RENA.

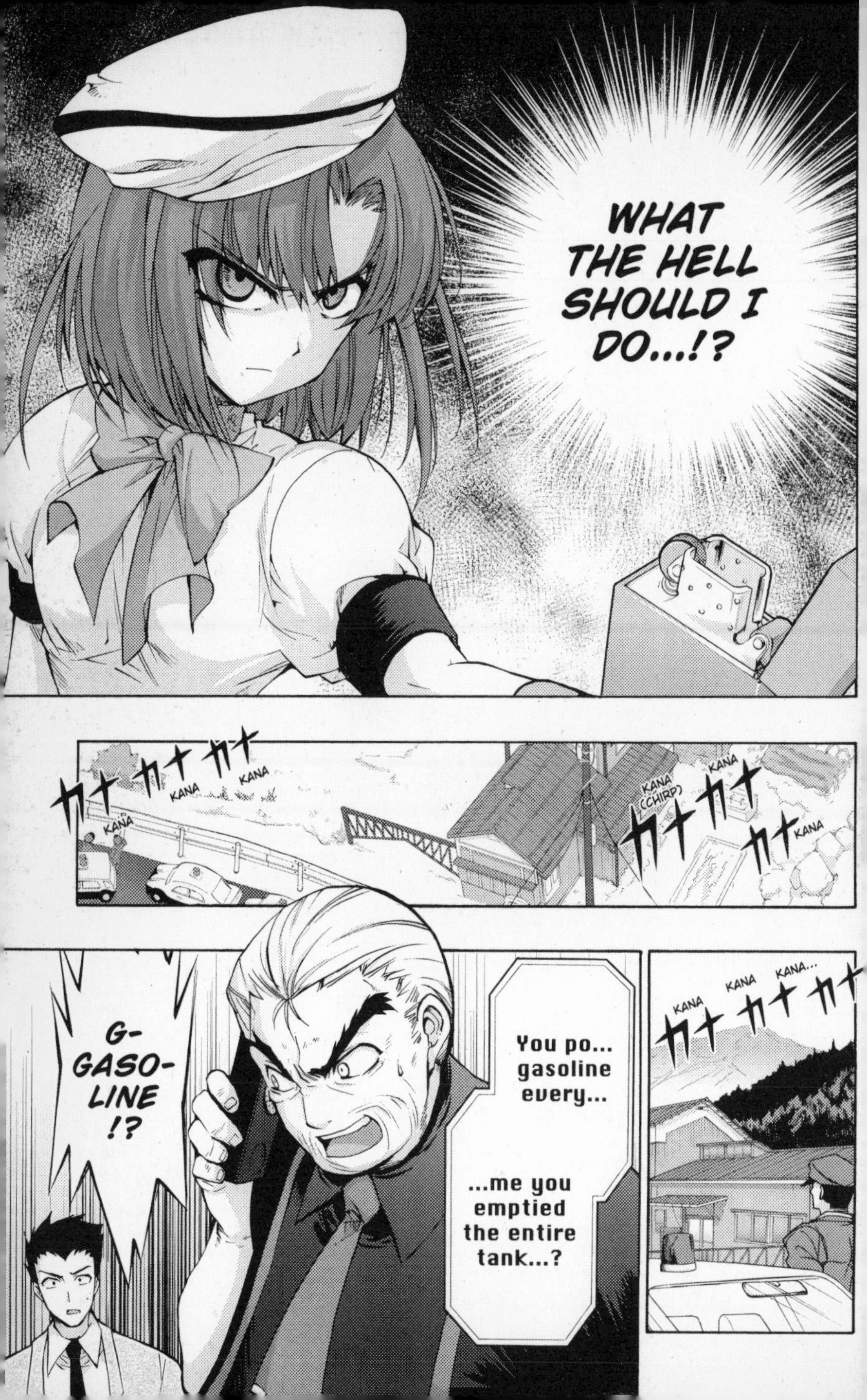
WHAT THE HELL SHOULD I DO...!?
KANA
KANA (CHIRP)
KANA
KANA
KANA
KANA
KANA...
KANA
KANA
You po... gasoline every...
...me you emptied the entire tank...?
G-GASO-LINE!?

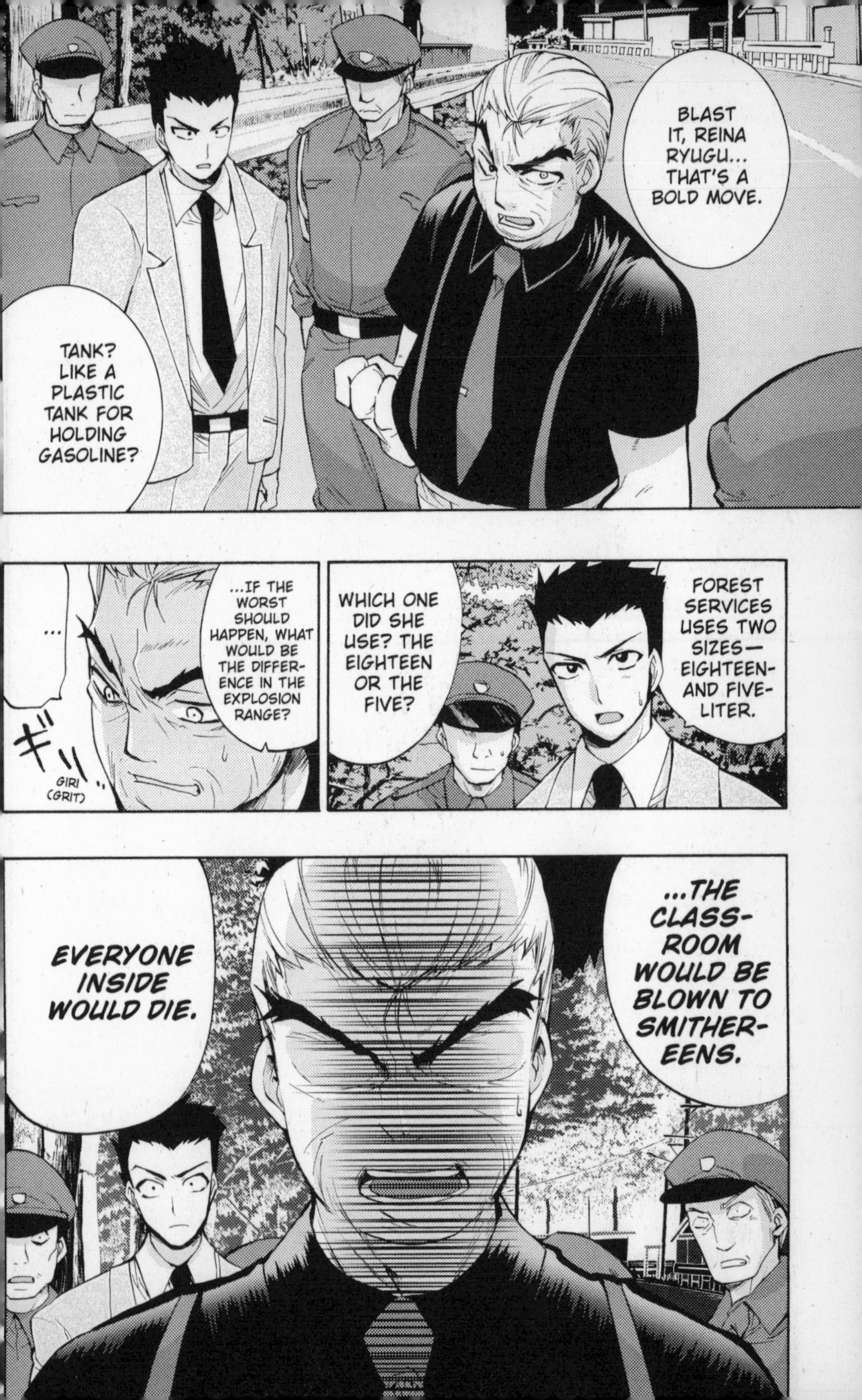
BLAST IT, REINA RYUGU... THAT'S A BOLD MOVE.
TANK? LIKE A PLASTIC TANK FOR HOLDING GASOLINE?
FOREST SERVICES USES TWO SIZES—EIGHTEEN- AND FIVE-LITER.
WHICH ONE DID SHE USE? THE EIGHTEEN OR THE FIVE?
...IF THE WORST SHOULD HAPPEN, WHAT WOULD BE THE DIFFERENCE IN THE EXPLOSION RANGE?
...
ギリ
GIRI (GRIT)
...THE CLASSROOM WOULD BE BLOWN TO SMITHEREENS.
EVERYONE INSIDE WOULD DIE.

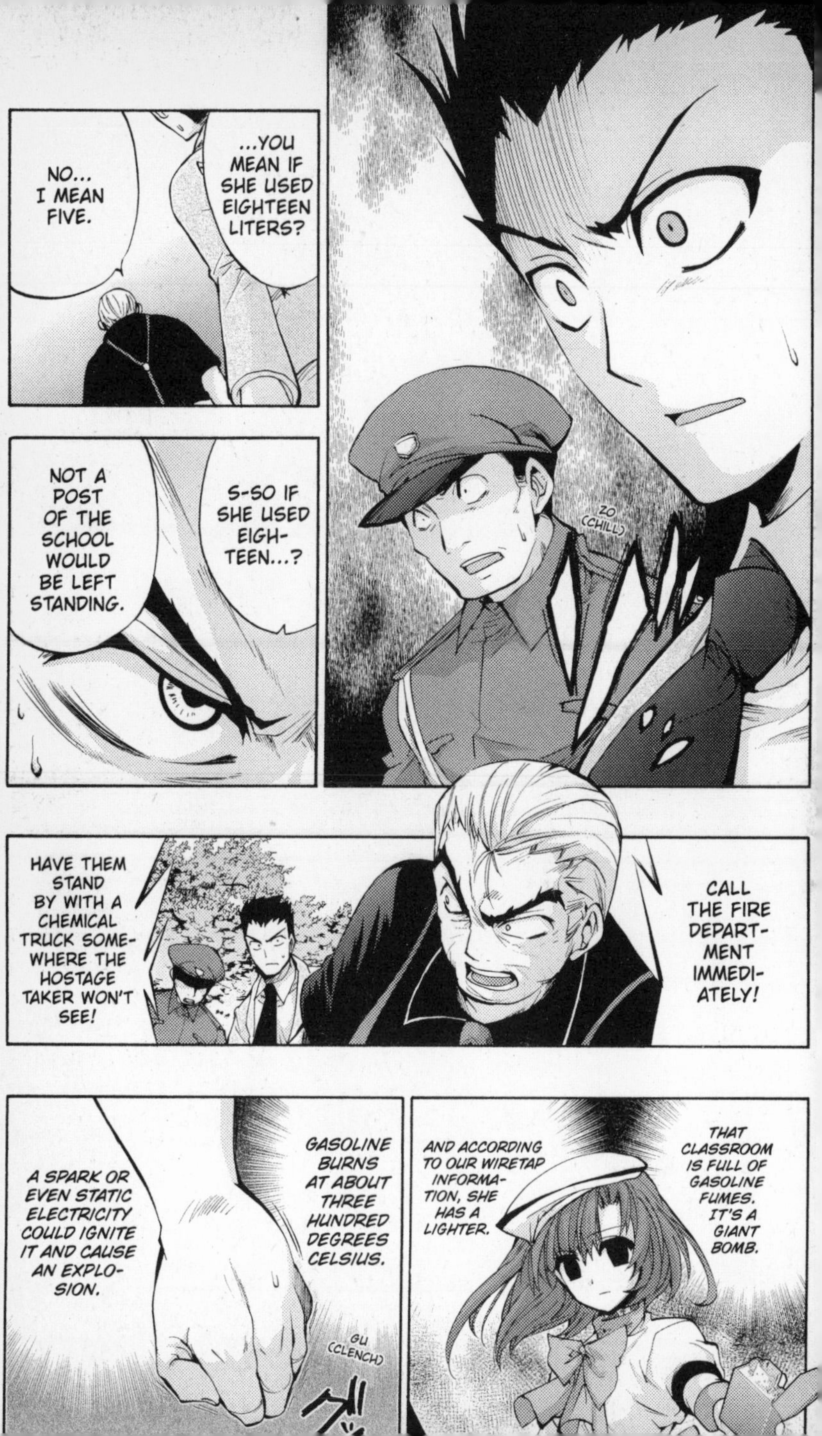
ZO (CHILL)
...YOU MEAN IF SHE USED EIGHTEEN LITERS?
NO... I MEAN FIVE.
S-SO IF SHE USED EIGH-TEEN...?
NOT A POST OF THE SCHOOL WOULD BE LEFT STANDING.
CALL THE FIRE DEPART-MENT IMMEDI-ATELY!
HAVE THEM STAND BY WITH A CHEMICAL TRUCK SOME-WHERE THE HOSTAGE TAKER WON'T SEE!
THAT CLASSROOM IS FULL OF GASOLINE FUMES. IT'S A GIANT BOMB.
AND ACCORDING TO OUR WIRETAP INFORMA-TION, SHE HAS A LIGHTER.
GASOLINE BURNS AT ABOUT THREE HUNDRED DEGREES CELSIUS.
A SPARK OR EVEN STATIC ELECTRICITY COULD IGNITE IT AND CAUSE AN EXPLO-SION.
GU (CLENCH)

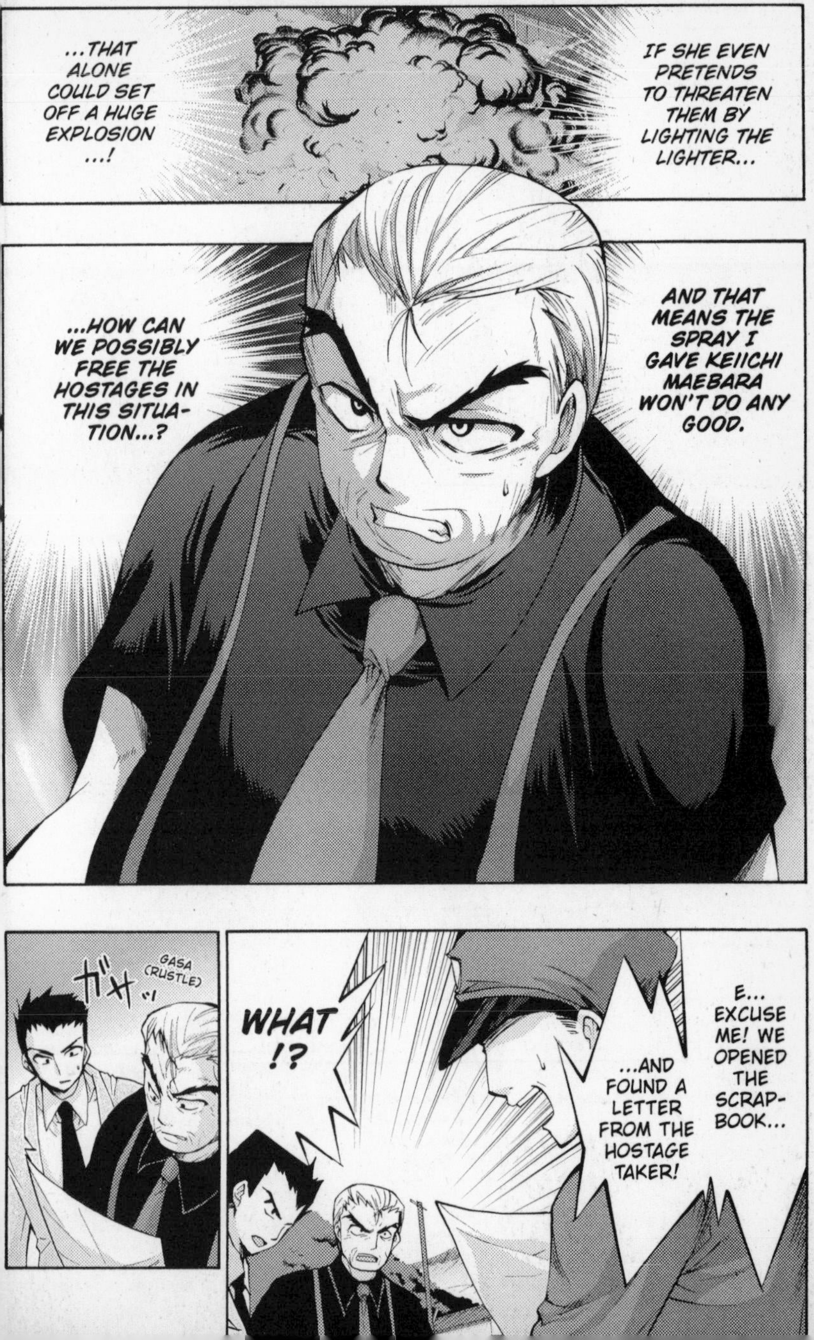
IF SHE EVEN PRETENDS TO THREATEN THEM BY LIGHTING THE LIGHTER...
...THAT ALONE COULD SET OFF A HUGE EXPLOSION ...!
AND THAT MEANS THE SPRAY I GAVE KEIICHI MAEBARA WON'T DO ANY GOOD.
...HOW CAN WE POSSIBLY FREE THE HOSTAGES IN THIS SITUATION...?
E... EXCUSE ME! WE OPENED THE SCRAPBOOK...
...AND FOUND A LETTER FROM THE HOSTAGE TAKER!
WHAT!?
ガサッ
GASA (RUSTLE)

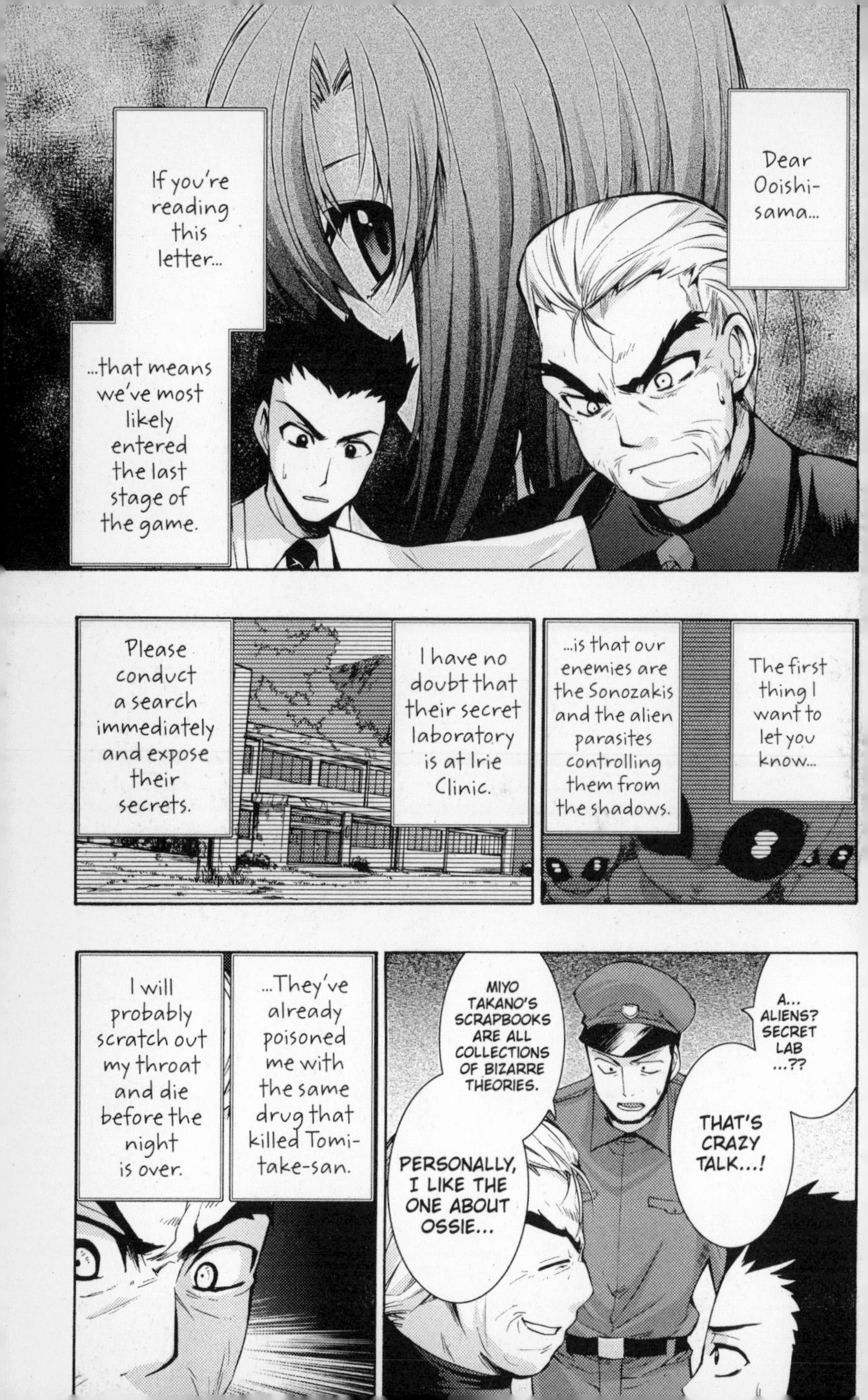
Dear Ooishi-sama...
If you're reading this letter...
...that means we've most likely entered the last stage of the game.
The first thing I want to let you know...
...is that our enemies are the Sonozakis and the alien parasites controlling them from the shadows.
I have no doubt that their secret laboratory is at Irie Clinic.
Please conduct a search immediately and expose their secrets.
A... ALIENS? SECRET LAB ...??
THAT'S CRAZY TALK...!
MIYO TAKANO'S SCRAPBOOKS ARE ALL COLLECTIONS OF BIZARRE THEORIES.
PERSONALLY, I LIKE THE ONE ABOUT OSSIE...
...They've already poisoned me with the same drug that killed Tomi-take-san.
I will probably scratch out my throat and die before the night is over.

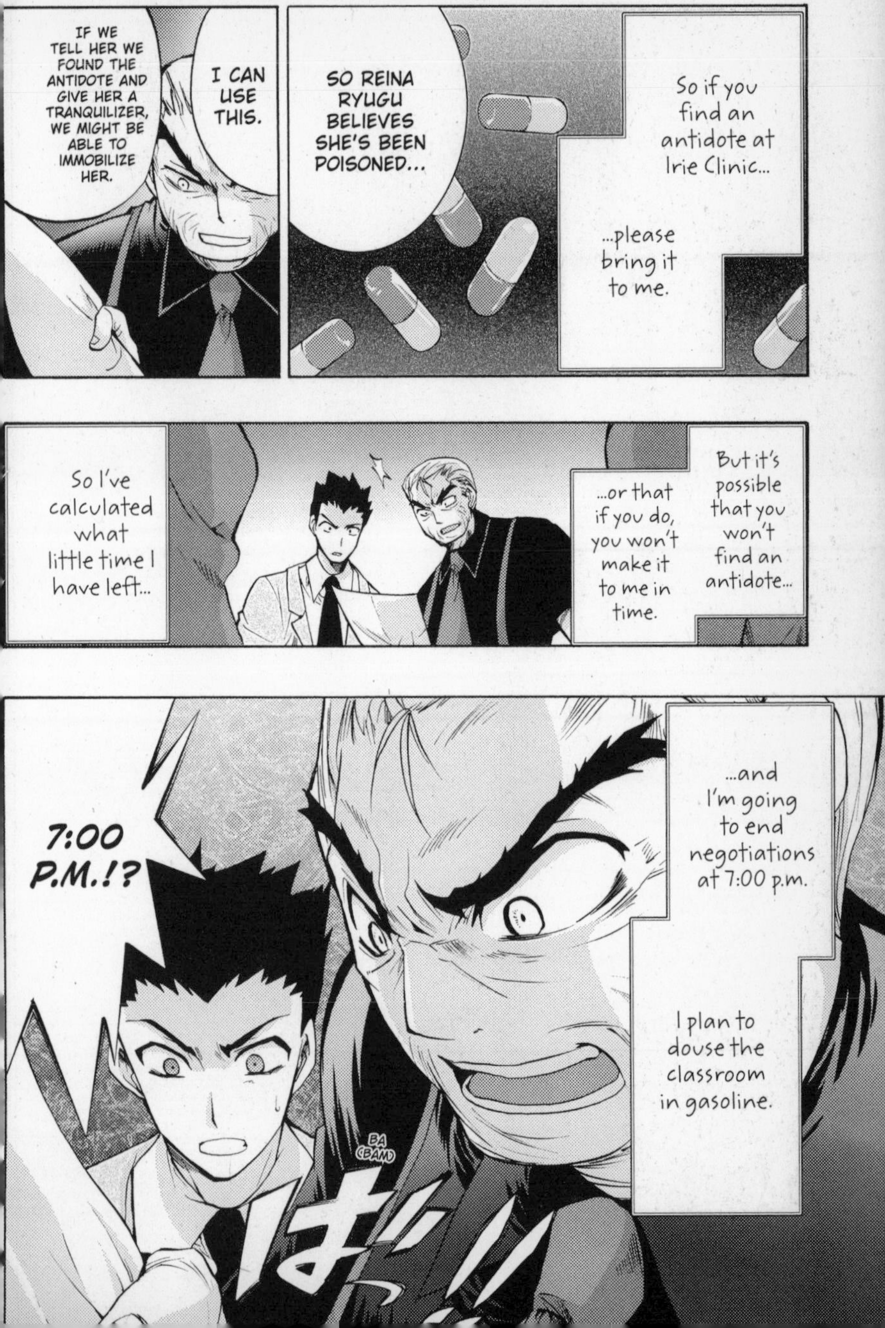
So if you find an antidote at Irie Clinic...
...please bring it to me.
SO REINA RYUGU BELIEVES SHE'S BEEN POISONED...
I CAN USE THIS.
IF WE TELL HER WE FOUND THE ANTIDOTE AND GIVE HER A TRANQUILIZER, WE MIGHT BE ABLE TO IMMOBILIZE HER.
But it's possible that you won't find an antidote...
...or that if you do, you won't make it to me in time.
So I've calculated what little time I have left...
...and I'm going to end negotiations at 7:00 p.m.
I plan to douse the classroom in gasoline.
7:00 P.M.!?
BA (BAM)

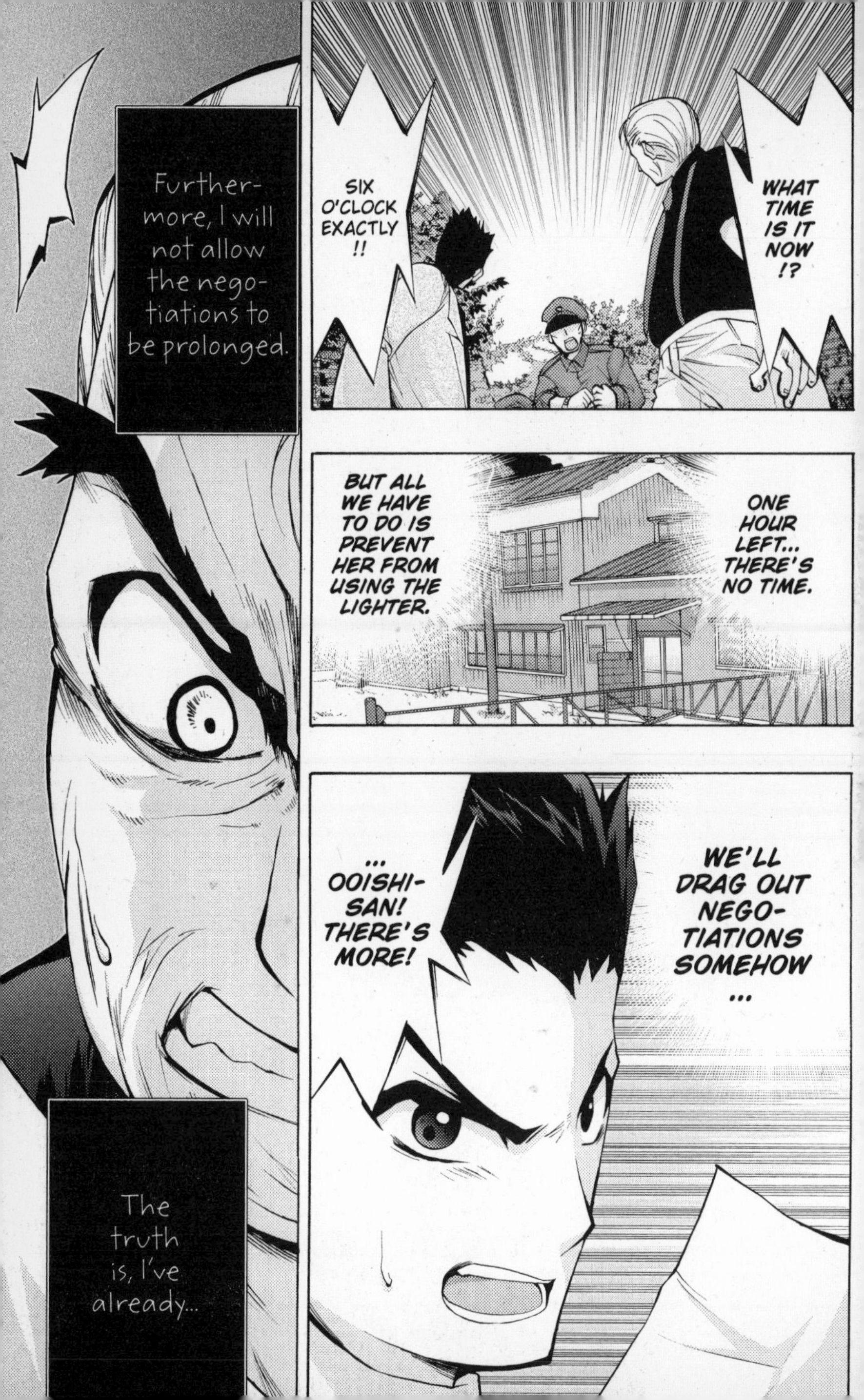
WHAT TIME IS IT NOW !?
SIX O'CLOCK EXACTLY !!
ONE HOUR LEFT... THERE'S NO TIME.
BUT ALL WE HAVE TO DO IS PREVENT HER FROM USING THE LIGHTER.
WE'LL DRAG OUT NEGO-TIATIONS SOMEHOW ...
... OOISHI-SAN! THERE'S MORE!
Further-more, I will not allow the nego-tiations to be prolonged.
The truth is, I've already...

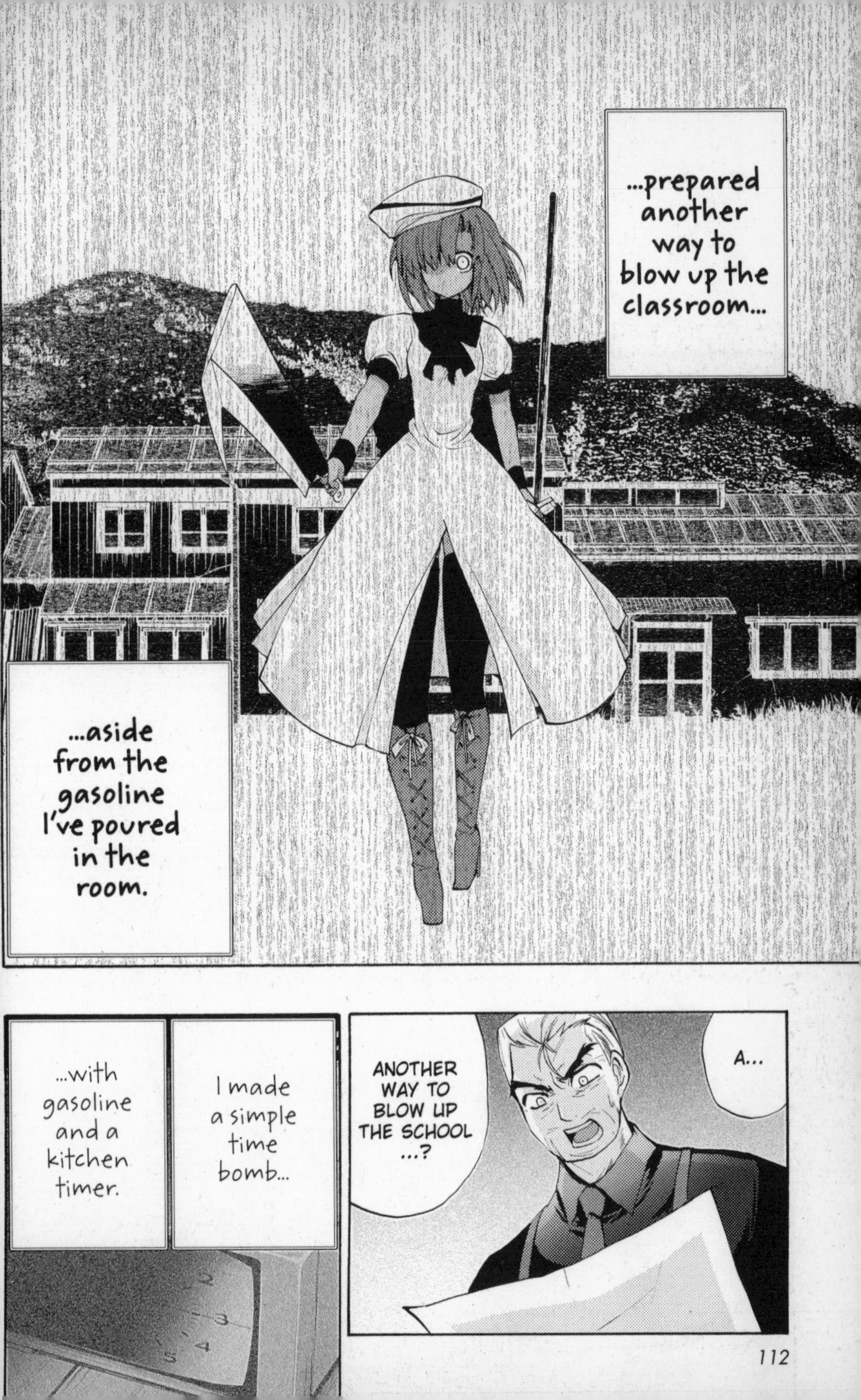
...prepared another way to blow up the classroom...
...aside from the gasoline I've poured in the room.
A...
ANOTHER WAY TO BLOW UP THE SCHOOL ...?
I made a simple time bomb...
...with gasoline and a kitchen timer.

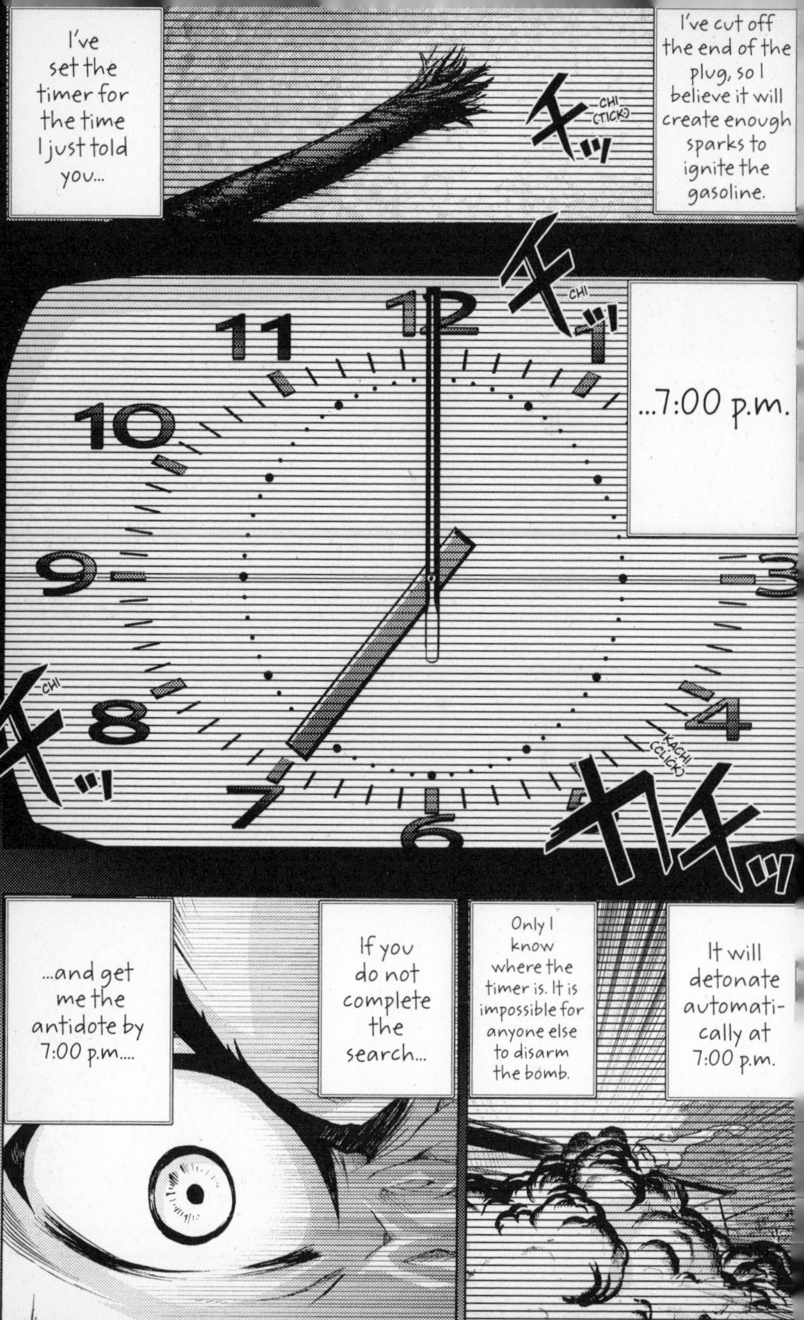
I've cut off the end of the plug, so I believe it will create enough sparks to ignite the gasoline.
CHI (TICK)
I've set the timer for the time I just told you...
CHI
...7:00 p.m.
CHI
KACHI (CLICK)
It will detonate automati-cally at 7:00 p.m.
Only I know where the timer is. It is impossible for anyone else to disarm the bomb.
If you do not complete the search...
...and get me the antidote by 7:00 p.m....

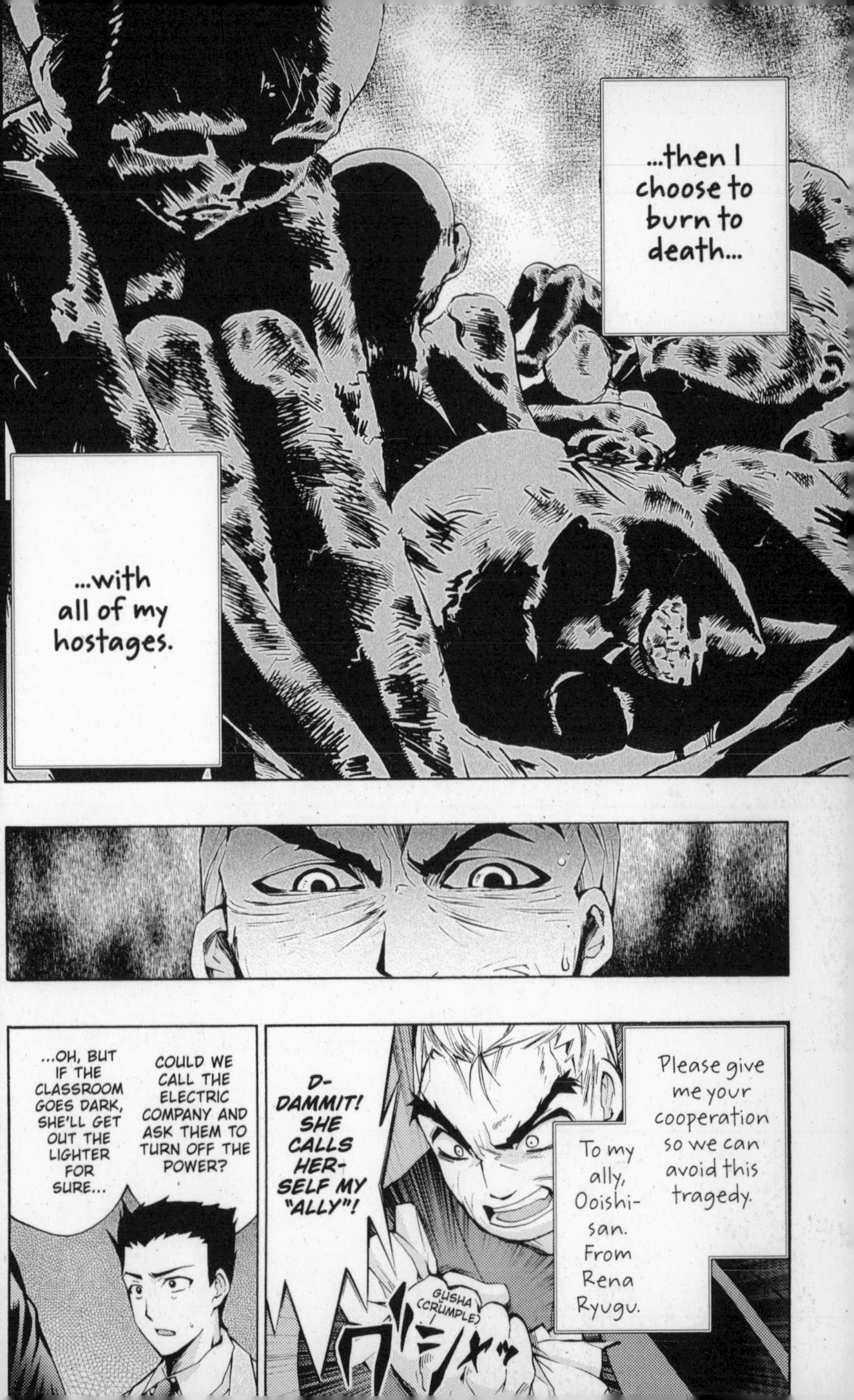
...then I choose to burn to death...
...with all of my hostages.
Please give me your cooperation so we can avoid this tragedy.
To my ally, Ooishi-san. From Rena Ryugu.
D-DAMMIT! SHE CALLS HER-SELF MY "ALLY"!
GUSHA (CRUMPLE)
COULD WE CALL THE ELECTRIC COMPANY AND ASK THEM TO TURN OFF THE POWER?
...OH, BUT IF THE CLASSROOM GOES DARK, SHE'LL GET OUT THE LIGHTER FOR SURE...

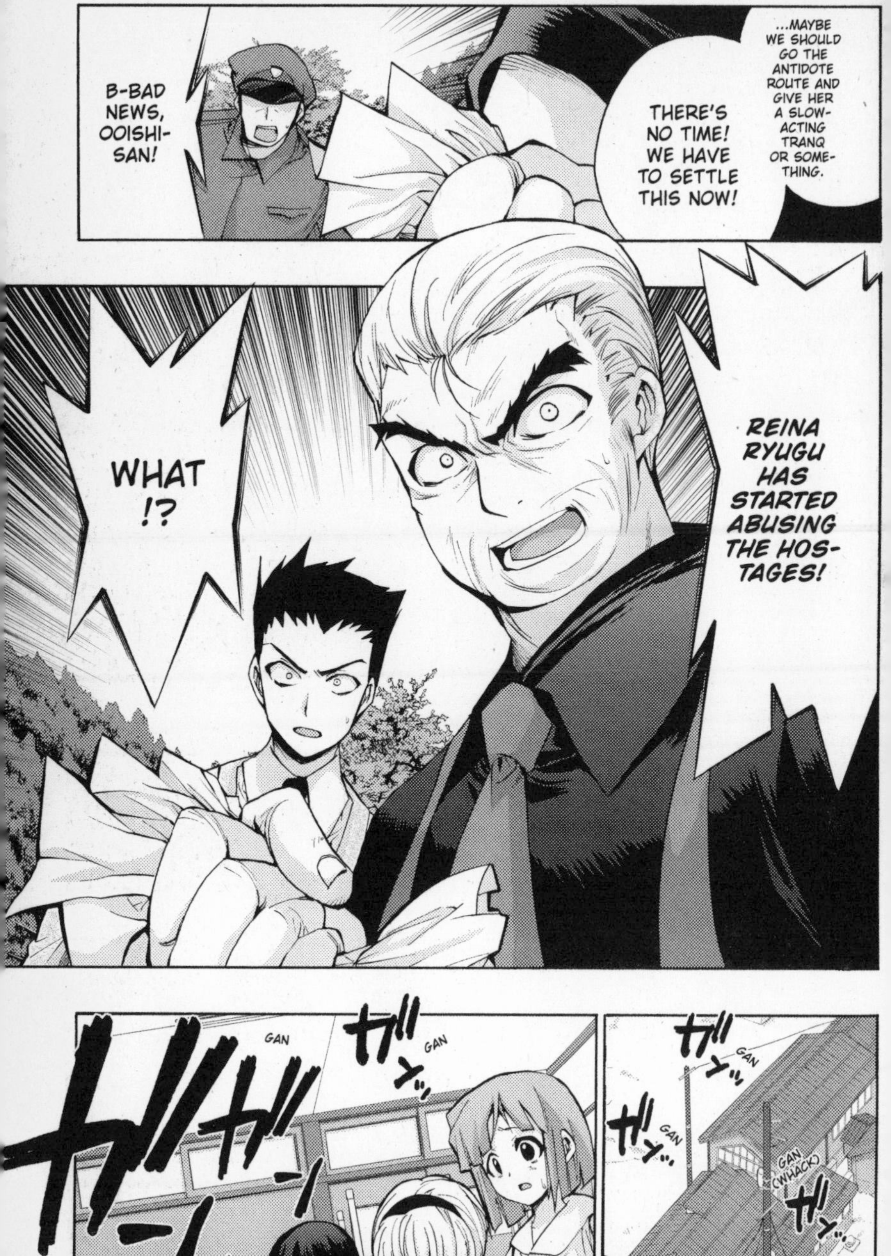

...MAYBE WE SHOULD GO THE ANTIDOTE ROUTE AND GIVE HER A SLOW-ACTING TRANQ OR SOMETHING.
THERE'S NO TIME! WE HAVE TO SETTLE THIS NOW!
B-BAD NEWS, OOISHI-SAN!
REINA RYUGU HAS STARTED ABUSING THE HOSTAGES!
WHAT !?
GAN
GAN
GAN (WHACK)
GAN
GAN
GAN

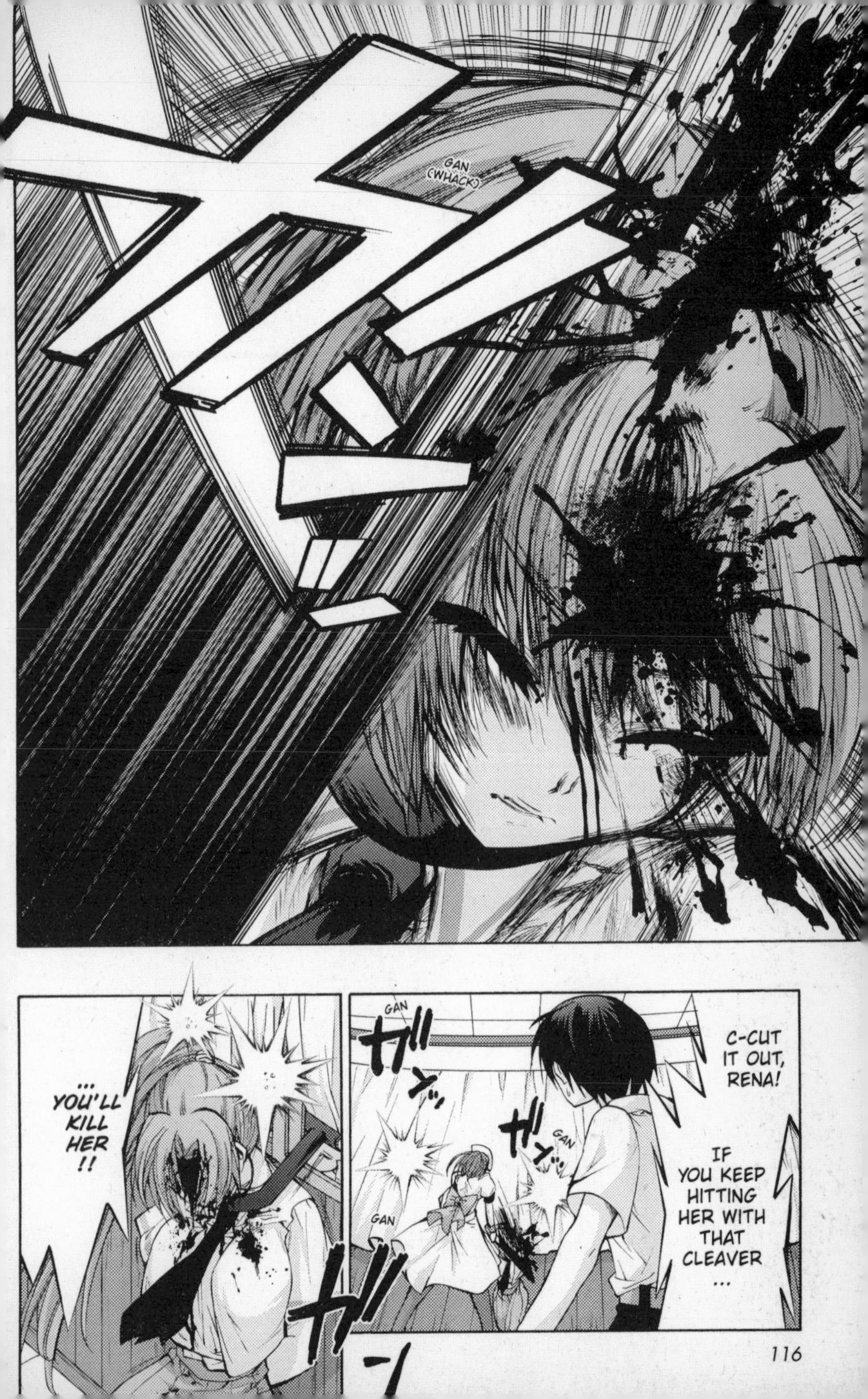
GAN
(WHACK)
GAN
C-CUT IT OUT, RENA!
GAN
IF YOU KEEP HITTING HER WITH THAT CLEAVER ...
GAN
... YOU'LL KILL HER !!

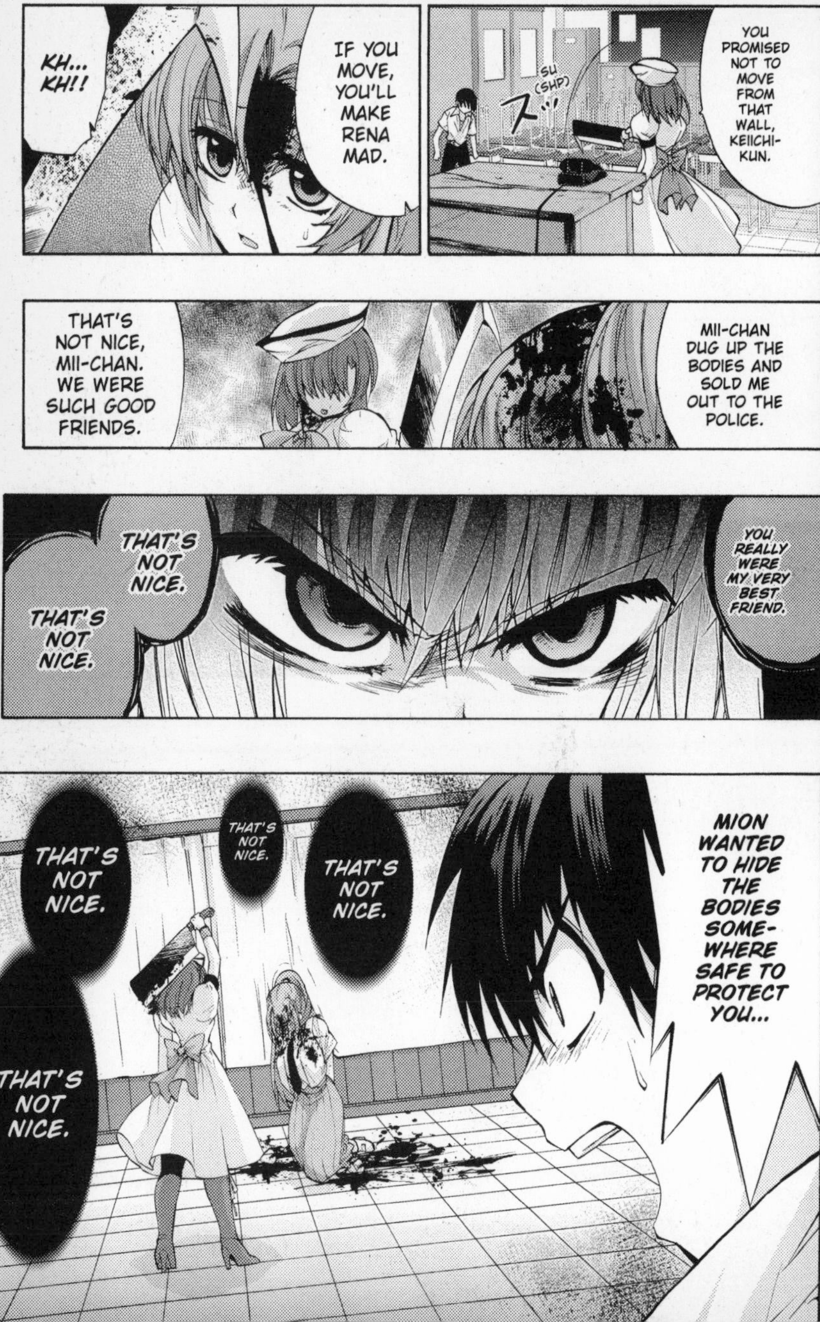
YOU PROMISED NOT TO MOVE FROM THAT WALL, KEIICHI-KUN.
SU (SHP)
ス
IF YOU MOVE, YOU'LL MAKE RENA MAD.
KH... KH!!
MII-CHAN DUG UP THE BODIES AND SOLD ME OUT TO THE POLICE.
THAT'S NOT NICE, MII-CHAN. WE WERE SUCH GOOD FRIENDS.
YOU REALLY WERE MY VERY BEST FRIEND.
THAT'S NOT NICE.
THAT'S NOT NICE.
MION WANTED TO HIDE THE BODIES SOME-WHERE SAFE TO PROTECT YOU...
THAT'S NOT NICE.
THAT'S NOT NICE.
THAT'S NOT NICE.
THAT'S NOT NICE.

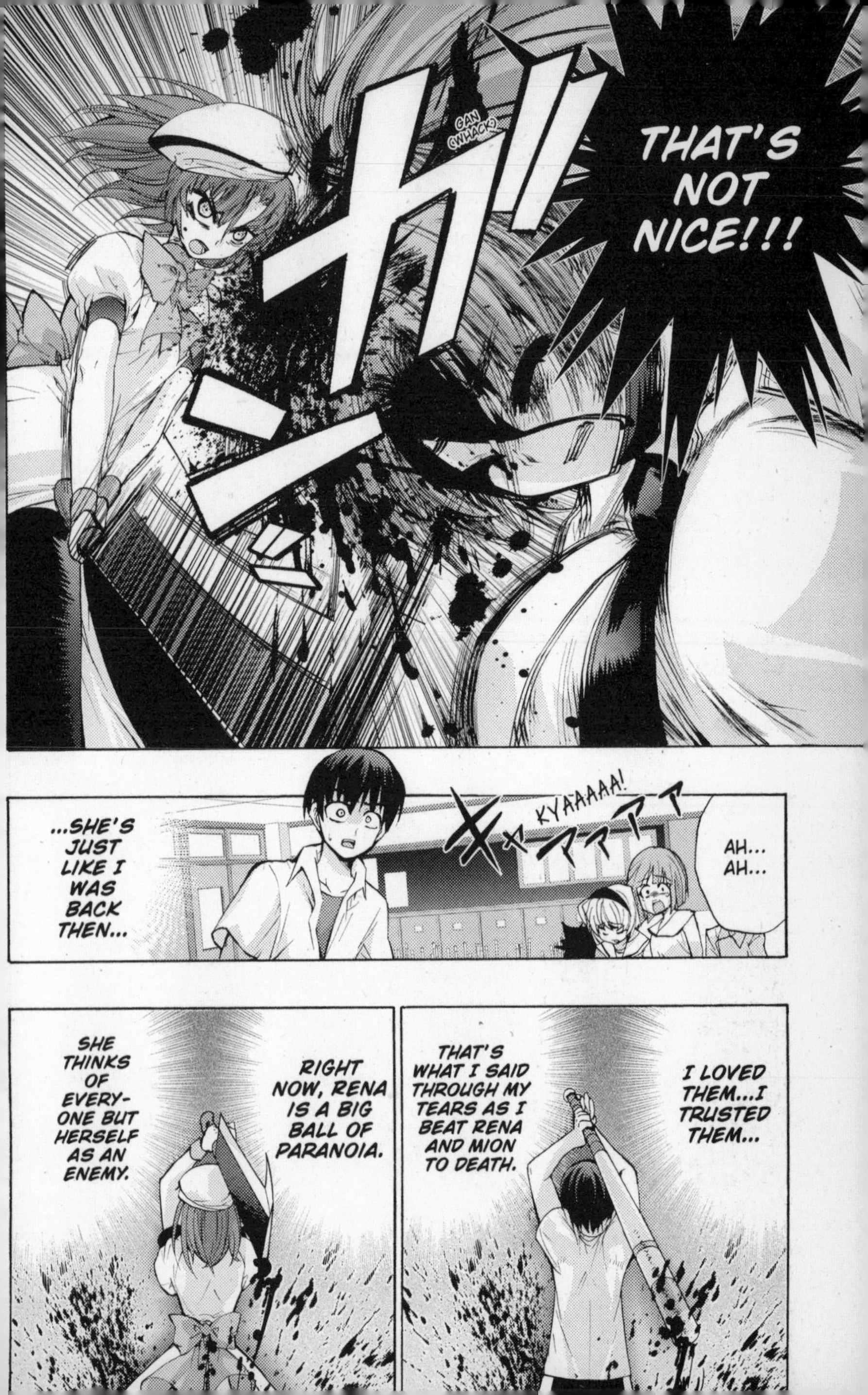
THAT'S NOT NICE!!!
GAN (WHACK)
AH... AH...
KYAAAAA!
...SHE'S JUST LIKE I WAS BACK THEN...
I LOVED THEM...I TRUSTED THEM...
THAT'S WHAT I SAID THROUGH MY TEARS AS I BEAT RENA AND MION TO DEATH.
RIGHT NOW, RENA IS A BIG BALL OF PARANOIA.
SHE THINKS OF EVERY-ONE BUT HERSELF AS AN ENEMY.

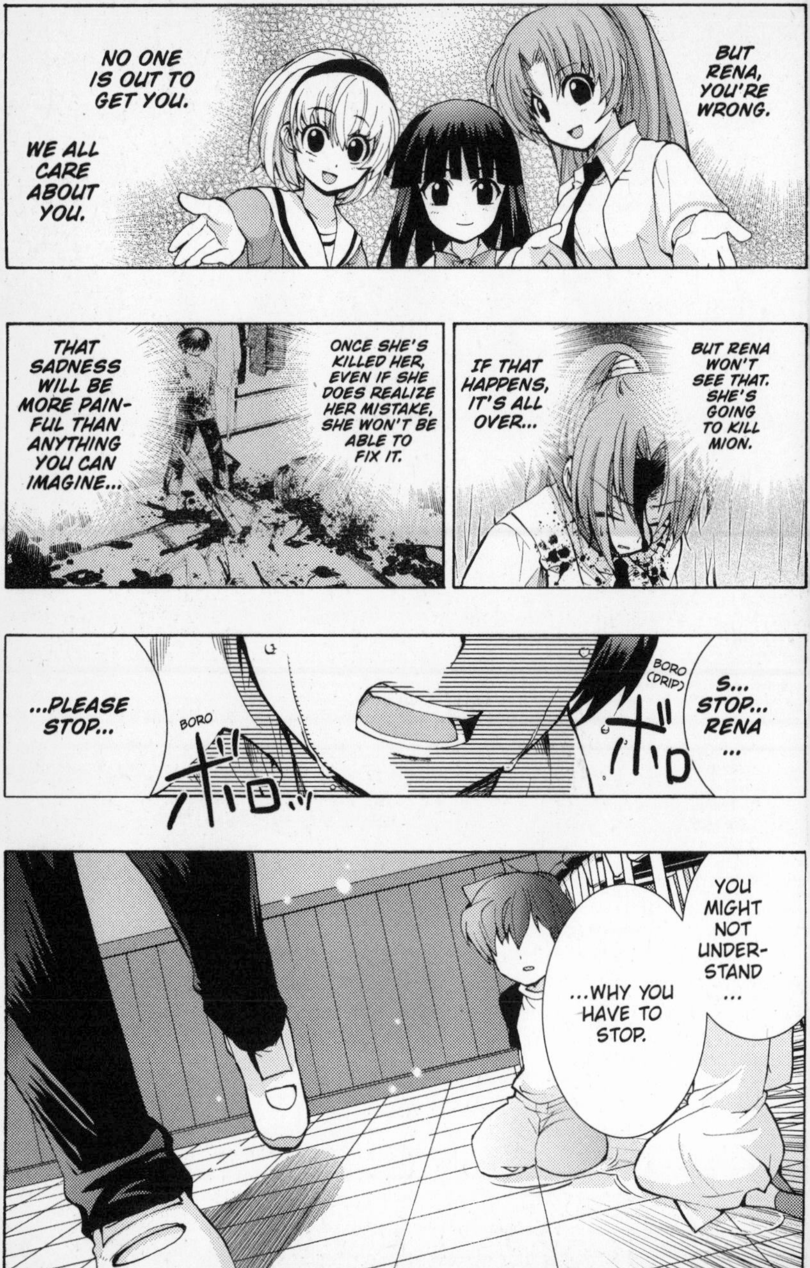
BUT RENA, YOU'RE WRONG.
NO ONE IS OUT TO GET YOU.
WE ALL CARE ABOUT YOU.
BUT RENA WON'T SEE THAT. SHE'S GOING TO KILL MION.
IF THAT HAPPENS, IT'S ALL OVER...
ONCE SHE'S KILLED HER, EVEN IF SHE DOES REALIZE HER MISTAKE, SHE WON'T BE ABLE TO FIX IT.
THAT SADNESS WILL BE MORE PAIN-FUL THAN ANYTHING YOU CAN IMAGINE...
S... STOP... RENA ...
BORO (DRIP)
ボロ
BORO
ボロッ
...PLEASE STOP...
YOU MIGHT NOT UNDER-STAND ...
...WHY YOU HAVE TO STOP.

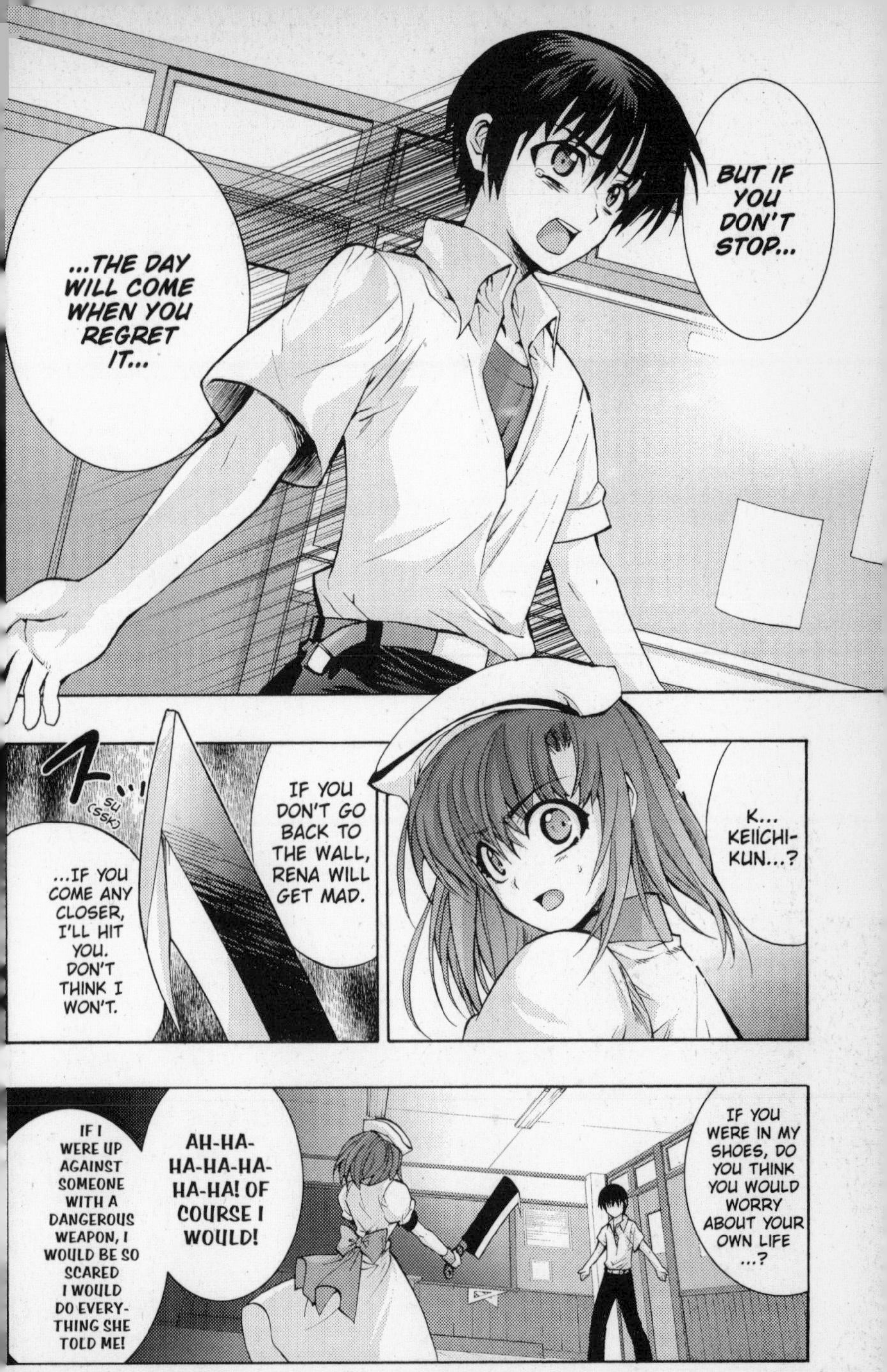
BUT IF YOU DON'T STOP...
...THE DAY WILL COME WHEN YOU REGRET IT...
K... KEIICHI-KUN...?
SU (SSK)
IF YOU DON'T GO BACK TO THE WALL, RENA WILL GET MAD.
...IF YOU COME ANY CLOSER, I'LL HIT YOU. DON'T THINK I WON'T.
IF YOU WERE IN MY SHOES, DO YOU THINK YOU WOULD WORRY ABOUT YOUR OWN LIFE ...?
AH-HA-HA-HA-HA-HA-HA-HA! OF COURSE I WOULD!
IF I WERE UP AGAINST SOMEONE WITH A DANGEROUS WEAPON, I WOULD BE SO SCARED I WOULD DO EVERY-THING SHE TOLD ME!

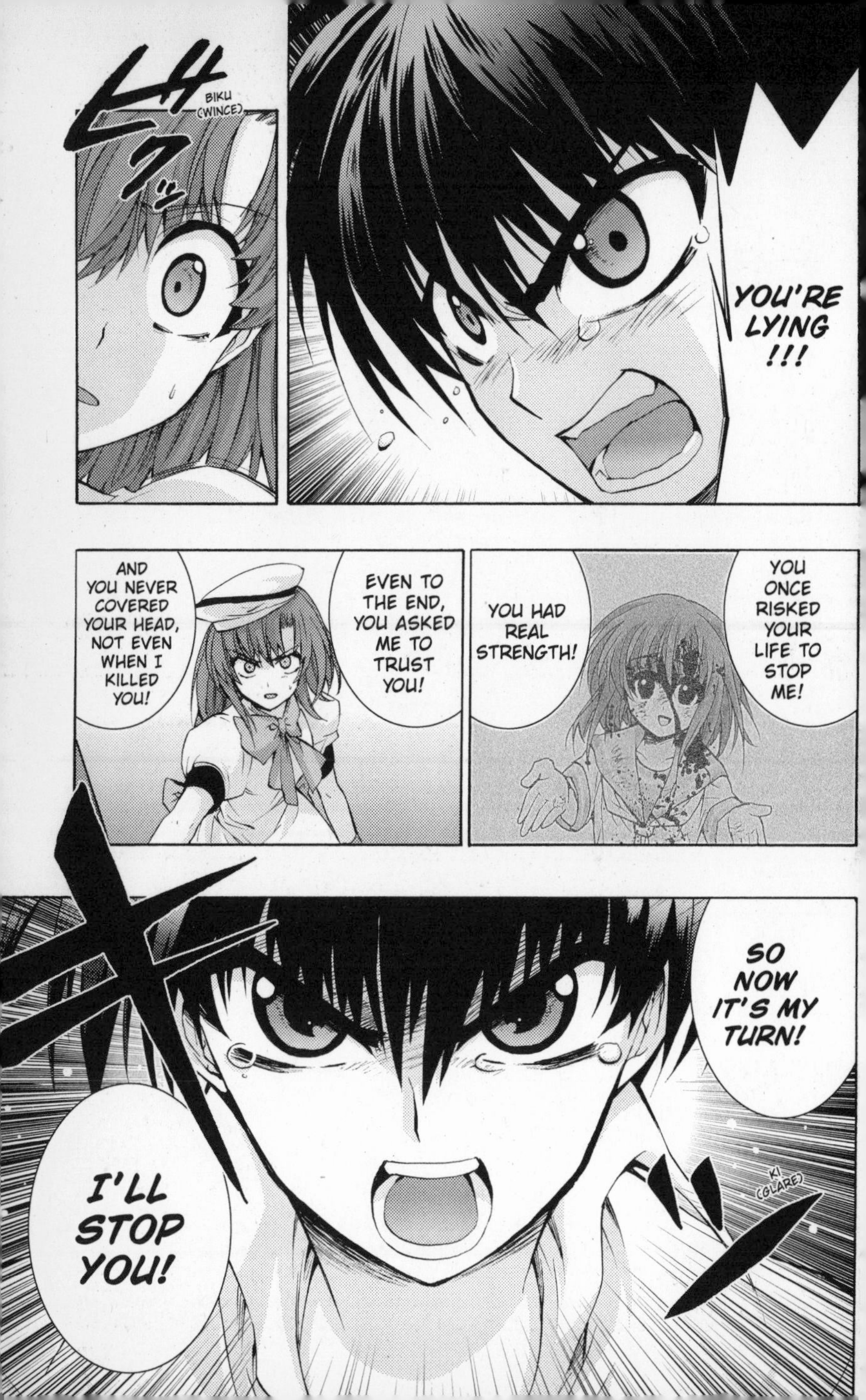
YOU'RE LYING !!!
BIKU (WINCE)
YOU ONCE RISKED YOUR LIFE TO STOP ME!
YOU HAD REAL STRENGTH!
EVEN TO THE END, YOU ASKED ME TO TRUST YOU!
AND YOU NEVER COVERED YOUR HEAD, NOT EVEN WHEN I KILLED YOU!
SO NOW IT'S MY TURN!
KI (GLARE)
I'LL STOP YOU!

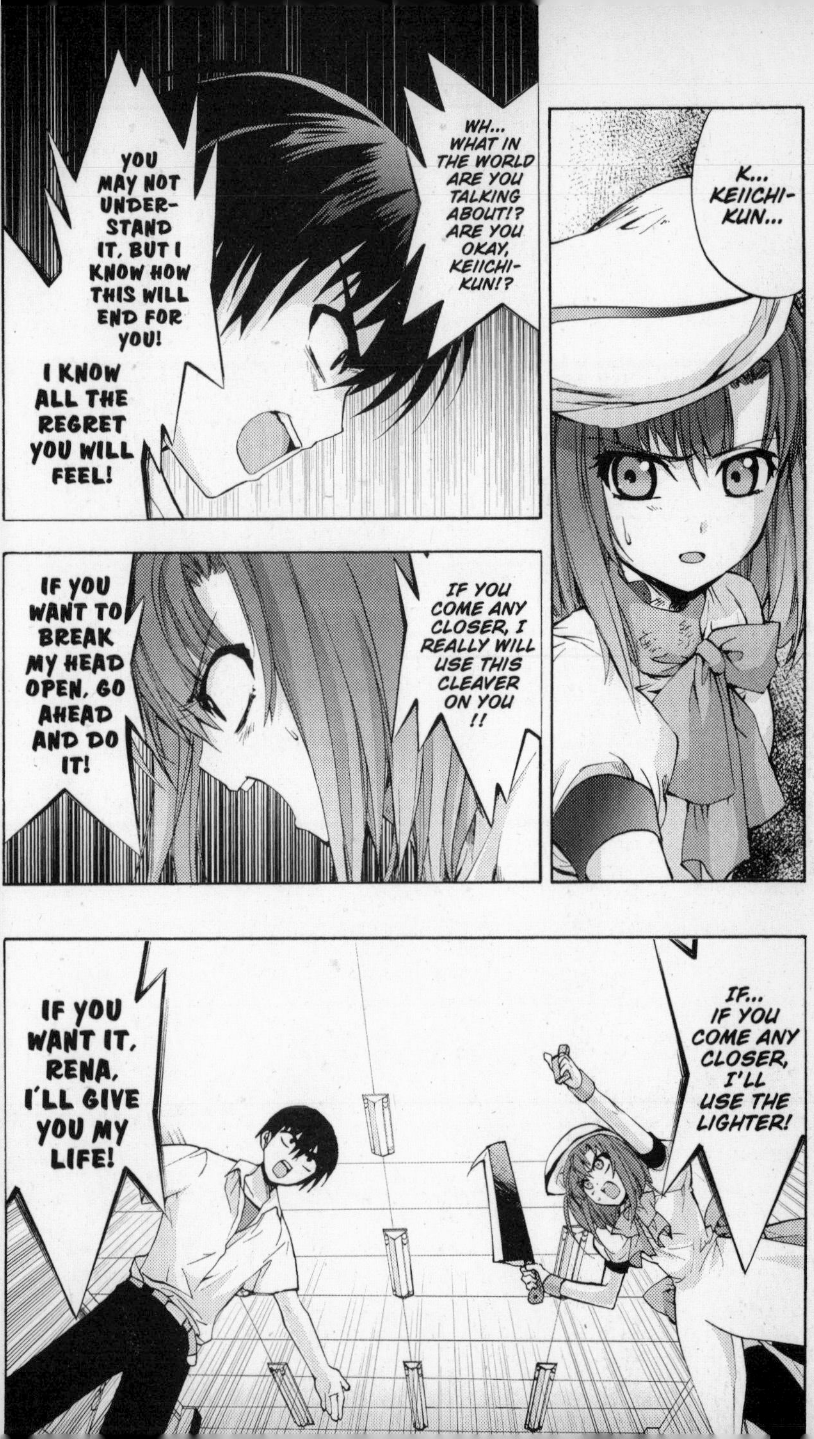
K... KEIICHI-KUN...
WH... WHAT IN THE WORLD ARE YOU TALKING ABOUT!? ARE YOU OKAY, KEIICHI-KUN!?
YOU MAY NOT UNDER-STAND IT, BUT I KNOW HOW THIS WILL END FOR YOU!
I KNOW ALL THE REGRET YOU WILL FEEL!
IF YOU COME ANY CLOSER, I REALLY WILL USE THIS CLEAVER ON YOU !!
IF YOU WANT TO BREAK MY HEAD OPEN, GO AHEAD AND DO IT!
IF... IF YOU COME ANY CLOSER, I'LL USE THE LIGHTER!
IF YOU WANT IT, RENA, I'LL GIVE YOU MY LIFE!

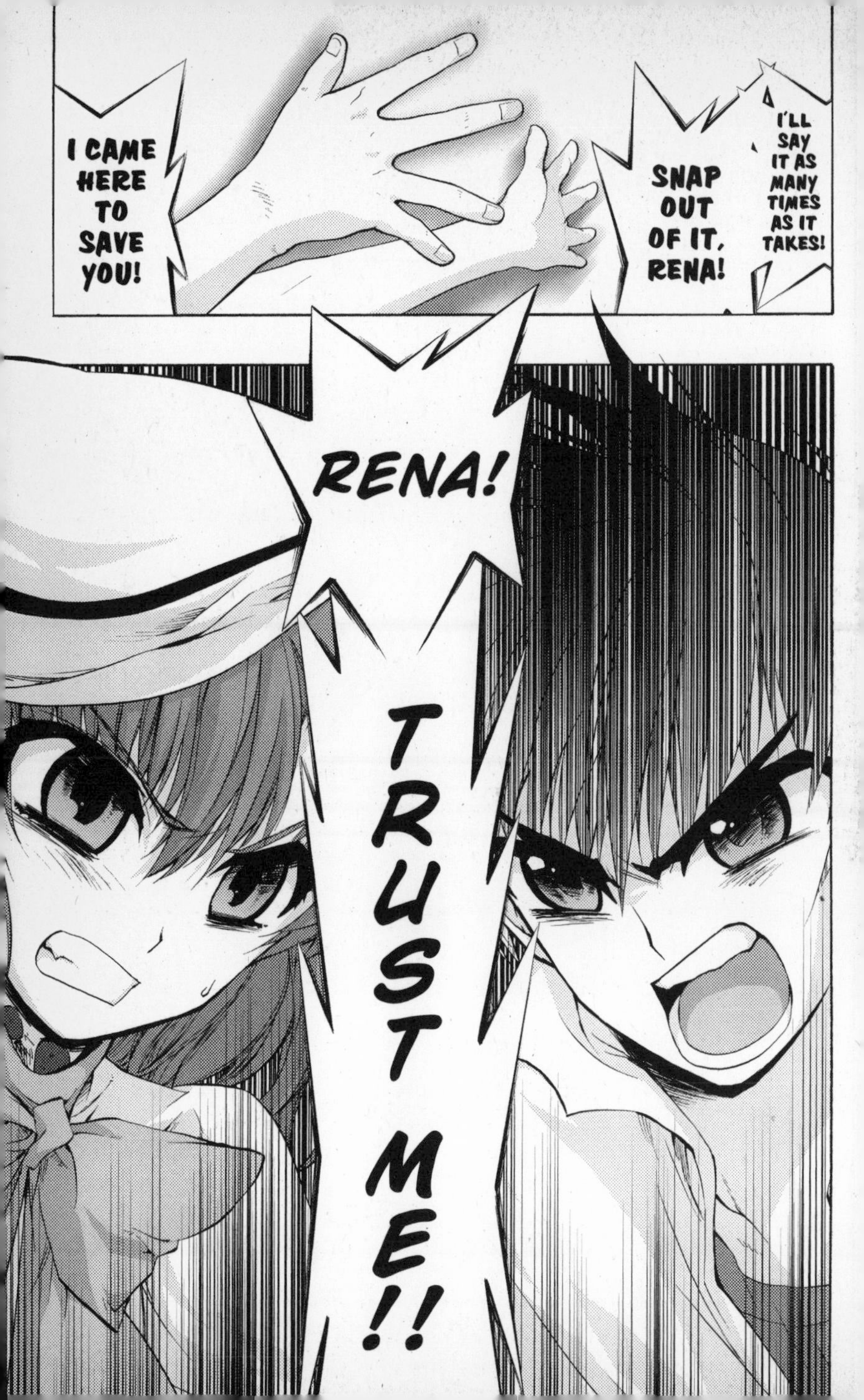
I'LL SAY IT AS MANY TIMES AS IT TAKES!
SNAP OUT OF IT, RENA!
I CAME HERE TO SAVE YOU!
RENA!
TRUST ME!!

GA
(WHACK)

EEP!!

KEIICHI-
SA—!

...POOR
KEIICHI-
KUN...

...THEY'RE
CONTROL-
LING YOU,
KEIICHI-
KUN.

HAA
CHUFF?

HAA

DO
(THUD)

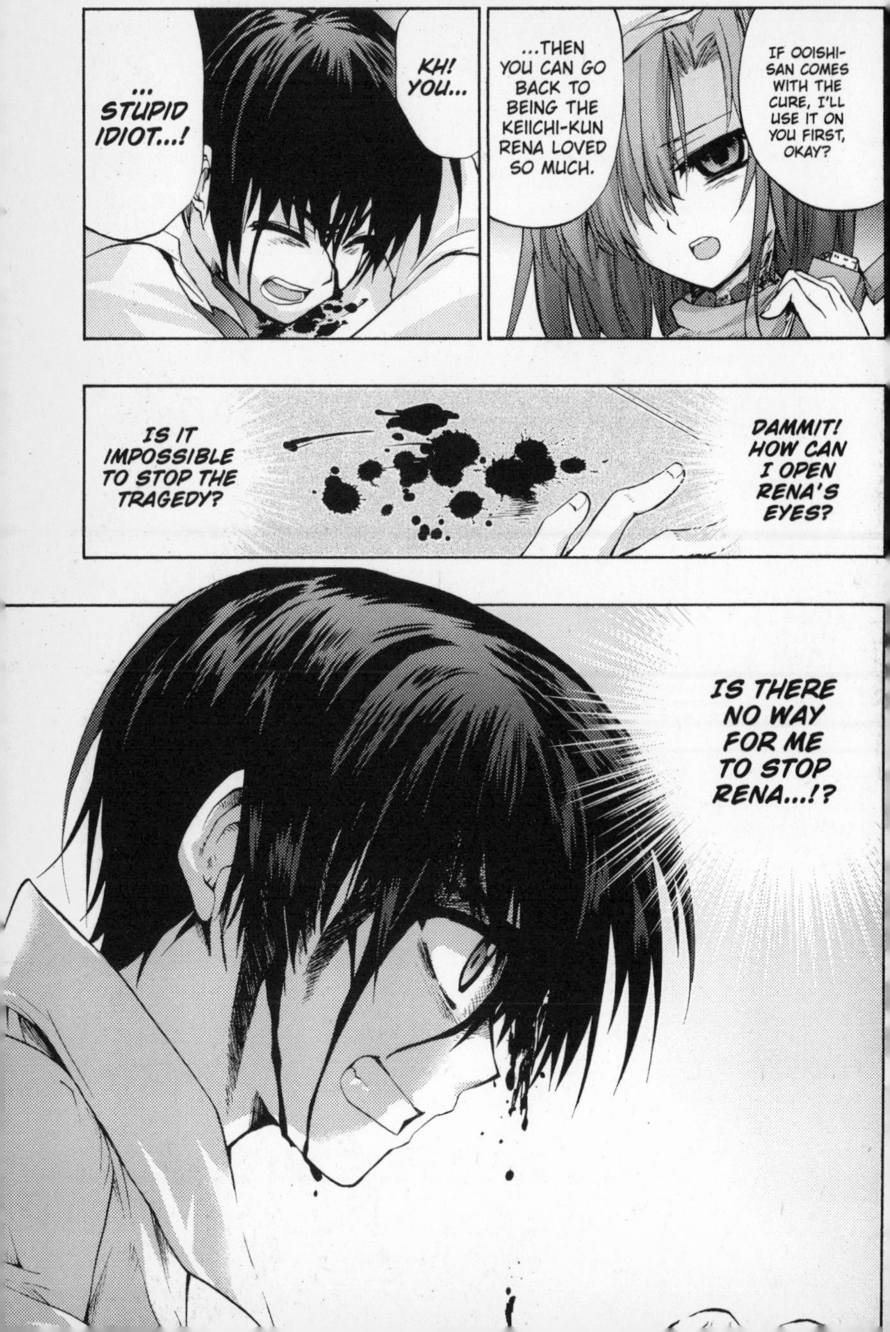
IF OOISHI-SAN COMES WITH THE CURE, I'LL USE IT ON YOU FIRST, OKAY?
...THEN YOU CAN GO BACK TO BEING THE KEIICHI-KUN RENA LOVED SO MUCH.
KH! YOU...
...STUPID IDIOT...!
DAMMIT! HOW CAN I OPEN RENA'S EYES?
IS IT IMPOSSIBLE TO STOP THE TRAGEDY?
IS THERE NO WAY FOR ME TO STOP RENA...!?

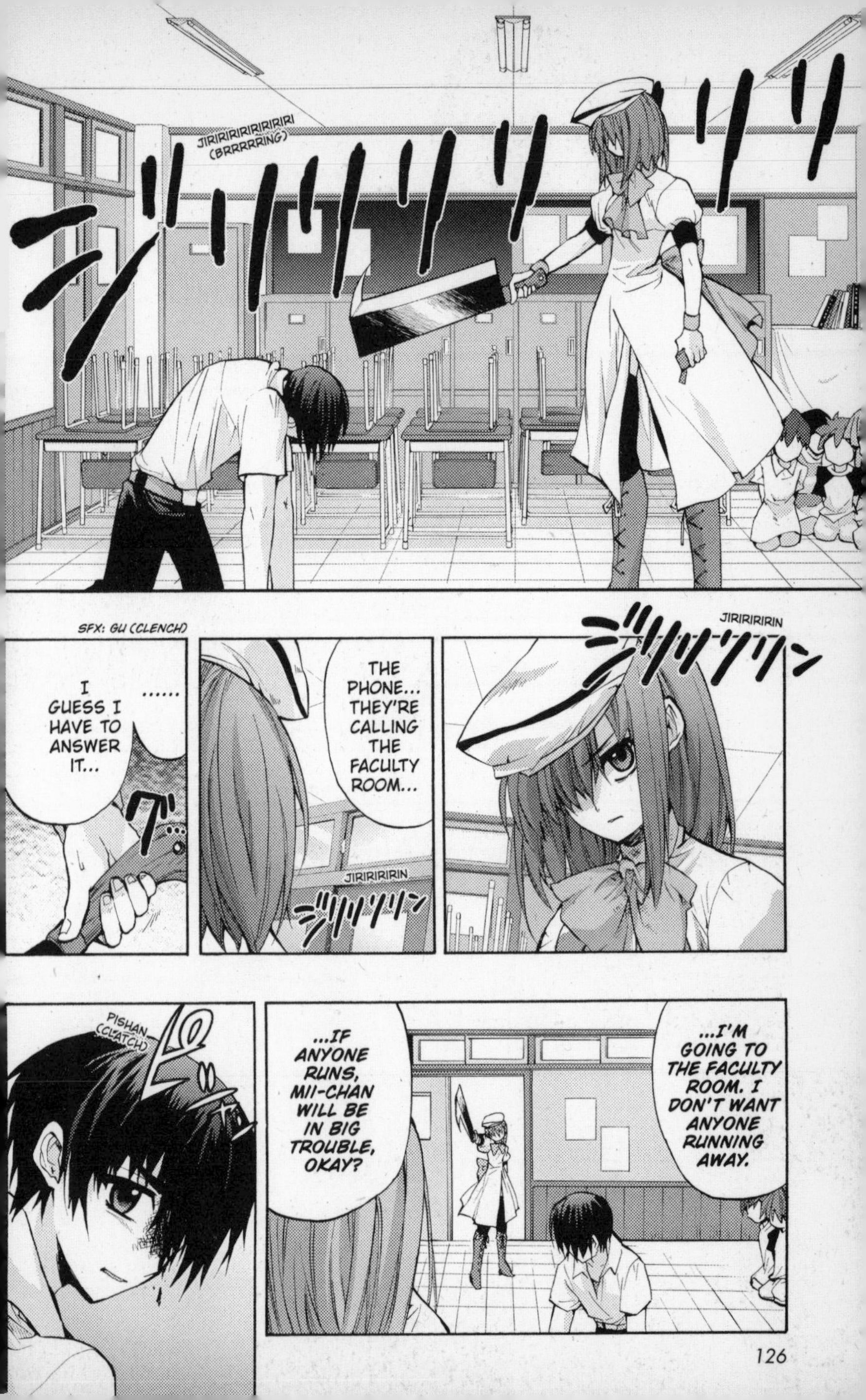
JIRIRIRIRIRIRIRI (BRRRRRING)
JIRIRIRIRIN
THE PHONE... THEY'RE CALLING THE FACULTY ROOM...
JIRIRIRIRIN
......
I GUESS I HAVE TO ANSWER IT...
SFX: GU (CLENCH)
...I'M GOING TO THE FACULTY ROOM. I DON'T WANT ANYONE RUNNING AWAY.
...IF ANYONE RUNS, MII-CHAN WILL BE IN BIG TROUBLE, OKAY?
PISHAN (CLATCH)

RENA...

GYU
(CLENCH)

プッ プー
PU-PUUU
(HON-HOOONK)

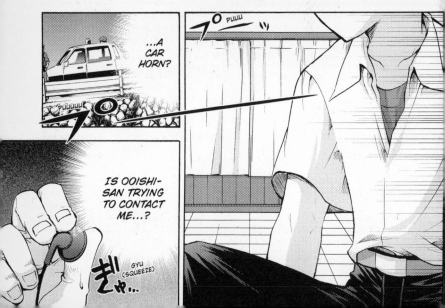

...A CAR HORN?

プー PUUU

プーッッ PUUUUU

IS OOISHI-SAN TRYING TO CONTACT ME...?

GYU
(SQUEEZE)

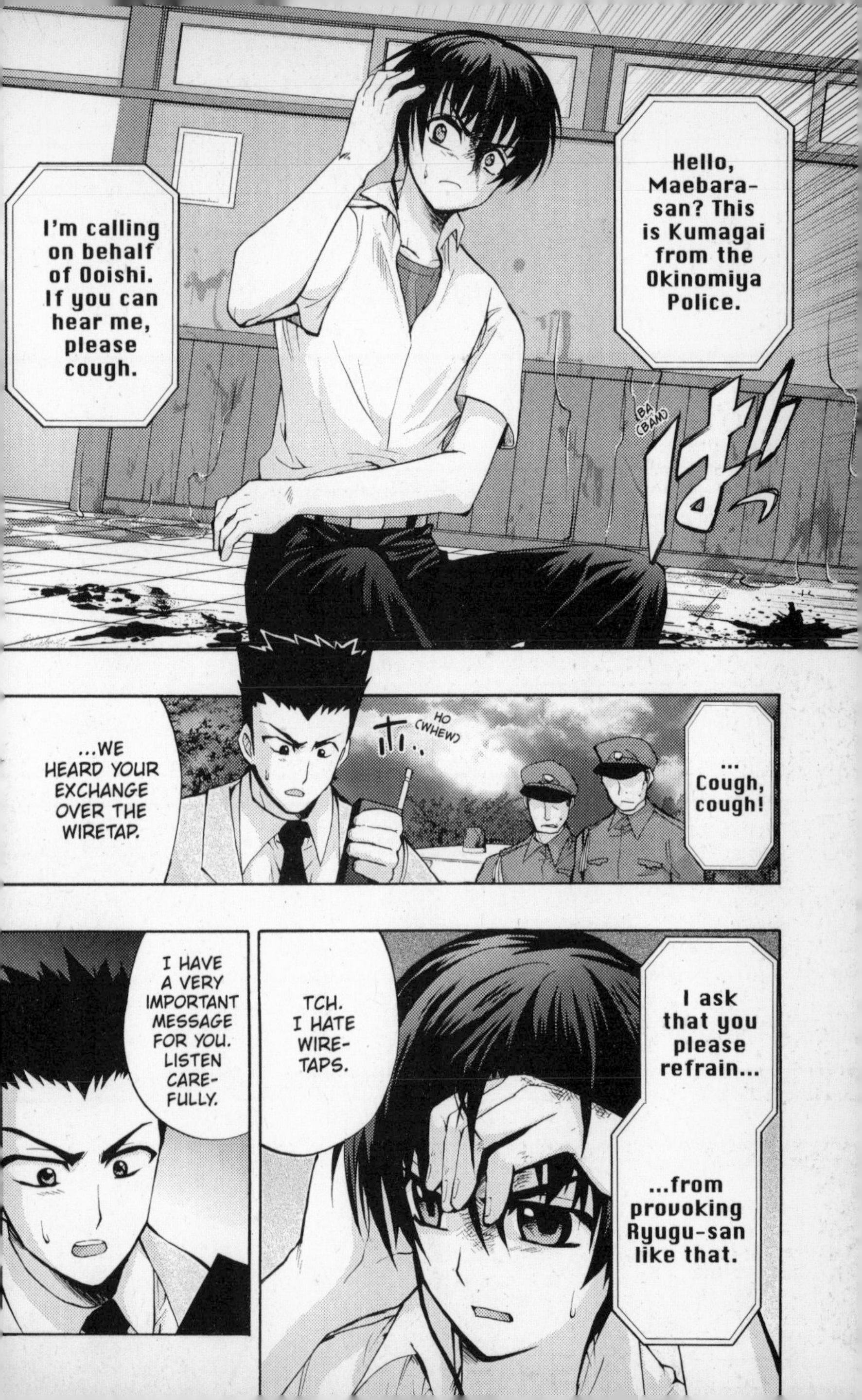
Hello, Maebara-san? This is Kumagai from the Okinomiya Police.
BA (BAM)
I'm calling on behalf of Ooishi. If you can hear me, please cough.
... Cough, cough!
HO (WHEW)
...WE HEARD YOUR EXCHANGE OVER THE WIRETAP.
I ask that you please refrain...
...from provoking Ryugu-san like that.
TCH. I HATE WIRE-TAPS.
I HAVE A VERY IMPORTANT MESSAGE FOR YOU. LISTEN CARE-FULLY.

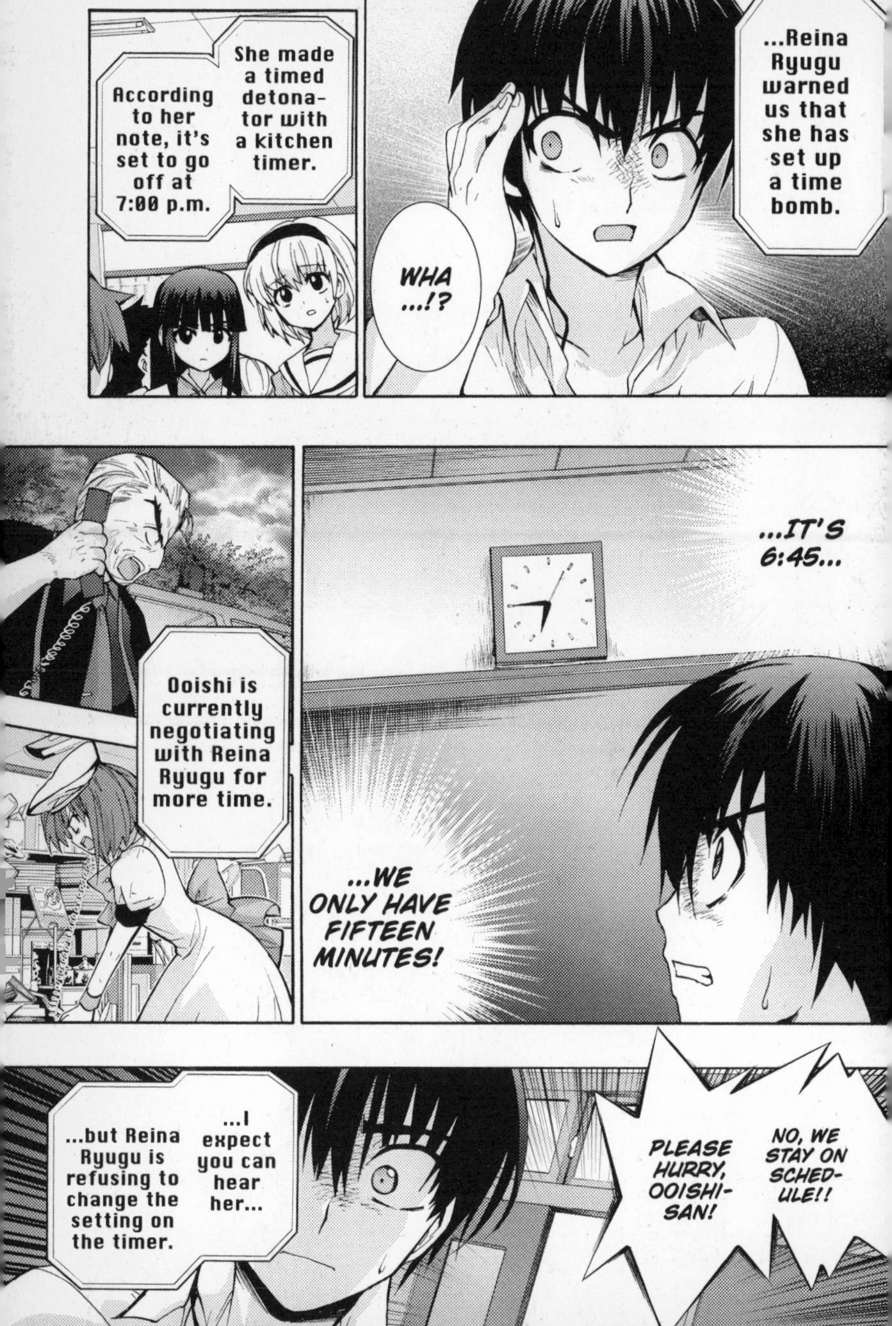
...Reina Ryugu warned us that she has set up a time bomb.
WHA ...!?
She made a timed detona-tor with a kitchen timer.
According to her note, it's set to go off at 7:00 p.m.
...IT'S 6:45...
...WE ONLY HAVE FIFTEEN MINUTES!
Ooishi is currently negotiating with Reina Ryugu for more time.
NO, WE STAY ON SCHED-ULE!!
PLEASE HURRY, OOISHI-SAN!
...I expect you can hear her...
...but Reina Ryugu is refusing to change the setting on the timer.

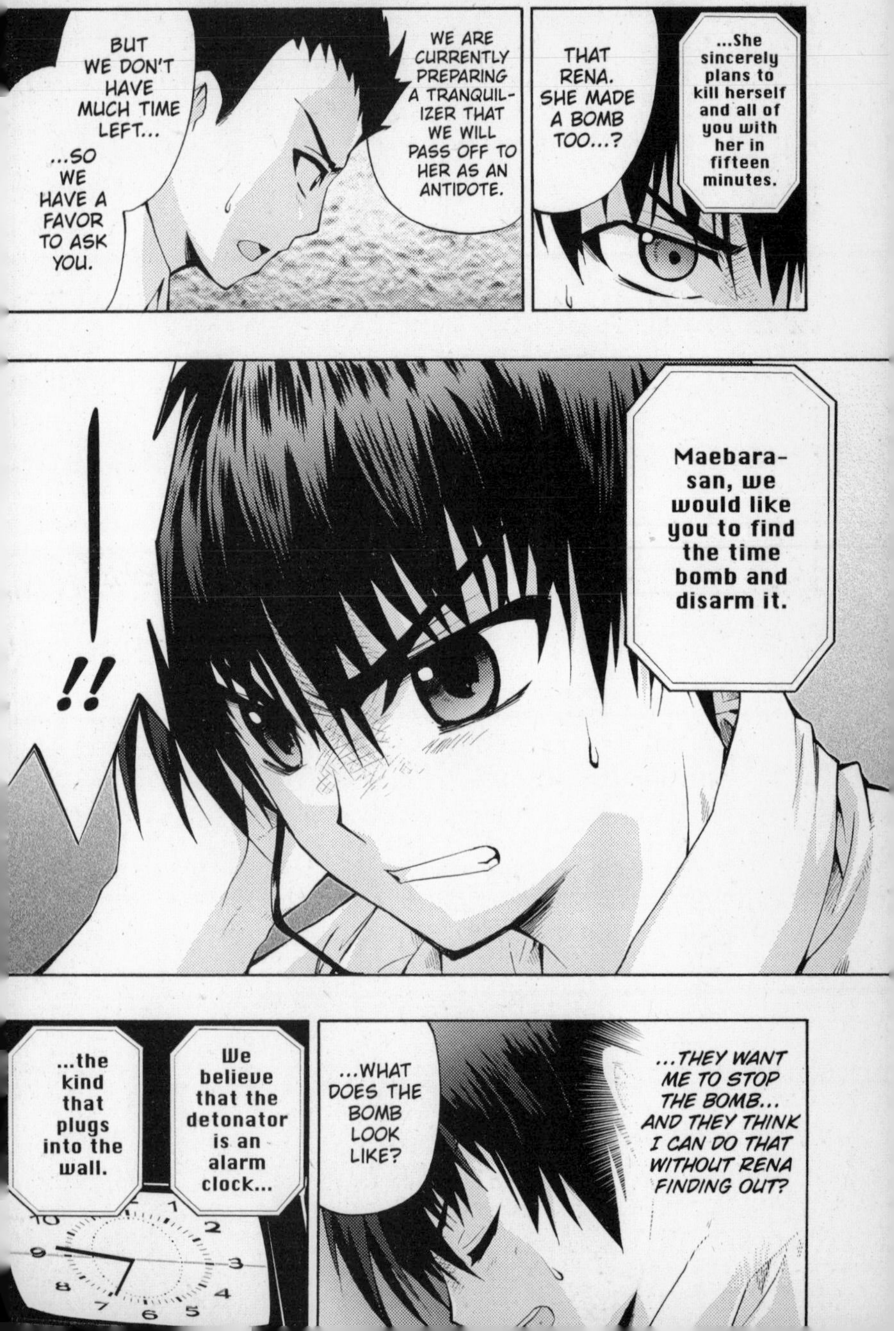
...She sincerely plans to kill herself and all of you with her in fifteen minutes.
THAT RENA. SHE MADE A BOMB TOO...?
WE ARE CURRENTLY PREPARING A TRANQUILIZER THAT WE WILL PASS OFF TO HER AS AN ANTIDOTE.
BUT WE DON'T HAVE MUCH TIME LEFT...
...SO WE HAVE A FAVOR TO ASK YOU.
Maebara-san, we would like you to find the time bomb and disarm it.
!!
...THEY WANT ME TO STOP THE BOMB... AND THEY THINK I CAN DO THAT WITHOUT RENA FINDING OUT?
...WHAT DOES THE BOMB LOOK LIKE?
We believe that the detonator is an alarm clock...
...the kind that plugs into the wall.

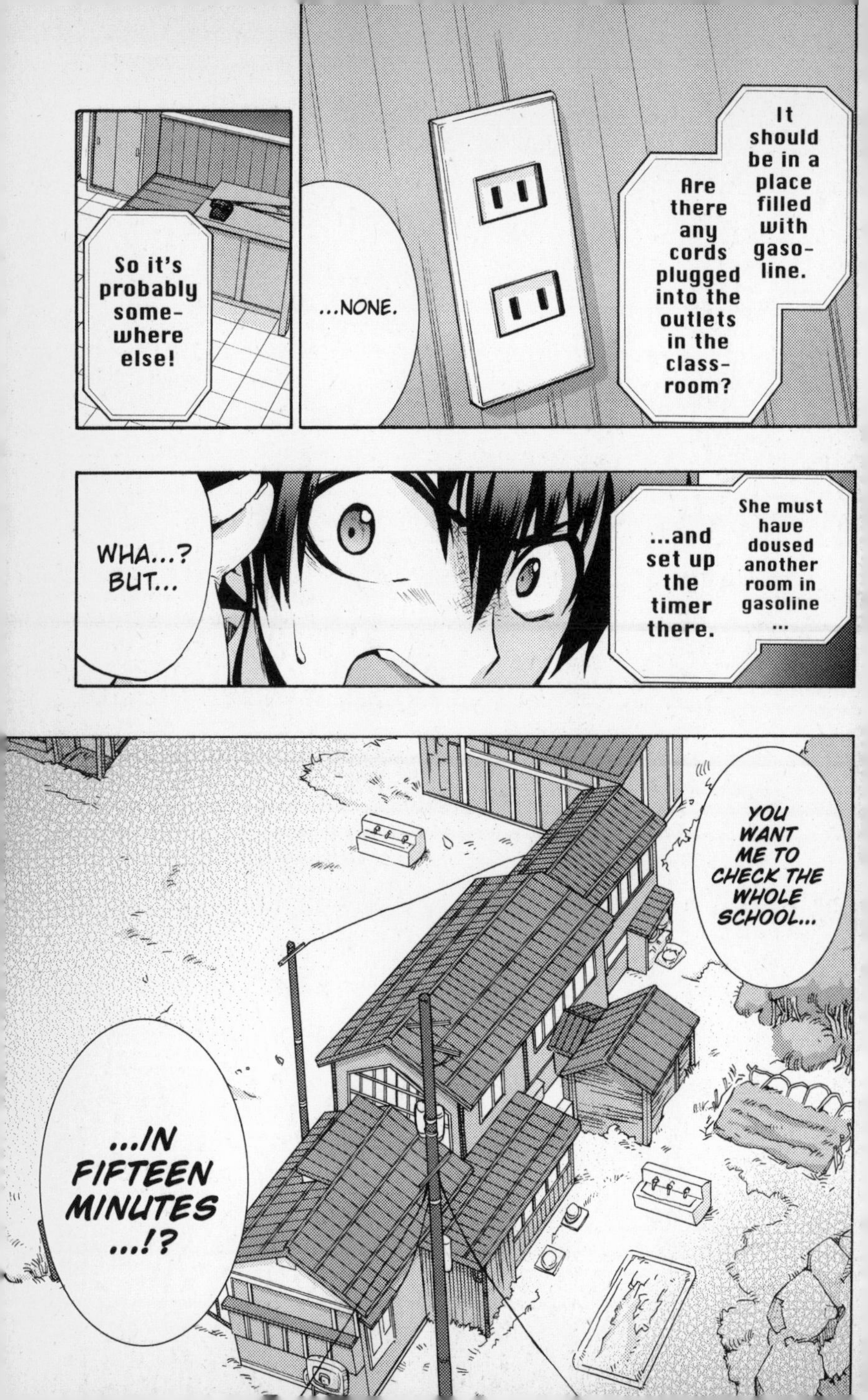
It should be in a place filled with gaso-line.
Are there any cords plugged into the outlets in the class-room?
...NONE.
So it's probably some-where else!
She must have doused another room in gasoline ...
...and set up the timer there.
WHA...? BUT...
YOU WANT ME TO CHECK THE WHOLE SCHOOL...
...IN FIFTEEN MINUTES ...!?

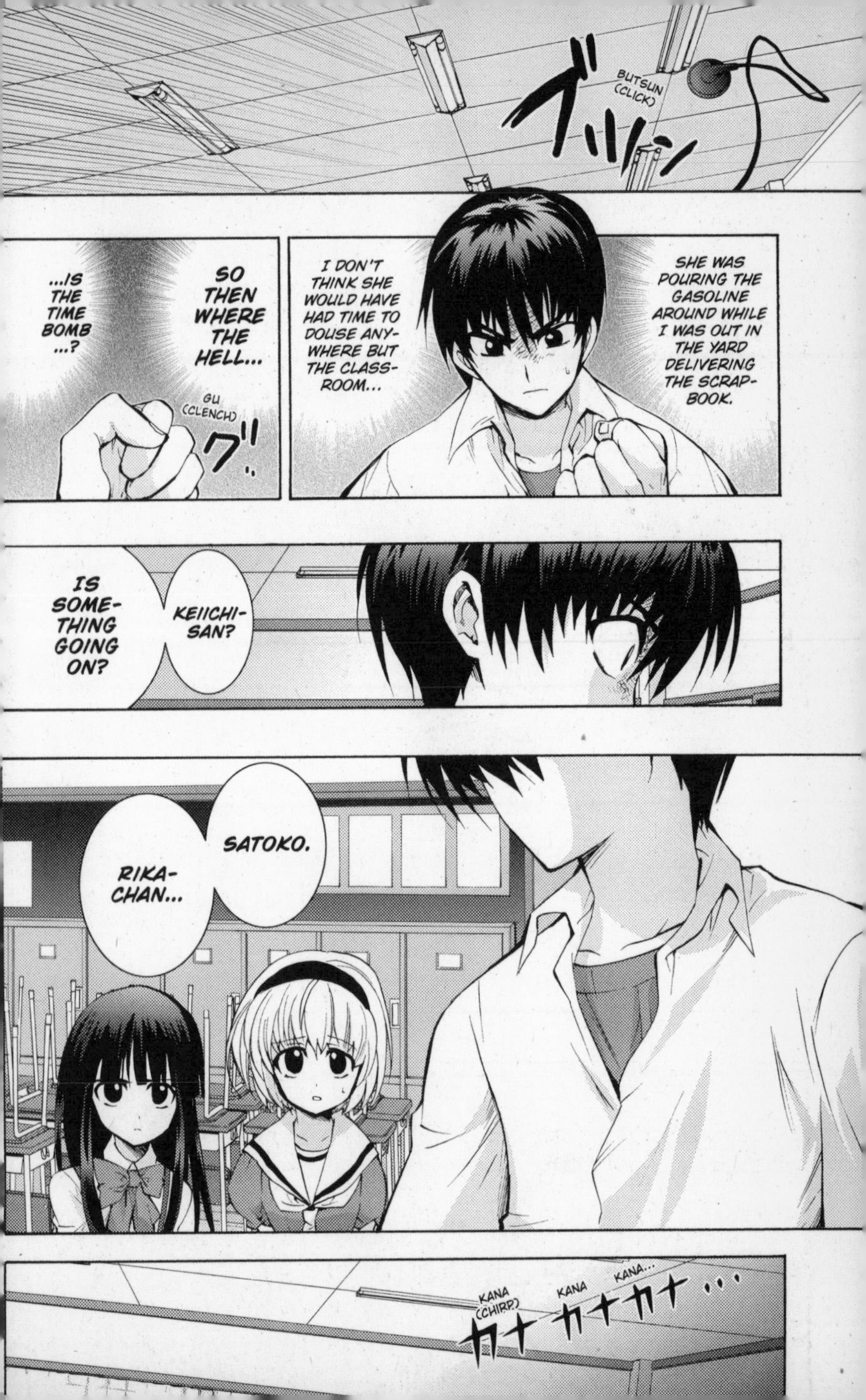
BUTSUN (CLICK)
SHE WAS POURING THE GASOLINE AROUND WHILE I WAS OUT IN THE YARD DELIVERING THE SCRAP-BOOK.
I DON'T THINK SHE WOULD HAVE HAD TIME TO DOUSE ANY-WHERE BUT THE CLASS-ROOM...
SO THEN WHERE THE HELL...
GU (CLENCH)
...IS THE TIME BOMB ...?
KEIICHI-SAN?
IS SOME-THING GOING ON?
SATOKO.
RIKA-CHAN...
KANA (CHIRP)
KANA
KANA...

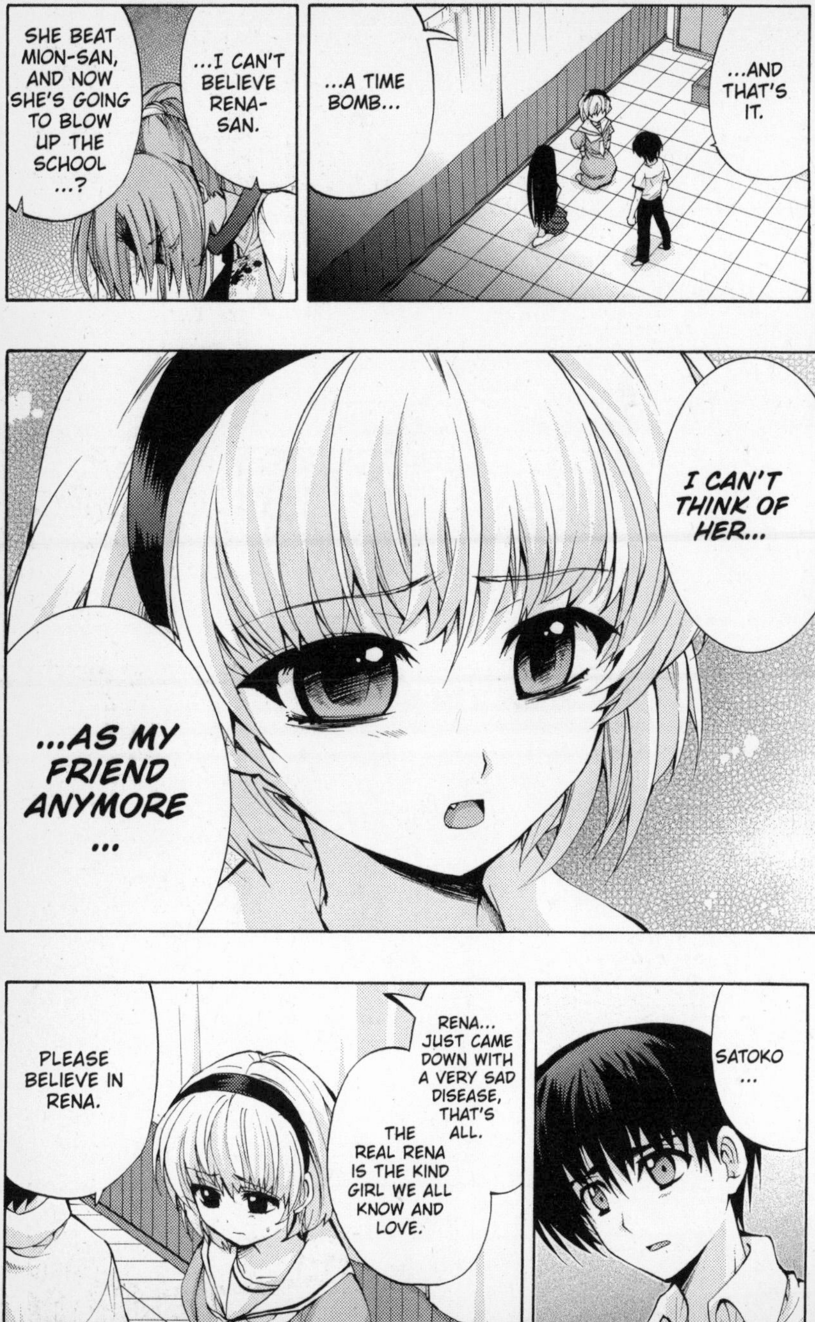
...AND THAT'S IT.
...A TIME BOMB...
...I CAN'T BELIEVE RENA-SAN.
SHE BEAT MION-SAN, AND NOW SHE'S GOING TO BLOW UP THE SCHOOL ...?
I CAN'T THINK OF HER...
...AS MY FRIEND ANYMORE ...
SATOKO ...
RENA... JUST CAME DOWN WITH A VERY SAD DISEASE, THAT'S ALL.
THE REAL RENA IS THE KIND GIRL WE ALL KNOW AND LOVE.
PLEASE BELIEVE IN RENA.

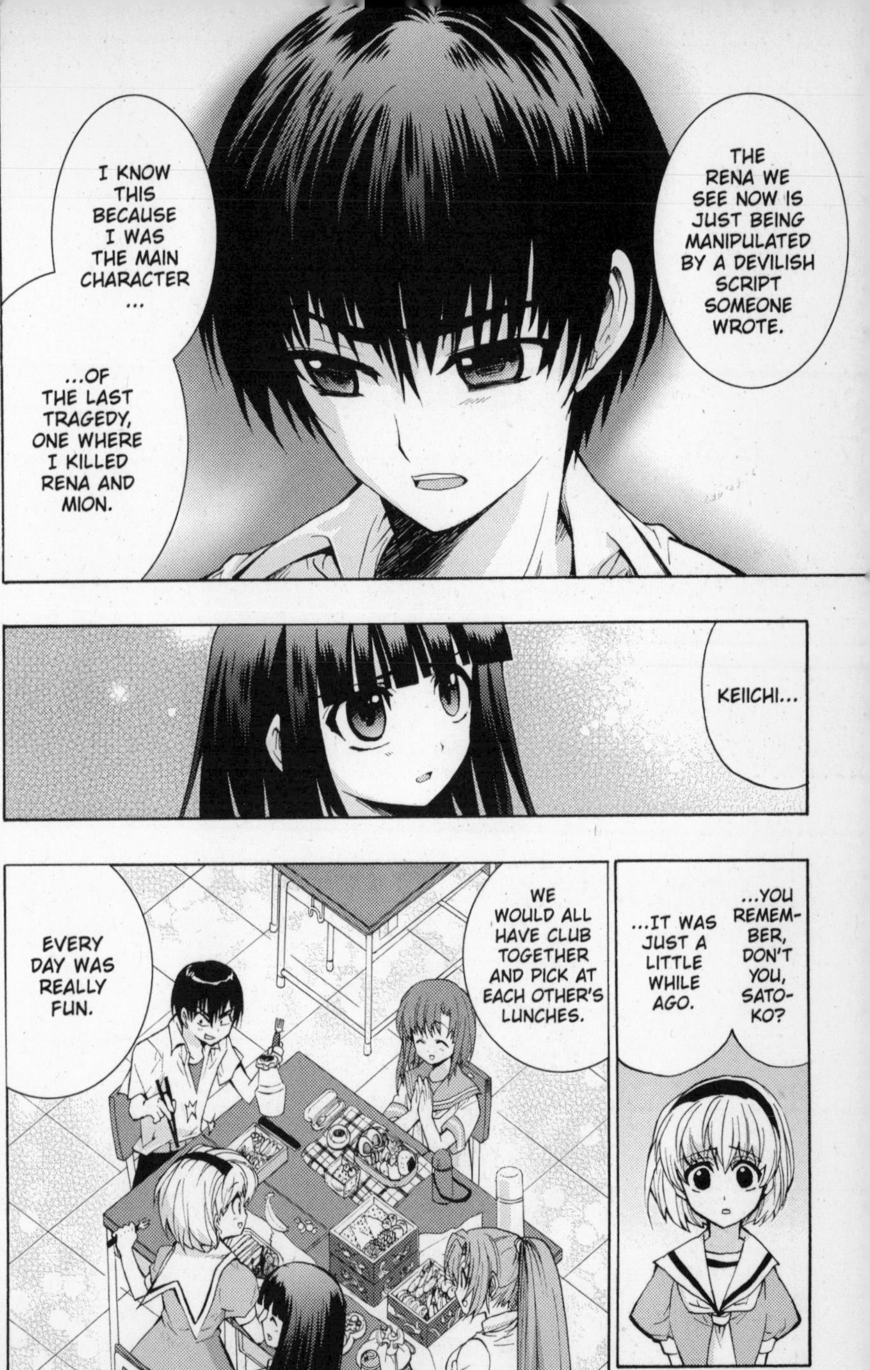
THE RENA WE SEE NOW IS JUST BEING MANIPULATED BY A DEVILISH SCRIPT SOMEONE WROTE.
I KNOW THIS BECAUSE I WAS THE MAIN CHARACTER ...
...OF THE LAST TRAGEDY, ONE WHERE I KILLED RENA AND MION.
KEIICHI...
...YOU REMEMBER, DON'T YOU, SATOKO?
...IT WAS JUST A LITTLE WHILE AGO.
WE WOULD ALL HAVE CLUB TOGETHER AND PICK AT EACH OTHER'S LUNCHES.
EVERY DAY WAS REALLY FUN.

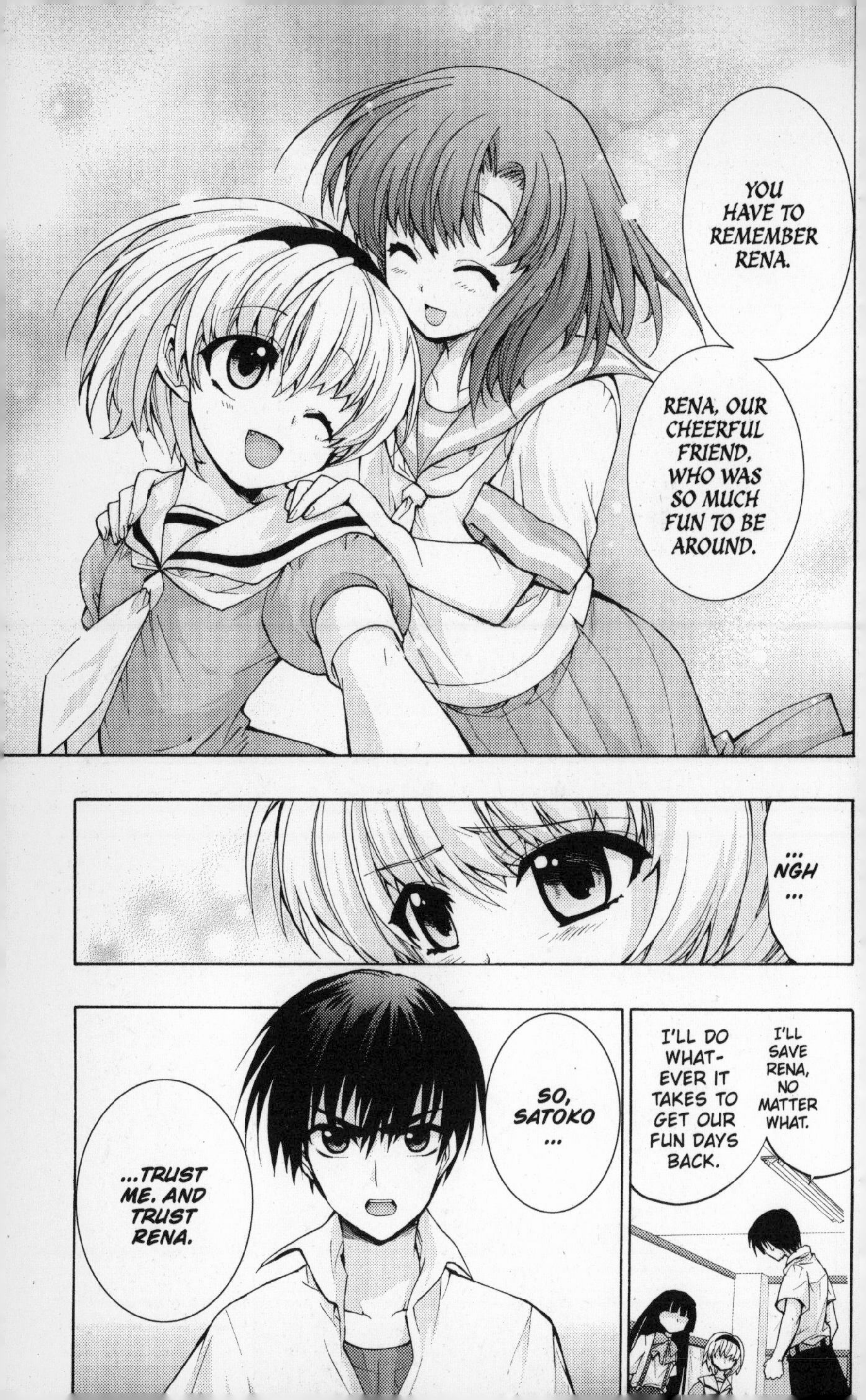
YOU HAVE TO REMEMBER RENA.
RENA, OUR CHEERFUL FRIEND, WHO WAS SO MUCH FUN TO BE AROUND.
...NGH...
I'LL SAVE RENA, NO MATTER WHAT.
I'LL DO WHAT-EVER IT TAKES TO GET OUR FUN DAYS BACK.
SO, SATOKO...
...TRUST ME. AND TRUST RENA.

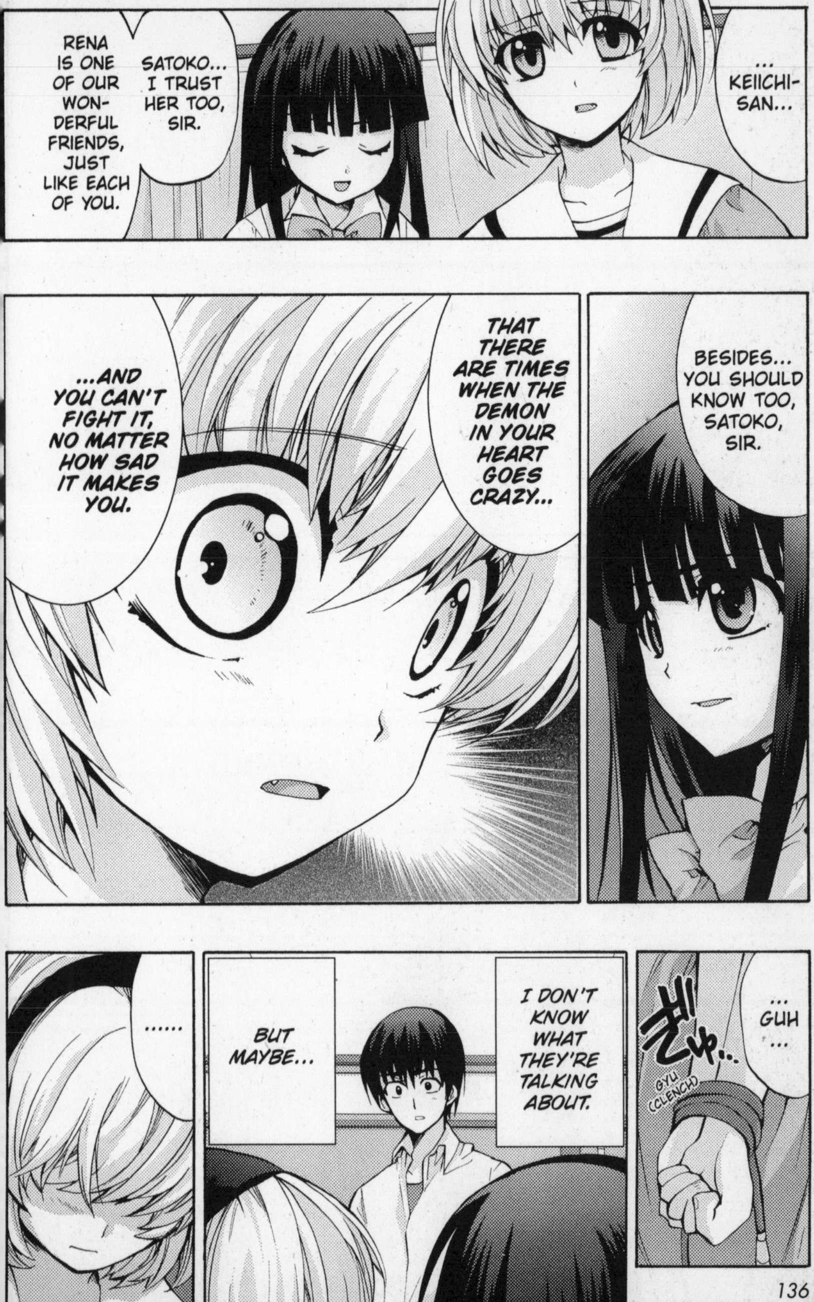
...KEIICHI-SAN...
SATOKO... I TRUST HER TOO, SIR.
RENA IS ONE OF OUR WONDERFUL FRIENDS, JUST LIKE EACH OF YOU.
BESIDES... YOU SHOULD KNOW TOO, SATOKO, SIR.
THAT THERE ARE TIMES WHEN THE DEMON IN YOUR HEART GOES CRAZY...
...AND YOU CAN'T FIGHT IT, NO MATTER HOW SAD IT MAKES YOU.
...GUH...
ぎゅ...
GYU (CLENCH)
I DON'T KNOW WHAT THEY'RE TALKING ABOUT.
BUT MAYBE...
......

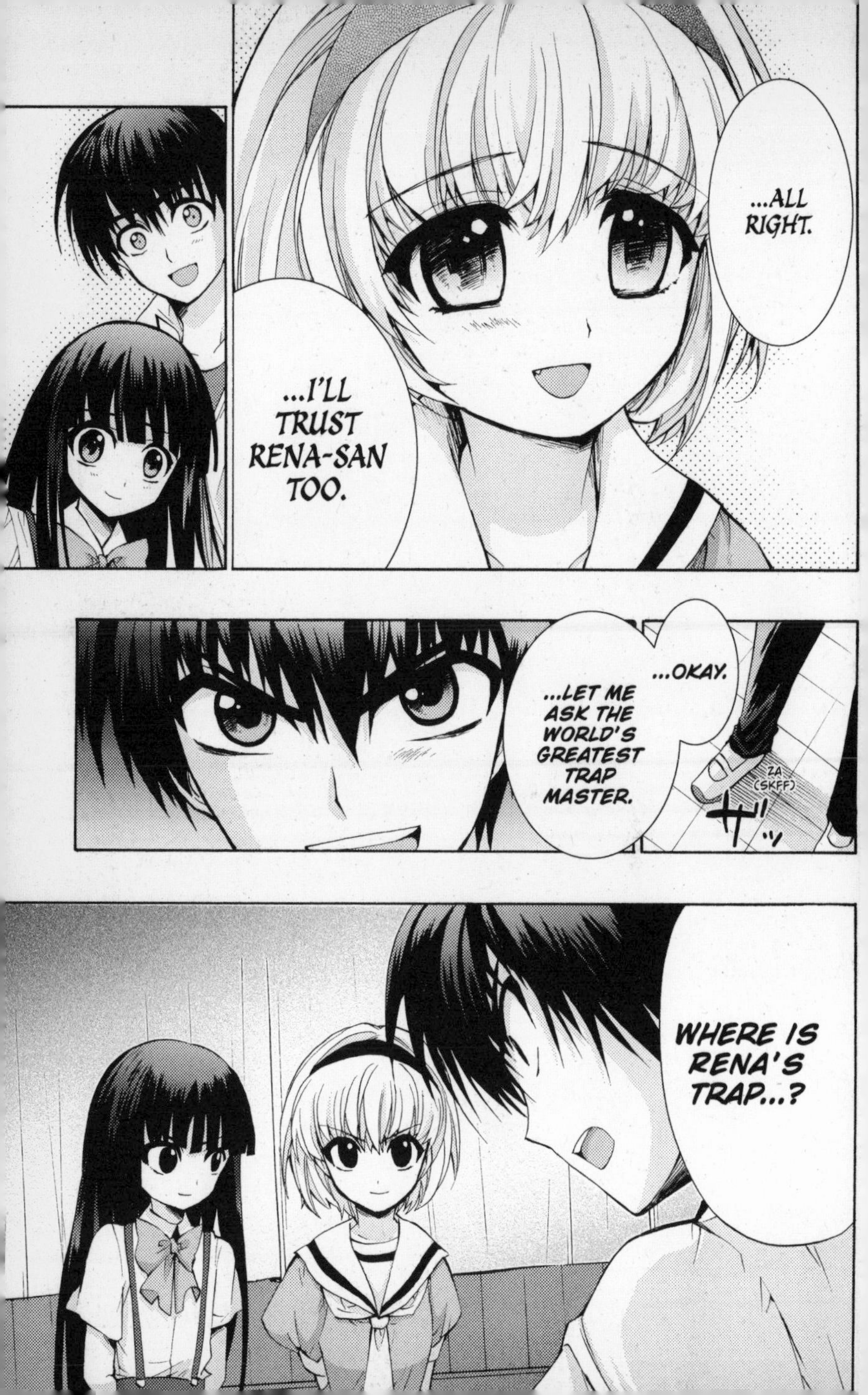
...ALL RIGHT.
...I'LL TRUST RENA-SAN TOO.
ZA (SKFF)
...OKAY.
...LET ME ASK THE WORLD'S GREATEST TRAP MASTER.
WHERE IS RENA'S TRAP...?

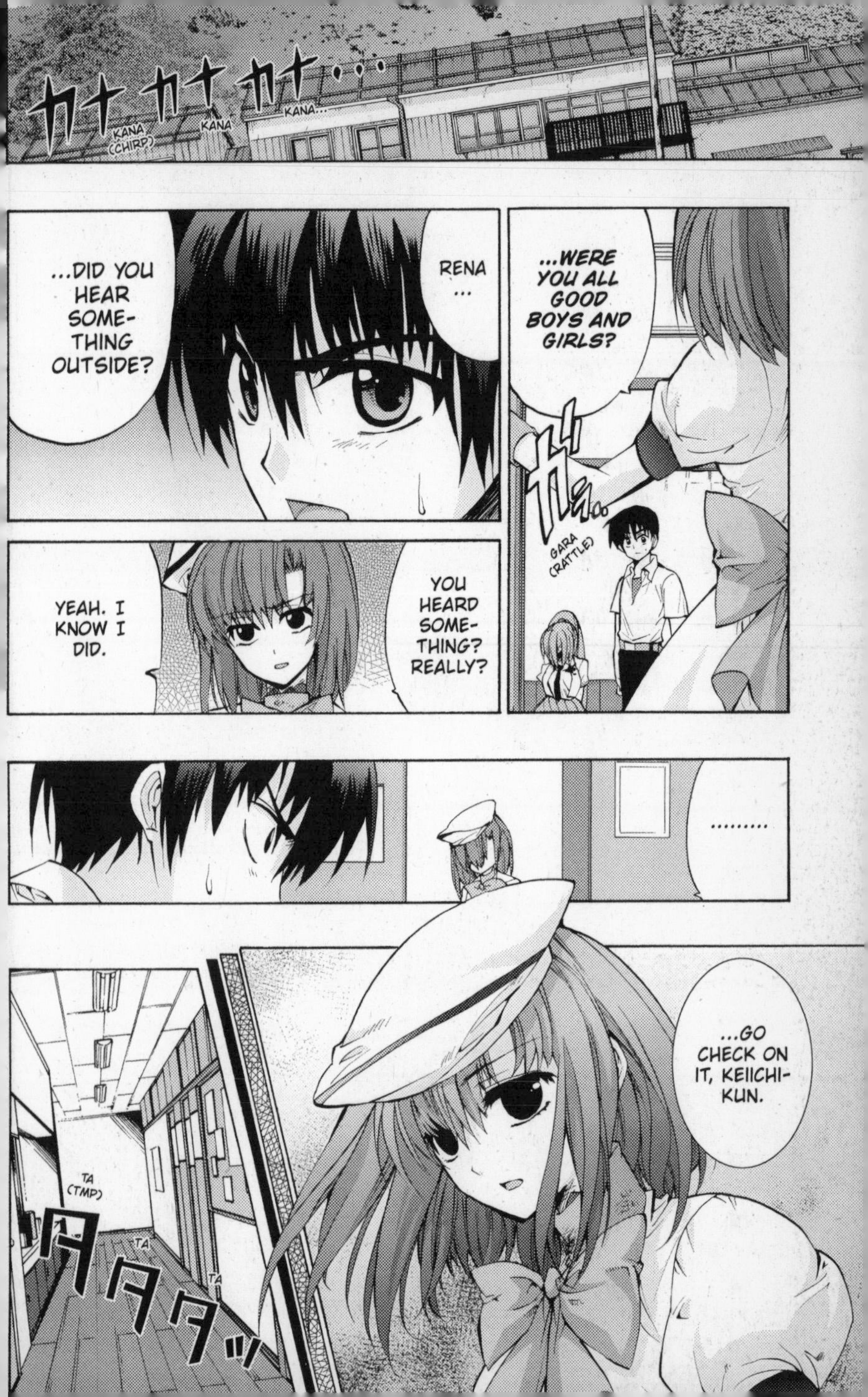
カナ カナ カナ・・・
KANA (CHIRP)
KANA
KANA...
...WERE YOU ALL GOOD BOYS AND GIRLS?
GARA (RATTLE)
RENA ...
...DID YOU HEAR SOME-THING OUTSIDE?
YOU HEARD SOME-THING? REALLY?
YEAH. I KNOW I DID.
....
...GO CHECK ON IT, KEIICHI-KUN.
TA (TMP)
TA
TA

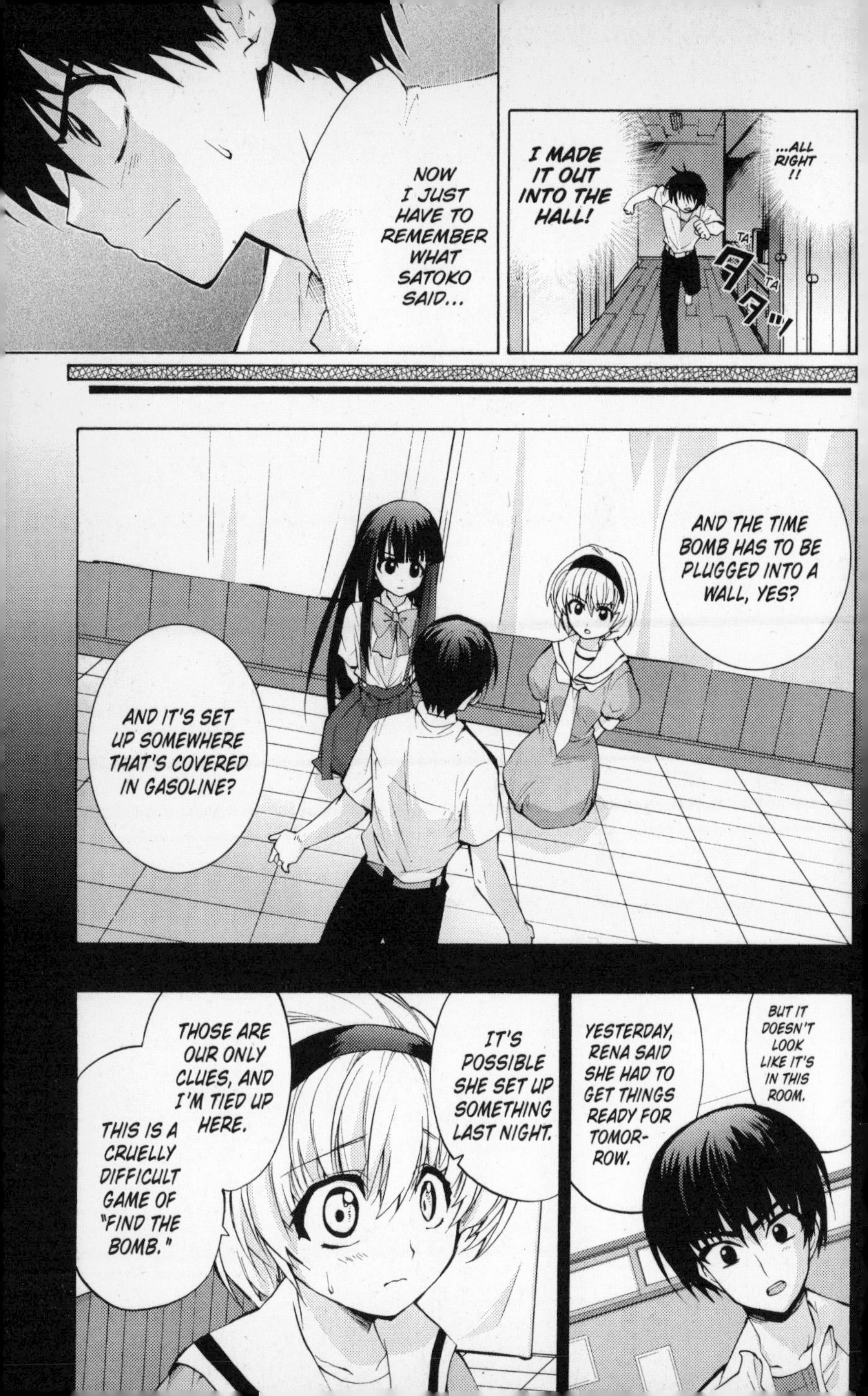
...ALL RIGHT !!
I MADE IT OUT INTO THE HALL!
TA
TA
NOW I JUST HAVE TO REMEMBER WHAT SATOKO SAID...
AND THE TIME BOMB HAS TO BE PLUGGED INTO A WALL, YES?
AND IT'S SET UP SOMEWHERE THAT'S COVERED IN GASOLINE?
BUT IT DOESN'T LOOK LIKE IT'S IN THIS ROOM.
YESTERDAY, RENA SAID SHE HAD TO GET THINGS READY FOR TOMOR-ROW.
IT'S POSSIBLE SHE SET UP SOMETHING LAST NIGHT.
THOSE ARE OUR ONLY CLUES, AND I'M TIED UP HERE.
THIS IS A CRUELLY DIFFICULT GAME OF "FIND THE BOMB."

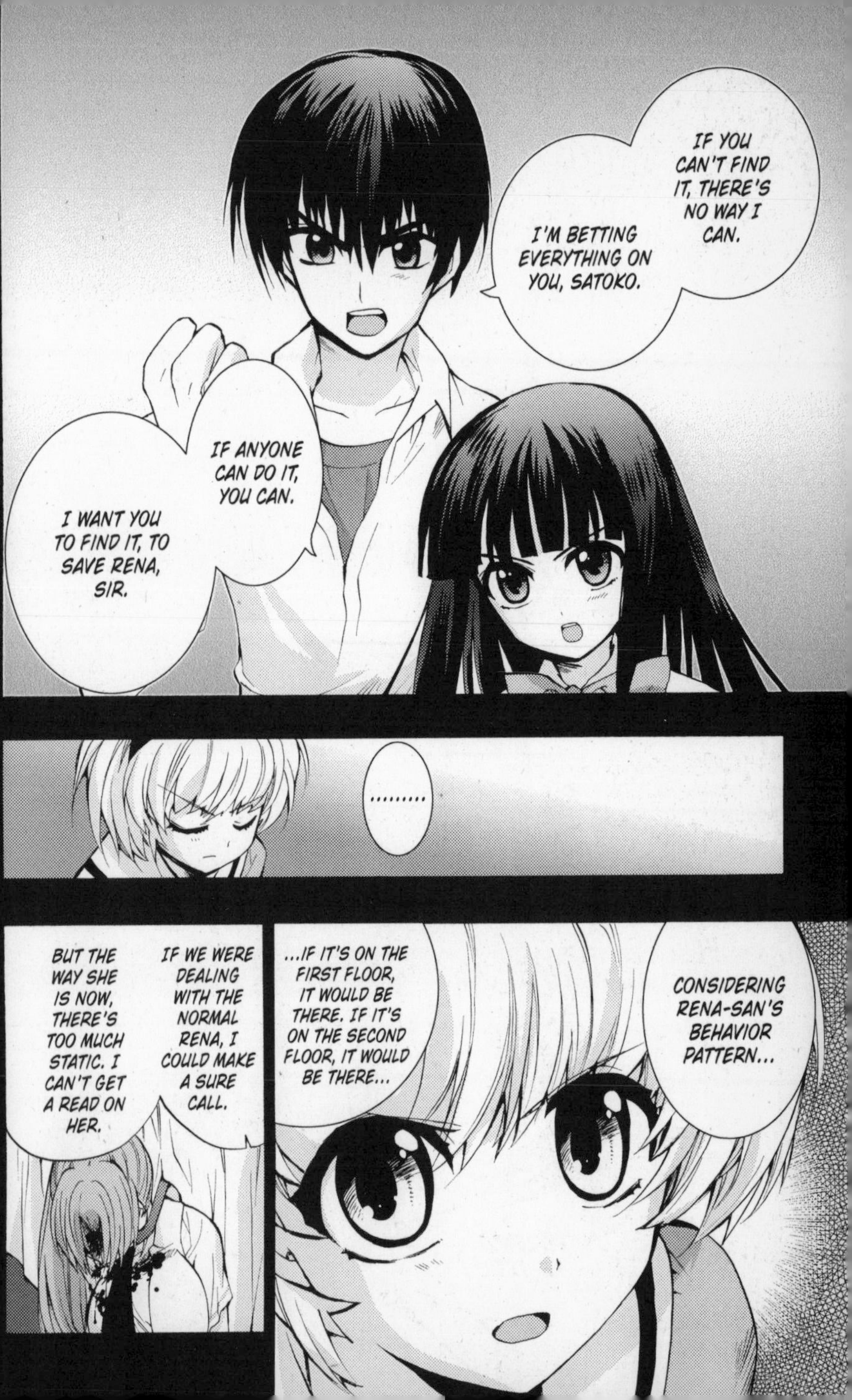
IF YOU CAN'T FIND IT, THERE'S NO WAY I CAN.
I'M BETTING EVERYTHING ON YOU, SATOKO.
IF ANYONE CAN DO IT, YOU CAN.
I WANT YOU TO FIND IT, TO SAVE RENA, SIR.
....
CONSIDERING RENA-SAN'S BEHAVIOR PATTERN...
...IF IT'S ON THE FIRST FLOOR, IT WOULD BE THERE. IF IT'S ON THE SECOND FLOOR, IT WOULD BE THERE...
IF WE WERE DEALING WITH THE NORMAL RENA, I COULD MAKE A SURE CALL.
BUT THE WAY SHE IS NOW, THERE'S TOO MUCH STATIC. I CAN'T GET A READ ON HER.

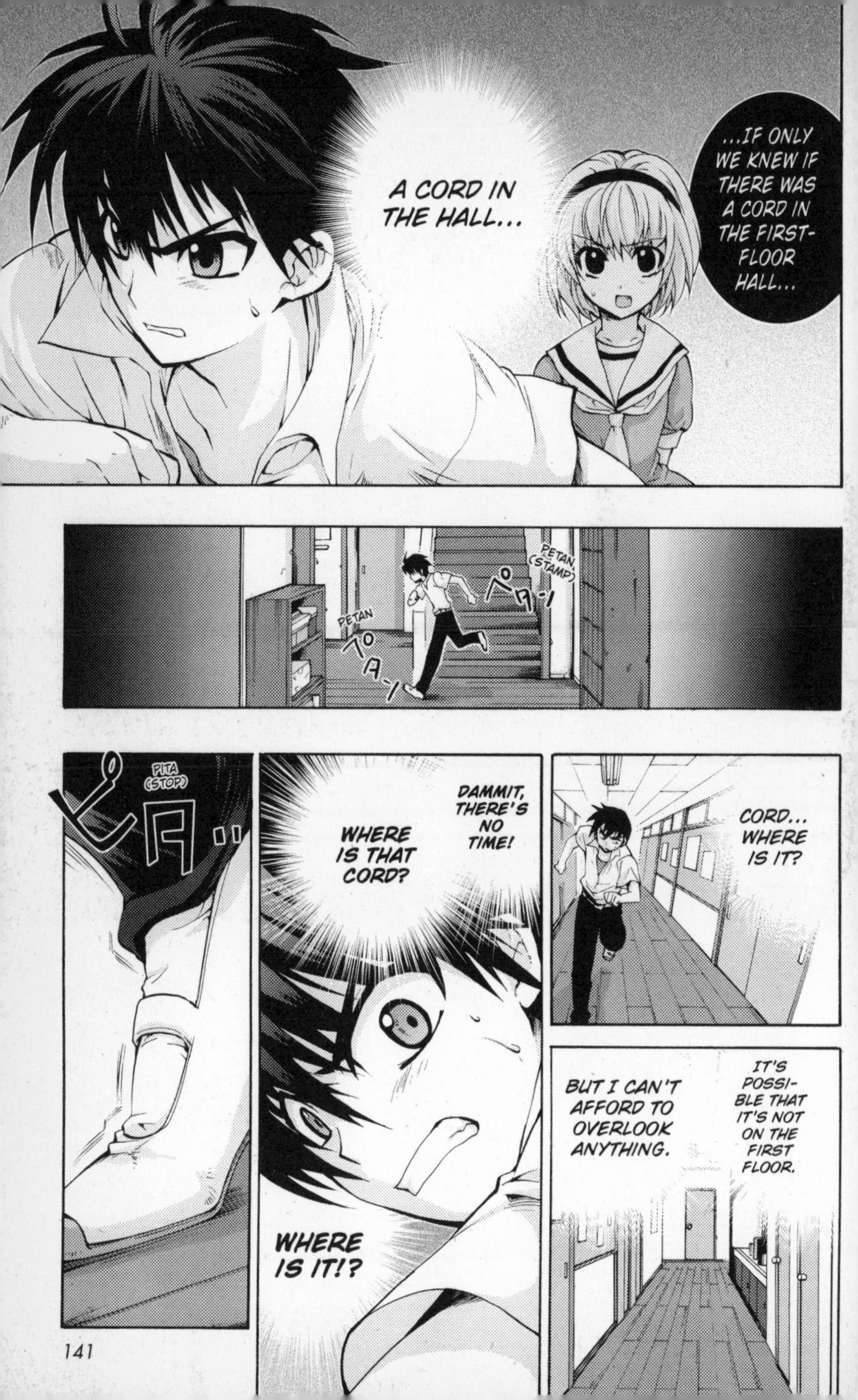
...IF ONLY WE KNEW IF THERE WAS A CORD IN THE FIRST-FLOOR HALL...
A CORD IN THE HALL...
PETAN (STAMP)
PETAN
CORD... WHERE IS IT?
IT'S POSSIBLE THAT IT'S NOT ON THE FIRST FLOOR.
BUT I CAN'T AFFORD TO OVERLOOK ANYTHING.
DAMMIT, THERE'S NO TIME!
WHERE IS THAT CORD?
WHERE IS IT!?
PITA (STOP)

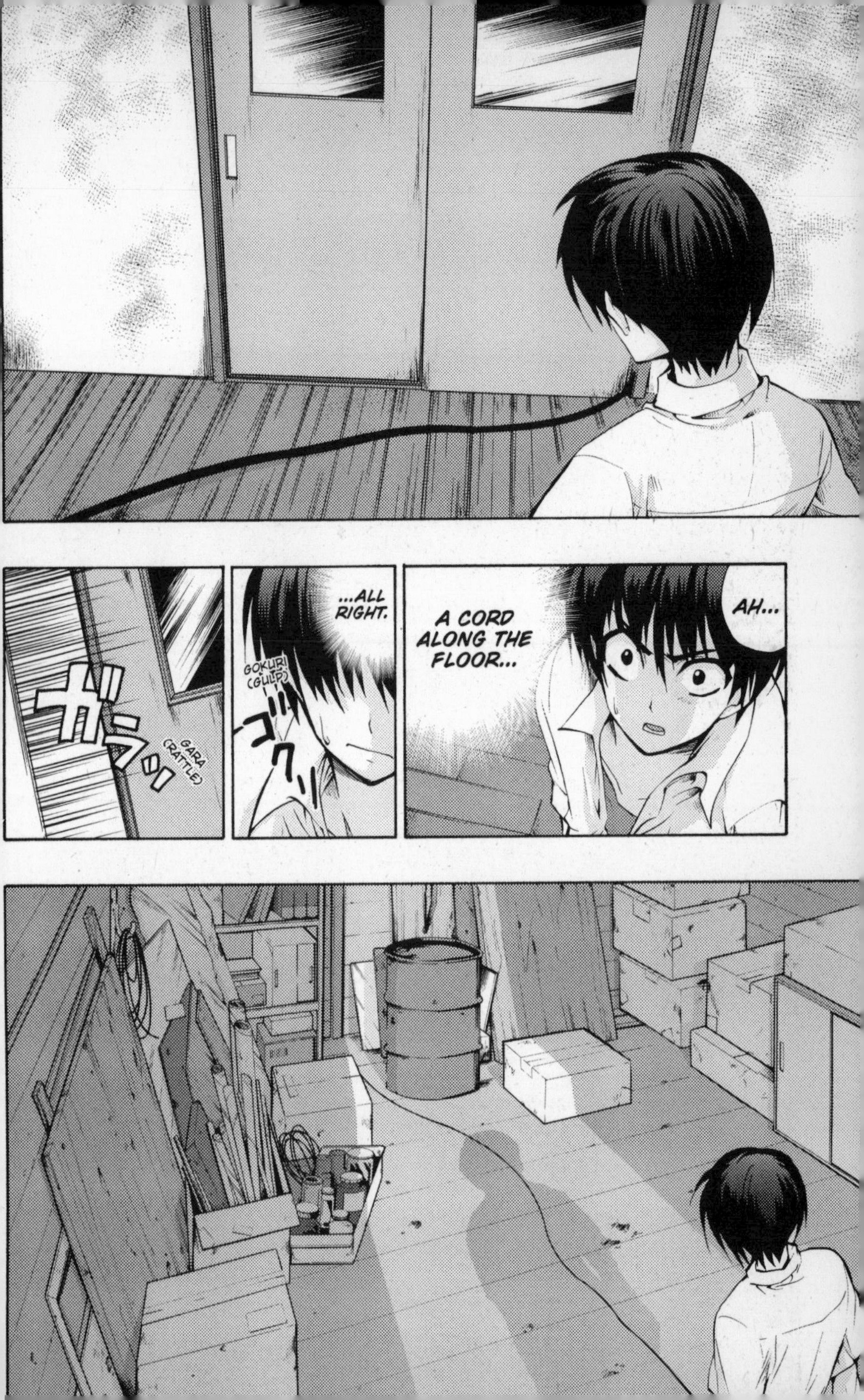
AH...
A CORD ALONG THE FLOOR...
...ALL RIGHT.
GOKURI (GULP)
ゴクッ
ガラッ
GARA (RATTLE)

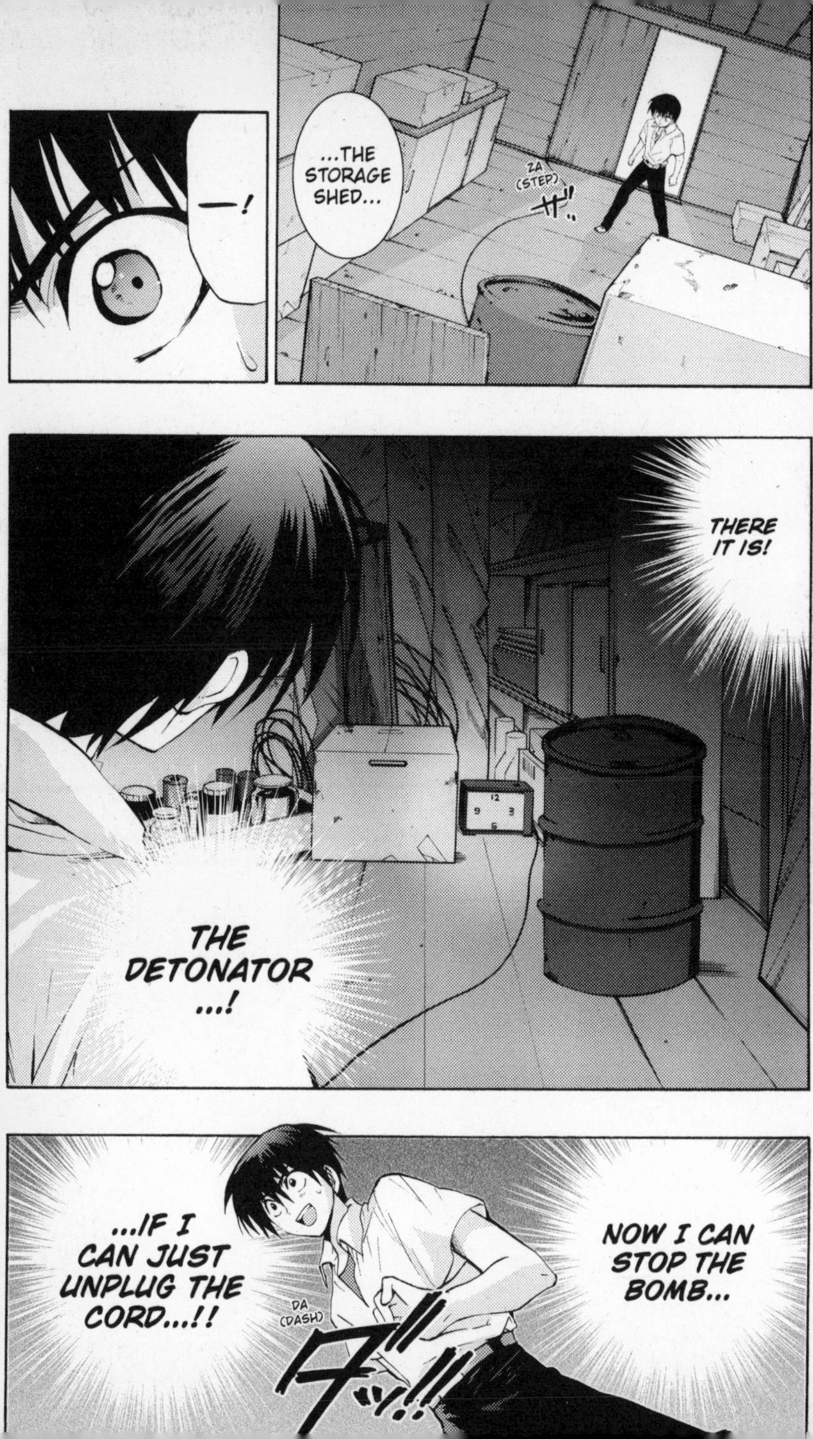
...THE STORAGE SHED...
ZA (STEP)
—!
THERE IT IS!
THE DETONATOR ...!
NOW I CAN STOP THE BOMB...
DA (DASH)
...IF I CAN JUST UNPLUG THE CORD...!!

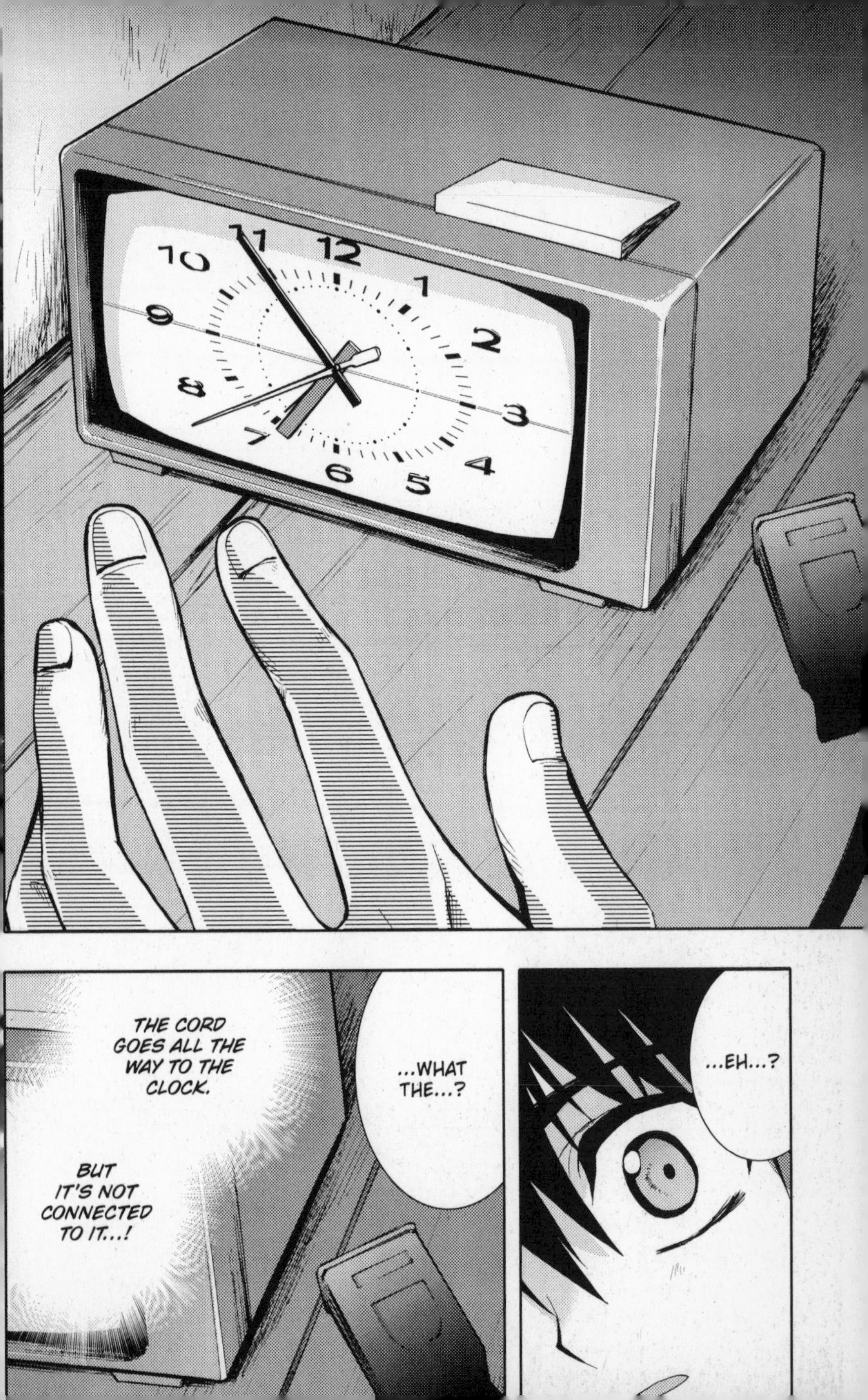
...EH...?
...WHAT THE...?
THE CORD GOES ALL THE WAY TO THE CLOCK.
BUT IT'S NOT CONNECTED TO IT...!

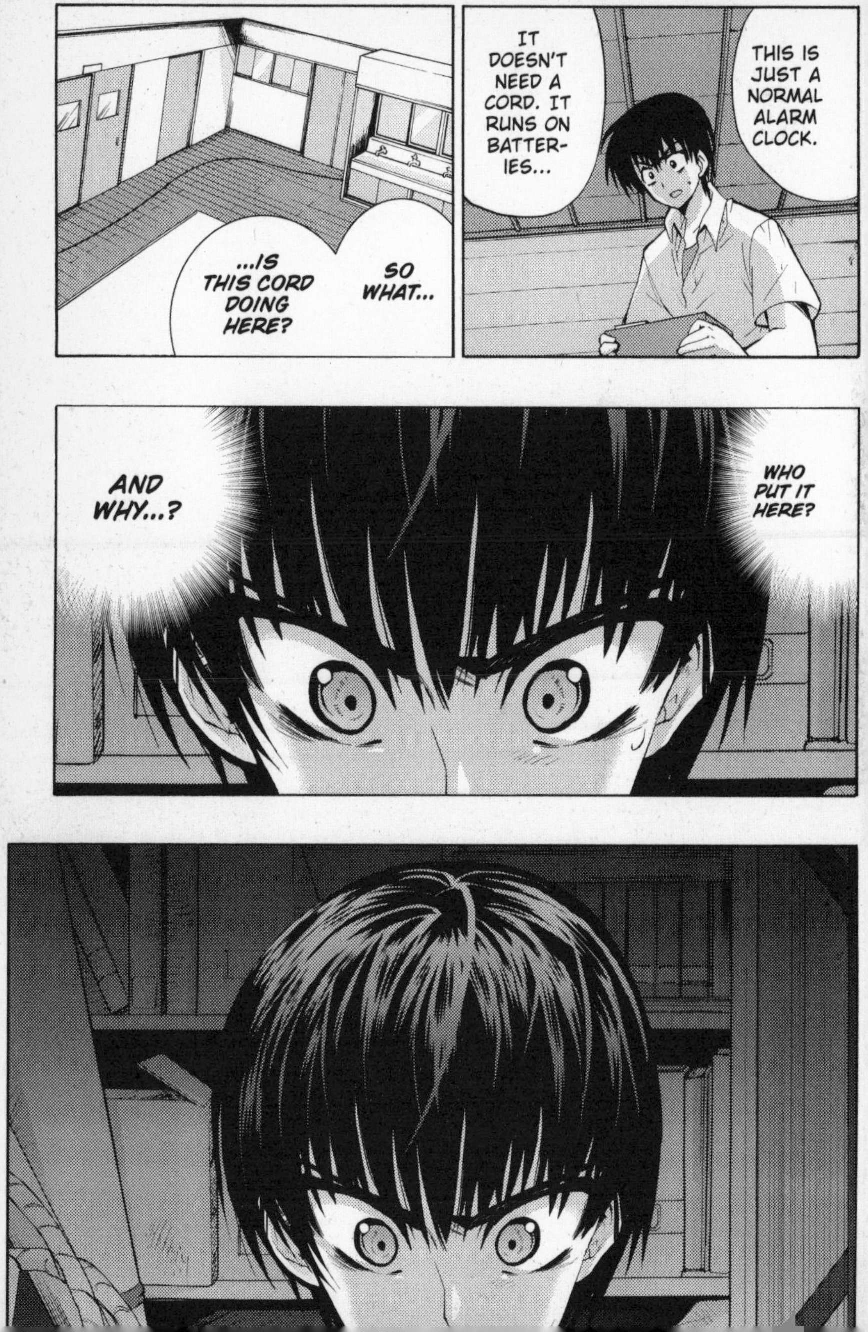
THIS IS JUST A NORMAL ALARM CLOCK.
IT DOESN'T NEED A CORD. IT RUNS ON BATTER-IES...
SO WHAT...
...IS THIS CORD DOING HERE?
WHO PUT IT HERE?
AND WHY...?

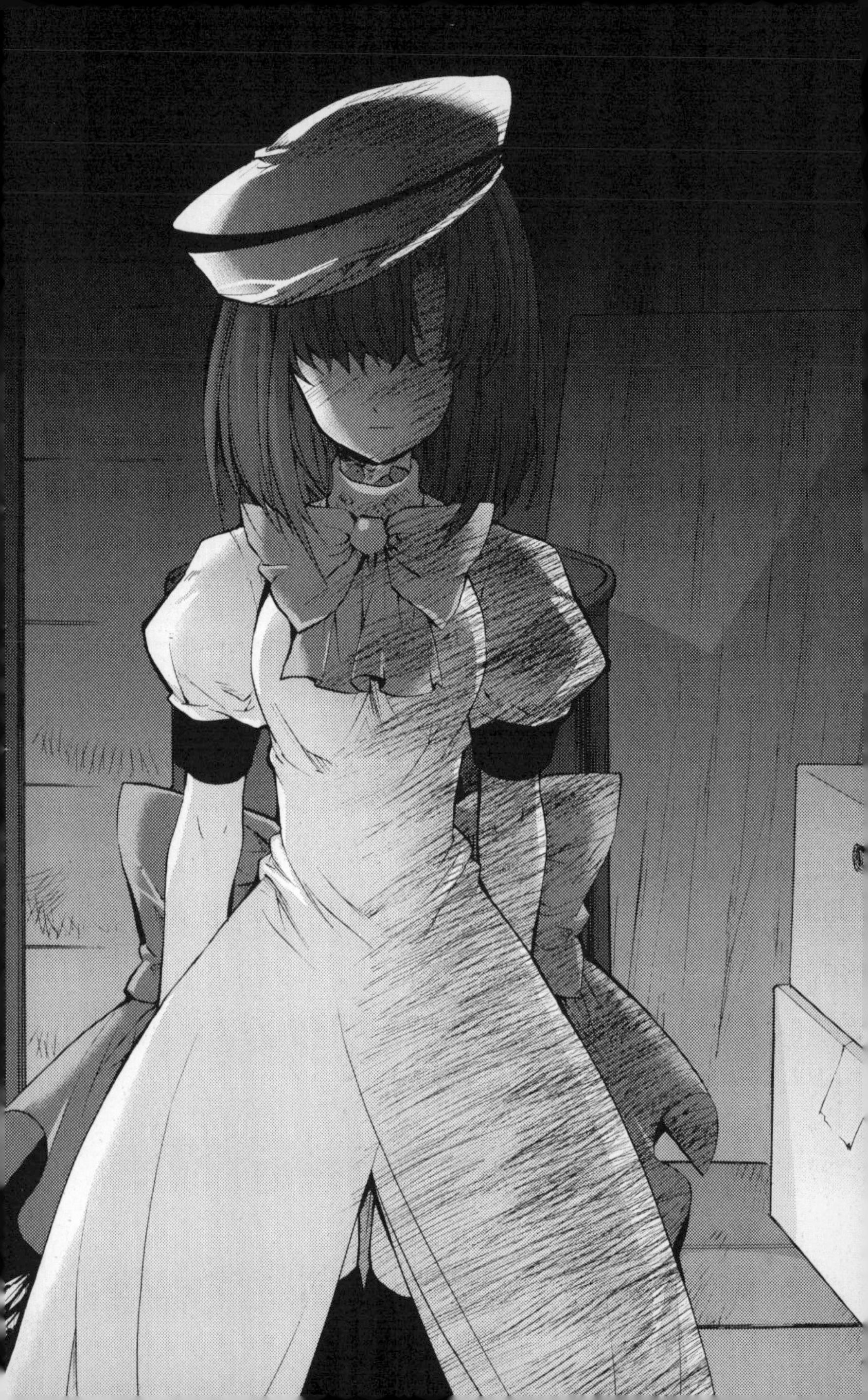

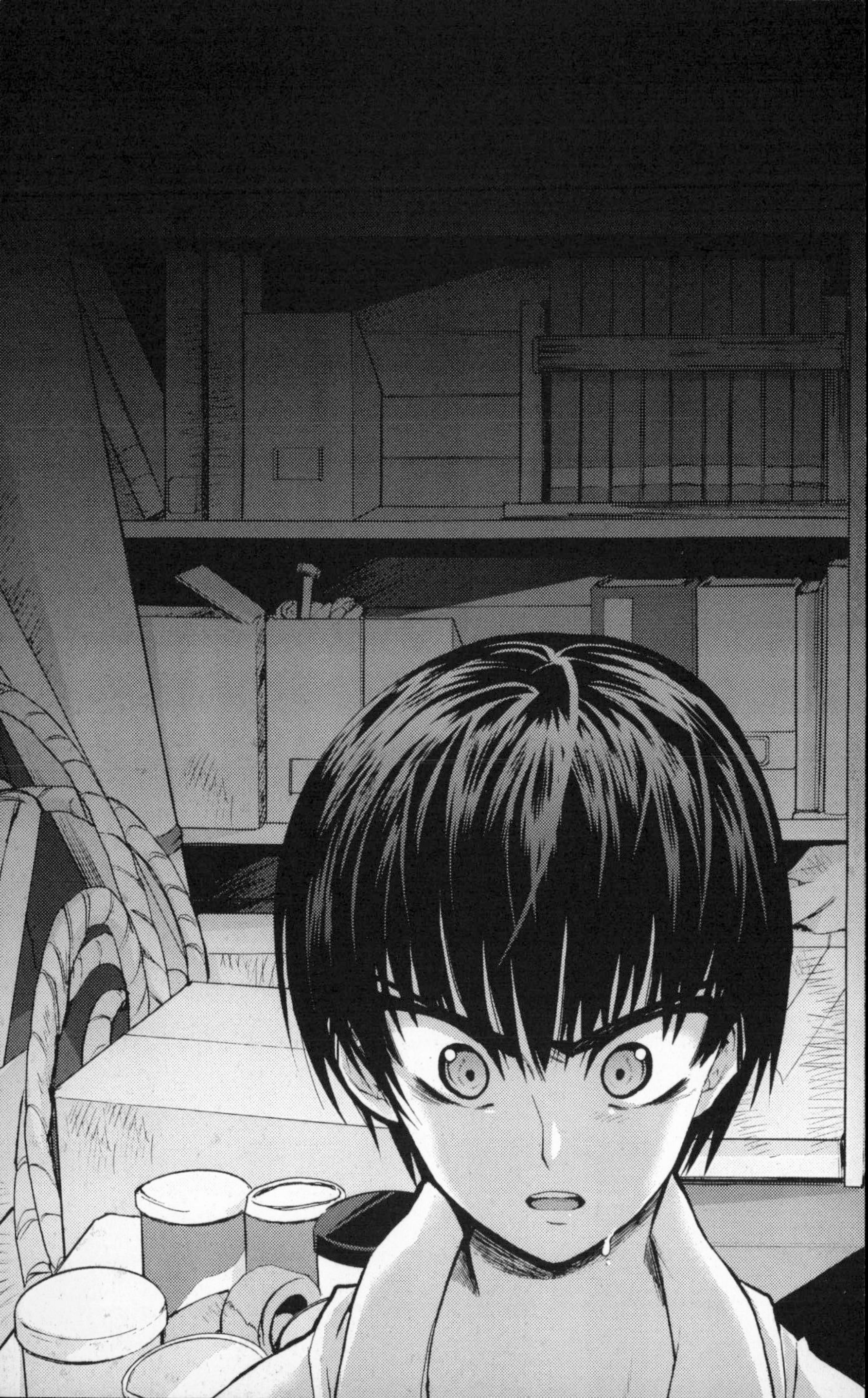

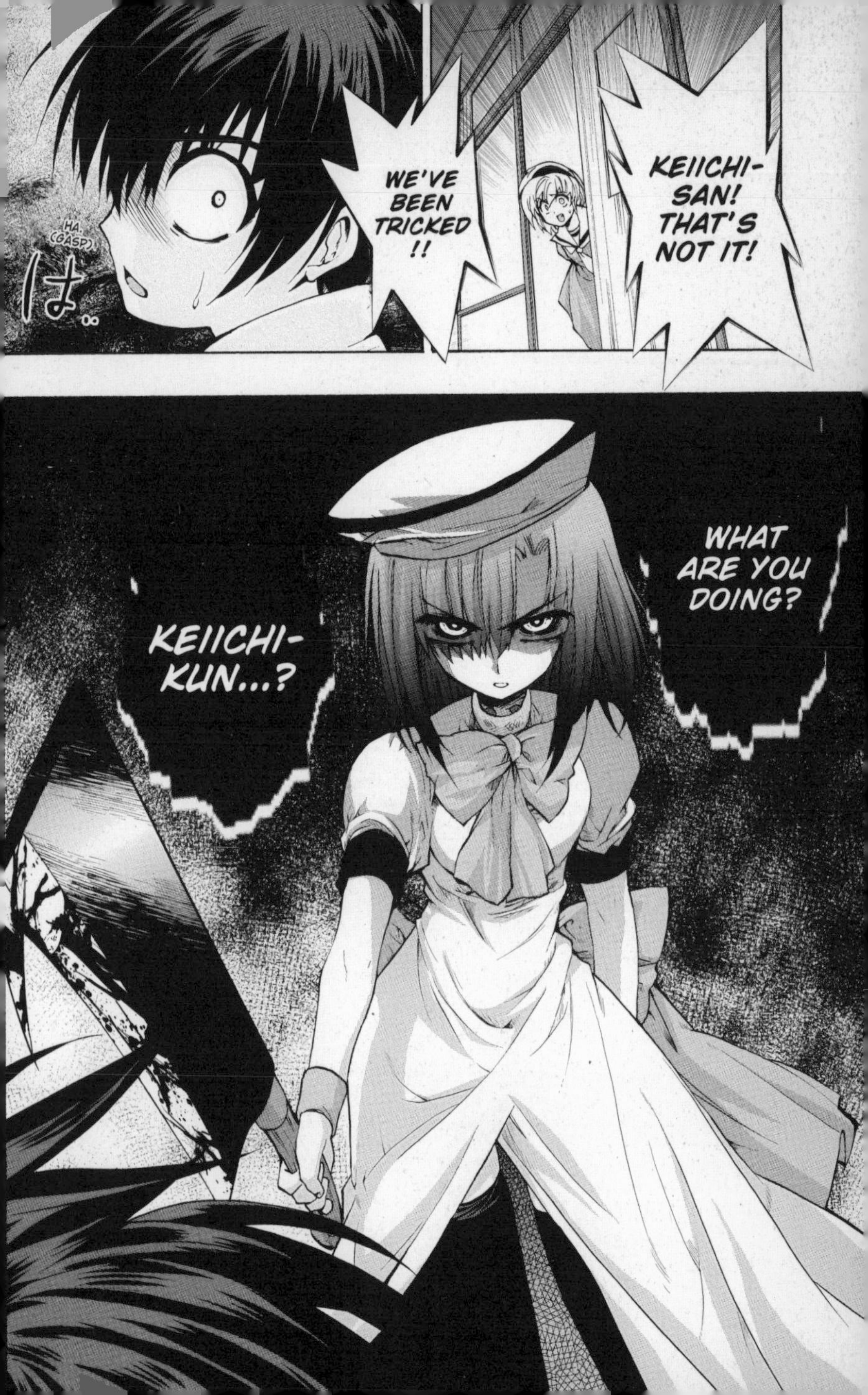
KEIICHI-SAN! THAT'S NOT IT!
WE'VE BEEN TRICKED!!
HA. (GASP)
は。
WHAT ARE YOU DOING?
KEIICHI-KUN...?

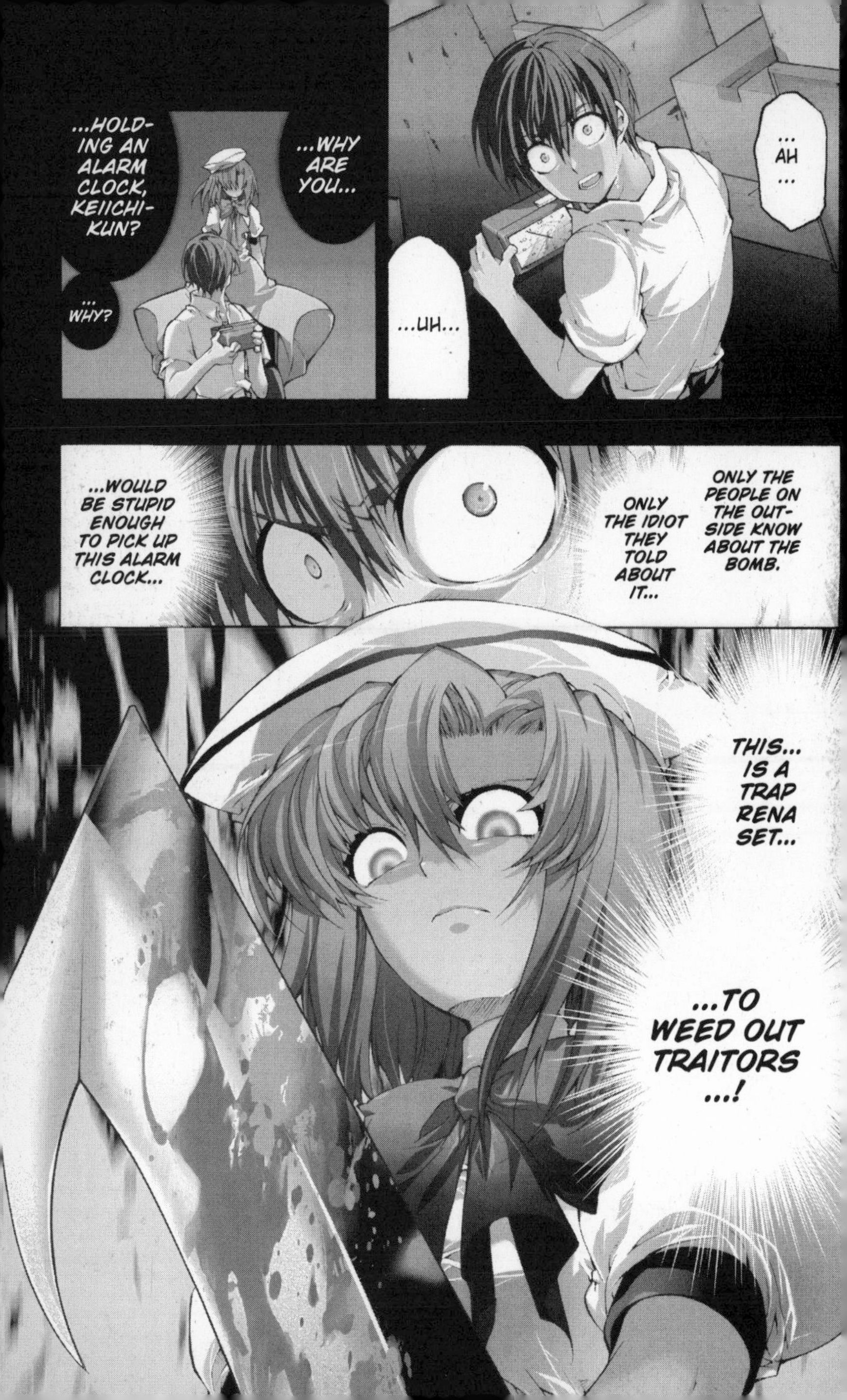
...AH...
...UH...
...WHY ARE YOU...
...HOLDING AN ALARM CLOCK, KEIICHI-KUN?
...WHY?
ONLY THE PEOPLE ON THE OUTSIDE KNOW ABOUT THE BOMB.
ONLY THE IDIOT THEY TOLD ABOUT IT...
...WOULD BE STUPID ENOUGH TO PICK UP THIS ALARM CLOCK...
THIS... IS A TRAP RENA SET...
...TO WEED OUT TRAITORS ...!

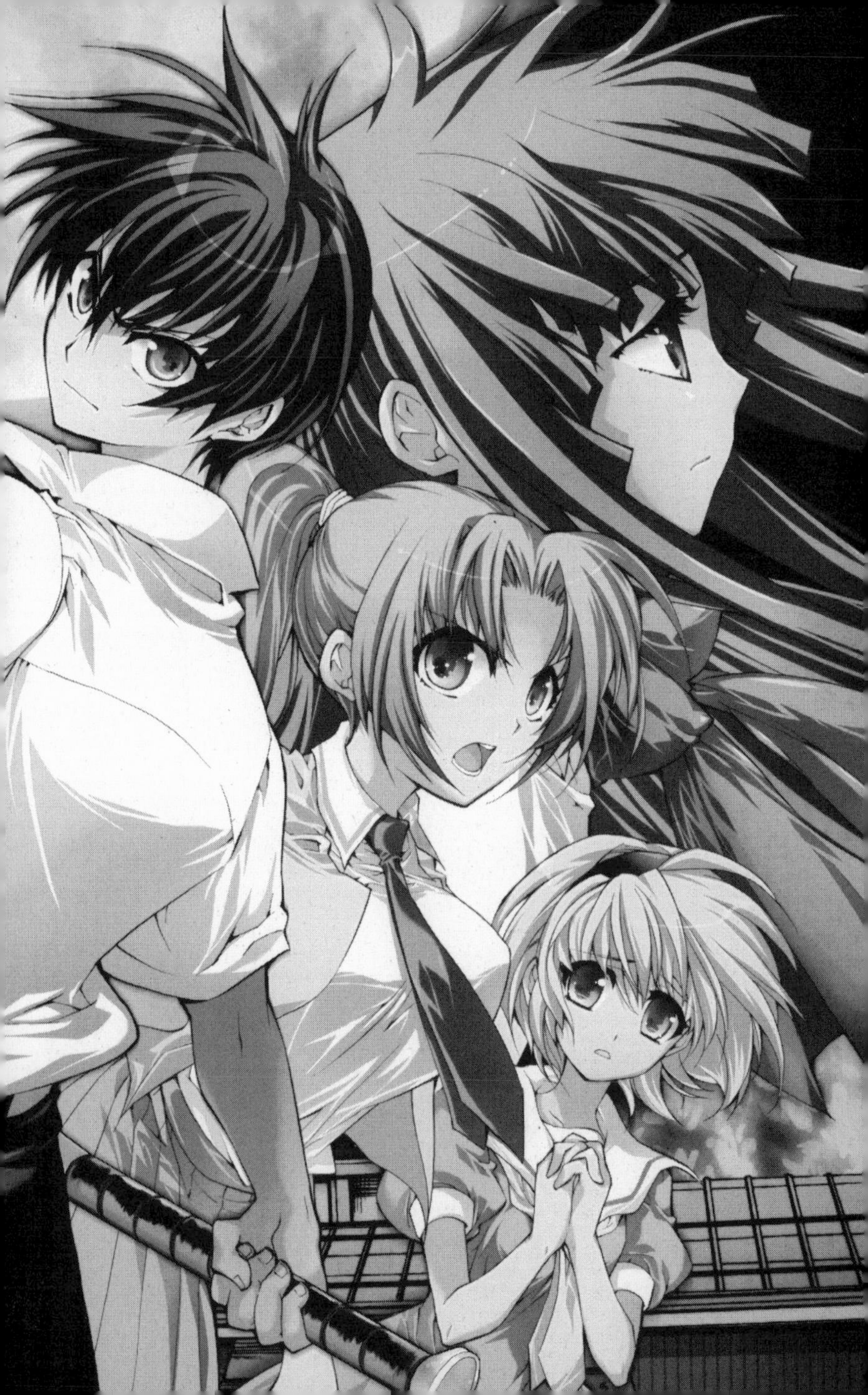

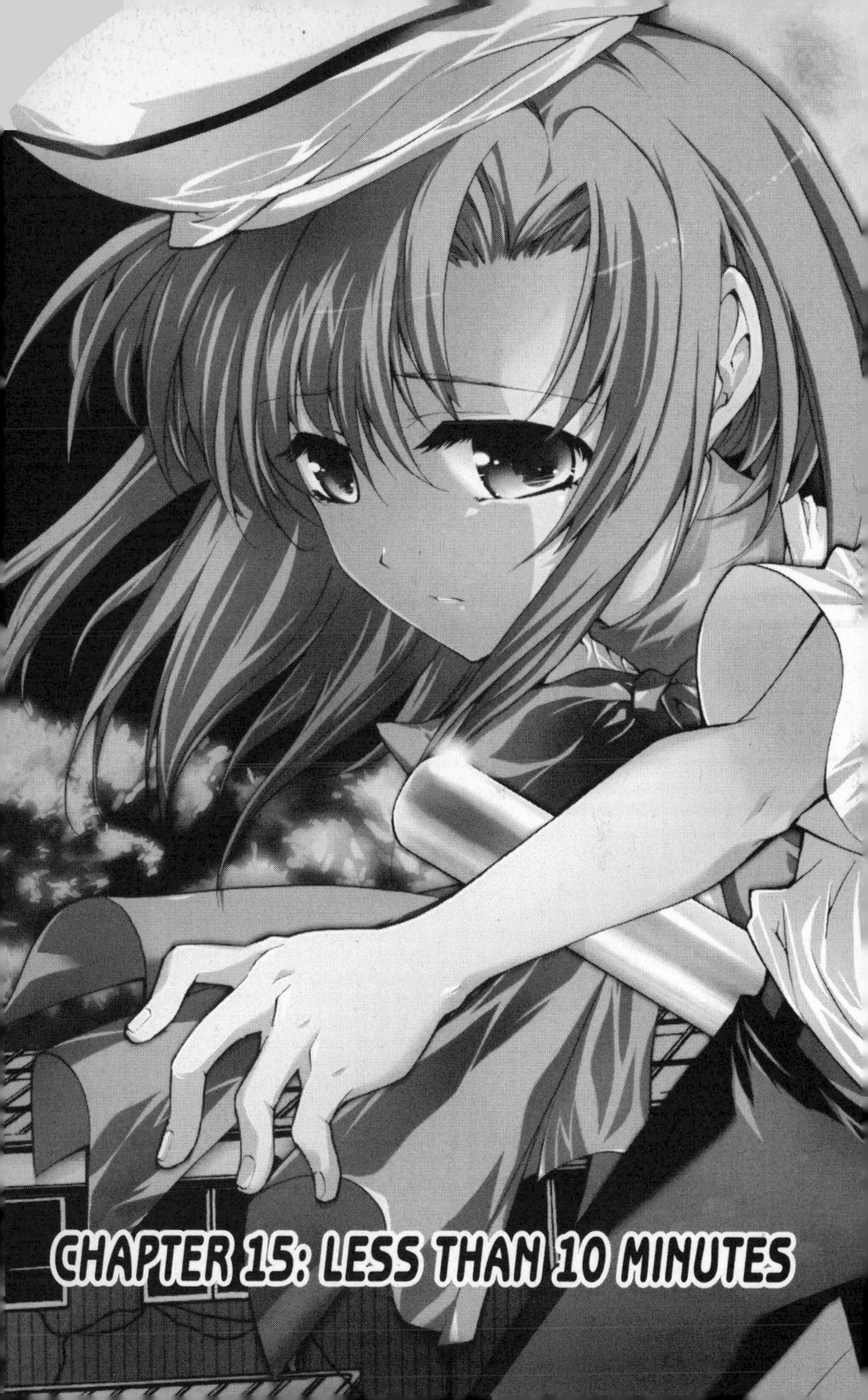

CHAPTER 15: LESS THAN 10 MINUTES

Higurashi
WHEN THEY CRY
ATONEMENT ARC

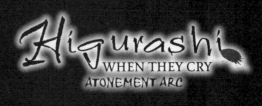

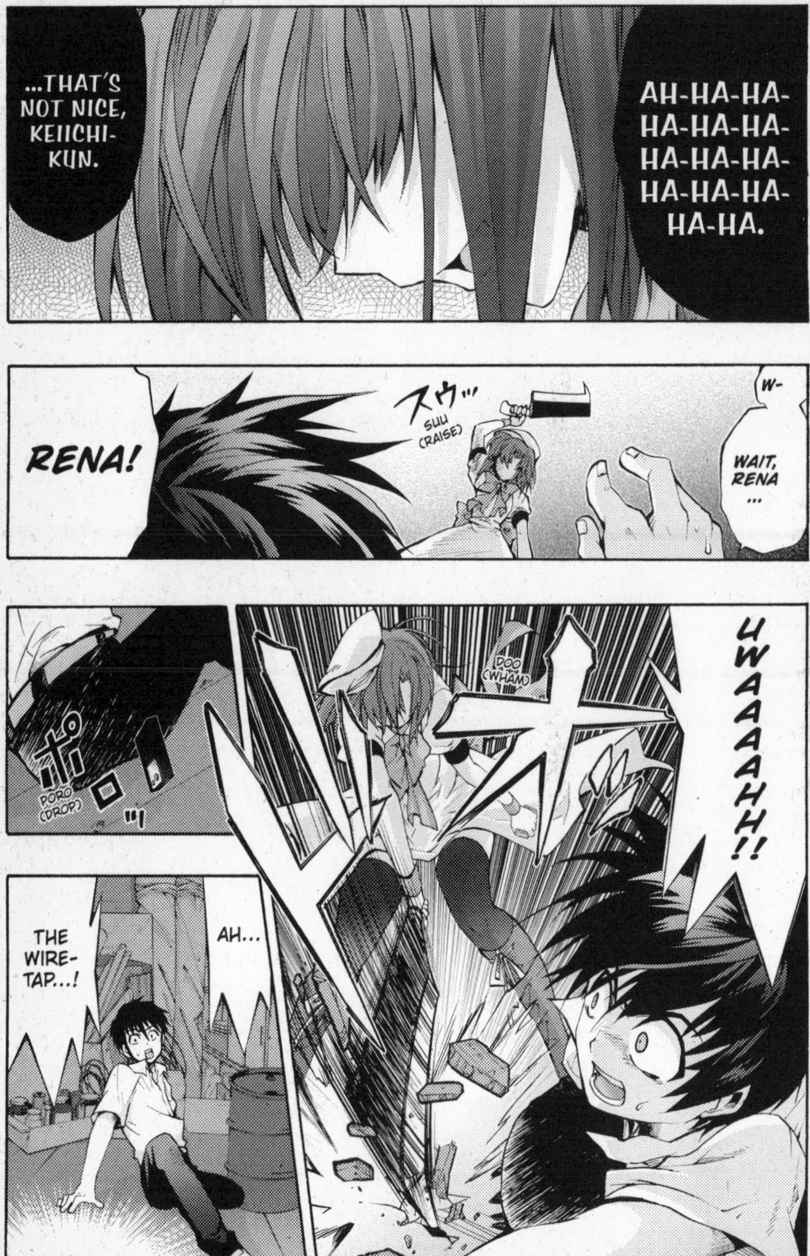
AH-HA-HA-HA-HA-HA-HA-HA-HA-HA-HA-HA-HA-HA.
...THAT'S NOT NICE, KEIICHI-KUN.
W-
WAIT, RENA...
スウッ
SUU (RAISE)
RENA!
UWAAAAAHH!!
DOO (WHAM)
ポロッ
PORO (DROP)
AH...
THE WIRE-TAP...!

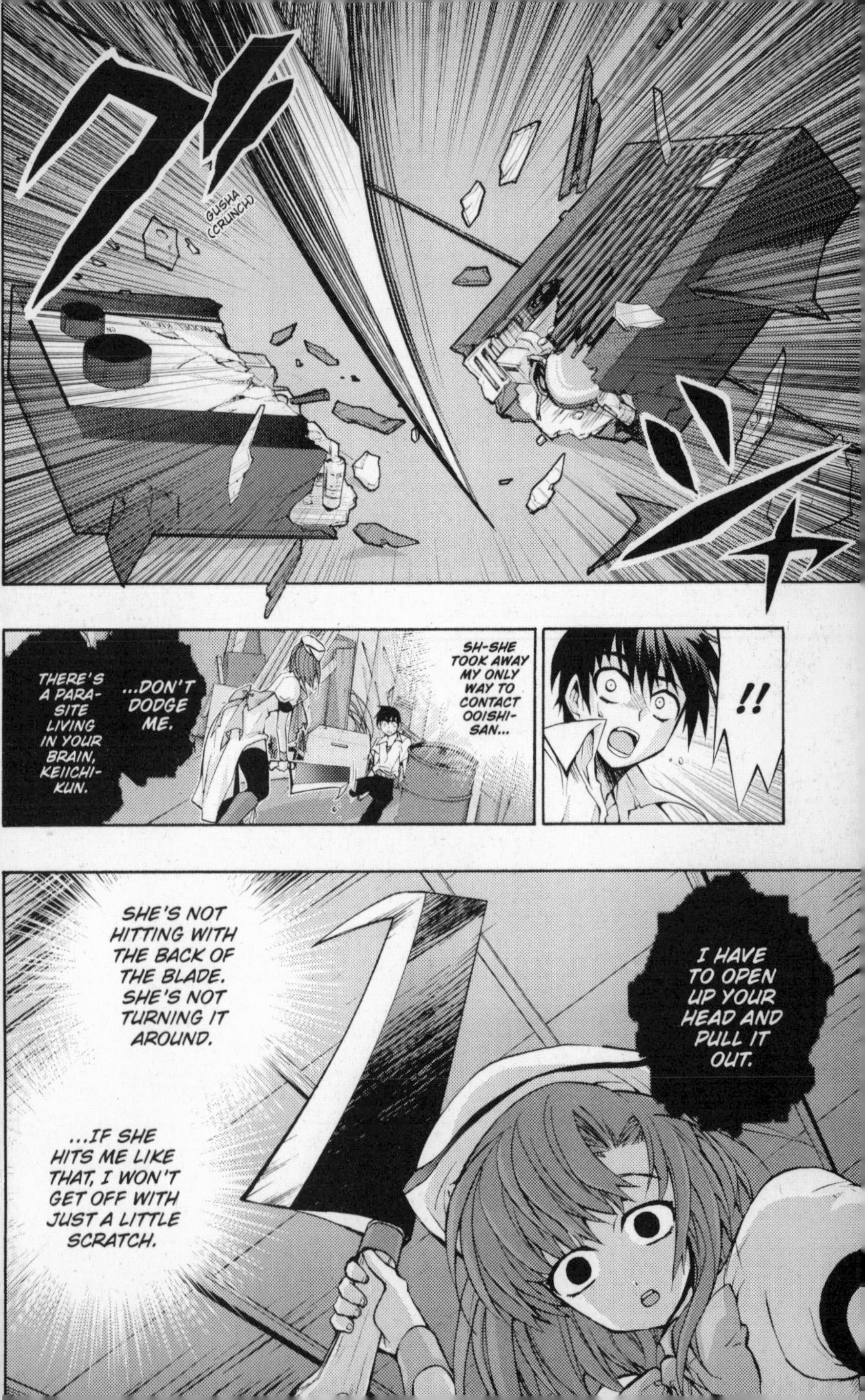
GUSHA (CRUNCH)
!!
SH-SHE TOOK AWAY MY ONLY WAY TO CONTACT OOISHI-SAN...
...DON'T DODGE ME.
THERE'S A PARASITE LIVING IN YOUR BRAIN, KEIICHI-KUN.
I HAVE TO OPEN UP YOUR HEAD AND PULL IT OUT.
SHE'S NOT HITTING WITH THE BACK OF THE BLADE. SHE'S NOT TURNING IT AROUND.
...IF SHE HITS ME LIKE THAT, I WON'T GET OFF WITH JUST A LITTLE SCRATCH.

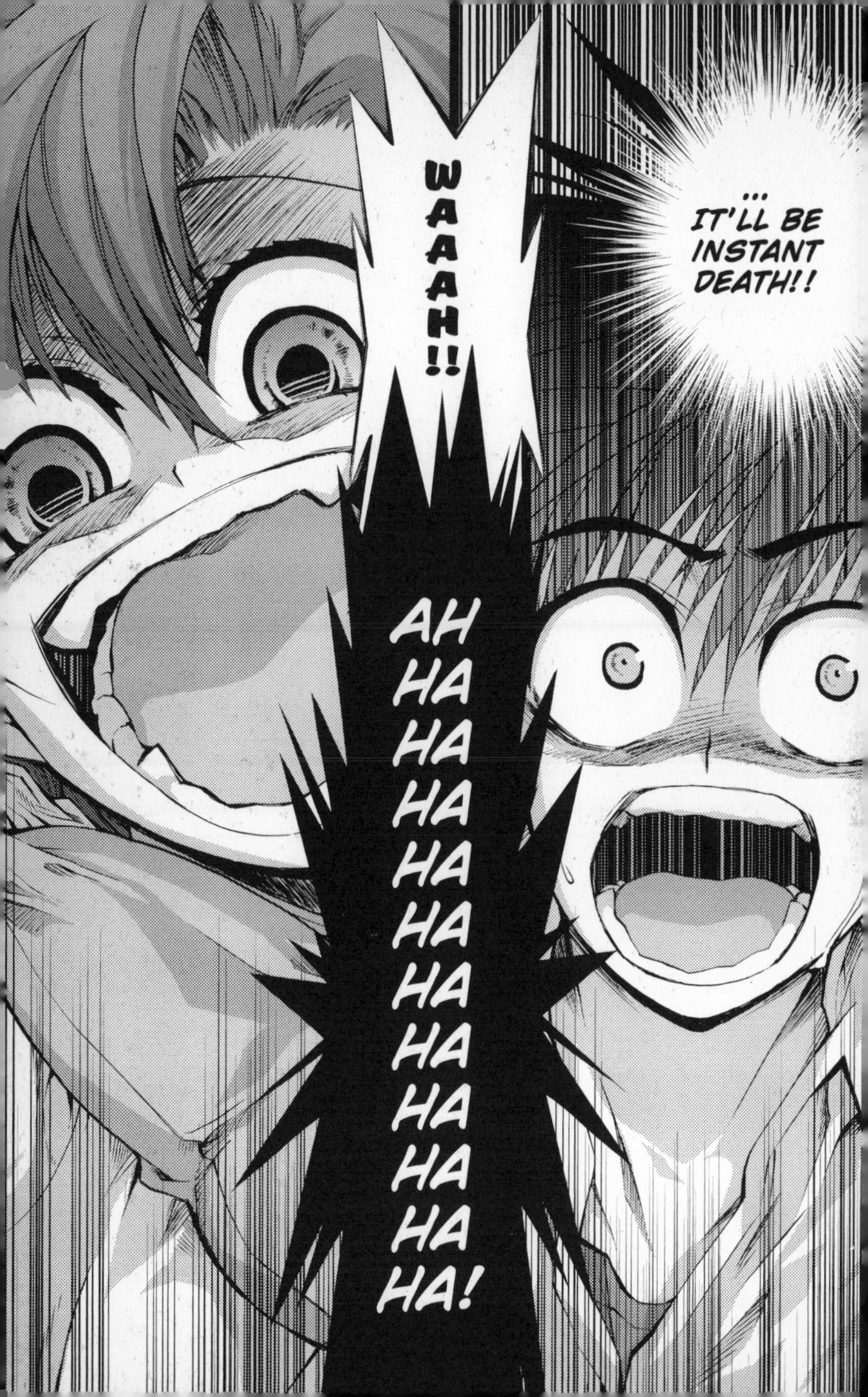
...IT'LL BE INSTANT DEATH!!
WAAAH!!
AH HA HA HA HA HA HA HA HA HA HA HA HA!

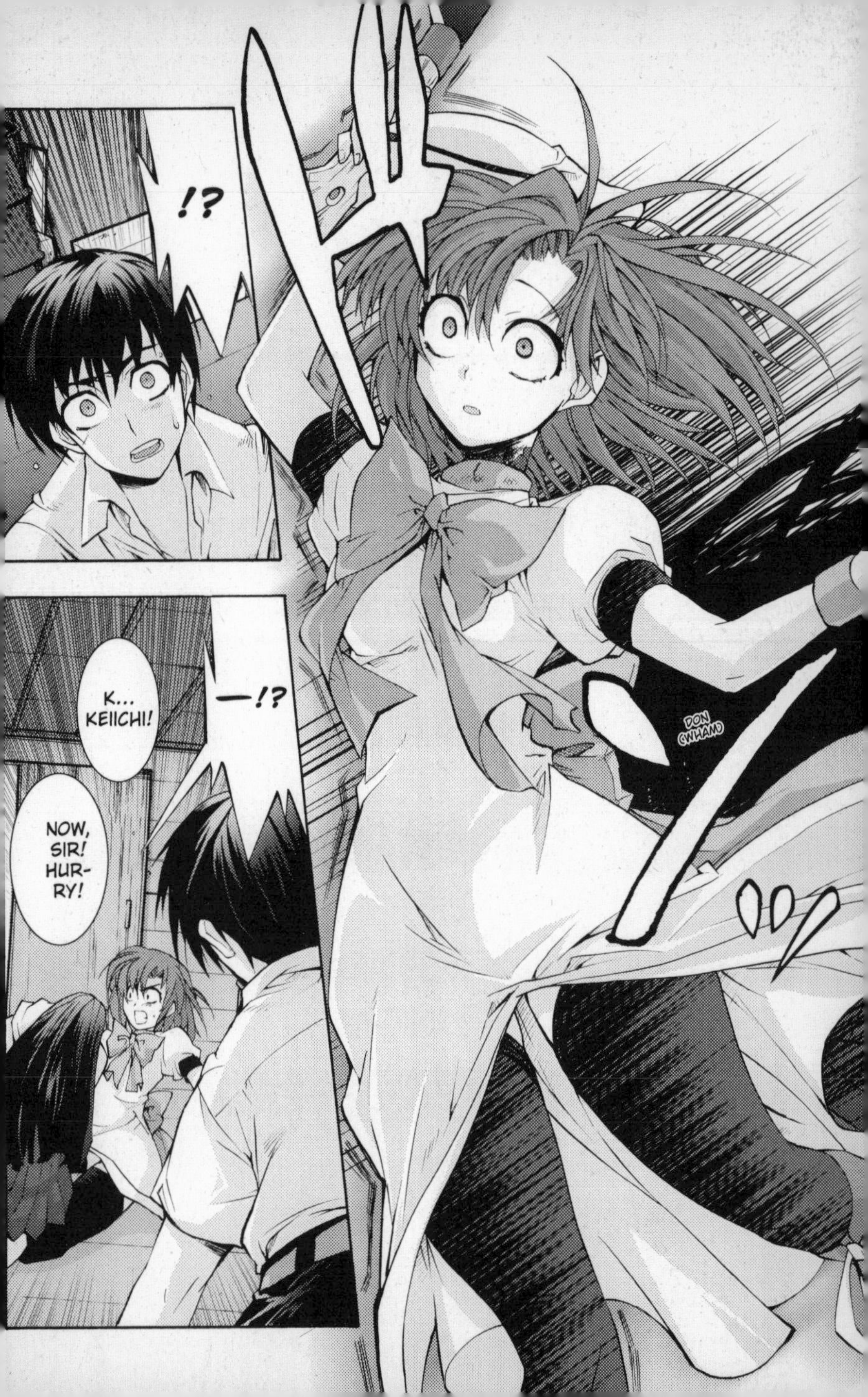
DON (WHAM)
!?
—!?
K... KEIICHI!
NOW, SIR! HURRY!

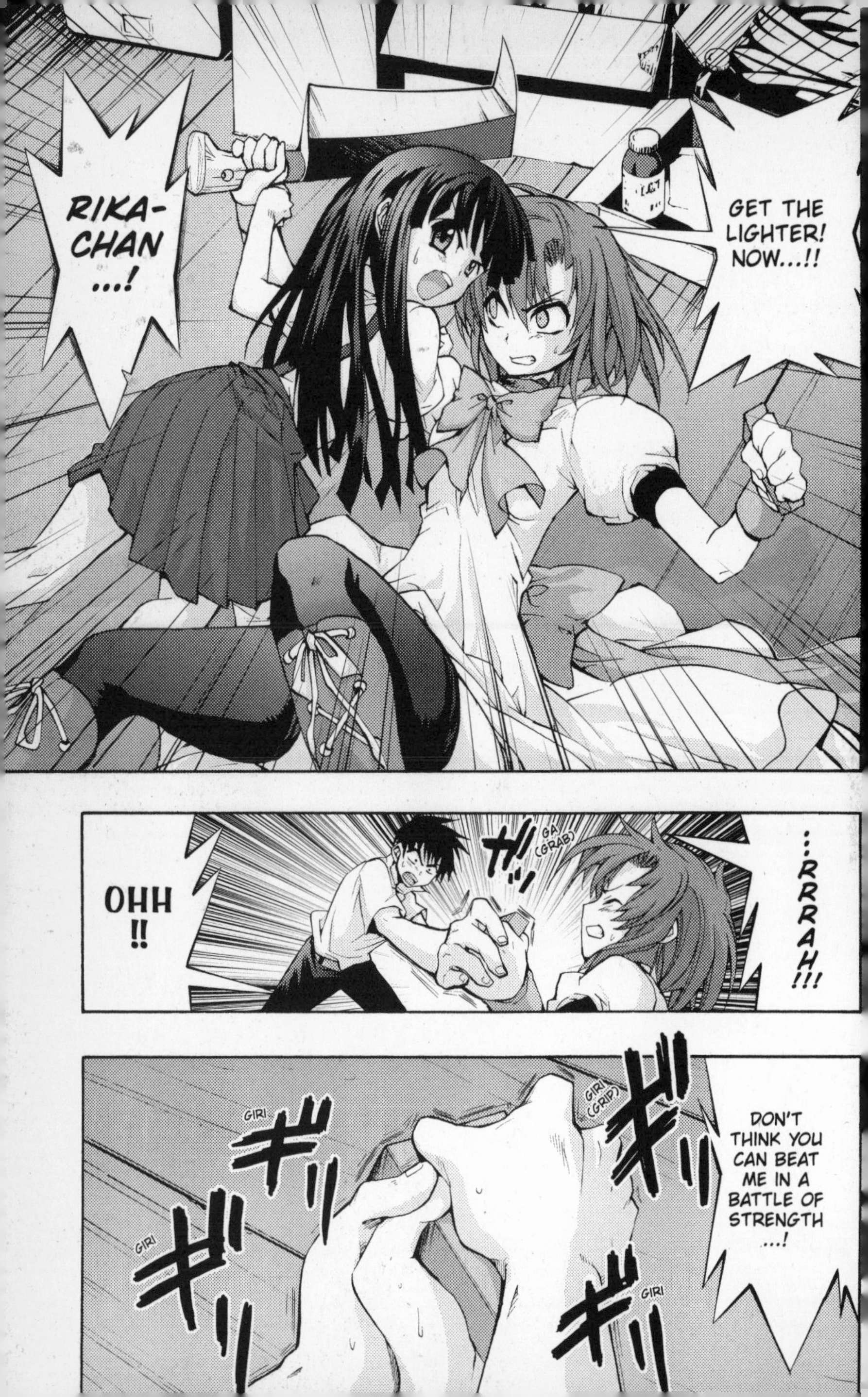
GET THE LIGHTER! NOW...!!
RIKA-CHAN ...!
...RRRAH!!!
GA (GRAB)
OHH !!
DON'T THINK YOU CAN BEAT ME IN A BATTLE OF STRENGTH ...!
GIRI (GRIP)
GIRI
GIRI
GIRI

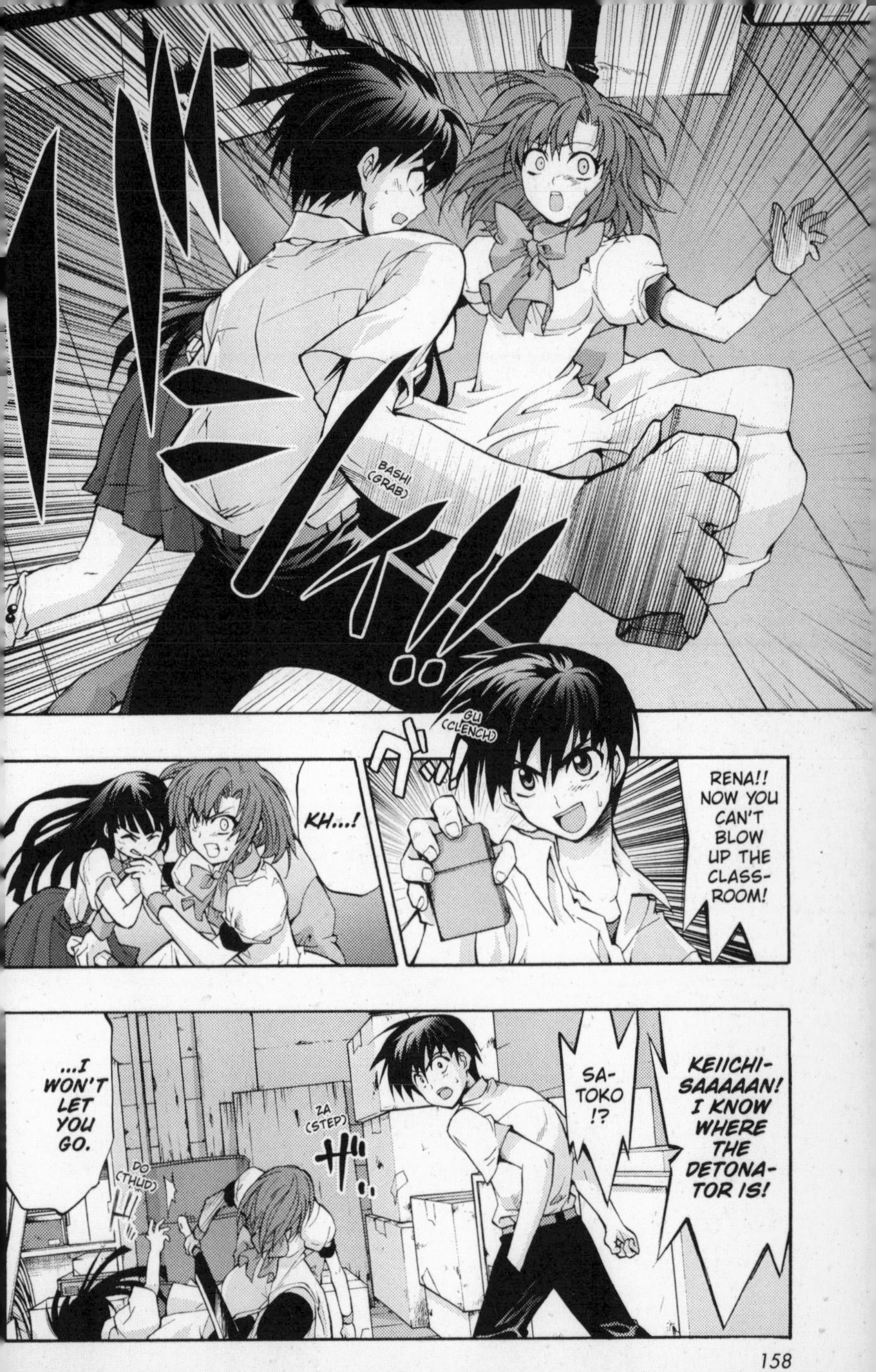
BASHI (GRAB)
GU (CLENCH)
RENA!! NOW YOU CAN'T BLOW UP THE CLASS-ROOM!
KH...!
KEIICHI-SAAAAAN! I KNOW WHERE THE DETONA-TOR IS!
SA-TOKO!?
ZA (STEP)
...I WON'T LET YOU GO.
DO (THUD)

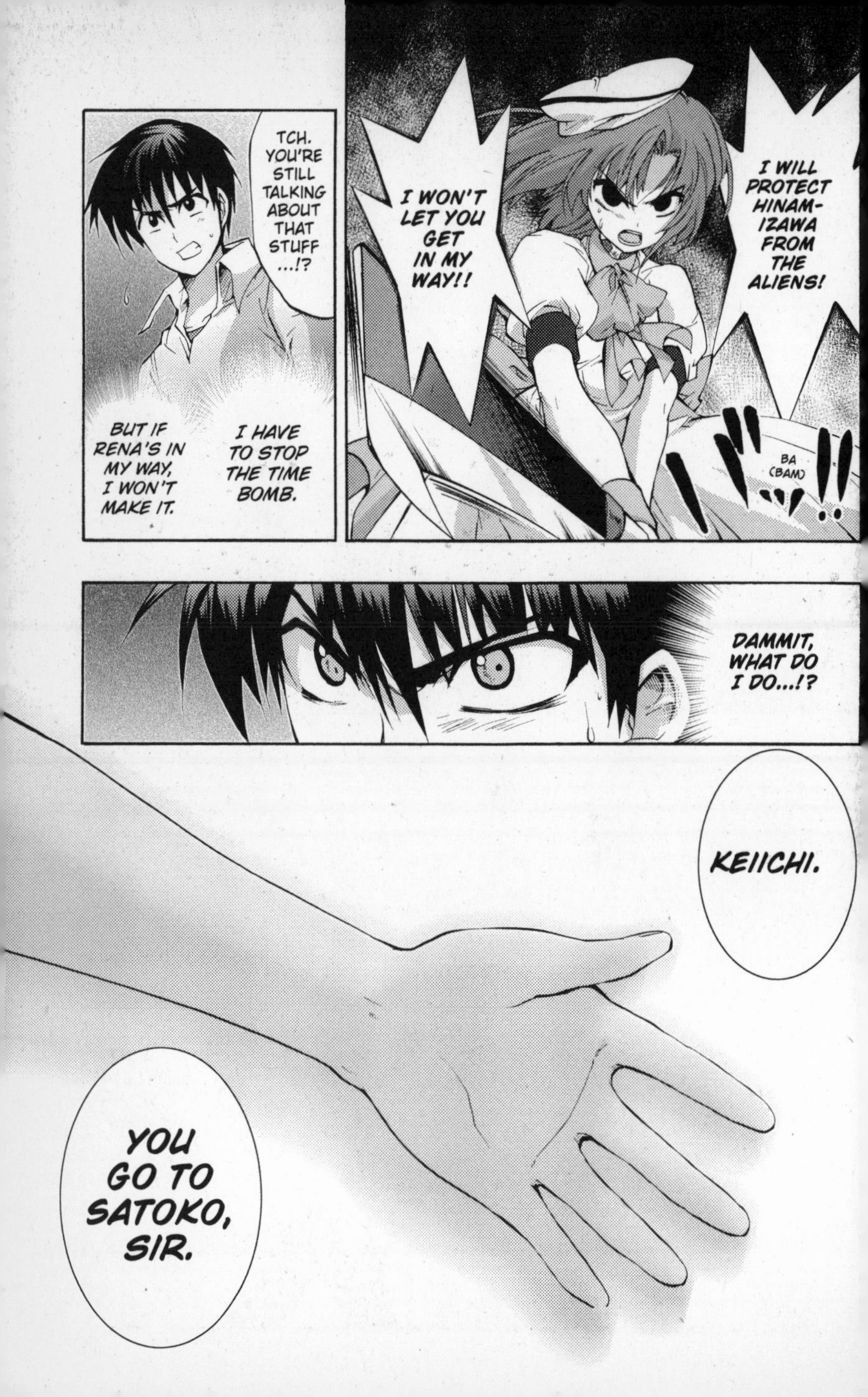
I WILL PROTECT HINAMIZAWA FROM THE ALIENS!
I WON'T LET YOU GET IN MY WAY!!
BA (BAM)
TCH. YOU'RE STILL TALKING ABOUT THAT STUFF...!?
I HAVE TO STOP THE TIME BOMB.
BUT IF RENA'S IN MY WAY, I WON'T MAKE IT.
DAMMIT, WHAT DO I DO...!?
KEIICHI.
YOU GO TO SATOKO, SIR.

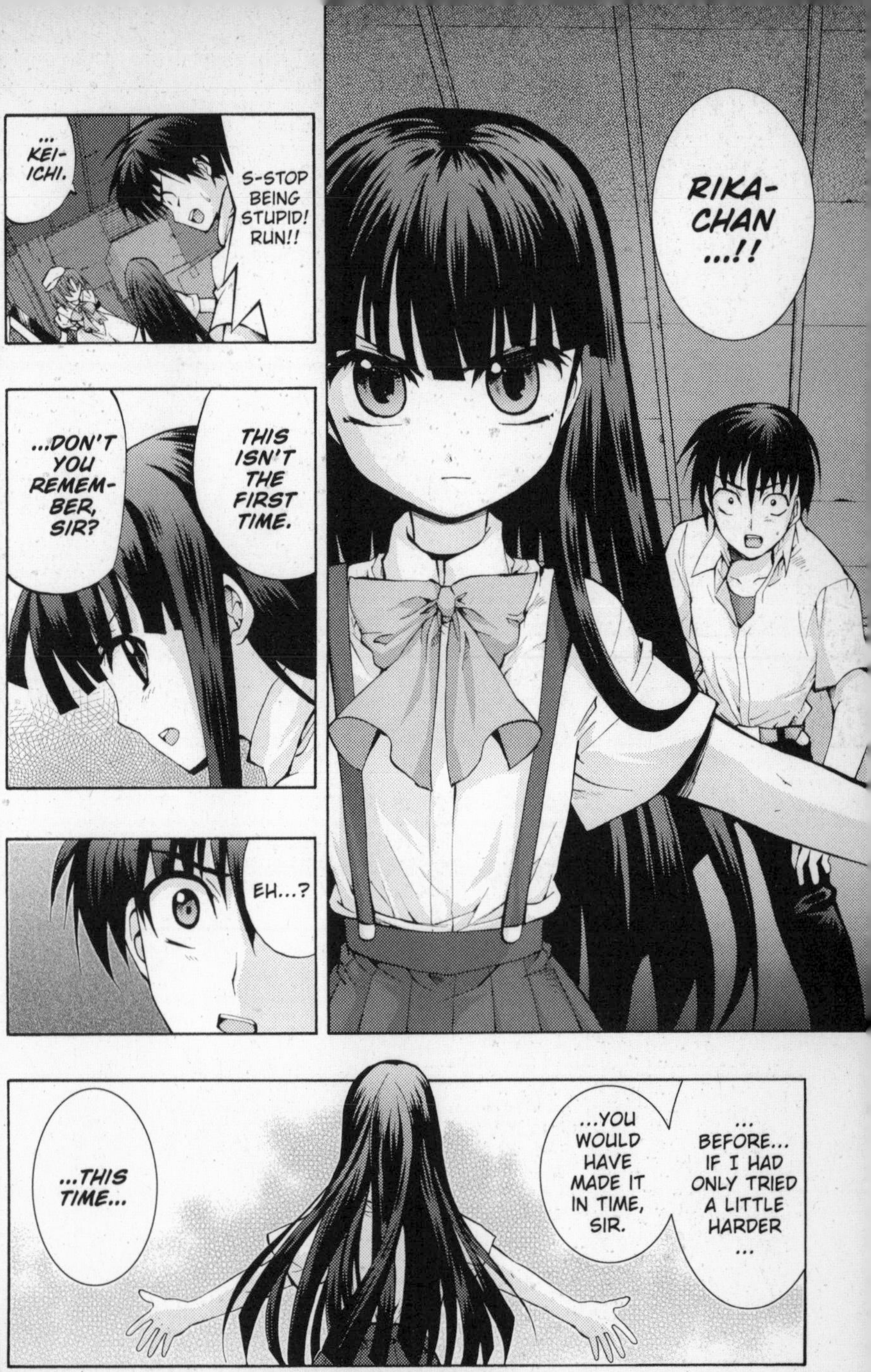
RIKA-CHAN ...!!
S-STOP BEING STUPID! RUN!!
... KEI-ICHI.
THIS ISN'T THE FIRST TIME.
...DON'T YOU REMEMBER, SIR?
EH...?
... BEFORE... IF I HAD ONLY TRIED A LITTLE HARDER ...
...YOU WOULD HAVE MADE IT IN TIME, SIR.
...THIS TIME...

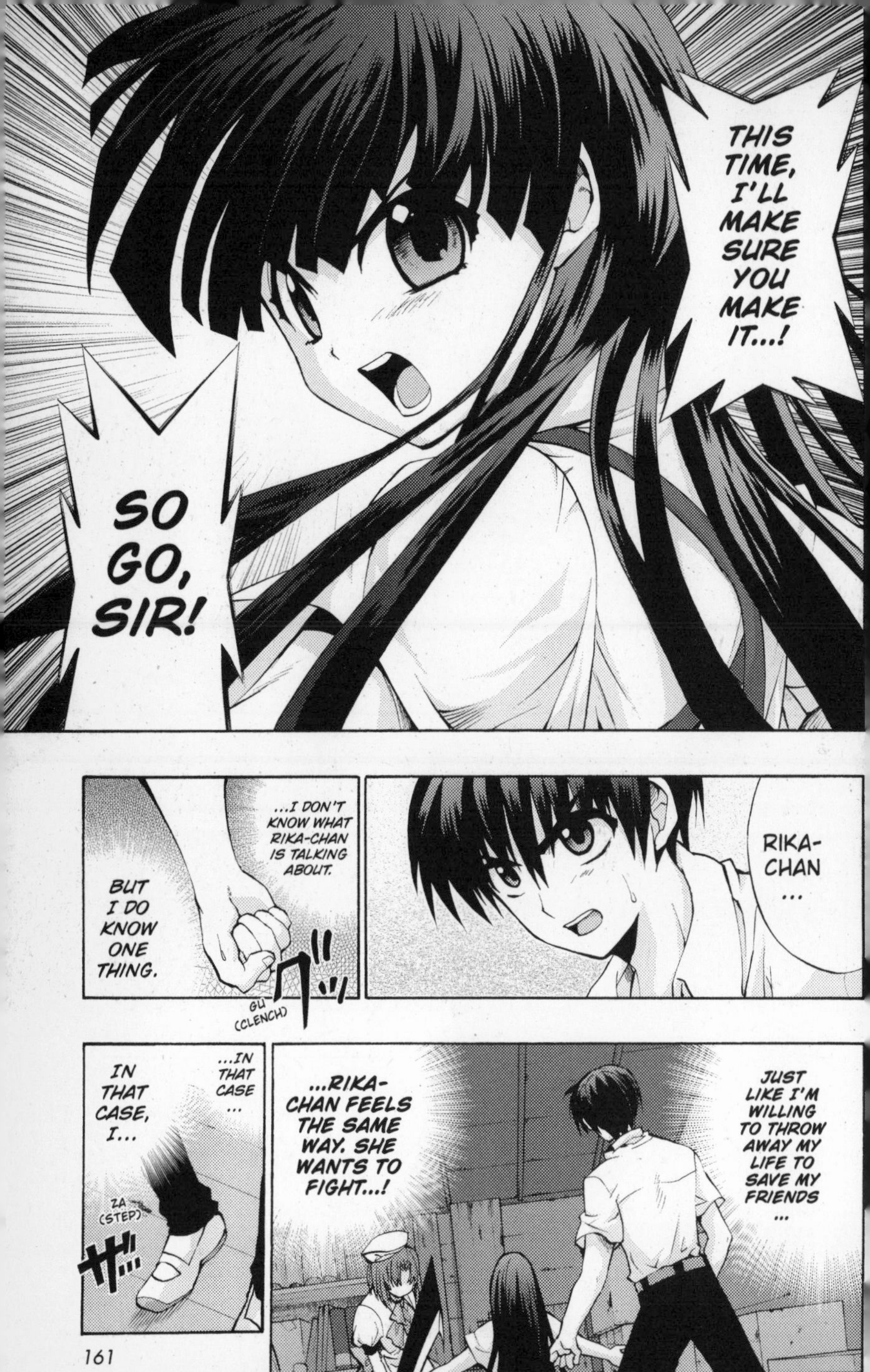
THIS TIME, I'LL MAKE SURE YOU MAKE IT...!
SO GO, SIR!
RIKA-CHAN ...
...I DON'T KNOW WHAT RIKA-CHAN IS TALKING ABOUT.
BUT I DO KNOW ONE THING.
GU (CLENCH)
JUST LIKE I'M WILLING TO THROW AWAY MY LIFE TO SAVE MY FRIENDS ...
...RIKA-CHAN FEELS THE SAME WAY. SHE WANTS TO FIGHT...!
...IN THAT CASE ...
IN THAT CASE, I...
ZA (STEP)

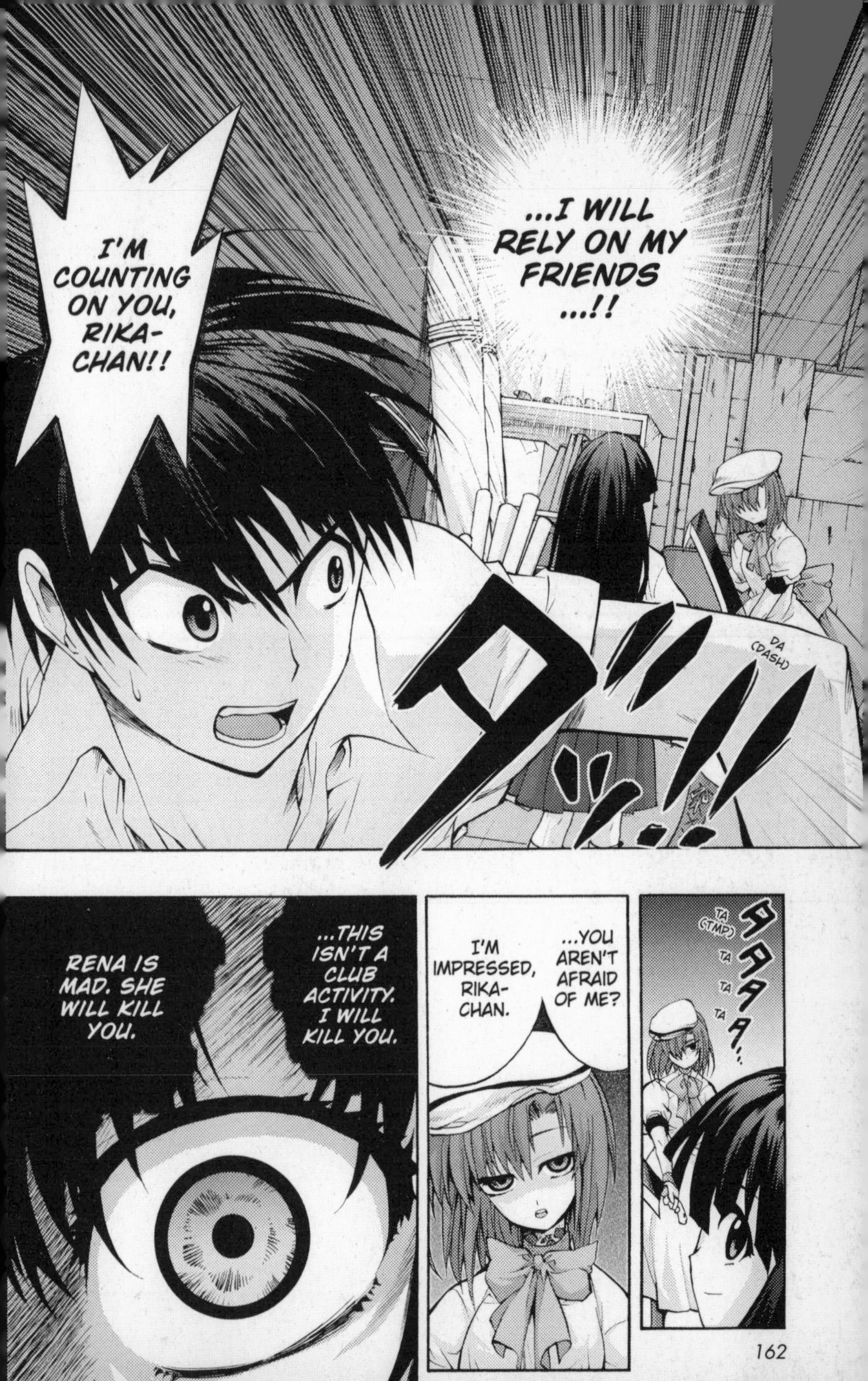
...I WILL RELY ON MY FRIENDS ...!!
I'M COUNTING ON YOU, RIKA-CHAN!!
DA (DASH)
TA (TMP) TA TA TA
...YOU AREN'T AFRAID OF ME?
I'M IMPRESSED, RIKA-CHAN.
...THIS ISN'T A CLUB ACTIVITY. I WILL KILL YOU.
RENA IS MAD. SHE WILL KILL YOU.

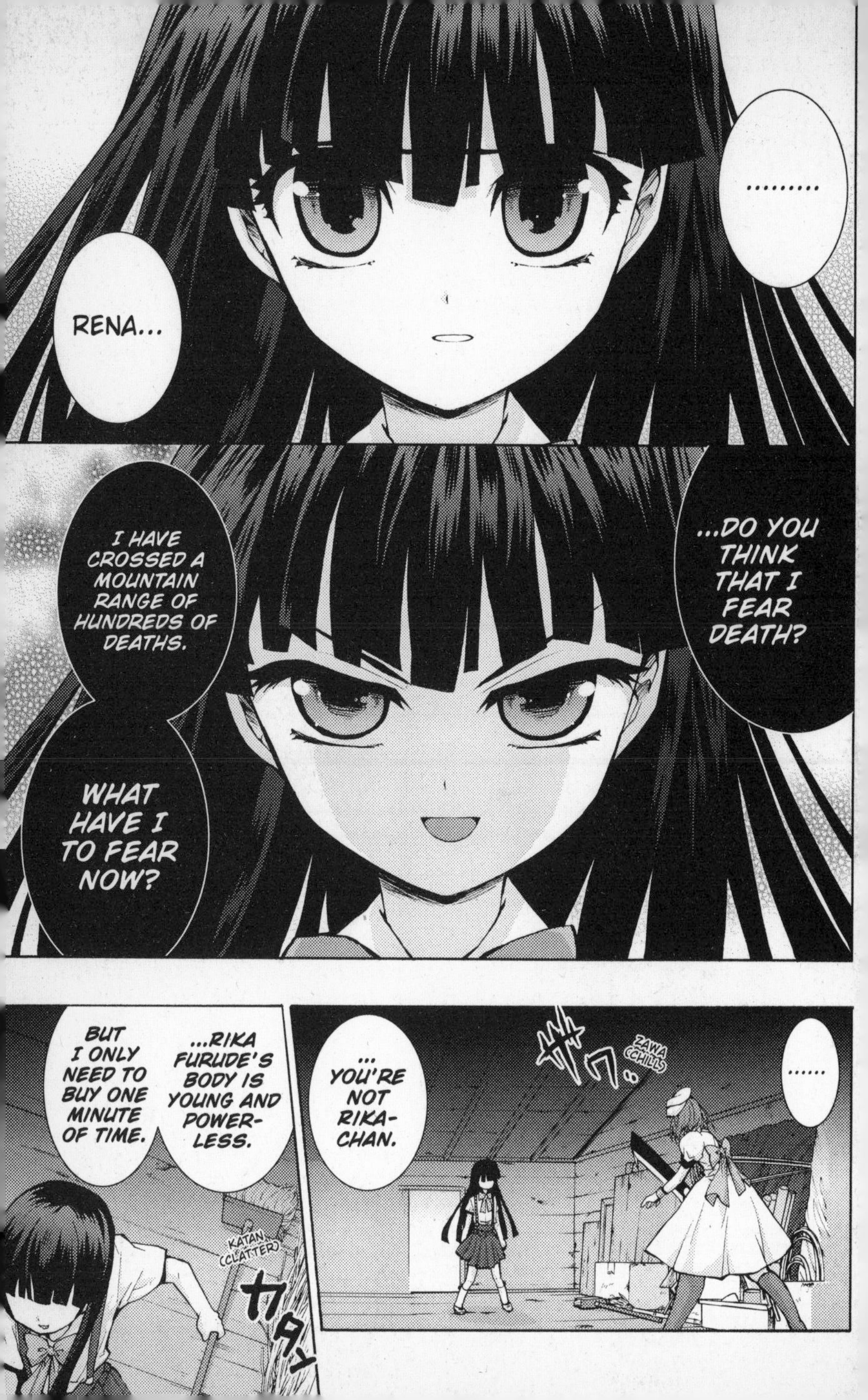
....
RENA...
...DO YOU THINK THAT I FEAR DEATH?
I HAVE CROSSED A MOUNTAIN RANGE OF HUNDREDS OF DEATHS.
WHAT HAVE I TO FEAR NOW?
......
ZAWA (CHILL)
... YOU'RE NOT RIKA-CHAN.
...RIKA FURUDE'S BODY IS YOUNG AND POWER-LESS.
BUT I ONLY NEED TO BUY ONE MINUTE OF TIME.
KATAN (CLATTER)

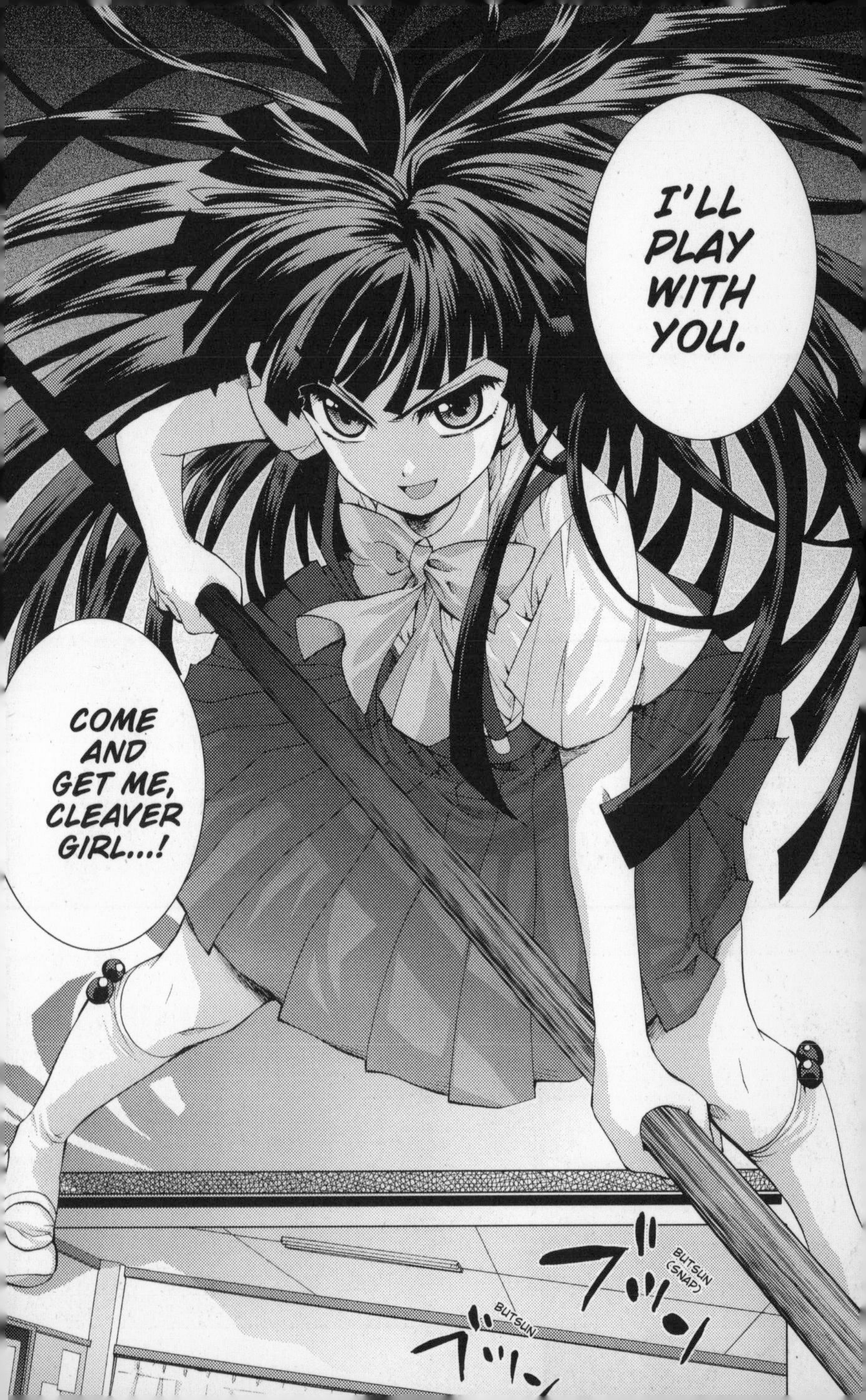
I'LL PLAY WITH YOU.
COME AND GET ME, CLEAVER GIRL...!
BUTSUN (SNAP)
BUTSUN

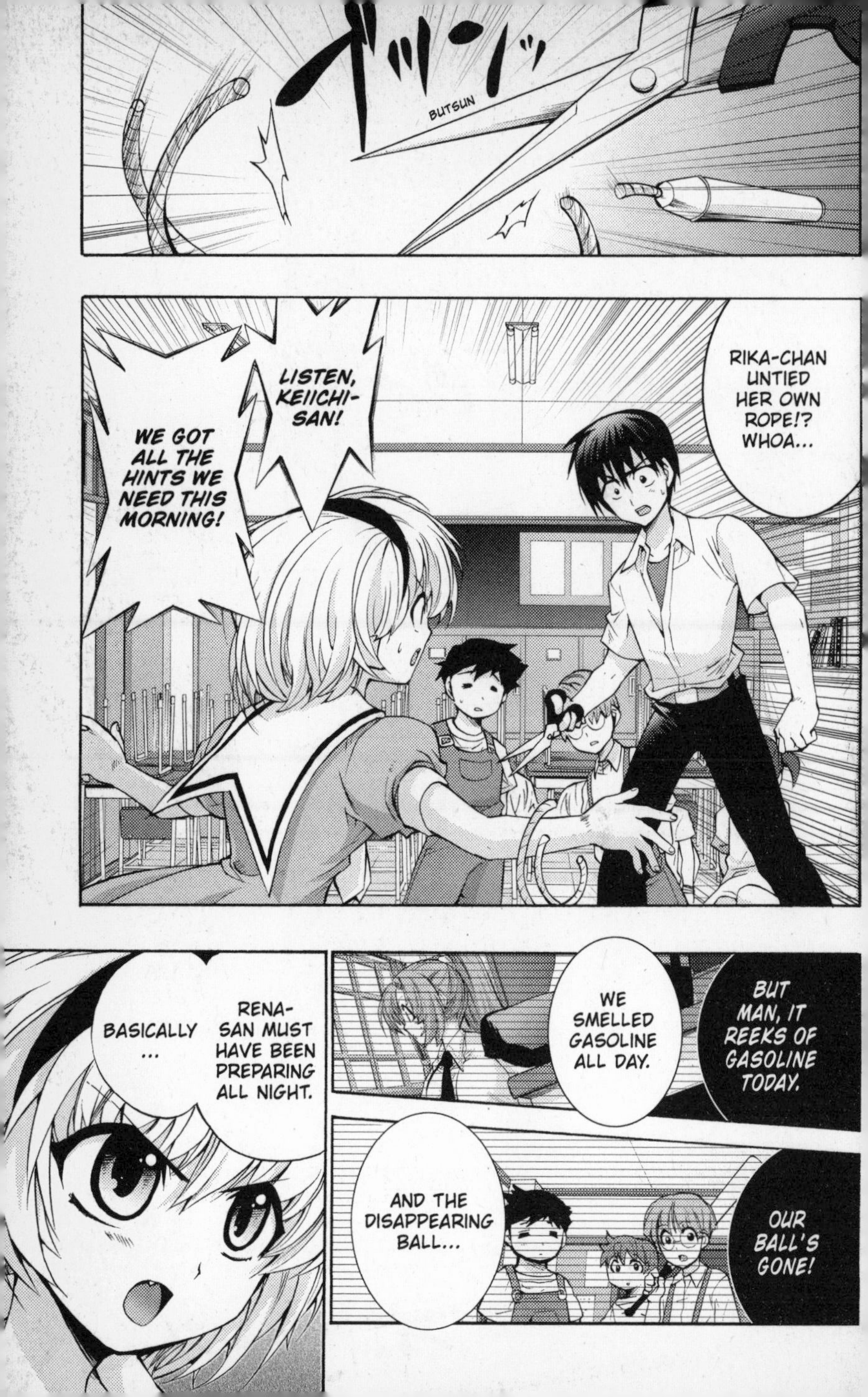
BUTSUN
RIKA-CHAN UNTIED HER OWN ROPE!? WHOA...
LISTEN, KEIICHI-SAN!
WE GOT ALL THE HINTS WE NEED THIS MORNING!
BUT MAN, IT REEKS OF GASOLINE TODAY.
WE SMELLED GASOLINE ALL DAY.
OUR BALL'S GONE!
AND THE DISAPPEARING BALL...
BASICALLY ...
RENA-SAN MUST HAVE BEEN PREPARING ALL NIGHT.

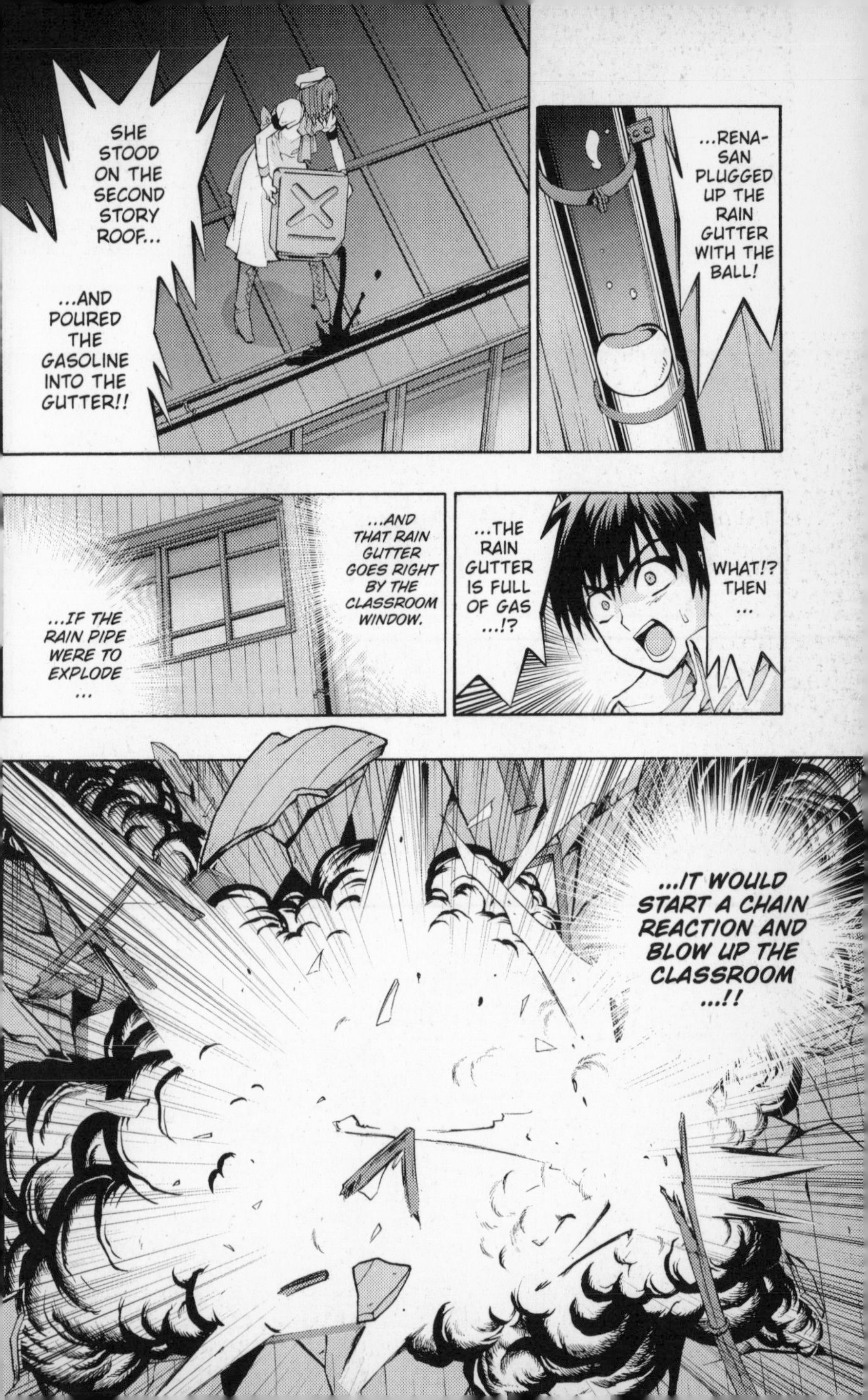
...RENA-SAN PLUGGED UP THE RAIN GUTTER WITH THE BALL!
SHE STOOD ON THE SECOND STORY ROOF...
...AND POURED THE GASOLINE INTO THE GUTTER!!
WHAT!? THEN ...
...THE RAIN GUTTER IS FULL OF GAS ...!?
...AND THAT RAIN GUTTER GOES RIGHT BY THE CLASSROOM WINDOW.
...IF THE RAIN PIPE WERE TO EXPLODE ...
...IT WOULD START A CHAIN REACTION AND BLOW UP THE CLASSROOM ...!!

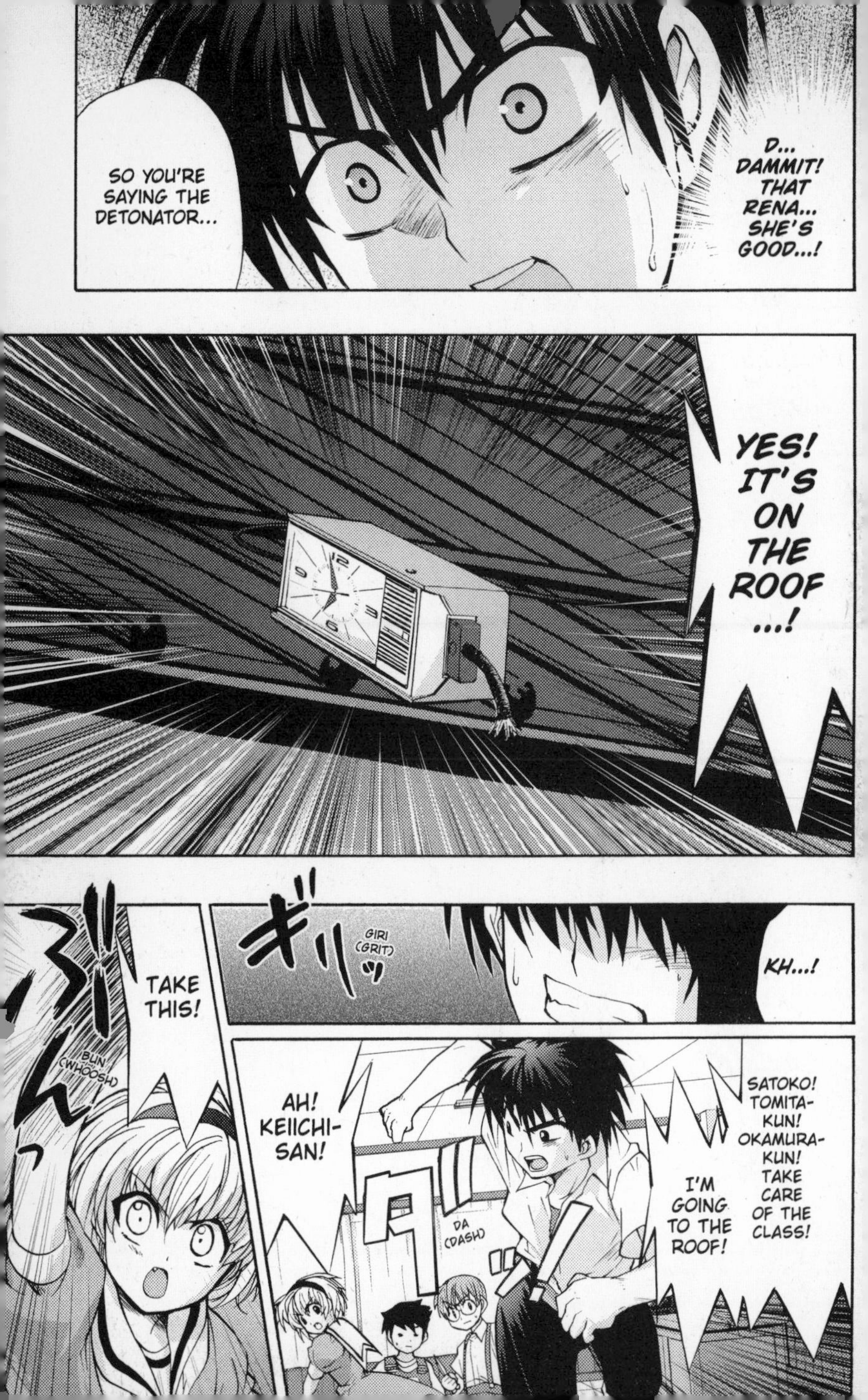
D... DAMMIT! THAT RENA... SHE'S GOOD...!
SO YOU'RE SAYING THE DETONATOR...
YES! IT'S ON THE ROOF ...!
KH...!
GIRI (GRIT)
SATOKO! TOMITA-KUN! OKAMURA-KUN! TAKE CARE OF THE CLASS!
I'M GOING TO THE ROOF!
DA (DASH)
AH! KEIICHI-SAN!
TAKE THIS!
BUN (WHOOSH)

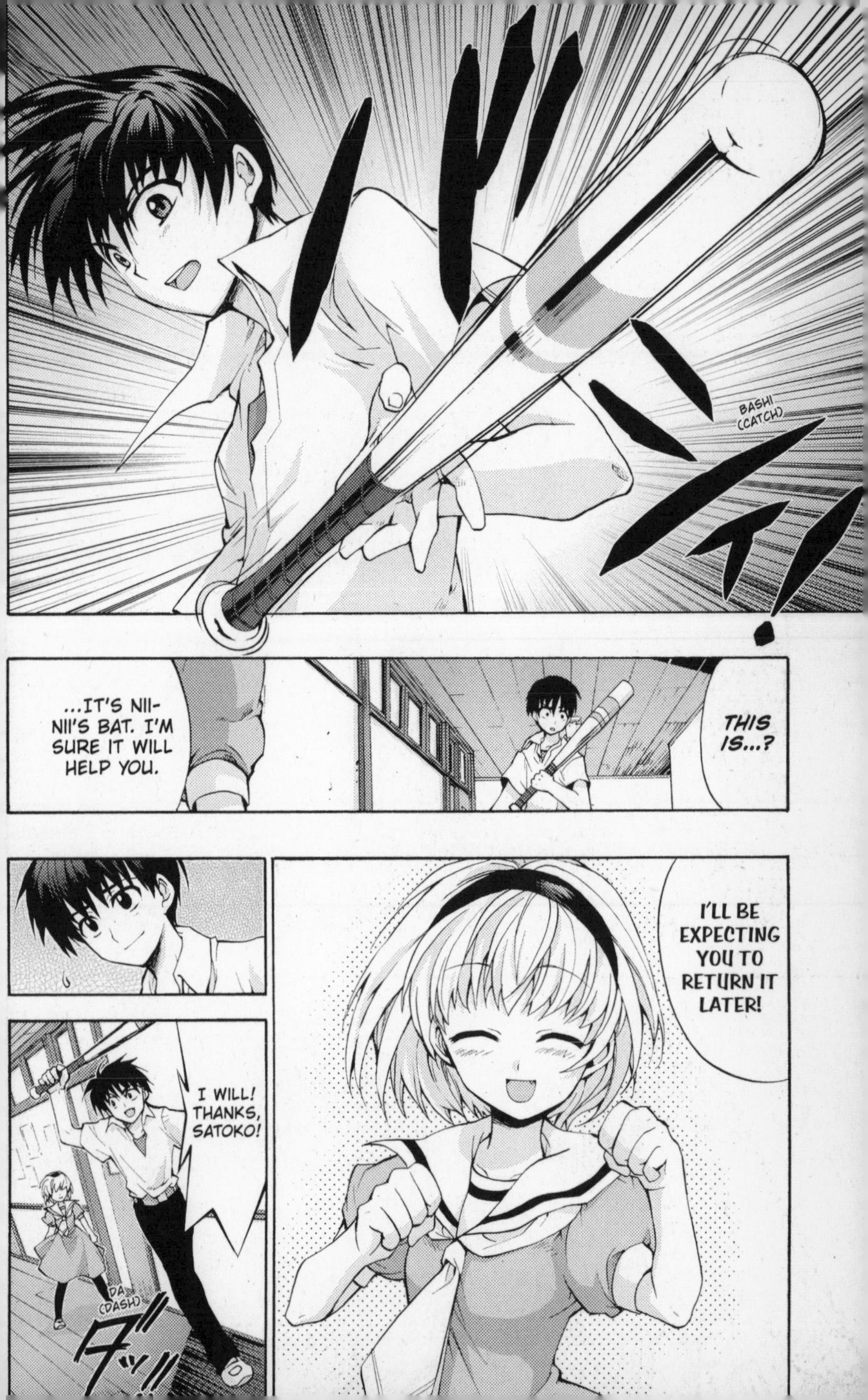
BASHI
(CATCH)
THIS IS...?
...IT'S NII-NII'S BAT. I'M SURE IT WILL HELP YOU.
I'LL BE EXPECTING YOU TO RETURN IT LATER!
I WILL! THANKS, SATOKO!
DA
(DASH)

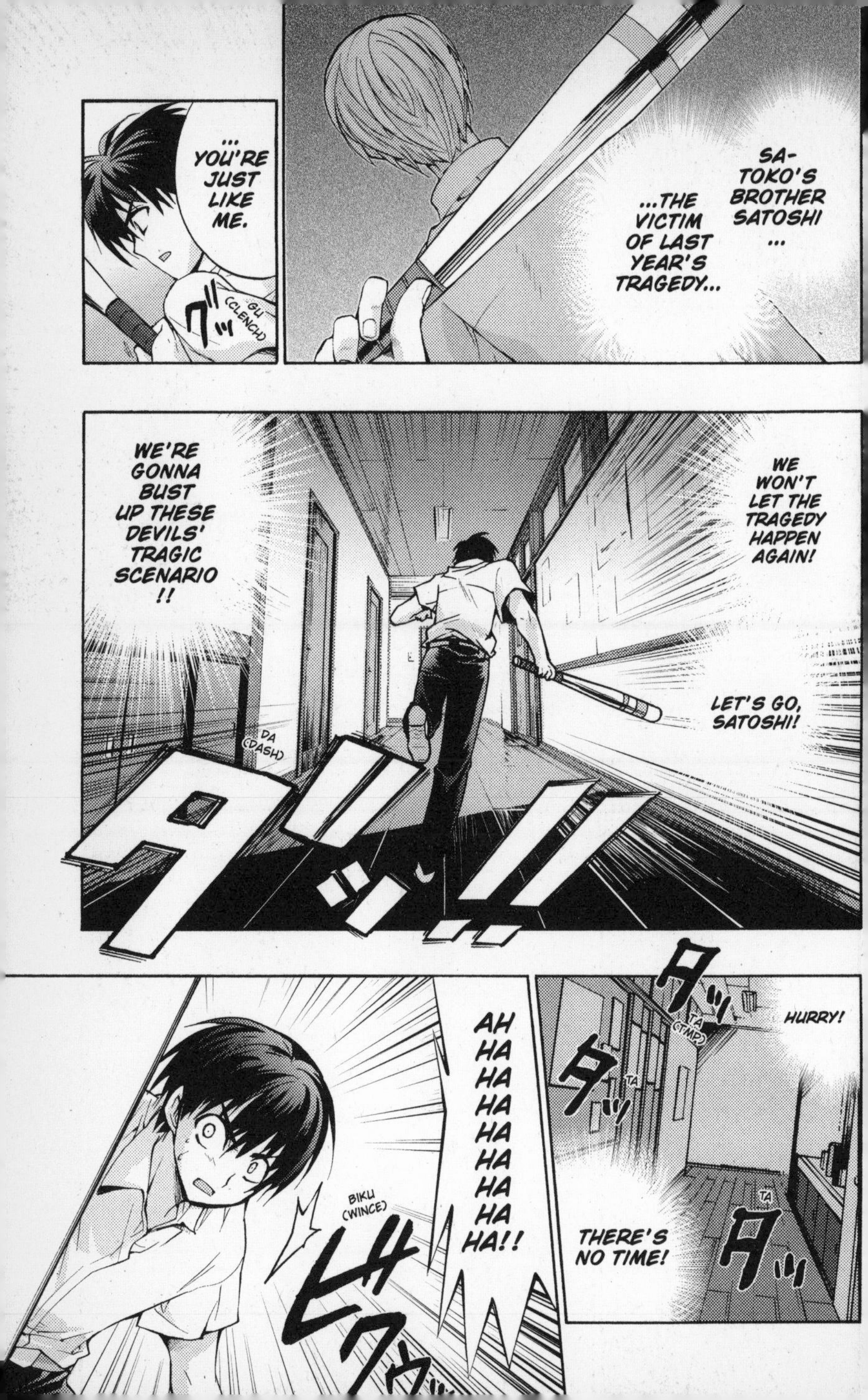
SA-TOKO'S BROTHER SATOSHI...
...THE VICTIM OF LAST YEAR'S TRAGEDY...
...YOU'RE JUST LIKE ME.
GU (CLENCH)
WE WON'T LET THE TRAGEDY HAPPEN AGAIN!
WE'RE GONNA BUST UP THESE DEVILS' TRAGIC SCENARIO!!
LET'S GO, SATOSHI!
DA (DASH)
TA (TMP)
HURRY!
TA
TA
THERE'S NO TIME!
AH HA HA HA HA HA HA HA HA!!
BIKU (WINCE)

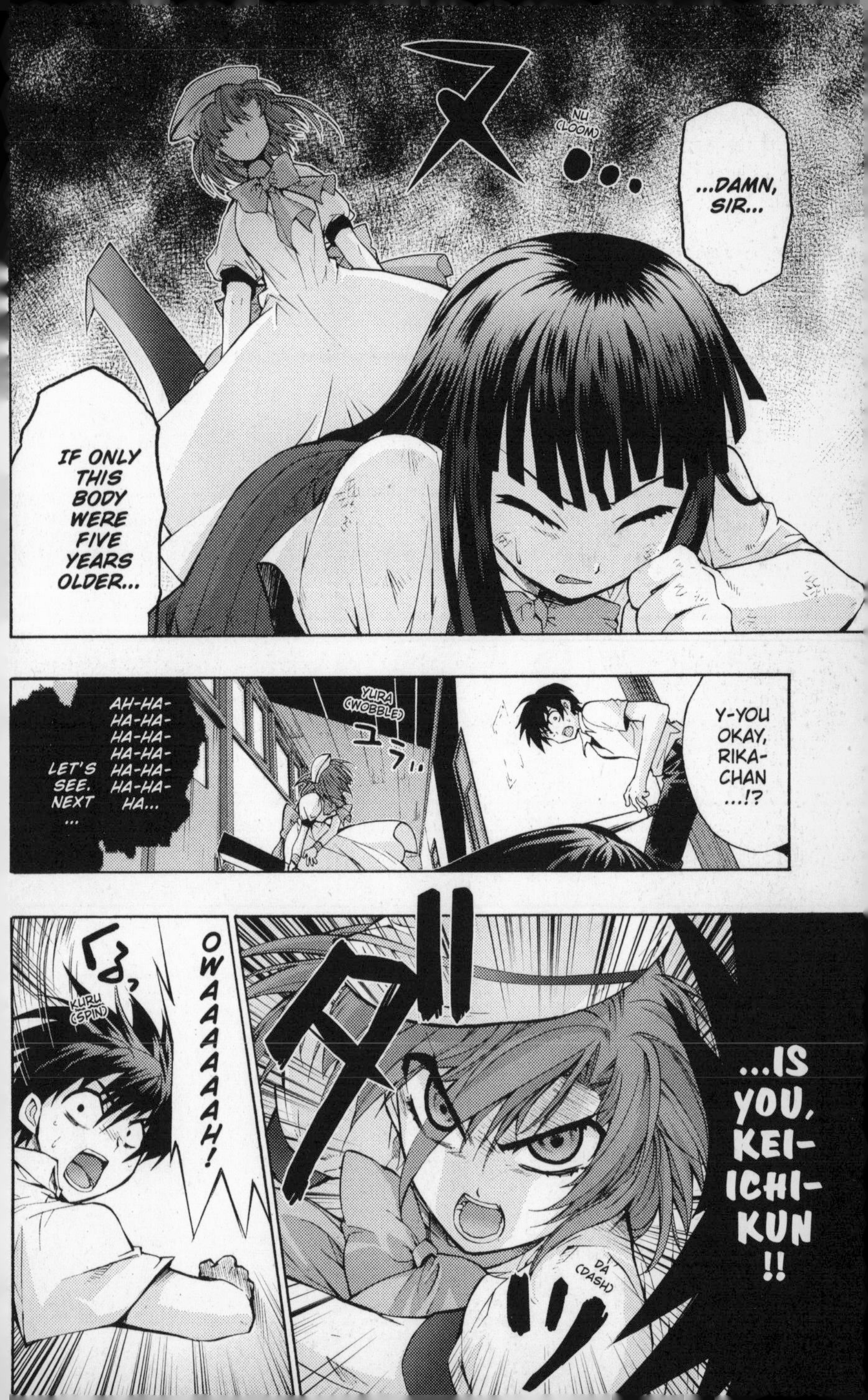

...DAMN, SIR...
NU (LOOM)
IF ONLY THIS BODY WERE FIVE YEARS OLDER...
Y-YOU OKAY, RIKA-CHAN ...!?
YURA (WOBBLE)
AH-HA-HA-HA-HA-HA-HA-HA-HA-HA-HA-HA-HA...
LET'S SEE. NEXT ...
...IS YOU, KEI-ICHI-KUN!!
DA (DASH)
OWAAAAAAAH!
KURU (SPIN)

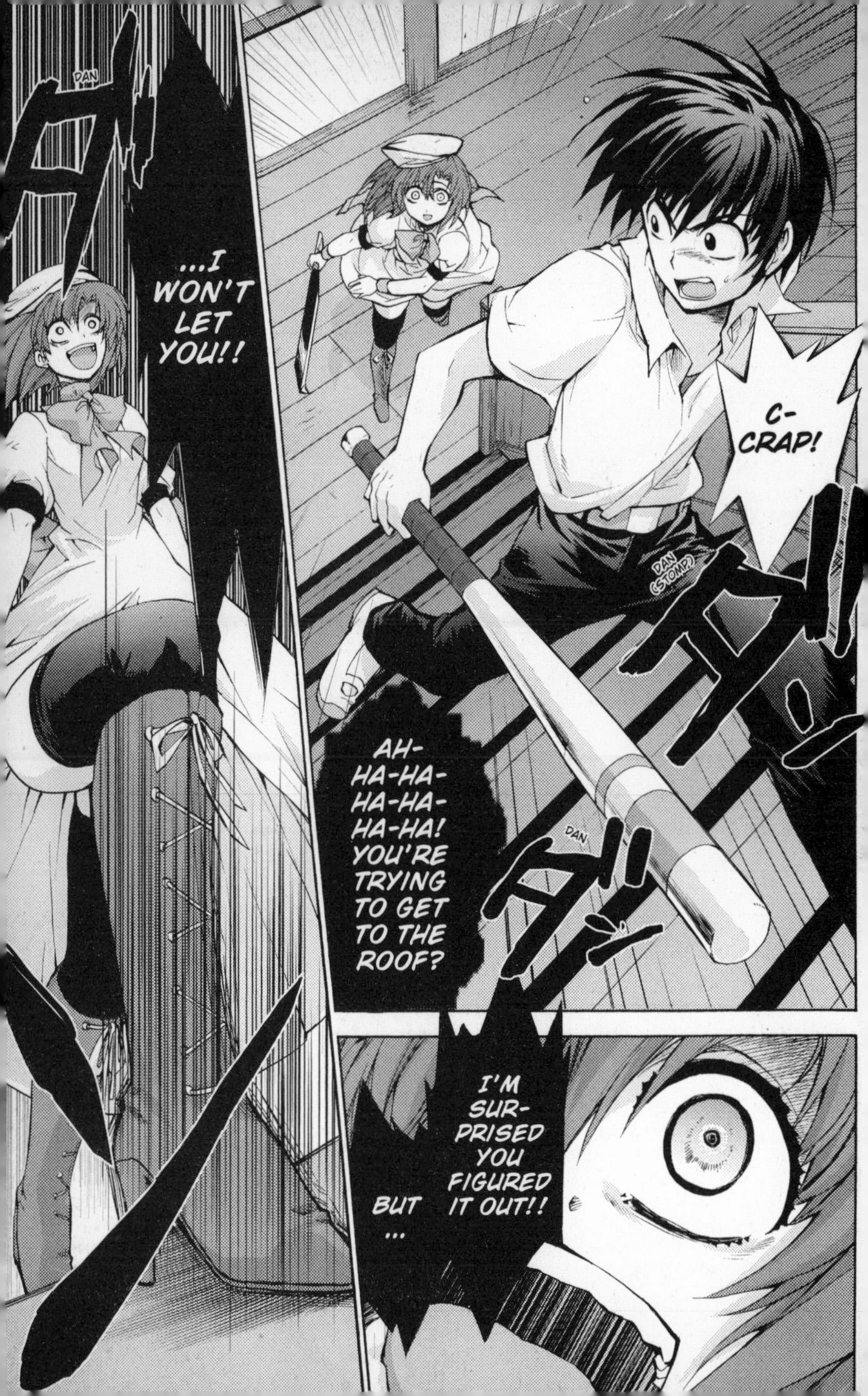
C-CRAP!
DAN (STOMP)
DAN
AH-HA-HA-HA-HA-HA-HA! YOU'RE TRYING TO GET TO THE ROOF?
I'M SURPRISED YOU FIGURED IT OUT!!
BUT ...
DAN
...I WON'T LET YOU!!

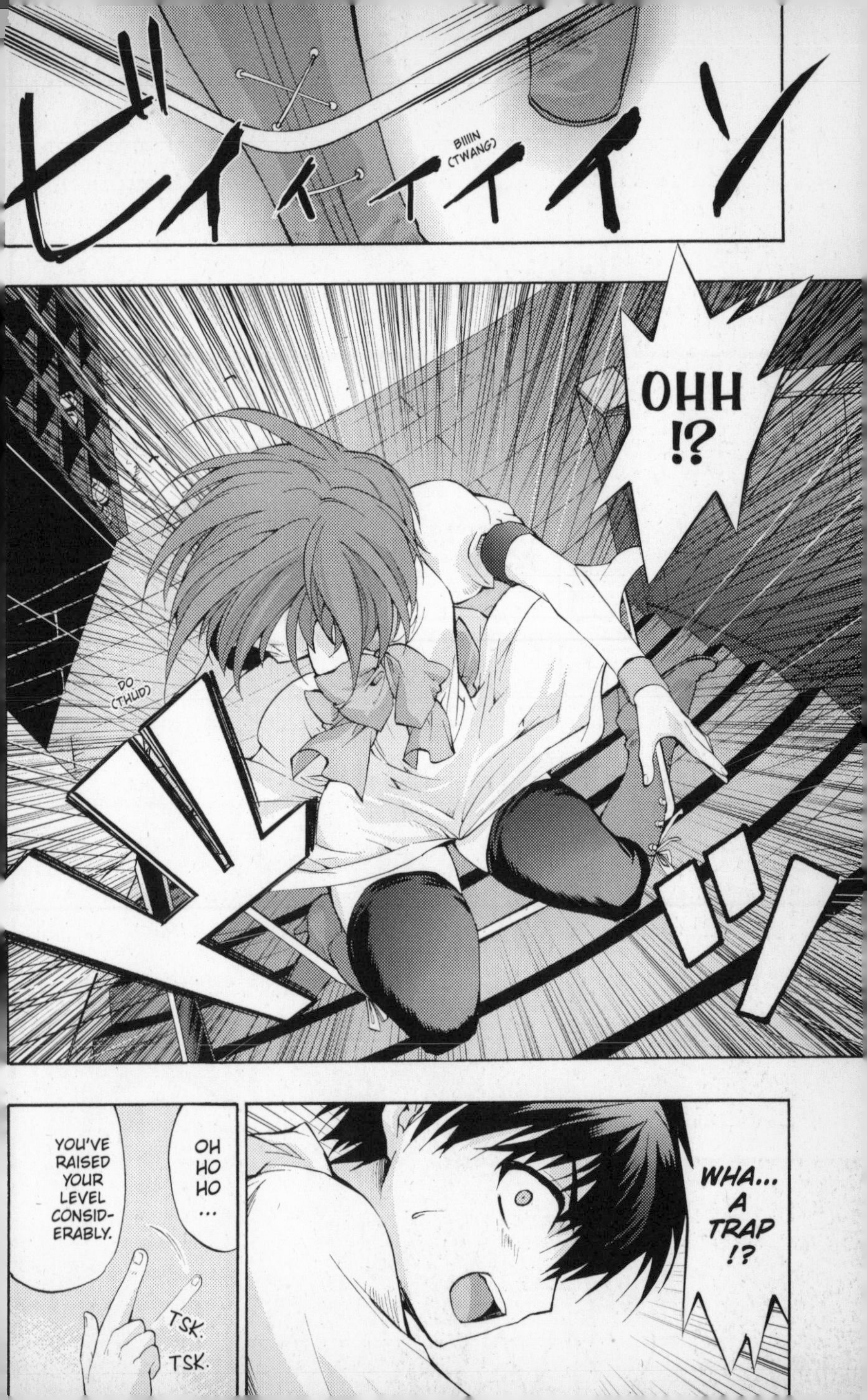
BIIIIN (TWANG)
OHH !?
DO (THUD)
WHA... A TRAP !?
OH HO HO ...
YOU'VE RAISED YOUR LEVEL CONSID-ERABLY.
TSK. TSK.

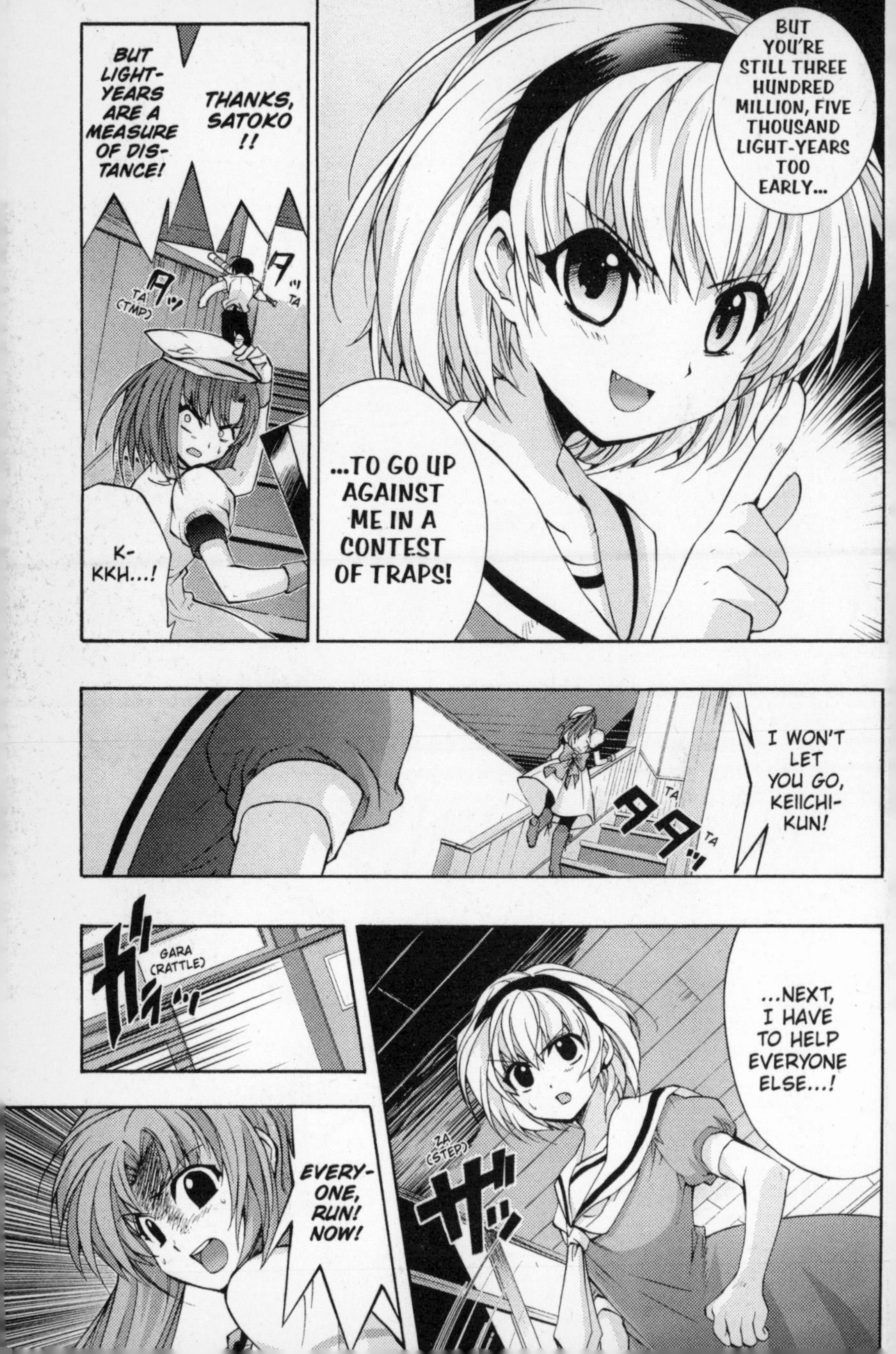
BUT YOU'RE STILL THREE HUNDRED MILLION, FIVE THOUSAND LIGHT-YEARS TOO EARLY...
...TO GO UP AGAINST ME IN A CONTEST OF TRAPS!
THANKS, SATOKO!!
BUT LIGHT-YEARS ARE A MEASURE OF DIS-TANCE!
TA
TA (TMP)
K-KKH...!
I WON'T LET YOU GO, KEIICHI-KUN!
TA
TA
...NEXT, I HAVE TO HELP EVERYONE ELSE...!
ZA (STEP)
GARA (RATTLE)
EVERY-ONE, RUN! NOW!

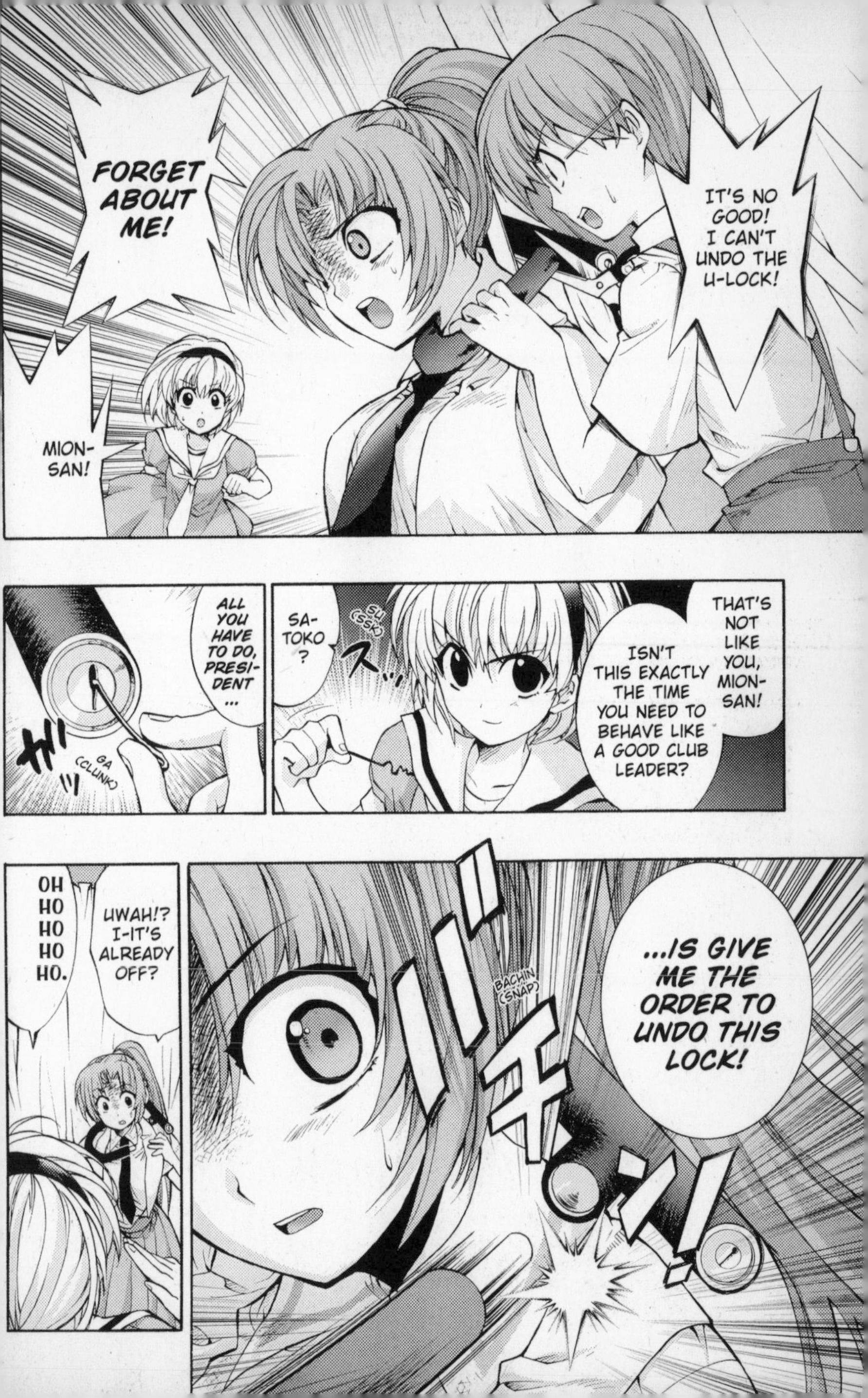
IT'S NO GOOD! I CAN'T UNDO THE U-LOCK!
FORGET ABOUT ME!
MION-SAN!
THAT'S NOT LIKE YOU, MION-SAN!
ISN'T THIS EXACTLY THE TIME YOU NEED TO BEHAVE LIKE A GOOD CLUB LEADER?
SU (SSK)
SA-TOKO?
ALL YOU HAVE TO DO, PRESIDENT...
GA (CLUNK)
...IS GIVE ME THE ORDER TO UNDO THIS LOCK!
BACHIN (SNAP)
UWAH!? I-IT'S ALREADY OFF?
OH HO HO HO HO.

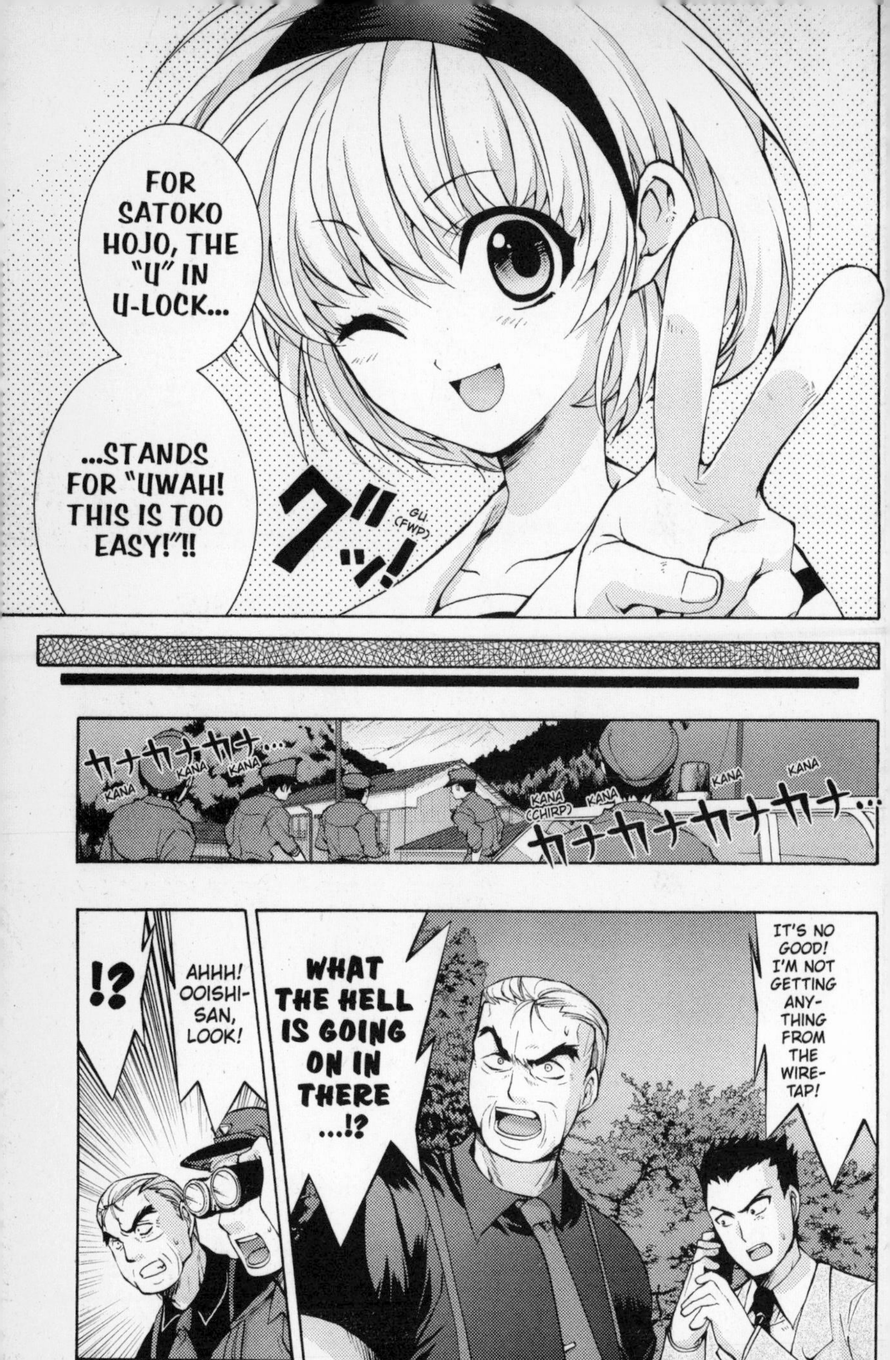
FOR SATOKO HOJO, THE "U" IN U-LOCK...
...STANDS FOR "UWAH! THIS IS TOO EASY!"!!
グッ!
GU (FWP)
カナカナカナ…
KANA
KANA
KANA
KANA
KANA
KANA (CHIRP)
カナカナカナカナ…
IT'S NO GOOD! I'M NOT GETTING ANY-THING FROM THE WIRE-TAP!
WHAT THE HELL IS GOING ON IN THERE ...!?
AHHH! OOISHI-SAN, LOOK!
!?

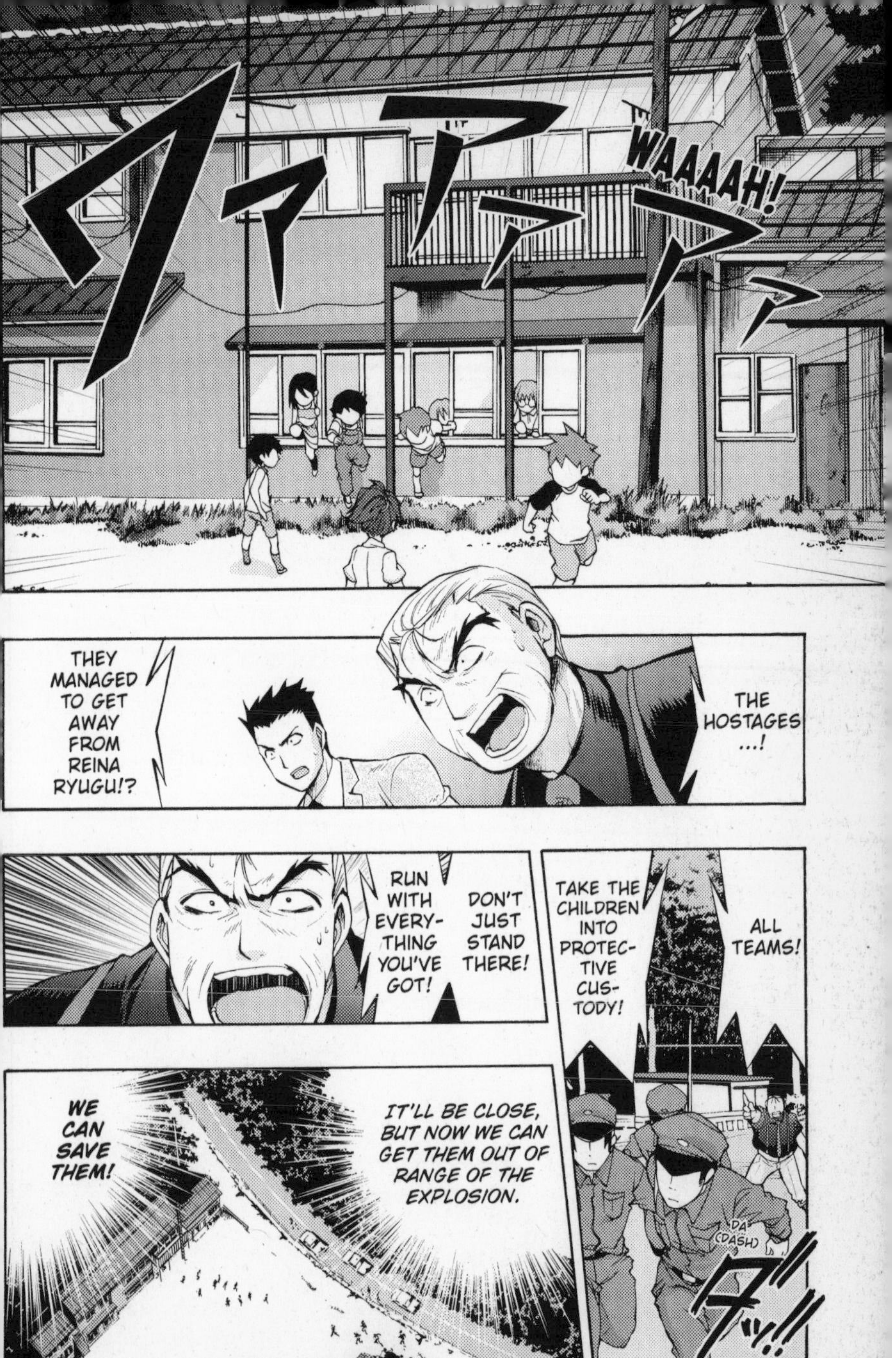
WAAAAH!
THE HOSTAGES...!
THEY MANAGED TO GET AWAY FROM REINA RYUGU!?
ALL TEAMS!
TAKE THE CHILDREN INTO PROTECTIVE CUSTODY!
DA (DASH)
DON'T JUST STAND THERE!
RUN WITH EVERYTHING YOU'VE GOT!
IT'LL BE CLOSE, BUT NOW WE CAN GET THEM OUT OF RANGE OF THE EXPLOSION.
WE CAN SAVE THEM!

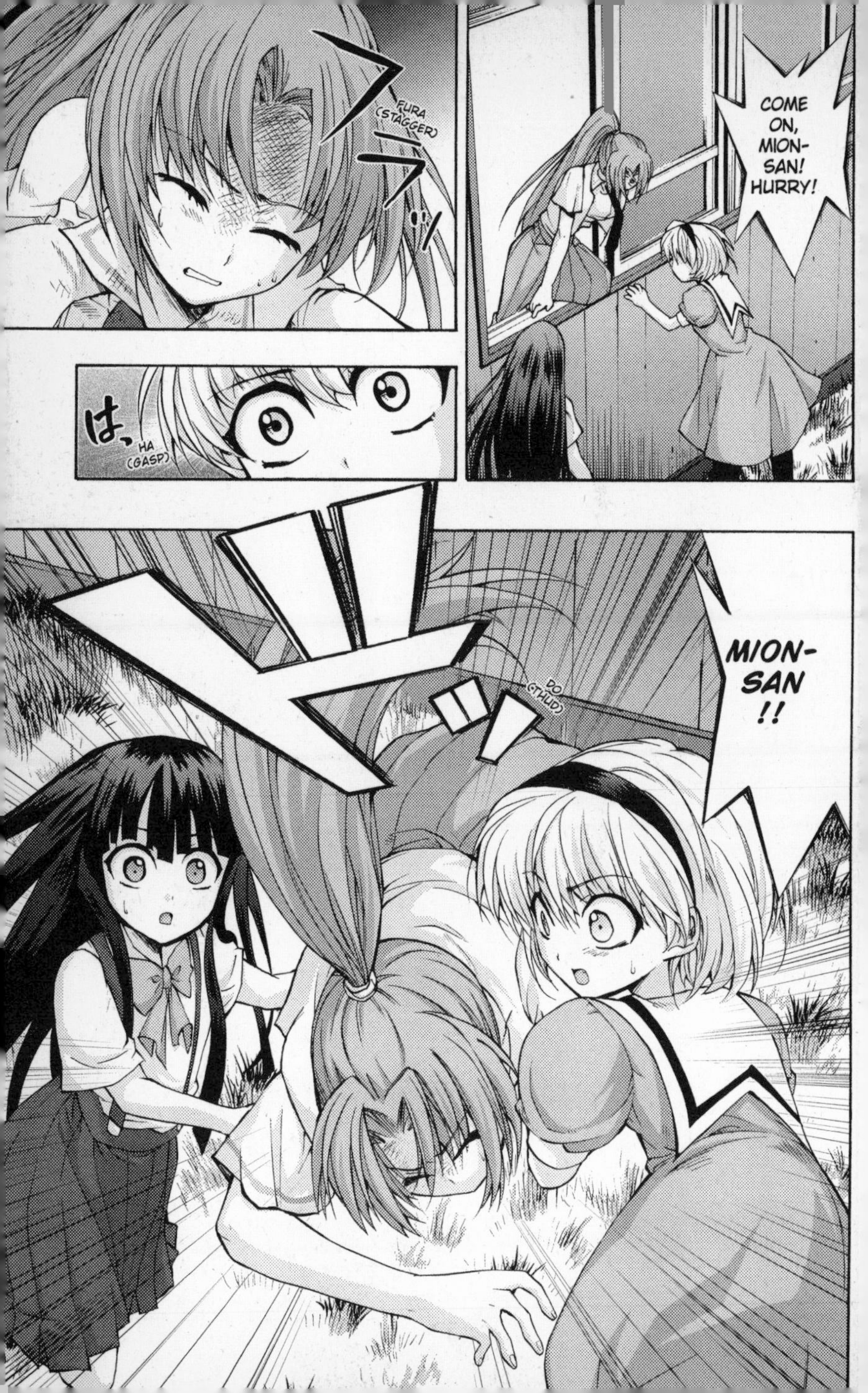
COME ON, MION-SAN! HURRY!
FURA (STAGGER)
は、
HA (GASP)
MION-SAN!!
DO (THUD)

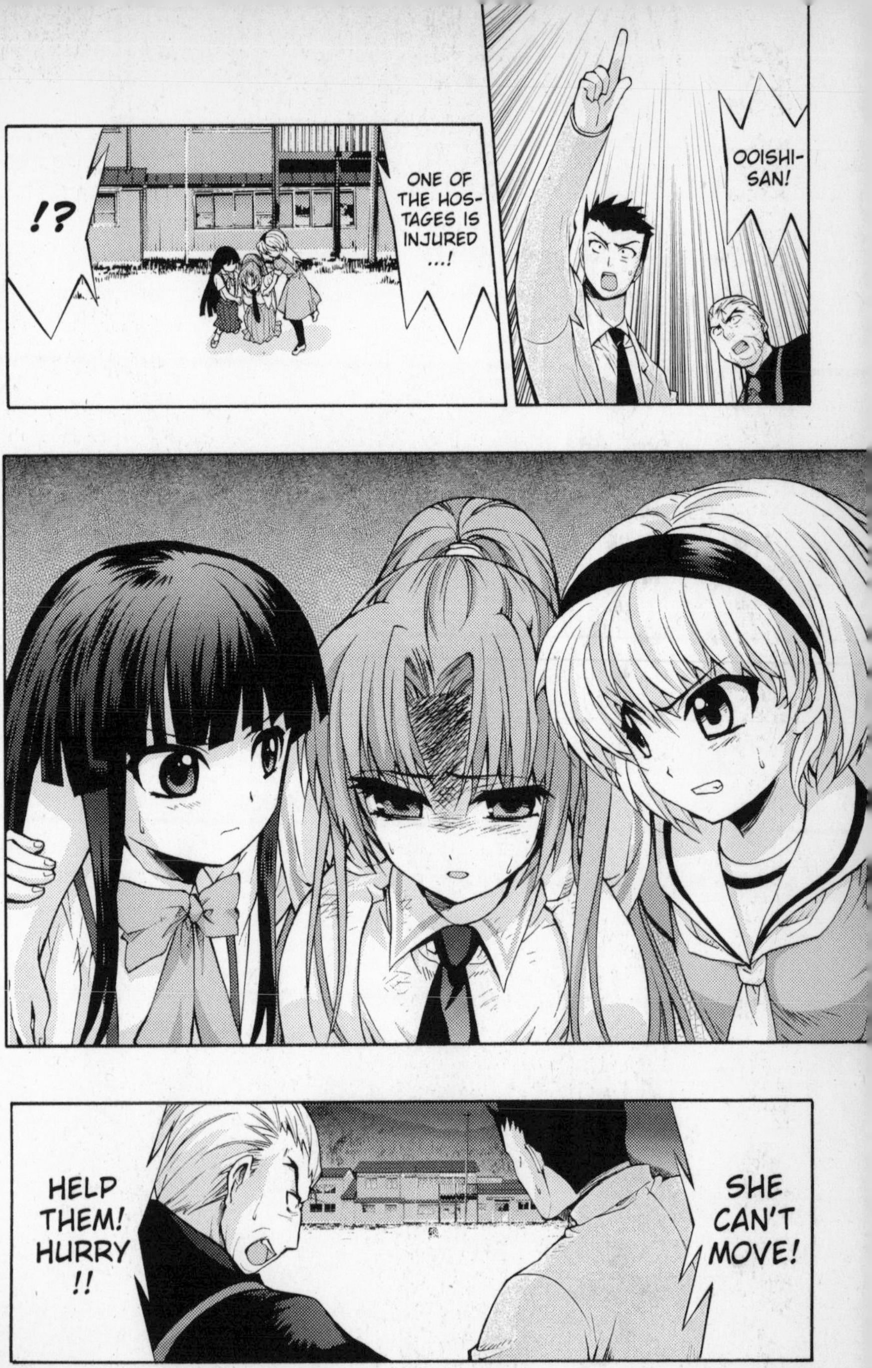
OOISHI-SAN!
ONE OF THE HOS-TAGES IS INJURED ...!
!?
SHE CAN'T MOVE!
HELP THEM! HURRY !!

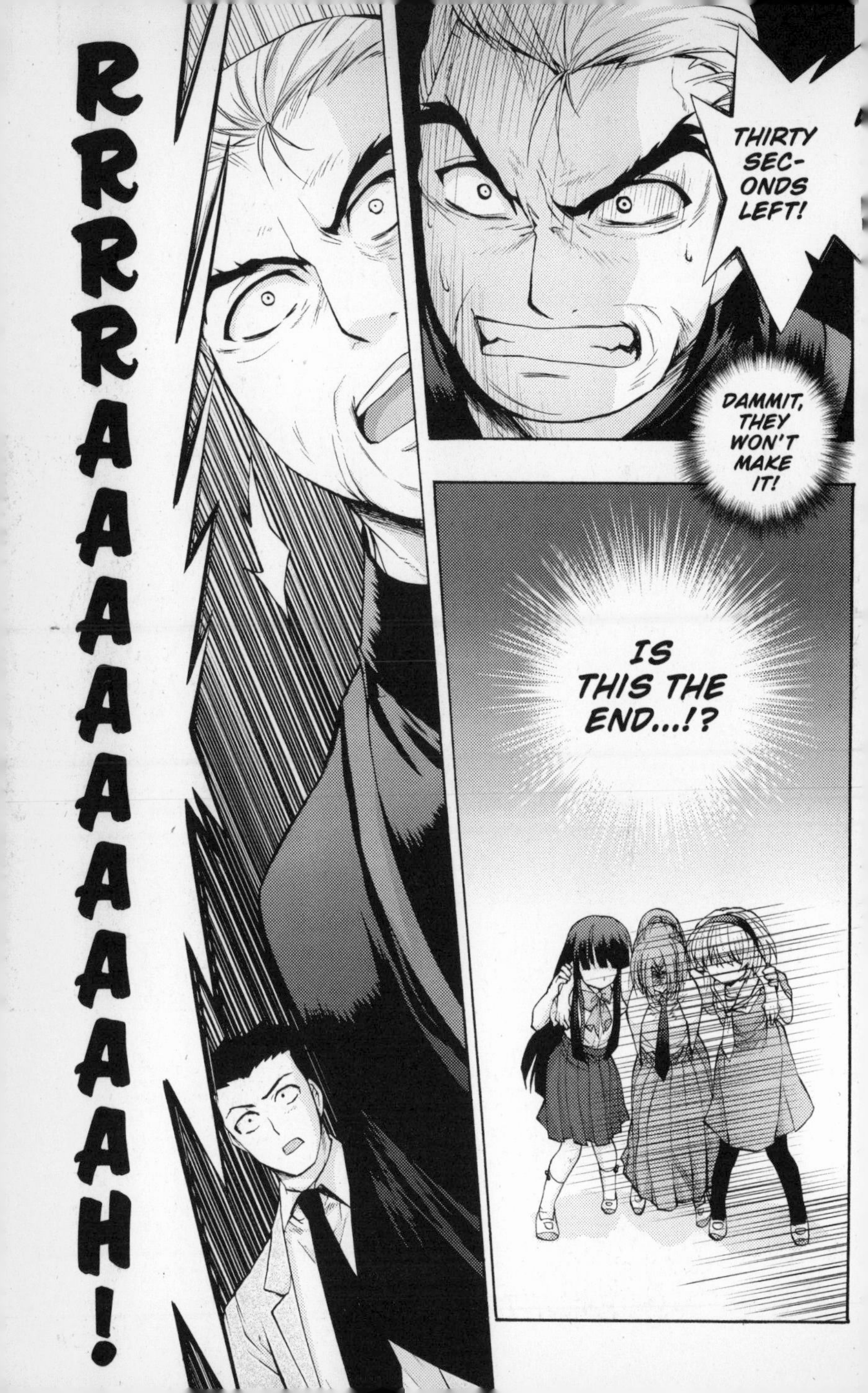
THIRTY SECONDS LEFT!
DAMMIT, THEY WON'T MAKE IT!
IS THIS THE END...!?
RRRRAAAAAAAAAAH!

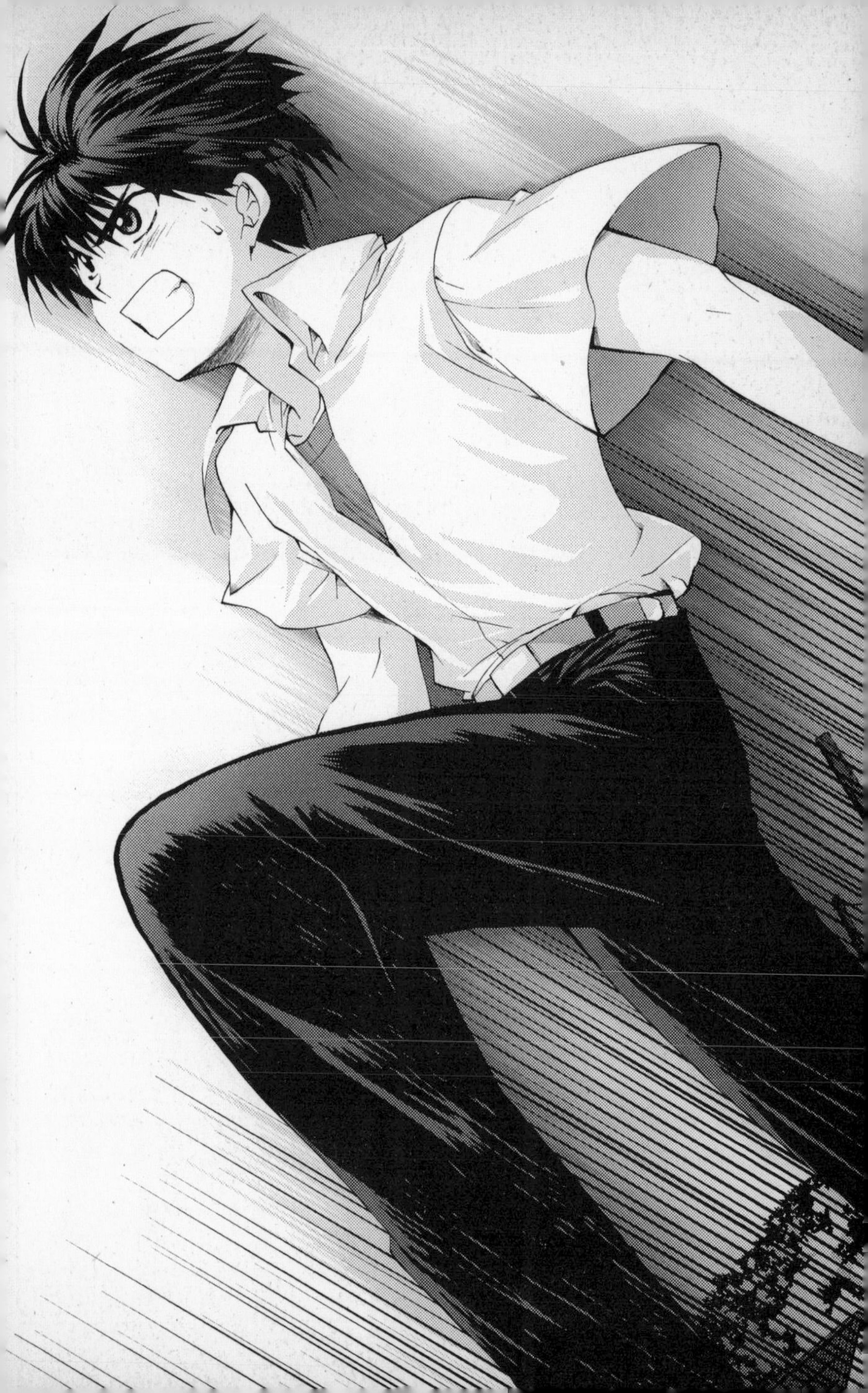

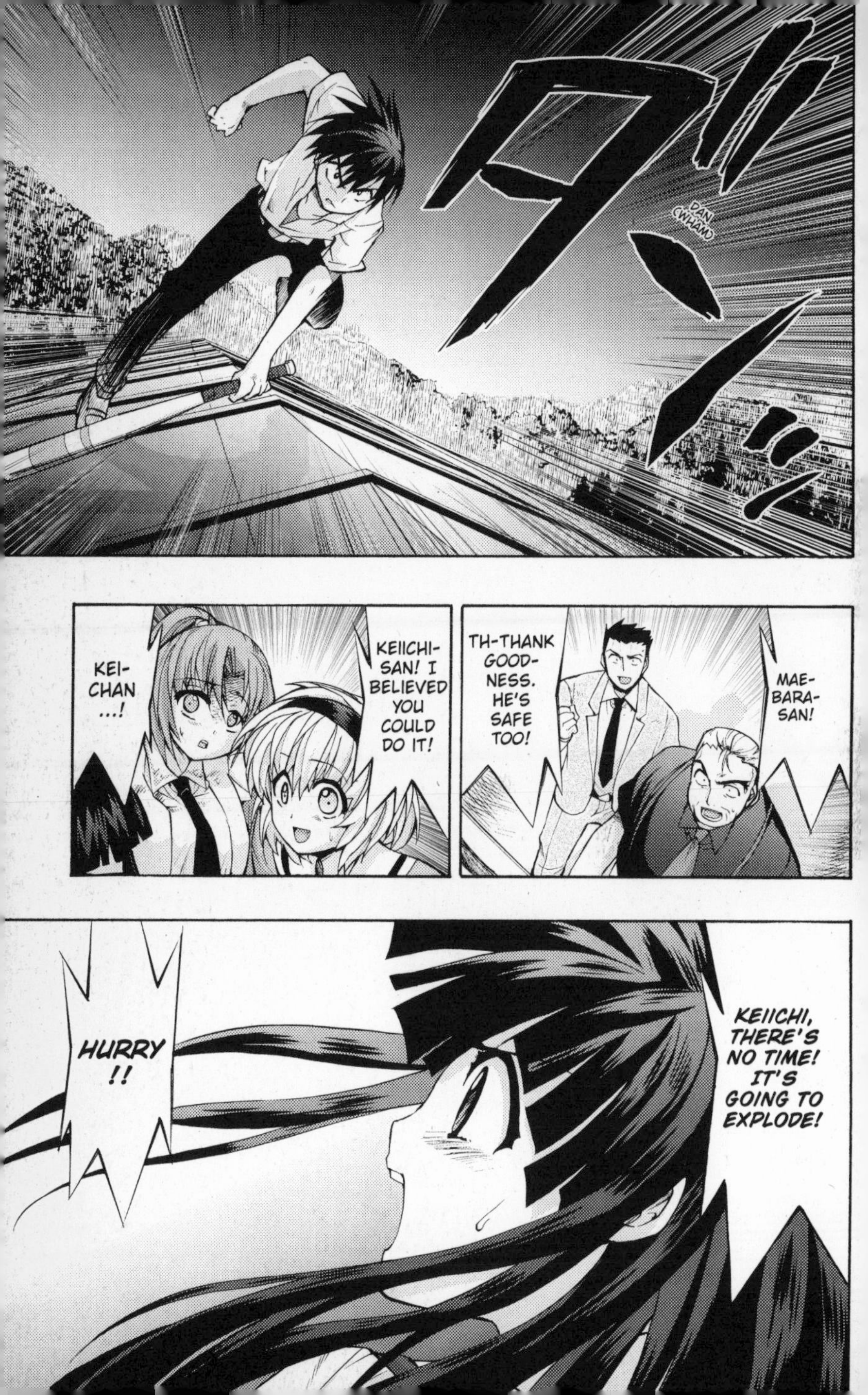
DAN (WHAM)
MAE-BARA-SAN!
TH-THANK GOOD-NESS. HE'S SAFE TOO!
KEIICHI-SAN! I BELIEVED YOU COULD DO IT!
KEI-CHAN ...!
KEIICHI, THERE'S NO TIME! IT'S GOING TO EXPLODE!
HURRY!!

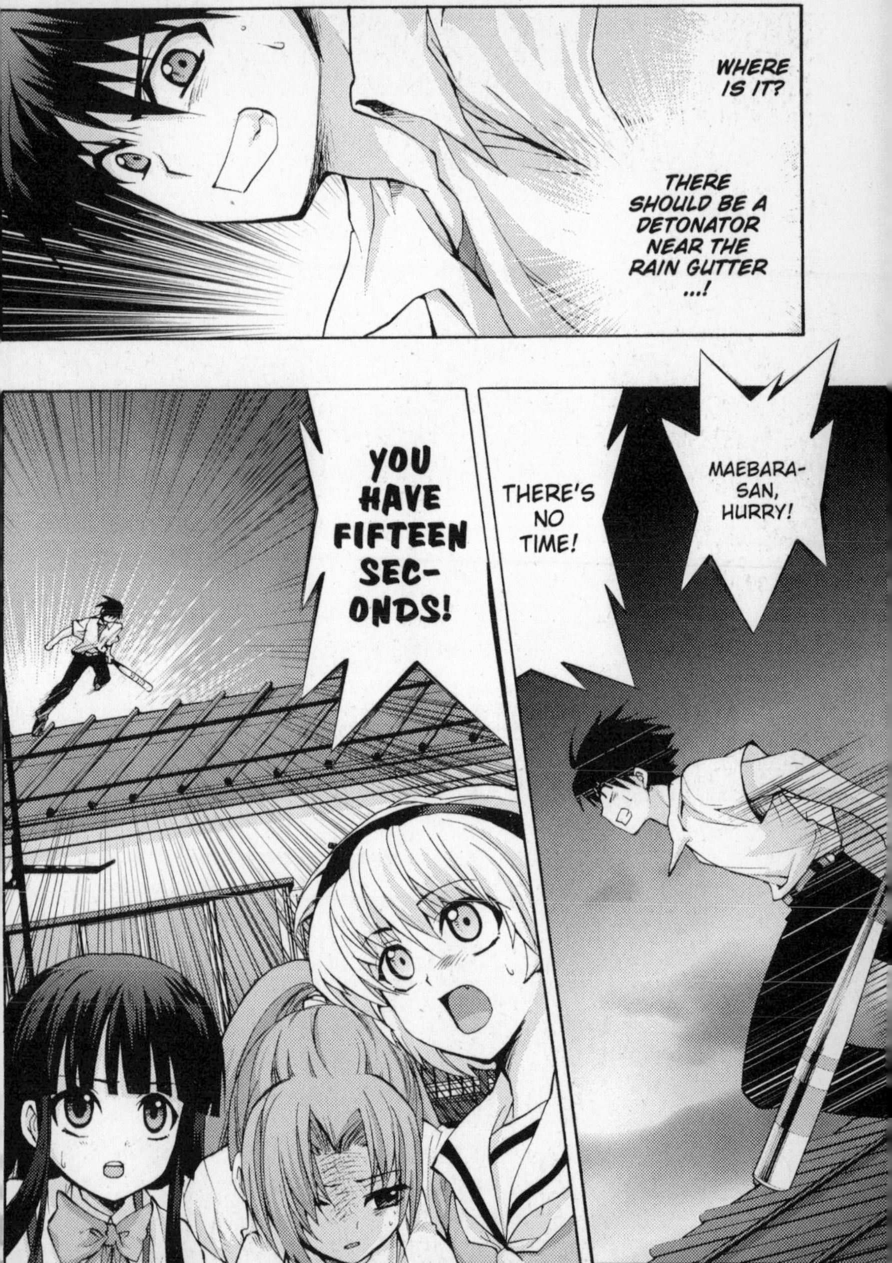
WHERE IS IT?
THERE SHOULD BE A DETONATOR NEAR THE RAIN GUTTER ...!
MAEBARA-SAN, HURRY!
THERE'S NO TIME!
YOU HAVE FIFTEEN SEC-ONDS!

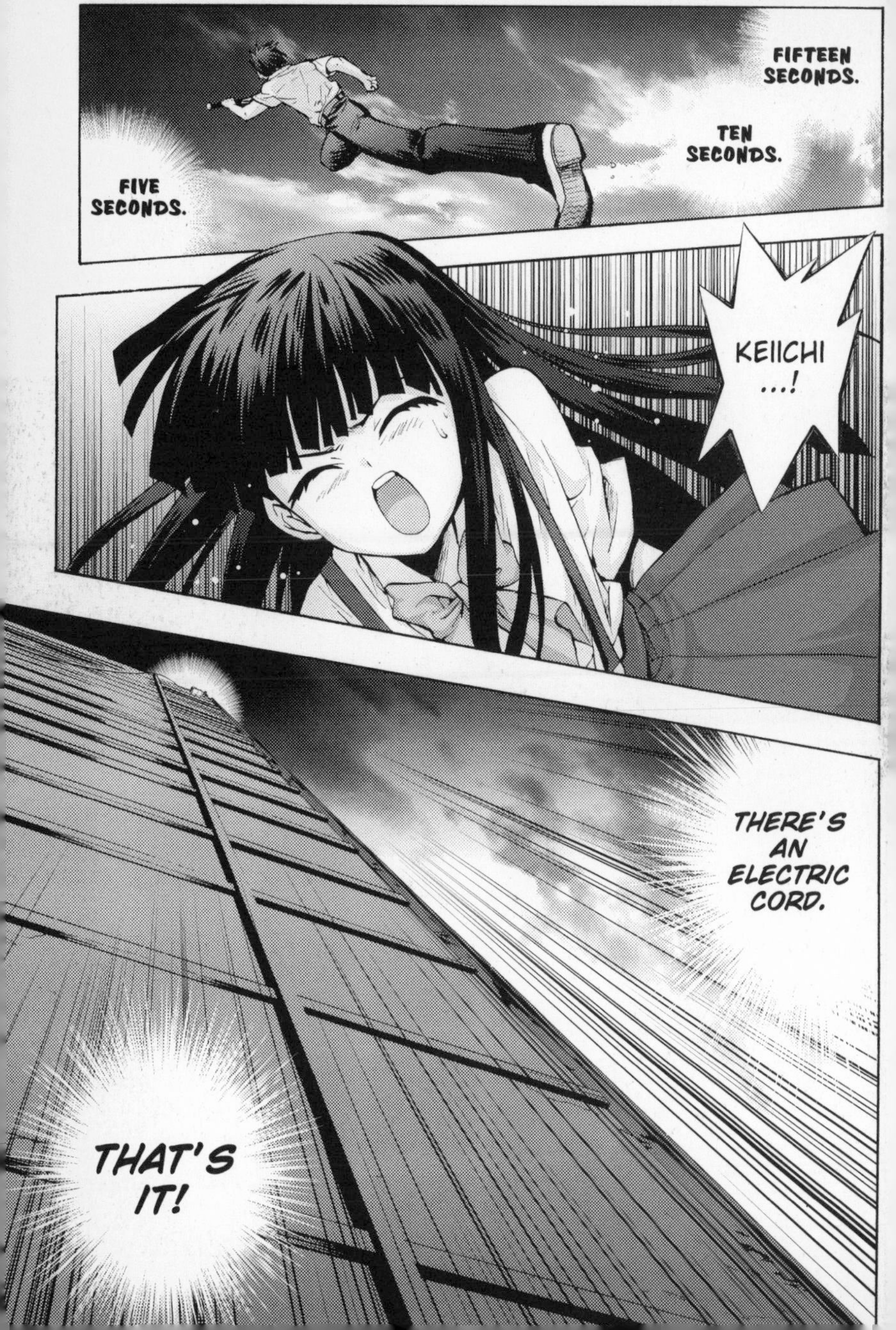
FIFTEEN SECONDS.
TEN SECONDS.
FIVE SECONDS.
KEIICHI ...!
THERE'S AN ELECTRIC CORD.
THAT'S IT!

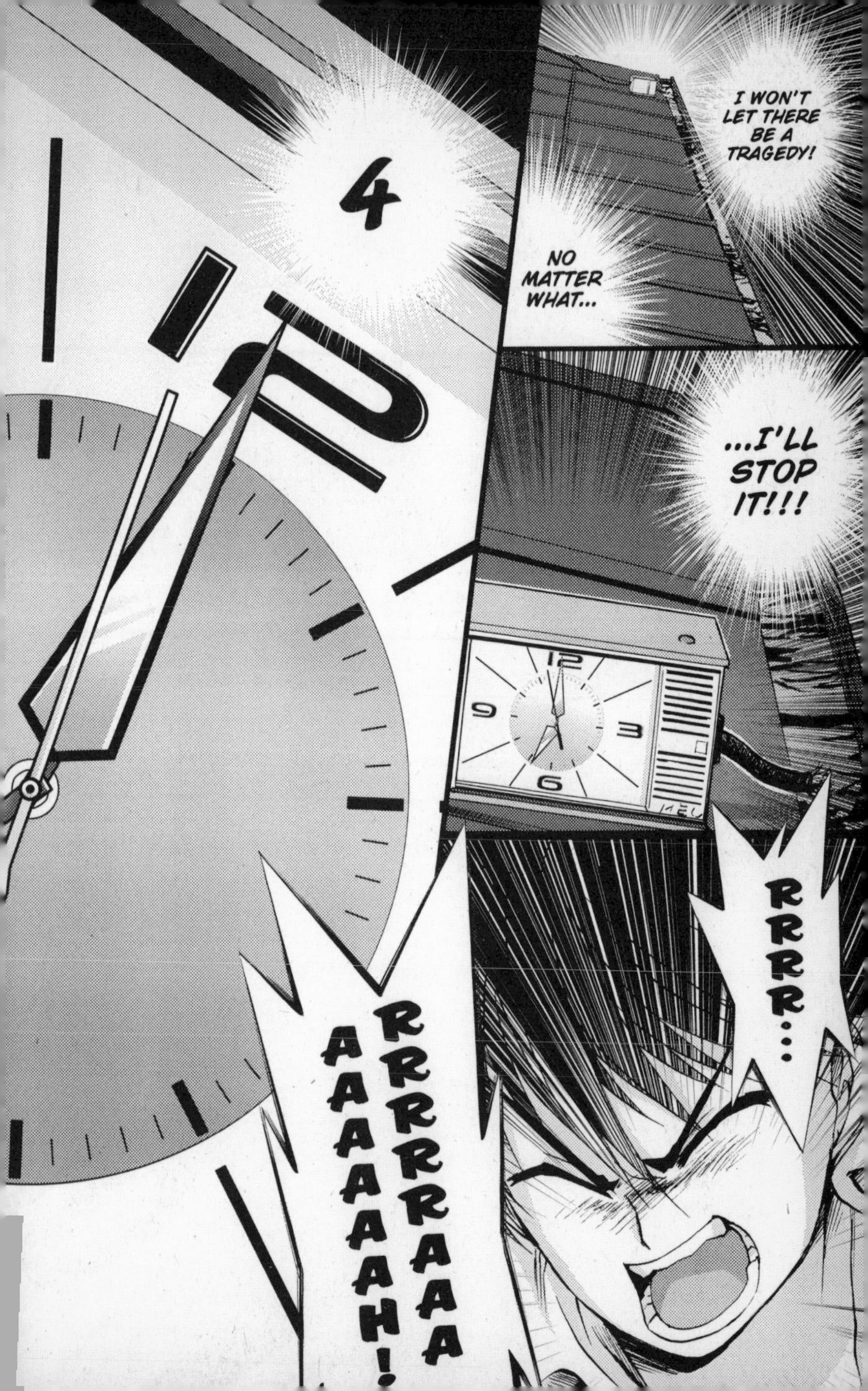
I WON'T LET THERE BE A TRAGEDY!
NO MATTER WHAT...
4
...I'LL STOP IT!!!
RRRR...
RRRRRRAAAA
AAAAAAAH!

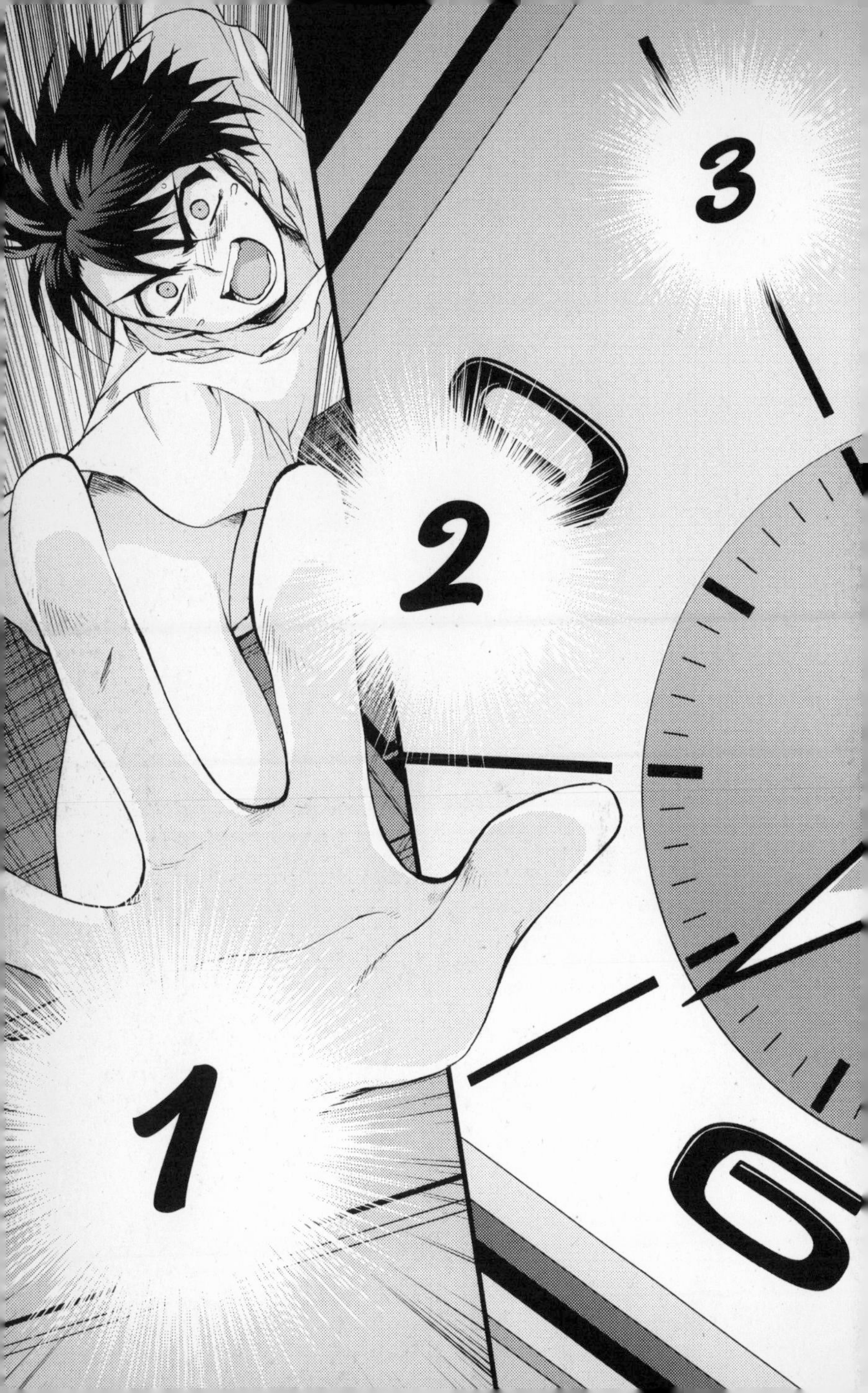
3
2
1

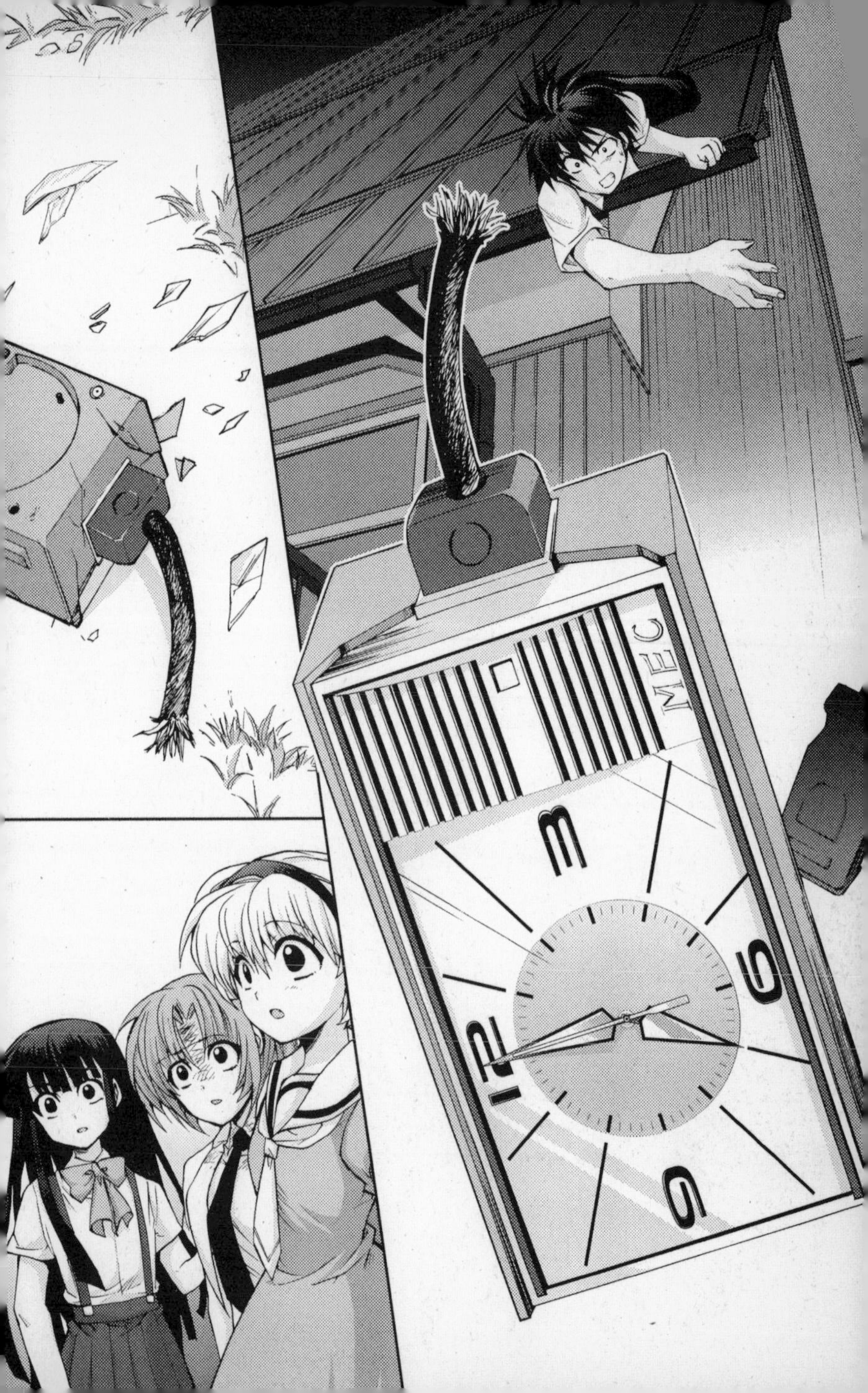
MEC

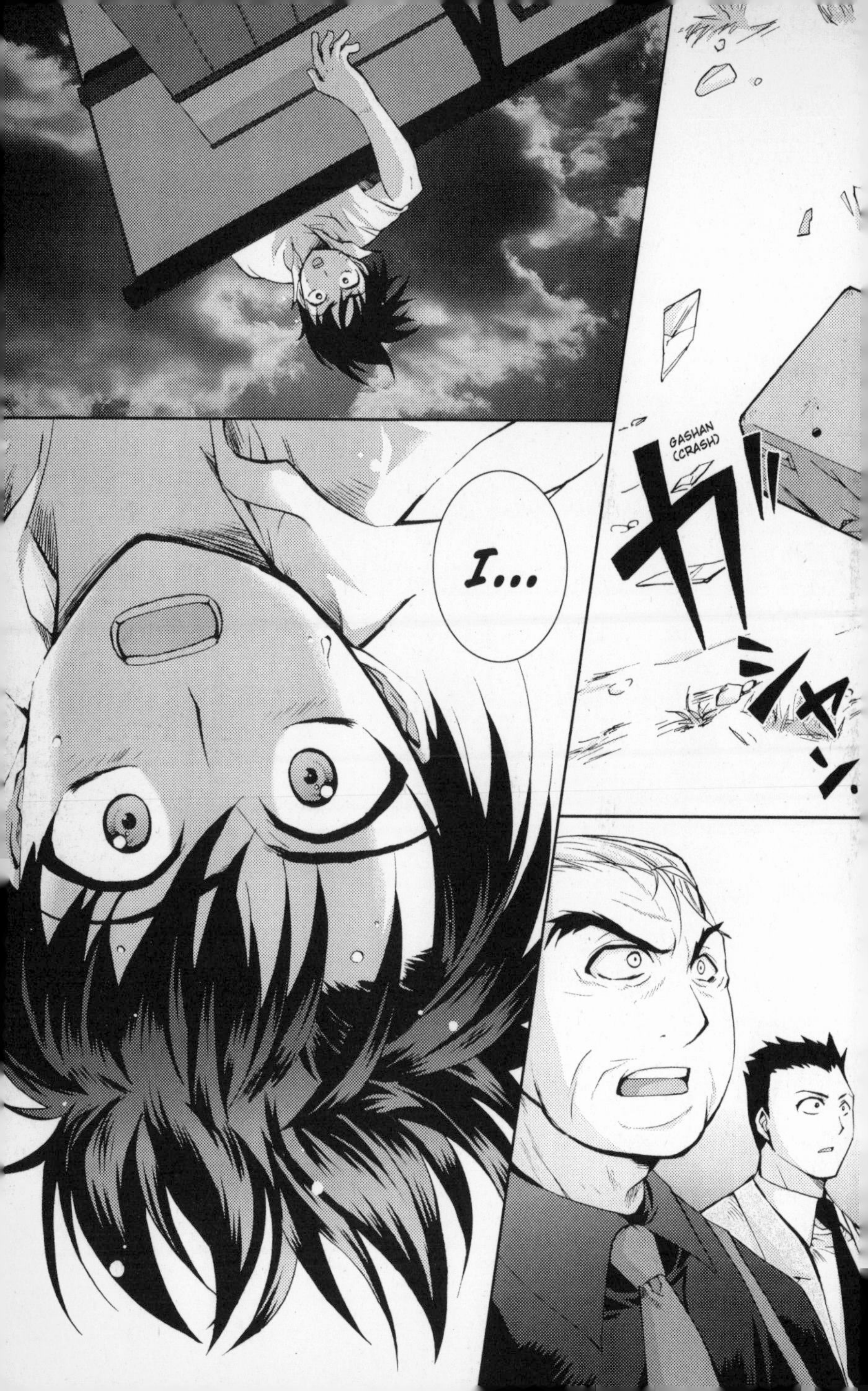
GASHAN (CRASH)
ガシャン
I...

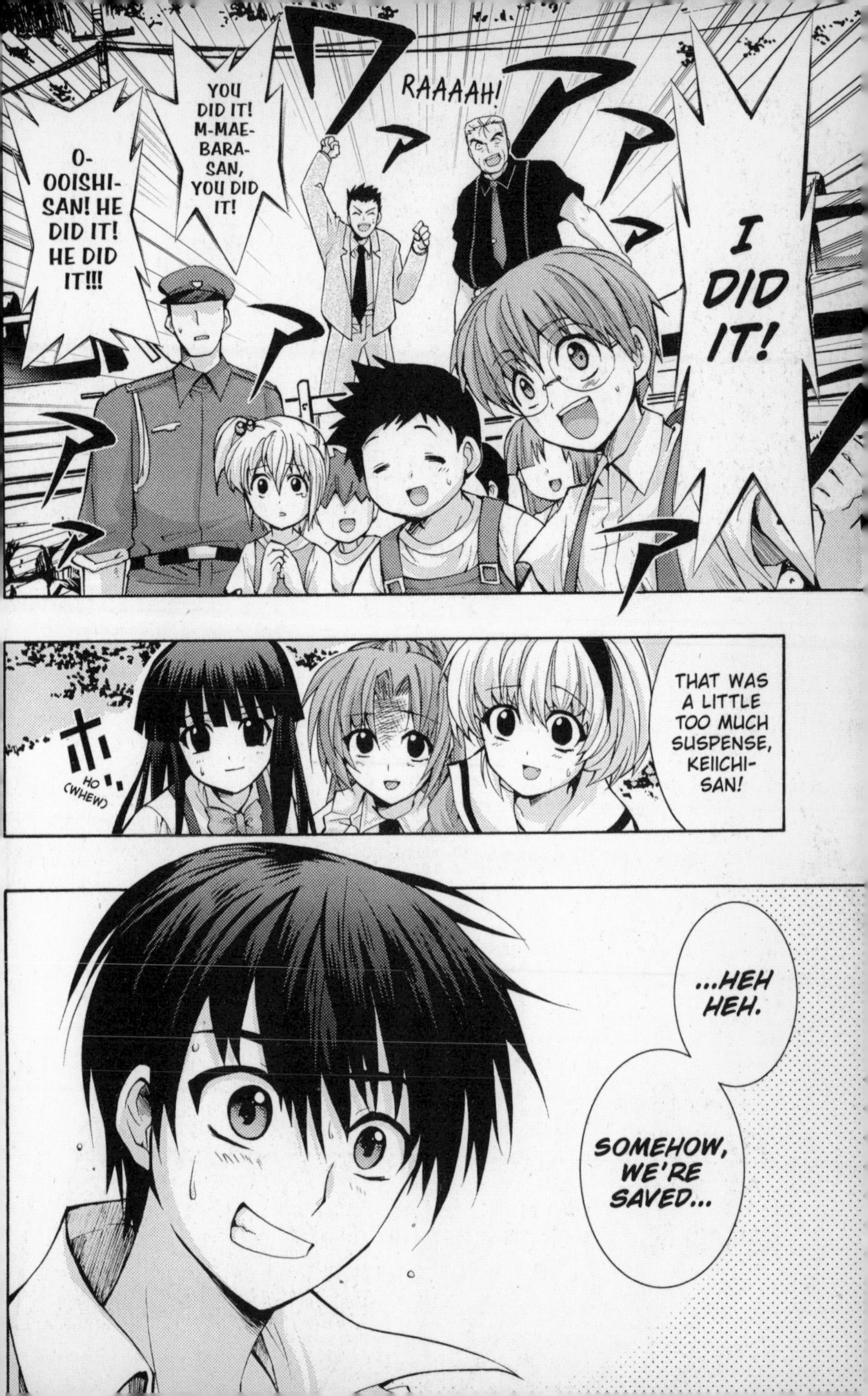
I DID IT!
RAAAAH!
YOU DID IT! M-MAE-BARA-SAN, YOU DID IT!
O-OOISHI-SAN! HE DID IT! HE DID IT!!!
THAT WAS A LITTLE TOO MUCH SUSPENSE, KEIICHI-SAN!
ホ、
HO (WHEW)
...HEH HEH.
SOMEHOW, WE'RE SAVED...

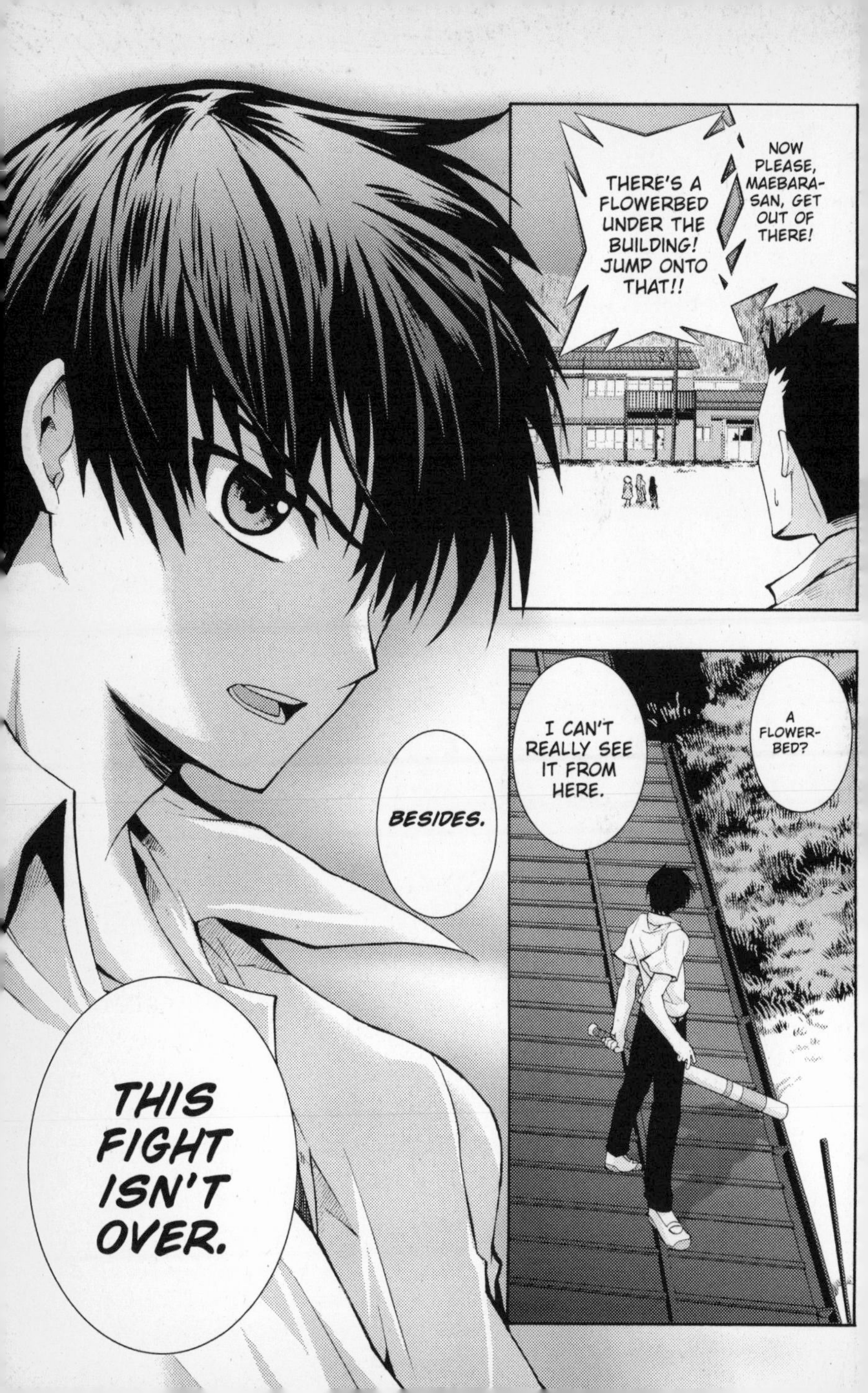
NOW PLEASE, MAEBARA-SAN, GET OUT OF THERE!
THERE'S A FLOWERBED UNDER THE BUILDING! JUMP ONTO THAT!!
A FLOWER-BED?
I CAN'T REALLY SEE IT FROM HERE.
BESIDES.
THIS FIGHT ISN'T OVER.

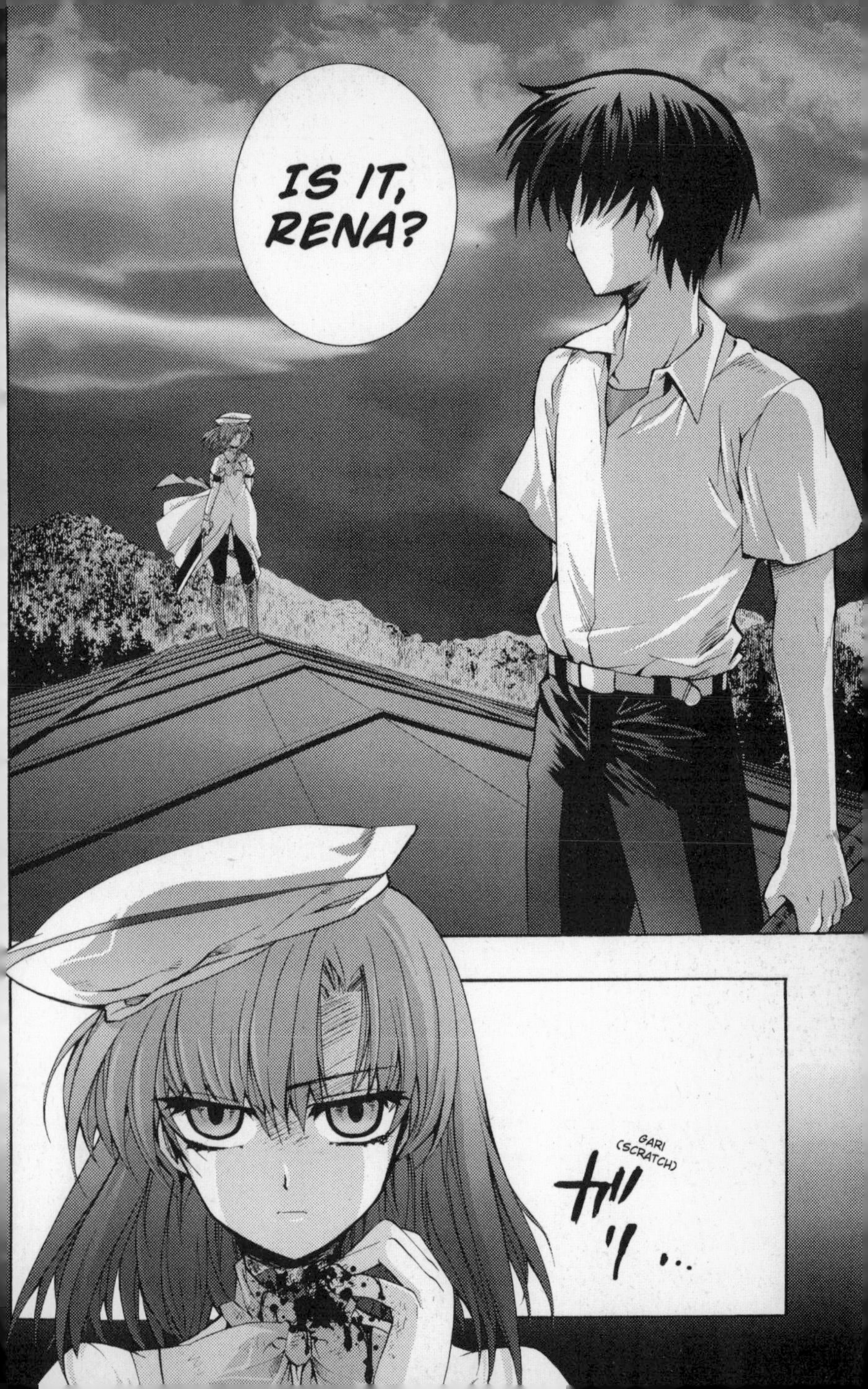
IS IT, RENA?
GARI (SCRATCH)
ガリ...

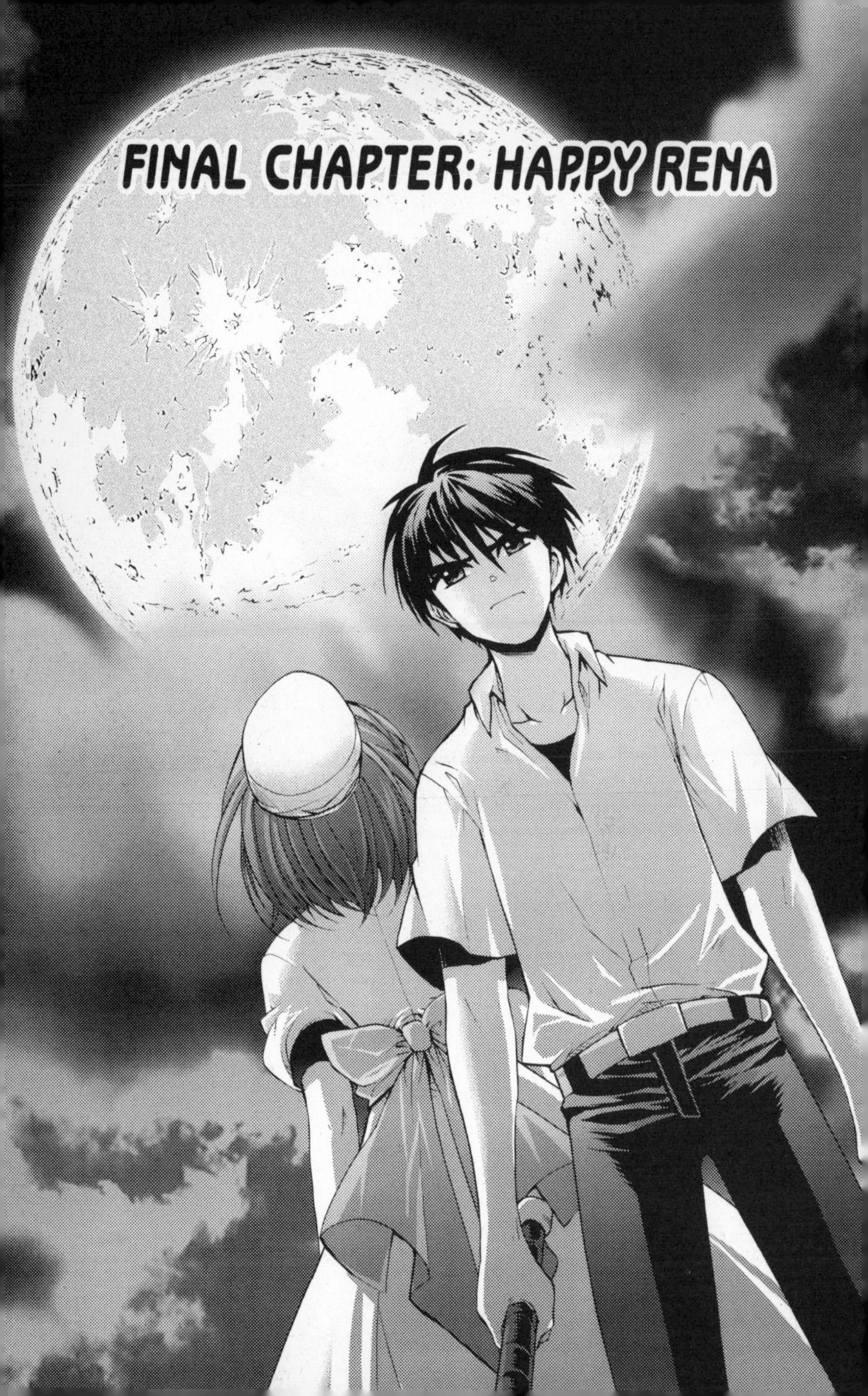
FINAL CHAPTER: HAPPY RENA

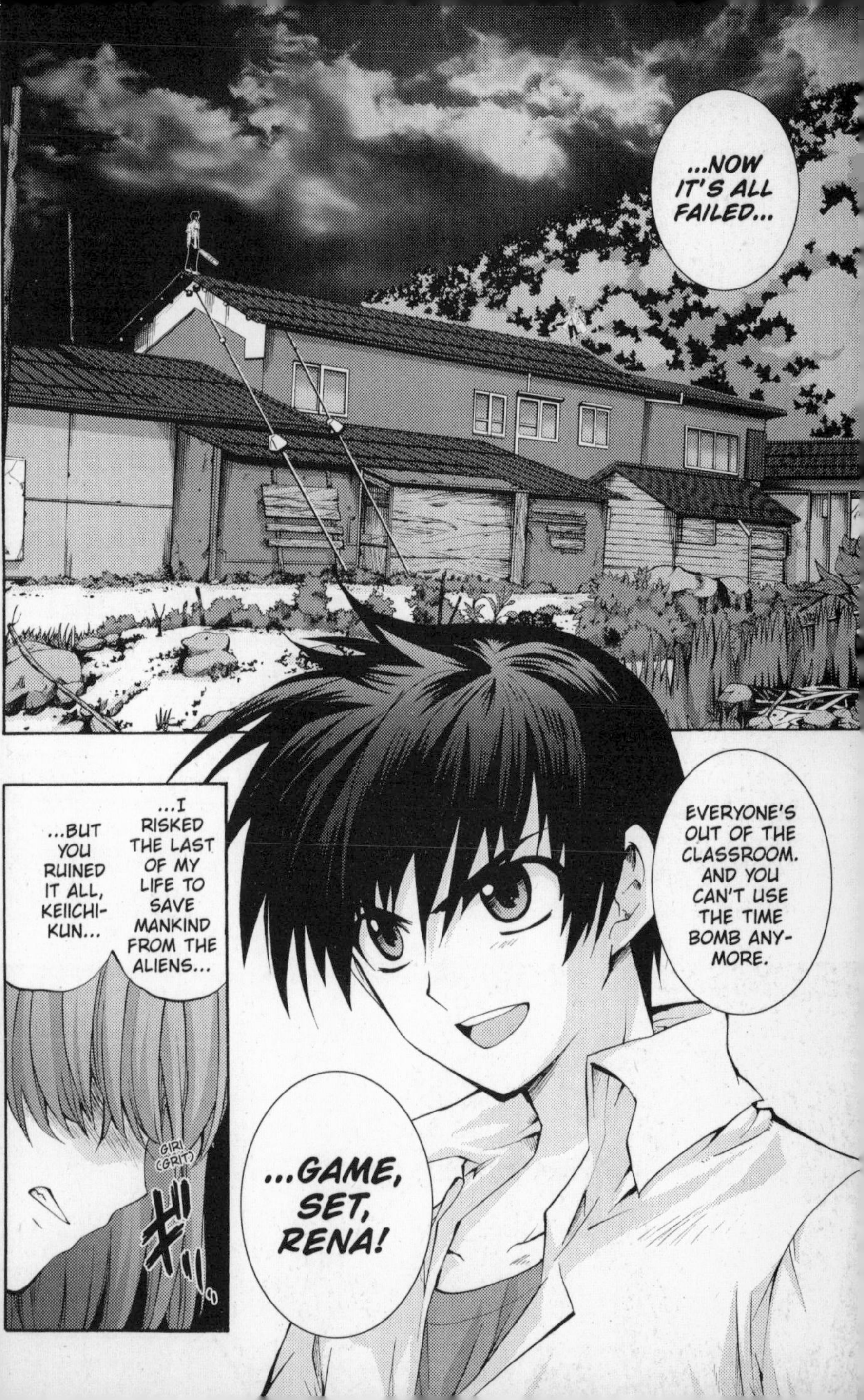
...NOW IT'S ALL FAILED...
EVERYONE'S OUT OF THE CLASSROOM. AND YOU CAN'T USE THE TIME BOMB ANY-MORE.
...I RISKED THE LAST OF MY LIFE TO SAVE MANKIND FROM THE ALIENS...
...BUT YOU RUINED IT ALL, KEIICHI-KUN...
...GAME, SET, RENA!
GIRI (GRIT)

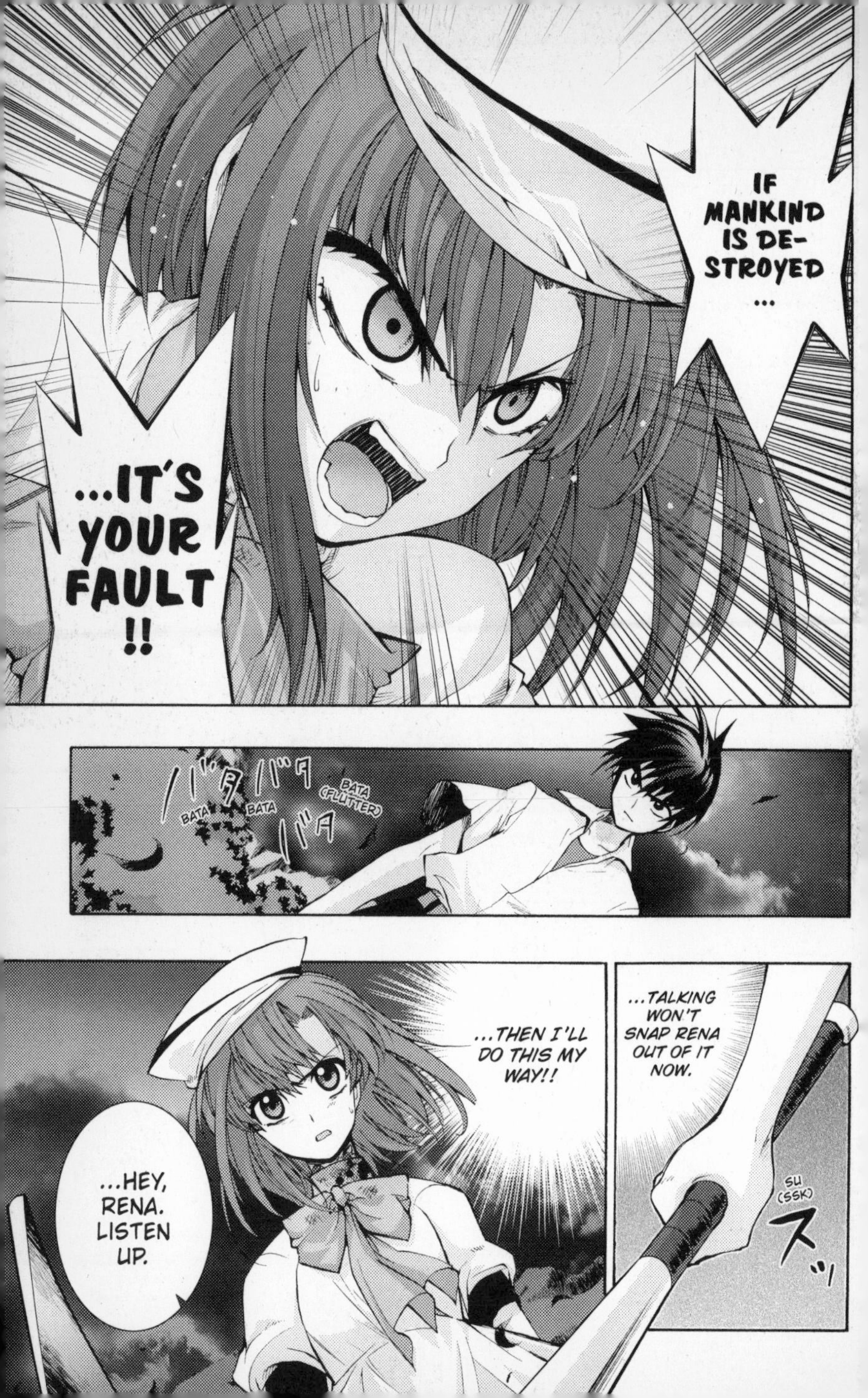
IF MANKIND IS DE-STROYED ...
...IT'S YOUR FAULT !!
バタバタバタ
BATA (FLUTTER)
BATA
BATA
...TALKING WON'T SNAP RENA OUT OF IT NOW.
SU (SSK)
スッ
...THEN I'LL DO THIS MY WAY!!
...HEY, RENA. LISTEN UP.

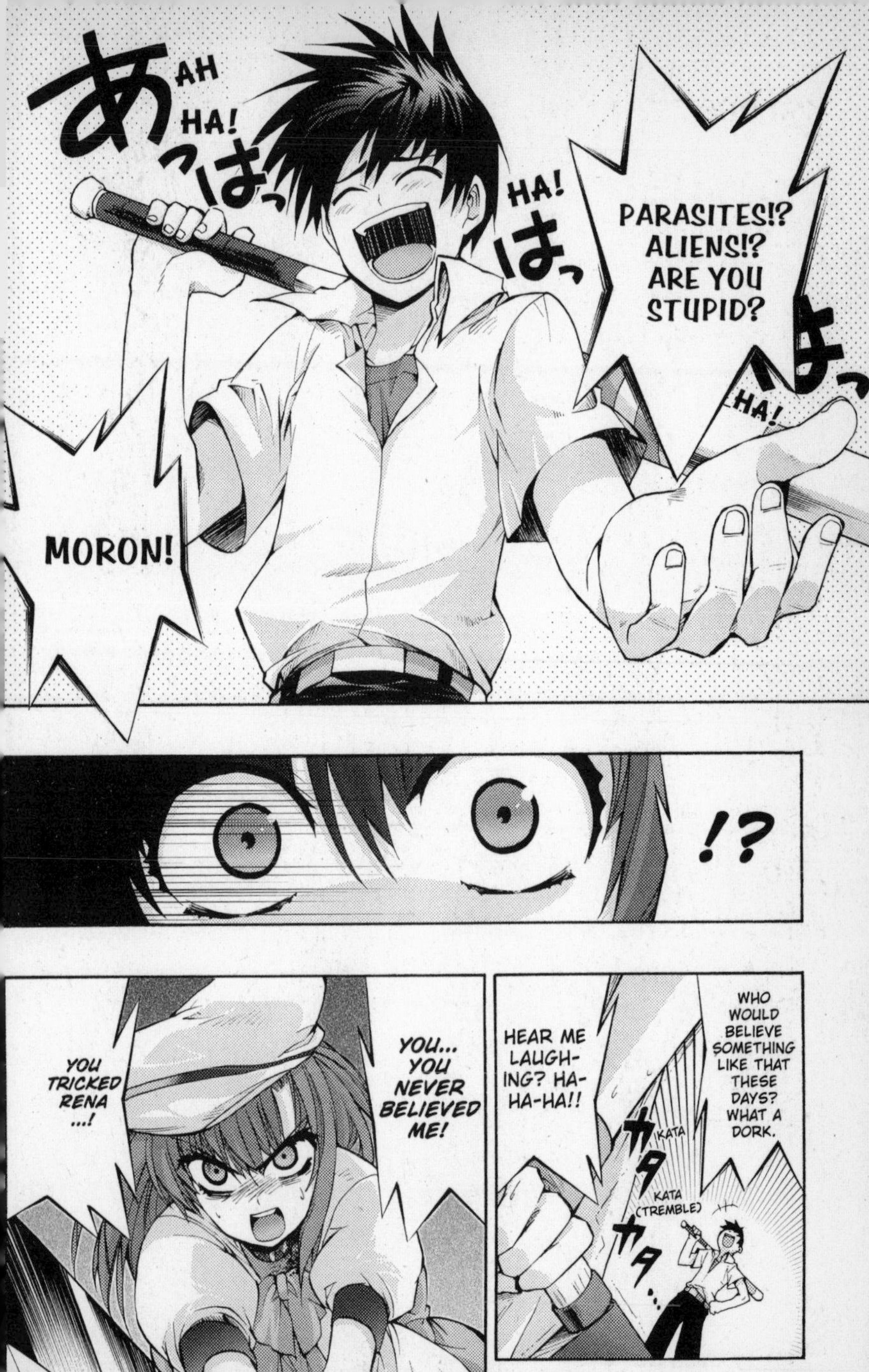

PARASITES!? ALIENS!? ARE YOU STUPID?
あっ AH
はっ HA!
はっ HA!
はっ HA!
MORON!
!?
WHO WOULD BELIEVE SOMETHING LIKE THAT THESE DAYS? WHAT A DORK.
HEAR ME LAUGHING? HA-HA-HA!!
カタ KATA
カタ KATA (TREMBLE)
...
YOU... YOU NEVER BELIEVED ME!
YOU TRICKED RENA ...!

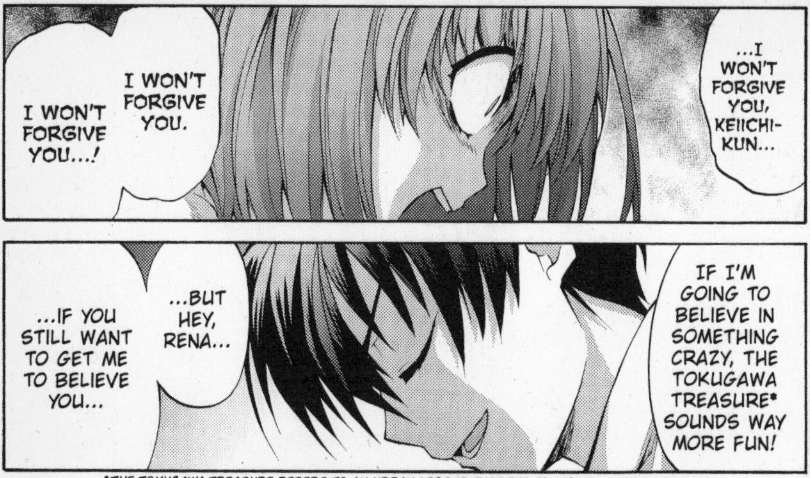
...I WON'T FORGIVE YOU, KEIICHI-KUN...
I WON'T FORGIVE YOU.
I WON'T FORGIVE YOU...!
IF I'M GOING TO BELIEVE IN SOMETHING CRAZY, THE TOKUGAWA TREASURE* SOUNDS WAY MORE FUN!
...BUT HEY, RENA...
...IF YOU STILL WANT TO GET ME TO BELIEVE YOU...

*THE TOKUGAWA TREASURE REFERS TO AN URBAN LEGEND THAT THE TOKUGAWA SHOGUNATE HID A VAST QUANTITY OF MONEY SOMEWHERE IN JAPAN. THERE HAVE BEEN MANY FAILED ATTEMPTS AT FINDING IT, AND TREASURE HUNTERS SEARCH FOR IT TO THIS DAY.

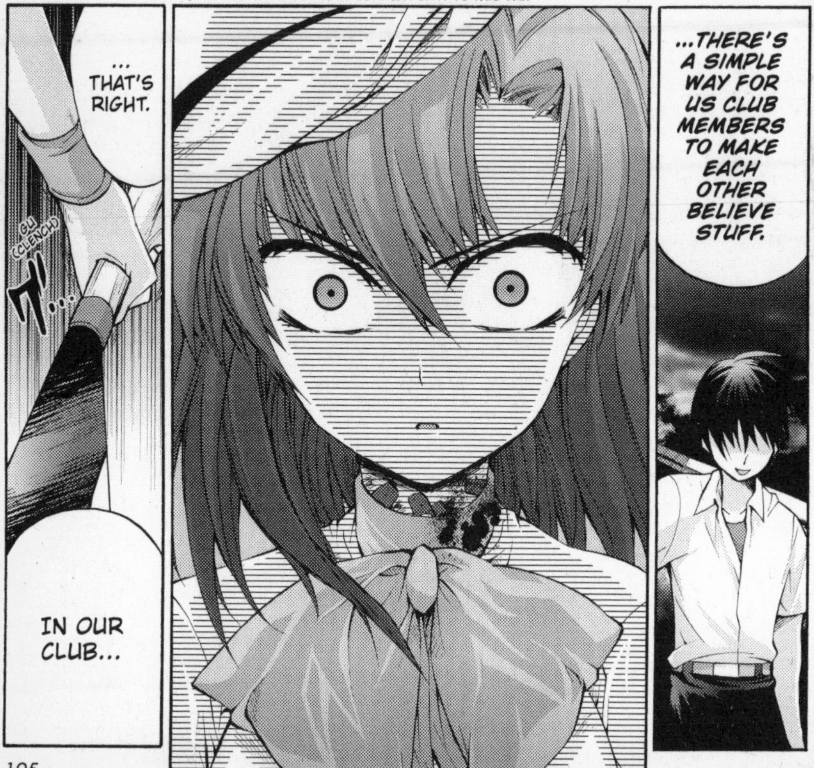
...THERE'S A SIMPLE WAY FOR US CLUB MEMBERS TO MAKE EACH OTHER BELIEVE STUFF.
... THAT'S RIGHT.
GU (CLENCH)
IN OUR CLUB...

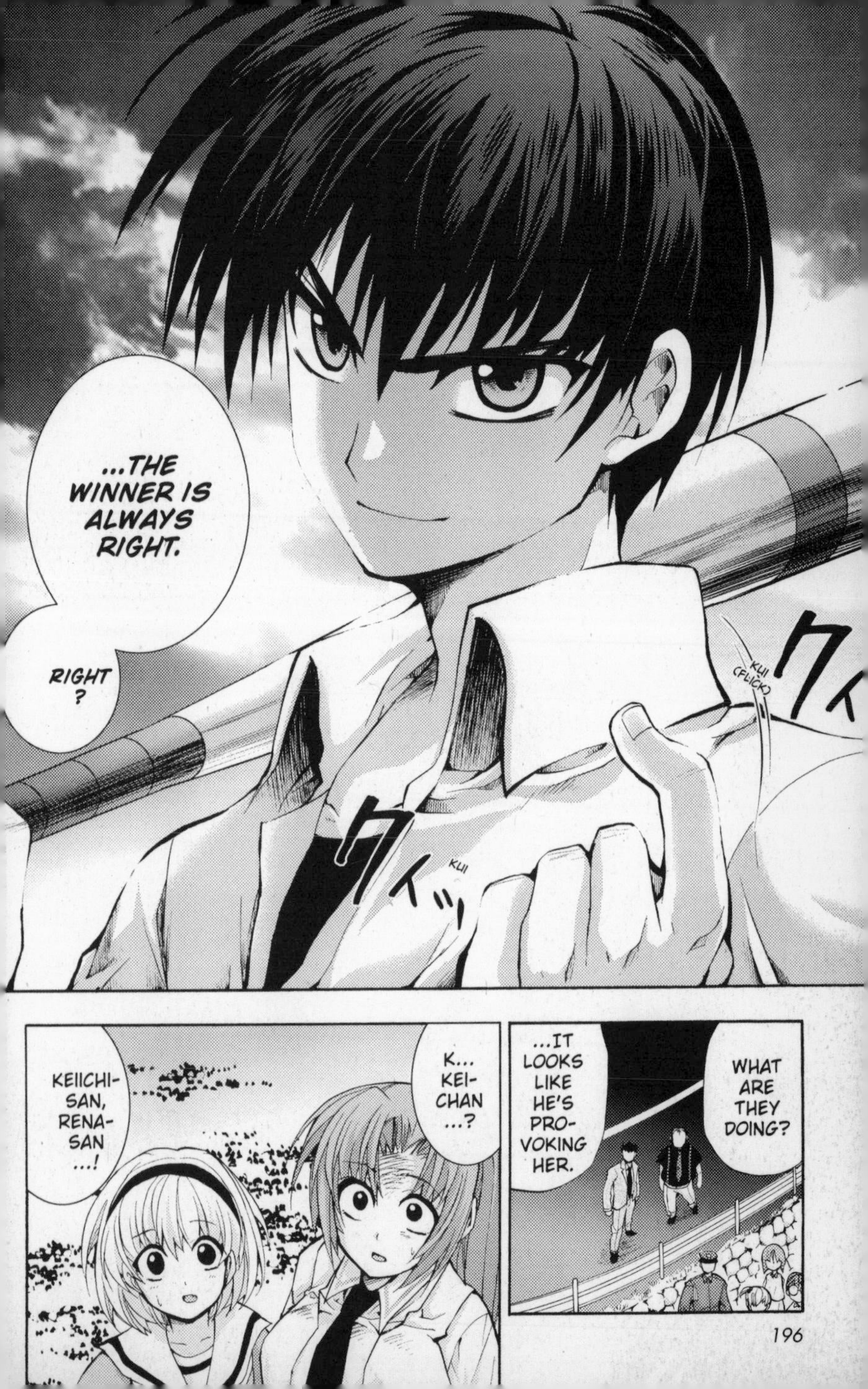
...THE WINNER IS ALWAYS RIGHT.
RIGHT?
KUI (FLICK)
KUI
WHAT ARE THEY DOING?
...IT LOOKS LIKE HE'S PRO-VOKING HER.
K... KEI-CHAN ...?
KEIICHI-SAN, RENA-SAN ...!

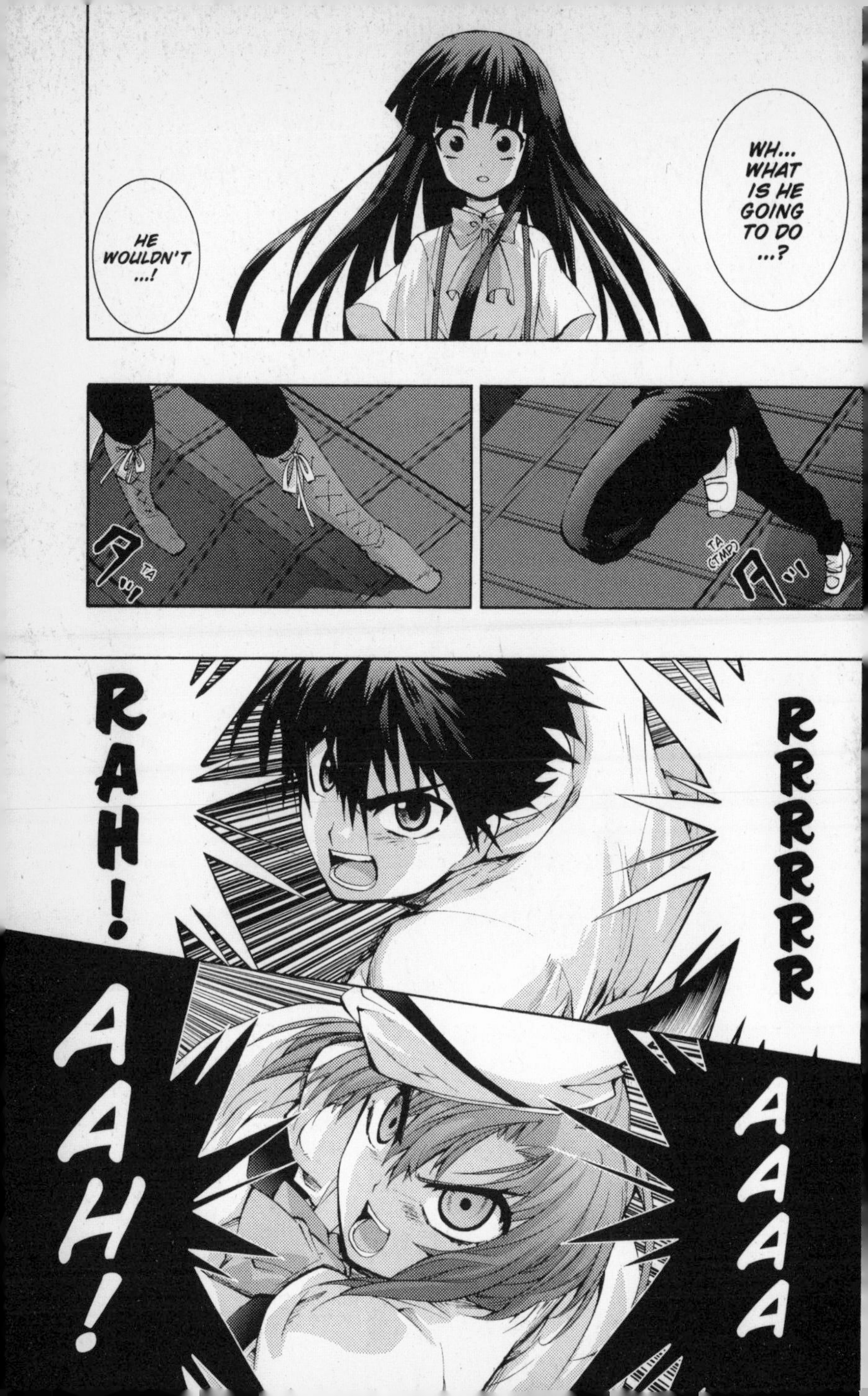
WH... WHAT IS HE GOING TO DO ...?
HE WOULDN'T ...!
TA (TMP)
タッ
TA
タッ
RRRRRR
RAH!
AAAA
AAH!

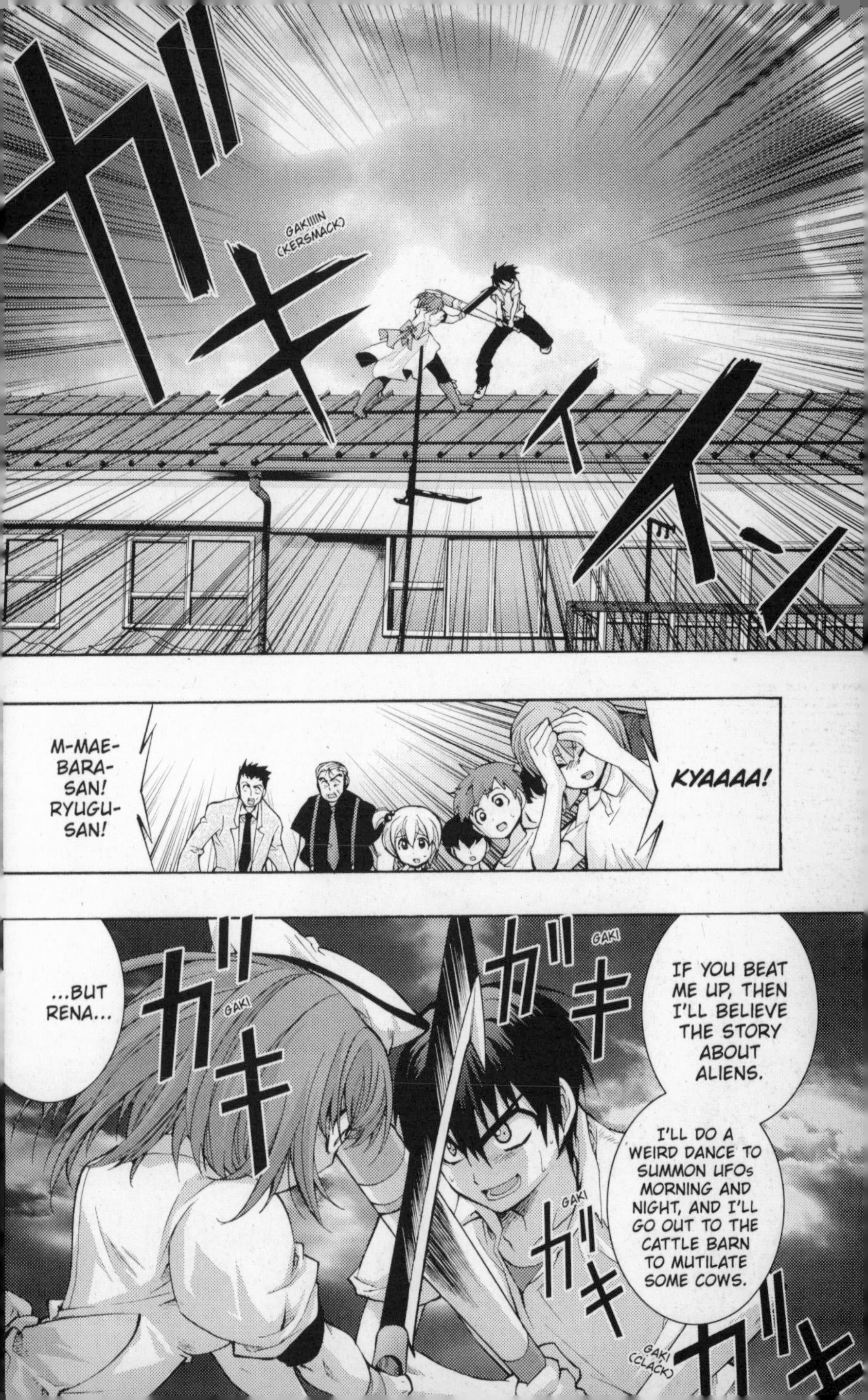
GAKIIIIN (KERSMACK)
KYAAAA!
M-MAE-BARA-SAN! RYUGU-SAN!
GAKI
IF YOU BEAT ME UP, THEN I'LL BELIEVE THE STORY ABOUT ALIENS.
I'LL DO A WEIRD DANCE TO SUMMON UFOs MORNING AND NIGHT, AND I'LL GO OUT TO THE CATTLE BARN TO MUTILATE SOME COWS.
GAKI (CLACK)
GAKI
GAKI
...BUT RENA...

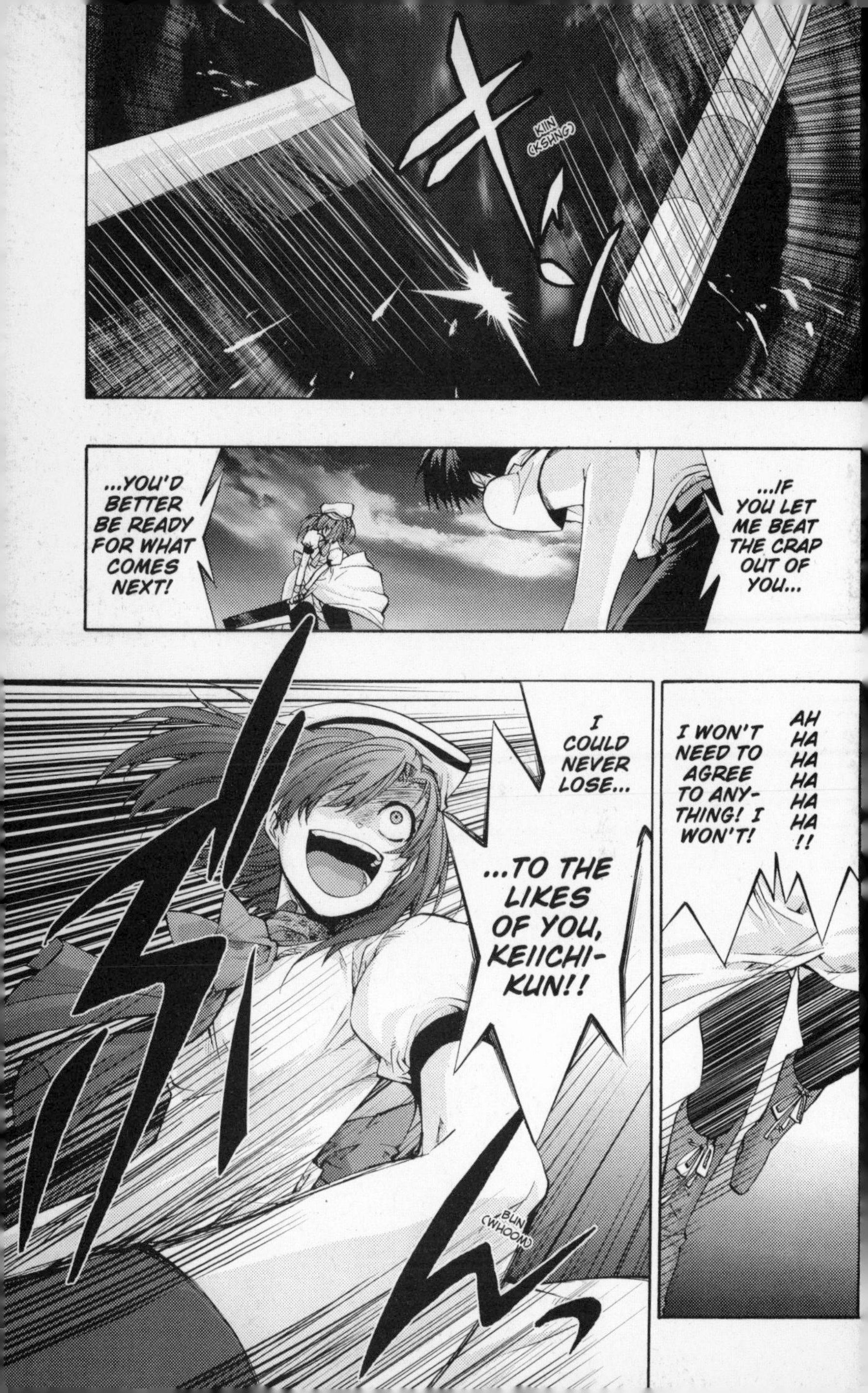
KIN (KSHNG)
...IF YOU LET ME BEAT THE CRAP OUT OF YOU...
...YOU'D BETTER BE READY FOR WHAT COMES NEXT!
AH HA HA HA HA HA!!
I WON'T NEED TO AGREE TO ANY-THING! I WON'T!
I COULD NEVER LOSE...
...TO THE LIKES OF YOU, KEIICHI-KUN!!
BUN (WHOOM)

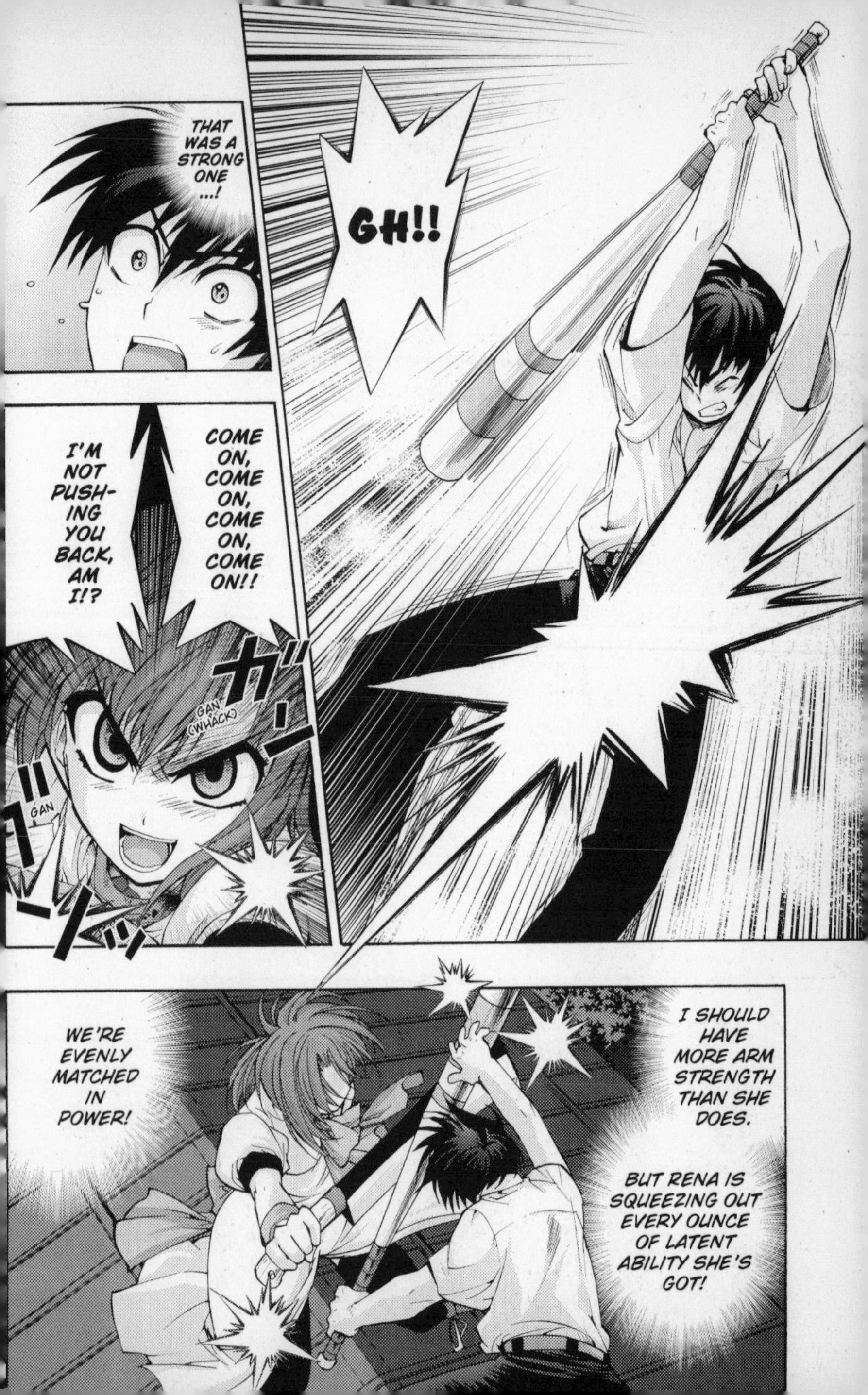

GH!!
THAT WAS A STRONG ONE ...!
COME ON, COME ON, COME ON, COME ON!!
I'M NOT PUSHING YOU BACK, AM I!?
GAN (WHACK)
GAN
I SHOULD HAVE MORE ARM STRENGTH THAN SHE DOES.
BUT RENA IS SQUEEZING OUT EVERY OUNCE OF LATENT ABILITY SHE'S GOT!
WE'RE EVENLY MATCHED IN POWER!

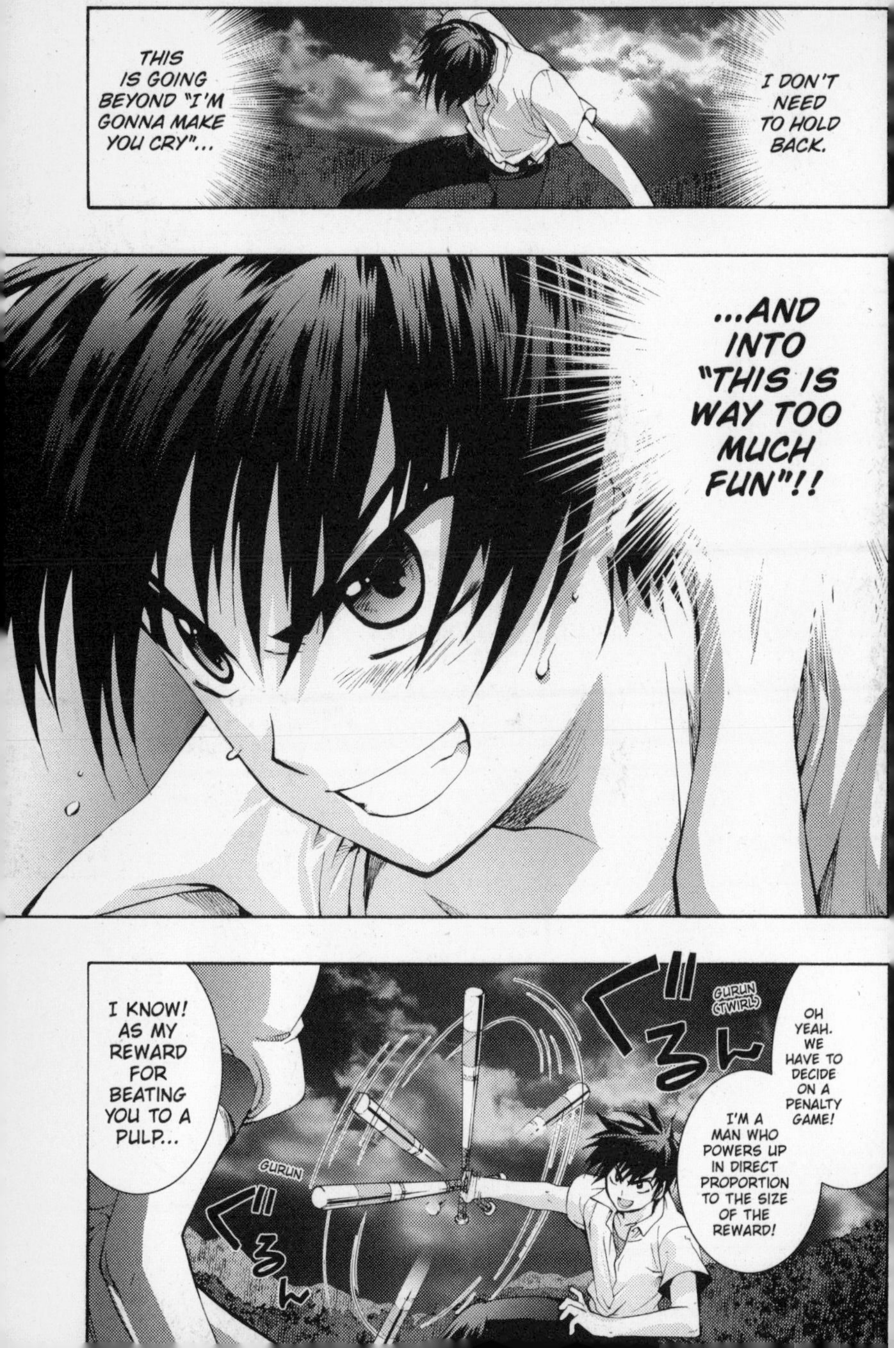
I DON'T NEED TO HOLD BACK.
THIS IS GOING BEYOND "I'M GONNA MAKE YOU CRY"...
...AND INTO "THIS IS WAY TOO MUCH FUN"!!
ぐるん
GURUN (TWIRL)
OH YEAH. WE HAVE TO DECIDE ON A PENALTY GAME!
I'M A MAN WHO POWERS UP IN DIRECT PROPORTION TO THE SIZE OF THE REWARD!
I KNOW! AS MY REWARD FOR BEATING YOU TO A PULP...
ぐるん
GURUN

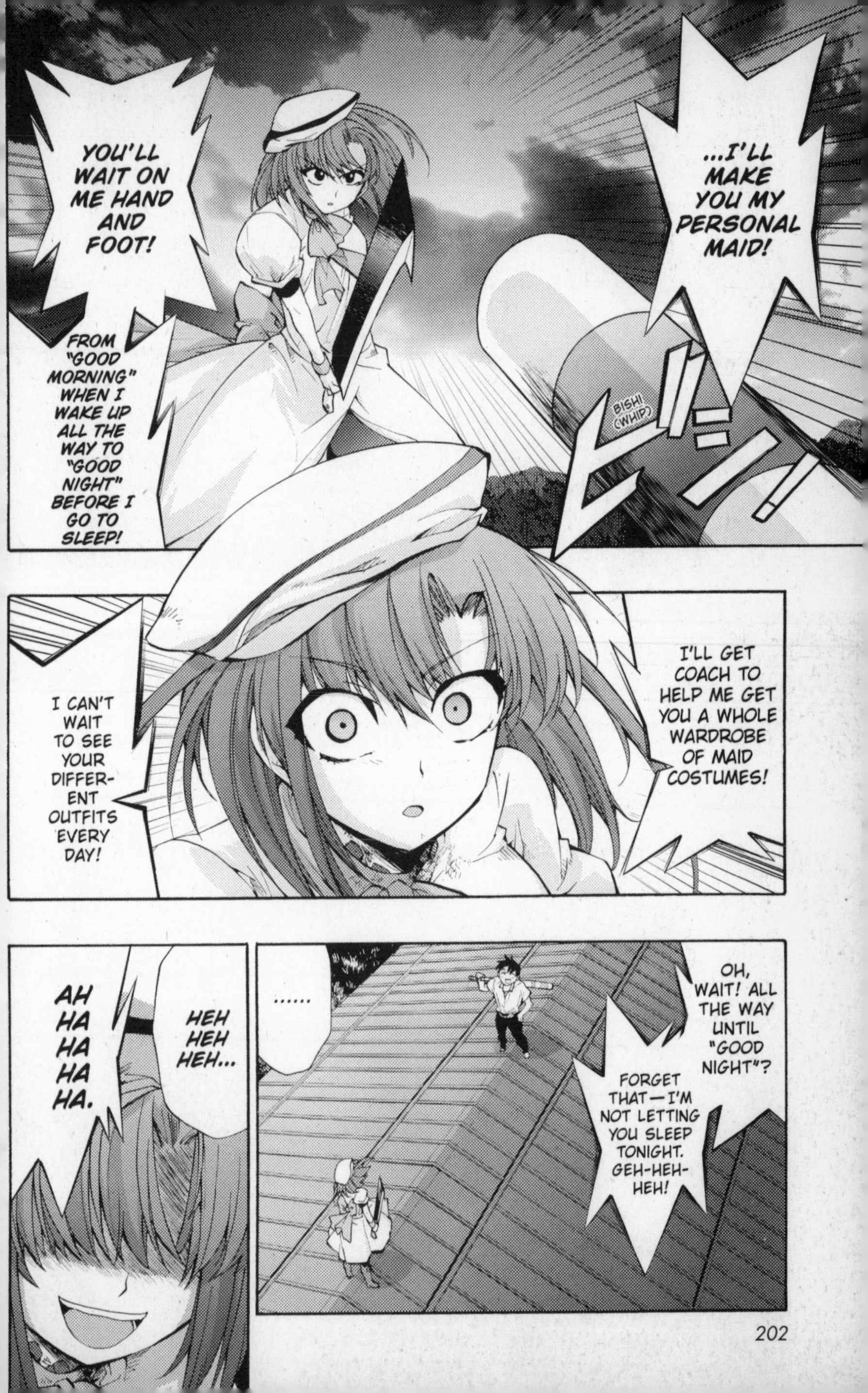
...I'LL MAKE YOU MY PERSONAL MAID!
BISHI (WHIP)
YOU'LL WAIT ON ME HAND AND FOOT!
FROM "GOOD MORNING" WHEN I WAKE UP ALL THE WAY TO "GOOD NIGHT" BEFORE I GO TO SLEEP!
I'LL GET COACH TO HELP ME GET YOU A WHOLE WARDROBE OF MAID COSTUMES!
I CAN'T WAIT TO SEE YOUR DIFFER-ENT OUTFITS EVERY DAY!
OH, WAIT! ALL THE WAY UNTIL "GOOD NIGHT"?
FORGET THAT—I'M NOT LETTING YOU SLEEP TONIGHT. GEH-HEH-HEH!
......
HEH HEH HEH...
AH HA HA HA HA.

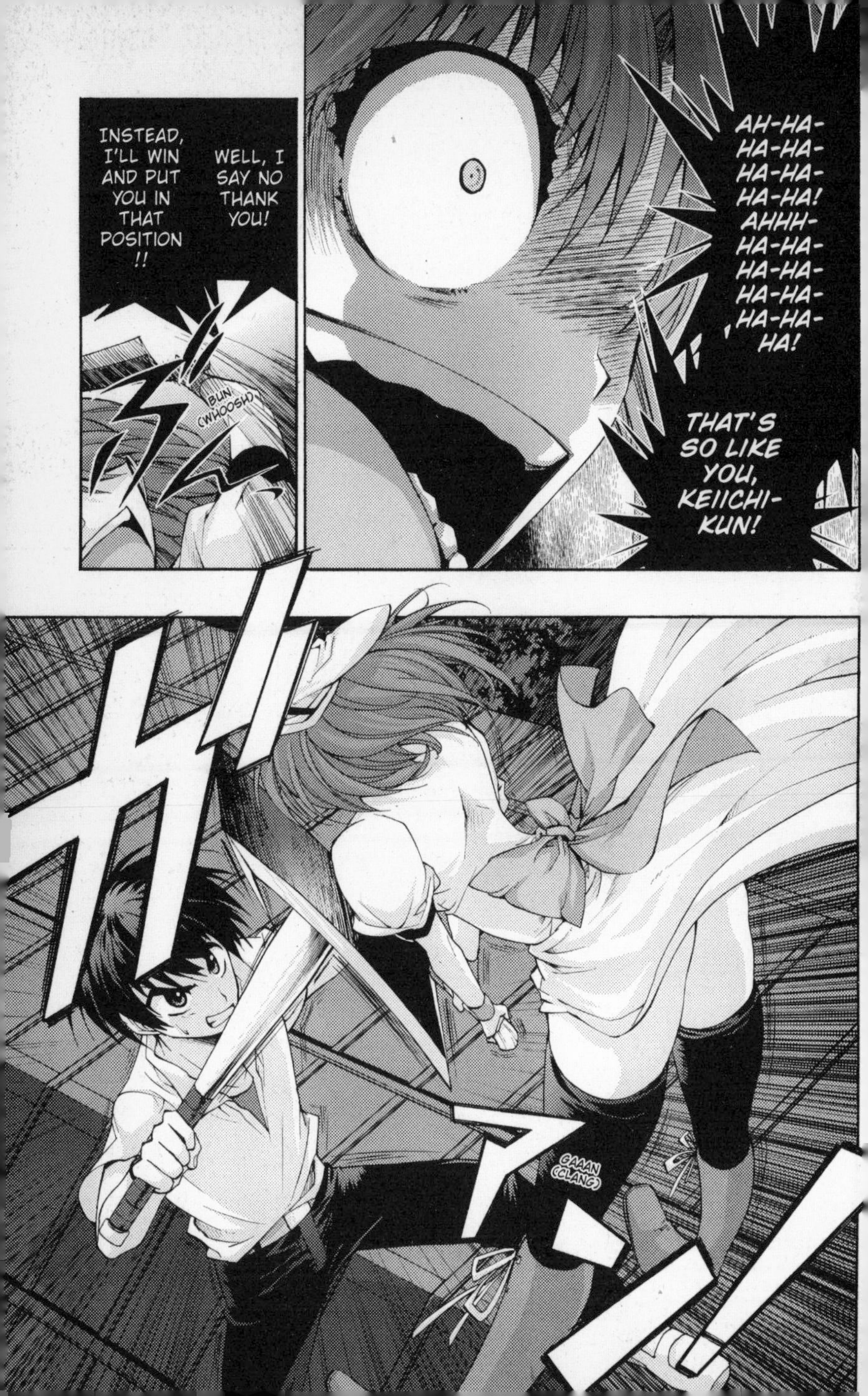
AH-HA-HA-HA-HA-HA-HA-HA! AHHH-HA-HA-HA-HA-HA-HA-HA-HA-HA!
THAT'S SO LIKE YOU, KEIICHI-KUN!
WELL, I SAY NO THANK YOU!
INSTEAD, I'LL WIN AND PUT YOU IN THAT POSITION!!
BUN (WHOOSH)
GAAAN (CLANG)

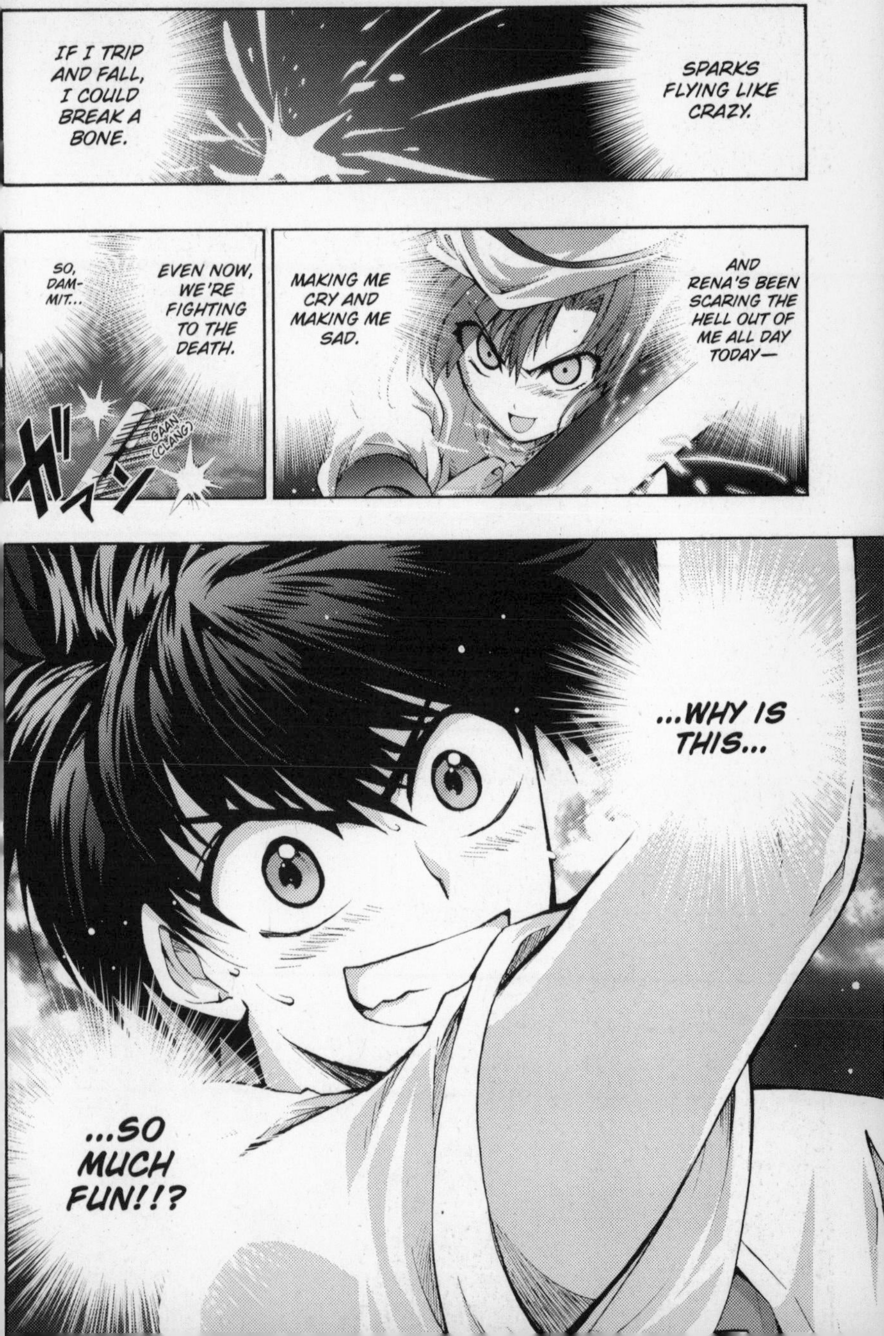
SPARKS FLYING LIKE CRAZY.
IF I TRIP AND FALL, I COULD BREAK A BONE.
AND RENA'S BEEN SCARING THE HELL OUT OF ME ALL DAY TODAY—
MAKING ME CRY AND MAKING ME SAD.
EVEN NOW, WE'RE FIGHTING TO THE DEATH.
SO, DAM-MIT...
GAAN (CLANG)
...WHY IS THIS...
...SO MUCH FUN!!?

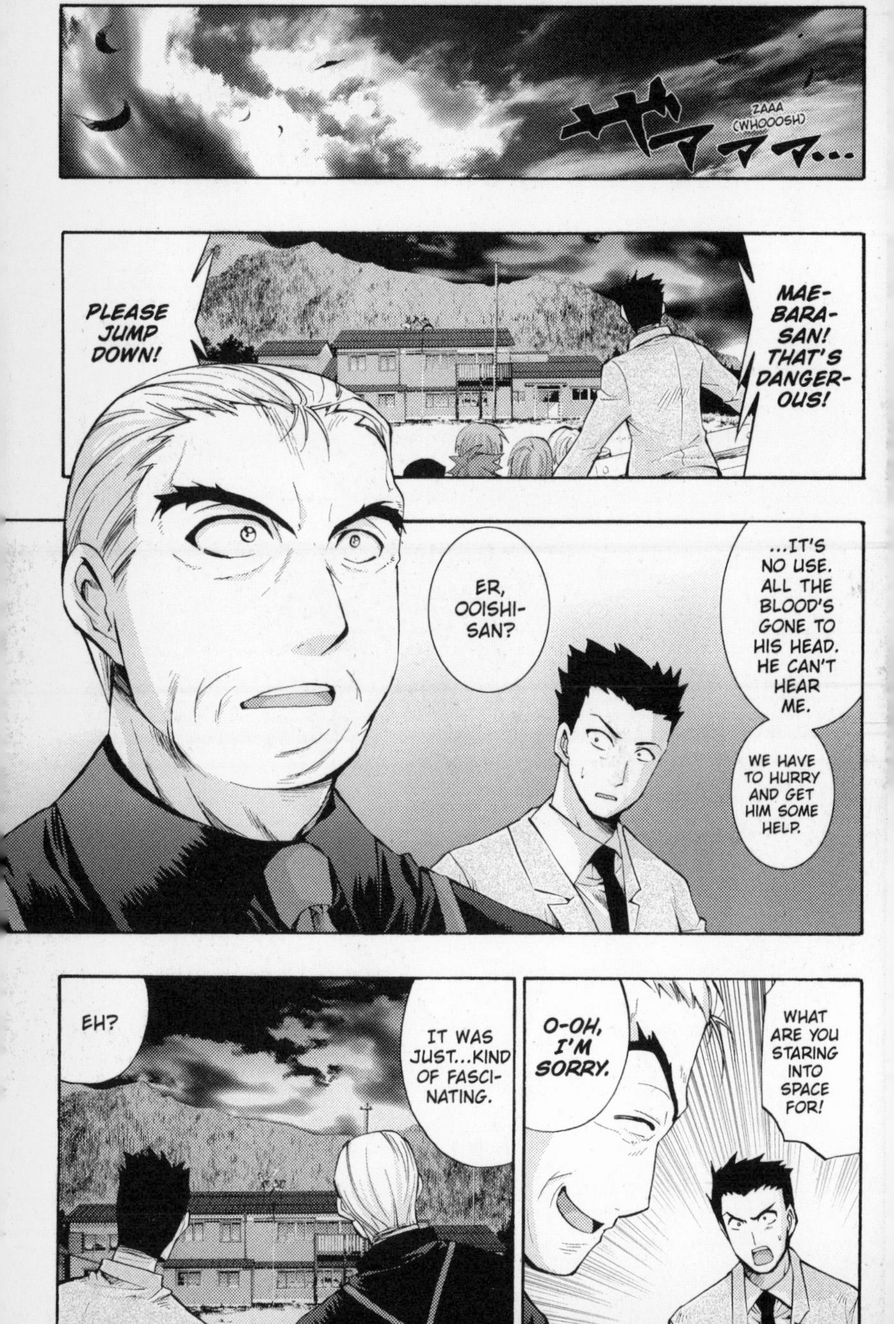
ZAAA (WHOOOSH)
ザアアア...
MAE-BARA-SAN! THAT'S DANGER-OUS!
PLEASE JUMP DOWN!
...IT'S NO USE. ALL THE BLOOD'S GONE TO HIS HEAD. HE CAN'T HEAR ME.
WE HAVE TO HURRY AND GET HIM SOME HELP.
ER, OOISHI-SAN?
WHAT ARE YOU STARING INTO SPACE FOR!
O-OH, I'M SORRY.
IT WAS JUST...KIND OF FASCINATING.
EH?

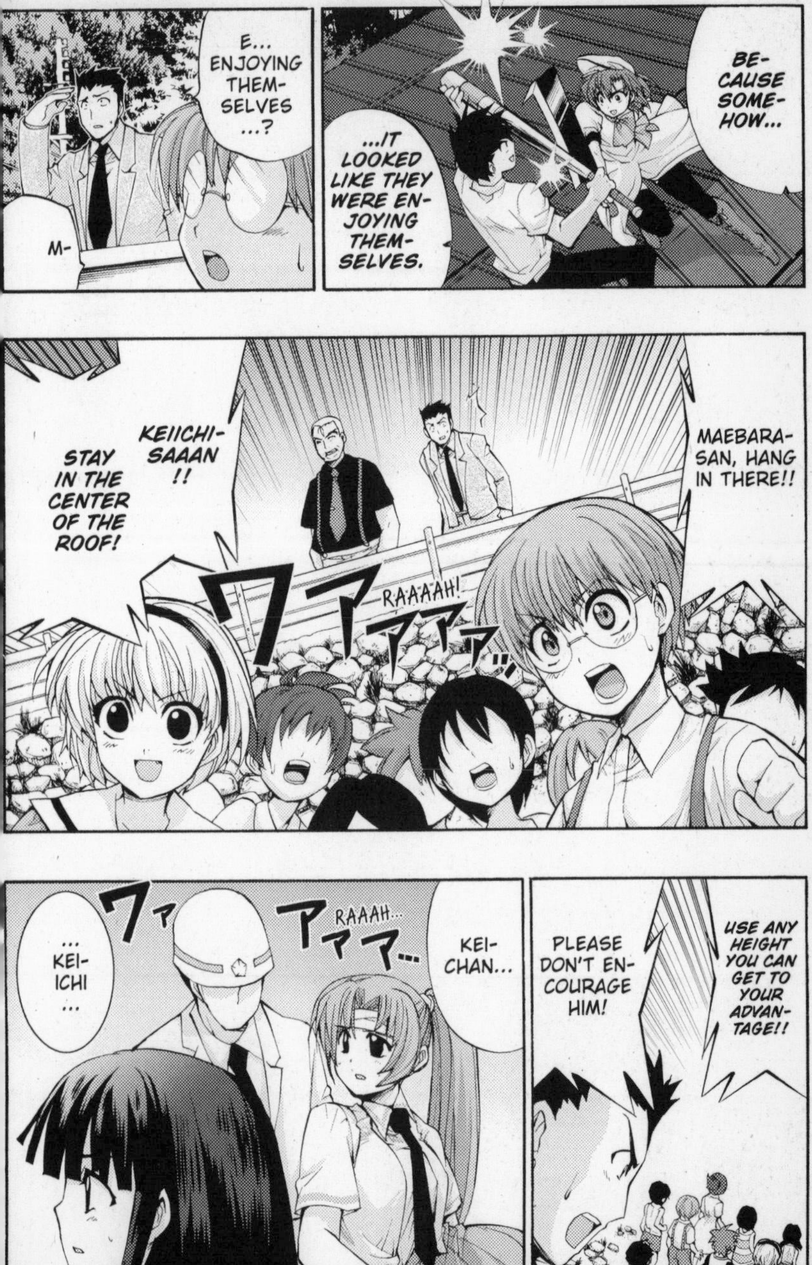
BE-CAUSE SOME-HOW...
...IT LOOKED LIKE THEY WERE EN-JOYING THEM-SELVES.
E... ENJOYING THEM-SELVES ...?
M-
MAEBARA-SAN, HANG IN THERE!!
RAAAAH!
KEIICHI-SAAAN !!
STAY IN THE CENTER OF THE ROOF!
USE ANY HEIGHT YOU CAN GET TO YOUR ADVAN-TAGE!!
PLEASE DON'T EN-COURAGE HIM!
KEI-CHAN...
RAAAH...
... KEI-ICHI ...

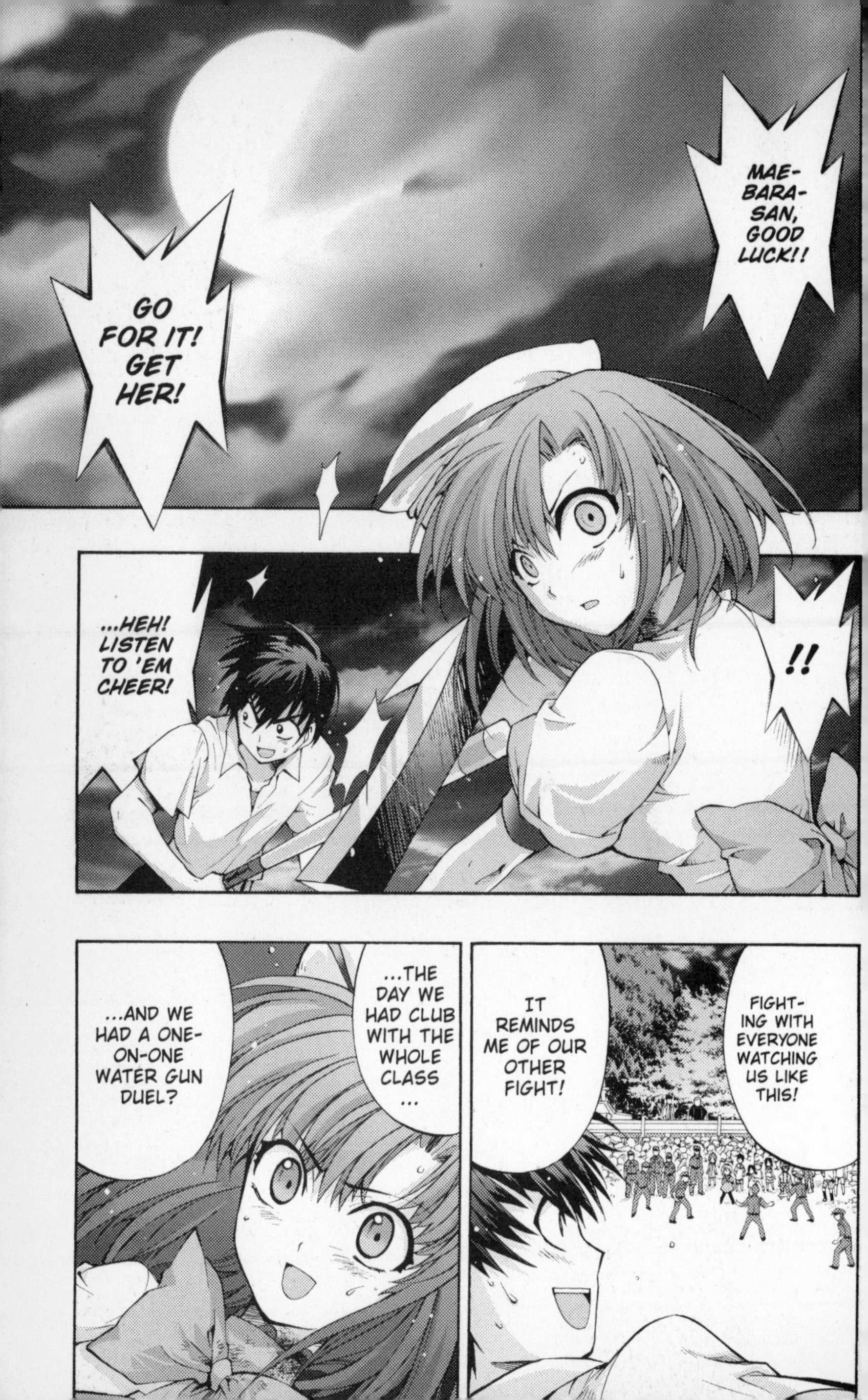
MAE-BARA-SAN, GOOD LUCK!!
GO FOR IT! GET HER!
!!
...HEH! LISTEN TO 'EM CHEER!
FIGHTING WITH EVERYONE WATCHING US LIKE THIS!
IT REMINDS ME OF OUR OTHER FIGHT!
...THE DAY WE HAD CLUB WITH THE WHOLE CLASS...
...AND WE HAD A ONE-ON-ONE WATER GUN DUEL?

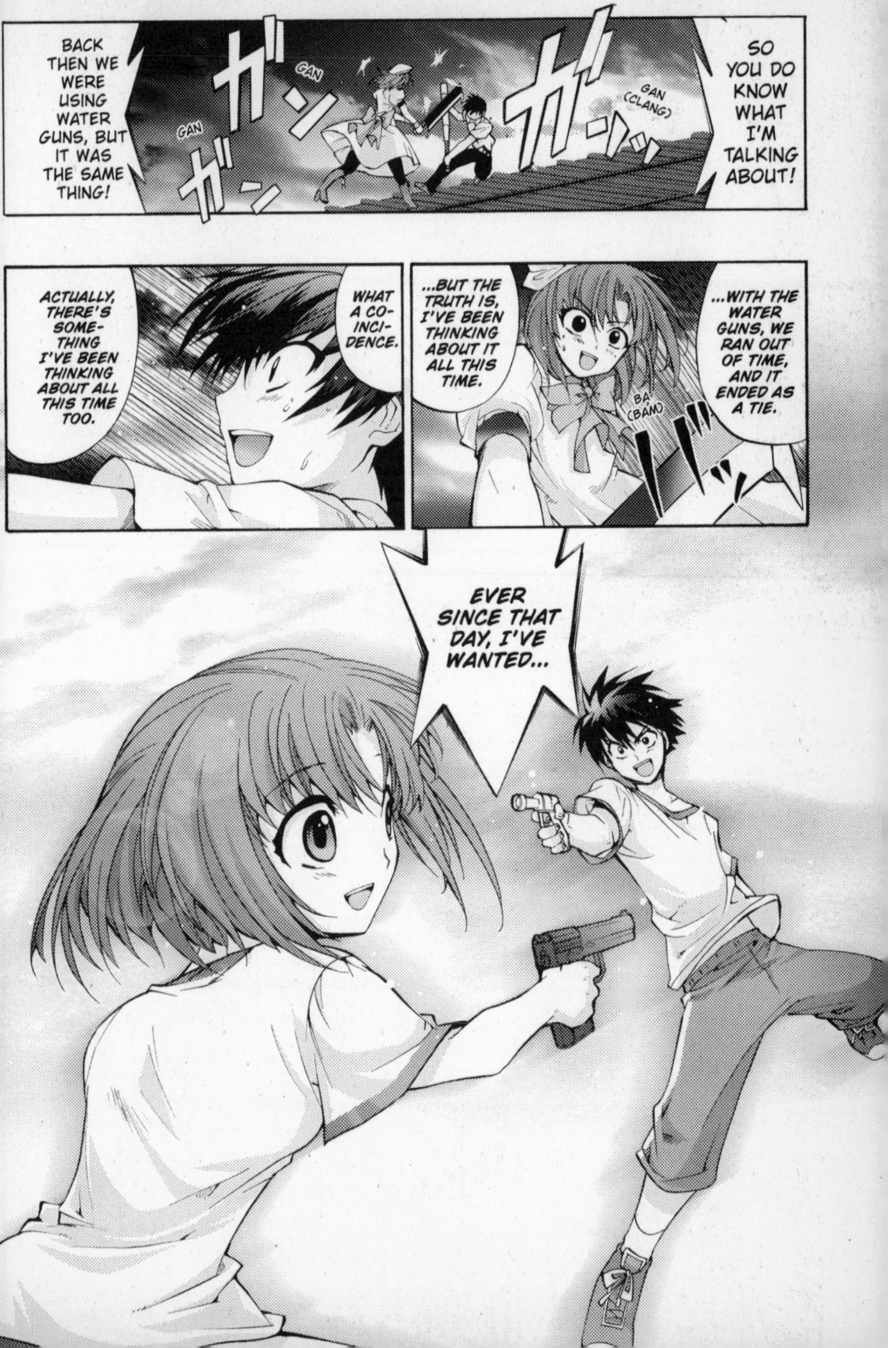
SO YOU DO KNOW WHAT I'M TALKING ABOUT!
GAN (CLANG)
GAN
GAN
BACK THEN WE WERE USING WATER GUNS, BUT IT WAS THE SAME THING!
...WITH THE WATER GUNS, WE RAN OUT OF TIME, AND IT ENDED AS A TIE.
BA (BAM)
...BUT THE TRUTH IS, I'VE BEEN THINKING ABOUT IT ALL THIS TIME.
WHAT A CO-INCI-DENCE.
ACTUALLY, THERE'S SOME-THING I'VE BEEN THINKING ABOUT ALL THIS TIME TOO.
EVER SINCE THAT DAY, I'VE WANTED...

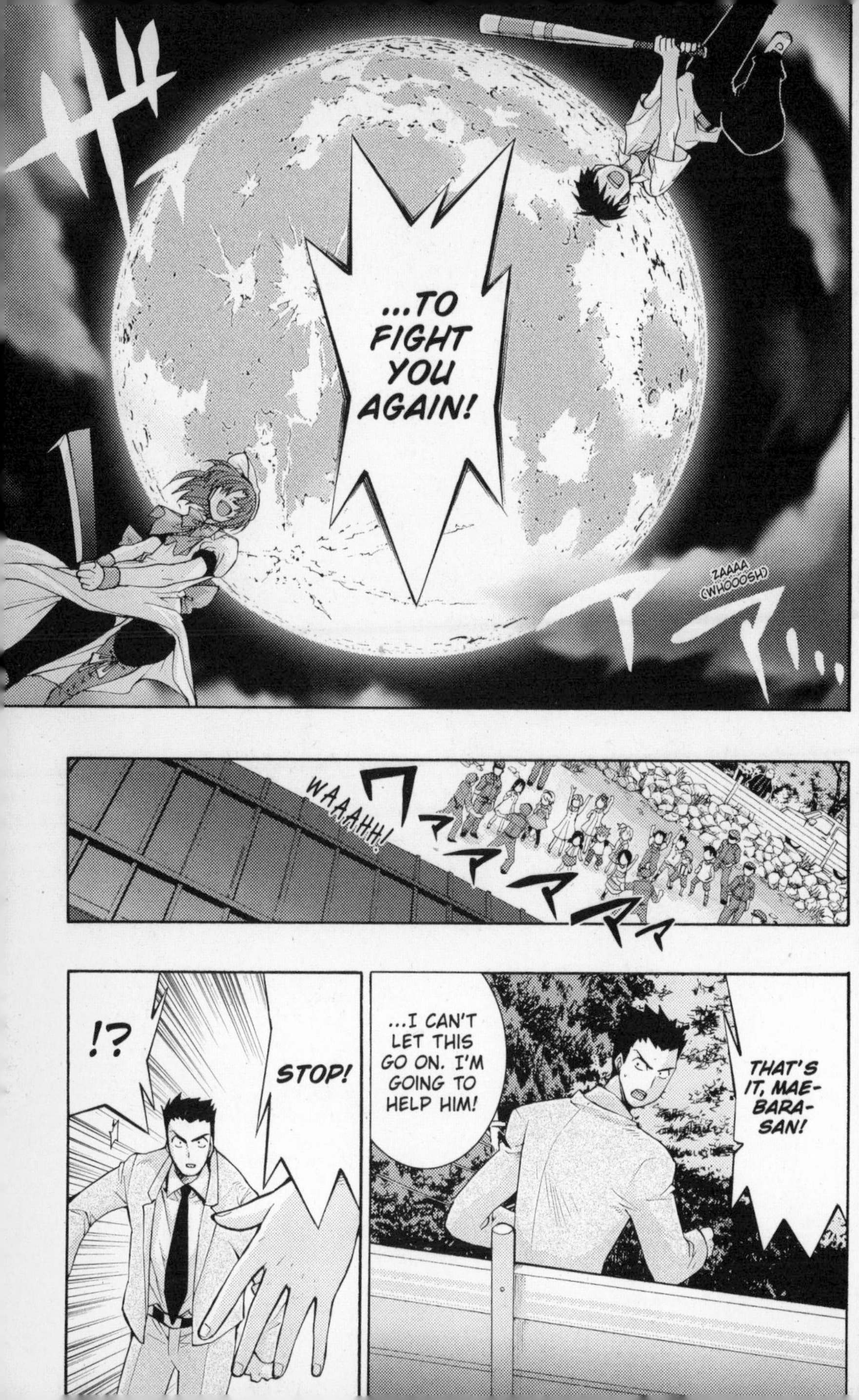
...TO FIGHT YOU AGAIN!
ZAAAA (WHOOOSH)
WAAAHH!
THAT'S IT, MAE-BARA-SAN!
...I CAN'T LET THIS GO ON. I'M GOING TO HELP HIM!
STOP!
!?

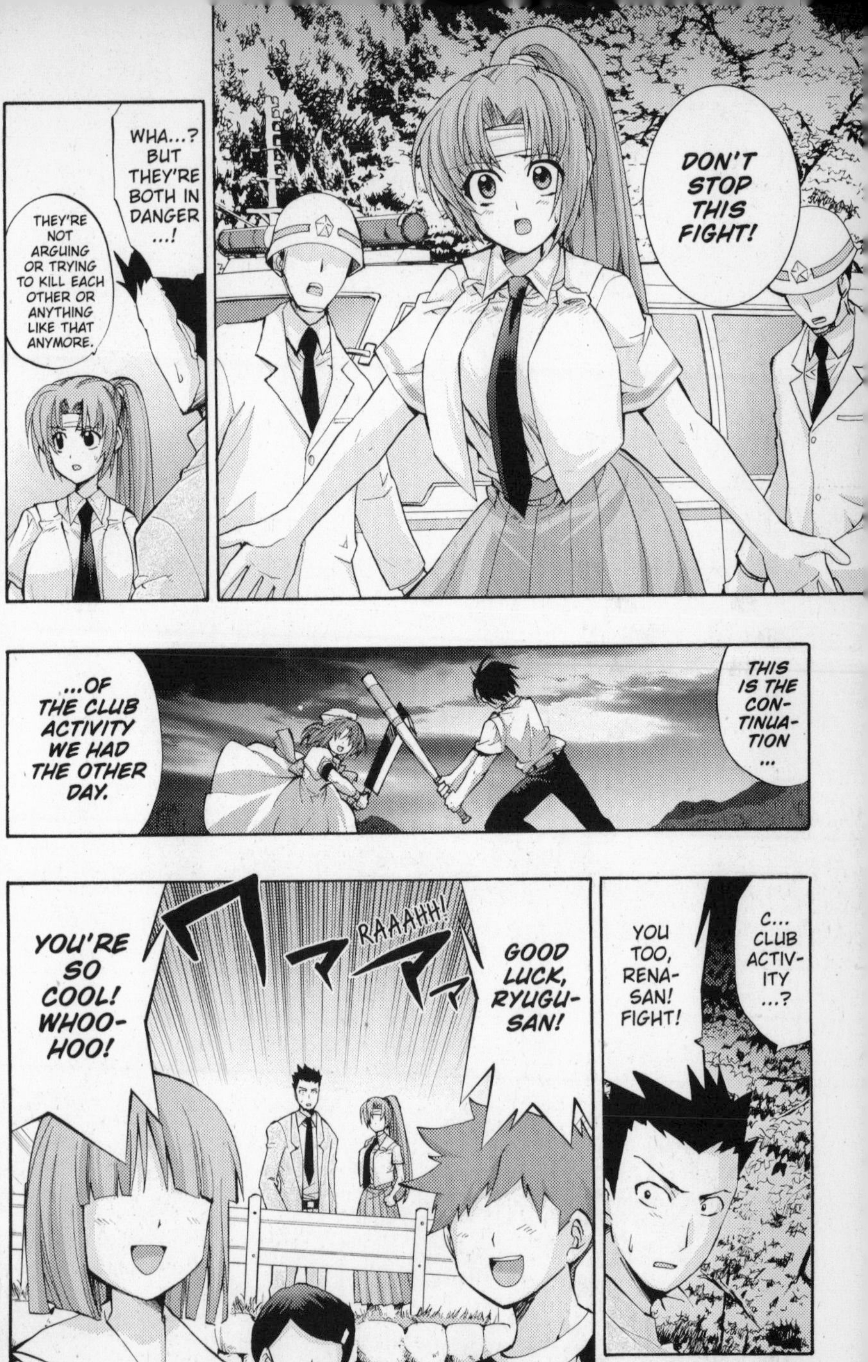
DON'T STOP THIS FIGHT!
WHA...? BUT THEY'RE BOTH IN DANGER ...!
THEY'RE NOT ARGUING OR TRYING TO KILL EACH OTHER OR ANYTHING LIKE THAT ANYMORE.
THIS IS THE CON-TINUA-TION ...
...OF THE CLUB ACTIVITY WE HAD THE OTHER DAY.
C... CLUB ACTIV-ITY ...?
YOU TOO, RENA-SAN! FIGHT!
GOOD LUCK, RYUGU-SAN!
RAAAHH!
YOU'RE SO COOL! WHOO-HOO!

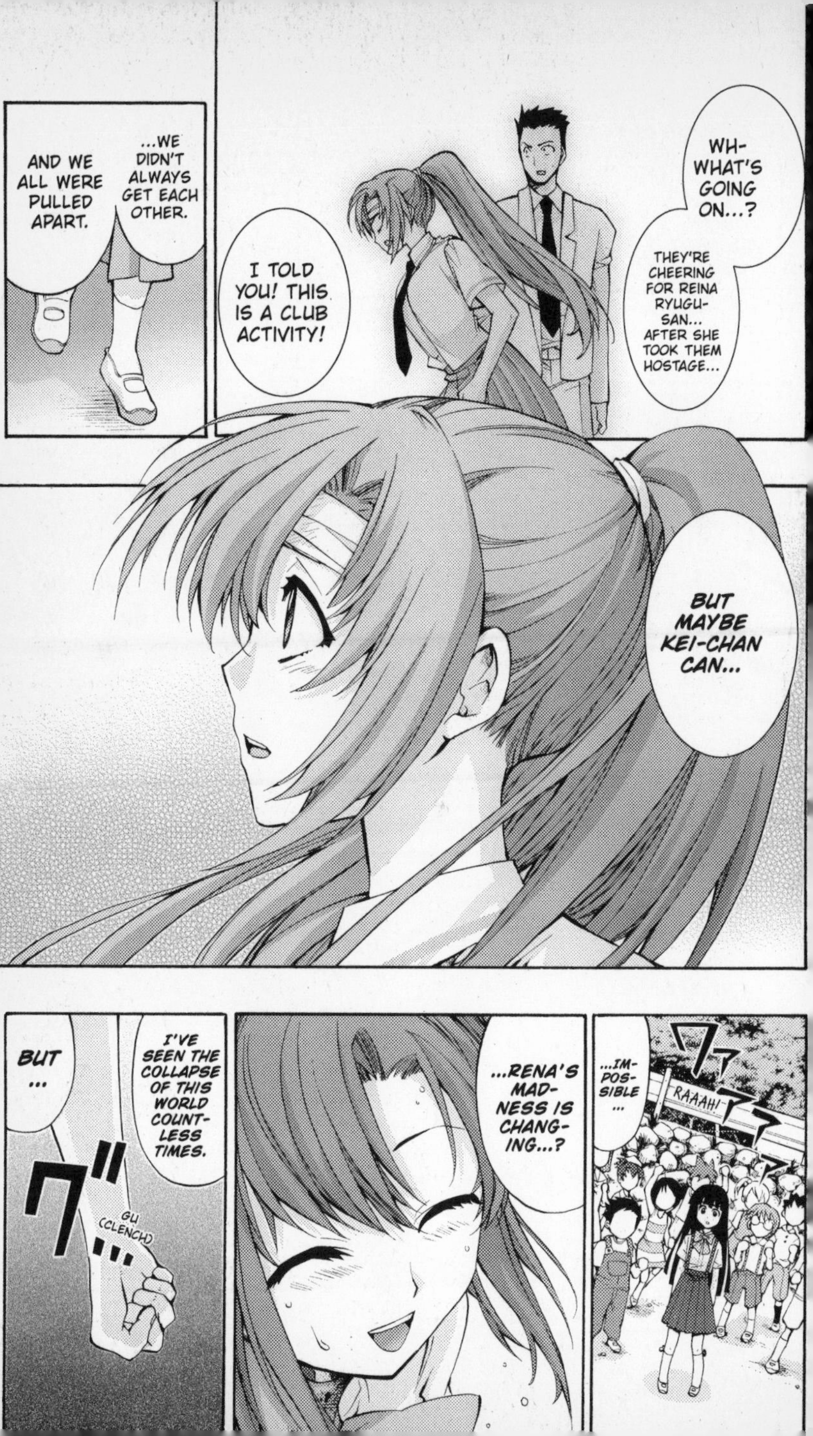
WH-WHAT'S GOING ON...?
THEY'RE CHEERING FOR REINA RYUGU-SAN... AFTER SHE TOOK THEM HOSTAGE...
I TOLD YOU! THIS IS A CLUB ACTIVITY!
...WE DIDN'T ALWAYS GET EACH OTHER.
AND WE ALL WERE PULLED APART.
BUT MAYBE KEI-CHAN CAN...
RA-AAH!
...IM-POSSIBLE...
...RENA'S MAD-NESS IS CHANG-ING...?
I'VE SEEN THE COLLAPSE OF THIS WORLD COUNT-LESS TIMES.
BUT ...
GU (CLENCH)

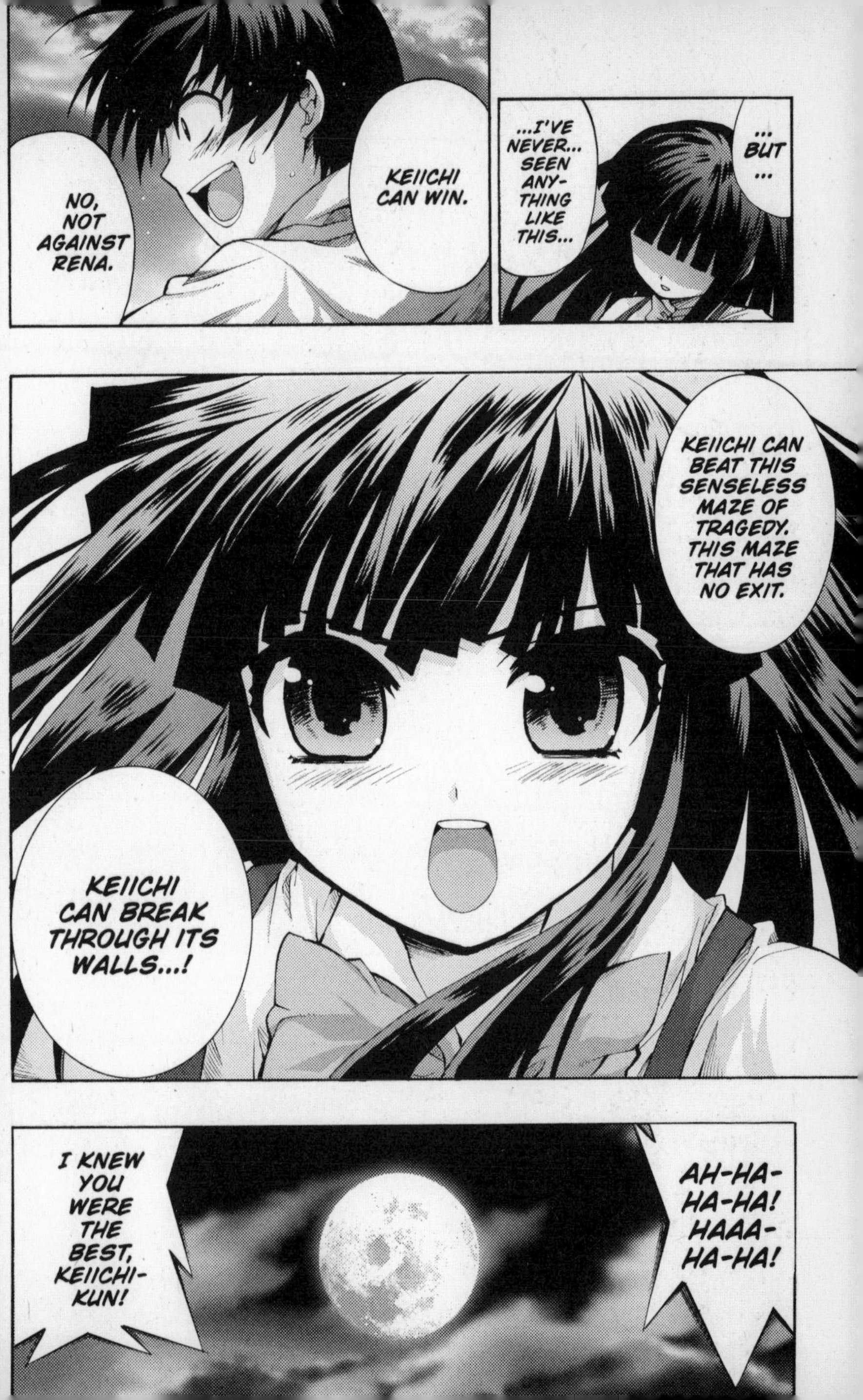
...BUT...
...I'VE NEVER... SEEN ANYTHING LIKE THIS...
KEIICHI CAN WIN.
NO, NOT AGAINST RENA.
KEIICHI CAN BEAT THIS SENSELESS MAZE OF TRAGEDY. THIS MAZE THAT HAS NO EXIT.
KEIICHI CAN BREAK THROUGH ITS WALLS...!
AH-HA-HA-HA! HAAA-HA-HA!
I KNEW YOU WERE THE BEST, KEIICHI-KUN!

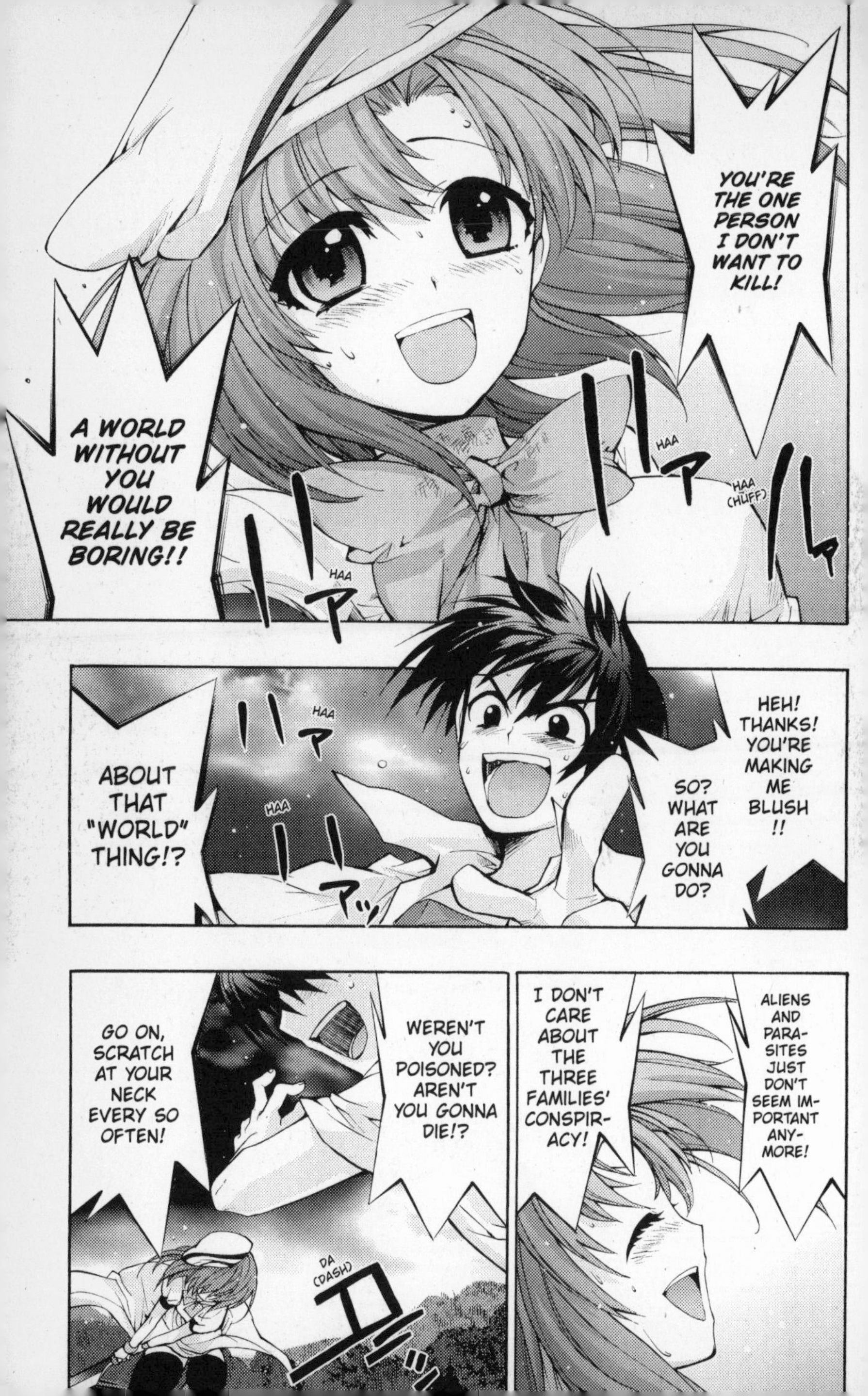
YOU'RE THE ONE PERSON I DON'T WANT TO KILL!
HAA
HAA (HUFF)
A WORLD WITHOUT YOU WOULD REALLY BE BORING!!
HAA
HEH! THANKS! YOU'RE MAKING ME BLUSH !!
SO? WHAT ARE YOU GONNA DO?
HAA
HAA
ABOUT THAT "WORLD" THING!?
ALIENS AND PARA-SITES JUST DON'T SEEM IM-PORTANT ANY-MORE!
I DON'T CARE ABOUT THE THREE FAMILIES' CONSPIR-ACY!
WEREN'T YOU POISONED? AREN'T YOU GONNA DIE!?
GO ON, SCRATCH AT YOUR NECK EVERY SO OFTEN!
DA (DASH)

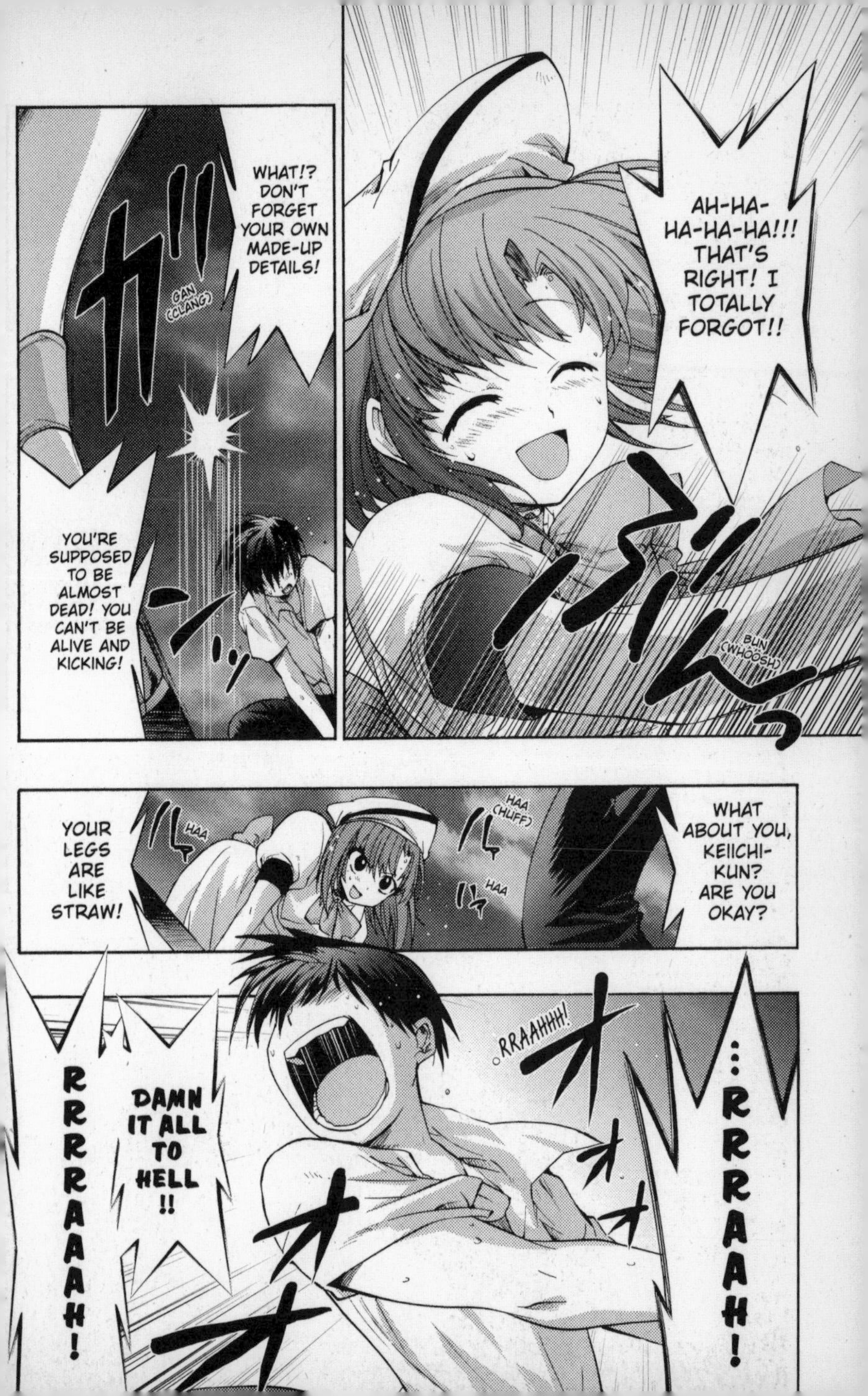
AH-HA-HA-HA-HA!!! THAT'S RIGHT! I TOTALLY FORGOT!!
BUN (WHOOSH)
WHAT!? DON'T FORGET YOUR OWN MADE-UP DETAILS!
GAN (CLANG)
YOU'RE SUPPOSED TO BE ALMOST DEAD! YOU CAN'T BE ALIVE AND KICKING!
WHAT ABOUT YOU, KEIICHI-KUN? ARE YOU OKAY?
HAA (HUFF)
HAA
HAA
YOUR LEGS ARE LIKE STRAW!
...RRRRAAAH!
RRAAHHH!
DAMN IT ALL TO HELL!!
RRRRAAAH!

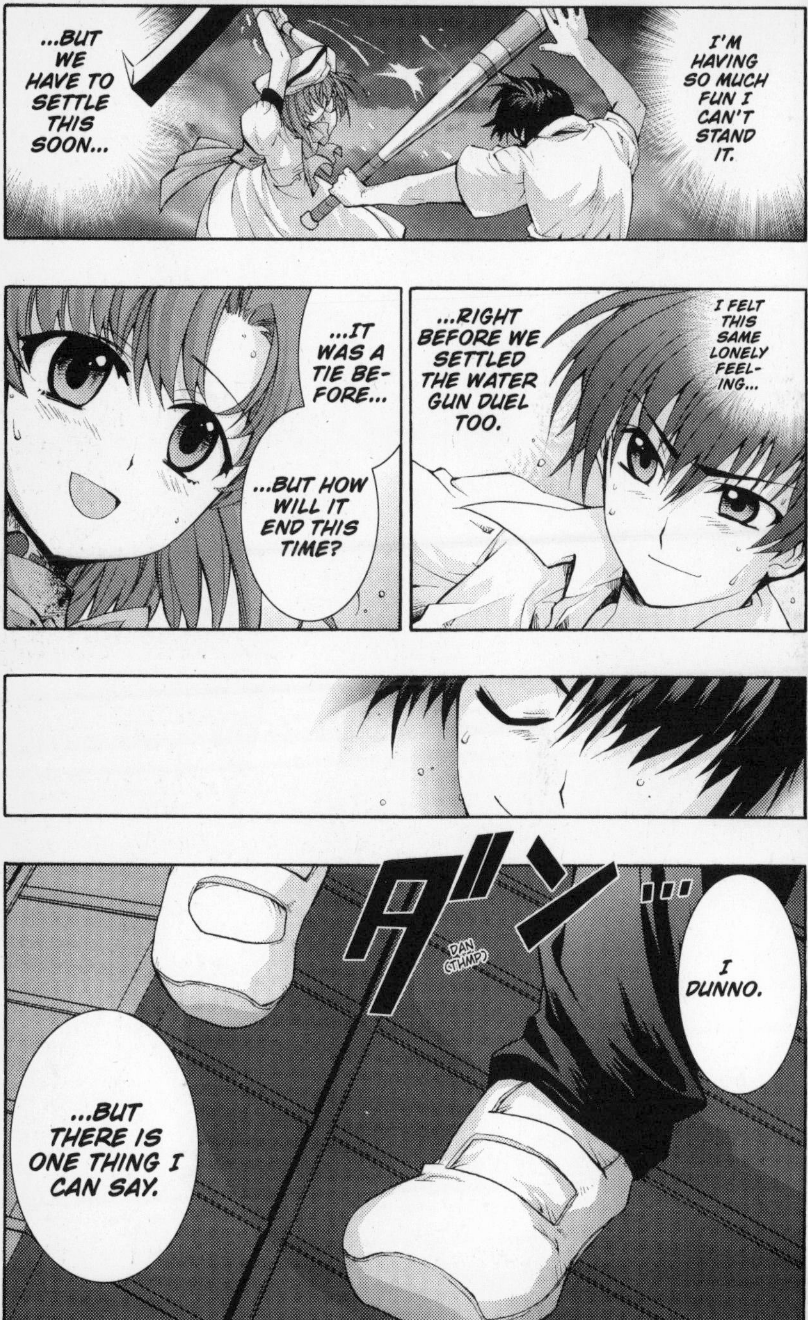
I'M HAVING SO MUCH FUN I CAN'T STAND IT.
...BUT WE HAVE TO SETTLE THIS SOON...
I FELT THIS SAME LONELY FEEL-ING...
...RIGHT BEFORE WE SETTLED THE WATER GUN DUEL TOO.
...IT WAS A TIE BE-FORE...
...BUT HOW WILL IT END THIS TIME?
DAN (THMP)
I DUNNO.
...BUT THERE IS ONE THING I CAN SAY.

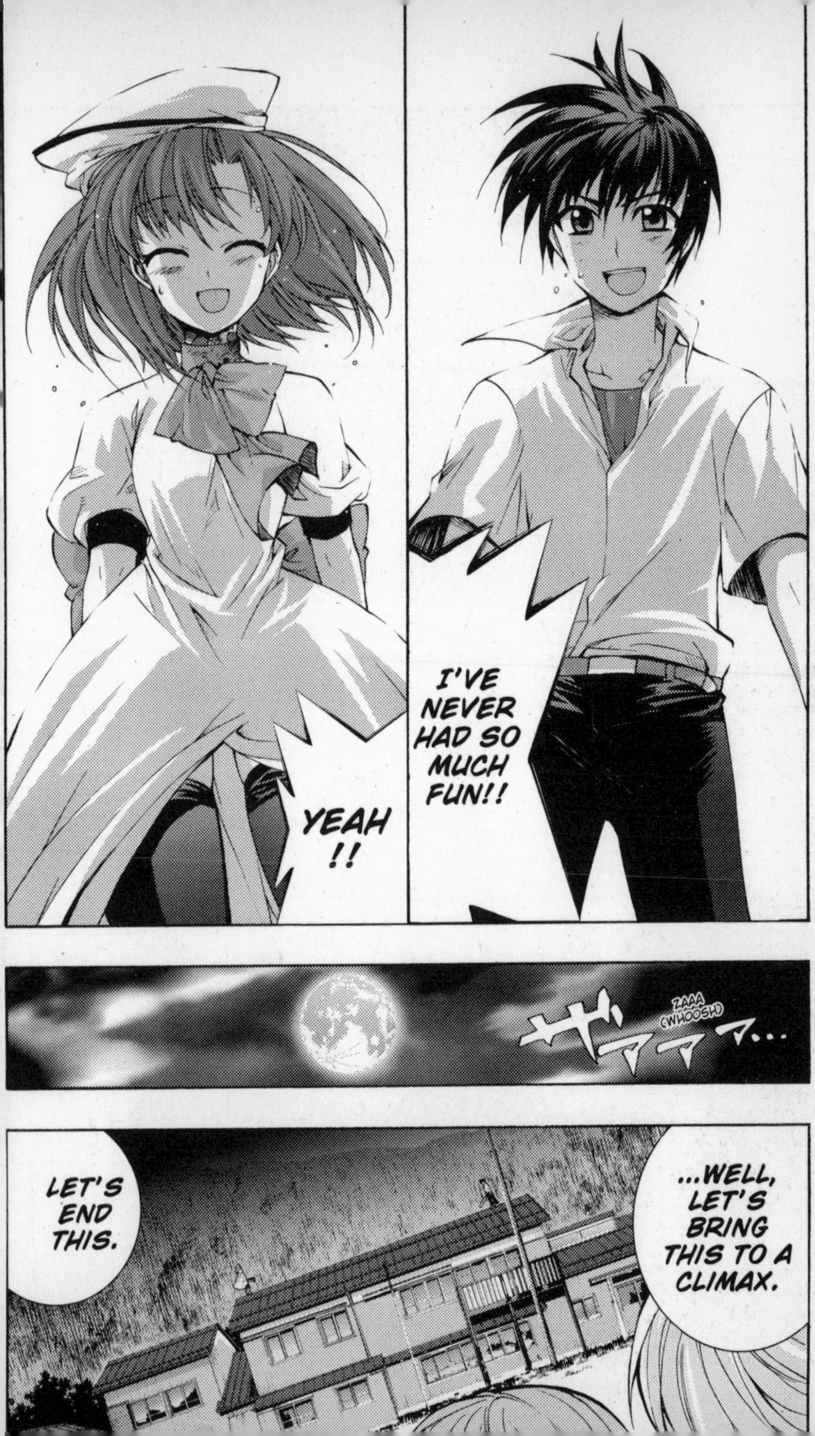
I'VE NEVER HAD SO MUCH FUN!!
YEAH !!
ザァァァ...
ZAAA (WHOOSH)
...WELL, LET'S BRING THIS TO A CLIMAX.
LET'S END THIS.

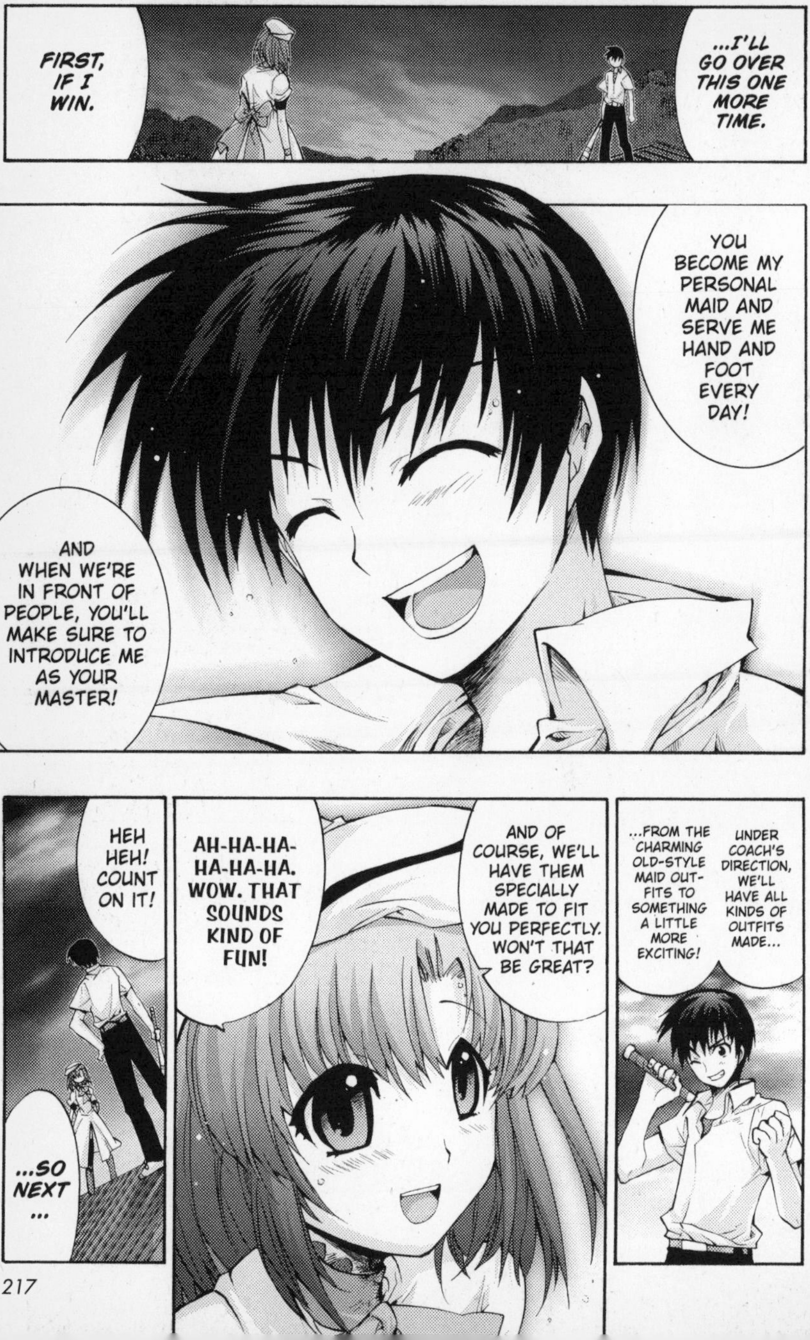
...I'LL GO OVER THIS ONE MORE TIME.
FIRST, IF I WIN.
YOU BECOME MY PERSONAL MAID AND SERVE ME HAND AND FOOT EVERY DAY!
AND WHEN WE'RE IN FRONT OF PEOPLE, YOU'LL MAKE SURE TO INTRODUCE ME AS YOUR MASTER!
UNDER COACH'S DIRECTION, WE'LL HAVE ALL KINDS OF OUTFITS MADE...
...FROM THE CHARMING OLD-STYLE MAID OUT-FITS TO SOMETHING A LITTLE MORE EXCITING!
AND OF COURSE, WE'LL HAVE THEM SPECIALLY MADE TO FIT YOU PERFECTLY. WON'T THAT BE GREAT?
AH-HA-HA-HA-HA-HA. WOW. THAT SOUNDS KIND OF FUN!
HEH HEH! COUNT ON IT!
...SO NEXT ...

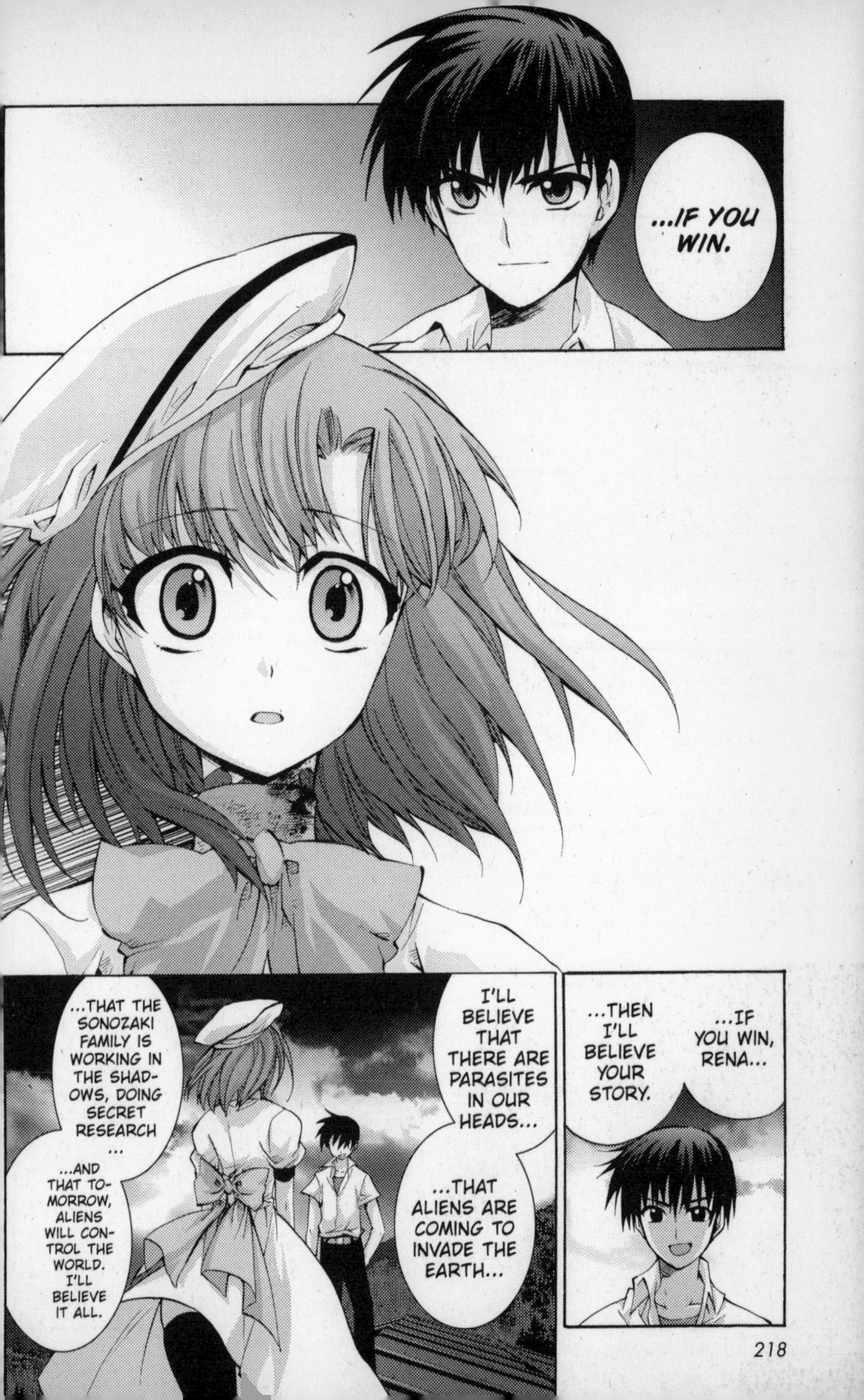
...IF YOU WIN.
...IF YOU WIN, RENA...
...THEN I'LL BELIEVE YOUR STORY.
I'LL BELIEVE THAT THERE ARE PARASITES IN OUR HEADS...
...THAT ALIENS ARE COMING TO INVADE THE EARTH...
...THAT THE SONOZAKI FAMILY IS WORKING IN THE SHAD-OWS, DOING SECRET RESEARCH...
...AND THAT TO-MORROW, ALIENS WILL CON-TROL THE WORLD. I'LL BELIEVE IT ALL.

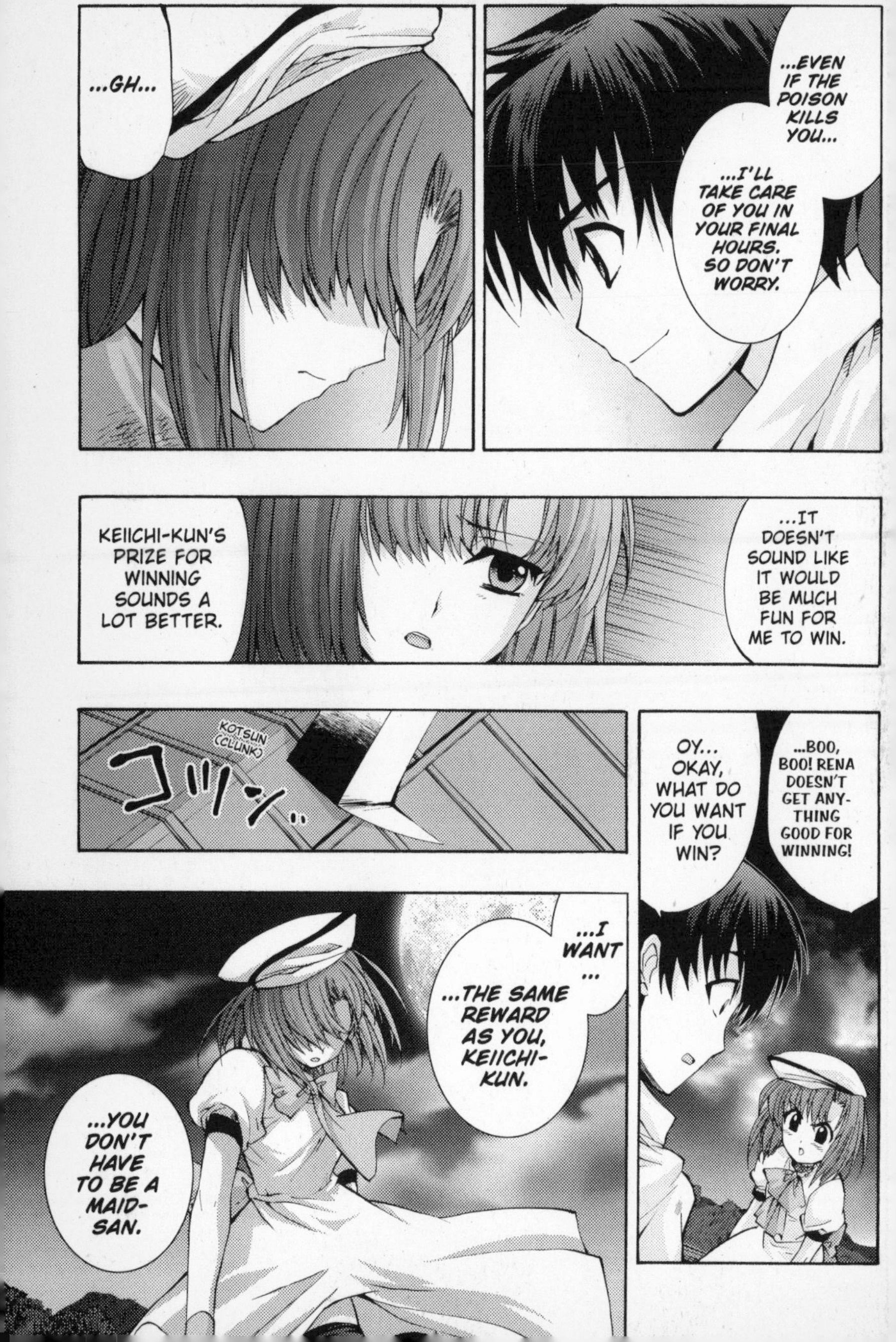
...EVEN IF THE POISON KILLS YOU...
...I'LL TAKE CARE OF YOU IN YOUR FINAL HOURS. SO DON'T WORRY.
...GH...
...IT DOESN'T SOUND LIKE IT WOULD BE MUCH FUN FOR ME TO WIN.
KEIICHI-KUN'S PRIZE FOR WINNING SOUNDS A LOT BETTER.
...BOO, BOO! RENA DOESN'T GET ANY-THING GOOD FOR WINNING!
OY... OKAY, WHAT DO YOU WANT IF YOU WIN?
KOTSUN (CLUNK)
...I WANT...
...THE SAME REWARD AS YOU, KEIICHI-KUN.
...YOU DON'T HAVE TO BE A MAID-SAN.

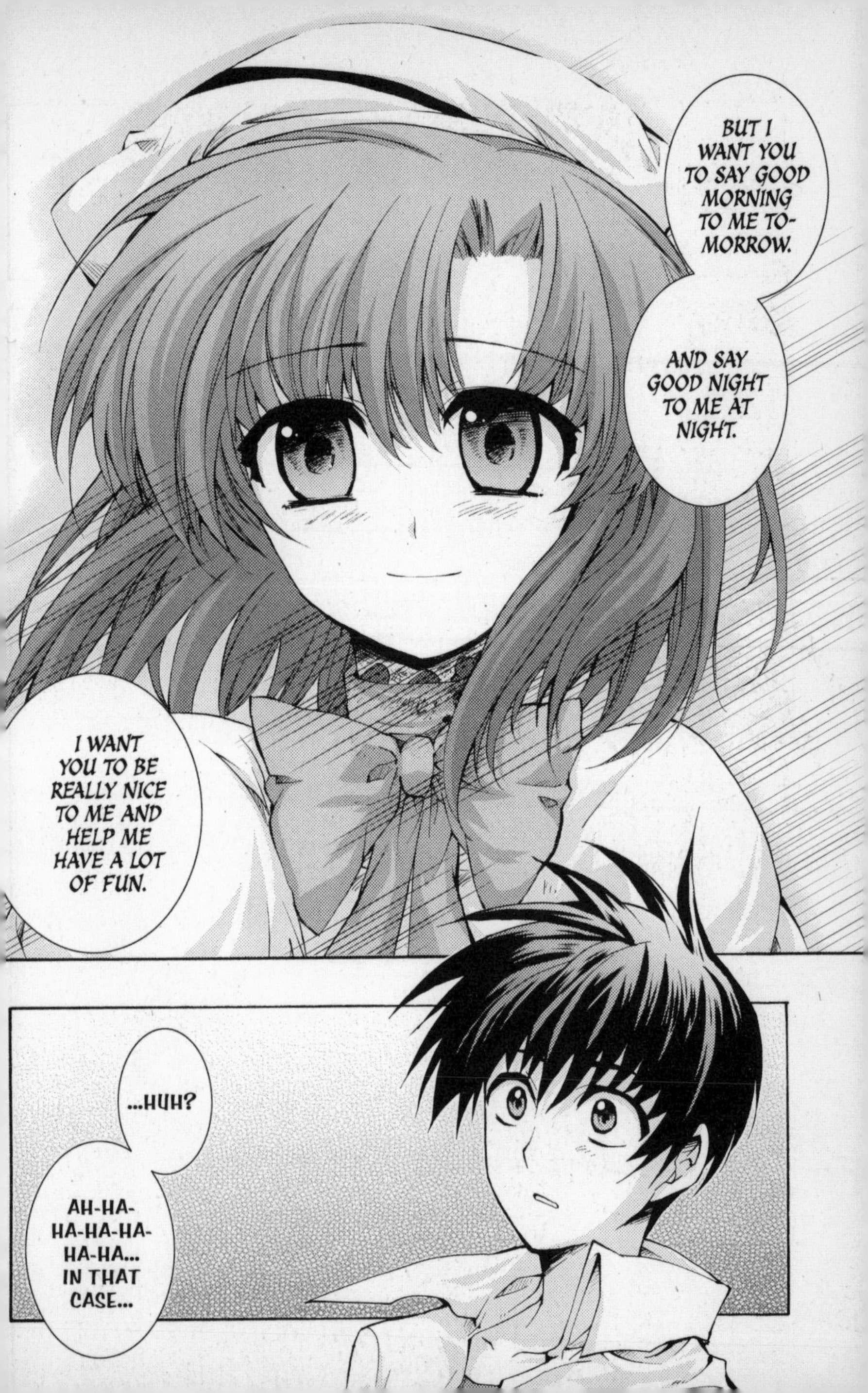
BUT I WANT YOU TO SAY GOOD MORNING TO ME TO-MORROW.
AND SAY GOOD NIGHT TO ME AT NIGHT.
I WANT YOU TO BE REALLY NICE TO ME AND HELP ME HAVE A LOT OF FUN.
...HUH?
AH-HA-HA-HA-HA-HA-HA... IN THAT CASE...

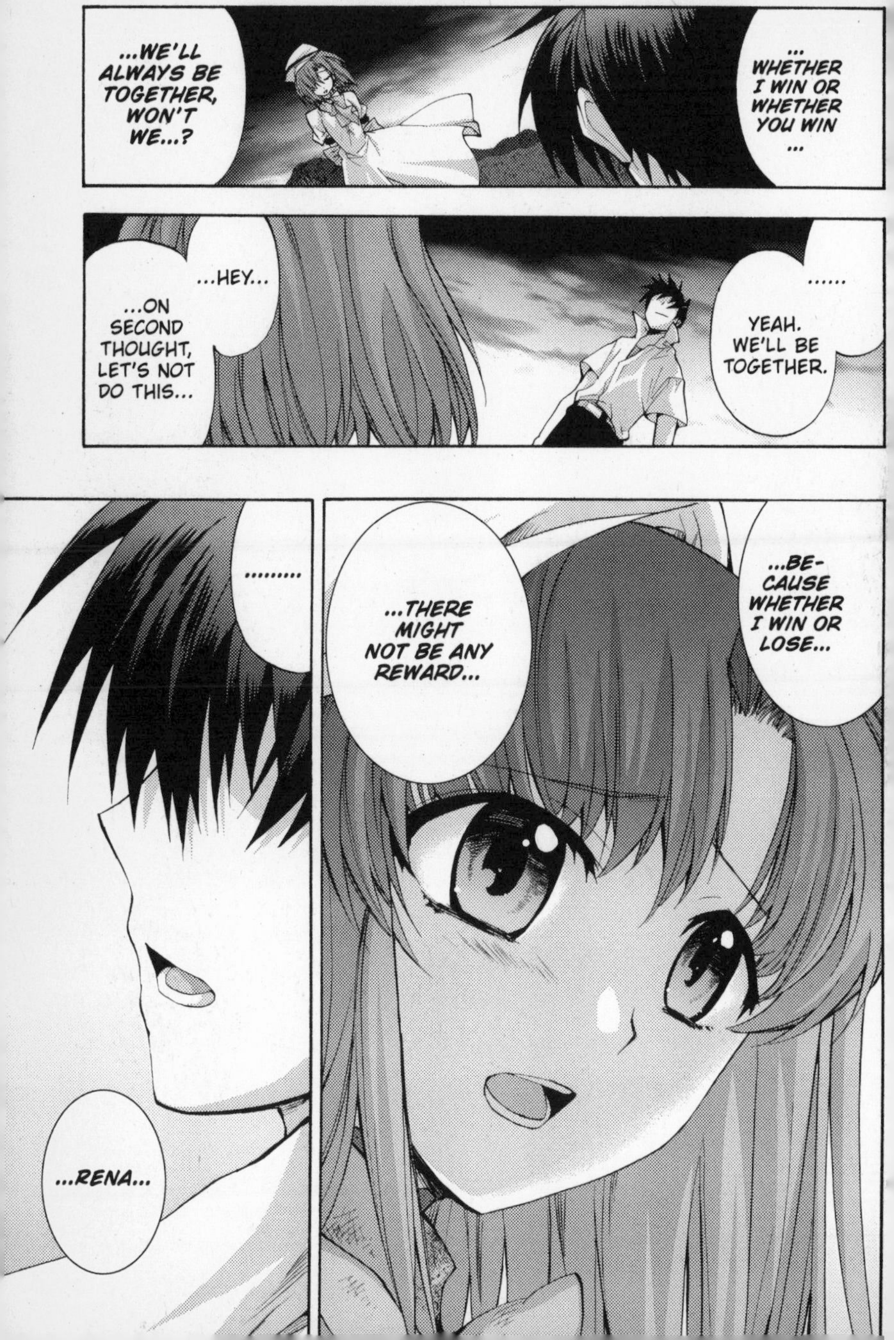
... WHETHER I WIN OR WHETHER YOU WIN ...
...WE'LL ALWAYS BE TOGETHER, WON'T WE...?
...... YEAH. WE'LL BE TOGETHER.
...HEY... ...ON SECOND THOUGHT, LET'S NOT DO THIS...
...BE-CAUSE WHETHER I WIN OR LOSE...
...THERE MIGHT NOT BE ANY REWARD...
....
...RENA...

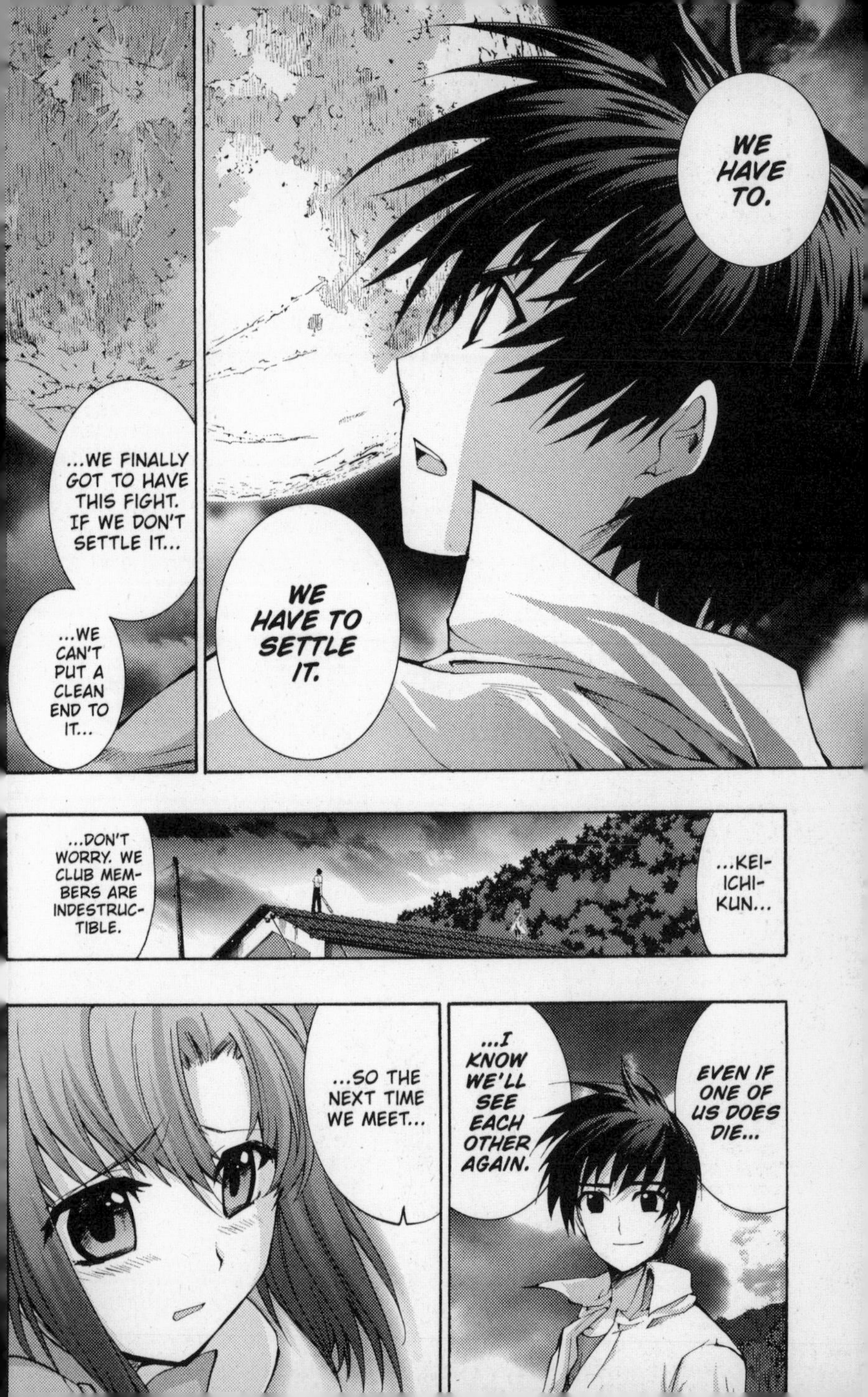
WE HAVE TO.
WE HAVE TO SETTLE IT.
...WE FINALLY GOT TO HAVE THIS FIGHT. IF WE DON'T SETTLE IT...
...WE CAN'T PUT A CLEAN END TO IT...
...KEI-ICHI-KUN...
...DON'T WORRY. WE CLUB MEM-BERS ARE INDESTRUC-TIBLE.
EVEN IF ONE OF US DOES DIE...
...I KNOW WE'LL SEE EACH OTHER AGAIN.
...SO THE NEXT TIME WE MEET...

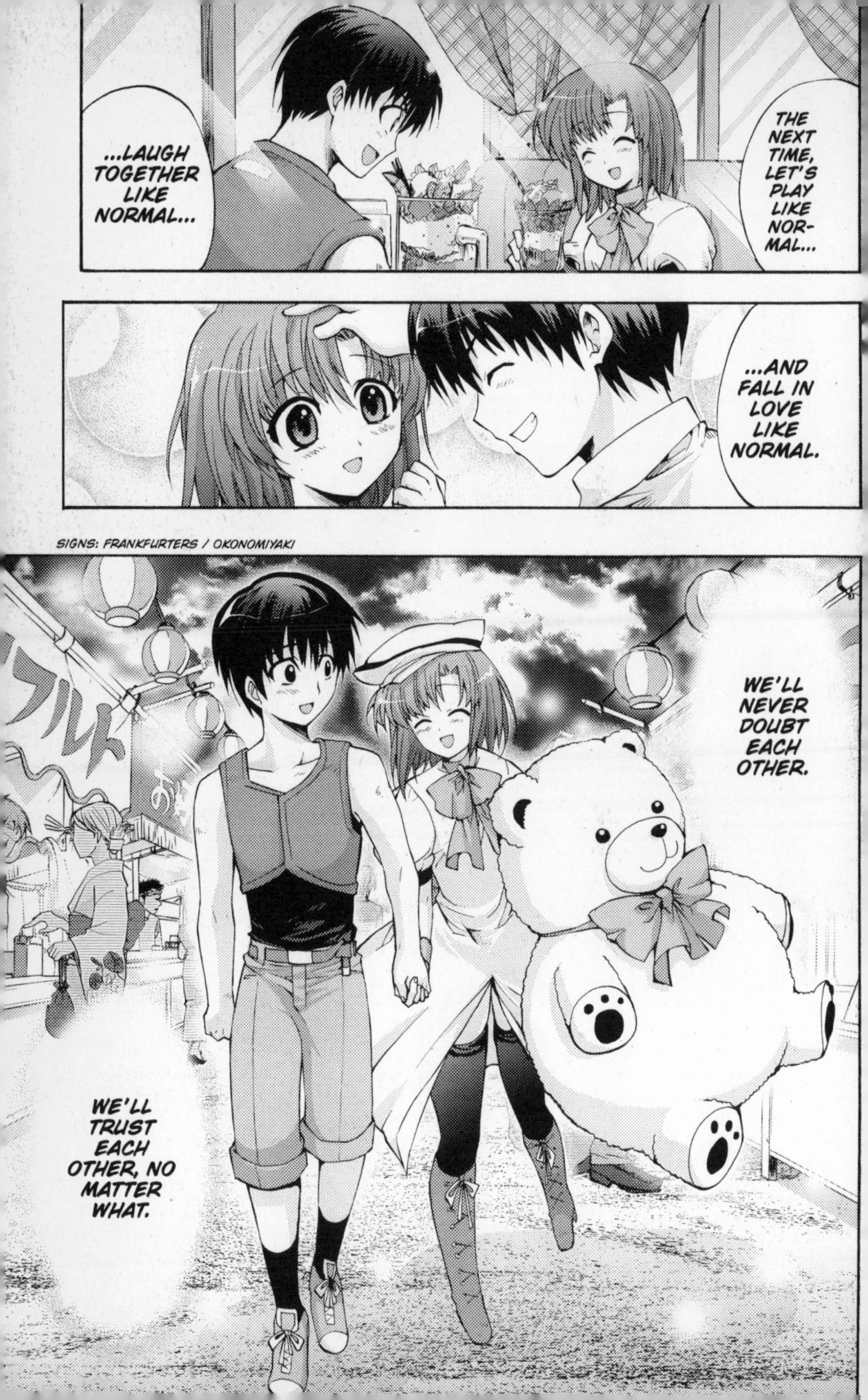
THE NEXT TIME, LET'S PLAY LIKE NOR-MAL...
...LAUGH TOGETHER LIKE NORMAL...
...AND FALL IN LOVE LIKE NORMAL.
SIGNS: FRANKFURTERS / OKONOMIYAKI
WE'LL NEVER DOUBT EACH OTHER.
WE'LL TRUST EACH OTHER, NO MATTER WHAT.

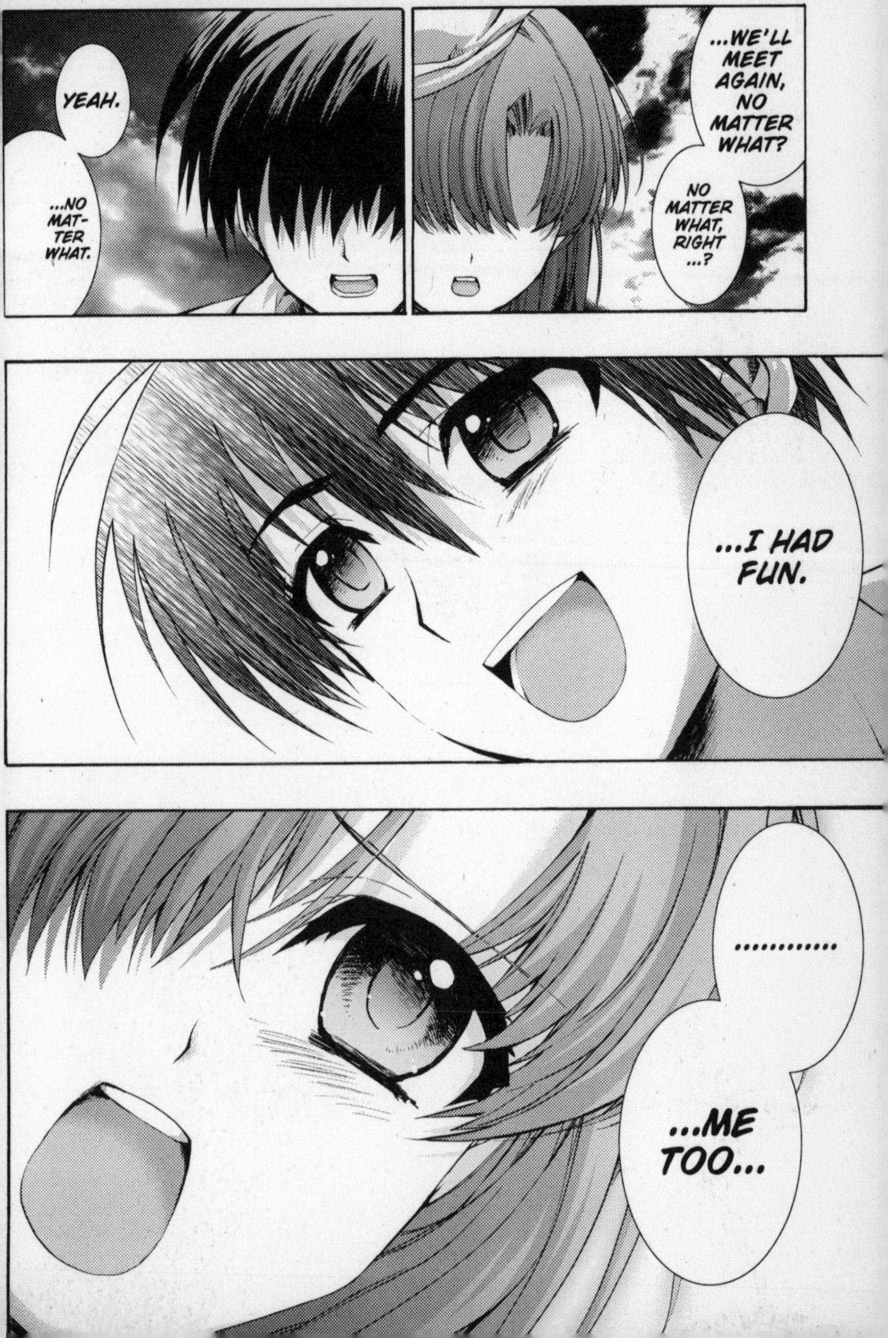
...WE'LL MEET AGAIN, NO MATTER WHAT?
NO MATTER WHAT, RIGHT ...?
YEAH.
...NO MAT-TER WHAT.
...I HAD FUN.
....
...ME TOO...

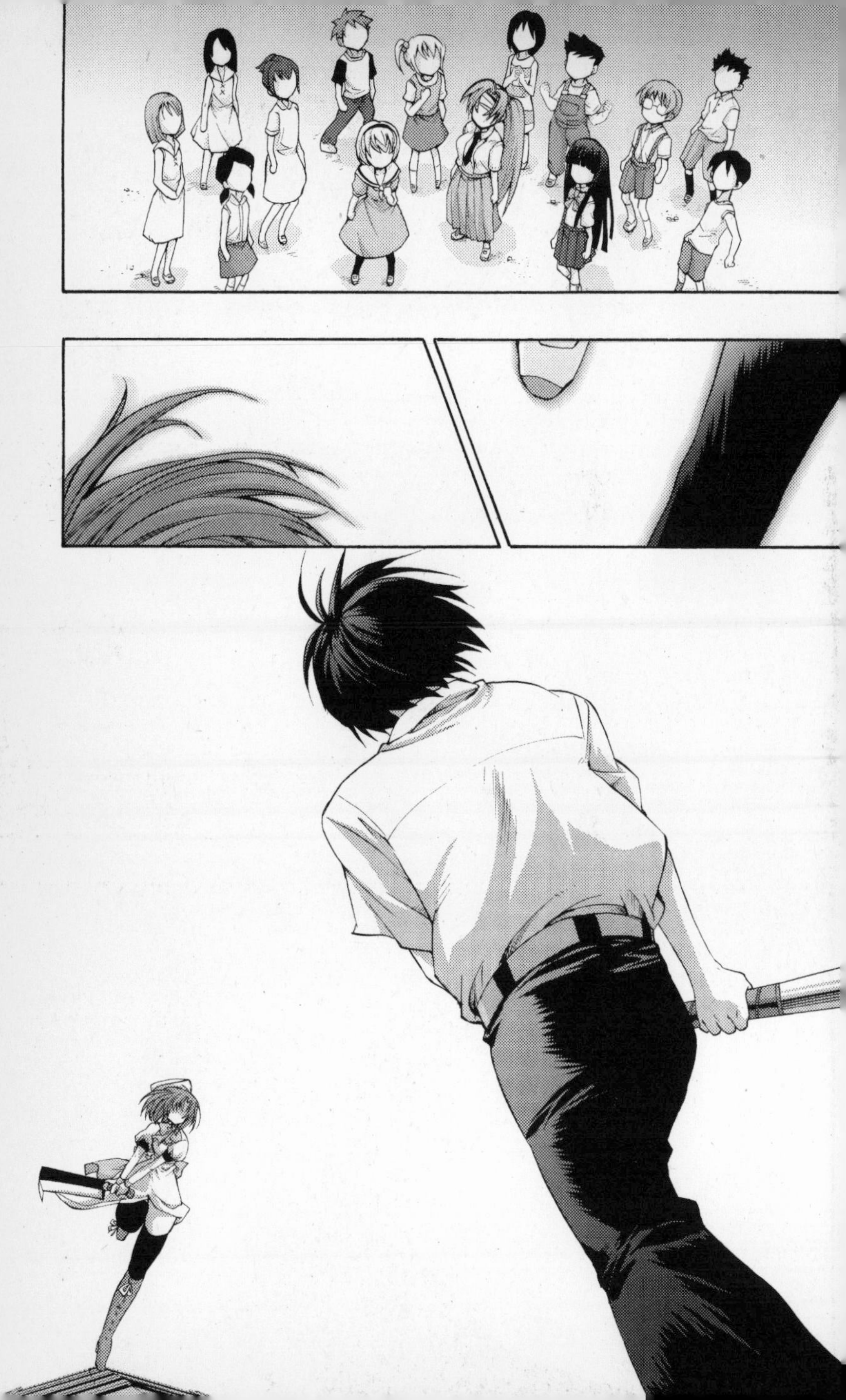

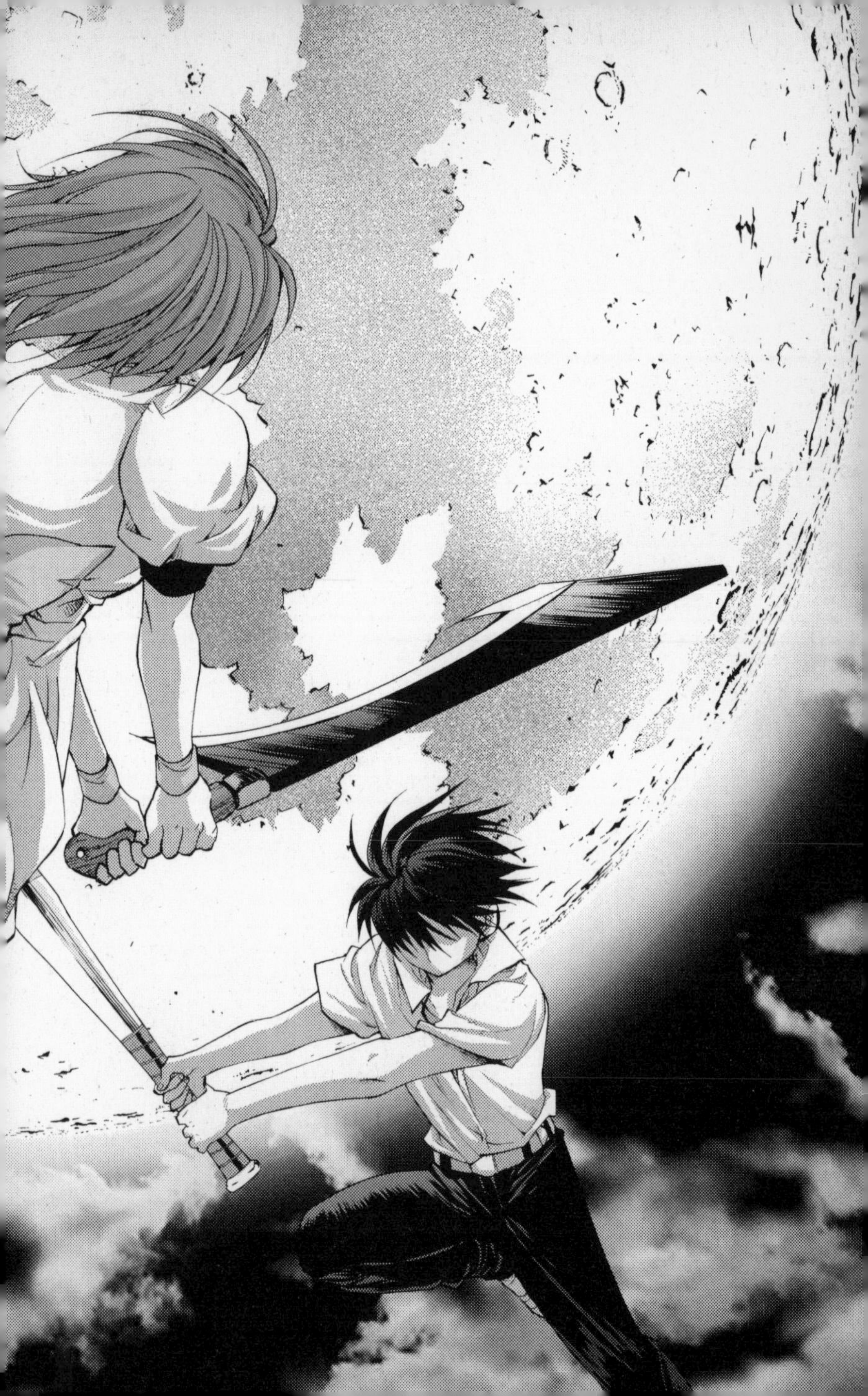

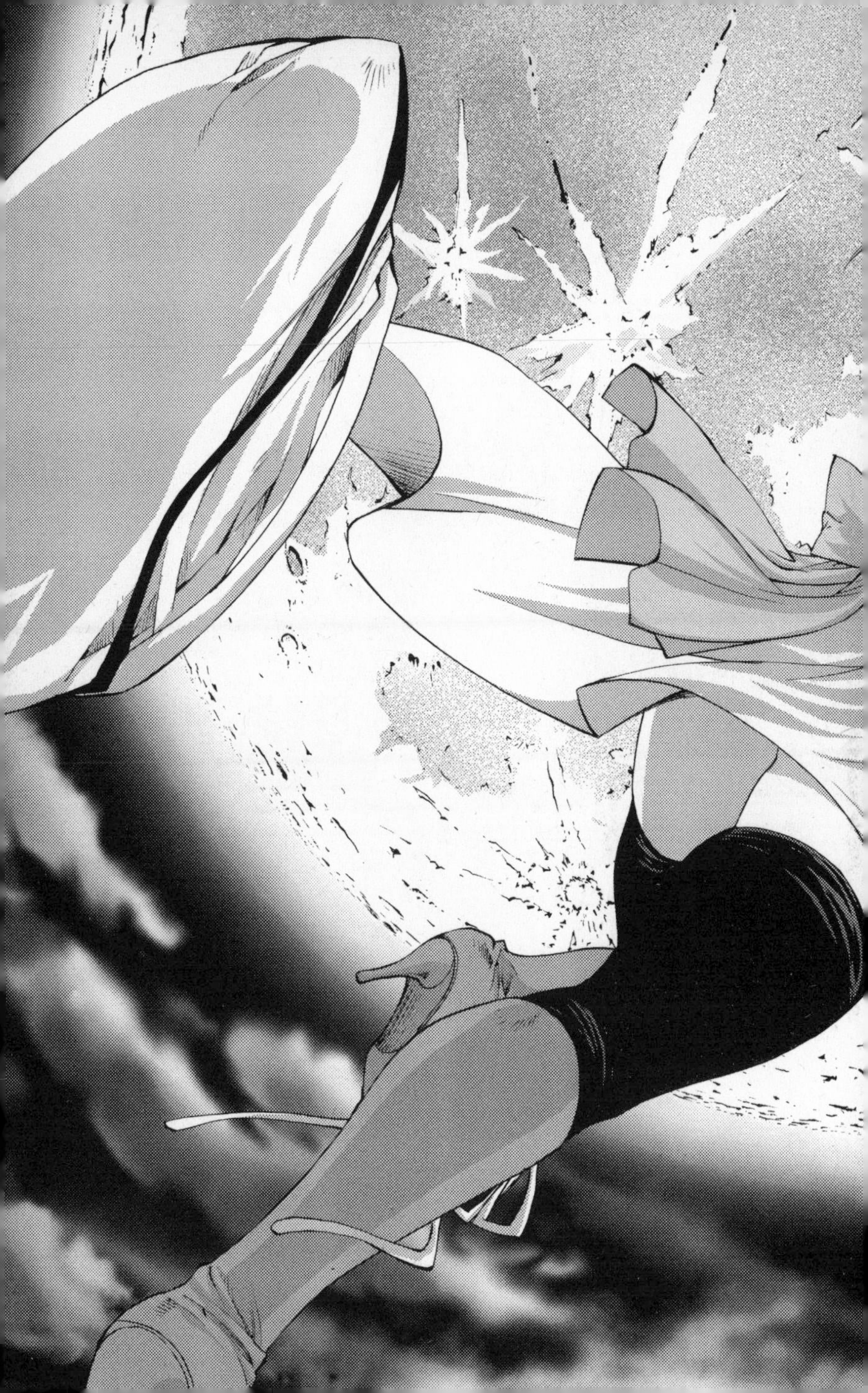

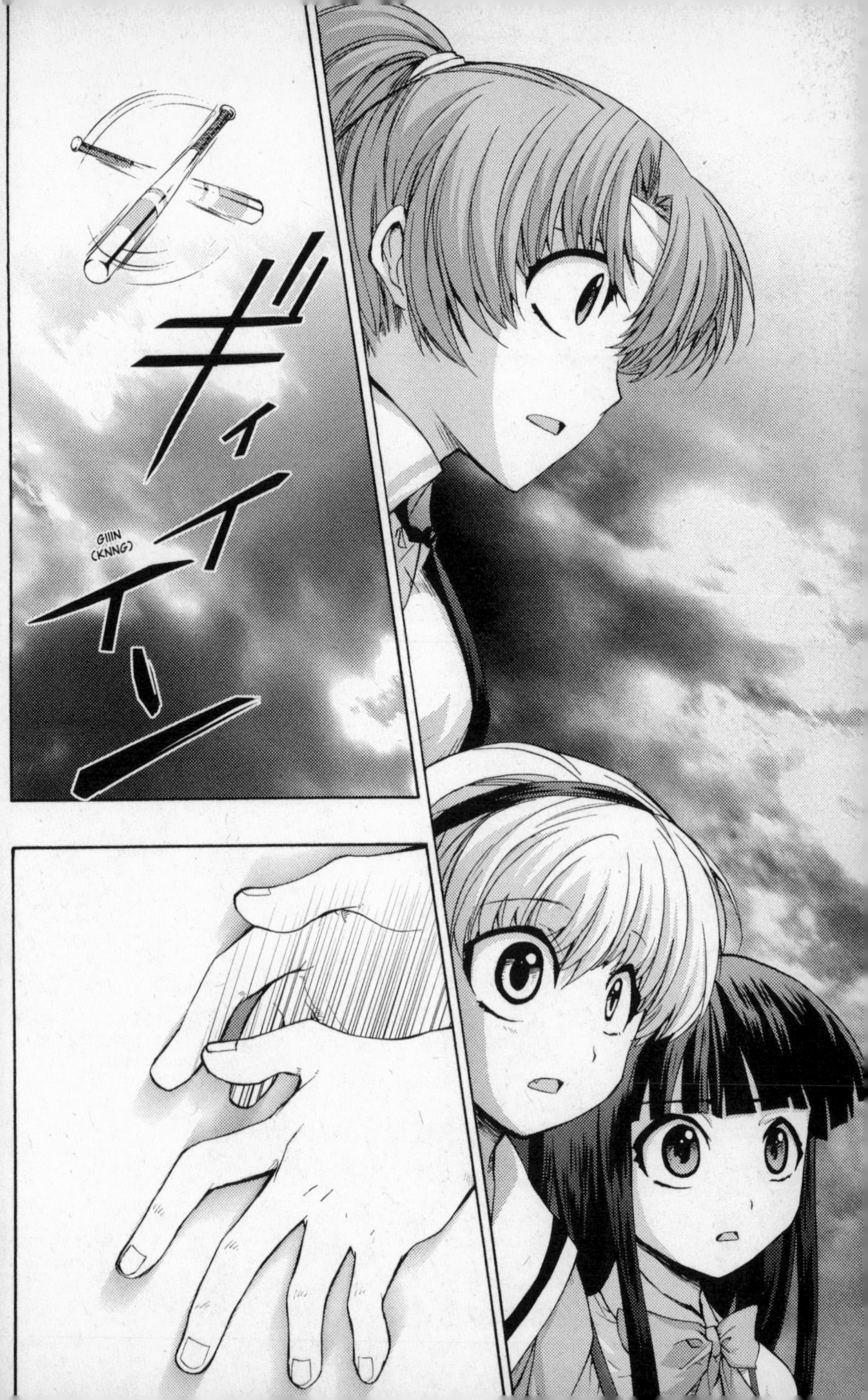
ギィイイーン
GIIIN
(KNNG)

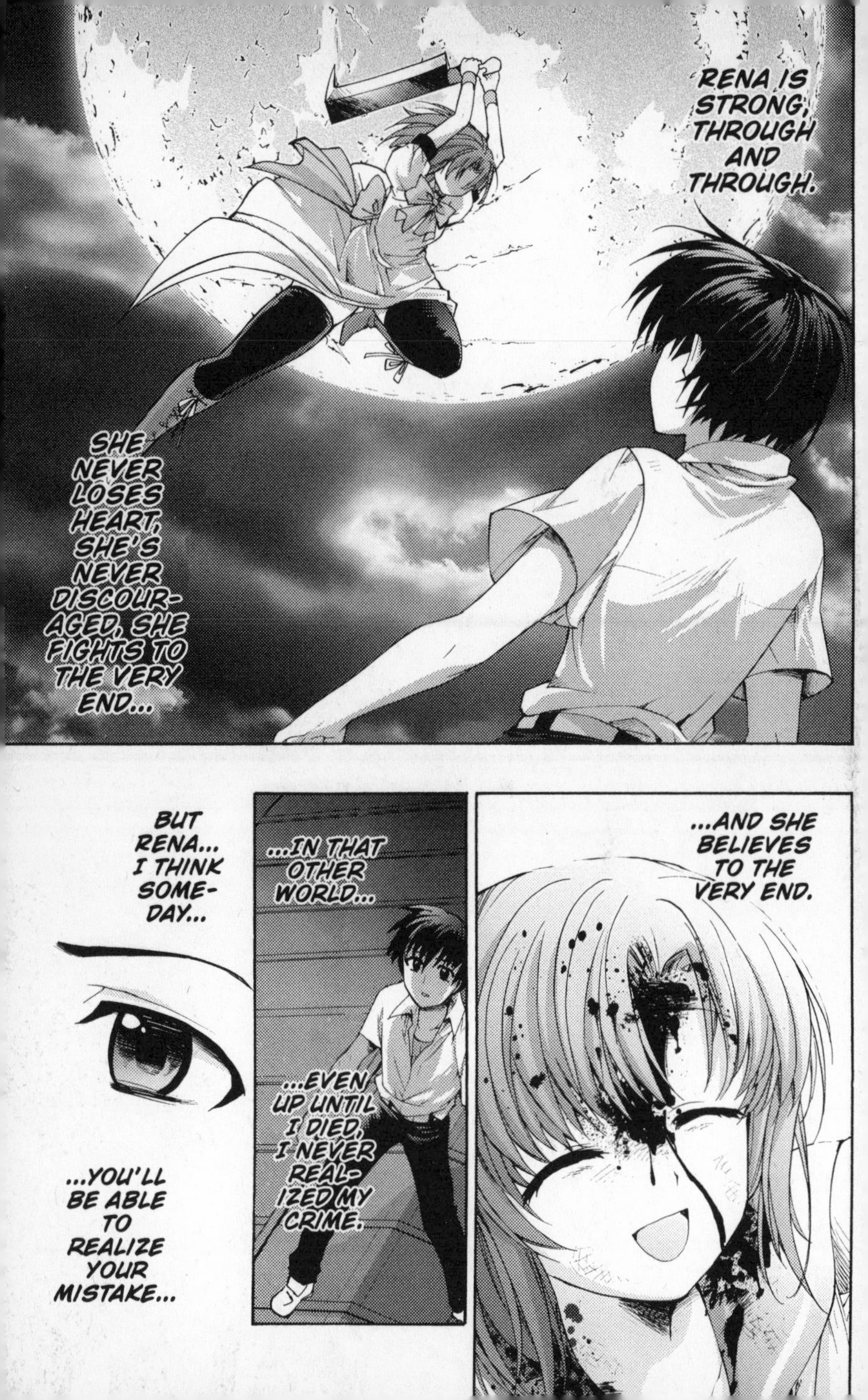
RENA IS STRONG, THROUGH AND THROUGH.
SHE NEVER LOSES HEART, SHE'S NEVER DISCOURAGED, SHE FIGHTS TO THE VERY END...
...AND SHE BELIEVES TO THE VERY END.
...IN THAT OTHER WORLD...
...EVEN UP UNTIL I DIED, I NEVER REALIZED MY CRIME.
BUT RENA... I THINK SOMEDAY...
...YOU'LL BE ABLE TO REALIZE YOUR MISTAKE...

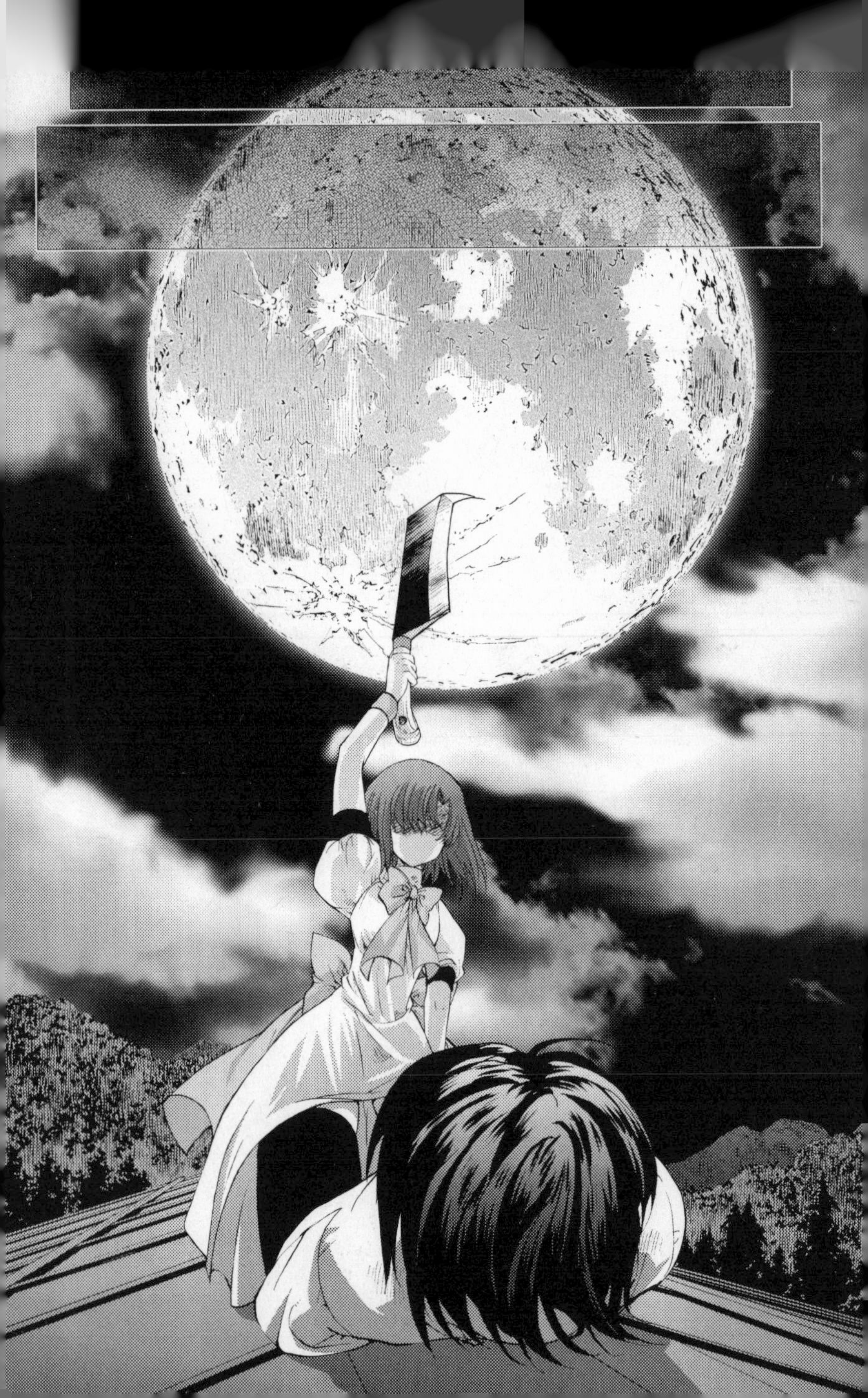

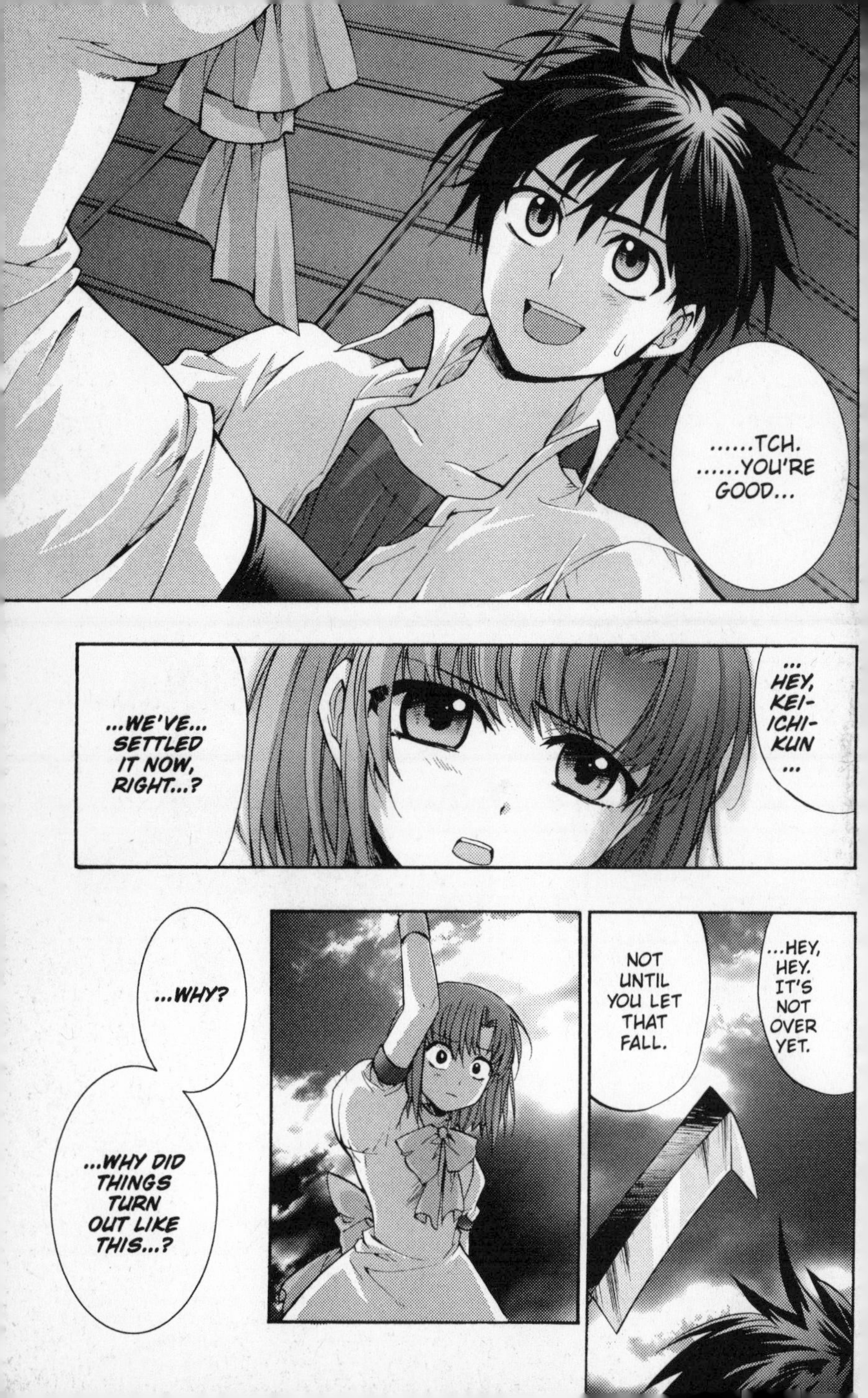
......TCH. ......YOU'RE GOOD...
... HEY, KEI-ICHI-KUN ...
...WE'VE... SETTLED IT NOW, RIGHT...?
...HEY, HEY. IT'S NOT OVER YET.
NOT UNTIL YOU LET THAT FALL.
...WHY?
...WHY DID THINGS TURN OUT LIKE THIS...?

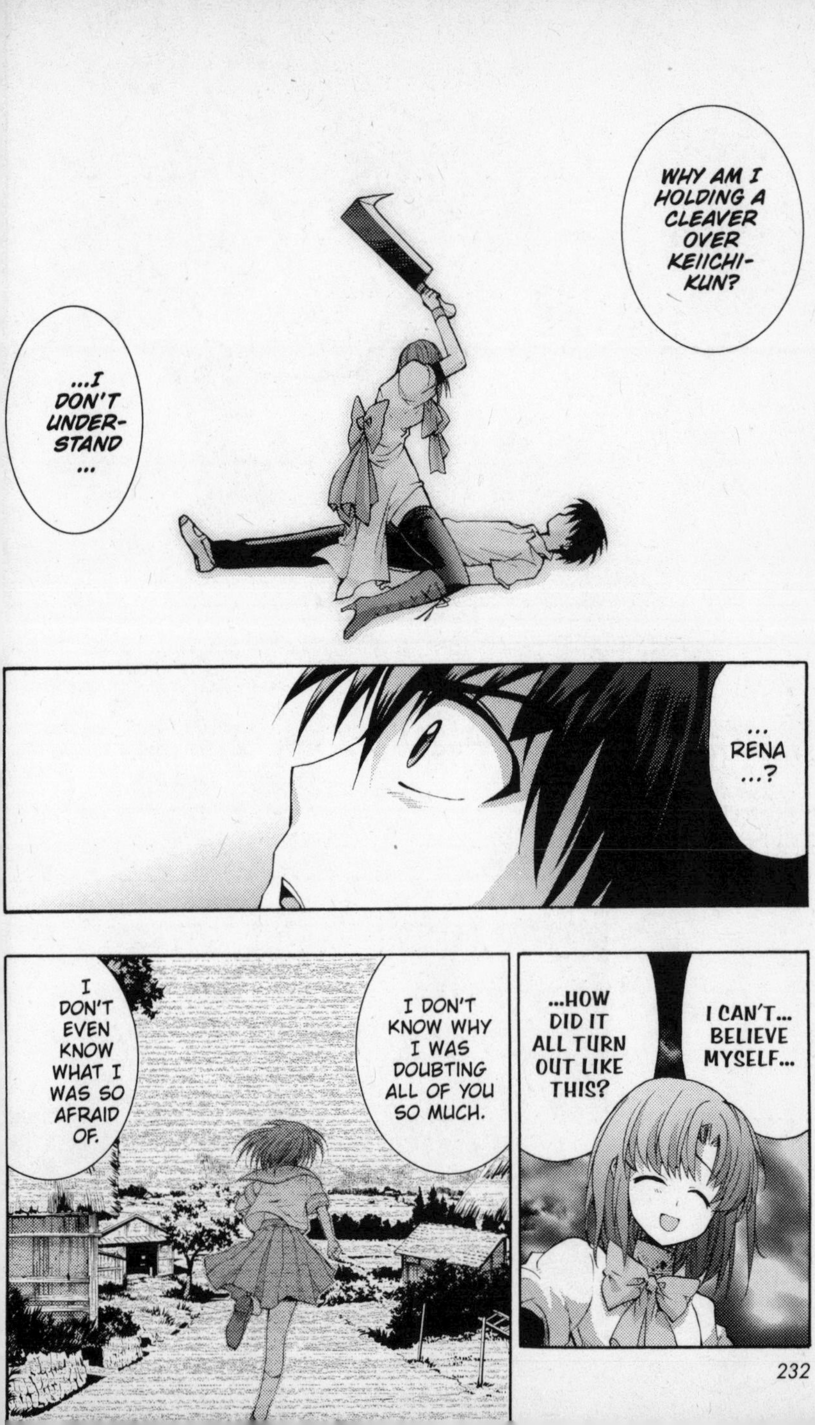
WHY AM I HOLDING A CLEAVER OVER KEIICHI-KUN?
...I DON'T UNDER-STAND...
...RENA...?
I CAN'T... BELIEVE MYSELF...
...HOW DID IT ALL TURN OUT LIKE THIS?
I DON'T KNOW WHY I WAS DOUBTING ALL OF YOU SO MUCH.
I DON'T EVEN KNOW WHAT I WAS SO AFRAID OF.

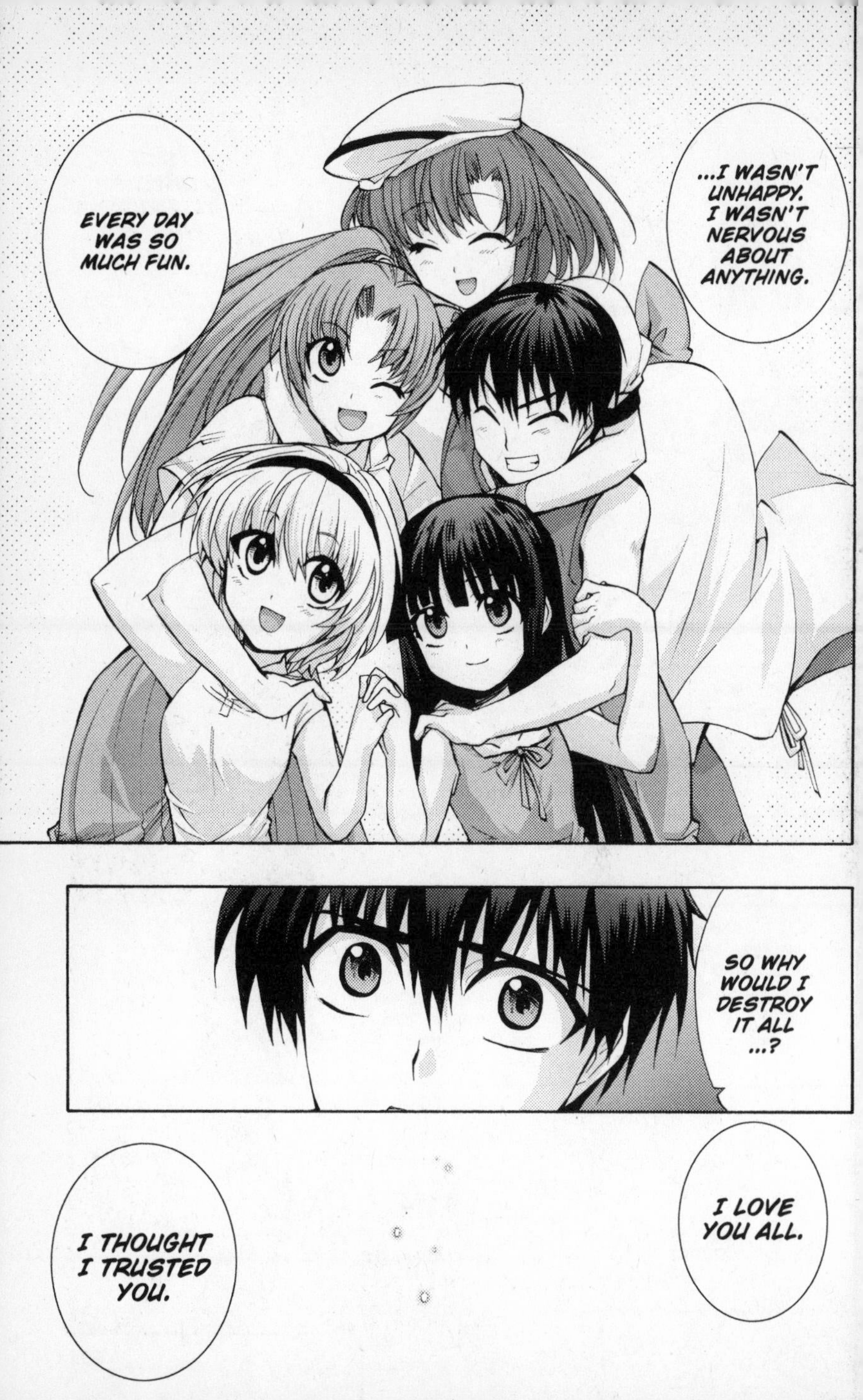
...I WASN'T UNHAPPY. I WASN'T NERVOUS ABOUT ANYTHING.
EVERY DAY WAS SO MUCH FUN.
SO WHY WOULD I DESTROY IT ALL ...?
I LOVE YOU ALL.
I THOUGHT I TRUSTED YOU.

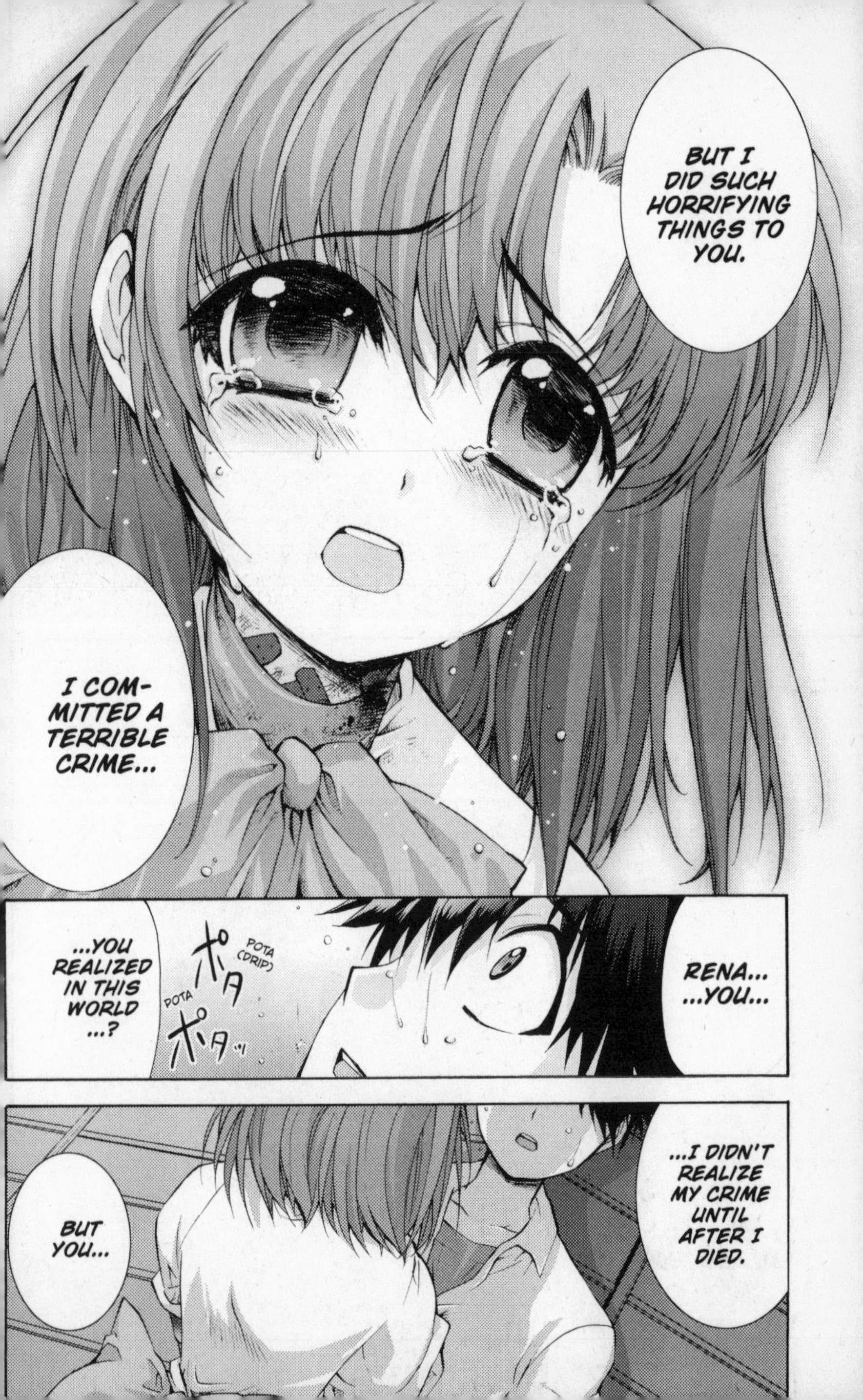
BUT I DID SUCH HORRIFYING THINGS TO YOU.
I COM-MITTED A TERRIBLE CRIME...
RENA... ...YOU...
ポタ POTA (DRIP)
ポタッ POTA
...YOU REALIZED IN THIS WORLD ...?
...I DIDN'T REALIZE MY CRIME UNTIL AFTER I DIED.
BUT YOU...

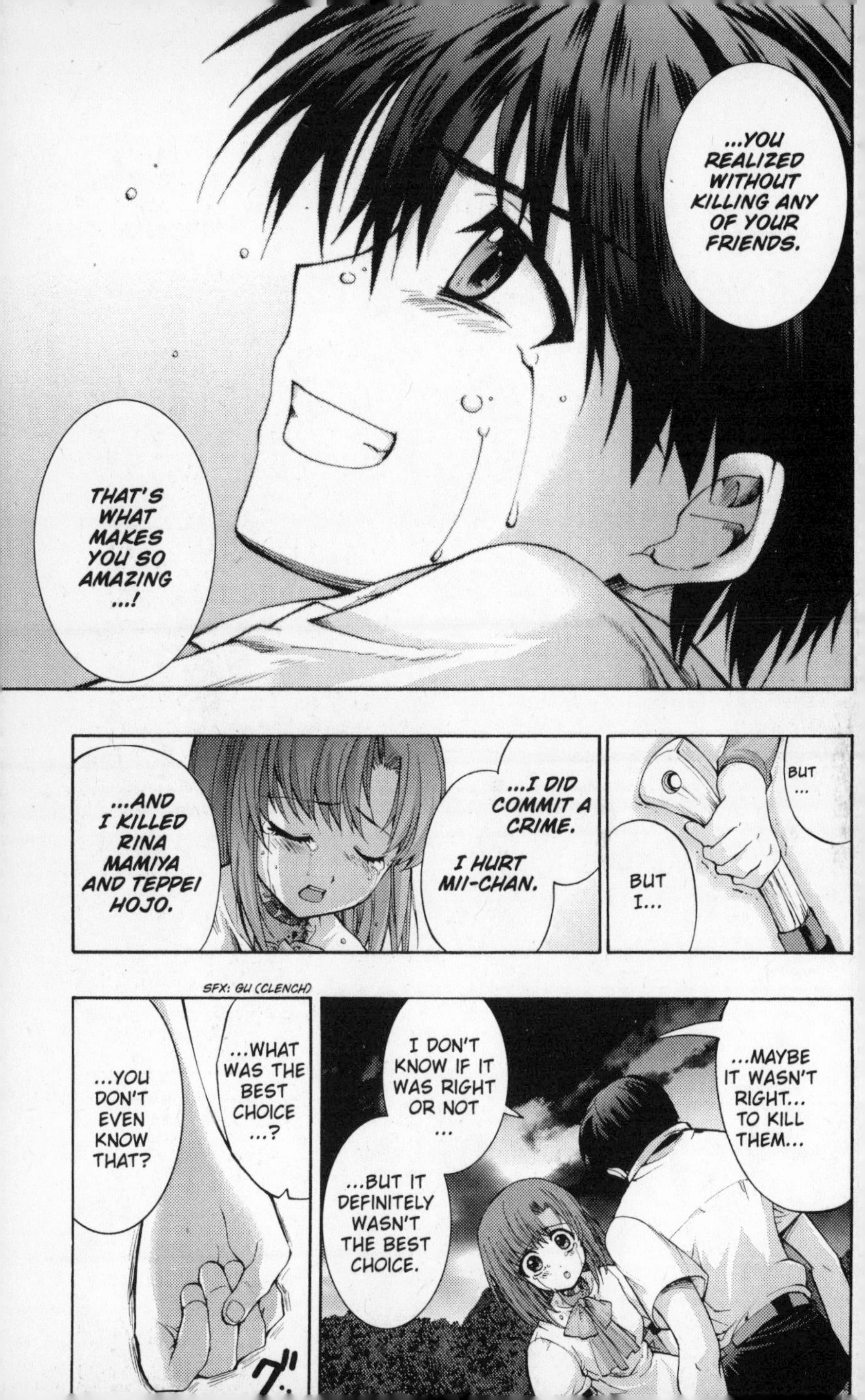
...YOU REALIZED WITHOUT KILLING ANY OF YOUR FRIENDS.
THAT'S WHAT MAKES YOU SO AMAZING ...!
BUT ...
BUT I...
...I DID COMMIT A CRIME.
I HURT MII-CHAN.
...AND I KILLED RINA MAMIYA AND TEPPEI HOJO.
...MAYBE IT WASN'T RIGHT... TO KILL THEM...
I DON'T KNOW IF IT WAS RIGHT OR NOT ...
...BUT IT DEFINITELY WASN'T THE BEST CHOICE.
...WHAT WAS THE BEST CHOICE ...?
...YOU DON'T EVEN KNOW THAT?
SFX: GU (CLENCH)
グッ

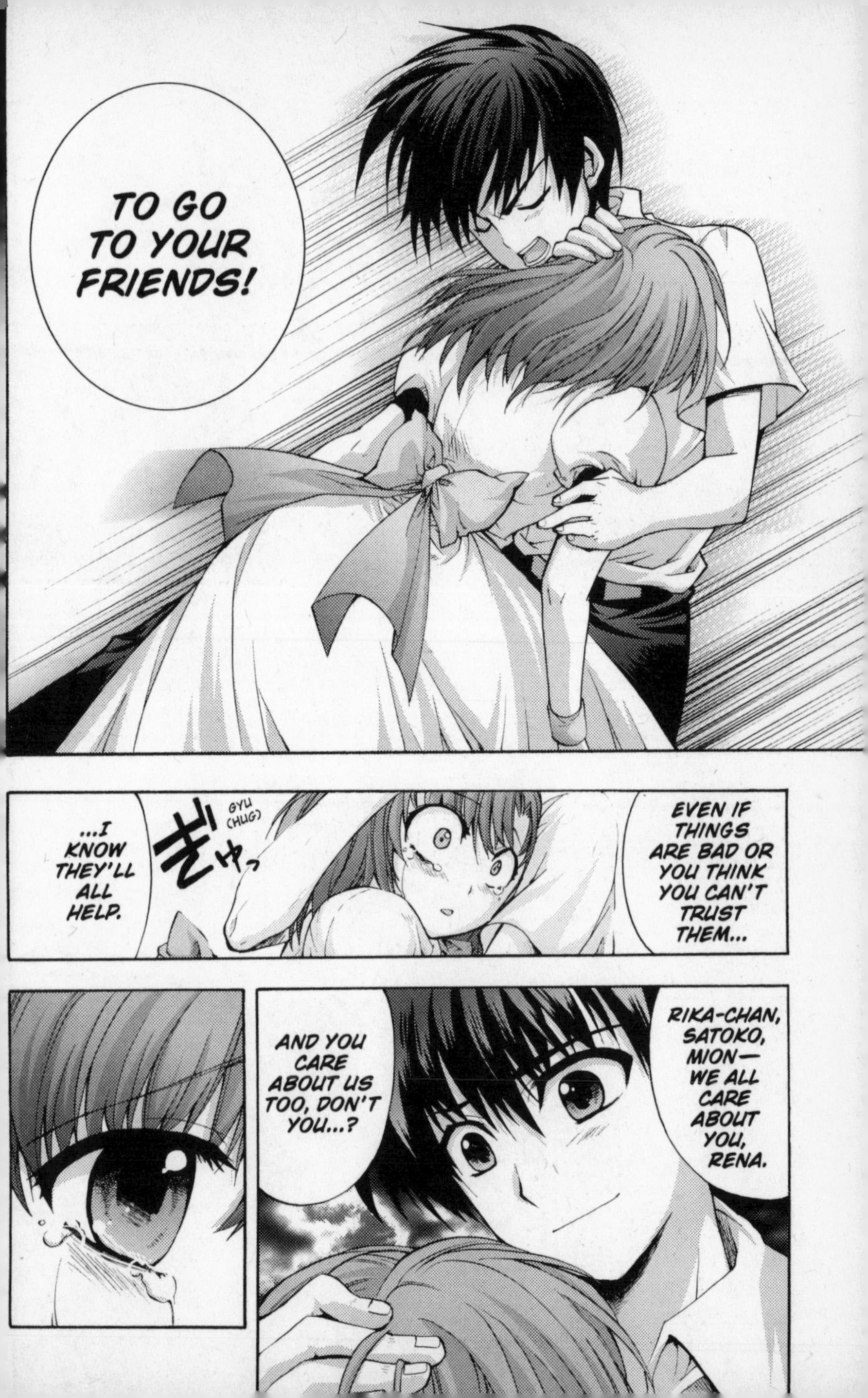
TO GO TO YOUR FRIENDS!
EVEN IF THINGS ARE BAD OR YOU THINK YOU CAN'T TRUST THEM...
ぎゅっ
GYU (HUG)
...I KNOW THEY'LL ALL HELP.
RIKA-CHAN, SATOKO, MION— WE ALL CARE ABOUT YOU, RENA.
AND YOU CARE ABOUT US TOO, DON'T YOU...?

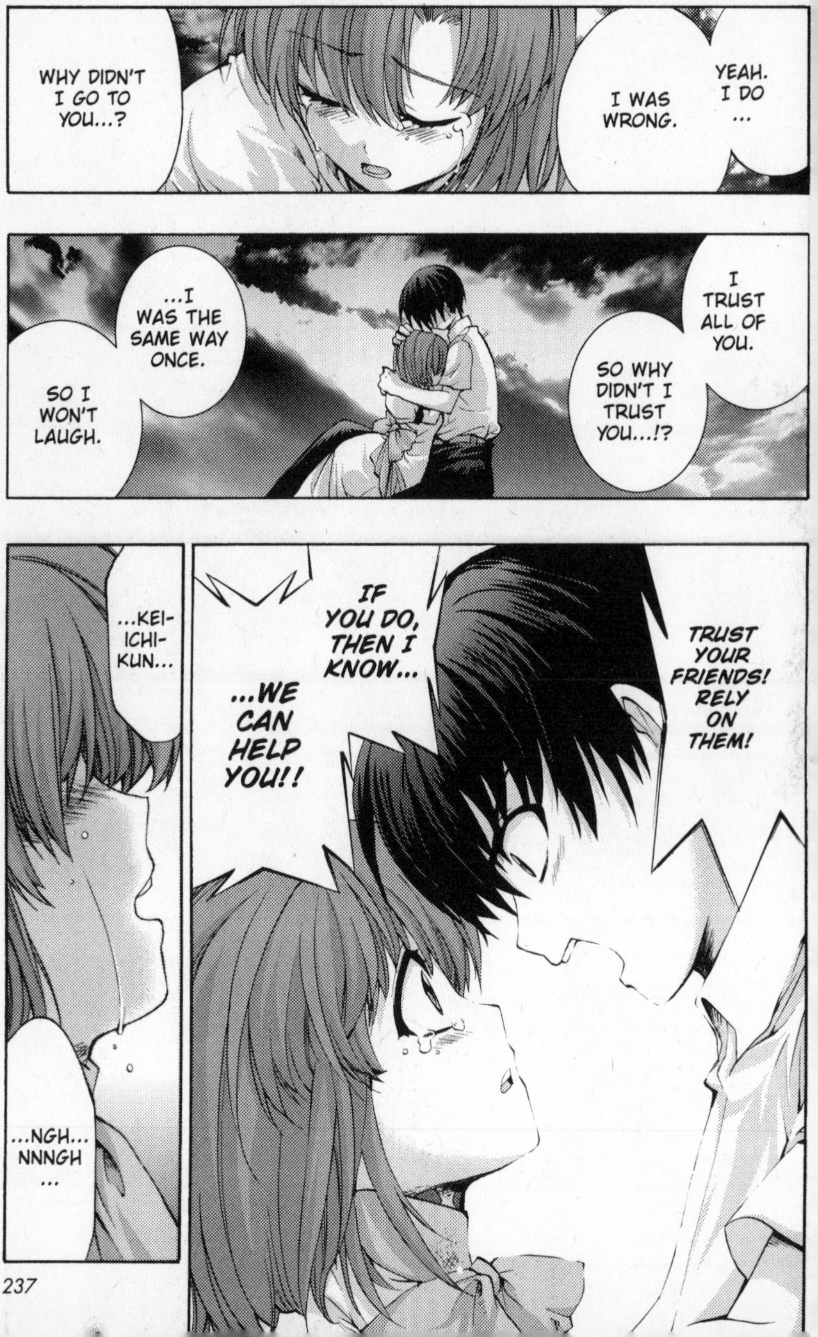
YEAH. I DO ...
I WAS WRONG.
WHY DIDN'T I GO TO YOU...?
I TRUST ALL OF YOU.
SO WHY DIDN'T I TRUST YOU...!?
...I WAS THE SAME WAY ONCE.
SO I WON'T LAUGH.
TRUST YOUR FRIENDS! RELY ON THEM!
IF YOU DO, THEN I KNOW...
...WE CAN HELP YOU!!
...KEI-ICHI-KUN...
...NGH... NNNGH ...

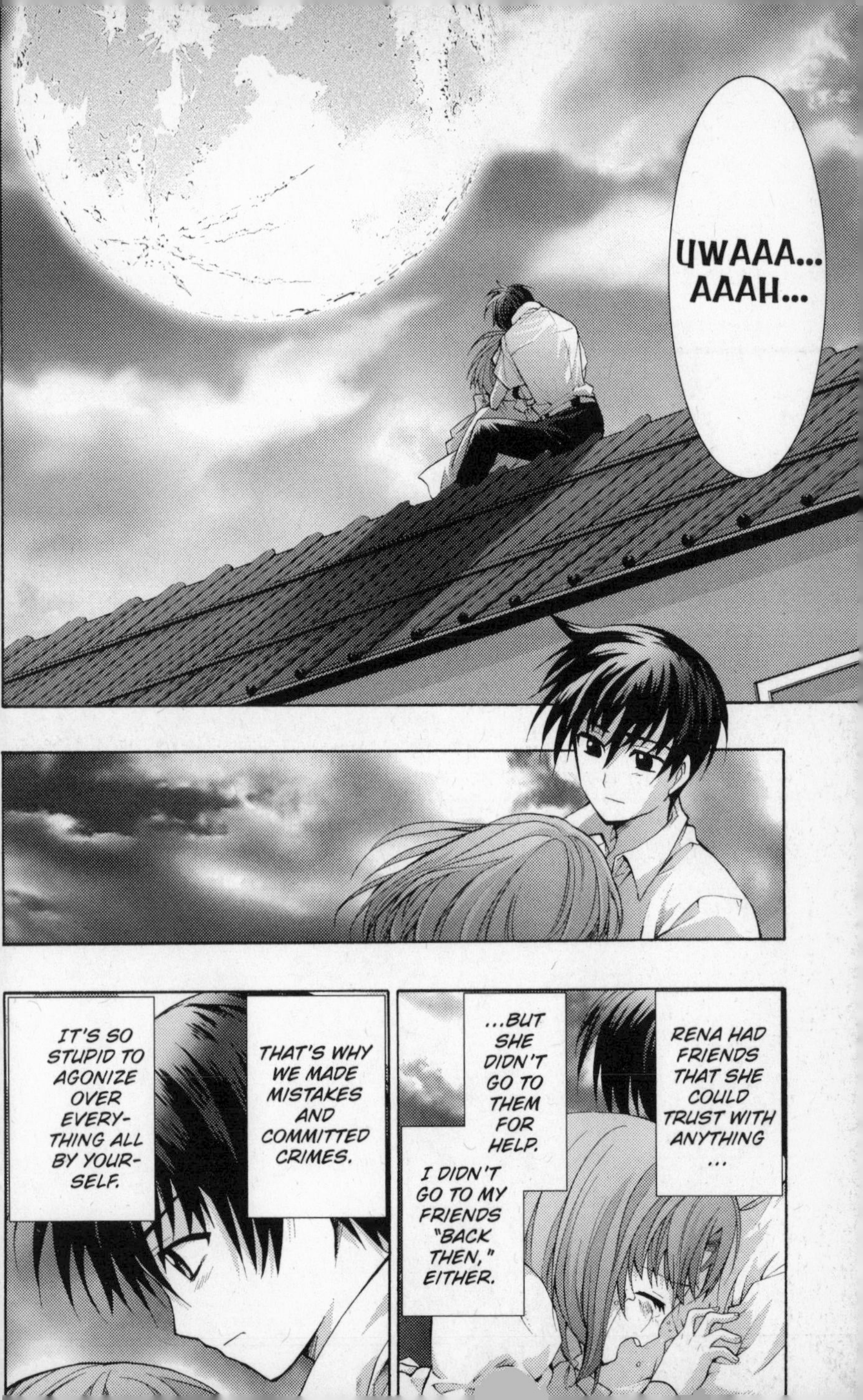
UWAAA... AAAH...
RENA HAD FRIENDS THAT SHE COULD TRUST WITH ANYTHING ...
...BUT SHE DIDN'T GO TO THEM FOR HELP.
I DIDN'T GO TO MY FRIENDS "BACK THEN," EITHER.
THAT'S WHY WE MADE MISTAKES AND COMMITTED CRIMES.
IT'S SO STUPID TO AGONIZE OVER EVERYTHING ALL BY YOURSELF.

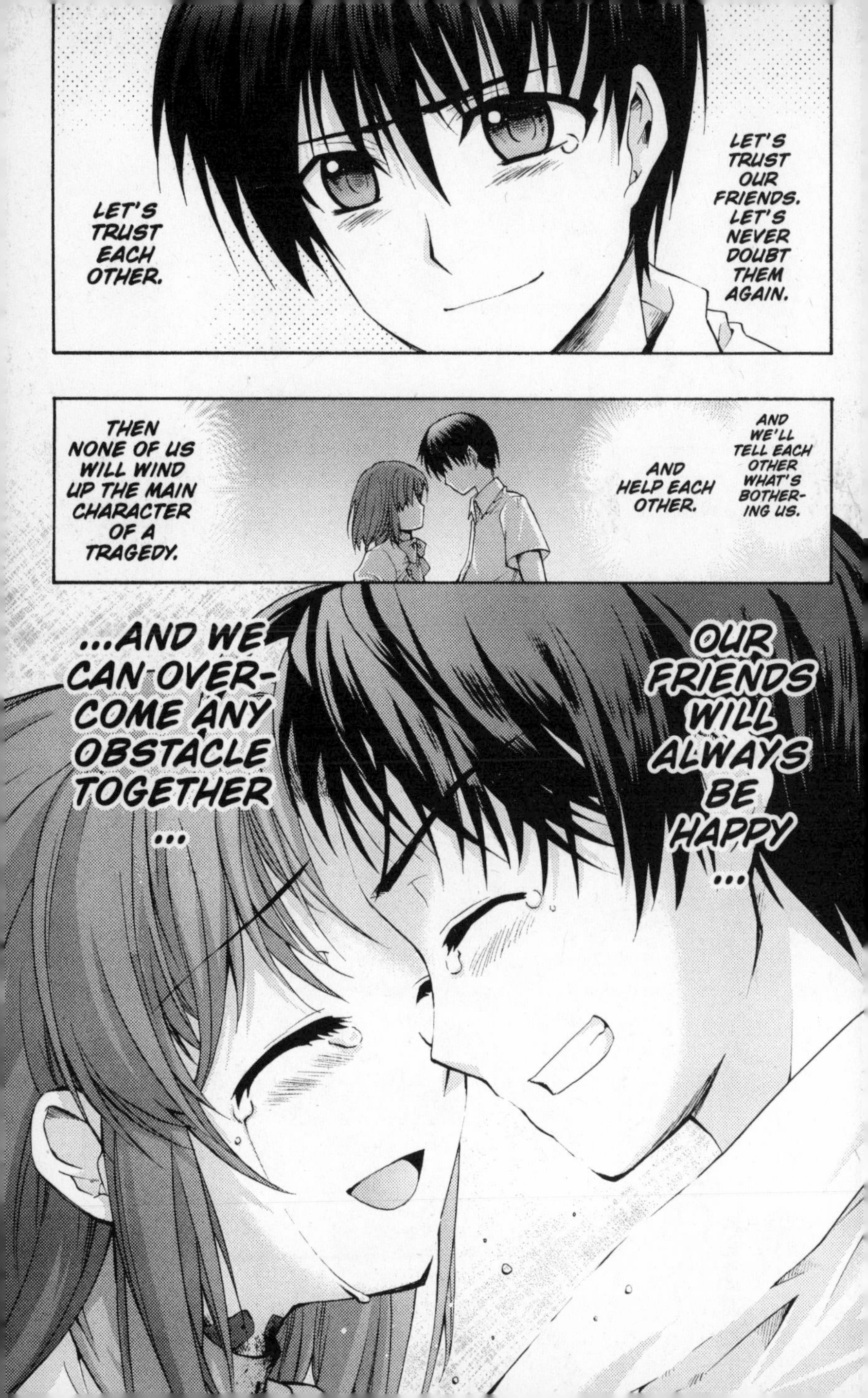
LET'S TRUST OUR FRIENDS. LET'S NEVER DOUBT THEM AGAIN.
LET'S TRUST EACH OTHER.
AND WE'LL TELL EACH OTHER WHAT'S BOTHER-ING US.
AND HELP EACH OTHER.
THEN NONE OF US WILL WIND UP THE MAIN CHARACTER OF A TRAGEDY.
OUR FRIENDS WILL ALWAYS BE HAPPY...
...AND WE CAN OVER-COME ANY OBSTACLE TOGETHER...

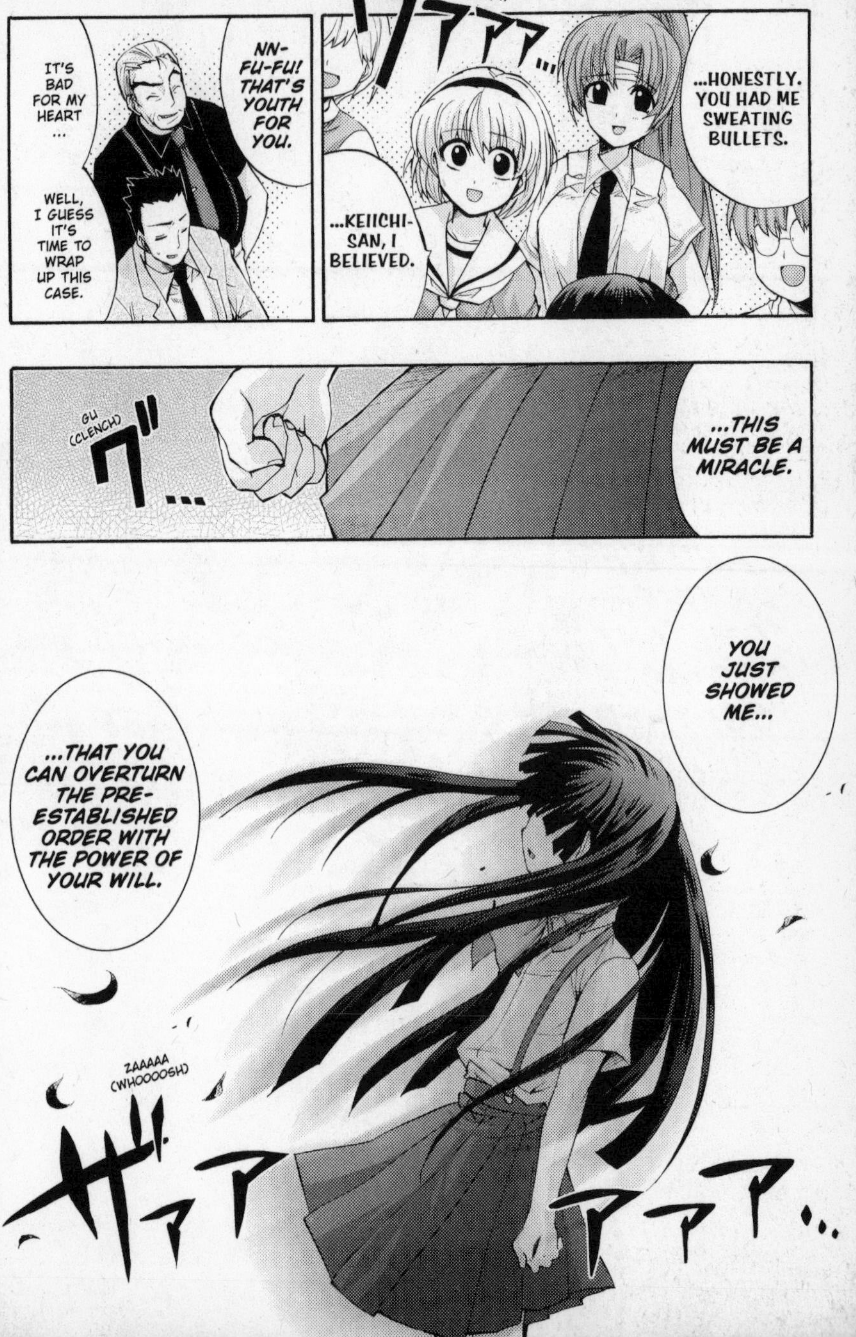
RAAAHH...
...HONESTLY. YOU HAD ME SWEATING BULLETS.
...KEIICHI-SAN, I BELIEVED.
NN-FU-FU! THAT'S YOUTH FOR YOU.
IT'S BAD FOR MY HEART ...
WELL, I GUESS IT'S TIME TO WRAP UP THIS CASE.
...THIS MUST BE A MIRACLE.
GU (CLENCH)
YOU JUST SHOWED ME...
...THAT YOU CAN OVERTURN THE PRE-ESTABLISHED ORDER WITH THE POWER OF YOUR WILL.
ZAAAAA (WHOOOOSH)

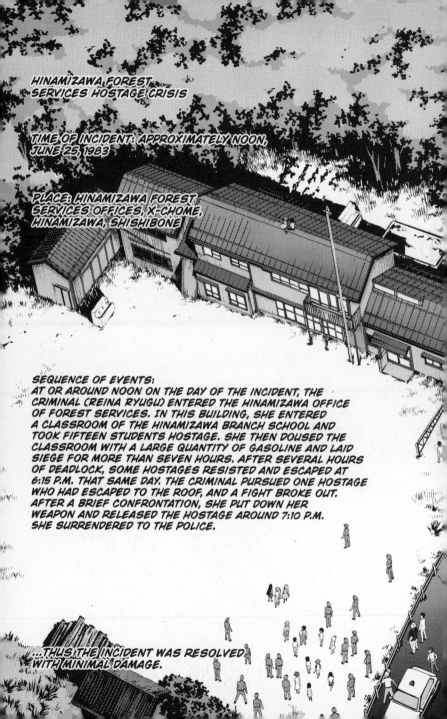

HINAMIZAWA FOREST
SERVICES HOSTAGE CRISIS

TIME OF INCIDENT: APPROXIMATELY NOON,
JUNE 25, 1983

PLACE: HINAMIZAWA FOREST
SERVICES OFFICES, X-CHOME,
HINAMIZAWA, SHISHIBONE

SEQUENCE OF EVENTS:
AT OR AROUND NOON ON THE DAY OF THE INCIDENT, THE
CRIMINAL (REINA RYUGU) ENTERED THE HINAMIZAWA OFFICE
OF FOREST SERVICES. IN THIS BUILDING, SHE ENTERED
A CLASSROOM OF THE HINAMIZAWA BRANCH SCHOOL AND
TOOK FIFTEEN STUDENTS HOSTAGE. SHE THEN DOUSED THE
CLASSROOM WITH A LARGE QUANTITY OF GASOLINE AND LAID
SIEGE FOR MORE THAN SEVEN HOURS. AFTER SEVERAL HOURS
OF DEADLOCK, SOME HOSTAGES RESISTED AND ESCAPED AT
6:15 P.M. THAT SAME DAY. THE CRIMINAL PURSUED ONE HOSTAGE
WHO HAD ESCAPED TO THE ROOF, AND A FIGHT BROKE OUT.
AFTER A BRIEF CONFRONTATION, SHE PUT DOWN HER
WEAPON AND RELEASED THE HOSTAGE AROUND 7:10 P.M.
SHE SURRENDERED TO THE POLICE.

...THUS THE INCIDENT WAS RESOLVED
WITH MINIMAL DAMAGE.

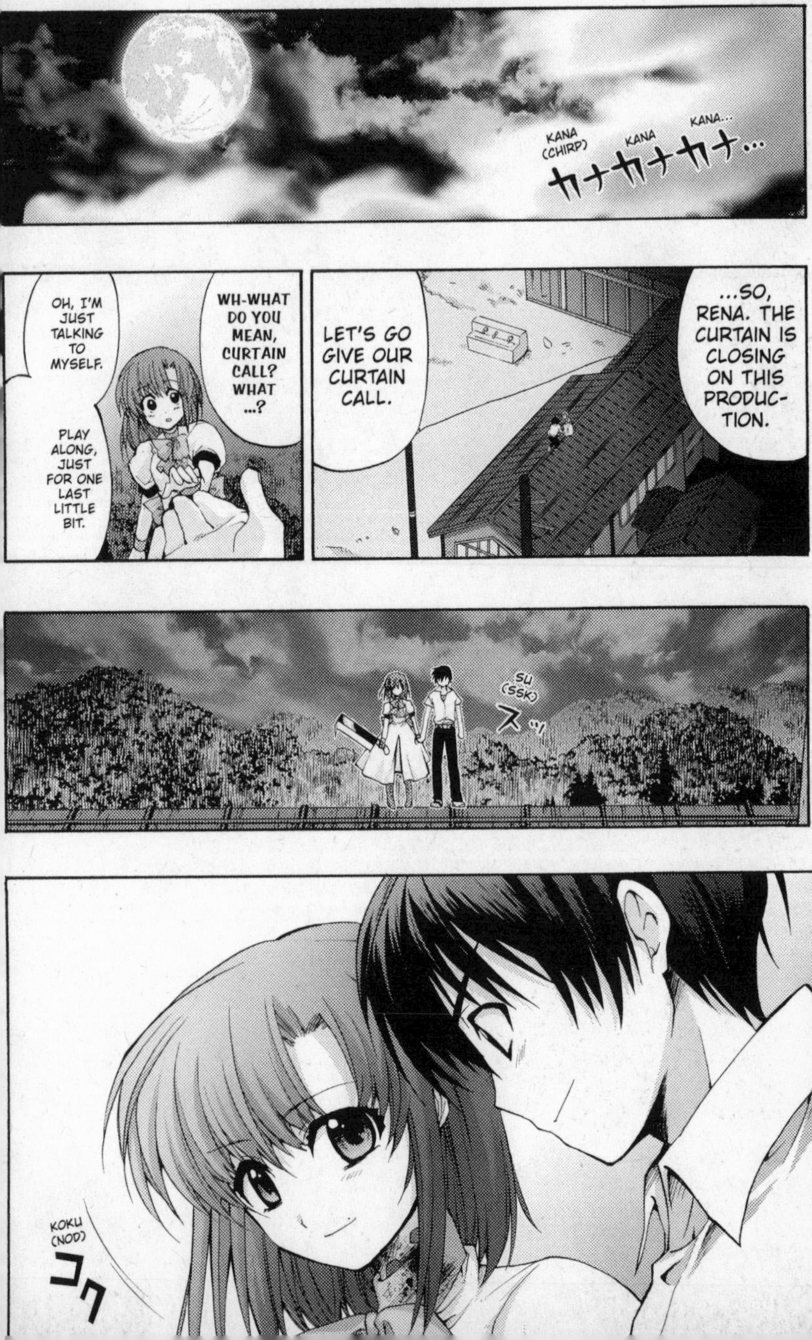
KANA (CHIRP) KANA KANA...
カナカナカナ…
...SO, RENA. THE CURTAIN IS CLOSING ON THIS PRODUC-TION.
LET'S GO GIVE OUR CURTAIN CALL.
WH-WHAT DO YOU MEAN, CURTAIN CALL? WHAT ...?
OH, I'M JUST TALKING TO MYSELF.
PLAY ALONG, JUST FOR ONE LAST LITTLE BIT.
SU (SSK)
スッ
KOKU (NOD)
コク

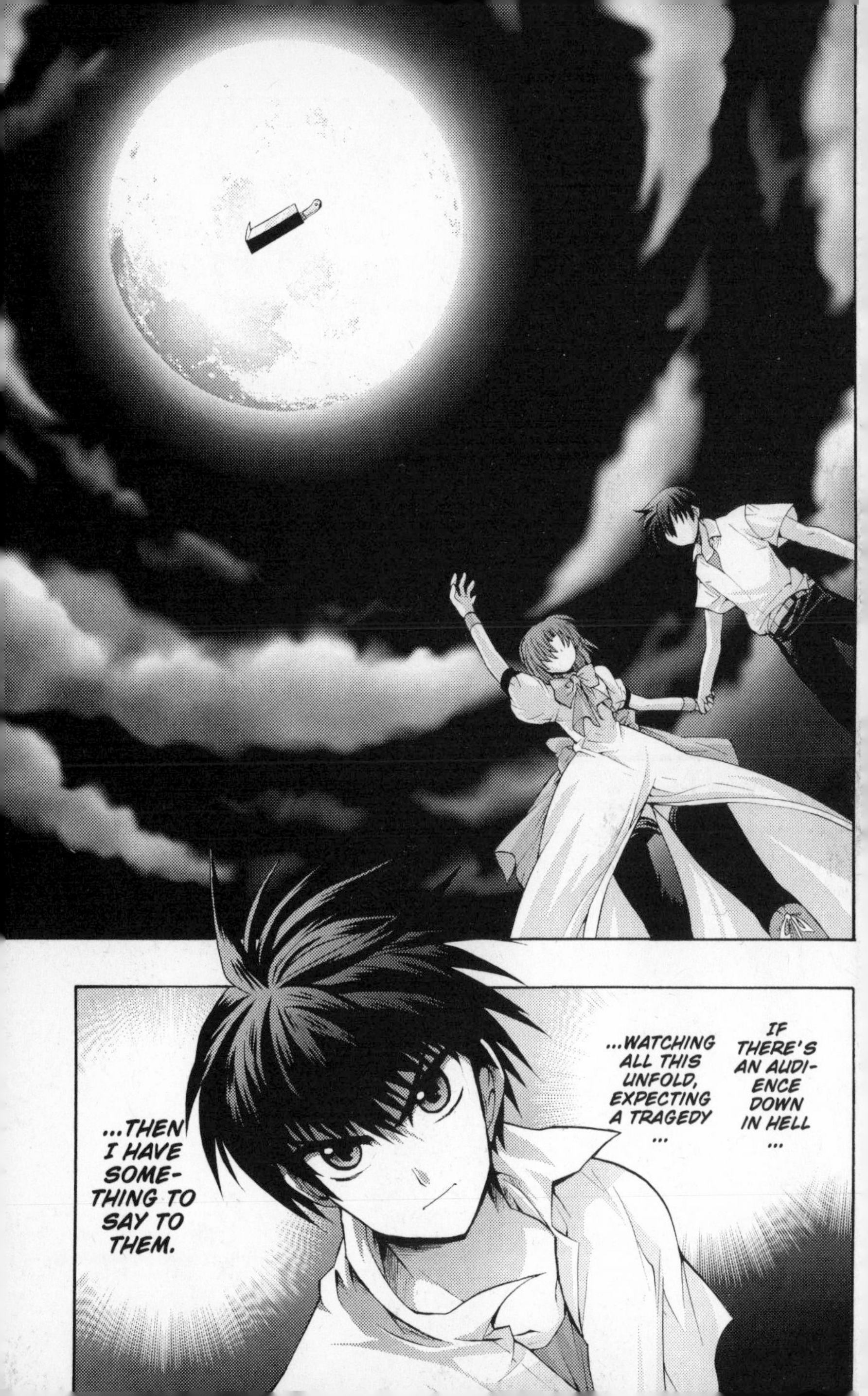
IF THERE'S AN AUDI-ENCE DOWN IN HELL...
...WATCHING ALL THIS UNFOLD, EXPECTING A TRAGEDY...
...THEN I HAVE SOME-THING TO SAY TO THEM.

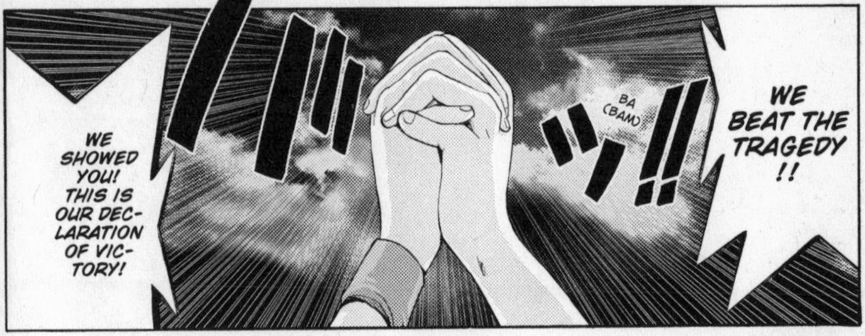
WE BEAT THE TRAGEDY !!
BA (BAM)
WE SHOWED YOU! THIS IS OUR DECLARATION OF VICTORY!

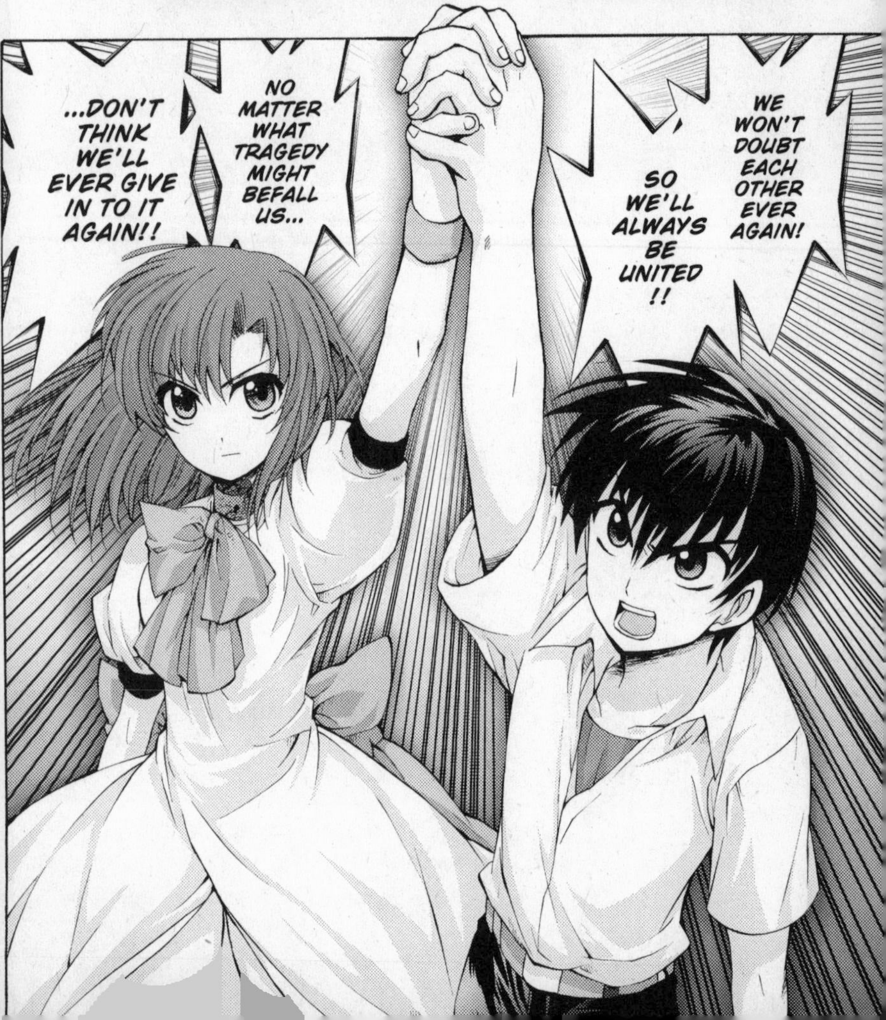
WE WON'T DOUBT EACH OTHER EVER AGAIN!
SO WE'LL ALWAYS BE UNITED !!
NO MATTER WHAT TRAGEDY MIGHT BEFALL US...
...DON'T THINK WE'LL EVER GIVE IN TO IT AGAIN!!

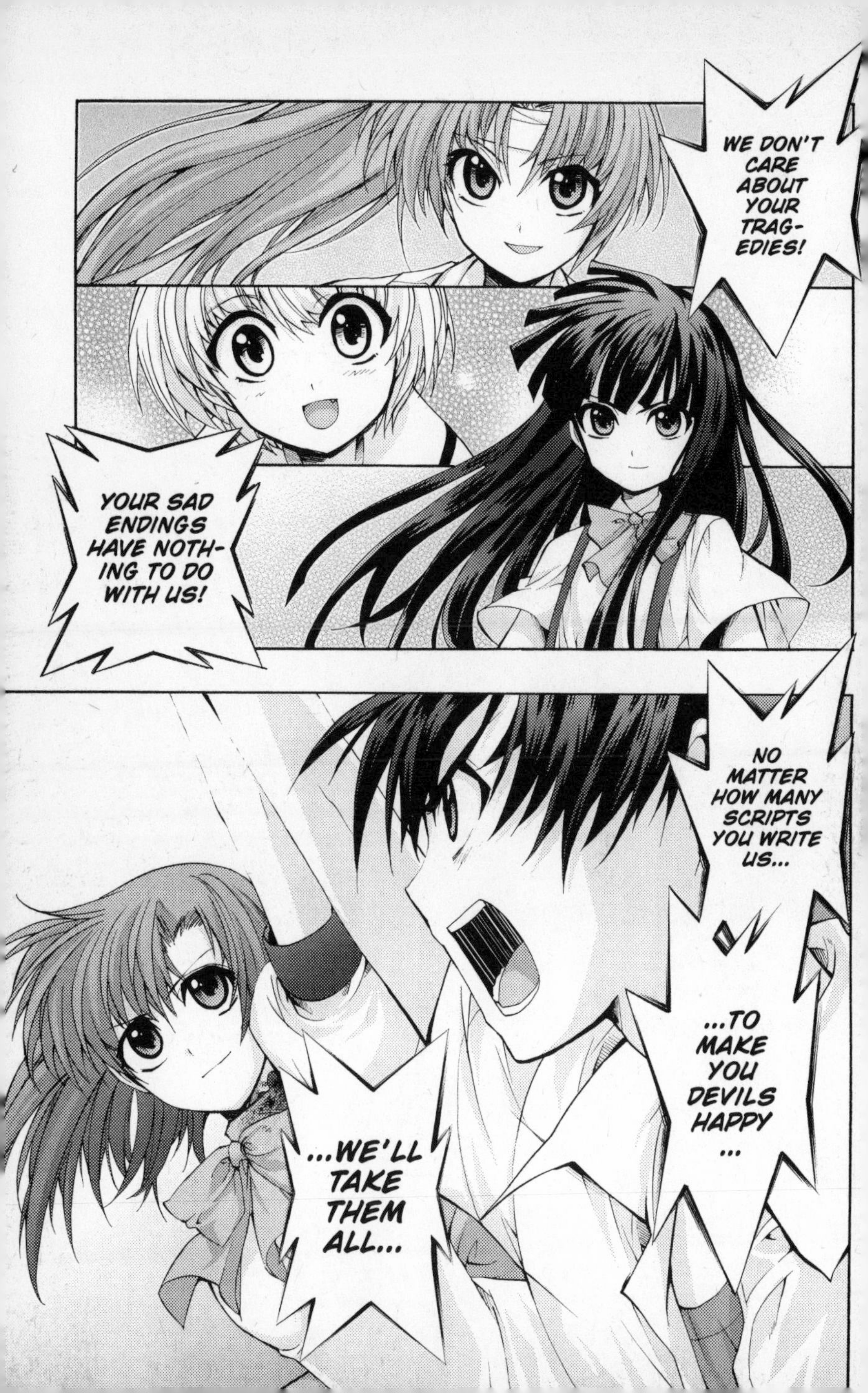
WE DON'T CARE ABOUT YOUR TRAG-EDIES!
YOUR SAD ENDINGS HAVE NOTH-ING TO DO WITH US!
NO MATTER HOW MANY SCRIPTS YOU WRITE US...
...TO MAKE YOU DEVILS HAPPY...
...WE'LL TAKE THEM ALL...

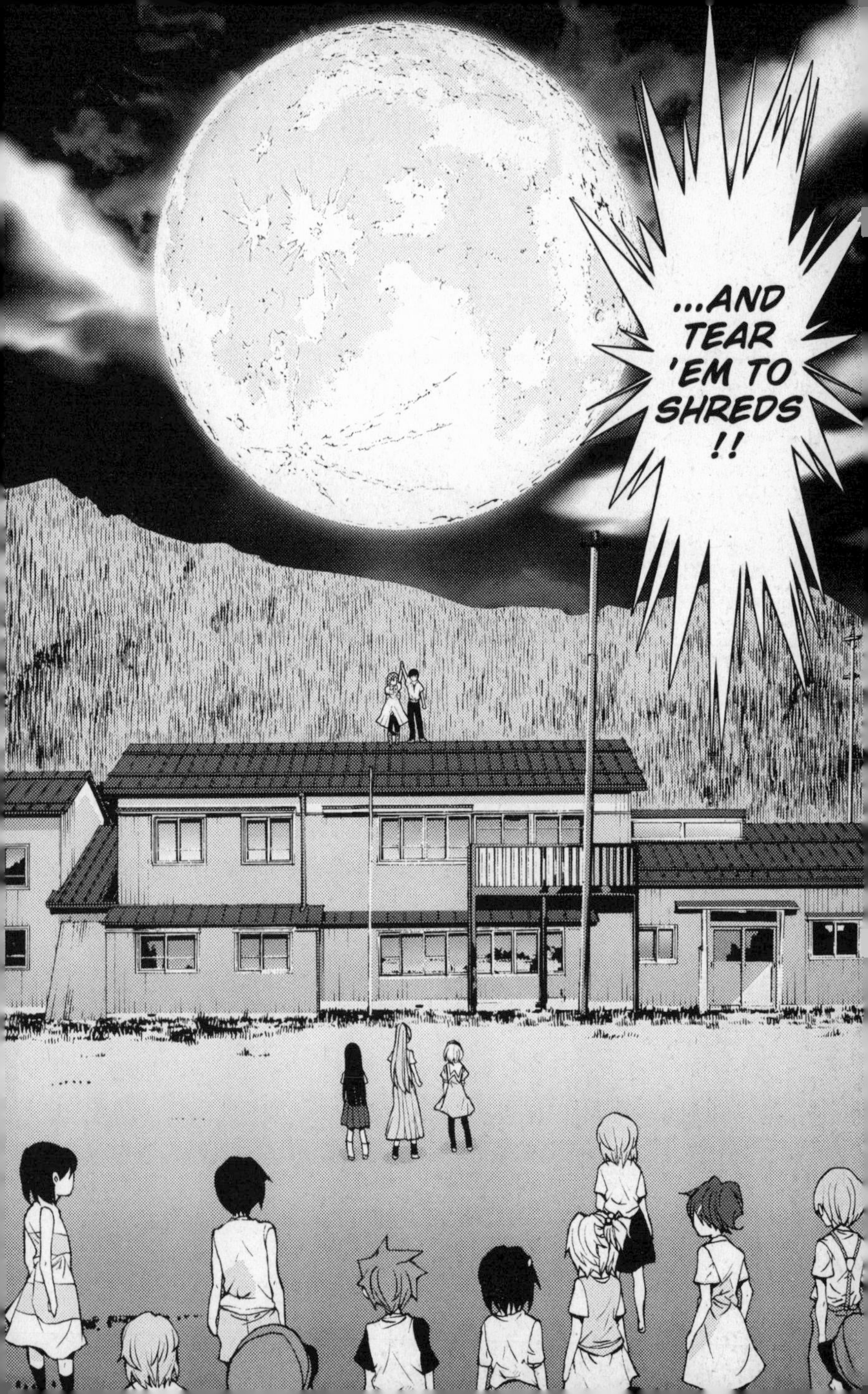
...AND TEAR 'EM TO SHREDS !!

Higurashi WHEN THEY CRY

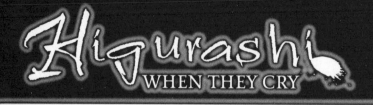

ATONEMENT ARC

FIN

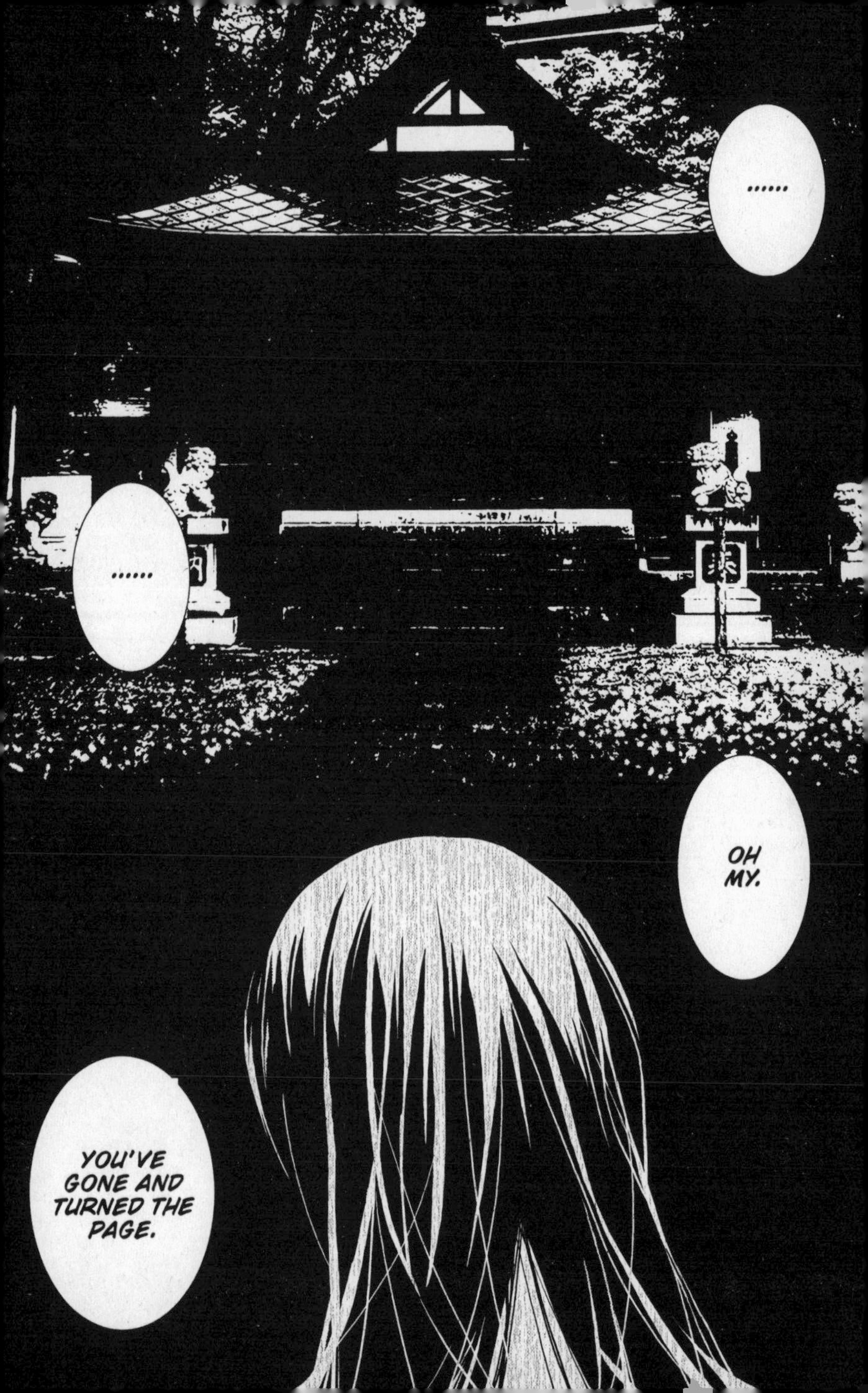
......
......
OH MY.
YOU'VE GONE AND TURNED THE PAGE.

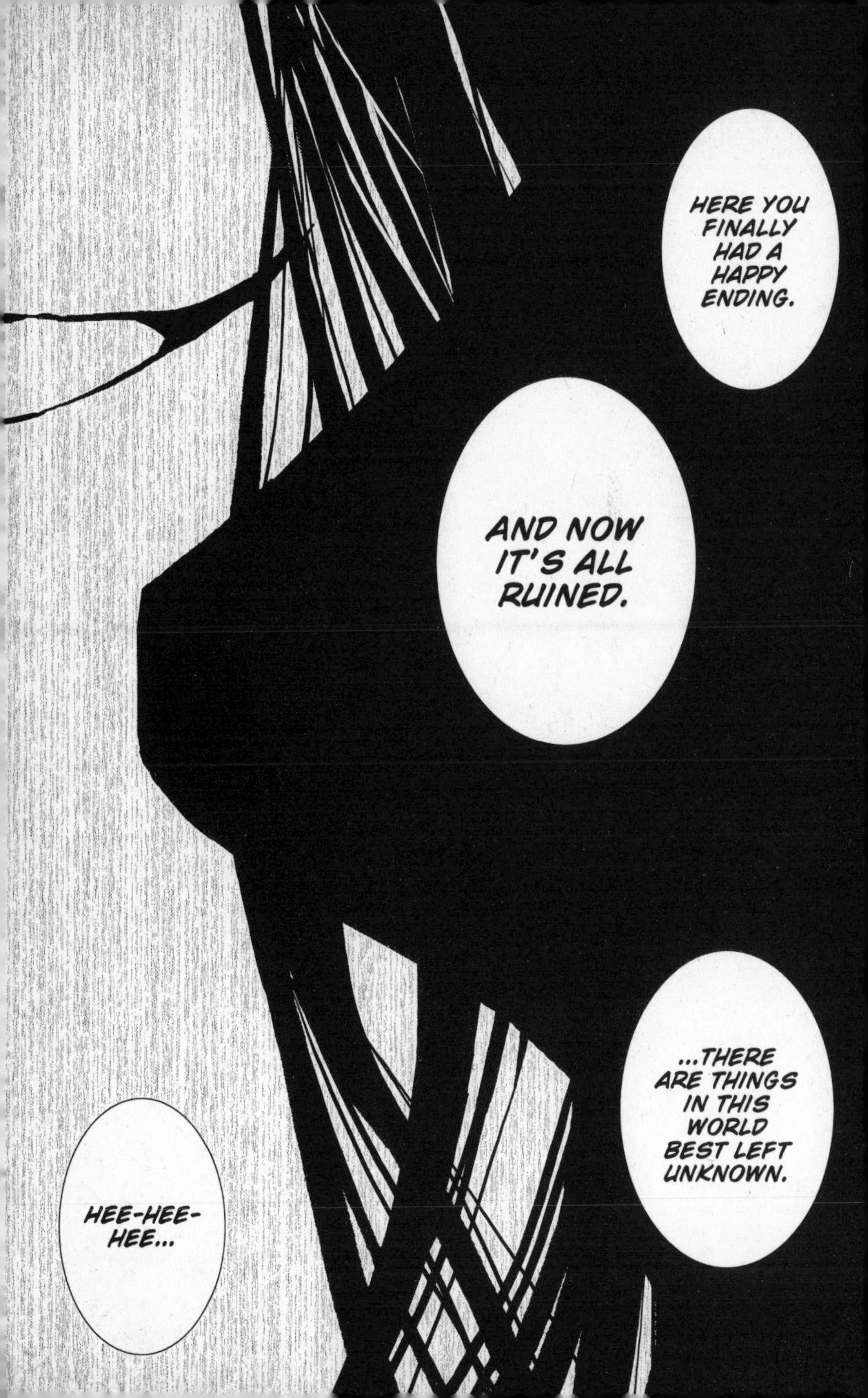
HERE YOU FINALLY HAD A HAPPY ENDING.
AND NOW IT'S ALL RUINED.
...THERE ARE THINGS IN THIS WORLD BEST LEFT UNKNOWN.
HEE-HEE-HEE...

22 YEARS AFTER THE INCIDENT

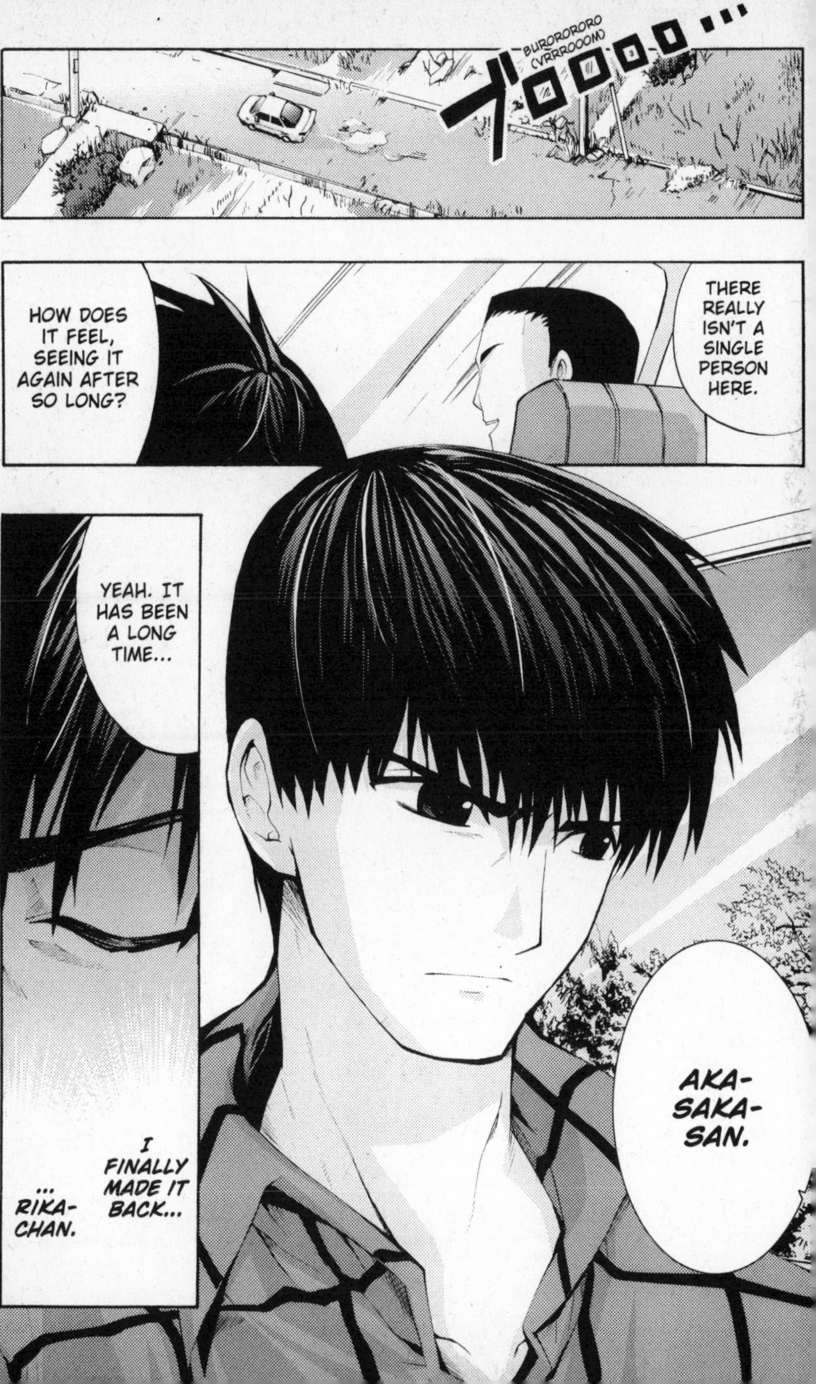
BUROROROROROBUROROROROROBUROROROROROBUROROROROROBURORORORORO
(VRRROOOM)
THERE REALLY ISN'T A SINGLE PERSON HERE.
HOW DOES IT FEEL, SEEING IT AGAIN AFTER SO LONG?
AKA-SAKA-SAN.
YEAH. IT HAS BEEN A LONG TIME...
I FINALLY MADE IT BACK...
...RIKA-CHAN.

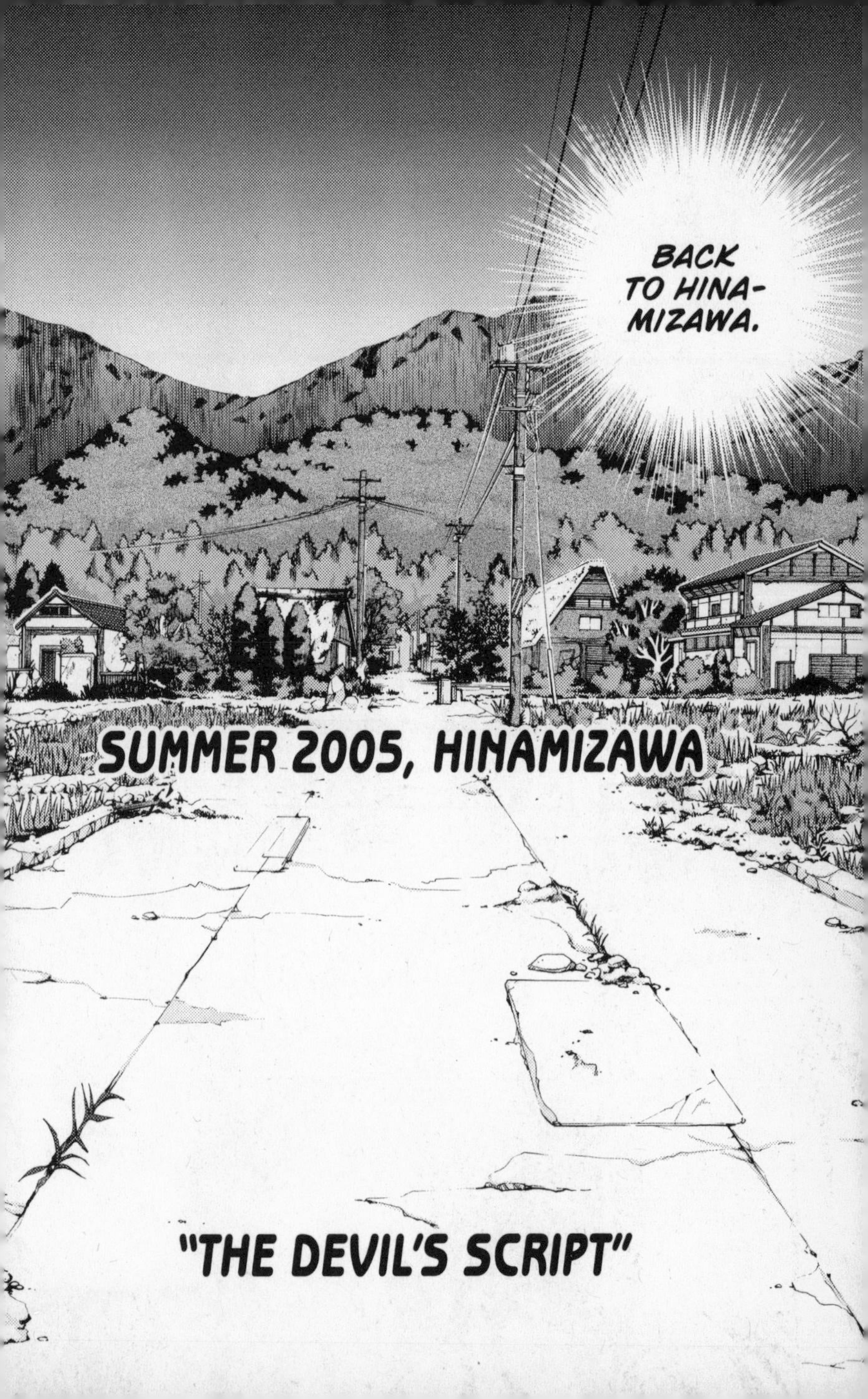
BACK TO HINA-MIZAWA.
SUMMER 2005, HINAMIZAWA
"THE DEVIL'S SCRIPT"

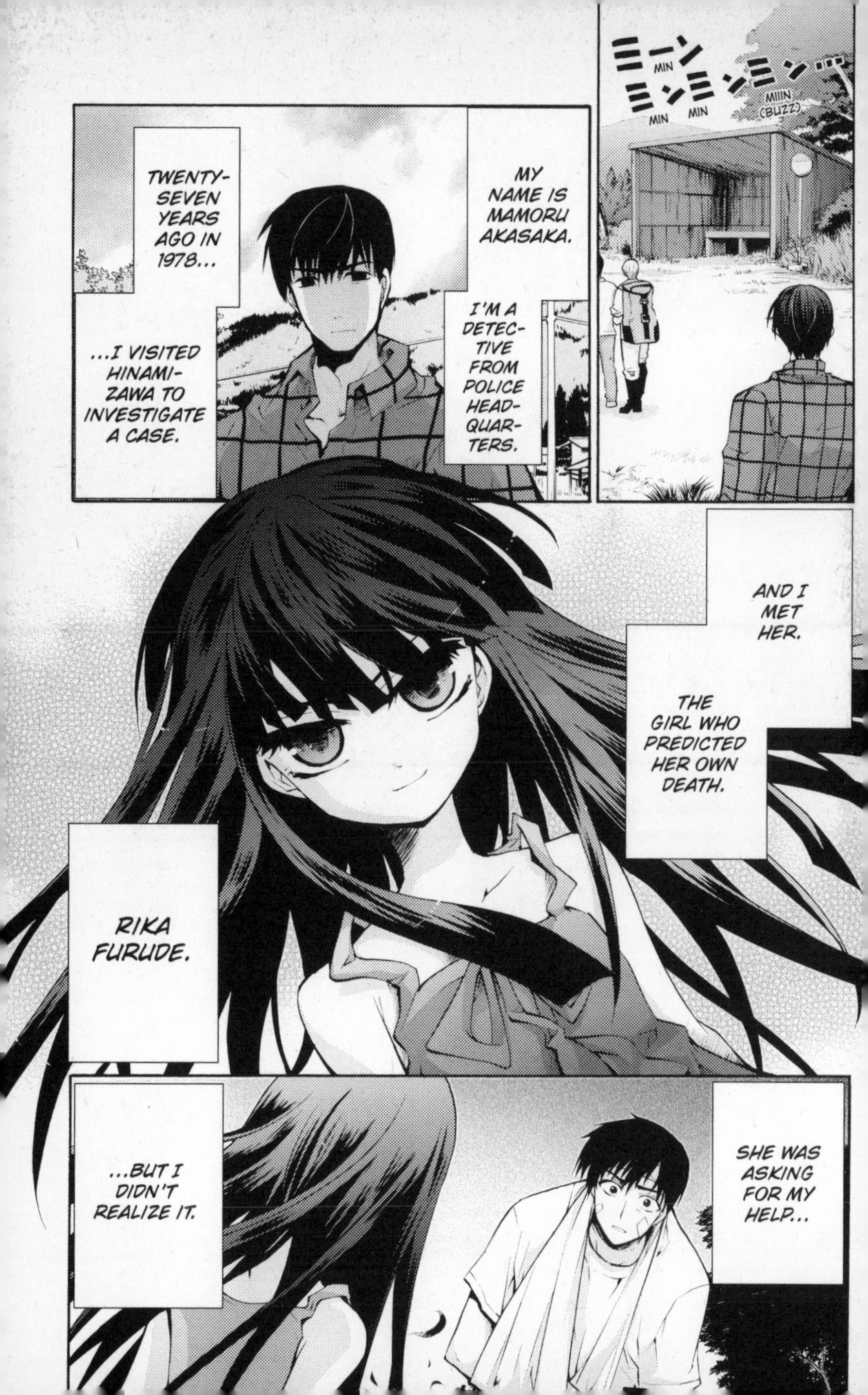
MIN
MIN
MIN
MIIIN (BUZZ)
MY NAME IS MAMORU AKASAKA.
I'M A DETECTIVE FROM POLICE HEADQUARTERS.
TWENTY-SEVEN YEARS AGO IN 1978...
...I VISITED HINAMIZAWA TO INVESTIGATE A CASE.
AND I MET HER.
THE GIRL WHO PREDICTED HER OWN DEATH.
RIKA FURUDE.
SHE WAS ASKING FOR MY HELP...
...BUT I DIDN'T REALIZE IT.

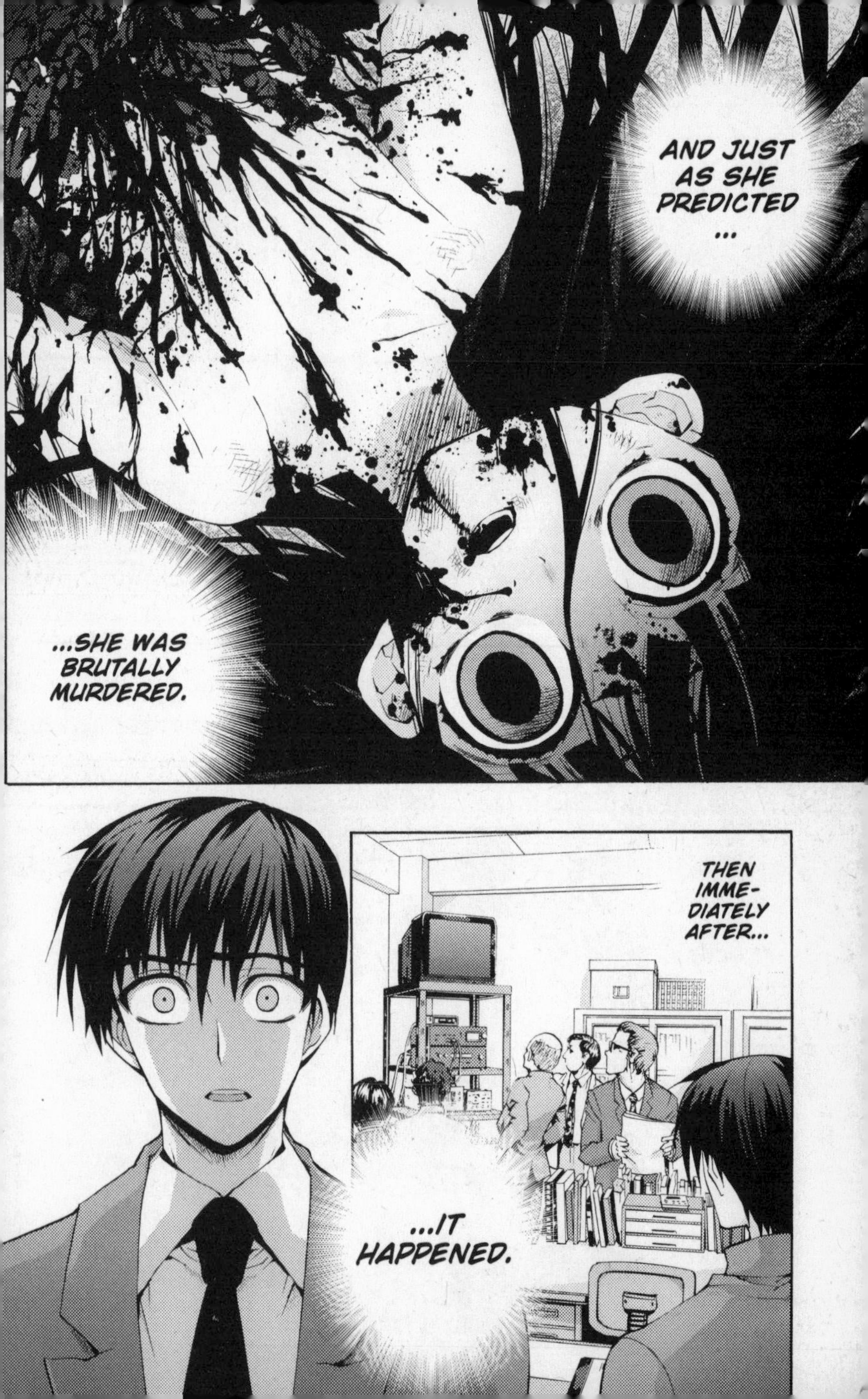
AND JUST AS SHE PREDICTED ...
...SHE WAS BRUTALLY MURDERED.
THEN IMME-DIATELY AFTER...
...IT HAPPENED.

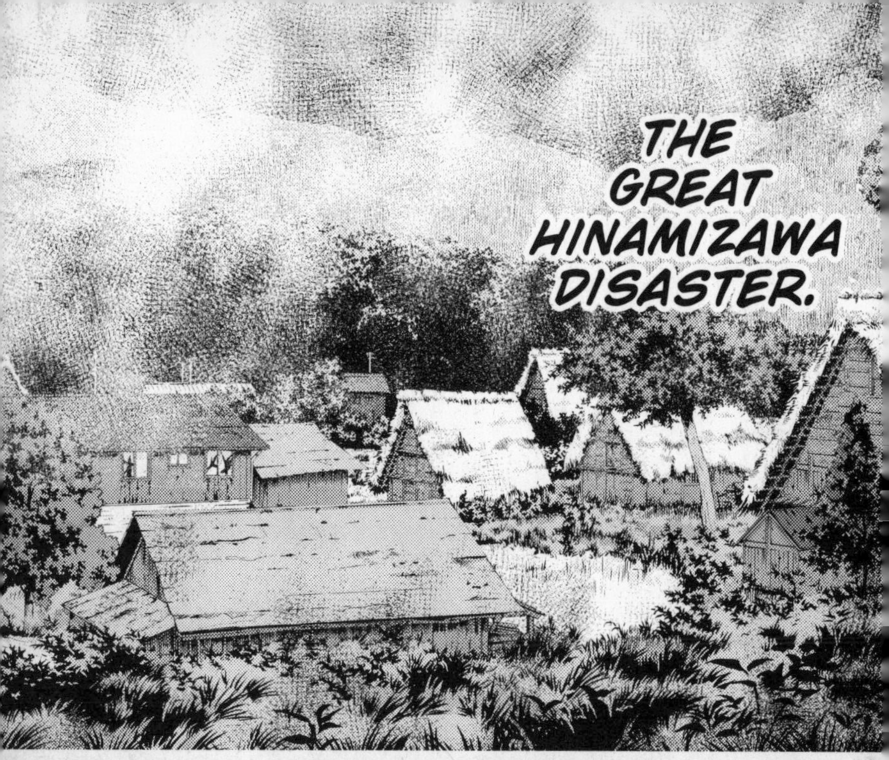
THE GREAT HINAMIZAWA DISASTER.
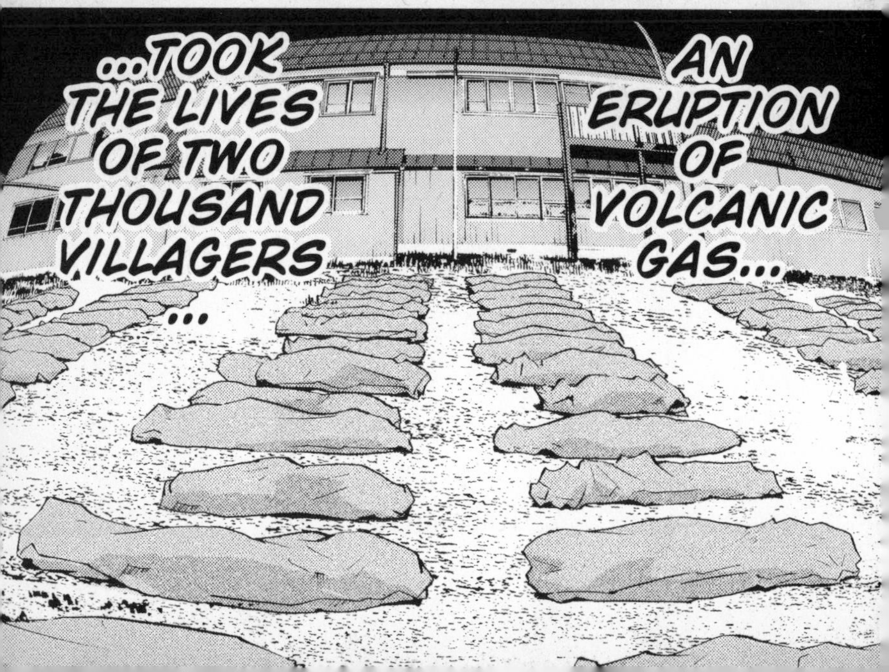
AN ERUPTION OF VOLCANIC GAS...
...TOOK THE LIVES OF TWO THOUSAND VILLAGERS...

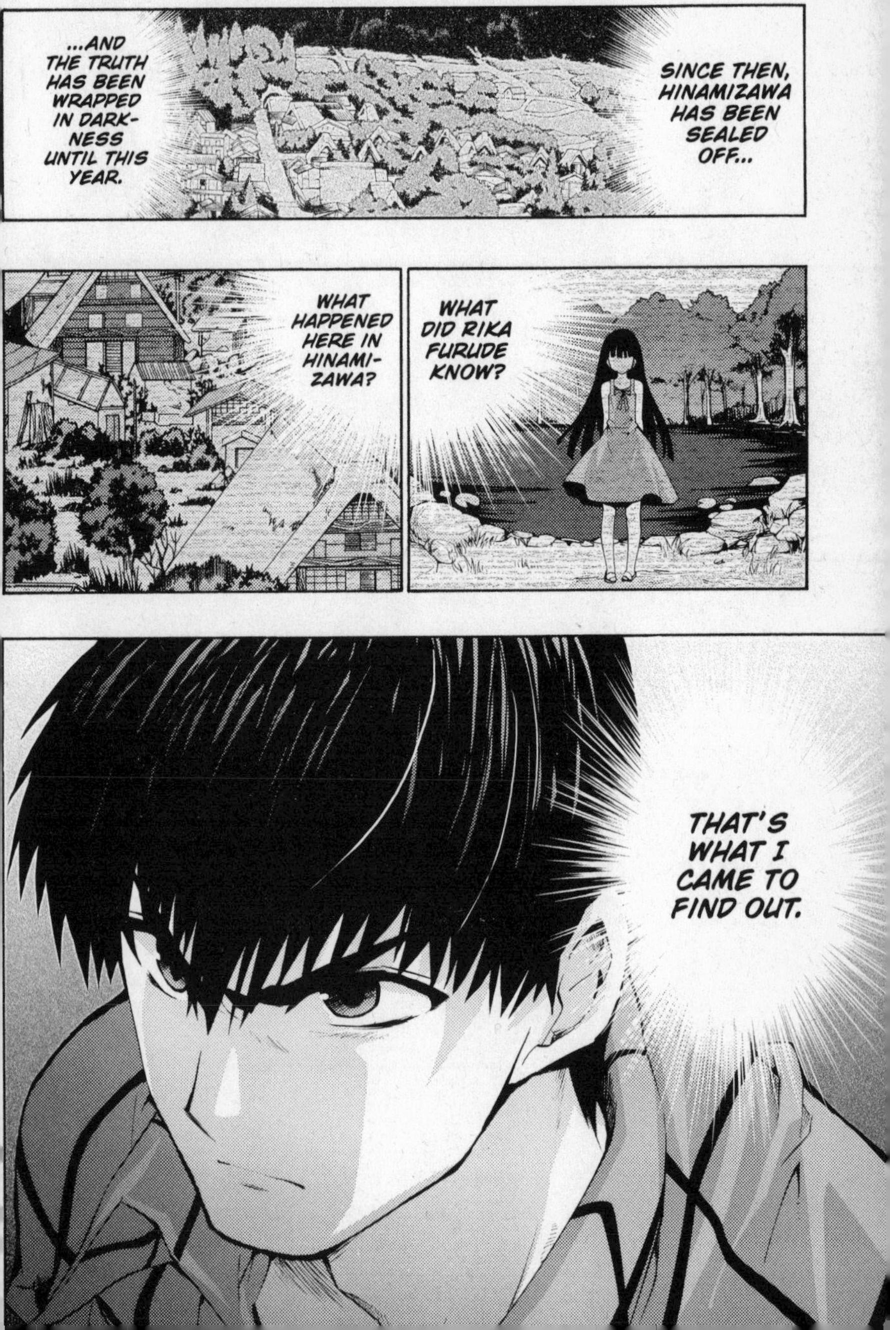
SINCE THEN, HINAMIZAWA HAS BEEN SEALED OFF...
...AND THE TRUTH HAS BEEN WRAPPED IN DARK-NESS UNTIL THIS YEAR.
WHAT DID RIKA FURUDE KNOW?
WHAT HAPPENED HERE IN HINAMI-ZAWA?
THAT'S WHAT I CAME TO FIND OUT.

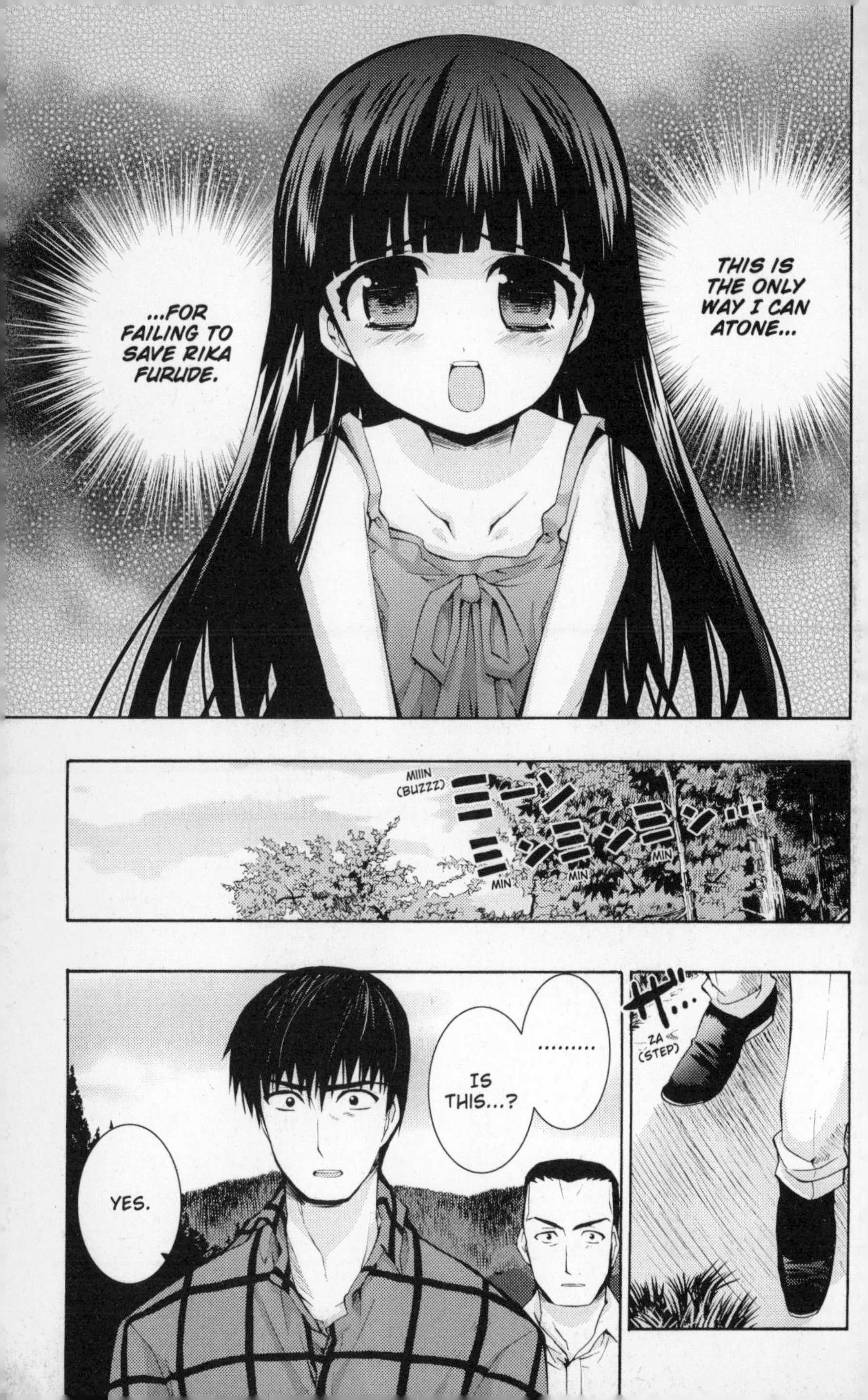
THIS IS THE ONLY WAY I CAN ATONE...
...FOR FAILING TO SAVE RIKA FURUDE.
MIIN (BUZZZ)
MIN
MIN
MIN
ZA (STEP)
....
IS THIS...?
YES.

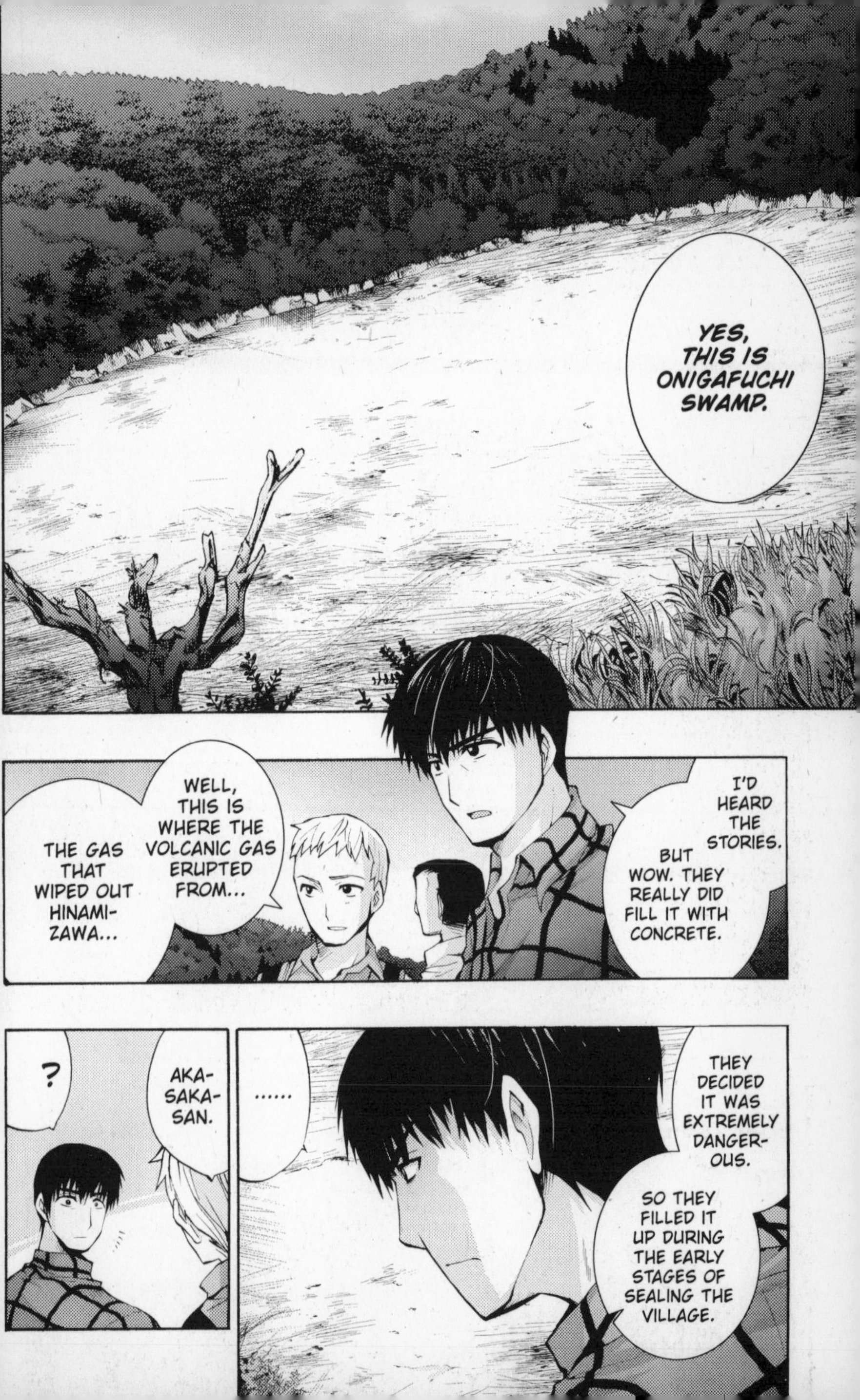
YES, THIS IS ONIGAFUCHI SWAMP.
I'D HEARD THE STORIES.
BUT WOW. THEY REALLY DID FILL IT WITH CONCRETE.
WELL, THIS IS WHERE THE VOLCANIC GAS ERUPTED FROM...
THE GAS THAT WIPED OUT HINAMI-ZAWA...
THEY DECIDED IT WAS EXTREMELY DANGER-OUS.
SO THEY FILLED IT UP DURING THE EARLY STAGES OF SEALING THE VILLAGE.
......
AKA-SAKA-SAN.
?

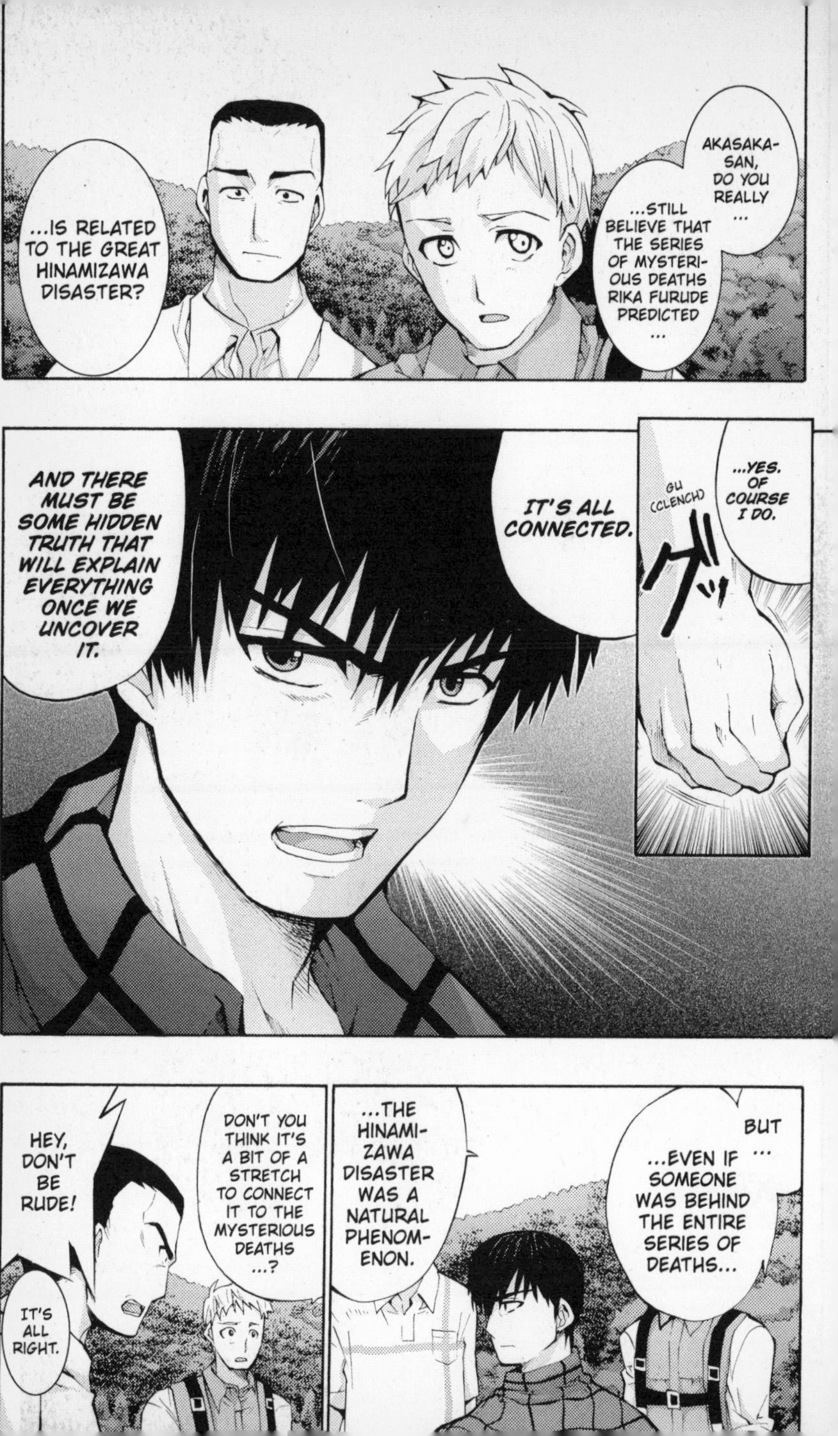
AKASAKA-SAN, DO YOU REALLY ...
...STILL BELIEVE THAT THE SERIES OF MYSTERIOUS DEATHS RIKA FURUDE PREDICTED ...
...IS RELATED TO THE GREAT HINAMIZAWA DISASTER?
...YES. OF COURSE I DO.
GU (CLENCH)
IT'S ALL CONNECTED.
AND THERE MUST BE SOME HIDDEN TRUTH THAT WILL EXPLAIN EVERYTHING ONCE WE UNCOVER IT.
BUT ...
...EVEN IF SOMEONE WAS BEHIND THE ENTIRE SERIES OF DEATHS...
...THE HINAMIZAWA DISASTER WAS A NATURAL PHENOMENON.
DON'T YOU THINK IT'S A BIT OF A STRETCH TO CONNECT IT TO THE MYSTERIOUS DEATHS ...?
HEY, DON'T BE RUDE!
IT'S ALL RIGHT.

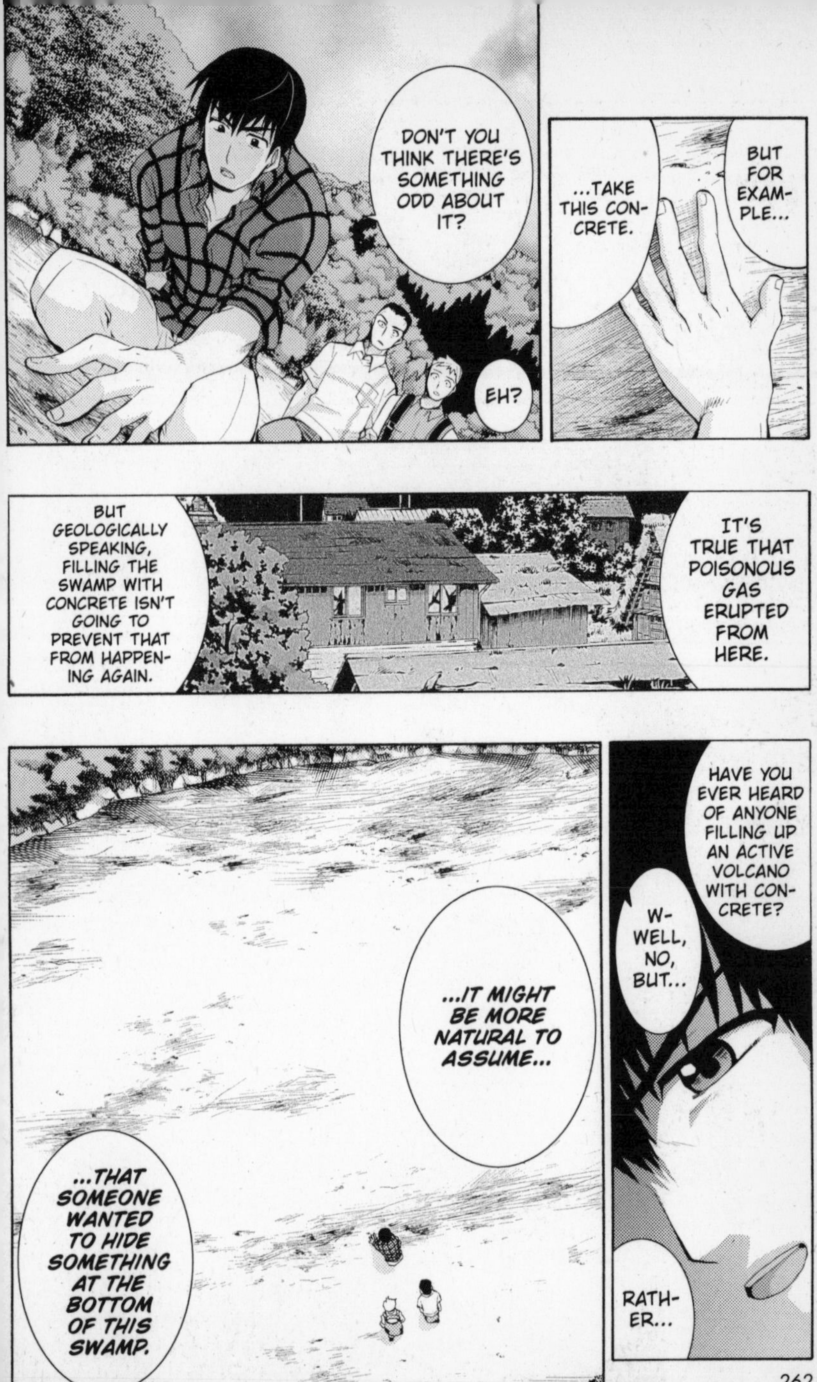
BUT FOR EXAMPLE...
...TAKE THIS CONCRETE.
DON'T YOU THINK THERE'S SOMETHING ODD ABOUT IT?
EH?
IT'S TRUE THAT POISONOUS GAS ERUPTED FROM HERE.
BUT GEOLOGICALLY SPEAKING, FILLING THE SWAMP WITH CONCRETE ISN'T GOING TO PREVENT THAT FROM HAPPENING AGAIN.
HAVE YOU EVER HEARD OF ANYONE FILLING UP AN ACTIVE VOLCANO WITH CONCRETE?
W-WELL, NO, BUT...
RATHER...
...IT MIGHT BE MORE NATURAL TO ASSUME...
...THAT SOMEONE WANTED TO HIDE SOMETHING AT THE BOTTOM OF THIS SWAMP.

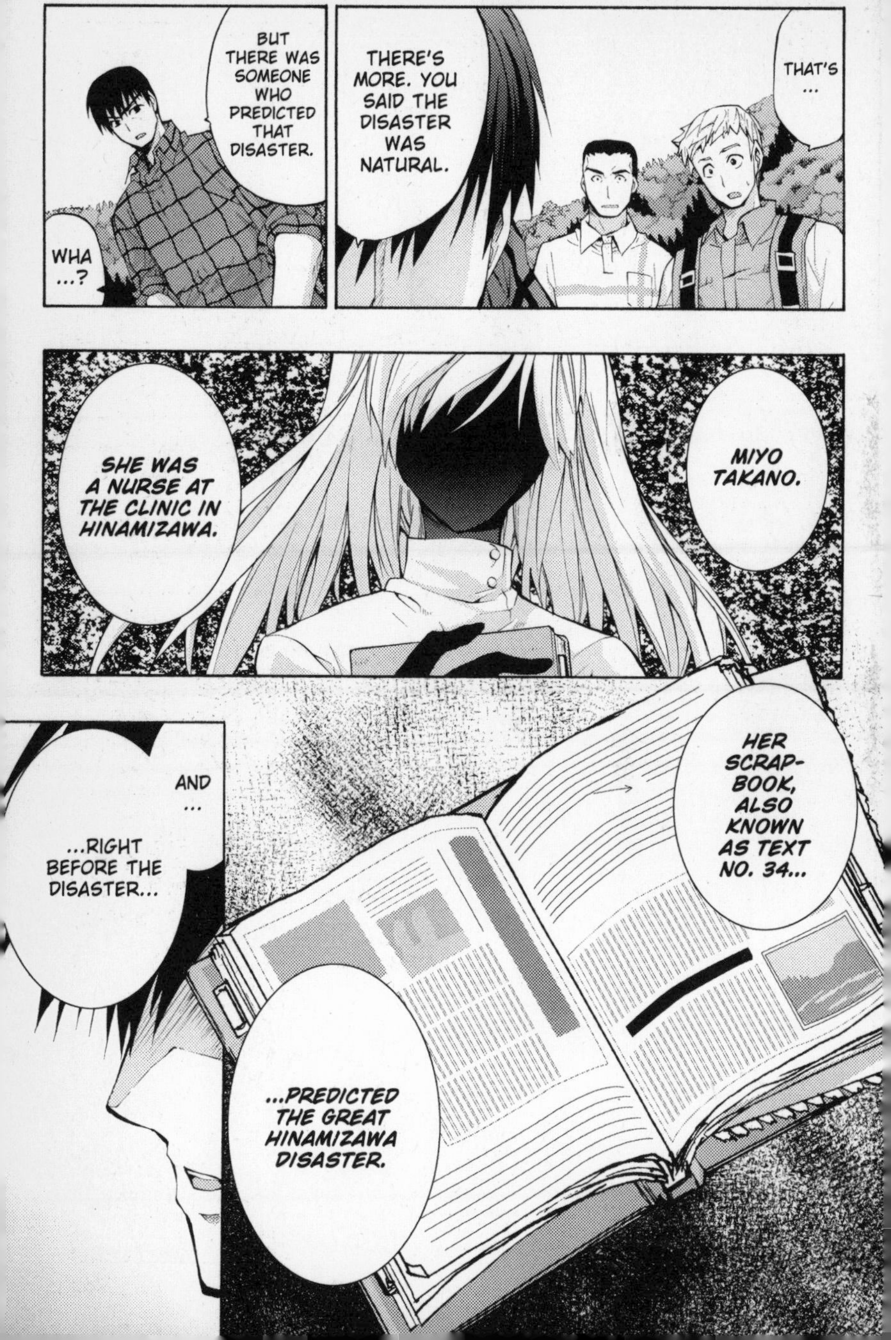
THAT'S ...
THERE'S MORE. YOU SAID THE DISASTER WAS NATURAL.
BUT THERE WAS SOMEONE WHO PREDICTED THAT DISASTER.
WHA ...?
MIYO TAKANO.
SHE WAS A NURSE AT THE CLINIC IN HINAMIZAWA.
HER SCRAP-BOOK, ALSO KNOWN AS TEXT NO. 34...
AND ...
...RIGHT BEFORE THE DISASTER...
...PREDICTED THE GREAT HINAMIZAWA DISASTER.

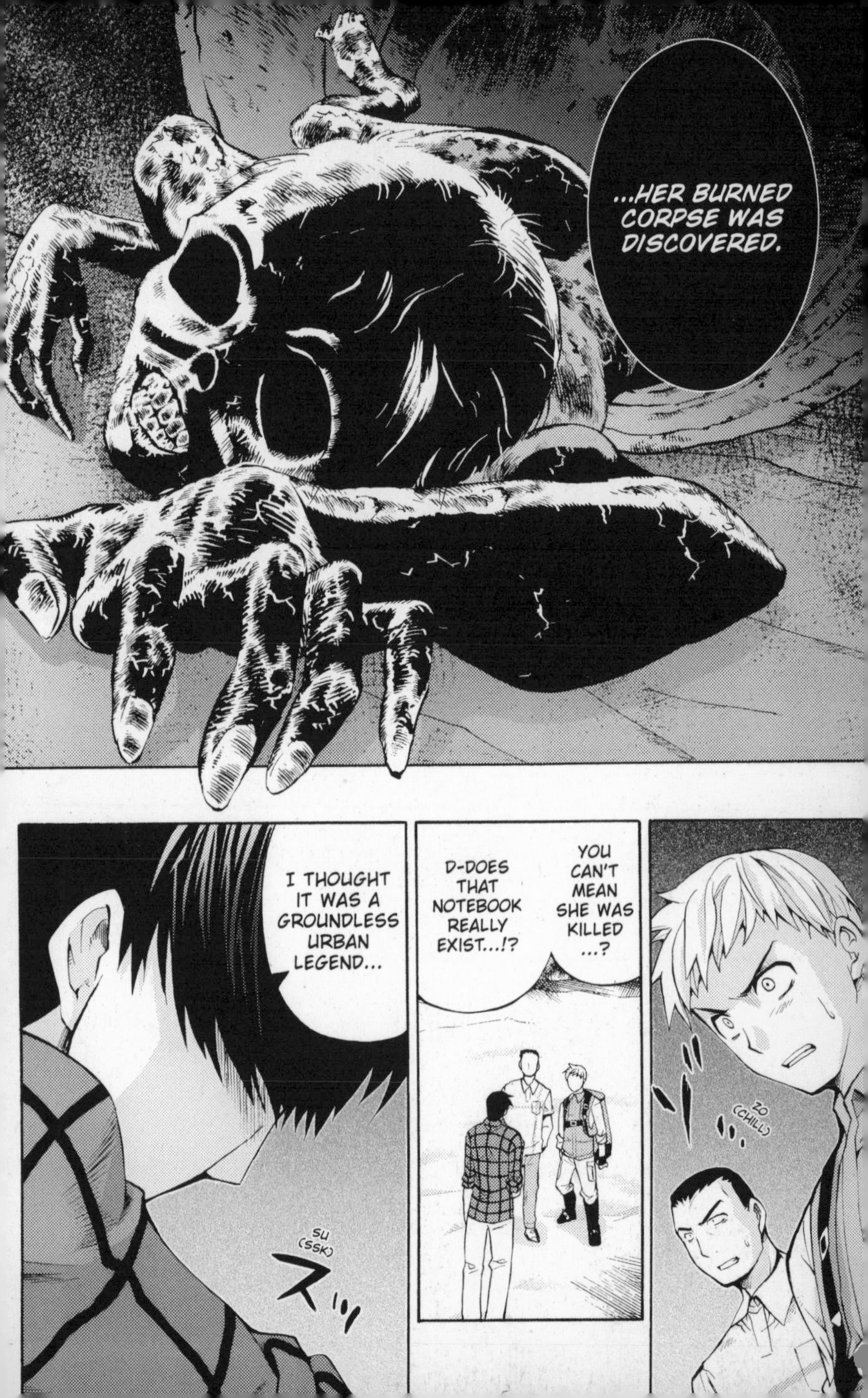
...HER BURNED CORPSE WAS DISCOVERED.
ZO (CHILL)
YOU CAN'T MEAN SHE WAS KILLED ...?
D-DOES THAT NOTEBOOK REALLY EXIST...!?
I THOUGHT IT WAS A GROUNDLESS URBAN LEGEND...
SU (SSK)

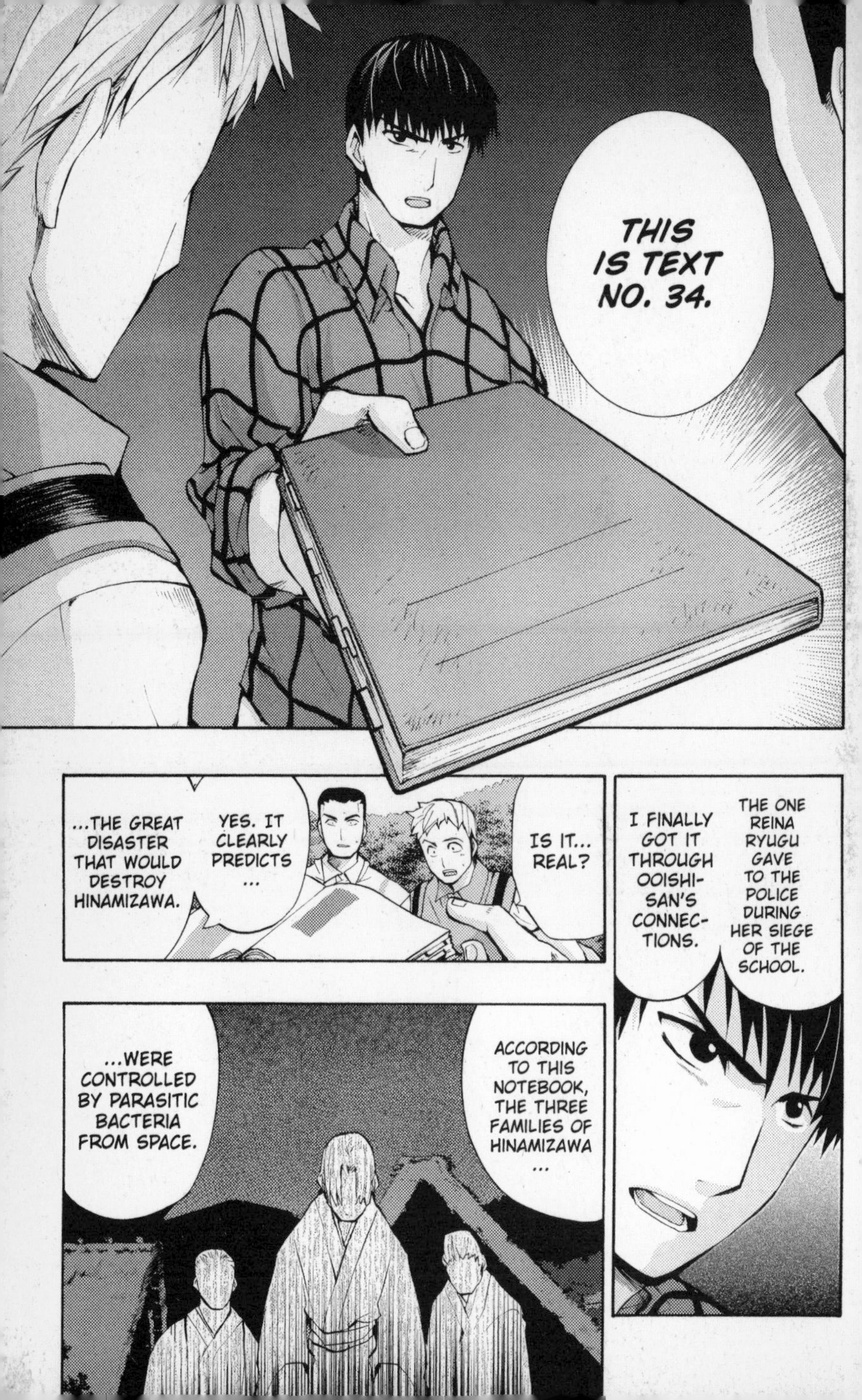
THIS IS TEXT NO. 34.
THE ONE REINA RYUGU GAVE TO THE POLICE DURING HER SIEGE OF THE SCHOOL.
I FINALLY GOT IT THROUGH OOISHI-SAN'S CONNECTIONS.
IS IT... REAL?
YES. IT CLEARLY PREDICTS...
...THE GREAT DISASTER THAT WOULD DESTROY HINAMIZAWA.
ACCORDING TO THIS NOTEBOOK, THE THREE FAMILIES OF HINAMIZAWA...
...WERE CONTROLLED BY PARASITIC BACTERIA FROM SPACE.

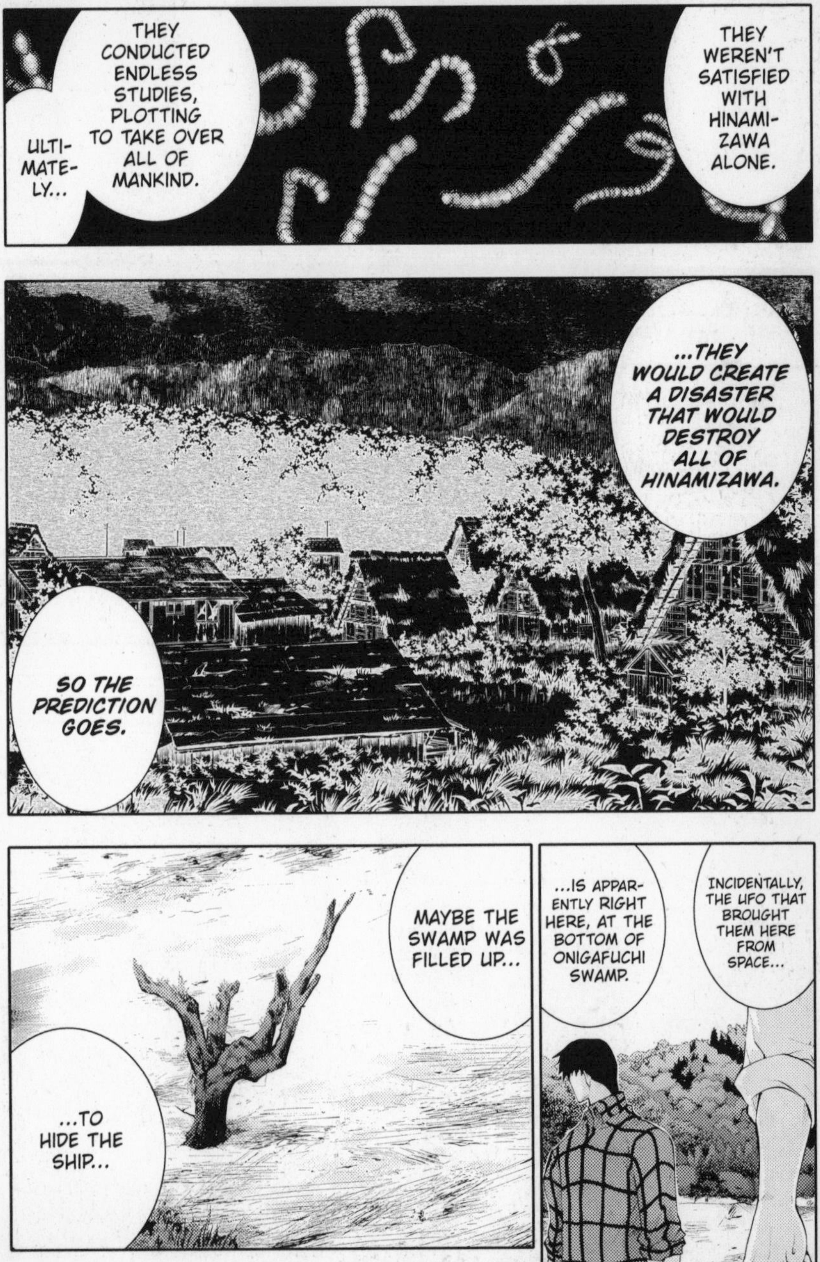
THEY WEREN'T SATISFIED WITH HINAMI-ZAWA ALONE.
THEY CONDUCTED ENDLESS STUDIES, PLOTTING TO TAKE OVER ALL OF MANKIND.
ULTI-MATE-LY...
...THEY WOULD CREATE A DISASTER THAT WOULD DESTROY ALL OF HINAMIZAWA.
SO THE PREDICTION GOES.
INCIDENTALLY, THE UFO THAT BROUGHT THEM HERE FROM SPACE...
...IS APPAR-ENTLY RIGHT HERE, AT THE BOTTOM OF ONIGAFUCHI SWAMP.
MAYBE THE SWAMP WAS FILLED UP...
...TO HIDE THE SHIP...

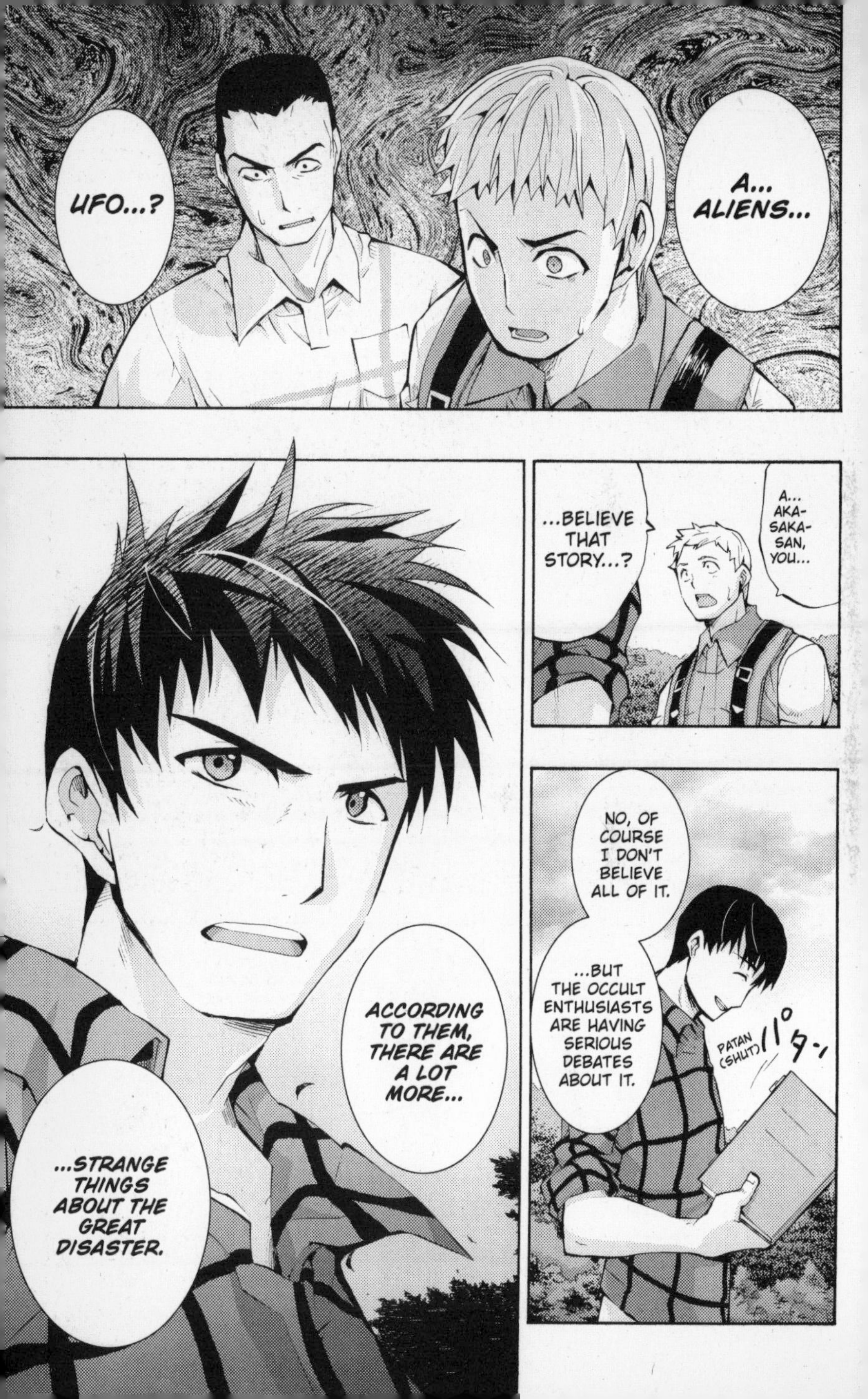
A... ALIENS...
UFO...?
A... AKA-SAKA-SAN, YOU...
...BELIEVE THAT STORY...?
NO, OF COURSE I DON'T BELIEVE ALL OF IT.
...BUT THE OCCULT ENTHUSIASTS ARE HAVING SERIOUS DEBATES ABOUT IT.
PATAN (SHUT)
ACCORDING TO THEM, THERE ARE A LOT MORE...
...STRANGE THINGS ABOUT THE GREAT DISASTER.

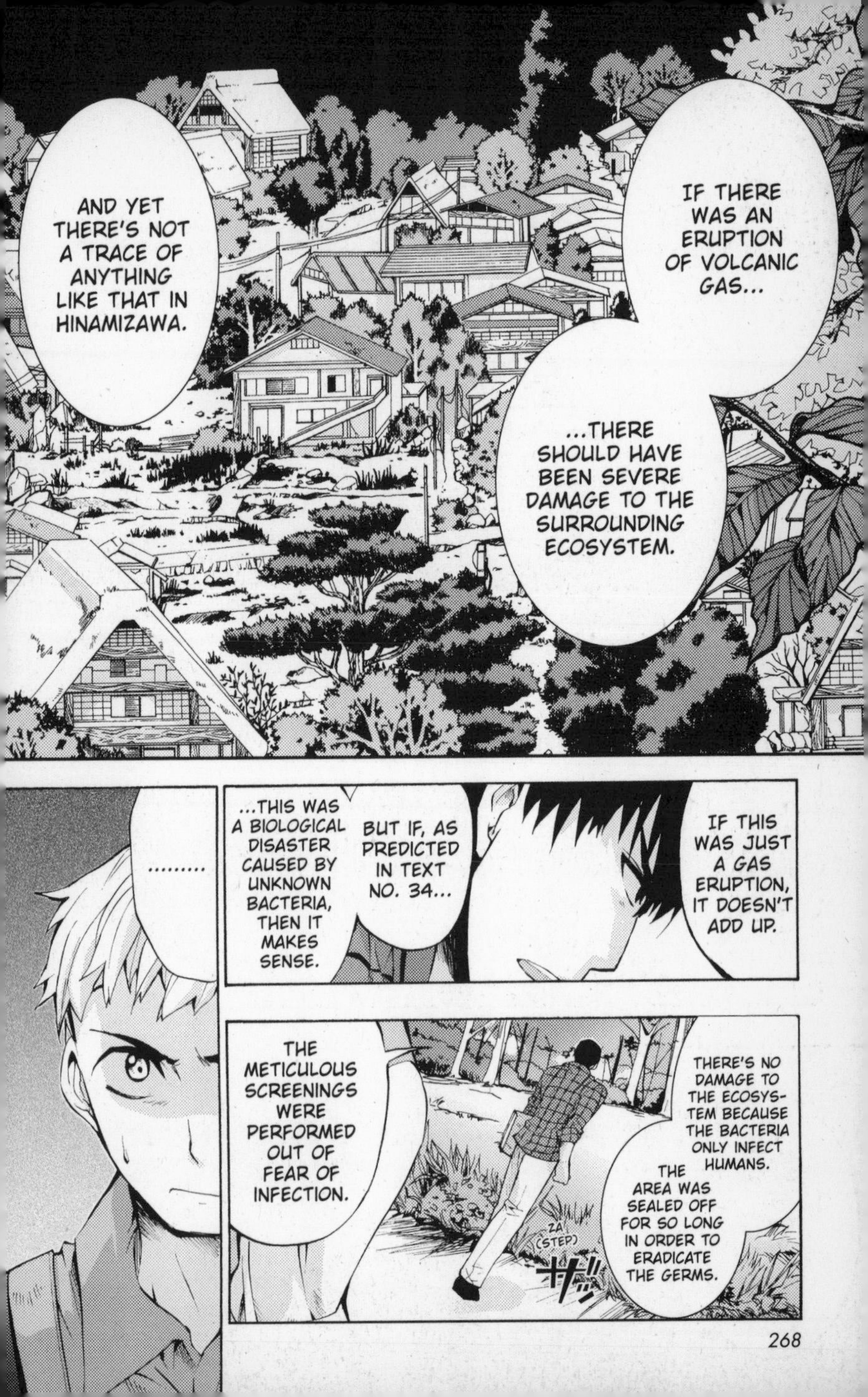
IF THERE WAS AN ERUPTION OF VOLCANIC GAS...
...THERE SHOULD HAVE BEEN SEVERE DAMAGE TO THE SURROUNDING ECOSYSTEM.
AND YET THERE'S NOT A TRACE OF ANYTHING LIKE THAT IN HINAMIZAWA.
IF THIS WAS JUST A GAS ERUPTION, IT DOESN'T ADD UP.
BUT IF, AS PREDICTED IN TEXT NO. 34...
...THIS WAS A BIOLOGICAL DISASTER CAUSED BY UNKNOWN BACTERIA, THEN IT MAKES SENSE.
THERE'S NO DAMAGE TO THE ECOSYSTEM BECAUSE THE BACTERIA ONLY INFECT HUMANS.
THE AREA WAS SEALED OFF FOR SO LONG IN ORDER TO ERADICATE THE GERMS.
ZA (STEP)
THE METICULOUS SCREENINGS WERE PERFORMED OUT OF FEAR OF INFECTION.
....

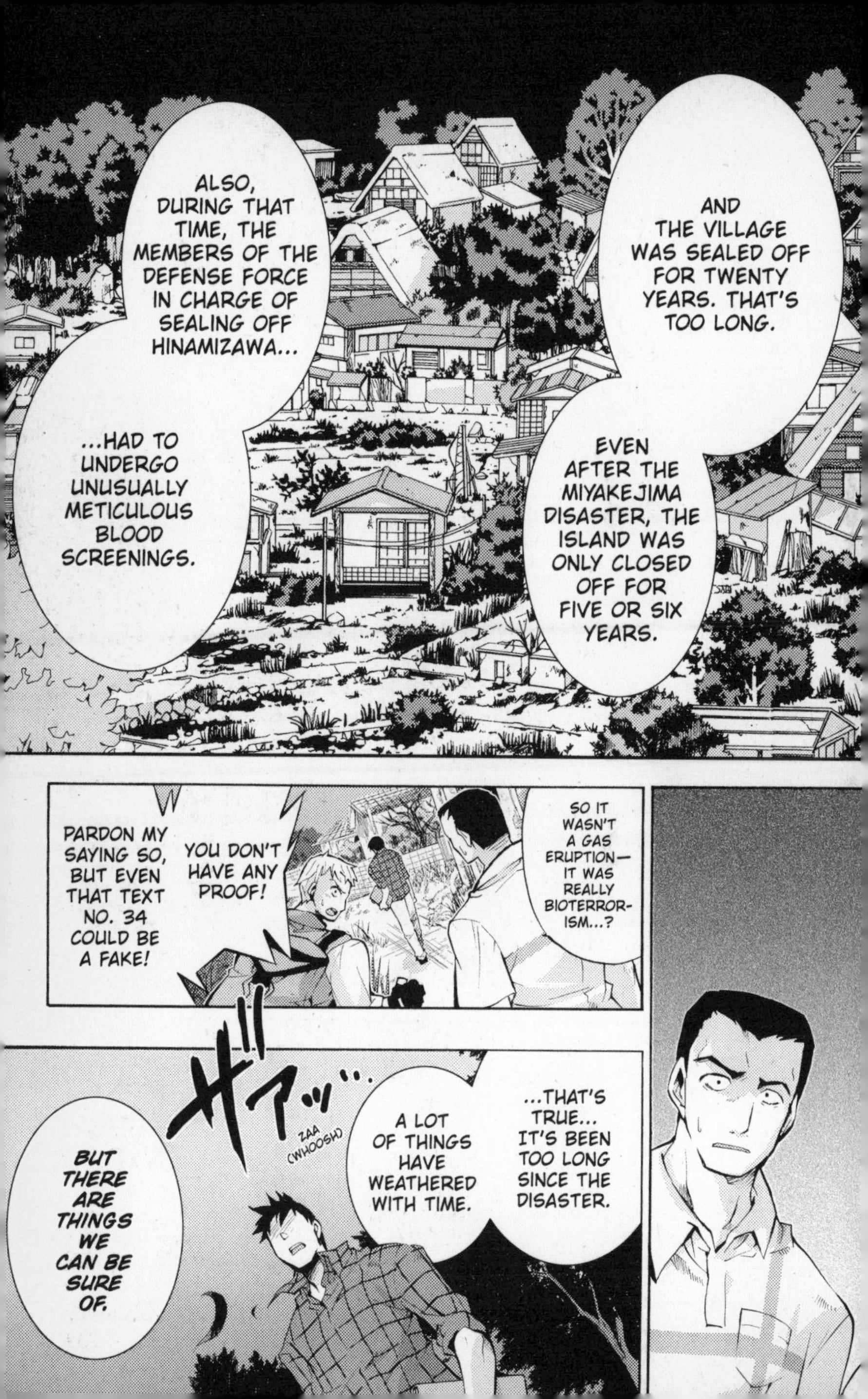
AND THE VILLAGE WAS SEALED OFF FOR TWENTY YEARS. THAT'S TOO LONG.
EVEN AFTER THE MIYAKEJIMA DISASTER, THE ISLAND WAS ONLY CLOSED OFF FOR FIVE OR SIX YEARS.
ALSO, DURING THAT TIME, THE MEMBERS OF THE DEFENSE FORCE IN CHARGE OF SEALING OFF HINAMIZAWA...
...HAD TO UNDERGO UNUSUALLY METICULOUS BLOOD SCREENINGS.
SO IT WASN'T A GAS ERUPTION—IT WAS REALLY BIOTERRORISM...?
YOU DON'T HAVE ANY PROOF!
PARDON MY SAYING SO, BUT EVEN THAT TEXT NO. 34 COULD BE A FAKE!
...THAT'S TRUE... IT'S BEEN TOO LONG SINCE THE DISASTER.
A LOT OF THINGS HAVE WEATHERED WITH TIME.
ZAA (WHOOSH)
BUT THERE ARE THINGS WE CAN BE SURE OF.

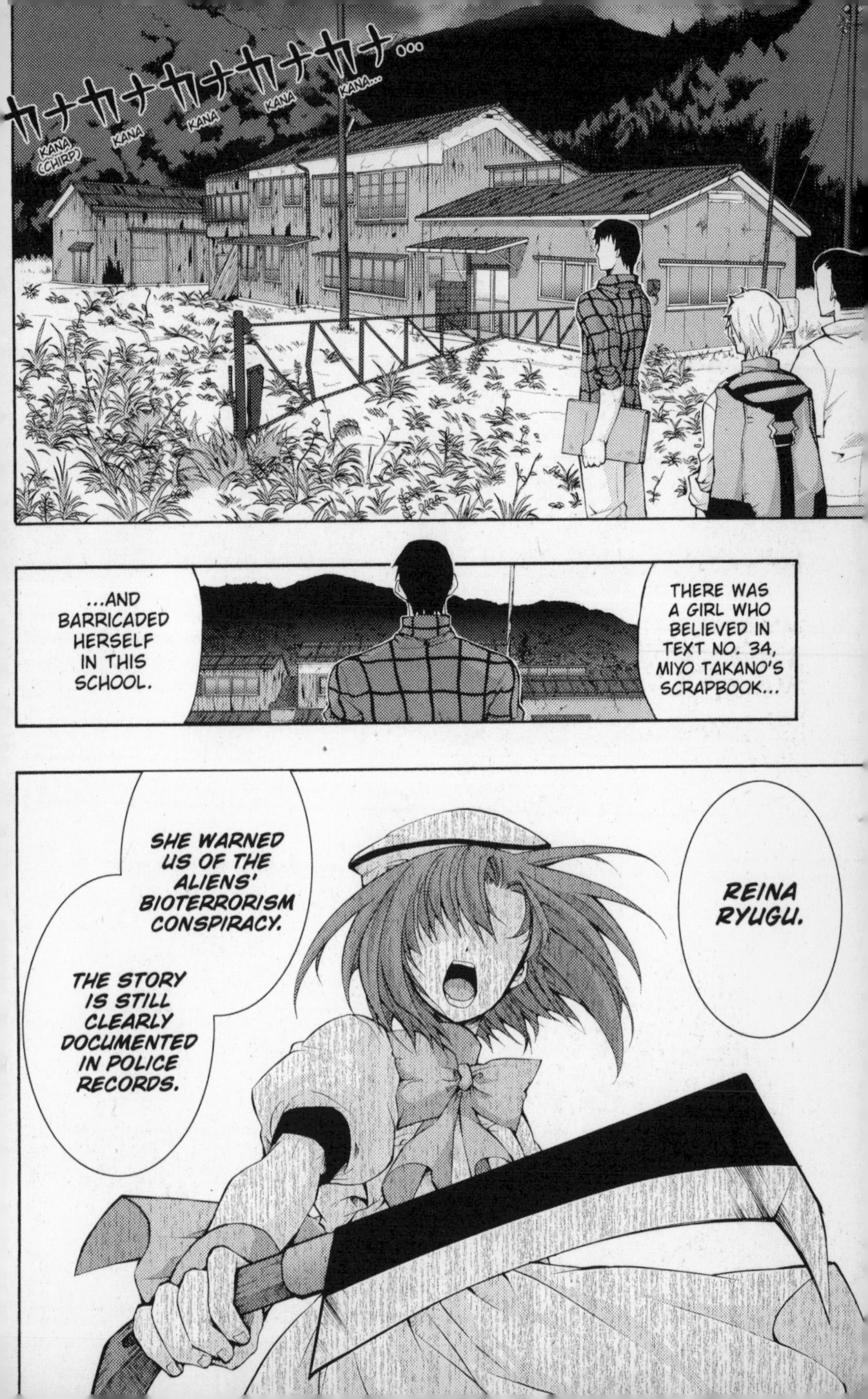

カナカナカナカナカナ…
KANA (CHIRP) KANA KANA KANA KANA...
THERE WAS A GIRL WHO BELIEVED IN TEXT NO. 34, MIYO TAKANO'S SCRAPBOOK...
...AND BARRICADED HERSELF IN THIS SCHOOL.
REINA RYUGU.
SHE WARNED US OF THE ALIENS' BIOTERRORISM CONSPIRACY.
THE STORY IS STILL CLEARLY DOCUMENTED IN POLICE RECORDS.

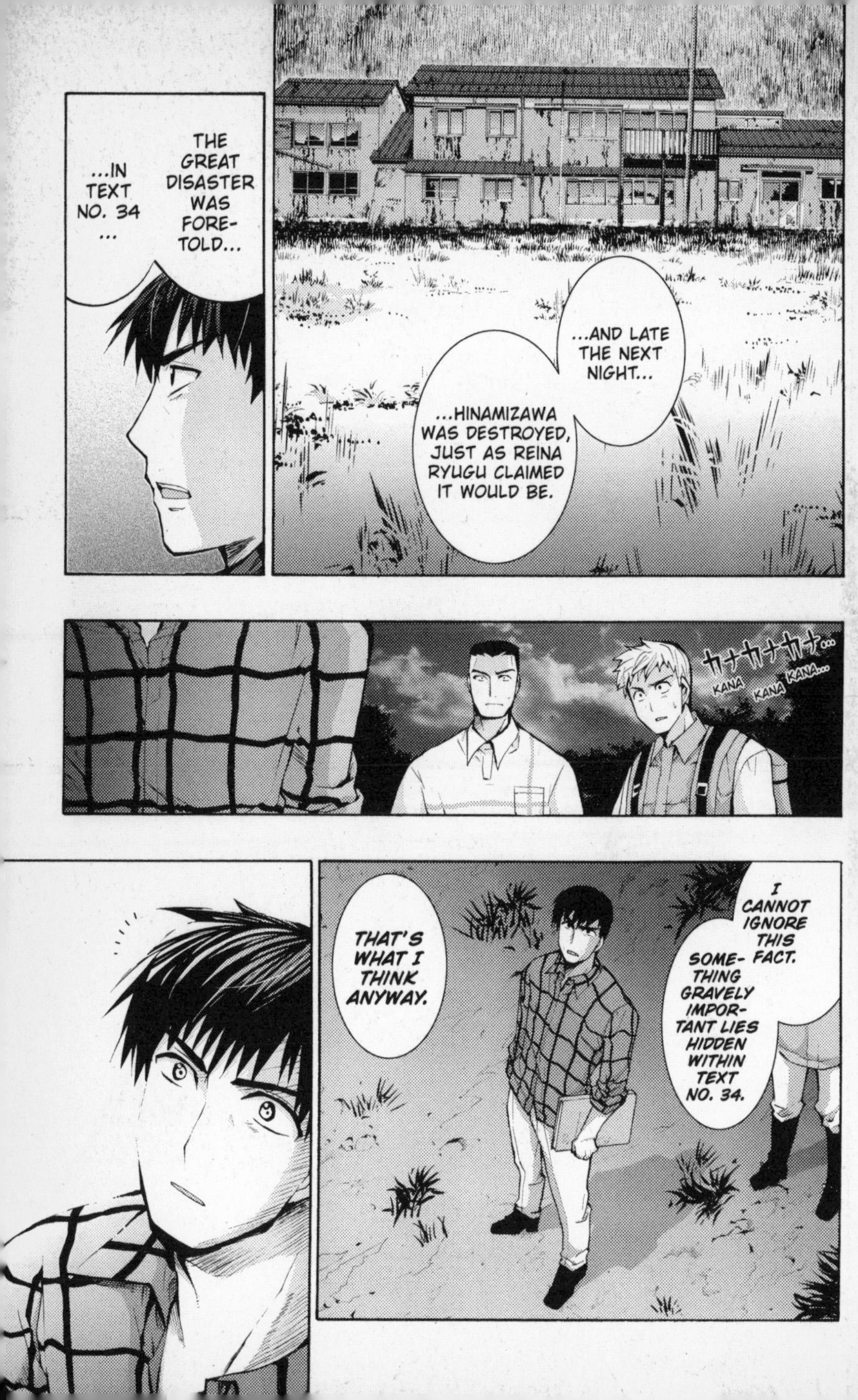
...AND LATE THE NEXT NIGHT...
...HINAMIZAWA WAS DESTROYED, JUST AS REINA RYUGU CLAIMED IT WOULD BE.
THE GREAT DISASTER WAS FORE-TOLD...
...IN TEXT NO. 34 ...
カナカナカナ…
KANA KANA KANA...
I CANNOT IGNORE THIS FACT.
SOME-THING GRAVELY IMPOR-TANT LIES HIDDEN WITHIN TEXT NO. 34.
THAT'S WHAT I THINK ANYWAY.

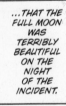

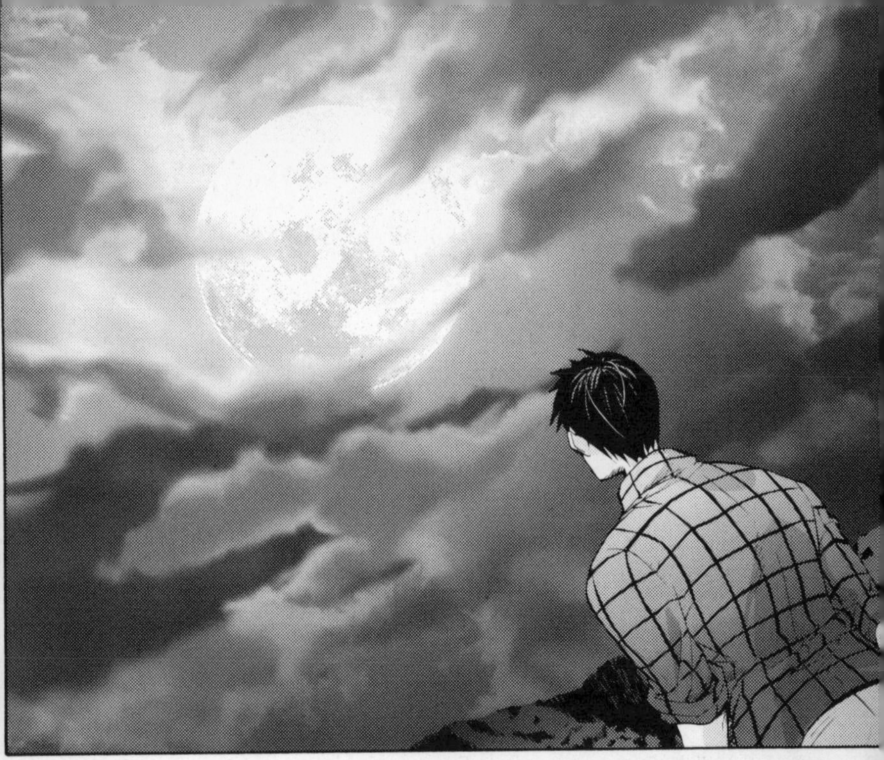
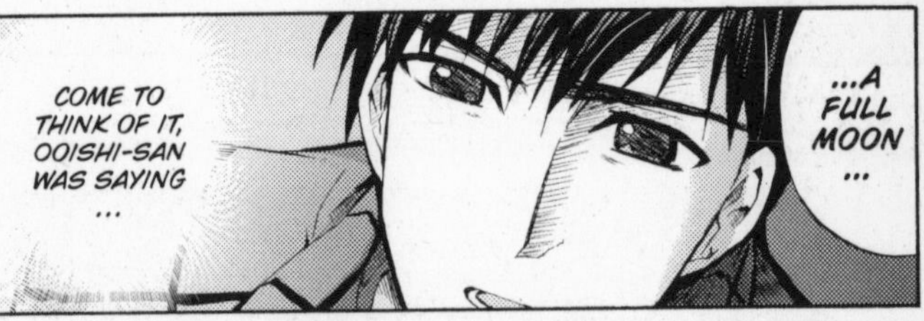
...A FULL MOON...
COME TO THINK OF IT, OOISHI-SAN WAS SAYING...
...THAT THE FULL MOON WAS TERRIBLY BEAUTIFUL ON THE NIGHT OF THE INCIDENT.
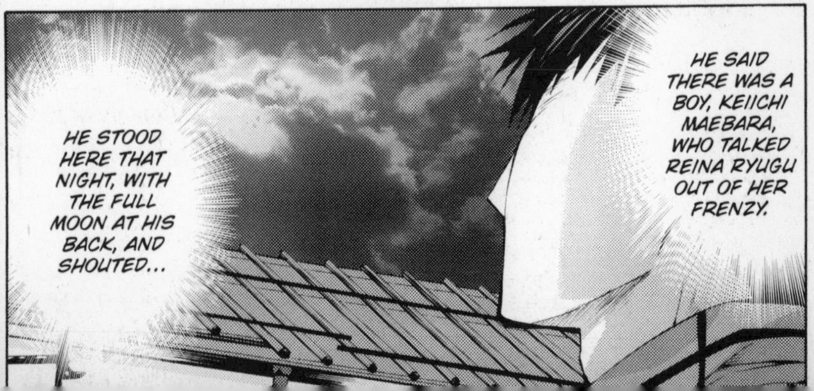
HE SAID THERE WAS A BOY, KEIICHI MAEBARA, WHO TALKED REINA RYUGU OUT OF HER FRENZY.
HE STOOD HERE THAT NIGHT, WITH THE FULL MOON AT HIS BACK, AND SHOUTED...

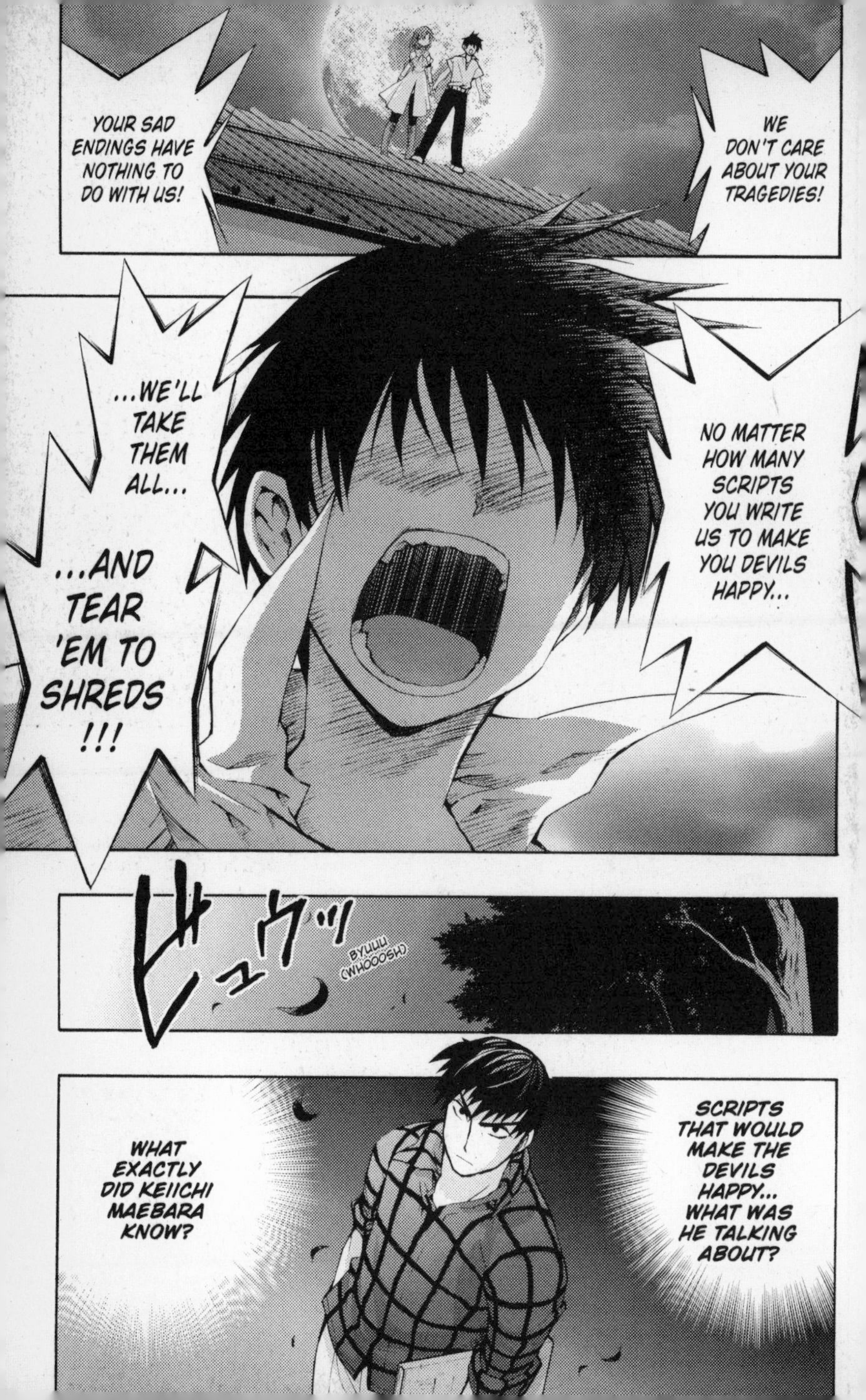
WE DON'T CARE ABOUT YOUR TRAGEDIES!
YOUR SAD ENDINGS HAVE NOTHING TO DO WITH US!
NO MATTER HOW MANY SCRIPTS YOU WRITE US TO MAKE YOU DEVILS HAPPY...
...WE'LL TAKE THEM ALL...
...AND TEAR 'EM TO SHREDS !!!
ビュウッ
BYUUU (WHOOOSH)
SCRIPTS THAT WOULD MAKE THE DEVILS HAPPY... WHAT WAS HE TALKING ABOUT?
WHAT EXACTLY DID KEIICHI MAEBARA KNOW?

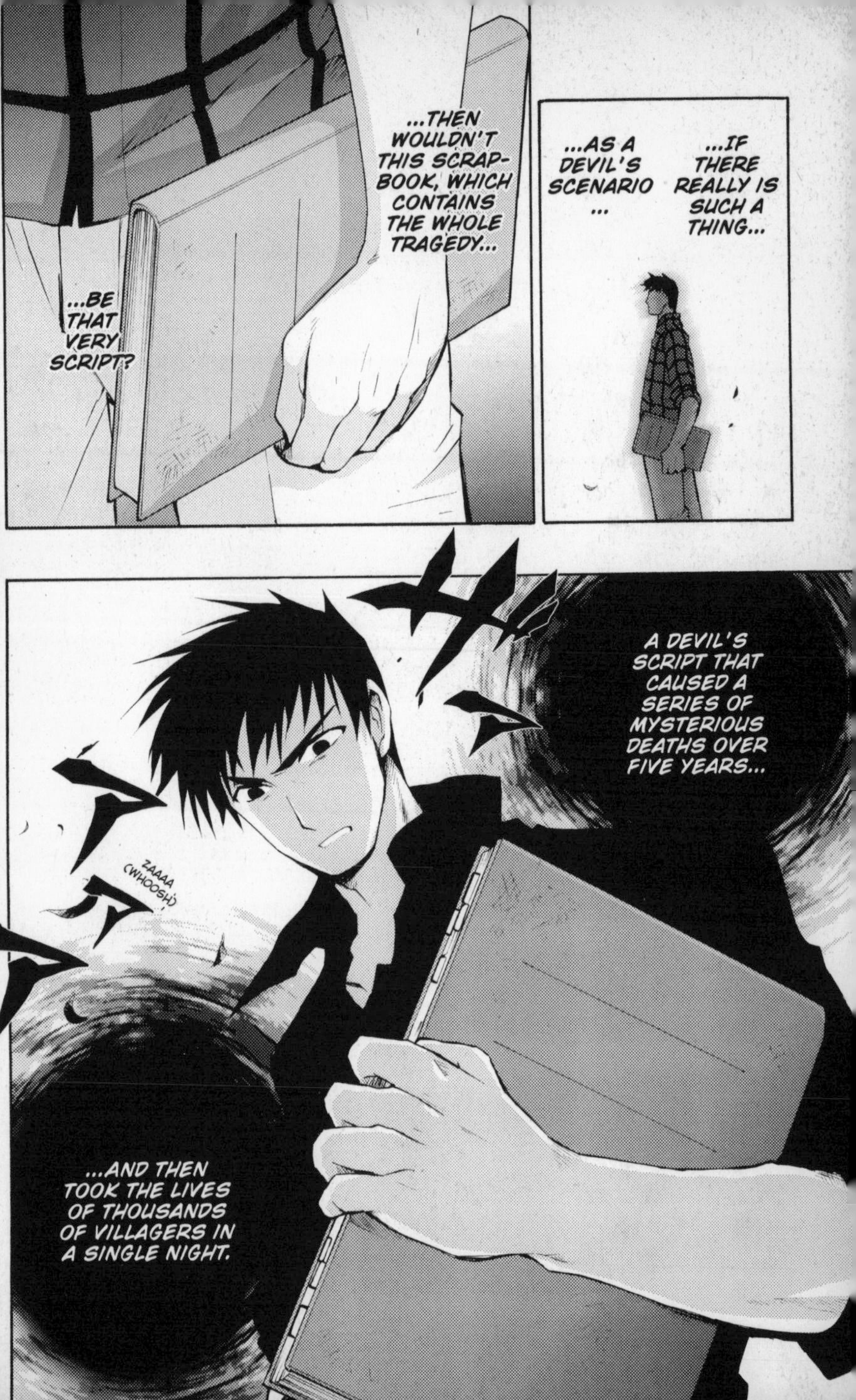
...IF THERE REALLY IS SUCH A THING...
...AS A DEVIL'S SCENARIO ...
...THEN WOULDN'T THIS SCRAP-BOOK, WHICH CONTAINS THE WHOLE TRAGEDY...
...BE THAT VERY SCRIPT?
A DEVIL'S SCRIPT THAT CAUSED A SERIES OF MYSTERIOUS DEATHS OVER FIVE YEARS...
ZAAAA (WHOOSH)
...AND THEN TOOK THE LIVES OF THOUSANDS OF VILLAGERS IN A SINGLE NIGHT.

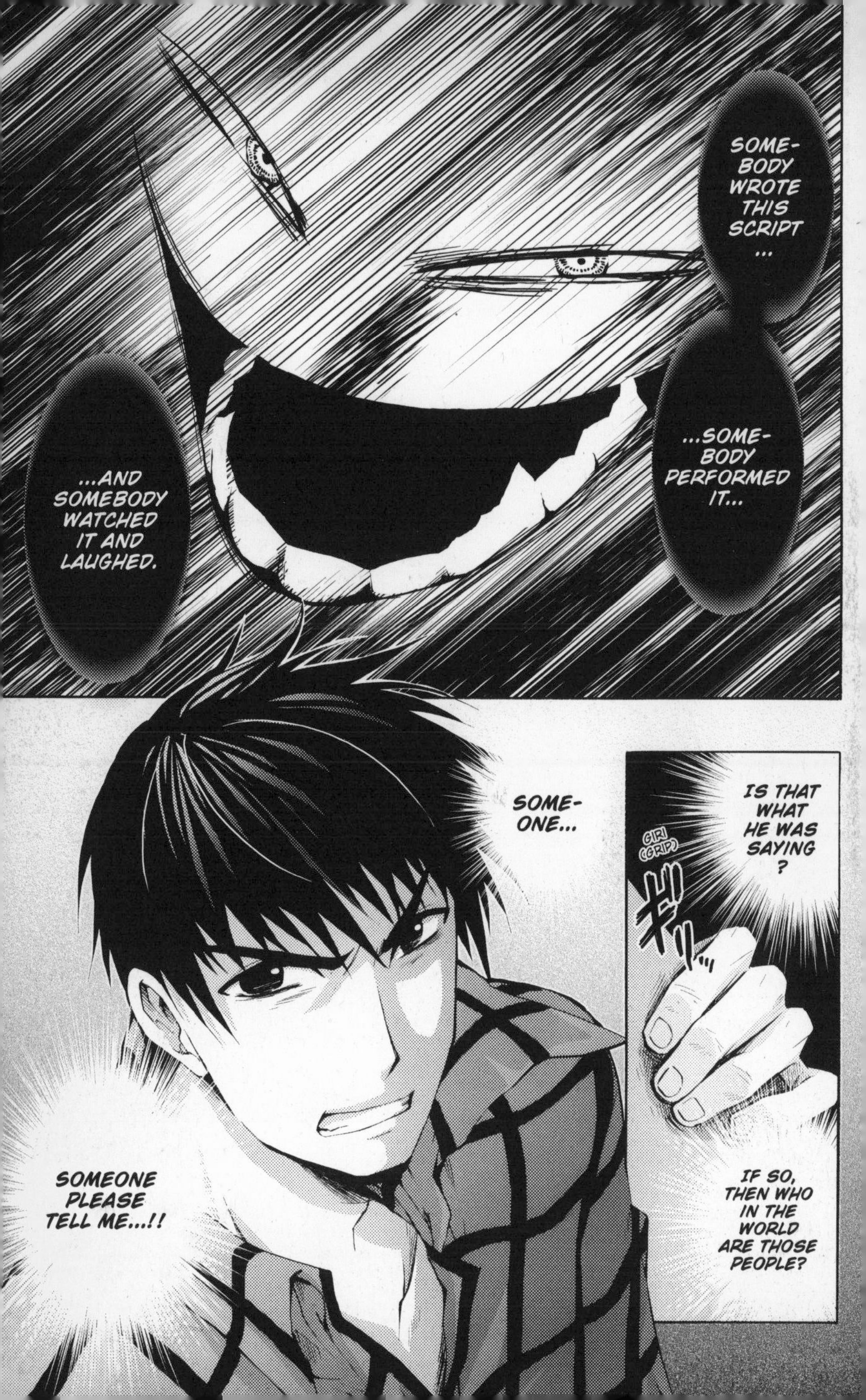
SOME-BODY WROTE THIS SCRIPT...
...SOME-BODY PERFORMED IT...
...AND SOMEBODY WATCHED IT AND LAUGHED.
IS THAT WHAT HE WAS SAYING?
SOME-ONE...
GIRI (GRIP)
IF SO, THEN WHO IN THE WORLD ARE THOSE PEOPLE?
SOMEONE PLEASE TELL ME...!!

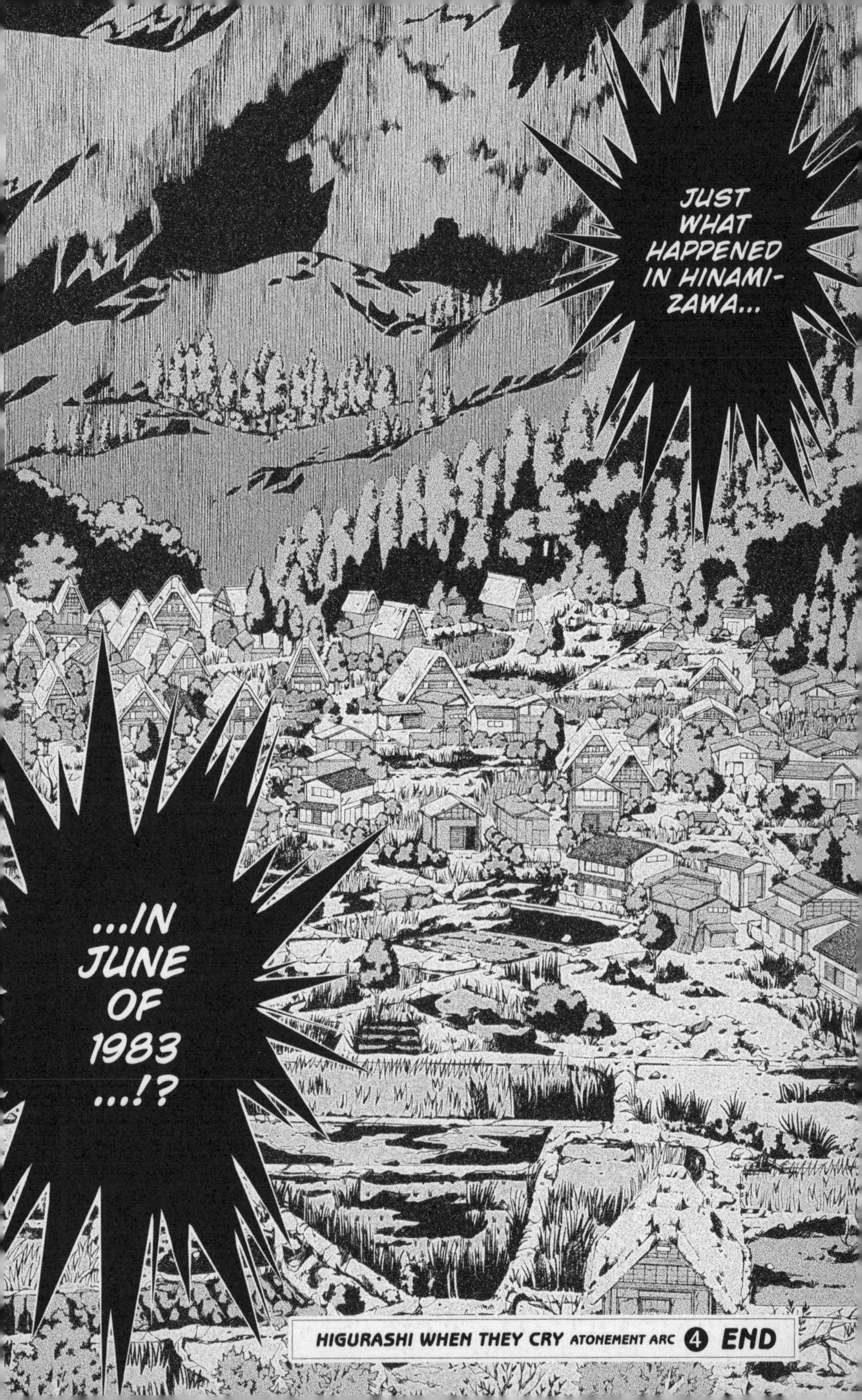
JUST WHAT HAPPENED IN HINAMI-ZAWA...
...IN JUNE OF 1983 ...!?
HIGURASHI WHEN THEY CRY ATONEMENT ARC 4 END

HIGURASHI WHEN THEY CRY

07th Expansion presents Welcome to Hinamizawa "WHEN THEY CRY"

WHAT IT MEANS TO CHALLENGE THE TRAGEDY, TO OPPOSE IT...

ORIGINAL STORY, SUPERVISOR: RYUKISHI07

ALL THE STORIES UNTIL NOW WERE ABOUT GETTING INVOLVED IN, AND HELPLESSLY FALLING PREY TO, TRAGEDIES THAT COULDN'T BE ANYTHING BUT INEVITABLE. AT LAST, THE MAIN CHARACTER SENDS UP A BEACON, ANNOUNCING HIS COUNTERATTACK AGAINST THE TRAGEDY...THAT IS THE IMAGE I HAD WHEN I CREATED THE "ATONEMENT ARC."

"CHALLENGING THE TRAGEDY" DOES NOT MEAN "FIGHTING THE TRAGEDIES THAT HAVE ALREADY HAPPENED." IT MEANS NOT CAUSING A TRAGEDY, OR RATHER, FIGHTING AGAINST THE IMPENDING TRAGEDY.

THINKING ABOUT IT, FROM THE "ABDUCTED BY DEMONS ARC" TO THE "CURSE KILLING ARC," THERE WAS ALWAYS A HASTY CONCLUSION CALLING FOR A VIOLENT SOLUTION, GETTING THE STORY LOST IN TRAGEDY...TO FIGHT AGAINST THE TRAGEDY MEANS NOT USING VIOLENT MEANS OF OPPOSITION, BUT TO OPPOSE THE VIOLENT MEANS THAT TURN THINGS INTO TRAGEDY.

IN THAT SENSE, MAYBE THE OPPOSITION TO THE TRAGEDY, WHERE KEIICHI AND RENA FACE OFF ON THE ROOF, WAS A FAILURE. MAYBE IT WOULD HAVE BEEN BEST TO TRY TO CLEAR UP THE MISUNDERSTANDINGS BEFORE RENA TOOK OVER THE SCHOOL...BUT FACED WITH AN INCIDENT THAT HAD ALREADY HAPPENED, KEIICHI THOUGHT ABOUT THE EVENTS AND CHALLENGED THEM IN THE BEST WAY HE KNEW HOW. AND IN THE VERY END, RENA WAS ABLE TO CHOOSE NOT TO LET THE CLEAVER FALL ON KEIICHI...AND MAYBE THAT IS KEIICHI AND RENA'S VICTORY AFTER OPPOSING THE TRAGEDY.

THAT'S EXACTLY WHY IN THAT LAST BATTLE ON THE ROOF, IF KEIICHI HAD DEFEATED RENA...IN THE CONTEXT OF THE STORY, THAT WOULD NOT HAVE BEEN A VICTORY.

TO CHALLENGE THE TRAGEDY. TO OPPOSE IT. THAT MEANS TO NOT LET A TRAGEDY HAPPEN. THAT IS THE KIND OF STORY THE "ATONEMENT ARC" IS.

THE "ATONEMENT ARC," WHICH COULD ALSO BE CALLED "THE TALE OF THE HARDEST RENA RYUGU HAS EVER WORKED IN HER LIFE," HAS MANAGED TO REACH ITS CONCLUSION IN VOLUME FOUR. IT'S BEEN A LONG, BUT SHORT TWO YEARS—THEY WERE OVER BEFORE I KNEW IT.

THOSE WHO HELPED ME AT THE BASIS OF THIS WORK, RYUKISHI07-SAMA, BT-SAMA, YATAZAKURA-SAMA, AND MY EDITORS, KOIZUMI-SAMA AND KOUNO-SAMA. MY STAFF: ERINA-SAMA, TASHIRO-SAMA, SHIGETOMO TANAKURA-SAMA, NAYU Y-SAMA, NIWAKO-SAMA, BANCHO-SAMA, TOMOKA FURUDA-SAMA, MOYOMOSO-SAMA, RICO-SAMA, YF-SAMA, YOSHUN-SAMA. AND EVERYONE WHO STUCK WITH ME THIS LONG. THANK YOU VERY MUCH.

THE MANGA VERSION OF *HIGURASHI WHEN THEY CRY* WILL CONTINUE WITH THE "MASSACRE ARC" AND THE "FESTIVAL ACCOMPANYING ARC." YOU MIGHT GET A PEEK AT SOME ACTION FROM THE MEMBERS OF THE *HIGURASHI* CAST WHO HAVEN'T HAD A CHANCE IN THE SPOTLIGHT YET AND AT THE OTHER SIDE OF THE *HIGURASHI* WORLD. IF YOU LIKE, PLEASE SEE IT THROUGH TO THE END.

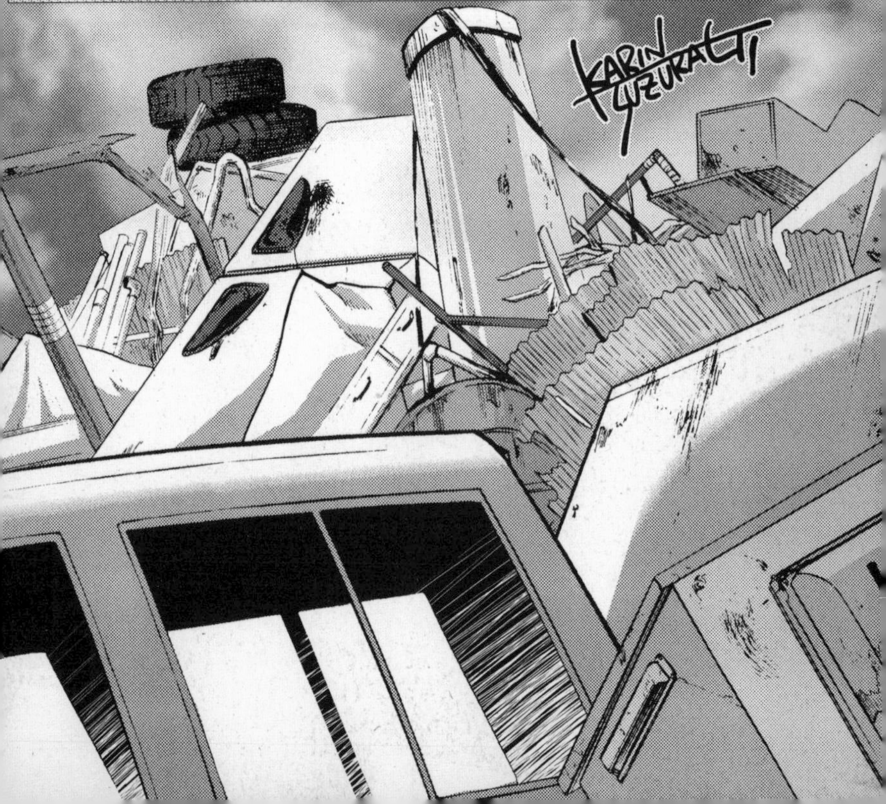
KARIN SUZURAGI

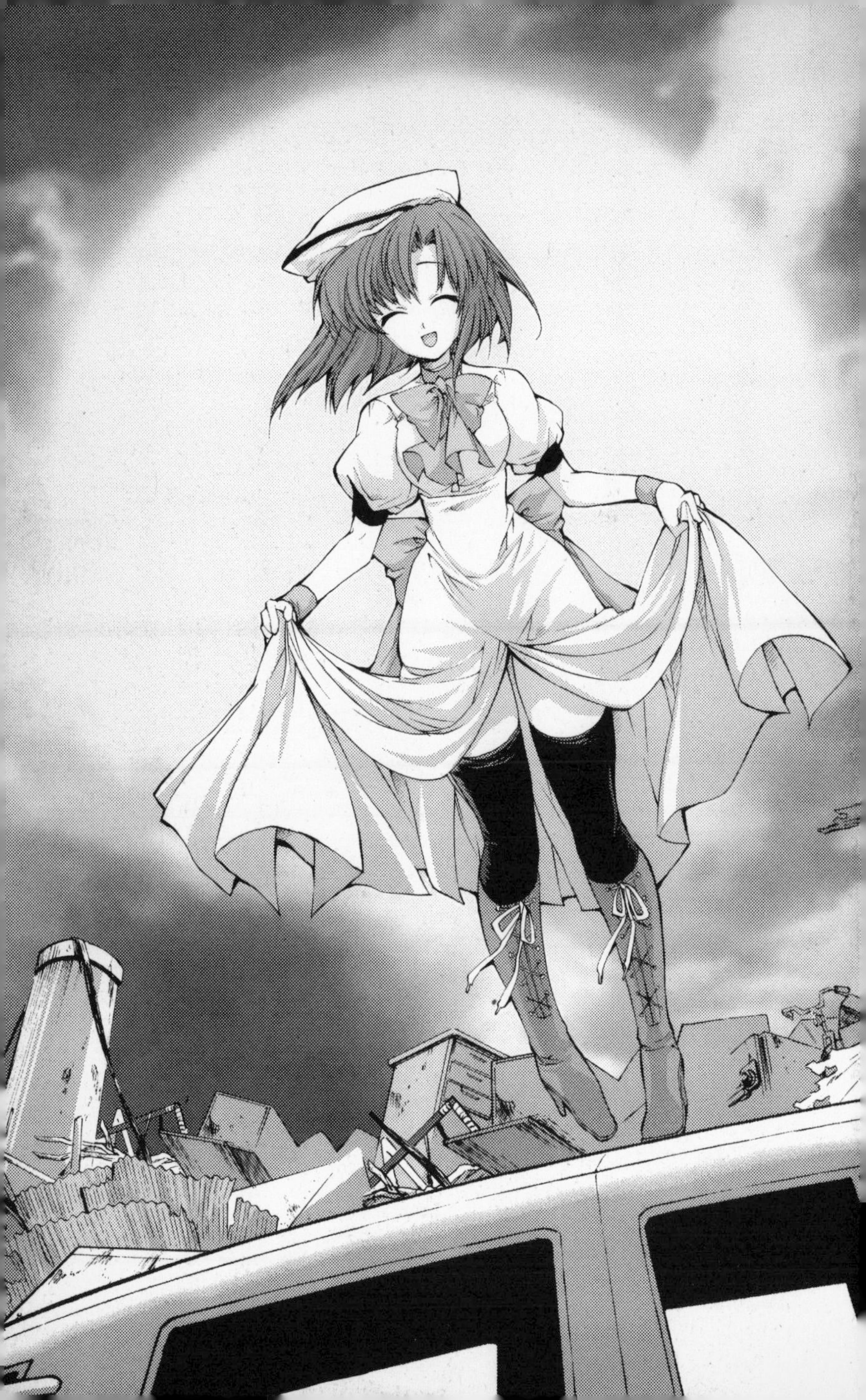

Can't wait for the next volume? You don't have to!

Keep up with the latest chapters of some of your favorite manga every month online in the pages of YEN PLUS!

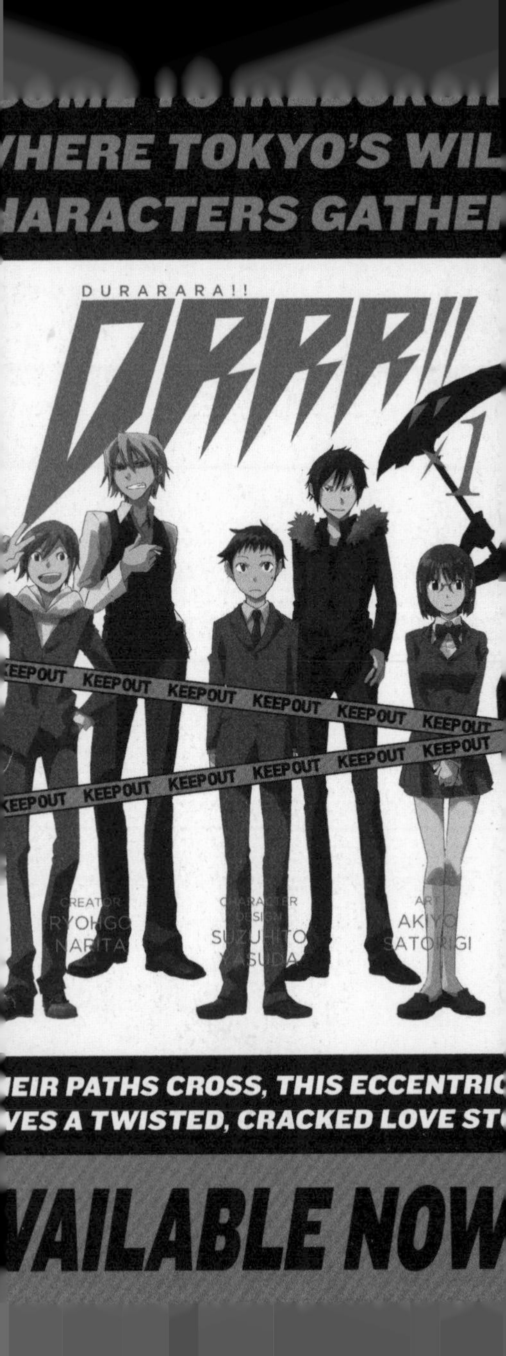

HERE TOKYO'S WIL
HARACTERS GATHE
DURARARA!!
DRRR!!
1
KEEPOUT
CREATOR
RYOHGO
NARITA
CHARACTER
DESIGN
SUZUHITO
YASUDA
ART
AKIYO
SATORIGI
EIR PATHS CROSS, THIS ECCENTRIC
VES A TWISTED, CRACKED LOVE ST
VAILABLE NOW

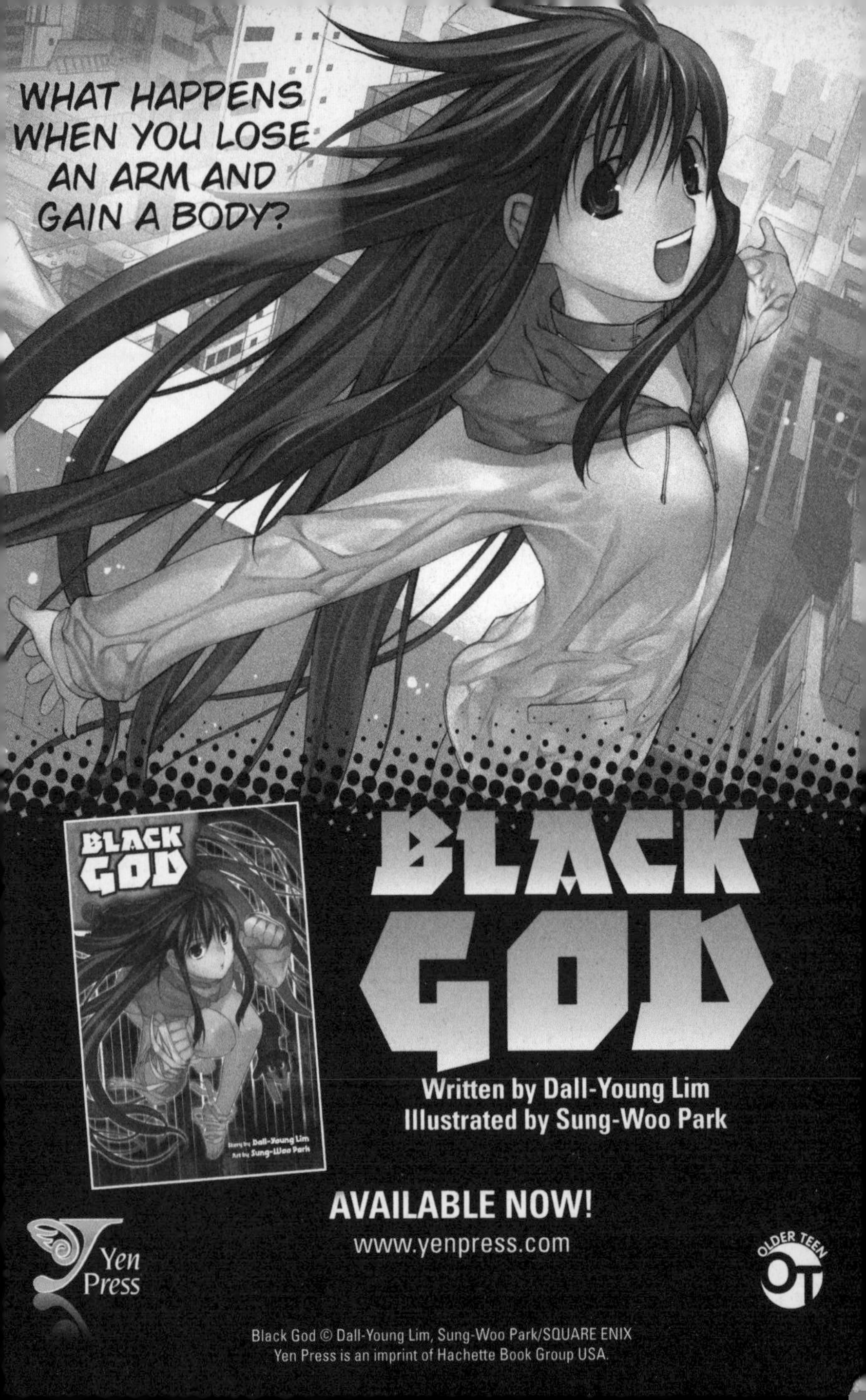
WHAT HAPPENS WHEN YOU LOSE AN ARM AND GAIN A BODY?
BLACK GOD
Story by Dall-Young Lim
Art by Sung-Woo Park
BLACK GOD
Written by Dall-Young Lim
Illustrated by Sung-Woo Park
AVAILABLE NOW!
www.yenpress.com
Yen Press
OLDER TEEN
OT
Black God © Dall-Young Lim, Sung-Woo Park/SQUARE ENIX
Yen Press is an imprint of Hachette Book Group USA.

The Phantomhive family has a butler who's almost too good to be true...

...or maybe he's just too good to be human.

Black Butler

YANA TOBOSO

VOLUMES 1-9 IN STORES NOW!

Yen Press
www.yenpress.com

BLACK BUTLER © Yana Toboso / SQUARE ENIX
Yen Press is an imprint of Hachette Book Group, Inc.

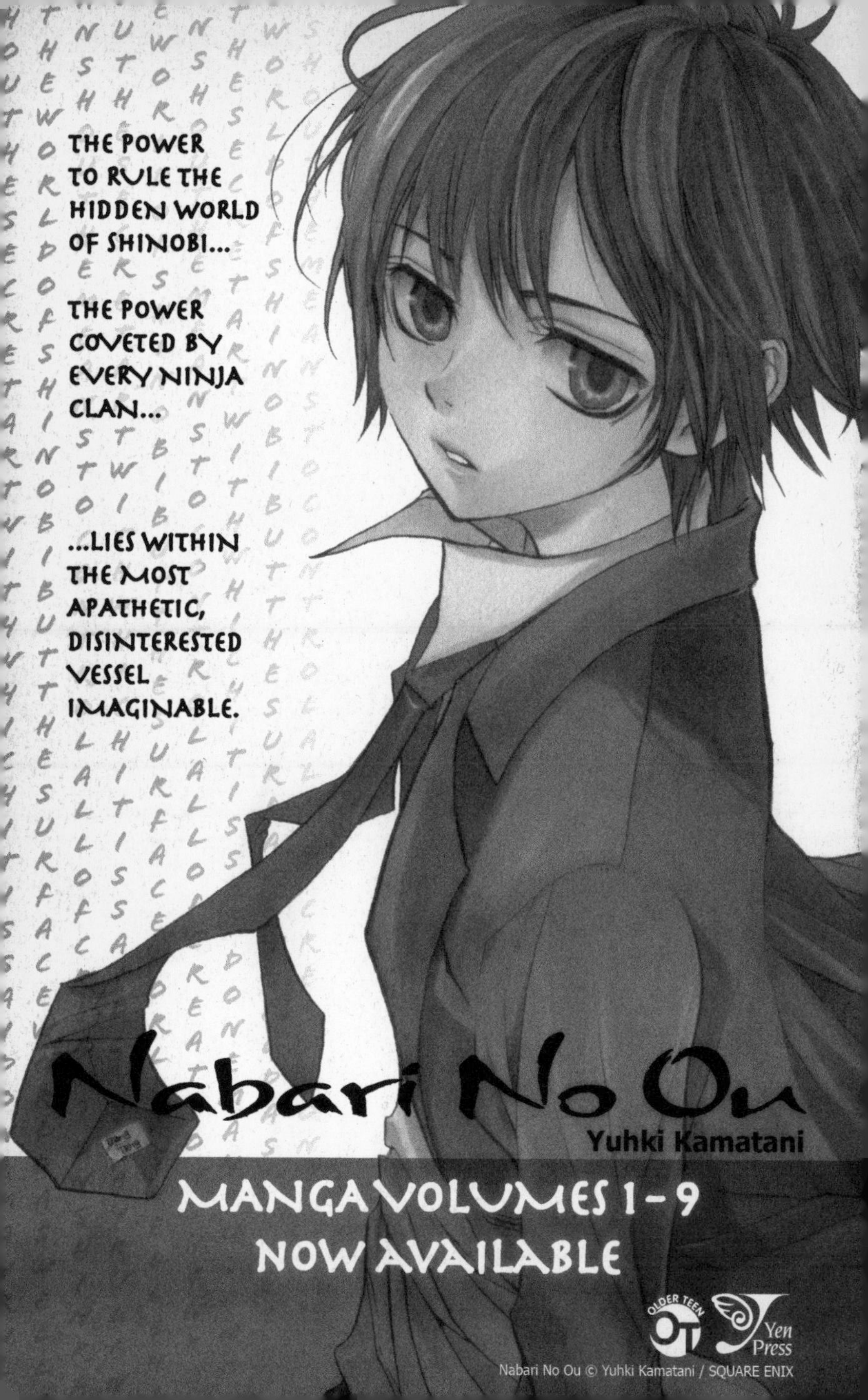
THE POWER TO RULE THE HIDDEN WORLD OF SHINOBI...
THE POWER COVETED BY EVERY NINJA CLAN...
...LIES WITHIN THE MOST APATHETIC, DISINTERESTED VESSEL IMAGINABLE.
Nabari No Ou
Yuhki Kamatani
MANGA VOLUMES 1-9
NOW AVAILABLE
OLDER TEEN OT
Yen Press
Nabari No Ou © Yuhki Kamatani / SQUARE ENIX

Kieli sees ghosts.
Harvey cannot die.
He will throw
her world into
chaos...
...and become her
one true friend.

STORY BY **Yukako Kabei**
ART BY **Shiori Teshirogi**

KIELI

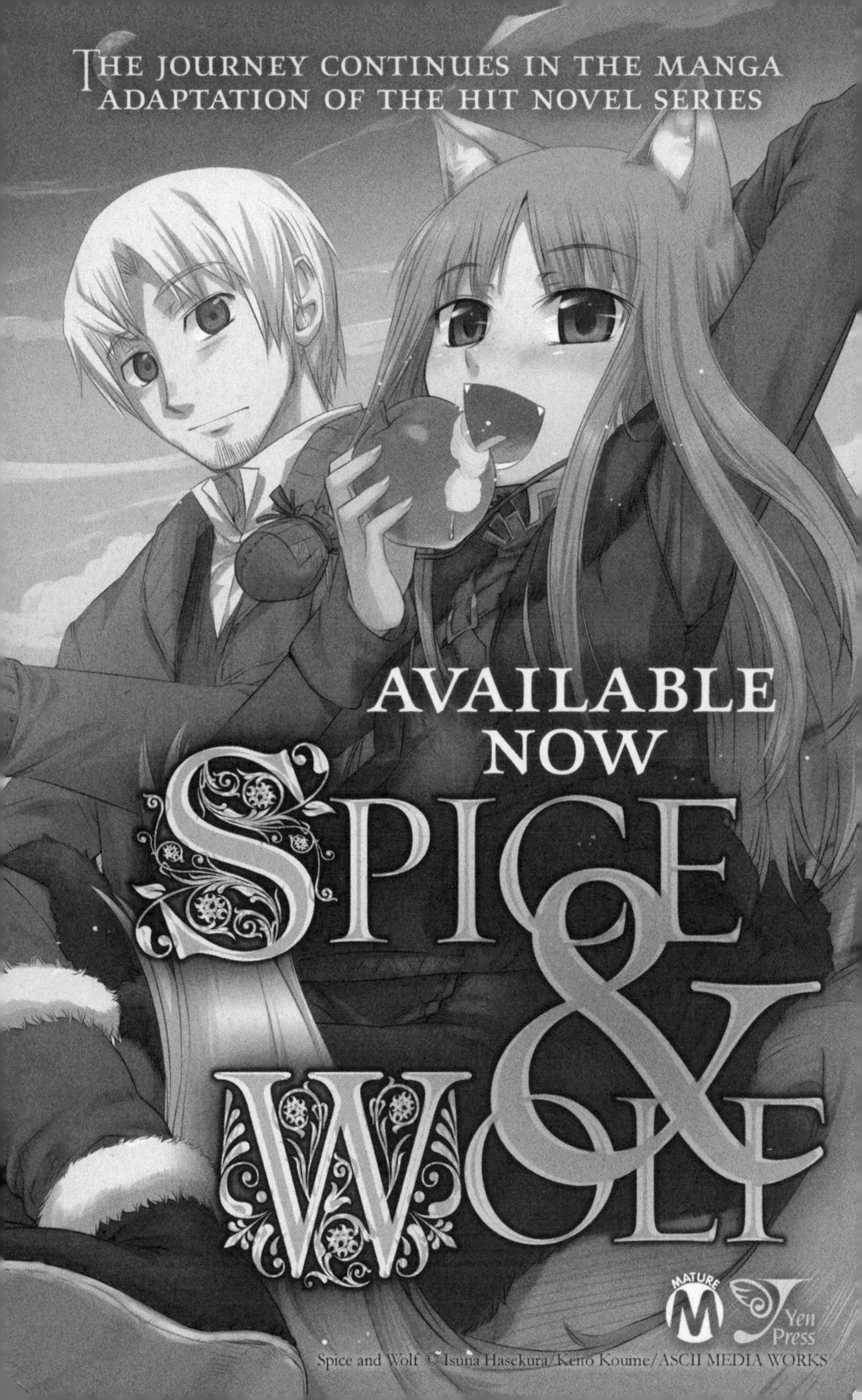
THE JOURNEY CONTINUES IN THE MANGA ADAPTATION OF THE HIT NOVEL SERIES
AVAILABLE NOW
SPICE & WOLF
MATURE
Yen Press
Spice and Wolf © Isuna Hasekura/Keito Koume/ASCII MEDIA WORKS

HIGURASHI
WHEN THEY CRY
ATONEMENT ARC ④

RYUKISHI07
KARIN SUZURAGI

Translation: Alethea Nibley and Athena Nibley

Lettering: AndWorld Design

Higurashi WHEN THEY CRY Atonement Arc, Vol. 4 © RYUKISHI07 / 07th Expansion © 2008 Karin Suzuragi / SQUARE ENIX CO., LTD. All rights reserved. First published in Japan in 2008 by SQUARE ENIX CO., LTD. English translation rights arranged with SQUARE ENIX CO., LTD. and Hachette Book Group through Tuttle-Mori Agency, Inc. Translation © 2012 by SQUARE ENIX CO., LTD.

Yen Press
Hachette Book Group
237 Park Avenue, New York, NY 10017

www.HachetteBookGroup.com
www.YenPress.com

Yen Press is an imprint of Hachette Book Group, Inc. The Yen Press name and logo are trademarks of Hachette Book Group, Inc.

First Yen Press Edition: April 2012

ISBN: 978-0-316-12388-4

10 9 8 7 6 5 4 3 2 1

BVG

Printed in the United States of America

AUG 3 0 2013